GLOBAL COMPETITIVENESS AND PRODUCTIVITY

GLOBAL COMPETITIVENESS AND PRODUCTIVITY

Editors

DR. B.S. BHATIA
Director
RIMT-Institute of Management and Computer Technology,
Mandi Gobindgarh
Distt. Fatehgarh Sahib (Punjab)

DR. BALRAM DOGRA
Director
Apeejay Institute of Management
Jalandhar (Punjab)

DEEP & DEEP PUBLICATIONS PVT. LTD.
F-159, Rajouri Garden, New Delhi - 110 027

GLOBAL COMPETITIVENESS AND PRODUCTIVITY

ISBN 81-7629-623-6

Printed in India at MAYUR ENTERPRISES,
WZ Plot No. 3, Gujjar Market, Tihar Village, New Delhi - 110 018.

Published by DEEP & DEEP PUBLICATIONS PVT. LTD.,
F-159, Rajouri Garden, New Delhi - 110 027 • Phone : 25435369, 25440916
E-mail : deep98@del3.vsnl.net.in • ddpbooks@yahoo.co.in
Showroom :
2/13, Ansari Road, Daryaganj, New Delhi - 110 002 • Telefax : 23245122

Editorial Committee

RAJESH VERMA
PARMINDER NATH
ASHU GUPTA
JASMINE BANSAL
ANURAG PAHUJA

Contents

Acknowledgements xi

List of Contributors xiii

Introduction xvii

SECTION I
CONCEPTUAL

1. *Balram Dogra and Rajesh Verma*
Productivity-Centric Global Competitiveness 3

2. *Paramjit Nanda and P.S. Raikhy*
Trends in Global Competitiveness of India
During Post-Liberalization Period 16

3. *B.S. Bhatia and Anurag Pahuja*
Corporate Reporting on Productivity 31

4. *Amarjit Singh Sethi*
Globalisation and the Changing Productivity
Performance in the Indian Economy—A Sectoral Analysis 40

5. *P.S. Raikhy and Paramjit Nanda*
Global Competitiveness—Issues Beyond Productivity 47

6. *Dyal Bhatnagar*
EVA as a Tool to Measure Productivity 53

7. *Narendra Singh and S.C. Davar*
Enhancing Indian Competitiveness through Knowledge 64

8. *Sonia Chawla*
Impact of Liberalization and Globalization : An Indian Perspective 73

Section II
MANUFACTURING SECTOR

9. *Raghbir Singh and Lalit Mohan Kathuria*
Competitiveness of the Indian Garment Export Sector after Multi-Fibre Arrangement (MFA) Phase-out 85

10. *B.S. Rathore and S.K. Dhameja*
Productivity Improvement of Industrial Sectors in Punjab 93

11. *Kuldip Kaur and Amandeep Kaur*
Extent of Competitiveness and Performance of Some Indian Industries 112

12. *Navjote Khara and Deependra Singh Garcha*
Export Competitiveness of Indian Manufacturing Industry 120

13. *Akepati S. Reddy*
Process-Based Management Systems and Productivity 134

14. *Ruchi Trehan and Sunil Kumar*
Productive Efficiency of Indian Textile Industry : A Non-Parametric Analysis 139

15. *V.K. Kohli*
Transforming Public Enterprises in India into Intellegent Organisations 154

16. *Sanjeev K. Sharma and K.K. Uppal*
Gaining Global Competitiveness : Lessons from Successful Companies 164

Section III
SERVICE SECTOR

17. *Ravinder Vinayek and Ravi Kumar Gupta*
Challenges and Strategies for Competitiveness, Productivity and Globalising Indian Insurance Market 175

18. *Urvashi Makkar and Ashok Shukla*
Achieving Global Competitiveness through Service Excellence and Total Customer Satisfaction 187

19. *Sanjay Kaushik*
Productivity in the Banking Industry with Special Reference to State Bank of India Group 208

20. *Monika Aggarwal*
Trends in Operational Poductivity of
Commercial Banks in India 228

21. *B.S. Bhatia and Swati Kumaria Puri*
Insurance Sector in India in Post-Liberalisation
Period : Challenges of Change 240

22. *Santosh Gupta*
Global Competitiveness in Health Sector 257

23. *Gaganjeet Kaur*
Competitiveness of Public Sector Banks in India
(Post-Liberalisation Scenario) 266

SECTION IV
AGRICULTURE SECTOR

24. *P.K. Vasudeva*
Globalisation, Competitiveness and Productivity in
Agriculture Sector 285

25. *P.S. Rangi*
WTO and Indian Agriculture with Special Reference to Punjab 300

26. *Sanjeev Gupta and R.S. Bawa*
Growth Performance of Productivity
in Indian Agricultural Sector 306

27. *Sukhbir Kaur and Harpinder Singh*
Natural Resource Management and Productivity
Enhancement through Organic Agriculture 314

28. *Dharminder Singh Ubha*
Agricultural Accounting : A Tool for Improving Productivity,
Efficiency and Efficacy in the Agriculture Sector 327

SECTION V
INFORMATION TECHNOLOGY

29. *Inderjeet Singh*
Structure of I.T. Industry and its Policy Implications 339

30. *Ashim Raj Singla and D.P. Goyal*
ERP Systems : Planning, Design and Implementation Model 358

31. *Rajinder Singh*
Role of Software Complexity Metrics in Productivity 369

32. *Dalbir Singh, Narender Singh and Hawa Singh*
CRM—An Additive Tool for Competitiveness 375

33. *H.J. Ghosh Roy*
IT Solutions for Service Providers in Education : A TQM Approach for Global Competitiveness 384

34. *Kulwant Kaur*
E-Governance for Productivity Improvement in Administration : An Indian Perspective 392

35. *Jasmine Bansal*
CRM : Increasing Organisational Competitiveness 406

36. *Deepak Kaushik*
E-Governance : A Tool for Increasing Government Productivity 417

37. *Shikha Kakkar*
Role of ERP Systems in Increasing Productivity and Competitiveness 428

38. *Manav Jindal, Sanjeev Bansal and Ruchi Jindal*
E-Business : A Must for Globalization 434

39. *Meera Bamba*
IT in Agriculture : An Effort for Improving Global Competitiveness of Indian Farmer 444

Index 449

Acknowledgements

This book owes its origin to the National Seminar on Global Competitiveness and Productivity in Indian Business organized at Apeejay Institute of Management, Jalandhar during March 2003.

The seminar received an overwhelming response from the academic and the industry in the shape of financial and academic inputs, which resulted in making the seminar a grand success.

The editors wish to acknowledge with thanks the financial support provided by All India Council of Technical Education, which made it possible to organize the event. During and after the seminar, a number of participants, academicians, managers and policy-makers, suggested putting together these ideas in the form of a book for wider dissemination and implementation of the recommendations made by various speakers. Many of the participants revised papers for the purpose of publication. We are grateful to the contributors to this volume for acceding to our request. Our thanks are also due to the seminar participants who made the seminar discussions fruitful and lively.

We are grateful to a number of colleagues and friends who provided support at various stages of this project. A special word of thanks is due to Shri O.P. Munjal, Co-Chairman, Hero Cycles Ltd., Ludhiana; Shri Vinod Sawhney, CEO, Bharti Mobile Ltd., Chandigarh, Shri S.C. Gupta, Income Tax Commissioner, Jalandhar, Dr. M.A. Zaheer, Professor Emeritus, Punjab Agricultural University, Ludhiana, Dr. H.L. Verma, Professor, Guru Jhambheshwar University, Hisar and Dr. Nachhatar Singh, Principal, Co-operative Bank Staff Training Institute, Jalandhar.

We appreciate very much the co-operation extended by the members of the faculty and the staff of Apeejay Institute of Management, Jalandhar.

B.S. BHATIA
BALRAM DOGRA

List of Contributors

Akepati S. Reddy : Thapar Institute of Engineering and Technology, Patiala.

Amandeep Kaur : Research Scholar, Punjab School of Economics, Guru Nanak Dev University, Amritsar.

Amarjit Singh Sethi : Professor, Punjab School of Economics, Guru Nanak Dev University, Amritsar.

Anurag Pahuja : Lecturer, Apeejay Institute of Management, Jalandhar.

Ashim Raj Singla : Asstt. Professor, IMT, Ghaziabad and Professor, IMT, Ghaziabad.

Ashok Shukla : Faculty, Department of Business Management and Entrepreneurship, Dr. R.M.L. Avad University, Faizabad.

B.S. Bhatia : Director, School of Management, Apeejay Institute of Technology, Greater Noida, U.P.

B.S. Rathore : Professor & Head, Entrepreneurship Development and Industrial Coordination Deptt., TTTI, Chandigarh.

Balram Dogra : Director, Apeejay Institute of Management, Jalandhar.

D.P. Goyal : Professor, IMT, Ghaziabad.

Dalbir Singh : Research Scholar, Deptt. of Commerce, Kurukshetra University, Kurukshetra.

Dayal Bhatnagar : Research Associate, University School of Management, Punjabi University Guru Kashi Campus, Talwandi Sabo, Bhatinda.

Deepak Kaushik : Lecturer, Apeejay Institute of Management, Jalandhar.

Deependra S. Garcha : Deptt. of Excise & Taxation, Punjab Civil Service.

Dharminder Singh Ubha : Head, Deptt. of Commerce, Mata Gujri College, Fatehgarh Sahib.

Gaganjeet Kaur : Lecturer, Apeejay Institute of Management, Jalandhar.

H.J. Ghosh Roy : Reader, IMSAR, Maharishi Dayanand University, Rohtak.

Harpinder Singh : Agriculture Development Officer, Deptt. of Agriculture, Punjab.

Hawa Singh : Reader, Deptt. of Commerce, Kurukshetra University, Kurukshetra.

Inderjit Singh : Professor of Economics, Punjabi University, Patiala.

Jasmine Bansal : Lecturer, Apeejay Institute of Management, Jalandhar.

K.K. Uppal : University Business School, Panjab University, Chandigarh.

Kuldip Kaur : Reader, Punjab School of Economics, Guru Nanak Dev University, Amritsar.

Kulwant Kaur : Head, Deptt. of Computer Science, Apeejay Institute of Management, Jalandhar.

Lalit Mohan Kathuria : Lecturer, Department of Humanities and Management, Beant College of Engineering & Technology, Pathankot Road, Gurdaspur, Punjab.

Manav Jindal : Lecturer in Management, Punjab Institute of Management and Technology, Mandi Gobindgarh.

Meera Bamba : Faculty, SBMNIMSAR, Asthal Bohar, Rohtak.

Monika Aggarwal : Lecturer, Hans Raj Maha Vidyalaya, Jalandhar.

Narendra Singh : Reader, Deptt. of Commerce, Kurukshetra University, Kurukshetra.

Navjote Khara : Lecturer, Apeejay Institute of Management, Jalandhar.

P.K. Vasudeva : Professor, College of Commerce & Management, Bharti Vidhya Bhawan, Chandigarh.

P.S. Raikhy : Professor, Punjab School of Economics, Guru Nanak Dev University, Amritsar.

P.S. Rangi : Senior Economist (Marketing), Deptt. of Economics and Sociology at Punjab Agriculture University, Ludhiana.

Paramjeet Nanda : Reader, Punjab School of Economics, Guru Nanak Dev University, Amritsar.

Raghbir Singh : Professor, Department of Commerce and Business Management, GNDU, Amritsar.

R.S. Bawa : Professor of Economics and Registrar, GNDU, Amritsar.

Rajesh Verma : Lecturer, Apeejay Institute of Management, Jalandhar.

Rajinder Singh : Reader, Deptt. of Computer Science and Application, M.D. University, Rohtak.

Ravi K. Gupta : Lecturer, SBMIMSAR, Asthal Bohar, Rohtak.

Ravinder Vinayek : Professor, Deptt. of Commerce, M.D.U., Rohtak.

Ruchi Jindal : Lecturer in Computer Science, Punjab Institute of Management and Technology, Mandi Gobindgarh.

Ruchi Trehan : Lecturer, Department of Commerce and Business Management, GNDU, Amritsar.

S.C. Davar : Reader, Deptt. of Commerce, Kurukshetra University, Kurukshetra.

S.K. Dhameja : Asstt. Professor, EDIC Deptt., TTTI, Chandigarh.

Sanjay Kaushik : Lecturer, Deptt. of Commerce, Kurukshetra University, Kurukshetra.

Sanjeev Bansal : Lecturer in Management, Punjab Institute of Management and Technology, Mandi Gobindgarh.

Sanjeev Gupta : Lecturer, Apeejay Institute of Management, Jalandhar.

Sanjeev K. Sharma : University Business School, Panjab University, Chandigarh.

Santosh Gupta : Senior Reader, Deptt. of Commerce, Jammu University, Jammu.

Shikha Kakkar : Lecturer, Deptt. of Business Studies, Guru Jambheshwar University, Hisar.

Sonia Chawala : Lecturer, Malout Institute of Management and Information Technology, Malout.

Sukhbir Kaur : Lecturer, Apeejay Institute of Management, Jalandhar.

Sunil Kumar : Lecturer, Punjab School of Economics, GNDU, Amritsar.

Swati Kumaria Puri : Lecturer, Apeejay Institute of Technology, School of Management, Greater Noida.

Urvashi Makkar : Director, Tilak Raj Chadha Institute of Management and Technology, Yamunanagar.

V.K. Kohli : Senior Project Officer, All India Council for Technical Education, New Delhi.

Introduction

In an era of rapid globalization and liberalizing economy, there has been an increase in the number of entrants into the world markets, leading to greater competition. Competitiveness in the market place is no longer seen as a matter of concern only for the companies competing in the market but also for the state. Because of the importance of competitiveness and productivity in the economic success, countries have started searching for policies and initiatives, which will spur the efforts of the business firms for improving their productivity and becoming competitive.

In the current global scenario, where geo-political boundaries are being replaced by geo-economic boundaries, the arc lights are now focused on recognizing and identifying the factors that could lead to enhanced productivity in various sectors of the economy as also in various organizations. Thus, productivity occupies an important place on the central stage in various economies. It is the focal point of current public interest in business and economic matters all over the world. In most of the contemporary discussions on business and economic affairs, productivity figures in one way or the other as a strategy for meeting the challenge of competition. No society/country can ignore the subject of productivity while discussing the formulation of policies and plans because the subject touches almost every sector of the society in one way or the other. The Government, the businessman, the working class, the economic analyst, all are interested in promotion of productivity in different sectors of the economy.

The concept, type and measurement of and the trends in productivity changes are among the important contemporary issues, which are being discussed in economic and business circles. There are different ways through which the subject is being approached. One of the most common approach to the analysis of the productivity is to measure and analyze the efficiency with which the inputs in a system are being utilized. It indicates the efficiency with which the capital and labour, the two principal inputs are being utilized. Their measurement is indicated by the capital output and labour output ratios. Another way of looking at productivity would be as an indicator of real wages and relative prices. Yet in another way, in the context of economic development of any society, productivity is considered as a major factor in the choice of technology and employment of labour.

Some of the critical issues about productivity, which must be addressed in any developing economy, relate to what productivity is? What are different forms/types of productivity? How is it measured? What are the implications of high or low rate of productivity promotion? How fast has it been growing? How fast should it grow? How should the gains of productivity be distributed in the society? What are the effects of productivity growth on income and wealth, etc.? A fruitful discussion on these issues is going to be the basis of economic and business planning. This book is addressed to some of these and may more related questions.

Traditionally, productivity is referred to as the ratio between output and input. However, a major flaw in this approach is that the inputs and outputs may not always carry a casual relationship. Therefore, a new concept of productivity known as Performance Objectives Productivity, is being adopted now-a-days. The model, termed as holistic approach advocates to the measurement of overall productivity of an organization considering it as a system comprising of sub-systems (and sub-sub-systems) with each sub-system to encompass key performance areas and each KPA with several performance objectives. The business history is full of techniques and approaches which have helped in the promotion of productivity. Taylor's Scientific Management, Elton Mayo's Hawthorne Experiments, Peter F. Drucker's Management By Objectives, Herbert Simon's Systems Approach are some of the important contributions, which helped in productivity movement from time to time. Many of these concepts are still being practiced world over in one way or the other.

In India, low productivity has characterized our investments in general and the industrial sector in particular. Our low growth rate is a result not of low investments but of poor policies resulting in a poor return from increased rate of investments. In this context, it is interesting to go through the observation of Myron Weiner as early as 1980s, "Had India's GDP grown as rapidly from 1960-80, as South Korea's, it would stand at $ 531 billion today rather than $ 150 billions, surpassing that of U.K., equal to that of France and more than twice that of China. India's per capita income would have been $ 740 instead of $ 260." Thus where countries like Taiwan and South Korea have grown much faster than India in the post-war period, with substantial impact on standard of living of their people, the Indian policy-makers are responding to this situation now.

During the last several years, economists and administrators in India have been debating and discussing the urgency and desirability of pegging up growth rate of economy to 6-8% per annum, so that over a period of 15-20 years, the Indian economy could occupy a reasonably respectable position in the world economies. But every time an effort was made in this direction, the target had to be revised due to constraints of resources. It is also recognized that with the present state of ill-developed infrastructure, the slow pace of economic reforms, the short-sighted economic and social policies and with present political scenario, a substantial growth in the inflow of foreign direct investments may not be possible. Since the growth is a function of capital formation, therefore, we continue to compromise with the slow growth of the economy due to resource constraints.

But there is another aspect which has perhaps not been given adequate attention. It is well known that output depends not only on the amount of capital, but also on capital-output ratio, that is productivity of capital. The economic planners seem to have assumed that this ratio is given and that, a substantial improvement in this ratio is not possible. A paradigm shift in our thinking is needed. A shift in the thinking that with alternative technologies, with changes in product design and with development of brand equity, productivity of capital can be improved. Thus, if business and economic policies collectively focus attention on improving capital-output ratio, then the rate of economic growth can be improved even with the existing capital stock.

Apart from the overall productivity of the economy, intra-sectoral and inter-sectoral comparison of productivity is also an important issue. For instance, productivity in general shows an increasing trend among a cross-section of industries. An analysis of trends would show rising labour productivity in individual industries in general. At the same time, variations in the rates of increase in productivity among industries are clearly visible. This is because in some industries, productivity has increased much more than in others. Similarly, within an industry or a group of industries, the productivity would differ with form of business, size of operations, technology employed, capacity utilization, level of training, competition and a host of other factors including the government regulations governing the industry.

Yet another area of serious concern is the low productivity in public sector, which plays an important role in the economy of our country. Till a decade ago, the Indian economy was highly protected economy with the public sector dominating each aspect of infrastructure development. Competition was scarce, resulting in little emphasis on important issues like competitive strategy, development of technology, increased returns and societal upliftment, which again are dependent on the productivity of an enterprise. The persistent problem of shortage of funds in these enterprises is also related to low level of productivity. So as to reverse the position, government adopted a plan of liberal economy, where the emphasis was laid on disinvestments of various public sector enterprises in order to generate funds for growth. In an environment of open economy healthy competition will prevail that will compel the organizations to optimize the utilization of capacity, improve technology, optimally utilize the resources and increase the productivity.

However, an important reason for poor productivity is the low morale of the working people at all levels. If the workers are not motivated, no amount of techniques and systems can speed up productivity. Even Elton Mayo's Hawthorne experiments are an indicator of this phenomenon. It is therefore imperative that the policies and wage structure are fair, merit and hard work is appreciated and adequately rewarded, conducive work environment is provided and healthy industrial relations are promoted. Essence of participation, fairness and justice would facilitate the efforts to augment productivity.

Finally, productivity is influenced to a large extent by the government policies. Ever since independence, for a long time the controls and restrictions led to stunted competition and hindered the growth of economy. With liberalization and globalization, these controls are being reduced thereby resulting in increased competition, better technology, optimal use of resources and a better economic and business environment. Thus, it is clear that a system is being developed where all the forces are working towards increasing the levels of productivity, both at macro as well as micro-levels. As per the systems approach, a plan can become effective only if all the related sub-systems are kept in mind. Therefore, all sectors of the economy should undergo a detailed scrutiny and proper analysis, if a meaningful program on productivity management is to be formulated. Thus, it is important to have a productivity policy at a national level and a programme of productivity improvement at the level of each organization. It was rightly stated by Peter F. Drucker, a few decades ago, "Without productivity goals, a business has no direction and without productivity measurement a business has no control."

This book covers an analysis of global competitive scenario and productivity trends and strategies for its improvement in all sectors of the economy, i.e., primary, secondary and tertiary sectors. Considering the global competitive scenario, India with low productivity levels in various sectors, stands at the cross-road in world markets. In this respect, the following observations of Dr. Satya Paul, Chairman, Apeejay Education Society not only provided the right direction but also are a source of great inspiration: ". . . it is not a disgrace if dreams are unfulfilled but it is, if we have no dreams to dream! It is not a calamity if we don't reach the stars, but it is, if we have no stars to reach".

B.S. BHATIA
BALRAM DOGRA

Section I

CONCEPTUAL

Productivity-Centric Global Competitiveness

BALRAM DOGRA AND RAJESH VERMA

INTRODUCTION

The globalization of the economy is going on at a fast pace. This rapid move towards greater integration of the world economy is fuelled by a number of distincts yet interdependent forces : the spreading political decisions of countries to move towards liberalization and adoption of market-oriented economies, the free flow of capital through direct foreign investments, the very rapid technological change especially in information and communication technology, and the vast improvements in transport systems.

The forces fuelling globalization are creating new production and market structure. The phenomenon of globalized manufacturing characterized by global commodity and value chains is getting widespread. The network form of enterprise, where the product or service is produced and distributed by a network of enterprises, each contributing to the production and distribution according to their respective core competencies, is the emerging production system. Flexible production processes and structure are increasingly required by very dynamic markets where product life is very short and where very discerning customers with higher purchasing power and more differentiated and international tastes are demanding much more product variety, high quality and value for money. Thus, in the increasingly globalized economy, competitiveness means the ability to constantly take the most advantageous position or niche in the rapidly changing market environment. The major determinants of the ability to sell products and services are no longer relative costs advantage alone but more and more, competitiveness is based on quality, speed, technical superiority, service and product differentiation. But the underlying determinant of competitiveness, whether at national, sectoral or enterprise level, remains raising total productivity which combines the notion of efficiency and effectiveness. It is no wonder then, that the factors that improve competitiveness of nations and enterprises are similar and parallel to the factors that are very important in improving total productivity.

COMPETITIVENESS OF ENTERPRISES

With globalization, enterprises are now faced with new competitiveness requirements. These are brought about by :

The Globalization of Competition

With the spreading trade liberalization and deregulation, there is now closer integration of domestic and international markets. Thus, enterprises not only face increased competition in their export markets but even in the domestic markets must cope with the competition from imported products that can now easily enter the country. The increasing significance of electronic commerce is also contributing to the rapid integration of markets.

Better Informed Customers

The advances in international communication, increased access to knowledge and information, and the increased integration of markets have led to internationalization of consumer's demands and preferences. This is resulting in very discriminating customers who are demanding more product differentiation and specialization. The fads and fashion not only spread rapidly across the globe but also shift and change very quickly. The rapid advance in information and production technology makes product obsolescence very fast. The product variety is thus increasing but the product life cycle is decreasing.

Increasing Number of Competitors

With countries moving towards trade liberalization and adopting export-oriented development—from import substitution strategies—many of their enterprises are entering international and the liberalized national markets.

Rapid Advances in Technological Capabilities

This enables more enterprises to adopt production and organizational systems that improve the capacity to produce products and services at lower costs, improve quality and increase speed of delivery.

Advances in New Scientific Fields

The fast developments in fields such as electronics, biotechnology, materials science, etc. are resulting in the increased flow of new products and services that substitute for or totally replace existing ones. This further accelerates product obsolescence mentioned earlier.

An enterprise's competitive advantage is developed through improvements in the way it organizes and performs its sourcing, production and distribution activities (Porter, 1990). It acquires strong competitive position by creating and offering products and services of better or superior value to its customers. This, it can achieve through better management and performance of what is called the value-chain of the enterprise : the sourcing and organizing of inbound inputs, the production operations which transform these inputs into products and services needed by the target markets, the organization and management of outbound distribution, marketing and sales, and the provision of after-sales services to ensure that customers enjoy the full value of its products and services.

In such an environment, speed, product differentiation, technical innovation, organizational flexibility, and good customer orientation are increasingly becoming important competitive tools in addition to costs and quality focus. To meet these new terms of competition, enterprises must build competitive advantage based on innovation in soft and hard technology, industrial upgrading, flexibility, agility and adaptability, and improved total productivity using strategies like customer orientation, better HRM policies, networking and alliances, etc.

Customer Orientation

The improvement of the enterprise's value chain start from determining what the customer wants. Thus, with the more discerning and demanding customers of varied and rapidly changing requirements, enterprises have realized the importance of increasing their customer orientation. They must always be able to meet the needs, desires and expectations of their customers. This may call for rapid product development, frequent changes in product models and types, a broader range of products, and even production according to specifications of a particular buyer. With the rapid change of technology, the needs and requirements of customers, whether it be industrial or end-consumers, is very dynamic and volatile. An enterprise must have the flexibility and competence to cater to this very dynamic market.

Flexibility and Agility

An enterprise develops and acquires the flexibility and competencies needed through strategies that involve :

(a) The development and strengthening of internal core competencies and capabilities, simplifying structures, improving lateral interactions and coordination and improving internal communication;

(b) The outsourcing of standard and specialized competencies through practices such as outright purchasing of standard parts and sub-contracting of specialized parts and services, including the use of business service suppliers, temporary workers, home-work and geographical relocation of particular jobs and activities; and

(c) The acquisition and quasi-internalization of complementary competencies and capabilities through various forms of cooperative relations with other enterprises such as partnership, networking and alliances.

Human Resource Management

Enterprise competitiveness is based more and more on the quality of the human resource of the enterprise. Good human resource management thus becomes an important cornerstone of an enterprise's competitiveness strategy. Being an integral part of the strategic management of the enterprise, the various HRM policies, functions and practices should contribute to the creation and sustenance of the enterprise's competitive advantage. Thus, the development of the culture of productivity and creativity, the building-up of mutual trust and shared values, initiative and self-management, multi-skilling and skills upgrading and continuous learning must always be priority goals of the various HRM functions of human resource planning, staffing, and allocation; human resource utilization; human resource development; and motivating and commitment-building.

Trust and shared values appear as central mechanism for work coordination and control in a flexible enterprise. When work is complex and constantly changing, direct control based on supervision becomes too expensive and unwieldy, and bureaucratic control based on work standardization and rigid systems and procedures and rules and regulations is not workable and can be counter-productive. Organizations must rely more on self-management. This form of internalized control is built on mutual trust and confidence, shared values, and common understanding and acceptance of the organization's or corporate objectives, philosophies, priorities and norms. In this sense, the importance of information sharing becomes very important. Committed, motivated and capable employees at all levels are essential to gaining sustained competitive advantage.

DEVELOPING DISTINCTIVE COMPETENCE AND PROPRIETARY TECHNOLOGIES

In an era of rapid technological development, enterprises gain competitive advantage through offering unique product and services, development of distinctive competence and proprietary technologies. A strategy towards productivity and competitiveness therefore is promoting organizational capacity and adaptability to exploit the full potential of new technology to improve efficiency, develop new products and services and unleash the creativity and innovation of the workforce. Efforts need not be just in research and development to develop cutting-edge technologies, but it must also be in the adaptation of already existing hard and soft technology to build-up distinctive technical competence and develop superior products and services. Introducing technology alone however, is not sufficient. More than ever before, people are the most important resource in the new knowledge-based economy. The benefits of new technology can only be fully realized if it is introduced together with new forms of work organization and continuous training.

Better Supply Chain Management

The product or service that an enterprise sells to a customer is the result of a series of activities that involve bringing together the inputs required, manufacturing these inputs into the enterprise's products, transporting these products to wholesalers and distributors, bringing them to the customer through retailing and other outlets, and providing after sales services as required. The supply chain is made-up of segments : the up-stream segments made-up of suppliers of raw-materials, components, services, consumables, etc., the internal supply-chain made-up of the various departments and units involved in the production of the products or services, and the down-stream segment made-up of distributors, wholesalers, retailers and providers of after-sale service. Improved value to customers can be achieved through the improvement in the various segments of the chain, as well as in completely redesigning the supply chain.

An enterprise can significantly improve its internal productivity by focusing on those things it can do well and sub-contracting or outsourcing the other activities to other firms who could do them better. In the situation where an enterprise relies on network of suppliers and service provider, the effectiveness and efficiency of the enterprise is very much affected and is very much dependent on the way it manages the supply chain. Improving collective productivity of an enterprise's supply chain requires (Poirier, 1997) :

- Carefully analysing the enterprise's business, and its operations strategy, how it can deliver the best value to its customer, and then deciding what to out-source and what products or parts to produce and/or activities to undertake internally within the enterprise;
- Careful selection of suppliers and down-stream distribution and sales channels;
- Establishing close collaboration and cooperation with suppliers and service providers to ensure that they meet the volume, quality and time requirements;
- Assisting in building the competencies of the various parties in the supply chain; and

- Ensuring that wastes in time, materials, money and other resources are minimized throughout the enterprise's supply chain.

Networking and Alliances

One way for enterprises to improve their flexibility, acquire new technical and managerial competencies, increase leverage of their internal resources, and achieve speed in bringing product to market from market research, product development to distribution and retailing is through entering into networks and alliances with other enterprises. Through cooperation and collaboration with other enterprises—even with those in the same business and competitors—an enterprise could access new market opportunities and sources of needed inputs; concentrate and perform only those activities and functions that it can do most productively and quickly; have better access to new technology and innovation; learn and access new managerial practices and organizational systems; increase speed of the product cycle; and improve overall productivity.

The networking relationships between and among firms can be formal or informal. It can be vertical relationships such as those formed by firms engaged in complementary activities and those that form supply chain relationships, and horizontal relationship involving firms engaged in similar or competing activities. Strategic alliances can be entered into, agreeing with other firms to combine efforts to pursue a competitive advantage that neither of the parties to the alliance could accomplish or achieve alone. The partners in the alliance contribute complementary products, market presence, distribution networks, production facilities, skills and technologies, etc. Strategic alliance is usually limited in space (e.g. for activities in a specific country), in time (i.e. for a specific period only), and purpose (e.g. they may be on technology but not on markets, or *vice versa*).

To obtain maximum benefits and minimize the risks and hidden costs of networking and alliances, the enterprises entering into the relationship must undertake careful analysis. They must address a number of critical questions such as what the enterprise's core competencies are, its strength and weaknesses and what peripheral capabilities must it seek from the external environment; how the network will be governed, share influence and responsibilities; and where the competitive advantage will be created through networking.

Sustaining the Enterprise's Competitive Advantage

The sustainability of the competitive advantage of an enterprise is dependent on the nature of the major source of its present advantage over the competitors. There is a hierarchy or level of sources of competitive advantage in terms of sustainability. Lower order sources of advantage such as low labour costs or cheap raw materials are relatively easy to imitate or acquire by competitors. Higher order advantages such as proprietary processes and technology, product differentiation based on unique product or services, brand reputation based on cumulative marketing efforts, and customer relationships protected by high costs to the customer of switching vendors, are more durable. These higher order advantages are created through sustained and cumulative investment in physical facilities, human resource development, research and development, and/or marketing activities. Competitive advantage is therefore sustained through constant improvement and upgrading. In order to sustain its competitive advantage, an enterprise must become a moving target, creating new advantages at least as fast as competitors can replicate old ones. To remain competitive, an enterprise must constantly destroy old advantages to create new, higher-order ones (Porter, 1990).

COMPETITIVENESS OF NATIONS

Nations do not compete as enterprises do. Rather, nations compete in creating the conditions that attract and encourage investors—foreign and domestic alike—to invest in productive and competitive enterprises within their borders (and even for local enterprise to invest abroad, if that will enhance international presence and market proximity and responsiveness). A country competes through creating the policy framework that encourage and enable its enterprise to constantly upgrade themselves and keep on improving their productivity, and by putting in place programmes and incentive packages that help and enable its enterprises to develop competitive advantages and pursue competitive strategies for successful participation in international markets.

Reports that rank countries according to competitiveness are getting widespread attention by policy-makers and economic actors in both developing and developed countries. The World Competitiveness Yearbook of the International Institute of Management Development based in Lausanne, Switzerland uses eight major groups of factors/principles to rank a nation's ability to encourage and sustain the competitiveness of its enterprises. Similarly, the Global Competitiveness Report published annually by the World Economic Forum also makes use of eight clusters of structural characteristics of national economies in constructing the competitiveness index used in ranking the competitiveness of the countries covered. The Report looks at international competitiveness as the ability of a nation's economy to make rapid and sustained gains in living standard (Sachs, J., Stone, G. and Warne, A., 1996). The competitiveness index thus aims to gauge the ability of a national economy to achieve sustained high rates of economic growth. It attempts to measure growth potential on a horizon of five to ten years, offering an assessment of economic conditions for medium-term growth.

A detailed scrutiny of the clusters of factors—and the sub-factors within them—used by the two competitiveness reports show that, over-all, the two cover the same general issues that are deemed to influence "national competitiveness" (O'Neill, 1997). These factors are :

(a) Internationalization or openness of the economy,
(b) Domestic economy and government involvement and policies including legal and regulatory environment and institutions of civil society,
(c) Financial institutions including their size and transparency, (physical infrastructure, environment and energy),
(d) Management skills,
(e) Science and technology capability and facilities, and
(f) People including skills and access to education, unemployment levels, working hours, welfare and social services, equality of opportunity, quality of life, and attitudes to work.

Systemic Competitiveness

The most competitive countries therefore have what Esser (1996) call systemic competitiveness. Industrial competitiveness is the result of the complex and dynamic interaction among factors at four social and economic levels in a national economy : at the meta, macro, meso and micro-levels.

At the meta-level are the socio-economic, cultural and political factors that are essential to competitiveness such as :

- A development-oriented cultural values which include social recognition of economic success, priority for long-term investment in knowledge and skills acquisition, a positive work ethics and pride in work and performance, and propensity to save;
- A basic consensus on the necessity of industrial development and competitive integration into the world market; and
- The ability of the social actors to jointly formulate visions and strategies and to implement agreed upon strategies and policies; this implies mechanisms and institutions for entrepreneurs, employers, workers and other concerned members of the society to develop shared visions on areas such as which position should be targeted in the international division of labour, which comparative advantage should be developed in the long-run, and how profits and costs of market integration should be distributed among social groups, etc.

At the macro-level, the key ingredient for competitiveness is a stable and predictable macro-economic framework. Such a framework should lead to the creation of well functioning markets that are essential for the effective and efficient allocation of resources. This policy framework includes a realistic exchange-rate policy, a general foreign trade policy that stimulate local industries, competition policy, and a fiscal and budgetary policy geared for growth and stability. The macro framework should encourage or require the country's enterprises to be effective and efficient.

At the meso-level, the key factors for competitiveness are specific policies and institutions that help industries to suit to their environment and create competitive advantage. There are two sets of meso-level factors :

- Meso-level institutions, both private and governmental, which offer services and support to enterprises and help build the development of human capital and technological infrastructure; and
- Selective and targeted policies aimed to shape and strengthen competitiveness of certain sectors (industrial structure, trade patterns, technology development and acquisition, human resource development, supportive infrastructures, etc.)

An important element at the meso-level is the legal and regulatory framework affecting the establishment and operations of enterprises. A legal and regulatory framework that imposes undue and excessive administrative and financial burden on enterprises affect adversely their capacity to compete. Another important element is effective channels and media of communication that facilitate the flow of information and exchange of ideas among key stakeholders and actors, relevant social groups, organizations and institutions.

At the micro-level, factors that determine enterprises competitiveness (in terms of costs, quality, product specificity, speed and responsiveness) are : entrepreneurial and managerial competencies; quality of the human resource; organization of production, including process and organizational innovations; organization of product development; organization of the value-chain; and cooperation networks and alliances, among others.

A MODEL OF THE RELATION BETWEEN FIRM'S COMPETITIVENESS STRATEGIES AND NATION'S COMPETITIVENESS

Theoretically, a competitive firm constantly monitors the environment in which it competes in order to learn the appropriateness of its offerings to its target customers. As the customers' needs and perceptions on the firm's and/or its competitors' offerings constantly change, it is imperative to routinely evaluate one's competitive status and make timely decisions on needed modifications to offerings. The net effect could be a reduction in the defection rate (percentage of customer switching to other service providers) as well as an increase in the capturing (new customer) rate.

With the right quality, customers will be more responsive by continuing patronage and spreading goodwill. Such responses enhance the effectiveness of a firm's operation and lead to customer satisfaction. It is expected that a competitive organization is aware of what customers want and enjoys a greater operating effectiveness because of quality offered and greater satisfaction to customers. Conversely, understanding what customers do not want can result in greater efficiency, reduce waste in management and manufacturing, and enhance competitive advantage. Operating effectiveness yields higher quality and customer loyalty. Cost efficiency leads to lower cost and competitive advantage in price. For most organizations, employees and assets are two major resources that managers can utilize to yield higher cost efficiency. A company may acquire cost advantage over its main competitors by utilizing its human and asset resources more efficiently. For example, an organization that can generate more sales from each employee than its competitors will enjoy higher cost efficiency and, possibly, higher profitability. Similarly, managers who create more sales or turnover from available assets will benefit from a cost advantage. As a resūlt, a favourable combination of operating effectiveness and cost efficiency will result in greater productivity for a competitive firm.

Through consistent cost effective operations and operating efficiency, customers will be more responsive by continuing patronage and spreading goodwill, which will attract new customers also. Further due to retention and addition of customers cash inflows to the company will be accelerated leading to increase in its earnings.

If firms in one industry are continuously competitive, promote a sustainable development of industry, which further provides competitiveness to the nation as shown in Figure 1.

STRATEGIES FOR ENHANCING NATIONAL PRODUCTIVITY AND COMPETITIVENESS

In the same vein, national productivity results from the intimate interaction of factors at the meta, macro, meso and micro-levels. At the meta-level are the socio-cultural factors that influence values and attitudes towards productive and quality work. It includes the capacity of the society to achieve strategic concentration towards common national development objectives. At the macro-level are the macro-economic policies that create the conducive and enabling economic environment that encourages and demands from the economic actors and enterprises to be productive and competitive. At the meso-levels are the supportive micro-economic policies and governmental and private institutions that are implementing programmes to help sectors and enterprises improve their productivity. At the micro-level are the enterprises who, through various efforts like managerial capability building, workers' skill and competency development, improvements in the production process and structures, alliances and networking, etc. are making productivity and competitiveness improvement a reality.

Many countries, faced with the opportunities created by globalization as well as by increased competition in the international and domestic markets are initiating national productivity movements or drives. These are concerted efforts aimed at creating the conditions for a sustained and continuing productivity improvement of the various economic activities of the country. National productivity movements or drives vary from country to country as they must address situations and priorities dictated by particular country's needs and development strategies. Invariably though,

Fig. 1.1
Model of the Relation between Firm's Competitiveness Strategies and Nation's Competitiveness

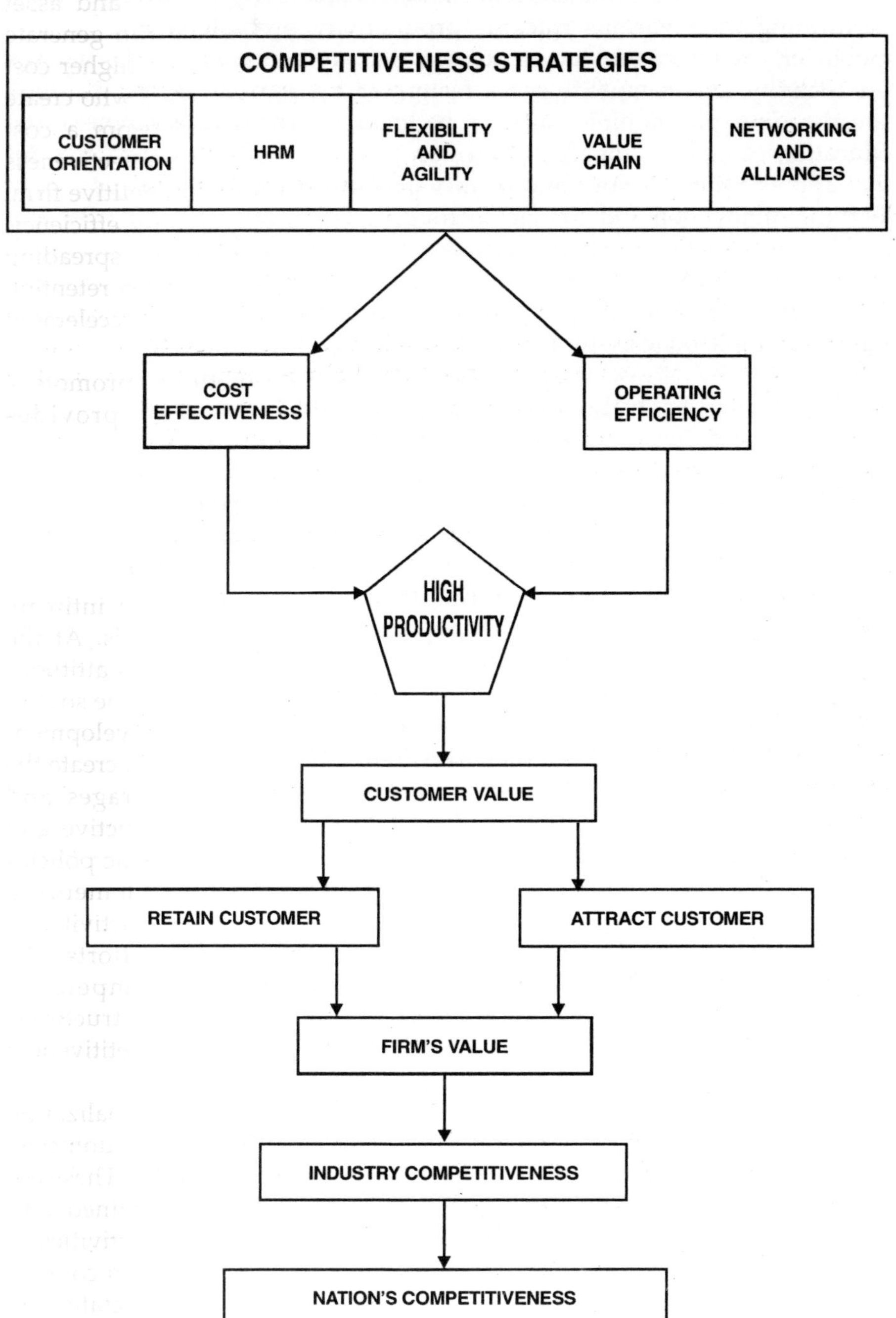

such a concerted action for productivity improvement must deal with the meta, macro, meso and micro-level factors important to productivity and competitiveness. Among the most important meso institutions are the National Productivity Councils and National Productivity Organizations. By performing their various roles as productivity promoters, catalyst and mobilizer, capability builder, etc. they in fact influence and strengthen the productivity and competitiveness factors at the various levels. Through spearheading programmes such as national productivity awareness and education campaigns they help develop the national values and attitudes that appreciate good work and quality performance and are supportive of learning, innovation and change. Through mobilization of a tripartite and multi-sectoral national productivity drive, they create the mechanisms and institution for national concerted efforts towards productivity improvement. By initiating and assisting in the review and formulation of macro and micro-economic policies, they help create the conducive and enabling policy environment. By networking and helping other institutions, they help build a strong supportive institutional infrastructure. And through their training, consulting and information services they help enterprises acquire the managerial and workers' capabilities to effect and implement the "high road" to productivity and competitiveness improvement. Through their pioneering of new productivity improvement approaches and capability building in industry, they help improve the production processes and build the human competencies essential to continuing productivity and competitiveness improvement. Through the promotion of participatory approaches to productivity improvement, they help improve the quality of jobs.

The specific roles and functions of a national productivity organization will vary from country to country and will depend on its assigned mandate, needs of its clients, stages in the countries economic development, cultural and social environment, and the quality of its leadership. However, despite the diversity across countries, it is possible and useful to identify the most common roles. These are :

(a) Those dealing with attitudinal change and developing awareness among people involved in productivity improvement;
(b) Improving the performance capability of enterprises through upgrading management competence, corporate organization and management systems, improving HRM and HRD and enhancing performance of the enterprise as a whole;
(c) Promoting productivity initiative among organizations through networking between research and educational institutions and enterprises, developing better cooperation between trade unions and employers, and promoting productivity improvement programmes to enterprises; and
(d) Helping create the policy and regulatory environment for productivity improvement through assessing economic and

business policies and regulations and their impact on productivity and competitiveness, providing advisory services on upgrading various productivity factors such as energy supply, transportation, technology and removing systemic barriers hindering productivity improvement.

References

Das, Ranjan (2000) : "Crafting the Strategy : Concepts and Cases in Strategic Management", Tata McGraw Hill, 2000.

Esser, K., Hillebrand, D., Messner, D. and Meyer-Stamer, J. (1996) : "Systemic Competitiveness : A New Challenge for Firms and for Governments", CEPAL Review, No. 59, August 1996, Economic Commission for Latin America, 1996.

Johnson, Gerry (1999) : "Exploring Corporate Strategy", 4th ed., Prentise Hall, 1999.

Kazmi, Azar (2002) : "Business Policy and Strategic Management", 2nd ed., Tata McGraw Hill, 2002.

O'Neill, H. (1997) : "Globalization, Competitiveness and Human Security : Challenges for Development Policy and Institutional Change", *The European Journal of Development Research*, Vol. 9, No. 1, June 1977, Frank Case, London.

Poirier, C. (1997) : "Evolving to the Ultimate Level of Performance through Supply Chain Management", *National Productivity Review*, John Wiley & Sons, Winter 1997.

Porter, M. (1990) : "The Competitive Advantage of Nations", The Free Press, 1990.

Sachs, J., Stone, G., and Warner, A. (1996) : "Why Competitiveness Counts", The Global Competitiveness Report, 1996, *World Economic Forum*, Geneva, 1996.

http ://europa.eu.int/comm/internal_market

http ://cber.nlu.edu/DBR

http ://www01.imd.ch/wcy/

Trends in Global Competitiveness of India During Post-Liberalization Period

PARAMJIT NANDA AND P.S. RAIKHY

The thrust of New Economic Policy (1991) is towards creating more competitive environment for improving productivity and efficiency in Indian economy. Industrial Policy changes were designed to bring about a greater competitive environment, domestically and the trade policy aimed to improve international competitiveness. The concept of competitiveness implies : (i) production of goods and services based on new technologies (ii) capacity to increase market share in world trade, and (iii) a move towards trade surplus. The competitiveness of country is affected by price as well as non-price factors. It is difficult to measure non-price factors (quality, design, marketing, consumer services, after sale services and delivery dates, etc.). An attempt has therefore been made in this chapter to study global competitiveness of India with respect to 14 competitors in respect of price factors during period 1984 to 1997 and to study the impact of global competitiveness on India's exports from 1984 to 2001-02.

The chapter has been divided into three sections. Section I is devoted to database and methodology. Section II examines global competitiveness of India with reference to its competitors in the light of different measures. Section III studies the impact of global competitiveness as measured by different indicators on export performance of India.

I

To measure global competitiveness of India, following measures have been considered.

1. Relative consumer price index,
2. Relative export unit value index,
3. Relative export unit value index of manufactured exports,
4. Relative wholesale price index,
5. Relative unit labour cost, and
6. Profitability index—Three measures of profitability index, viz. export profitability index, manufactured export profitability index and import substitution index have been considered.

For the purpose of comparability, data are in relative terms, in index form and in common currency dollar (except profitability index, which is in Rs. terms). Fourteen competitors have been considered on the basis of share in world's exports and share in manufactured exports during the period 1996 to 1999. These competitors are : Belgium, China, Hong Kong, Canada, France, Germany, Italy, Japan, Korea Rep., Mexico, Netherlands, Singapore, U.K. and USA. The study period relates to pre-Liberalization period, i.e. from 1984 to 1990 and post-liberalization period (1990 to 1997) so as to bring out the impact of liberalization policies.

Various indicators of global competitiveness have been explained as under :

1. Relative Consumer Price Index

$$RCP = \frac{CP_i}{CPc} \times 100$$

where CP_i = Consumer price index of India,
and CPc = Geometric weighted average of consumer price index of selected competitors.

2. Relative Unit Value Index of Exports

$$RUVX = \frac{UVX_i}{UVMXc} \times 100$$

where UVX_i = Export unit value index of India,
and UVMXc = Geometric weighted average unit value index of exports of selected competitors.

3. Relative Unit Value Index of Manufactured Exports

$$RUVMX = \frac{UVMX_i}{UVMX_C} \times 100$$

where $UVMX_i$ = Unit value index of manufactured exports of India,
and UVMXc = Geometric weighted average of Unit value index of manufactured exports of selected competitors.

4. Relative Wholesale Price Index

$$RWP = \frac{WP_i}{WP_C} \times 100\ WP_C$$

where WP_i = Wholesale price index of India,
and WP_C = Geometric weighted average of wholesale price index of selected competitors.

5. Relative Unit Labour Cost in Manufacturing

$$RULCM = \frac{ULCM_i}{ULCM_C} \times 100$$

where $ULCM_i$ = Unit labour cost in manufacturing of India,
and $ULCM_C$ = Geometric weighted average of unit labour cost in manufacturing of selected competitors.

Unit labour cost in manufacturing has been calculated by quotient of labour cost per worker in manufacturing to value-added per worker in manufacturing.

6. Relative Profitability Index (RP)

Three measures of "relative profitability index" of India have been calculated in following ways :

(i) $$RP = \frac{UVMX_i}{WPM_i} \times 100$$

where $UVMX_i$ = Unit value index of manufactured exports of India,
and WPM_i = wholesale price index of manufactured goods of India.

(ii) $$RP = \frac{UVMM_i}{Wp_i} \times 100$$

where $UVMM_i$ = Unit value index of Imports of manufactures of India
and Wp_i = Wholesale price index of India

(iii) $$RP = \frac{UVX_i}{Wp_i} \times 100$$

where UVXi = Unit value index of exports of India,
and Wp_i = Wholesale price index of India. The indices of relative profitability use in Rs. terms.

Geometric weighted average index of each variable of selected competitors has been calculated in following way :

$$\Sigma w_n \sqrt{(P_1^1/P_0^1)\, w_1 * (P_1^2/P_0^2)\, w_2 * (P_1^3/P_0^3) w_3 (P_1^n/P_0^n) w_n)}$$

where P_i and P_0 represent the value of an index in current year and the base year and 1, 2, 3 .... n is number of countries and w_1, w_2, w_3 ... w_n is weight. To calculate weight, average of three years (1996-97 to 1999-00) trade flows of India to these selected competitors was considered. From the total average of trade flows of these competitors, the share of each competitor has been calculated for estimating its respective weight.

TREND CO-EFFICIENT

Linear trends in each relative index of global competitiveness of India were worked out by fitting function of type

$$Y_{it} = A + Bt$$

where Y—Relevant index of global competitiveness of India, t—time (1984 to 1990 and 1990 to 1997), and B= trend value.

II

Global competitiveness of India in terms of different variables and its trend values have been explained as under :

1. Relative Consumer Price Index

An analysis of relative consumer price index of India and its competitors given in Table 2.1 shows that India and China were found to be most competitive in terms of consumer price index during eighties. But the trend was reversed during nineties. These two nations became least competitive during nineties (China during late nineties). Maxico was found to be least competitive in terms of consumer price index (Value ranging between 123 in 1991 to 364 in 1997). Relative consumer price index of India with preference to fourteen competitors has been continuously increasing, indicating decrease in global competitiveness of India. Index increased from 79.93 in 1994 to 108.96 in 1991 and further to 156.59 in 1997. Trend coefficient is also found to be positive and significant (at 1% level) in both periods, indicating that India lost global competitiveness at a significant rate.

2. Export Unit Value Index

Table 2.2 shows that India, which was globally most competitive in terms of export unit value index during 80's turned out to be least

TABLE 2.1
Trends in Relative Consumer Price Indices of India and its Competitors

(In Dollar terms) 1990=100

Countries	1984	1985	1986	1987	1988	1989	1990	1991	1992	1993	1994	1995	1996	1997
India	63	66	72	78	85	92	100	114	121	136	150	165	180	193
Belgium	89	92	93	93	94	97	100	103	106	109	111	113	115	117
Canada	80	83	87	91	91	95	100	106	107	109	109	112	114	115
China	53	60	64	70	85	99	100	105	113	133	166	194	210	—
Hong Kong	69	71	73	77	83	91	100	112	122	133	143	156	165	175
France	82	86	89	91	170	177	100	103	106	108	110	112	114	115
Germany	—	—	—	—	—	—	100	100	105	110	113	115	117	119
Italy	69	76	80	84	88	94	100	106	112	117	121	128	133	136
Japan	92	93	94	94	94	97	100	103	105	106	107	137	107	109
Korea Republic	75	77	79	81	87	92	100	109	116	122	129	135	142	148
Mexico	—	—	—	—	66	79	100	123	142	156	166	125	202	364
Netherlands	94	97	98	55	97	98	100	103	106	109	112	114	117	119
Singapore	94	94	93	53	95	97	100	103	106	108	112	114	115	117
UK	70	75	77	80	85	91	100	106	110	112	114	118	121	125
USA	79	82	84	87	91	95	100	104	107	111	113	117	120	125
Global Competitiveness of India in terms of Consumer Price Index														
a.	—	—	—	—	—	—	100	109.24	114.63	120.64	126.79	3i.73	144.99	156.46
b.	79.93	80.78	85.44	90. 64	91.87	34.62	100	108.86	116.86	120.32	125.61	i:c.26	144.65	156.59

Trend Co-efficients	Pre-liberalization Period	Post-liberalization Period
a.	—	7.61214* US = 11
b.	3.3685* (13.849)	7.63536* (22.869)

Note : a denotes all fourteen countries, b excludes Germany. Figures in parenthesis indicate t-values, * significant at 1 percent level.
Source : United Nations, *Statistical Year Book* (1995 and 2000).

TABLE 2.2

Trends in Relative Export Unit Value Indices of India and its Competitors

(In Dollar terms) 1990=100

Countries	*1984*	*1985*	*1986*	*1987*	*1988*	*1989*	*1990*	*1991*	*1992*	*1993*	*1994*	*1995*	*1996*	*1997*
India	55	58	56	76	78	93	100	111	142	155	168	167	157	—
Belgium	104	106	94	90	96	103	100	98	97	95	94	97	97	101
Canada	93	94	94	93	98	101	100	96	99	103	110	119	120	120
China	—	—	—	—	—	—	—	—	—	—	—	—	—	—
Hong Kong	—	—	—	—	93	98	100	103	104	103	105	108	108	106
France	95	98	94	93	96	102	100	100	97	94	100	102	102	103
Germany	97	102	98	96	96	101	100	99	99	94	93	95	93	94
Italy	83	90	86	87	92	98	100	103	104	115	120	131	179	178
Japan	115	115	97	91	90	97	100	100	100	96	95	94	101	105
Korea Republic	73	71	75	79	103	97	100	104	109	111	114	116	104	—
Mexico	—	—	—	—	—	—	100	92	92	89	—	—	—	—
Netherlands	117	121	102	93	94	101	100	98	95	92	92	94	94	100
Singapore	129	113	97	101	100	100	100	88	86	83	82	81	80	88
UK	94	99	91	95	92	97	100	101	103	116	118	125	128	116
USA	89	87	88	90	97	99	100	101	101	101	104	109	109	108
Global Competitiveness of India in terms of Export unit value index														
a.	—	—	—	—	100	111.27	142.29	154.56	—	—	—	—	—	
b.		—	—	81.95	93.7	100	—	—	—	164.5	157.68	145.53	—	
c.	57.02	59.61	61.57	81.82	93.68	100	111.47	142.71	154.29	168.55	157.87	145.95	—	

*Trend Co-efficients**	*Pre-liberalization Period*	*Post-liberalization period*
c.	7.7617 (8.377)	9.1603 (2.851)

Note : a excludes China, b excludes China and Mexico, c excludes China, Hong Kong and Mexico. Figures in parentheses indicate t-values, * significant at 1 percent level.

Source : United Nations, *Statistical Year Book* (1995 and 2000).

competitive during 90's. However, lesser competitive nations like Netherlands, Germany (after 1986) and Singapore during 80's turned out to be most competitive during 90's. Japan, France and Belgium were also found to be least competitive during 80's. Relative export unit value index of India with respect to its competitors has been increasing since 1984 (except 1995 and 1996). The value of index increased from 57.02 in 1984 to 168.55 in 1994 and then decreased to 145.53 in 1996, indicating loss in global competitiveness in this variable. Trend coefficient was positive and significant during pre-liberalization period, but positive and non-significant during post-liberalization period, indicating that global competitiveness of India was lost at significant rate during pre-liberalization period and at non-significant during post-liberalization period.

3. Export Unit Value Index of Manufactures

In terms of export unit value index of manufactured exports indicated in Table 2.3 shows that India was found to be most competitive throughout the study period. Japan and USA have remained least competitive since 1984. Canada was found to be least competitive during eighties, while Singapore and UK during nineties. Relative export unit value index of manufacturers of India with respect to its competitors increased by the end of eighties but declined afterwards, indicating erosion of global competitiveness of India during this period and improvement in global competitiveness during nineties. Index increased from 61.77 in 1984 to 100 in 1990 and decreased to 77.82 in 1997. Trend Co-efficient was found to be positive and significant (at 10 percent level) during pre-liberalization period and negative but insignificant during post-liberalization period, indicating that global competitiveness was eroded during pre-liberalization period but improved at non-significant rate during post-liberalization period.

4. Relative Wholesale Price Index

Global competitiveness measured in terms of wholesale price index given in Table 2.4 reflects that most globally competitive India in terms of wholesale price index indicator during eighties turned out to be least competitive during nineties. Least competitive nations, namely, Japan and Singapore during eighties turned to be most competitive during nineties. Korea and Italy were found to be other less competitive nations during nineties. Relative wholesale price index of India with respect to its competitors has been continuously increasing since 1987 (except 1994, when there was marginal decrease). Index increased from 90.51 in 1987 to 179 in 1997 indicating loss in global competitiveness of India. Trend co-efficient is found to be positive and significant during post-liberalization period, indicating that global competitiveness decreased at significant rate.

5. Relative Unit Labour Cost in Manufacturing

Table 2.5 showing labour cost per unit of output in manufacturing of India and its competitors, reflects that China is found to be globally most

TABLE 2.3

Trends in Relative Export Unit Value Indices of Manufactured Exports of India and its Competitors

(In Dollar terms) 1990=100

Countries	*1984*	*1985*	*1986*	*1987*	*1988*	*1989*	*1990*	*1991*	*1992*	*1993*	*1994*	*1995*	*1996*	*1997*
India	45	48	51	58	69	91	100	80	92	89	88	86	—	—
Belgium	56	58	74	84	90	89	100	97	99	90	93	110	105	96
Canada	91	87	87	89	97	101	100	99	91	88	84	80	83	77
China	—	—	—	—	—	—	100	—	—	—	—	—	—	—
Hong Kong	—	—	—	—	—	—	100	102	104	104	105	108	108	104
France	60	62	73	85	88	86	100	96	100	94	98	111	107	96
Germany	53	55	73	86	88	87	100	98	103	93	94	108	101	87
Italy	54	54	68	80	85	86	100	99	105	89	86	96	98	90
Japan	71	70	84	93	102	101	100	108	115	124	134	144	133	126
Korea Republic	—	—	—	—	—	—	100	101	97	96	98	102	86	85
Mexico	—	—	—	—	—	—	100	—	—	—	—	—	—	—
Netherlands	57	57	71	83	87	86	100	96	102	92	92	100	102	—
Singapore	—	—	—	—	—	—	100	101	103	99	108	112	109	102
UK	58	60	70	81	91	88	100	100	102	98	103	114	113	113
USA	83	85	88	90	95	98	100	102	103	103	104	107	106	108
Global Competitiveness of India in terms of Export Unit Value Index of Manufactured Exports														
a.	—	—	—	—	—	—	100	79.57	89.43	89.69	85.16	78.10	—	—
b.	61. 77	61.10	48.38	58.36	72.48	94.55	100	79.68	89.25	89.86	85.28	77.82	—	—

Trend Co-efficients	*Pre-liberalization period*	*Post-liberalization Period*
a.		-2.6420 (1.572)
b.	7.34607 *** (3.192)	-2.6711 (1.587)

Note : a excludes Mexico and China, b excludes Singapore, Mexico, Korea, China and Hong Kong.
Figures in parenthesis indicate t-values, *** significant at 10 percent level.

Source : United Nations, *Statistical Year Book* (1995 and 2000).

TABLE 2.4

Trends in Relative Wholesale Price Indices of India and its Competitors

(In Dollar terms) 1990=100

Countries	1984	1985	1986	1987	1988	1989	1990	1991	1992	1993	1994	1995	1996	1997
India	—	—	—	78	84	90	100	113	125	135	152	164	172	179
Belgium	—	—	—	93	93	99	100	99	99	98	99	102	102	104
Canada	—	—	—	—	—	—	—	—	—	—	—	—	—	—
China	—	—	—	—	—	—	—	—	—	—	—	—	—	—
Hong Kong	—	—	—	—	—	—	—	—	—	—	—	—	—	—
France	—	—	—	—	—	—	—	—	—	—	—	—	—	—
Germany	—	—	—	—	—	—	100	101	102	102	104	104	105	103
Italy	—	—	—	84	88	93	100	105	107	113	117	130	232	134
Japan	—	—	—	95	95	97	100	100	99	96	95	94	93	95
Korea Republic	—	—	—	92	94	96	100	105	107	109	112	117	121	125
Mexico	—	—	—	—	—	—	—	—	—	—	—	—	—	—
Netherlands	—	—	—	98	95	98	100	93	92	89	87	87	88	87
UK	—	—	—	—	—	—	—	—	—	—	—	—	—	—
USA	—	—	—	88	92	96	100	100	101	102	104	107	110	110
Global Competitiveness of India in terms of Whole Sale Price Index														
a.	—	—	—	90.51	93.94	95.26	100	111.13	124.6	136.5	145.75	144.84	166.5	171.75
b.	—	—	—	—	—	—	100	111	124.32	136.20	145.58	144.88	166.65	172.56

Trend Co-efficients	*Pre-liberalization Period*	*Post-liberalization Period*
a .	—	10.1079* (15.098)
b.	—	10.2051* (15.564)

Note : a excludes China, Hong Kong, Canada, France, Mexico, Netherlands and UK; b excludes China, Hong Kong, Canada, France, Mexico; Netherlands, UK and Germany. Figures in parenthesis indicate t-values, * significant at 1 percent level.

Source : United Nations, *Statistical Year Book*, (1995 and 2000.

TABLE 2.5
Trends in Relative Labour Cost per Unit of Output in Manufacturing of India and its Competitors

(Dollars)

Countries	1980-84	1990-94	1995-99
India	0.4909	0.3822	0.3822
Belgium	0.2182	0.4897	0.4112
Canada	0.4799	0.4668	0.4681
China	0.1541	0.1504	0.2526
Hong Kong	0.5233	0.6931	0.6931
France	0.6911	0.6375	—
Germany	0.4495	—	0.4173
Italy	—	—	0.6867
Japan	0.3571	0.4331	0.3422
Korea Republic	0.2714	0.3866	0.2625
Mexico	0.2161	0.2361	0.2933
Netherlands	0.6871	0.7018	0.6043
Singapore	0.3391	0.5294	0.5240
UK	0.4614	0.4730	0.3553
USA	0.4040	0.3930	0.4330
Global Competitiveness in terms of Unit Labour Cost of India			
a.	—	—	93.49
b.	129.86	—	—
c.	—	88.04	—
d.	119.2	88.04	96.58
Trend Co-efficient			
Post-liberalization Period	-11.3100 (0.87)		

Note : a excludes France, b excludes Italy, c excludes Germany and Italy, d excludes France, Germany and Italy.

Source : Calculated from data given in World Development Indicators, World Bank (1998, 1999 and 2001).

competitive throughout the study period. During eighties, three competitors, namely, Hong Kong, France and Netherlands were found to be least competitive. Mexico was found to be globally competitive during nineties, while Korea and Japan became globally competitive during late nineties. Relative labour cost index of India with respect to its competitors decreased from 119.2 during eighties to 96.58 during late nineties indicating some improvement in global competitiveness of India in terms of labour cost per unit of output. Trend Coefficient is negative but non-significant indicating that global competitiveness improved at non-significant rate.

6. Profitability Index

Of the three measures of profitability index, first measure of profitability index, i.e. ratio of export unit value index of manufactures to wholesale price index of manufactures provides an incentive to manufactured exporters (if export unit value index is higher than wholesale price index or if value of index is greater than 100). Table 2.6 shows that export profitability index has always remained at low level (value being less than 100) from 1984 to 1996 (except 1991 and 1993), indicating low export profitability of India as compared to domestic profitability. Index showed signs of improvement till 1993 but again declined afterwards. Trend Coefficient was positive and significant during pre-liberalization period, indicating that export profitability increased at a significant rate during this period, while trend coefficient was found to be negative during post-liberalization period, indicating decrease in export profitability during this period.

TABLE 2.6
Profitability Index of India

Year	*I*	*II*	*III*
1984-85	71.3	62.9	88.58
1985-86	71.22	61.66	85.32
1986-87	72.85	52.55	84.81
1987-88	77.42	64.53	84.24
1988-89	83.62	79.94	94.25
1989-90	99.59	97.25	104.50
1990-91	100	100	100.00
1991-92	109.65	95.72	111.00
1992-93	98. 64	125.48	114.90
1993-94	107.59	102.87	119.70
1994-95	95.99	99.82	111.11
1995-96	96.32	122.59	100.59
1996-97	89.23	154.67	100.33
1997-98	—	—	
Trend Coefficients			
Pre-liberalization Period	5.4932* (5.713)	7,4953** (3.951)	2.9307 (2.949)
Post-liberalization Period	-2.20071 (2.048)	6.8603 (2.173)	-0.8435 (-0.526)

Note : Figures in parenthesis indicate t-values, * significant at 1 percent level, ** significant at 5 percent level.

Source : United Nations, *Statistical Year Book,* (1995 and 2000), R.B.I., *Report on Currency and Finance,* GOI, *Economic Survey* (Various Issues).

Second measure of profitability index, i.e., ratio of import unit value of manufactures to domestic wholesale price index indicates incentive for import substitution. Low value of index indicates an improvement in competitiveness, while high value of index indicates an incentive for import substitution. This measure of profitability index has been fluctuating, but has tendency to increase, indicating an incentive for import substitution. The index increased from 62.9 in 1984 to 125.48 in 1991 and further to 154.67 in 1996. Trend coefficient was found to be positive and significant at 5 percent level, indicating erosion of global competitiveness during pre-liberalization period while trend coefficient was positive and non-significant, indicating that global competitiveness was eroded at a non-significant rate during post-liberalization period.

Third measure of profitability index (i.e., ratio of export unit value index to wholesale prices), after showing signs of improvement from 1986 to 1993, declined afterwards (index declined to 100 in 1996), indicating erosion in export profitability during late nineties. Trend co-efficient was found to be positive but non-significant during pre-liberalization period, but negative and non-significant during post-liberalization period, indicating improvement in global competitiveness during pre-liberalization period but erosion during post-liberalization period.

Thus, as compared to pre-liberalization period, during the post-liberalization period, global competitiveness of India improved at a non-significant rate in case of one indicator only, i.e., relative export unit value index of manufactures.

The examination of relationship between different indicators of global competitiveness and quantum index of exports of manufactures, showed that three measures of global competitiveness (relative consumer price index/wholesale price index and relative export unit value index of manufactures) are positively related with quantum index of exports of manufactures, (correlation co-efficient being 0.98, 0.50 and 0.97) indicating that loss in global competitiveness in these variables (i.e., increase in value of these variables) can also lead to increase in quantum index of manufactured exports.

III

India is a marginal player in world trade. Share of India in world exports improved from 0.48 in 1984 to 0.53 in 1986, but experienced only marginal changes till 1996. However, during 1997-99 the share improved at somewhat satisfactory pace. India has not been able to achieve even one percent share in world export. The share of the country in world imports has been fluctuating and reached at highest level in 1998 (0.84 percent) and was at the same level in 1999 as in 1984. India's trade share has increased mainly due to increase in import share as compared to export share (Table 2.7). Share of manufactured exports in India's exports increased from 58.5 percent in 1985-86 to 72.91 percent in 1990-91, 75 percent in 1995-96 and

TABLE 2.7
India's Share in World Exports and Imports

(Percentage)

Year	Exports	Imports	Trade
1984	0.48	0.79	1.27
1985	0.47	0.82	1.29
1986	0.53	0.70	1.23
1987	0.53	0.65	1.18
1988	0.56	0.65	1.21
1989	0.59	0.67	1.26
1990	0.56	0.70	1.26
1991	0.52	0.58	1.10
1992	0.55	0.59	1.14
1993	0.58	0.60	1.18
1994	0.57	0.61	1.18
1995	0.59	0.65	1.24
1996	0.59	0.64	1.23
1997	0.61	0.67	1.28
1998	0.63	0.84	1.47
1999	0.67	0.79	1.46

Source : United Nations, *Statistical Year Book,* 1995 and World Bank, *World Development Report* (Different Issues).

78.98 percent in 2001, indicating that only marginal change has occurred during post-liberalization period. The trade scenario does not appear optimistic, if we consider the rate of increase of exports in dollar terms. Exports could increase at double digit rate only in eight years from 1984-85 to 2001-02, declined in 1985-86, 1991-92 and in 1998-99 while increased at very low rates in 1996-97 and in 1997-98. Export performance is rather poor in post-liberalization period as compared to pre-liberalization period in dollar terms (though in Rs. terms, exports could increase at double digit rate except 1997-98 and 1998-99).

Thus, the study reveals that global competitiveness of India has improved in terms of relative export unit value index of manufactures, ratio of export unit value index to wholesale prices, ratio of export unit value index of manufactures to wholesale price of manufactures during post-liberalization period as compared to pre-liberalization period.

The impact analysis of global competitiveness on exports showed that India has not been able to increase its share in world exports. Moreover,

TABLE 2.8
India's Exports

(Percentage)

Year	Exports in Rupee terms (Rs. Cr.)	Percent Increase in Rupees Terms	Exports in Dollar terms (million $)	Percent Increase in Dollar terms
1984-85	11744	20.2	9878	—
1985-86	10895	-7.2	8904	-9.9
1986-87	12452	14.3	9745	9.4
1987-88	15674	25.9	12089	24.1
1988-89	20232	29.1	13970	15.6
1989-90	27658	36.7	16612	18.9
1990-91	32553	17.7	18143	9.2
1991-92	44041	35.3	17865	-1.5
1992-93	53688	21.9	18537	3.8
1993-94	69751	29.9	22238	20.0
1994-95	82674	18.5	26330	18.4
1995-96	106353	28.6	31797	20.8
1996-97	118817	11.7	33470	5.3
1997-98	130100	9.5	35006	4.6
1998-99	139752	7.4	33218	-5.1
1999-00	159561	14.2	36822	10.8
2000-01	203571	27.6	44560	21.1
2001-02	209018	2.7	43827	-1.6

Source : Government of India, *Economic Survey* (2002-03).

indicators of global competitiveness are not associated with quantum index of exports of manufactures. Thus to increase exports, non-price factors may be given more emphasis. Non-price factors assume importance today in view of imposition of existing as well as new non-tariff barriers (in the form of environment and labour standards) by developed countries in exports of agricultural commodities (fish, meat), textiles (carpets and readymade garments), engineering goods and leather manufactures, use of anti-dumping measures by developed countries and growing tendency towards bilateral agreements. It is feared that India will lose comparative advantage in exports based on factor endowments and in labour-intensive export goods. There is need to strengthen export efforts based on competitive environment. Marketing is most important constituent of export promotion strategy. Exports have to be geographically diversified. There is need to export new products to those markets from where country is facing threats as new products will be less prone to protectionist measures. There is need, for greater customer orientation, high quality, after sale service, reliability, timeliness and competitive prices. To create awareness about quality, variety and price of Indian products, market surveys/exhibitions, show rooms and trade fairs, etc. be organized and trade delegates be sent to prospective markets. Anti-dumping cell should be strengthened so as to take timely and adequate measures to prevent dumping. To meet the challenges of sanitary and phyto-sanitary standards in agriculture sector, Indian exporters should be made fully aware of these standards and these standards should be adopted at initial levels. Eco-friendly products should be produced to meet the requirements. For this purpose, services should be strengthened in areas of information, testing eco-quality control, technical assistance, R & D, education and training of staff and environment management system. In this context, the approach based on BATNEEC (Best Available Technology Not Entailing Excessive Cost) (Sharma, Mahesh, 1994) has been termed as most suitable.

References

CMIE, *Foreign Trade and Balance of Payments*, July 2000.
Government of India, *Economic Survey* (Various Issues).
RBI, *Report on Currency and Finance* (Various Issues).
Sharma, Mahesh (1994), 'Status of Processing of Eco-Textiles in India', Eco-Friendly Textile Challenges to the Textile Industry, Textile Committee, GOI, Ministry of Textiles, Mumbai, p. 61.
United Nations, *Statistical Year Book*, 1995 and 2000.
World Bank, World Development Indicators (Various Issues).

Corporate Reporting on Productivity

B.S. Bhatia and Anurag Pahuja

INTRODUCTION

The ongoing process of liberalization in Indian economy and its rapid integration with the global economy has left Indian industry in a state where either it must excel or exit. If any industrial unit wants to survive, it has to compete successfully both with national and multinational competitors. If one cannot do this, the market forces would show the exit door to such lethargic units. This is because of the growing competition in the corporate world, with competitive forces such as threat of new entrants with substitute products and services, bargaining power of suppliers as well as buyers and rivalry among the existing competitors. So as to have a competitive edge over the competitors, the buzzword is productivity.

Productivity is the measure of how well resources are brought together in an organization and utilized for accomplishing a set of results. It is the highest level of performance with least expenditure of resources.

According to George Kaper, productivity can be expressed as combination of effectiveness and efficiency. Efficiency is related to resource utilization and depicts the relationship between input and output. The effectiveness, on the other hand, is related to the performance and expresses the relationship between output and stated objectives. The productivity measure called Productivity Index may be expressed as :

$$\text{Productivity Index} = \frac{\text{Output obtained}}{\text{Input expensed}}$$

$$= \frac{\text{Performance achieved}}{\text{Resources consumed}}$$

$$= \frac{\text{Effectiveness}}{\text{Efficiency}}$$

In the competitive environment, continuous increase in productivity seems to be an absolute necessity for any organization to survive, be it a manufacturing organization, a service sector organization or even one relating to agriculture sector. Increasing productivity reduces the cost of output, which enables the producers to supply the goods and services at lower prices to the customers without compromising the quality, which can be used as a powerful tool against the competitors. The reason behind the United States competence in the world market has been its productivity.

Business organizations, as an organ of society, have a lot of societal stake in the form of capital, employees and utilization of scarce resources, etc. Its failure will involve huge social and economical cost to the society. On the other hand, its success reflected in its profits will be shared by all the stakeholders, be it the shareholders, employees, customers, government or society in general. So there is always a dire need for not only improving productivity but also to disclose it to various stakeholders particularly society as they are always eager to know about the measures an organization is taking to enhance productivity.

WHY CORPORATE DISCLOSURES?

Today, in the post-liberalization era, business has become a highly complex and collective affair in contrast to simple individual effort requiring a small amount of capital affecting the interest of single individual in the earlier days of its origin. The corporate organizations raise their capital from the public and providers of the capital expect to get fair and adequate disclosure of the state of affairs from the management. This is done through corporate disclosures. The need of disclosure, a process through which a business enterprise communicates with external parties, has grown over a period of time because of the divorce between the ownership and management in the corporate sector enterprises, the increasing complexities and size of organization, the growing awareness of public and their keen interest in the working of business enterprise and the changing socio-economic and potential environment in the country. This disclosure of corporate affairs and its management is done by the companies through their annual reports.

PRESENT REPORTING FRAMEWORK IN INDIA

In India, Companies Act, 1956, the Bureau of Public Enterprises and the Institute of Chartered Accountants of India have laid down some guidelines and are making efforts in effecting improved reporting practices in Indian corporate sector. The financial reporting has become more or less mandatory in the annual reports with specified contents to be disclosed. Thus, reporting of financial performance provides information to various parties interested in making sound financial decisions. But over the time, it has been realized that a company is a social organization and social obligations of a company are as important as its statutory obligations. With this realization, social performance reporting, though not mandatory, started showing its presence in few annual reports. There is no specific provision in the companies Act, 1956, requiring companies to provide social performance reporting in annual report but Sachar Committee has recommended certain items to be included in Director's report.

In continuation, there arose a need for corporate governance (depicting an environment of trust, ethics, moral values and confidence) reporting in annual reports. The corporate governance is expected to result in the creation of a set of transparent relationships between an institution's management, its board, shareholders and other stakeholders. The recommendation of Kumar Mangalam Birla Committee on Corporate Governance have been made mandatory by SEBI in February 2000 through insertion of a new clause 49 in the listing agreement. All listed companies are required to give effect to these mandatory provisions within a time schedule extending up to March 31, 2003.

OBJECTIVES OF THE STUDY

Considering the importance of Productivity reporting, it was decided to take up the issue for detailed investigation of the conceptual and procedural aspects. This paper deals specifically with the following questions related to varied aspects of Productivity Reporting :

- To examine the conceptual aspects relating to Productivity reporting.
- To examine the procedure relating to measurement and presentation of productivity so as to make it useful to management and various stakeholders.
- To identify the scope of Productivity Reporting.
- To develop a suitable format for reporting productivity.

This chapter tends to examine the above issues in the subsequent sections.

Meaning of Productivity Reporting

Productivity reporting aims at ensuring accountability of corporate management towards various stakeholders. It means submitting an appropriate report on the changes in the level of overall productivity as well as various variables responsible for that change. This would require development of an appropriate framework, which is capable of depicting different aspects of productivity in an analytical manner.

Productivity Accounting

Productivity measures an organization's ability to convert labour, capital and material inputs into valued goods and services but the ultimate challenge being faced today is to turn this concept of measurement into a useful framework which management can make use of. The framework will link productivity changes to resources and hence to profitability. Discussing the importance of Productivity measurement, Peter F. Drucker has rightly said, "Without productivity goals a business has no direction and without productivity measurement, a business has no control." Traditional measures of performance have tended to view productivity and profitability as rivals, vying for the attention of management. Accountants have focused solely on profitability, ignoring any attempts to link and integrate productivity measures into their financial systems.

Productivity represents the organization's ability to create wealth (while prices are merely the vehicle for distributing it). Whereas productivity measures are ordinarily based on quantities (of products and resources), profit is based on money values. Here comes the term 'Productivity Accounting' to our rescue. Productivity Accounting offers a mechanism for linking these directly. 'Productivity Accounting measures' the change in total resource productivity, which includes in its purview, labour productivity, materials productivity, capital productivity and energy productivity and the effect of these changes on the corresponding changes in business profitability. Thus, Productivity Accounting seeks to link the change in profit to its underlying causes and change in profit can be described as the sum of two elements :

Change in Profit = Change in Productivity + Change in Price Recovery

$$\text{where, Productivity} = \frac{\text{Product Quantity (Output Quantity)}}{\text{Resource Quantity (Input Quantity)}}$$

$$\text{Price Recovery} = \frac{\text{Product Price (Output Price)}}{\text{Resource Price (Input Price)}}$$

From above, it is clear that the productivity is the measure of the ability to efficiently turn inputs into outputs. A Company with superior process execution has very little waste, i.e., it efficiently utilizes its inputs to give maximum outputs. Whereas price recovery is a measure of structural position or the degree to which a firm is able to capture value it creates through pricing power, i.e., to what an extent it can recover its price. The methodology rests on isolating the quantity and price components of monetary changes for both revenues and costs and then showing directly the separate rupee contributions that productivity and prices are making to profits or profitability.

To compete in the hyper competitive market the firm must enhance both productivity and price recovery, as these two are the sources of economic competitiveness to guide the overall strategy of the firm.

Nine-Box Diagram

Anthony J. Hayzen and James M. Reeve in their paper, "Examining the Relationships in Productivity Accounting" have tried to explain the complete and analytical relationship between productivity and profit in a nine-box diagram as explained below :

FIG. 3.1
Nine Box Diagram

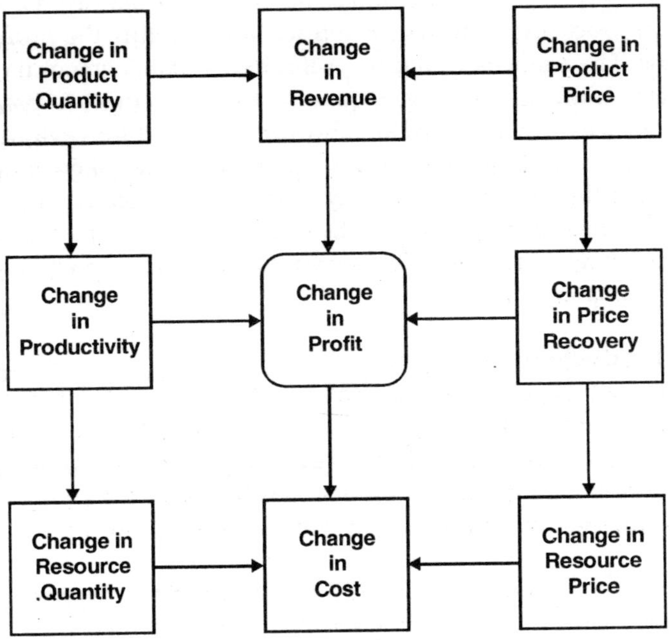

Conventional financial analysis defines profit as the difference between an organization's revenues and its costs, as shown by the center column of the diagram. The left-hand column identifies productivity as the ratio between product and resource quantities. A productivity level exists for each and every resource utilized by the business : labour, materials, energy and most importantly, capital.

A similar relationship exists between product and resource prices; it is called price recovery. Resource prices would include material prices, labour rates, electricity tariffs, interest rates and replacement prices for capital goods. Since the quantity and price movements are derived from the revenue and cost streams, it is a fairly simple exercise to show directly, in rupees terms, the contribution that productivity and price recovery are making to bottom-line financial performance (the center row of the diagram).

Profit, by itself, provides little managerial guidance. Rather, the manager needs information that identifies the causes for change in profit. Using the productivity accounting approach, one can take the change in productivity and the change in price recovery and relate them to the change in profit. If we now analyze the change in product quantities and change in resource quantities we get the change in productivity. If, in addition, we analyze the change in product prices and change in resource prices we get the change in price recovery. Price indexes may be used in situations where it is difficult to access detailed price and quantity information.

Together the measures give the manager a comprehensive analysis of how the changes in product quantity and resource quantity, as well as the change in product price and resource price, are affecting the profitability of the business. The analysis would be useful to the management if changes in the product quantity and resources quantity as also changes in product price and resource price are analyzed suitably and reported for each major input resource so that appropriate relevant action could be taken. Further, it is important that the output : input equation and the price equation for each input resource be compared against the standard laid down. In other words, the application of variance analysis would be of great help in ensuring productivity improvements.

Scope of Productivity Reporting

A company, which produces good quality products at a reasonable cost and with minimum of inputs is generally said to have high productivity level. This can be used as a tool to have a competitive edge over rivals and ensure a continuous presence in the market. But its social commitment and its social accountability requires that it must not be found to :

- directly or indirectly polluting environment through dumping waste in open, releasing obnoxious gases into the atmosphere or by any other means, which result in deterioration of surrounding environment.
- utilizing the perishable natural resources in a thrift manner so as to exhaust them. In other words, the organization must also help conserving scarce resources for future generation of society.

The scope of productivity reporting, therefore, include not only reporting of physical quantity (productivity) and monetary value (Price recovery) associated with it, but also reporting on various measures taken by an organization to upgrade environment or prevent environmental degradation. Also reporting on sustainable development must be a part of productivity reporting.

If a company is committed to improve productivity, the management has to adopt a holistic approach to decision-making in which all dimensions of productivity improvement, i.e., the technical efficiency in terms of input-output analysis the price recovery, the sustainability development, the eco-efficiency and the environmental factors are also given due consideration.

Format of Productivity Reports

There is no clear-cut format yet prescribed for productivity reports by accountants all over the world. The issues relate to the question whether this report should be covered in the annual report or be made a part of financial statement or be issued on a stand-alone basis. The other issue is that there are no specific guidelines issued for presentation of the productivity reports. So the companies providing the information on the productivity generally use different formats. The practices include reporting under social performance reporting or through Director's report or Chairman's speech on various related aspects of the productivity. As the practices are different there is a need to bring harmonization in reporting framework.

Another important issue relates to the class of users for such reports. In case of financial statement, investors are defined as the class of users of financial reports. A productivity report is also in the form of a financial report as investors may make economic decisions based on its contents. But productivity report has, in addition to investors, various other users also viz., customers, employees and society in particular. Therefore, reporting framework must take their needs also in one way or the other.

There are several issues like the measure of productivity, the scope of productivity reporting, the format for reporting, etc. which are needed to be seriously discussed and developed. Though there are objections to productivity reporting on the grounds that an organization's confidential information may have to be disclosed which will be detrimental to the interests of the organization. But in view of serious interests of Indian organizations, in productivity improvement in the wake of the emergence of global markets, the subject can not be ignored any more. It is recommended that the Institute of Chartered Accountants of India (ICAI) and the Institute of Cost and Works Accountants of India (ICWAI) must recommend, the framework and issue guidelines within which information related to productivity and related aspects is to be presented. This framework must provide for information contents for the productivity report, viz. qualitative, quantitative as well as supplementary information and the ways and manners in which it is to be presented.

The reporting on productivity should be made a part of corporate governance. Corporate Governance depicts an environment of trust, ethics, moral values and confidence and is a synergistic effort of all the constituents of society. The stakeholders including government through legislative measures, professionals through their value-added and independent services, service providers and the corporate sector through their thrust to grow and flourish, contribute to good governance level.

Good corporate governance framework has to adopt a holistic approach, taking care of three important P's – Profit (economical), Productivity (Quantitative as well as qualitative aspects) and People (including various stakeholders and environment affecting them) as shown in the Figure 3.2.

FIG. 3.2
Holistic Approach to Corporate Governance

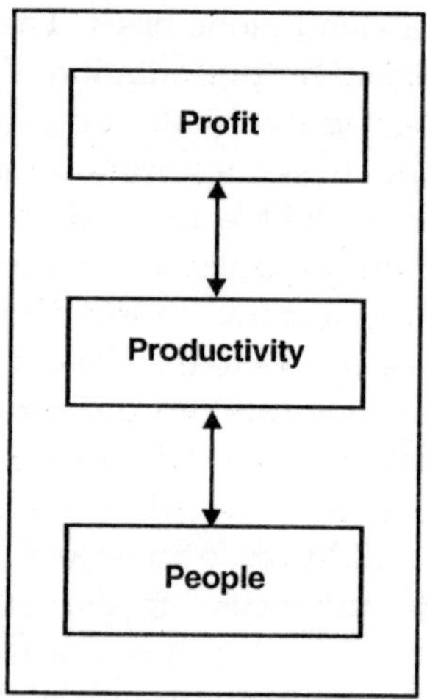

The approach indicates the directions in which the gains of productivity should be distributed. A part of the gains of incremental productivity should be reflected in terms of profits, another part should take care of the interests of the various stakeholders like government, customers, employers, etc. The increased profits must ensure reinvestment of additional resources into the organization apart from improved return to the shareholders.

CONCLUSION

It has been a maiden attempt to discuss the subject that seems to be untouched despite the importance attached to it. As it is evident from the paper itself that productivity leads to profitability, the subject cannot be ignored by any of the organization. The ultimate objective of all the organizations is to maximize the wealth of shareholders, whilst not hampering the interest of other stakeholders. All the parties attached directly or indirectly to the organization are interested in knowing the profitability and indirectly the productivity. So there is a need for proper and adequate disclosure of productivity in the annual reports. The measures of productivity, the aspects to be covered and the format of reporting still stand as the issues that need to be debated and discussed to arrive at a conclusion so as to develop a uniform framework for productivity reporting all over the world. There is a need for a serious thinking on the subject here in India too.

References

Banerjee, Bhabatosh, "Corporate Financial Reporting Practices in India", *Indian Journal of Accounting*, Vol. xxxii, December 2001, pp. 1-17.

Dashora, M.L., "New Dimensions in Accounting Discipline : Social Accounting"; Developments in Accounting, ed. by Bhatia, B.S. , Verma, H.L., 1994 ,Vol. 2, pp. 335-45.

Garg, Lakshmi Kant, "Assurance on Sustainability Reporting", *The Chartered Accountant*, September 2002, pp. 234-37.

Hayzen, Anthony J., "Examining the Relationships in Productivity Accounting", *Management Accounting Quarterly*, Summer, 2000.

Murthy, K.R.S., "Corporate Governance : A Sociological Perspective", ASCI, *Journal of Management* (1998), Vol. 27.

Parsons, John, Corrigan, John, "Productivity Accounting : Measuring for Competitive Advantage", *Australian CPA*, April 1998.

Ubha, Dharmender Singh, "Corporate Disclosure Practices : Text and Case Studies", Deep & Deep Publications (Pvt.) Ltd., New Delhi, 2001.

Vasal, V.K., "Corporate Reporting on Intangibles in India", *Productivity*, Vol. 42, No. 4, January-March, 2002, pp. 618-29.

Internet sites

1. www.mamag.com/summer00/su00hayzen.htm
2. www.cpaonline.com.au/Archive/9804/pg_aa9804_productivi.html

Globalisation and the Changing Productivity Performance in the Indian Economy—A Sectoral Analysis

AMARJIT SINGH SETHI

Economic growth of a nation is indicated not merely through the absolute expansion in the nation's output, but also through growth in productivity—a concept used for measuring efficiency of various input factors, such as capital, labour, etc., taken singly or jointly. In other words, along with an increase in the bulk of factor inputs, productivity improvement appears as an additional dimension in the value formation. The concept of productivity is thus fundamental to growth.

In its simplest version, productivity refers to the value of output per unit of time. In order to study whether efficiency in the use of factor inputs and in the overall allocation of resources in a country has been rising over a period of time or not, the analysis of productivity growth could play an important role. A precise decomposition of the growth of output into the contribution of changes in factor inputs and that of residual (or what is also known as Total Factor Productivity—a measure of technological progress) can be carried out by following Denison's (1962) Factors Share approach. Measurement of total factor productivity (TFP) can play a two-fold role : (1) it helps in knowing as to whether technological changes happen to be an important source of economic growth and, if yes, to what an extent; and (2) as to whether the technological changes have been labour-saving or capital-saving. According to Denison, different sources of growth varied in importance from time to time and from place to place.

India adopted a set of policy measures and regarding experienced 'U'-turn in its policies (being followed since 1950-51) of control, regulation, import substitution, public sector development, etc. in June 1991, though a beginning regarding liberalisation in policies was made with effect from 1984-85. The analysis of changes in sources of growth during the pre-reforms and reforms period is expected to bring out important implications about the future pattern of growth and need for corrective measures, if any. Against this back-drop, the objective of the present paper is to examine the sources of economic growth in India during pre-reforms and the on-going reforms periods, so as to bring out implications for second generation reforms. In this chapter, an attempt has been made to measure in quantitative terms, the differential role played by technological progress as a source of economic growth in major sectors of the Indian economy from pre-globalisation period (i.e., from 1960-61 to 1983-84) to the ongoing globalisation period (i.e. from 1984-85 to 1999-2000). The study was based on secondary time series data for 40 years on India's real Net Domestic Product, Net Fixed Capital Stock, Distributive Shares of Factors in National Income, and Working Force compiled in respect of Primary sector, Secondary sector, Tertiary-I sector, Tertiary-II sector, Aggregated Tertiary sector and the Overall economy. From the appropriate series generated (on Relative Shares of Wages and Salaries of Employees in National Income, and Real Wage Rates of Workers), partial productivities of both labour and capital, K-L and K-0 ratios were worked out. Further, through the Denison's Factor Shares' Approach, the indices of Total Factor Productivity (TFP) were estimated through both Solow and Translog Divisia methods. Through dummy variable technique, differentials in TFP growth during pre-globalisation period *vis-a-vis* that during the on-going globalisation period were tested for their significance in respect of each of the six sectors.

An important aspect of measuring the structural changes is to examine the sources of economic growth, which may change in importance due to changes in policy emphasis and, in turn, have significant implications for future rate and pattern of economic growth. Denison made a path-breaking contribution about sources and rates of economic growth in U.S. economy by identifying more than 20 independent sources, and observed that different sources of growth varied in importance from time to time and from place to place. In the context of the Indian economy, Dholakia made a pioneering study about various sources of economic growth, measured their contribution and concluded that the relative contribution of different sources varied considerably during different sub-periods. The relative importance of capital was observed to be increasing steadily due to increased investment efforts.

Though the liberalisation policies were adopted in a big way in 1991, yet the liberalization period in the present study has been taken to be 1984-85 to 1997-98, so as to provide a fairly long time period for estimating the statistical and econometric functions.

DATA BASE AND METHODOLOGY

The study was based on secondary data collected primarily from various issues of National Accounts Statistics (NAS) of India during post-independence era. Time series information was compiled in respect of the following economic variables for various sectors and sub-sectors of the economy :

(a) Domestic Product (NDP, Y) at 1980-81 prices for 50 years' period (1950-51) through (1999-00);
(b) Net Fixed Capital Stock (K), again at 1980-81 prices for 50 years' period (1950-51 through 1999-00);
(c) Comparable estimates of Working Force (L) at four points in time, viz., 01.10.1960, 01.10.1970, 01.10.1980 and 01.10.1993. Information on Working Force engaged in each sector for the intervening periods was generated under the assumption of compound growth rate behaviour, thereby getting continuous time series information on working force; and
(d) Distributive Shares of Factor Incomes at current prices. Broadly, three series on."

Factor Incomes were compiled from various issues of NAS with different constituents. These were : (i) for 25 years' period (from 1960-61 through 1984-85) available with NDP of each sector divisible into 5 components—Compensation to employees, Rent, Interest, Profits and Dividends, and Mixed Income of Self-Employed; (ii) for 16 years' period (from 1980-81 through 1995-96) available with of each sector divisible into Compensation to Employees, Rent, Interest, Imputed Bank Charges (IBC) and Mixed Income of Self-Employed; (iii) for 7 years' period (from 1993-94 through 1999-00) available with NDP of each sector divisible in to Compensation to Employees, Rent, Interest, Financial Intermediary Services Measured (FISIM) and Mixed Income of Self-Employed. With the objective to attain comparability among the three distinct series, NDP for each sector/ sub-sector was expressed as the sum total of only three components, viz., Compensation to Employees (CE), Property Income (PI = Rent + Interest + Profits and Dividends/IBC/FISIM) and Mixed Income of Self-Employed (MI). Making use of the overlapping years, the three series were back-spliced with the latest series of 7 years as the base, thereby getting a continuous series on Factor Incomes for 40 years' period (i.e., from 1960-61 through 1999-00).

For the present study, time series in respect of all the variables were obtained in terms of 5 comparable main aggregates, viz. Primary (consisting of Agriculture, Forestry and Logging, Fishing, and Mining and Quarrying), Secondary (consisting of Manufacturing—Registered and Un-Registered, Construction, and Electricity, Gas and Water Supply), Tertiary-I (consisting of Trade, Hotels and Restaurants, Railways, Transport by Other Means,

Storage, and Communication), Tertiary-II (consisting of Banking and Insurance, Real Estate, Ownership of Dwellings and Business Services, Public Administration and Defence, and Other Services), Aggregated Tertiary (consisting of Tertiary-I and Tertiary-II) and Overall Total. The so-obtained time series on income, capital stock and working force were then expressed in terms of index numbers with 1960-61 as the base period. For each of the aggregates, relative shares w and k of CE and PI respectively were computed. Real wage rate of employees in a given sector during a specific year was then obtained as WR = wY/L. Such wage rates, too, were expressed in terms of index numbers with 1960-61 as the base year.

Partial productivities of labour and capital were obtained as Y/L and Y/K. For making an assessment of the extent of capital intensiveness, K/L ratios were computed for each of the sectors. For estimating relative contribution of the three main sources of growth, viz., Labour, Capital and Total Factor Productivity (TFP) in each of the aggregates, two different models—Solow and Translog (Divisia)—were adopted As per the Solow's model, which assumes a Cobb-Douglas production process, the TFP growth was obtained as :

$$\Delta T/T = \Delta Y/Y - [\ \alpha\Delta L/L + (1 - \alpha)\Delta K/K\ ]$$

where AY/Y stands for the discrete approximation to the rate of growth in income during successive years, etc. By taking T(0) =1, a time series for Solow's index of TFP was generated as :

$$T(t+1)=T(t)+ \Delta T/T;\ t = 0, 1, \dots , n-1.$$

As per the Divisia model, which makes use of a more versatile Translog production function allowing variable elasticity of substitution, the basic equation for estimating TFP growth could be expressed as :

$$\ln (T_1 \sqrt{} T_{t-1}) = \ln (Y_1 \sqrt{} Y_{t-1}) - [\ \bar{\alpha} \ln (L \sqrt{} L_{t-1}) + \bar{\beta} \ln (K_1 / K_{t-1})] = g^{TL\ (say)}$$

where in stands for natural logarithm, and $\bar{\alpha}$ and $\bar{\beta}$ represent average (over two consecutive years) shares of labour and capital respectively. The Translog index of TFP was then generated as $T_(= T,.\backslash \exp(g^{TL})$ by taking T_0 to be equal to unity.

With a view to examine whether liberalisation policy has induced significant impact on relative importance of the sources of growth, the analysis was carried out not only over the entire study period (1960-61 through 1999-00) of 40 years but over two sub-periods as well—pre-liberalisation (1960-61 through 1983-84) and liberalisation period (1984-85 through 1999-00). Furthermore, the TFP indices obtained through the analysis over the entire study period were subjected to the estimation of the functional form : $X_{t=}$ $bob_1{}^{t} / b_2{}^{Dt}$, where D stands for the dummy variable assuming values of 0 and 1 during pre-liberalisation and liberalisation periods respectively. Estimation of the function was carried-out through *ordinary least-squares technique* as applied to its log-linear version. Rates of growth in TFP indices during the two periods were estimated as GR_1=— (b_1 –1)*100 and GR_2 = (b_1 + b_2 –2)*100. Student's t-ratios for the b-coefficients and *the coefficient of multiple determination* (R^2) were also computed. Statistical significance of the coefficient 02 (as revealed through Student's t-test) was taken to imply that the two rates of growth were really different. Such analyses of differential growth rates were similarly carried out in respect of the other indices, too.

MAIN FINDINGS

- During globalisation regime, share of 'compensation to employees' has decreased in secondary sector, and has remained virtually constant in both primary and tertiary sectors.

Regarding Single Factor Productivities and Capital Intensity

- *In the overall economy,* capital productivity has shown a slight improvement during globalisation period in comparison to that during pre-globalisation period. Labour productivity has continued to grow but at diminishing rates. And, the capital intensity has also continued to increase during globalisation regime.
- *Primary sector* has experienced a slight improvement in capital productivity during globalisation period *vis-a-vis* that during pre-globalisation period. However, labour productivity as well as the capital intensity showed a declining trend during globalisation period.
- *In secondary sector,* capital productivity continued declining whereas capital intensity continued increasing rapidly during globalisation period. However, the pattern was just the opposite in respect of *aggregated tertiary sector.* Notably, labour productivity in both secondary and tertiary sectors showed an improvement during globalisation regime, which was indicative of some improvement in efficiency. The improvement in Tertiary-II was comparatively better than that in Tertiary-I sector.
- There has been an improvement in growth rates of capital productivity during liberalisation period as compared to the earlier period in all sectors and the overall economy. The differential in growth rates was significant in respect of secondary, tertiary-I and tertiary-II sector and the overall economy.

Regarding Solow and Translog Indices of Productivity Growth

- Both the indices depicted, more or less, identical results.
- As per the indices, there was an indication of productivity improvement during globalisation regime *vis-a-vis* the earlier regime in the aggregated economy. However, the sector-wise

analysis revealed that the improvement was largely due to that in tertiary sector. In respect of all the sectors (except that in Tertiary-I sector), the rates of growth during globalisation regime were significantly smaller than the corresponding rates during pre-globalisation regime. In tertiary-I sector, the rate of growth was 0.59 percent during globalisation regime which was significantly higher than the rate of 0.43 percent during the pre-globalisation regime.

Regarding Growth Accounting Analysis

For the aggregated economy, contribution of labour as a source of growth increased (from 36 to 52 percent) while that of capital decreased (from 43 to 32 percent) during globalisation period. As a result, contribution of Total Factor Input increased by nearly 5% (from 79 to 84 percent) and correspondingly that of Total Factor Productivity (TFP) decreased (from 21 to 16 percent). Significant reductions in the contributions of TFP in growth rates were observed in respect of secondary sector (from 18.3 to 7.1 percent), Tertiary-II sector (from 57 to 22 percent) and aggregated tertiary sector (from 41 to 22 percent). On the other hand, Primary sector (to some extent) and Tertiary-I sector (from 4.3 to 21.0 percent) were the only exceptions to have registered improvements in the contributions of TFP in growth during globalisation regime.

The findings thus reveal that the opening up of the Indian economy has resulted in declining share of wages and salaries (compensation to employees) in secondary sector, overall consistency in share of wages and salaries, increase in capital intensity in secondary sector as well as in overall economy, decline in TFP growth and decline in the contribution of TFP to economic growth. Growth in TFP has shown retardation in all sectors of the economy (as well as in the overall economy) except that in the Tertiary-I sector. Thus, the process of globalisation has induced an impetus to the activities like Trading (both at domestic and international levels), and Transport and Communication. A retardation in the productivity growth in the all-important industrial sector calls for an urgent need for the adoption of suitable measures such as strengthening of indigenous technology through R and D, human resource development, improved marketing systems, etc., so as to cope up with the increased competitiveness under the global scenario. Thus, the impacts of globalisation measures as gauged through their impact on real wage rates of workers, labour-productivity and TFP have not turn out to be encouraging. Evidently, the measures have failed to bring in increased efficiencies, which otherwise were very much expected via dismantling of the controls and regulations, reduced role of public sector, improvement in technology and increased competitiveness of the economy. Therefore, other suitable measures such as regarding population check, strengthening of indigenous R & D so as to boost the all important industrial sector, curbing the unrestrained race for adopting foreign technology irrespective of its suitability to the local conditions, strengthening of agro-processing and marketing units, adoption towards human resource development measures, promotional steps towards domestic and international trade, etc. are needed. In nut-shell, an improvement in efficiency in the functioning of different sectoral and sub-sectoral programmes constitutes the basis for the improvement in productivity and, hence, in a rapid growth of the country, and second generation reforms must address to these issues on priority basis.

REFERENCES

Todaro, M.P. (1989), *Economic Development in the Third World,* London, Orient Longman.

Chenery, H., Ahluwalia, M.S., Bell, C.L.G., Duloy, J.H., and Jolly, R. (1974), *Redistribution with Growth,* London, Oxford University Press.

Sethi, A.S. (1997), *Dynamics of National Income,* New Delhi, Deep and Deep Publications.

Denison, E.F. (1967), *The Sources of Economic Growth in the United States and the Alternatives Before US,* New York, Committee for Economic Development.

Dholakia, B.H. (1974), *The Sources of Economic Growth in India,* Baroda, Good ! Companions.

Solow, R.M. (1957), "Technical Change and the Aggregate Production Function", *Review of Economics and Statistics, 39* : 312-20.

Christensen, L.R. (1973), "Transcendental Logarithmic Production Frontiers", *Review of Economics and Statistics,* 55(1) : 28-55.

Global Competitiveness—Issues Beyond Productivity

P.S. Raikhy and Paramjit Nanda

With the Intensification of reforms process in most of the developing countries; there is much wider scope of GATT-94 far beyond tariff and non-tariff barriers. With WTO becoming the watchdog of trade in goods and services and flow of investment and finance the world economy started becoming structurally interdependent at a fast pace. The concept of 'global' has become more acceptable and justifiable in place of 'international' (Dunning, 1997). This closer integration of the world economy is leading to shrinkage of the world into 'global neighbourhood' or 'global village' and is heading towards 'world without borders'. In this very context, the concept of 'international competitiveness' has been substituted by 'global competitiveness'. The concept of 'comparative advantage', affecting the cost of production, productivity of factors and prices of the commodities and services has been widened into 'competitiveness' to include the non-price factors such as delivery schedules, packaging, quality and reliability, after sales service and customer relations, etc. However, as most of the non-price factors are difficult to quantify, therefore, the studies have generally concentrated on productivity and resulting price competitiveness. The objective of the present chapter is to highlight the role of non-price factors in addition to productivity and go beyond to 'market access conditions', which translate competitiveness into sales. The chapter has been divided into three sections. In Section I productivity-competitiveness link has been brought out and importance of non-price factors has been highlighted.

Section II discusses the issues beyond productivity and Section III brings out the implications for India in the light of the issues.

I

Trade-productivity link can be examined from two angles. In one sense, degree of openness of the economy affects productivity and economic growth. When there is exposure to foreign competition, adoption rate of technological innovations is accelerated, there are increasing returns to scale and returns to entrepreneurial efforts also increase (Tybout, 1992). Openness to trade provides access to imported inputs, which embody new technology and as a result production process becomes more efficient and productivity increases. Even when trade remains neutral, openness leads to greater capacity utilization and thus leads to improvement in productivity. Moreover, under the challenges of foreign competition, there arises strong pressure for reduction in cost inefficiencies, which further leads to productivity gains.

The empirical studies about trade-productivity relationship in India, using both firm and industry level data, reported positive impact of the trade liberalization on productivity growth. Krishna and Mitra (1998) and Balakrishnan, Pushpangadan and Babu (2000), using firm level data, brought out contradictory results of trade liberalization on Total Factor Productivity (TFP) growth, due to difference in methodologies; while the former reported positive impact, the latter observed negative impact of trade liberalization on TFP growth. However, three recent studies by Das (2001), Goldar and Kumari (2002) and Chand and Sen (2002), on the basis of industry level data, reported positive effect of trade liberalization on TFP growth.

In reality, competitiveness depends upon micro-economic fundamentals based on internal competition of the firms and the quality of local business environment. Thus, even when sources of competitiveness may be there at the economy level, these are basically to be identified at the level of the industry and firms. The reaction of an industry or a firm to global competitiveness depends upon its inner strength and its comparative advantage, which may get reflected into productivity growth under the competitive pressure. If an industry or firm has no inner strength, trade liberalization or competitiveness may further weaken it instead of strengthening. It is in this sense that no country can be competitive in producing all goods and services, hence industry competitiveness and particularly firm competitiveness are more relevant concepts. Firm competitiveness lays down the foundation of industry competitiveness. However, the government can only help firms compete.

Productivity in the strict sense affects the cost of production and hence relates to price competitiveness. However, now-a-days non-price factors have at least equal role in affecting competitiveness. Consumer especially in developed countries, has become extremely quality conscious. Going far beyond consumer sovereignty, consumer has been assigned the status of god and producers now leave no stone unturned in pleasing the god by introducing new features in the products. Product life cycle has drastically reduced and marginal utility of even durable products is reduced to zero by introducing new products with new features. Packaging has also assumed much more importance in view of its significant impact on shelf life of the products. Buyers, especially in the foreign countries have become sensitive to delivery schedules. They start searching for new sources of supply even when there is remote possibility of disruption in it. The image of the country and reliability of producers also matters a lot which are reflected in rejection rate of the supplies. A study conducted by Canadian Department of Industry has reported that delivery and reliability and quality were ranked higher by the consumers with scores of 9.2 and 9.0, while the price factor was ranked third with a score of 8.8 (on a 10 point scale). It was concluded that while price was important, it was not sufficient factor in getting export orders (Shanbhag and Nair, 2000). These non-price factors are very difficult to quantify and are generally not reflected in the cost effectiveness and productivity measurements. Thus, the concept of global competition has extended beyond productivity dimensions.

II

The concept of competitiveness is relevant so long as competition is fair competition. Competition requires rules, but these rules have to be conceived and practised within the framework of some normative values. GATT 94 framed rules, which were claimed to provide 'level playing field' to all the countries. However, there are two main problems with these rules. First, the rules are distorted to suit the interests of developed countries. Second, the rules generally have not kept in view the differences in capacity to compete. Though, the developing countries have been given some relaxations in tariff and subsidy reduction, keeping in view their level of development, yet the developed countries themselves provide huge subsidies to their agricultural products, which they justify on the pretext of green and blue box policies. These subsidies amount to $327 billion annually (Anderson, 2002) and a large part of these subsidies are provided by United States, European Union and Japan. Still, on the other hand, developing countries are expected to further reduce the meager subsidies provided by them, after terming these WTO-incompatible. In reality, the developed countries are not prepared to open their markets to the developing countries.

Another important component of GATT-94 was elimination of non-tariff barriers (NTBs) to trade like the Quantitative Restrictions (QRs) and Multi Fibre Arrangement (MFA) and to convert these into tariffs, which were to be reduced further. Developing countries have been made to do away with the QRs and most of them, including India, have withdrawn the QRs. However, the developed countries, the proponents of the free trade, do not practice free trade when it comes to safeguarding their own interests and have evolved new instruments of NTBs in the form of Environmental and Labour Standards, Technical Barriers to Trade (TBT) and Sanitary and Phyto-Sanitary (SPS) measures, etc. to deny the advantages of comparative advantage and market access to developing countries. Japan alone has imposed 36 categories of NTBs, covering thousands of commodities. Specific NTBs have been imposed in case of genetically modified organism, specified risk materials, pesticide residues, use of azo-dyes along with imposition of other SPS and Environmental and Labour Standards. In addition to these measures, anti-dumping and countervailing measures have also been resorted to mostly by developed countries. It has been estimated that in 1996-97, India's exports worth Rs. 27188.45 crores were subjected to various NTBs by United States, European Union and Japan (CMIE, 1998). It may be pointed out that NTBs have far more distortionary effects than the tariffs. While the tariffs are certain, NTBs introduce element of uncertainty on export front, which causes undue harm to productive capacity and exports. The foreign buyers start searching for new suppliers when there is fear of disruption in supplies. Moreover, the credibility of the quality of the product is lost. Ultimately even when no substantive proof may be found and no action may be taken, but by the time immense damage is done.

Developing countries are not generally against quality standards and other environmental and SPS measures. But there are four main problems. One, the standards are set at much higher level than are scientifically required and these may be beyond the approach of developing countries. Second, the testing facilities may not be available in different parts of the country and may more than exhaust the comparative advantage being enjoyed by these countries. Third, there is lack of knowledge about these standards to the exporters. Fourth, appropriate technology and raw material may not be available to meet the standards.

To quote a few examples : even when tea is one of the oldest export items from India, Australia requires radiation test, which is conducted by Bhaba Atomic Research Corporation only. Peanut exports require different SPS tests, which cost Rs. 6000 per test. For export of mango pulp, test regarding pesticide residues is required, which costs Rs. 3000 per test (Kaushik and Saquib, 2001). Similarly, food products require different certifications under Codex Food Code (CFC) and Hazard Analysis Critical Control Point (HACCP). India's exports of marine products, meat, spices, fruit juice, mushrooms and other processed foods, etc. have faced many such NTBs and resulting cost escalations and uncertainties in the recent past.

In case of textile and garment exports, different labelling-eco-labels, eco-packing and social-labelling is required to prevent the rejection of exports. In carpet, footwear and sports goods exports from India, labelling like Rugmark, Kaleen, Pro-child, Care and Fair, etc. have been introduced to indicate that child labour has not been employed. ISO-14000 series reflect adherence to technical regulations, technical standards and environmental standards. Government of India introduced 'Eco-Mark' in 1991, but it has not achieved desired results so far.

The major problem about these standards is non-transparency and stringency. The standards differ from country to country and go on changing. For example, electronic industry was known to be free from ecological hazards but now there is increasing worry about disposal of electronic waste. European Union directives in this context are expected to be implemented by 2008, which will have serious implications for electronic exports to ED. The lack of awareness of exporters of the standards, and of internationally accepted agencies for certification of fulfilment of the standards have become the major hurdles in translating the competitiveness of developing countries into growth of exports.

III

As per the World Investment Report, 2002, USA had 13.2 percent world export market in 2000, followed by Germany, Japan, China and France with 8.2, 7.7, 6.1 and 4.8 percent shares. During the period 1985-2000, China increased its market share by 4.5 percent, USA by 1.7 percent, Korea and Mexico by 1.1 percent each and Malaysia by 0.8 percent (UNCTAD, 2002). However, the world export share of India stagnated around 0.6 percent during the past 10 years. It indicates that India could not translate its competitiveness potential into increase in exports.

The competitiveness of a firm or industry largely depends upon availability of quality and cheaper raw material, cheap labour, technological capabilities and marketing strategies. The comparative advantage of India in producing cheaper food grains and other raw material has been dissipated, as presently the international prices of these are lower. No doubt, the wages in the country are lower but productivity of labour is much lower. As a result, labour cost per unit of output in India has been much higher than in China, Korea, Japan and many other countries. The technological capabilities of the country in the industrial sector are desperately poor. Therefore, to increase the share of the country in world exports, multi-pronged strategy with focused approach needs to be adopted. The country should identify sectors and specific activities with comparative advantage and technological potential and start innovation chains there. While technology acquisition be liberalized, domestic R & D be aggressively promoted so as to improve technological capabilities. Labour laws be amended to improve work culture and more emphasis be laid on human resource development.

To get the benefit from export-oriented FDI, linkages should be established between domestic suppliers of material and foreign affiliates. There should be much more emphasis on quality infrastructure and institution building, like setting up of export promotion zones, export promotion councils, industrial parks, institutions of testing, certification and standards, and for providing market information. Internal market should be liberalized to match with external liberalization. The export basket should be steadily diversified so that competitiveness becomes sustainable. State must play a proactive role in all these aspects.

On the external policy front, India should take up the role of leader of developing countries on international economic issues so as to strengthen the bargaining power in the meetings of WTO bodies. There is need for consensus among developing countries regarding Technical Barriers to Trade, Environment and Labour Standards and Sanitary and Phyto-Sanitary measures, which may be arrived at through consultations. Then effective bargaining be made at the international forum to have an extended time table for introducing these standards and having greater transparency about these standards. Foreign direct investment be allowed only in those sectors which contribute to income generation, employment creation and more exports. In this context, Multilateral Agreement on Investment (MAI), allowing MNCs legal right to invest in the sectors of their choice in the host countries without any restrictions, should not be accepted under any circumstances. Last, regional co-operation be increased by strengthening SAARC and setting up Asian Economic Community for increased co-operation in trade, investment, technology and skills.

References

Anderson, P.P. (2002), *Emerging Issues in Trade and Technology : Implications for South Asia*, ICRIER, New Delhi, April 24.

Balakrishnan, P., K. Pushpangadan and M.S. Babu (2000), "Trade Liberalization and Productivity Growth in Manufacturing : Evidence from Firm Level Panel Data", *Economic and Political Weekly*, October 7, pp. 3679-82.

Chand, S. and K. Sen (2002), "Trade Liberalization and Productivity Growth : Evidence from Indian Manufacturing", *Review of Development Economics*, Vol. 6, No. 1.

CMIE, *India Trades*, 1998.

Das, O.K. (2001), *Some Aspects of Productivity Growth and Trade in Indian Industry*, Ph.D. Thesis (Unpublished), Delhi School of Economics, University of Delhi.

Dunning, J.H. in Dunning, J.H. and K.A. Hamdani (eds.) (1997), *The New Globalism and Developing Countries*, Bookwell, Delhi.

Goldar, B.N. and A. Kumari (2002), *Import Liberalization and Productivity Growth in Indian Manufacturing Industries in the 1990s*, Working Paper E/219/2002, Institute of Economic Growth, Delhi.

Kaushik, Atul and Mohammad Saquib (2001), *Environmental Requirements and India's Exports : An Impact Analysis*, Rajiv Gandhi Institute for Contemporary Studies, New Delhi.

Krishna, P. and D. Mitra (1998), "Trade Liberalization, Market Discipline and Productivity Growth : New Evidence from India", *Journal of Development Economics*, Vol. 56, pp. 447-62.

Shanbhag, V. and A.K.G. Nair (2000), *Winning Ways for the Future Apparel Business*, Global Business Press, New Delhi.

Tybout, J.R. (1992), "Linking Trade and Productivity : New Research Directions", *The World Bank Economic Review*, Vol. 6, No. 2, pp. 189-211.

UNCTAD (2002), *World Investment Report, 2002*, United Nations, New York.

EVA as a Tool to Measure Productivity

DYAL BHATNAGAR

INTRODUCTION

The primary objective of any enterprise is to create wealth and not only to cut the costs. The traditional measurements of wealth creation do not take this fact into account. In other words, a concern has not only to portray the liquidation value of the enterprise rather it has to be managed as a going concern, that is for wealth creation. To do that requires information that enables executives to make informed judgments. It requires four sets of diagnostic tools : foundation information, productivity information, competence information, and information about the allocation of scarce resources. In the present study, the focus is on the role of productivity information in measuring the value-added to the shareholders' wealth.

Up-to World War-II, the productivity of a concern was measured with reference to the manual labour. However, it was realized that it is not sufficient to take into account only labour productivity for investigating whether some value has been added to the market value of shares or not. Rather, we need data on total-factor productivity.

That explains the growing popularity of economic value-added analysis. EVA is based on something we have known for a long time. The EVA of the company is just a measure of the incremental return, the investment earns over the market rate of return. In simple terms, it can be stated that EVA measures the profitability net of cost of capital raised. As someone has aptly remarked, you only get richer if you invest money at a higher return than the cost of money to you. Every body knows this but many seem to forget it. Thus, EVA can be taken as the net operating profit minus an appropriate charge for the opportunity cost of all the capital invested in an enterprise. As such, EVA is an estimate of true economic profit or the amount by which earnings exceed or fall short of the required minimum rate of return that shareholders and lenders could get by investing in other securities of comparable risk.

By measuring the value added overall costs, including the cost of capital, EVA measures, in effect, the productivity of all factors of production. It does not, by itself, tell us why a certain product or a certain service does not add value or what to do about it but it shows us what we need to find out and whether we need to take remedial action. EVA should also be used to find out what works. It does show which product, service, operation, or activity has unusually high productivity and adds unusually high value.

Theoretically, a continuous rise in EVA will push up the market value of company. That is why the level of EVA is not what really matters; rather it is the incremental value of EVA, which is more significant.

The discussion about the concept of EVA does not seem to be complete without taking into consideration another significant measure of financial performance of a company, that is, 'Market Value Added' (MVA). According to Stewart, if the total market value of a company is more than the amount of capital invested in it, the company has managed to create shareholder value. On the other hand, if the market value is less than the capital invested, the company has destroyed shareholder value. This difference between the company's market and book value is termed as 'Market Value Added'. Thus :

MVA = Market Value of Equity — Book Value of Equity

Book value of equity refers to all equity equivalent items like reserves, retained earnings and provisions. In other words, in this context, all the items that are not debt (interest bearing or non-interest bearing) are classified as equity.

The concept of 'Market Value Added' tells us how much value a company has added to or subtracted from its shareholders' investments. The successful companies add their MVA and thus increase the value of capital invested in their companies. On the other hand, unsuccessful companies decrease the value of the capital originally invested in the company. Whether a company succeeds in creating MVA (increasing shareholders' value) or not, depends on its rate of return. If the rate of return of a company exceeds its cost of capital, the company will sell on the stock markets with a premium compared to the original capital, which shows that it has a positive MVA. On the other hand, companies that have rate of return smaller than their cost of capital, sell with discount compared to the original capital invested in the company, which shows a negative MVA. Whether a company has positive or negative MVA depends upon the level of rate of return compared to the cost of capital. All this applies to EVA also. Thus, positive EVA also means positive MVA and *vice-versa.*

OBJECTIVES

The main objective of the present study is to investigate the efficacy and appropriateness of EVA as a method of measuring productivity of a concern as compared to some traditional methods of measuring productivity like Kp and Lp.

In the financial management literature it is considered that market price of a company's share reflects the wealth of its shareholders. It is believed that a company's effort to maximize its productivity is reflected in its shares. This means that market assesses the firm on the basis of long-term productivity.

In this context another objective of the study is to analyze whether there is any association between share prices of a concern and it's various productivity measures viz., Kp, Lp and EVA.

The specific objectives of the study have been listed below :

1. To identify (and compute) various financial variables, which may have a probable effect on company's 'Market Value Added'.
2. To arrange these financial variables; viz., MVA, EVA, Kp and Lp, company-wise (for all the years) separately and check for any relationship among these financial variables with MVA, for each company.
3. To arrange all the financial variables, year-wise (for all the companies) separately and check for any relationship among these financial variables with MVA, over a period of time.

METHODOLOGY

For the purpose of analysis, the sample of 56 companies has been taken from the list of companies whose shares are actively traded on Bombay Stock Exchange (List A shares). List A shares have been considered more appropriate for the purpose of present study because the prices of these shares are more sensitive to the productivity of the organization. Banks and other financial institutions have not been included in the sample because the format of their financial statements is different from that of the business concerns.

The financial data of the sample companies have been collected from the 'Official Bombay Stock Exchange Directory'. The data available from this directory pertains to ten years and accordingly the time frame of the present study has been restricted to ten years, that is, from 1988-89 to 1997-98. Although the time frame adopted in the present study is of ten years, the financial variables viz., EVA, MVA, Kp, and Lp, have been calculated for nine years due to the nature of calculations. EVA has been calculated on the basis of invested capital in the previous year. Thus, data for the period 1989-90 have been used as the starting point, restricting the calculated values of EVA only to nine years.

The calculation procedure for the various financial variables has been described in the ensuing paragraphs.

EVA has been calculated by applying the following formula :

$$EVA^t = (r - c) \times \text{Invested Capital } (t-1)$$

where, r = Net Operating Profit After Tax (NOPAT)/Invested Capital × 100

c = Weighted Average Cost of Capital (WACC)

Invested Capital = Total Borrowings + Net Worth

t = Time period

NOPAT = (Interest + Operating profit) × (1–Effective tax rate)

The data for the purpose of tax rates has been collected from the Income Tax Office, Patiala. The tax rates pertaining to the companies in which public are substantially interested have been procured from the ITO, Patiala for a period of ten years, that is, 1988-89 to 1997-98.

WACC has been calculated by assigning weights according to the book value of borrowings and the book value of shares to cost of debt and cost of equity respectively. Cost of debt (Kd) has been computed as :

$$Kd = (\text{Total interest expenses}) \times (1 - \text{Effective tax rate}) / \text{Beginning total borrowings}$$

While calculating beginning borrowing all short-term as well as long-term borrowings have to be included as all debts are interest bearing. Therefore, interest paid in the financial year has been considered as total interest expenses.

To find out cost of equity (Ke), Capital Asset Pricing Model (CAPM) has been used. According to this model, Ke is the shareholders' expected rate of return and this expected rate of return (Rj) is calculated as follows :

$$Rj = Rf + \beta \times (Rm - Rf)$$

where, Rf = Risk free rate of return,

Rm = Market rate of return, and

β = Sensitivity of the share price in relation to the market index.

The weighted average of domestic term deposit interest rates of nationalized banks has been considered as a proxy for risk free rate of return. The weight has been decided as per the number of months for which a particular rate of interest has remained valid in a particular financial year.

The market rate of return has been calculated by using Index Numbers of Security Prices (Mumbai) from year to year basis. The source of procuring the index numbers has been the RBI Bulletin published monthly by the Reserve Bank of India. The yearly return of the index numbers has been computed by using the following formula :

Rm = [(Index number for current year – Index number for previous year)/(Index number for previous year)] × 100

The x-coefficient in a standard regression equation (referred to as Beta in this case) measures the sensitivity of dependent variable to a per unit change in the independent variable(s). For the purpose of ascertaining the cost of equity, the individual security prices have been taken as the dependent variable and the return on the market (computed as yearly return of security market index) has been taken as the independent variable. To find out the responsiveness of individual security's expected return (taken as proxy for the cost of equity) to the market rate of return, the Beta coefficient has been calculated as follows :

$$\beta_i = cov_{im}/\sigma^2_m$$

where, β_i is the Beta of the security in the question,
cov_{im} stands for covariance between the return of security and return of market, and
σ^2_m stands for the variance of market return.

Finally, EVA is calculated on the basis of invested capital of the previous year. Thus, it is obvious that EVA is based on two dimensions, that is, the 'spread' (r–c) and the 'invested capital'.

MVA depicts the value added to a particular share over its face value. It tells how much value a shareholder has added to this wealth, which he has invested in that share. Thus, a company with an objective of enhancing the shareholders' wealth should try to maximize its MVA. MVA can be calculated by subtracting the book value of shares from the market value of shares. It is understood that EVA helps in pushing up the MVA of an organization. Thus, EVA can be considered as an internal measure and MVA as the external measure of a company's performance. They should, therefore, move together in one direction. For the purpose of analysis in the present study MVA has been considered as the dependent variable, that is, its value depends on other independent financial variables viz., EVA, Kp and Lp. A brief explanation of each of these variables has been given in the ensuing paragraphs.

Banerjee and Jain (1999), used two new measures, that is, Kp and Lp to gauge labour and capital efficacy in addition to EVA, which can have a significant bearing on MVA. A brief explanation of these variables is as follows :

Capital Productivity (Kp)

It is defined as (Net sales + Changes in stock – Stock consumed – Direct manufacturing expenses)/Net fixed assets. Net fixed assets are equal to Gross Block – Depreciation. Kp tells that how efficiently and productively the fixed assets of the firm have been utilized. It is believed that value of shares will go up if the capital productivity goes up. In simple words, if fixed assets are efficiently used, they would generate wealth for equity shareholders in an organisation.

Labour Productivity (Lp)

This is defined as (Net sales + Changes in stock – Stock consumed – Direct manufacturing expenses)/Wage costs. Thus, Lp tells that how efficient is the work-force of the organisation. Lp will improve if the efficacy of workers improves or if same amount of value is generated with less number of workers. It has been observed that there is a positive relationship between Lp and MVA.

Thus, Lp and Kp can be two relevant independent financial measures, which can be checked for having any bearing on the shareholders' value.

Stewart claims that EVA has a strong positive correlation with MVA. By taking EVA as an independent financial variable, it is checked whether EVA is a superior productivity measure as compared to other traditional measures. Thus, the hypothesis of our study is that among the chosen independent financial variables EVA is the most explanatory variable.

The Scheme of Analysis

In the analysis phase, multiple regression has been calculated for each year in case of year-wise arrangement of the variables and for each company in case of company-wise arrangement of the variables, taking MVA as the dependent variable and EVA, Kp, and Lp, as the independent financial variables. The regression statistics reveals that to what extent a particular independent financial variable is related to the dependent variable and how statistically significant the relationship is? The multiple regression has also been calculated for all the years together to know which independent financial variable was most significantly related to the dependent variable during the whole time-span of the study.

In the regression analysis the following regression measures were computed-regression coefficients for x-variables (independent variables) which depict the nature of relationship between the dependent and a particular independent variable; t-statistics to find out the level of significance, if any, between the dependent and a particular independent variable; intercept, which completes the regression equation; multiple r^2, which indicates the extent of variation in the dependent variable which can be explained by independent variables; and Standard Error of Y estimation, which depicts the limits within which the estimated value of the dependent variable is expected to lie. The t-statistics is calculated by dividing the regression coefficient for each independent variable by the Standard Error for that particular variable.

RESULTS AND DISCUSSION

Based on the analysis of data pertaining to 56 companies, the results have been presented in the ensuing pages.

Table 6.1 depicts the number of times a particular independent variable has been statistically significant in its relationship with the dependent variable, i.e., MVA in all the companies under study. Table 6.1 indicates that there is very little variation between the various independent variables in the context of their statistical relationship with the dependent variable, i.e., MVA. The percentage of companies in which independent variables were significantly related to MVA varied between 23 to 27%. Therefore, it can not be inferred that any one of the independent variables is capable of explaining the movement in the dependent variable.

TABLE 6.1
Company-wise Composite Extent of Relationship among Dependent and Independent Variables

Independent Variables	*No. of Companies in which significantly related to MVA*	*No. of companies in which not significantly related to MVA*	*Total No. of Companies*
EVA	15 (26.78)	41 (73.22)	56 (100)
Kp	14 (25.00)	42 (75.00)	56 (100)
Lp	13 (23.21)	43 (76.79)	56 (100)

Further, an attempt was made to find out the level of significance in the relationship between independent and dependent variables in the sample companies. The results are shown in Table 6.2. Table 6.2 shows that in case of a majority of the companies the independent variable had a significant relation with the dependent variable at 1% level of significance.

TABLE 6.2
The Level of Significance of Relationship among Dependent and Independent Variables

Independent Variables	*Significant at 1% level*	*Significant at 5% level*	*Total*
EVA	12 (80.00)	3 (20.00)	15 (100)
Kp	11 (78.58)	3 (21.42)	14 (100)
Lp	11 (84.62)	2 (15.38)	13 (100)

However, as the variation in the independent variables which have a significant relationship with the dependent variable either at 1% or 5% level was not apparent in the company-wise analysis, an attempt has been made to find out the multiple regression for various years separately for all the companies. The multiple regression results for different years under study have been pooled together to find out the extent of relationship between the independent variables and the dependent variables for all the years taken together. This composite analysis has been presented in Table 6.3. Table 6.3 reveals that it was in a very high proportion (77.78%) of instances that EVA has emerged as the independent variable, which had a statistically significant relationship with MVA. None of the other independent variables had any statistically significant relationship with the dependent variable even once. Thus, it can be inferred that EVA was the most significant explanatory independent variable which could account for movement in MVA.

TABLE 6.3
Year-wise Composite Extent of Relationship among Dependent and Independent Variables

Independent Variables	*Significantly related to MVA (%)*	*Not Significantly at related to MVA (%)*	*Total No. of years (%)*
EVA	7 (77.78)	2 (22.22)	9 (100)
Kp	—	9 (100)	9 (100)
Lp	—	9 (100)	9 (100)

Further, an attempt was made to find out the level of significance in the relationship between dependent and independent variables for the year-wise analysis. The results are presented in Table 6.4. Table 6.4 indicates that in all the cases (100%) EVA had a significant relationship with MVA at 1% level of significance. Thus, this analysis further substantiates that EVA is the most significant independent variable, which can account for the movement in MVA even at a more rigorous level of significance.

TABLE 6.4
The Level of Significance of Relationship among Dependent and Independent Variables

Independent Variables	*Significant at 1% level (%)*	*Significant at 5% level (%)*	*Total (%)*
EVA	7 (100)	—	7 (100)
Kp	—	—	—
Lp	—	—	—

The analysis has been carried further to present a composite picture by pooling the data for the total time span of the study and applying the regression model on this combined data to ascertain the overall extent of significance in the relationship among dependent and independent variables. The result of this analysis has been presented in Table 6.5. The regression analysis presented in the table indicates that only EVA was positively related with the dependent variable.

TABLE 6.5
Multiple Regression Results for the Total Time Span of the Study

Regression Measures	*Independent Variables*		
	EVA	*Kp*	*Lp*
X-Coefficient (in lakhs)	0.00169*	-306	-751
t-Statistics	11.435**	-0.151	-0.997

Intercept (in lakhs) : 51670
Multiple r^2 : 0.330
$S.E._{Y\ est}$: 20339120618

*denotes significance at 5% level of significance.
**denotes significance at 1% level of significance.

The t-statistics for the regression coefficients revealed that only EVA had a statistically significant relationship with MVA at 1% level of significance. Thus, EVA is the only independent variable, which could explain any movement in MVA.

The $S.E._{Y\ est}$ indicated that in 68% cases of Y estimation the predicted value of the dependent variable would be within a range of ±20339120618 and for the remaining cases the predicted value of MVA could be beyond the aforesaid estimated range.

The multiple r^2 (0.330) indicated that 33% of the variation in the dependent variable could be explained by the independent variables.

The composite analysis presented above by pooling the data for the total time span for the study has clearly depicted that EVA was the only independent variable which had a significant bearing on the dependent variable, i.e., MVA.

CONCLUSIONS

The analysis leads to the following conclusions :

1. The company-wise multiple regression results indicated that there exists very little variation in the dependent variable (MVA) *vis-a-vis*

the independent variables chosen for the study. As such, it could not be inferred as to which independent variable(s) was/were capable of explaining the movements in MVA. Therefore, it was thought to make a similar analysis year-wise for all the companies taken together.

2. The year-wise composite multiple regression analysis saw EVA emerging as the single largest variable, which was significantly related to MVA. Kp and Lp did not prove to be statistically significant in explaining the movement in MVA.
3. The multiple regression exercise was also conducted by pooling the entire data for the total time span of the study. EVA turned out to be the only variable which was highly significant in having a bearing on MVA. This result proved beyond doubt that EVA is a significant measure of financial performance.

Thus, the regression analysis amply demonstrates the significance of EVA as a measure of total factor productivity. This analysis based on the empirical data also validates the theoretical formulation about EVA as the most explanatory variable which is capable of accounting for the pattern of changes in the share prices.

References

Ansof, H., Igor (1965), *Corporate Strategy*, Penguin.

Anand, Manoj; Garg, Ajay; Arora, Asha (1999), "Economic Value Added : Business Performance Measure of Shareholder Value." *The Management Accountant*, May 1999, pp. 351-56.

Banerjee, Ashok (1999), "Economic Value Added and Shareholder Wealth : An Empirical Study of Relationship," *Paradigm*, Vol. 3, No. 1, January-June, 1999.

Banerjee, Ashok; Jain, S.C. (1999), "Measuring Performance", *The Chartered Accountant*, February 1999, pp. 34-40.

Banerjee, Ashok (2000), "Linkage between Economic Value Added and Market Value : An Analysis," *Vikalpa*, Vol. 25, No. 3, July-September, 2000, pp. 23-36.

Harihar, T.S. (1999), "Evaporating Myths," *Chartered Financial Analyst*, November 1999, pp. 8-9.

Kumar, Satheesh, (2000), "Economic Value Added—A Critique," *Indian Management*, March 2000, pp. 57-62.

Lahiri, Arjun (1998), "All about EVA," *Business India*, September 21-October 4, pp. 32-33.

Marshal, Alferd, *The Principles of Economics*, 1890, Chapter 4.

Pattanayak, J.K., Mukherjee, K. (1998), "Adding Value to Money," *The Chartered Accountant*, February 1998, pp. 8-12.

Rajeshwar, C. (1997), "Economic Value Added : Rediscovery Value, *Analyst*, December 1997, pp. 39-44.

Ravishankar, T.J. (1999), "Value for Money, Sir," *The Economic Times* (Corporate Dossier), 26 March - 1 April, 1999, p. 1.

Ravishankar, T.J. (1999), "EVA Analysis is no Gospal Truth," *The Economic Times*, 19 January, 1999.

Stewart, G. Bennet (1993), "EVA™ : Fact and Fantasy," *Journal of Applied Corporate Finance*, 1993, pp. 6-19.

Stewart, Bernett, G. (1995), "EVA Works—But not if you make these Common Mistakes." *Fortune*, May 1, 1995.

Stern-Stewart & Co. (1996), EVA—The Real Way to Creating Wealth.

Thenmoshi, M. (1999), "Economic Value Added as a Measure of Corporate Performance," *The Indian Journal of Commerce*, Vol. 52, No. 4, October-December 1999, pp. 72-85.

Tully, Shawn (1997), "Adding Value," *Business Today*, Sept. 22-Oct. 6, 1997, pp. 68-73.

Enhancing Indian Competitiveness through Knowledge

NARENDRA SINGH AND S.C. DAVAR

The expansion of global markets and dismantling of protective barriers to trade and commerce has enhanced the growth opportunities for the Indian economy. However, while international trade opportunities will grow, the protection that a large domestic market offered to Indian industries would decline in importance. The ability of India to penetrate both domestic and world markets would depend on its relative competitive strength *vis-a-vis* other nations. India is destined to become the major power house of the world economy (Manmohan Singh, 2000). This is neither going to happen overnight nor is it going to happen like a miracle. We have to synchronize our efforts and need to focus our resources and energy strategically in the right direction where we have competitiveness and cost advantage. Competitiveness has become a prominent business and government concern in the era of globalization. The new environment has put extra burden on the shoulder of corporate and industrial India so as to play more crucial role as an engine of growth. There is an urgent need to inject much seeded vitality into the economic system. This could be achieved by making industry, corporate houses and ultimately the entire nation globally competitive.

FACTORS AFFECTING THE COMPETITIVENESS

Competitiveness is the most discussed topic these days at various forums including of managers, academicians, government officials or media.

It can be defined as the relative standing of one competitor against other competitors. The key factors determining the competitiveness are listed below :

Labour

It affects the competitiveness from two angles—*Cost and Productivity.* If in a country wages are low, the labour-intensive production can enhance their competitiveness. Moreover, the productivity of labour, which in turn depends upon their skill, training, work culture, efficiency, attitude toward change and learning affects the competitiveness of the industry where they are employed.

Government

The sensitivity of the government and the pace with it takes decisions has a direct bearing on the competitiveness of any country's business. Domestic companies can be helped by their government's industrial policies by making available low cost funds for technology upgradation, product development research (venture capital), and marketing (brand equity funds). Usually, States provides fiscal incentives in terms of lower taxes or exempting certain industries from tax. The role of the government can also become negative if there is over-regulation and/or high taxes.

Exchange Rate

In the international markets, prices charged are substantially affected by the exchange rates. A low-value currency enhances the competitiveness and compels the manufacturers to shift their production to such countries. On the other hand, in case a currency gets stronger, it is hard to sell overseas. Moreover, the stronger currencies make the import cheaper.

Technology

A company that launches an advanced technology product first, and get it protected legally (by patent rights, copy rights, etc.) may enjoy competitive advantages over the rivals.

Cost of Capital

If the cost to borrow money or raise equity capital is less, a company can invest more and accept lower returns.

Management and Governance

This includes varieties of skills, including manufacturing skills and marketing skills as well ability to organize world-wide operations. Good governance inspires leadership, promote teamwork, reduce layers, and clarify accounting in the different facets. This may help in the overall competitiveness.

Country-specific Factors

A better educated population, with a culture that stress hard work, savings, and an un-equivocal concern for society is likely to make a country competitive in world markets. (Terpestra *et. al.*, 2000)

Infrastructure

The level of infrastructure of a market affects the operational efficiency of a concern and thus the competitiveness. Well-developed roads, ports, airports, banking and insurance facilities, media and adverting agencies are known to reduce the cost of production.

COMPARATIVE COMPETITIVENESS OF SELECTED COUNTRIES

As a nation it is important to understand where we stand in comparison to our Asian-Pacific counterparts. A study by Mashelkar (1998) as reflected in Table 7.1, shows that we are far behind them on most of the parameters viz., domestic economic strength, internationalization, government, finance, management, science and technology. In infrastructure we are 41st out of 42. In science and technology in which we pride ourselves we are 29th. This is because science and technology are measured not in terms of mere generation of new knowledge, but by the ability of our science and technology to create new products and new wealth.

Table 7.1
Comparative Competitiveness Ranking of Selected Countries in Asia Pacific

Country	*Domestic Economic Strength*	*Internationalization*	*Government*	*Finance*	*Infra-structure*	*Management*	*S & T*
Hong Kong	4	3	2	3	17	4	20
India	22	33	27	27	41	33	29
Indonesia	25	34	24	30	32	36	30
Japan	3	8	19	5	24	1	1
Malaysia	6	14	4	13	18	14	24
Singapore	2	2	1	2	16	7	8
Taiwan	5	17	11	20	27	21	15
Thailand	9	21	8	14	33	23	31

(Mashelkar, 1998).

INDICATORS OF FUTURE COMPARATIVE ADVANTAGE

The future scenario indicates that the sources and nature of competitive strength of nations will be characteristically different from those in the past. During the last century, the world business leaders mostly derived their competitive strength from the above factors besides breakthroughs in major scientific inventions and their slow dissemination across countries. In the twenty-first century, scientific innovations will not be based on capital alone or on monopolistic position of a few nations. Both capital and technology are fluid today. It is the disembodied technology rather than the hardware, which is moving faster across countries in bridging technological gaps. Apart from technological leadership, the competitive strength of nations would depend more and more on the strategic behaviour of the firms, their adaptability to the changing world environment and how they promote their core competence in several spheres (Jalan, 1999).

BUILDING INDIAN COMPETITIVENESS THROUGH KNOWLEDGE

Apart from the large size of different natural-resources, India can boast of its human resources. Human resources, particularly the large young population, are the unique core strength of the country. 70% of the Indian population is young. Therefore, we can adopt changing technologies faster and design a knowledge-led growth strategy for our economy. The nation needs young leaders who can command the change for transformation of India into a developed nation embedded with a knowledge society front now on to 20 years (Kalam, 2003).

Knowledge is the future of the business and economy. After agriculture and industrial revolution, *knowledge* is the *third wave revolution in wealth* creation and is more deeply rooted than most people could imagine. The *third wave revolution* in one of the major impacts driving globalisation as well as mounting backlash against globalisation. After all, all those people protesting against globalisation are using the Internet to do so. Something new is arising on the planet and it doesn't fit into the assumptions and paradigm left over from the *second wave*. The *third wave* knowledge economy threatens the core institutions and power arrangements of the industrial age. Many of these institutions are still dominant in traditional industrialized countries including France and Germany. This new wealth-creation system not only holds the potential for providing gigantic leap forward, but also for increased conflict both within and among societies (Toffler, 2003). We are seeing the beginning of bio-digital convergence. We now have clues to the digital manipulation of some sort of intelligence. Day after day discoveries are pouring from different laboratories. They also present us with profound moral issues. In the first phase, IT revolutionized biology. In the next phase, biology will revolutionize IT. Together, this represents turning points in human history.

INDIA'S COMPETITIVENESS IN KNOWLEDGE

The greatest heritage and assets of India is the power of its mind. Every nation has its own special attributes. The special attribute of Germany is its organization, of USA its enterprise, of Japan its adaptability and of Great Britain its balance. The hallmark of India has been the power of its mind (Jagmohan, 2003). Unless this power is regenerated, India can neither exploit its potential to the full nor evolve a distinct style of its own. This power of mind also found expression in the words of world scholars. For example, Will Durant a celebrated American historian says, "India was the mother of our philosophy; mother of much of our mathematics; mother, (through the Buddha) of the ideals embodied in Christianity; mother, through the village community, of self-government and democracy. Mother India is in many ways the mother of us all."

We need to introspect our unrealized potent strength of knowledge to make India a developed nation. Our Honorable Prime Minister declared on August 15, 2002 from the Red Fort that India would become a developed nation by 2020. The knowledge-led development of several countries suggests that India would follow the model for its developments and thus, it could become a major economy. In the 21st century, new societies are emerging which recognize knowledge as—a prime resource for the production of goods and services. Erstwhile, resources such as capital and labour are going to play a subservient role in the development planning of different countries. The information and communication technology (ICT) sector is one such area where it directly contributes 7-8 percent to the GDP of most of the developed nations. It is expected that by 2010 in these countries, ICT will account for 25 per cent of the GDP either directly (by way of sale of hardware and software) or indirectly. The indirect effects are visible through the connectivity for improved productivity of industries and improved efficiency in daily life through e-governance. Even India can boast of the fact that ICT accounts for nearly 2 per cent of gross domestic product of India. (Kalam, 2003)

Technology has brought access to colossal amount of information at desktops everywhere. Innovation at the right time is the order of the day. Corporate leaders need the benefit of the best thinking in order to focus on the right global strategies. Though India has made steady progress towards merging into global market and economy, it may not be adequate to become a global player. Shift in priorities needs to occur for corporations as well as for defining policy framework to realize India's potential. As global competition is shifting from an infrastructure intensive to a knowledge intensive environment, we need to know how to capitalize on our human capital and its pool of knowledge. We give brief account of selected measures and issues associated with such measures that can help improve the competitiveness of India Inc.

1. Innovation-based Education

If we are going to have a knowledge economy, we need to have knowledgeable people. Education is the critical component. Presently, we have a mass production education system in which kids are subjected to routine processing. They are not dealt with as individuals. This is not the model for the innovative people that the economy of the future requires people capable of working at home, capable of thinking (Toffler, 2003). Mere knowledge cannot be useful. It must help to create wealth and social good out of it through a process of innovation. We have to move from inhibition and imitation to innovation. To inculcate innovation, India needs an environment, which could upset the mind-set significantly. The fundamental issue is the transformation of institutions so that they are able to recognize breakthroughs.

In the knowledge society, minds and vision will be the dominating influences for competitive strengths. Human minds must, therefore, be unleashed to innovate, to interact, to co-operate and produce wealth for the ultimate good of society. India has just embarked on this innovative path as it approaches the new millennium. (Mashelkar, 1999).

2. Creating and Organizing Knowledge

The role of knowledge management is to promote and nurture innovation and creativity (Bowonder, 2001). Generating knowledge requires, innovative resolution of problems, generation of new ideas, discussion threads and meeting with customers, and new events (Banerjee, 2001). In the present changing environment, it is very important for business to continuously search for new avenues of knowledge. Creating new knowledge is of utmost significance, as the obsolescence is very fast. Knowledge can be created by simple techniques of creativity and structured dialogue or using sophisticated technique of simulation. According to Prof. A. Neelmeghan (Ojha, 2001), Knowledge is embodied in objects, a body of ideas, social and cultural systems and values. There are several paths that lead to knowledge discovery, including the important ones of observing the unusual in the usual, finding and formulating a principle or theory that explains observed phenomena in different fields, and relating an observation in one situation to different situations. Organizational knowledge consists of a combination of the knowledge of all individuals in an organization. It emerges out of a process of conscious and/or unconscious negotiations among all members of the organization (Ojha, 2001)

For the knowledge to be of maximum use to the organization, it must be accessible to different people when they need them and be transferable to those parts of the organization where they can be applied for creating greater value. India's leading FMCG Company HLL's sustained performance is the result of strong brands, but also of leveraging its collective knowledge of brand management, logistics and distribution management (Krishnan, 2001).

3. Networking and Partnering

Effective use of networking and partnering is a significant issue in achieving faster and steady technological development. They can be internal as well as external. Studies focused on internal networking and partnering found that "on the average the best source of information for an R & D engineer is a colleague in his own organization". But in case of complex projects, the inner team cannot sustain itself and work effectively without constantly importing new information from the outside world (Allen, 1985). The partnering result into Complex interactions between different partners resulting in synergy that produce value (Porter, 2002).

Degree of collaboration/integration between functional units, such as marketing and R & D, has a profound influence on the success/failure outcome of innovative projects in industrial settings (Suman, 2002). The technological leaders have the highest level of R & D cooperation with other companies, but these firms regard external technological resources as complementary and not as a substitute and they prefer stable and formal co-operation agreement; External R & D cooperation with other companies is clearly a matter of firm size. Large companies cooperate more often than small ones. Customer-focused developers cooperate more with research institutes and universities than firm following other strategies (Gemiindea r *et. al*, 1995).

4. Protecting the Knowledge

Protecting knowledge is even more important than merely creating it. It is awful that the knowledge created by us on neem, turmeric, or ginger is being monopolized by American companies, by patenting the products. Similarly, Microsoft is leading the world in software products. The Indians constitute significant portion of pool of its employees. Therefore, we must develop sensitive system of protecting our intellectual property and check the brain drain.

Additional protection for valuable knowledge is gained by converting it to a form protectable by (IRP) law. This includes designs, patents copyrights and trade mark. Active IRP management involves the registering of this intellectual property and rigorously pursuing redress against violators of the owner's rights. Knowledge origination must maintain proper documentation. Chronological progress of an invention must be maintained. It is necessary to legally prevent competitor to exploit it.

5. Business Process Re-engineering

Small companies, as is true of large companies, must resort to the business process re-engineering. The expanse of widely available information technologies with immense power of advanced analysis can help even small and specialized companies to improve the processes of manufacture, delivery and service. Let innovations be not a monopoly of

MNC's. If Japanese companies can mastermind, why it can't be true for Indian companies. In India the problem is of management of R & O and not of the lack of people and—technology. Our industry's lack of contribution to R & D shows their narrowness of vision and time frame. In global environment a long-term perspective is key to good performance. The future may belong to neither large nor small companies perse but rather—to those societies that can innovate and create appropriate organizations to meet the needs of 21st century business. Improving professionalism and organizational effectiveness applies both to private and public sectors and this is where India's social values will play an important role in shaping its future competitiveness. In order to face increased global competition, it is important to concentrate on India's long-term competitive strength and to gear its research developments, technological and managerial strength towards that end.

India has rich heritage. It has come through difficult challenges with many achievements. It has a strong industrial base, highly educated and skilled professionals, rich technological capabilities, entrepreneurial skill and a mature democracy with a sound rule of law. Management challenges for the present century are in the fields of technology, organizational restructuring, skill development and public policy. India's position in these spheres, though impressive, require further strengthening in order to enable it to face the new environment with confidence. In the open world economy, it is relative competitive strength that would matter.

CONCLUSION

In the changing uncertain environment, knowledge will play a key role for the success of any business. The organization needs to embed knowledge in every sphere of activity for its effectiveness in global market. Every organization generates or has potential to generate knowledge, but due to lack of any established system of its management, it goes into drain. Knowledge management is generally associated with decentralized decision-making and a belief in specialization and the value of deep expertise. Many Indian organizations would therefore, have to change their whole way of thinking, structure and culture to make it work to their benefit. India is rich in traditional knowledge and skills that have been accumulated over centuries in the past and these should be nurtured for posterity and to enhance our competitiveness.

REFERENCES

Alien, T.J., Managing the Flow of Technology, Cambridge, Massachnsetts : MIT Press, 1985.

Dawar, Subhash, "Competing is Easy", *Indian Management*, 2001, June.

Gemiinden, H.G. and Hydebrecky, P., The Influence of Business Strategies on Technological Network Activity, *Research Policy*, 24(6), 1995, pp. 834-49.

Kalam, A.P.J. Abdul, Vision for 2020 : It is the knowledge societies that will transform—India into a Developed Nation, *India Today*, March 17, 2003, pp. 23-26V.

Porter, Michael E., "What is Strategy", In MucTicato, Mariana (Rd.X Strategy for Sage Publications, New Delhi, 2002, pp. 10-31.

Jagmohan, "Power of Indian Mind : Our Heritage and Asset", *The Tribune*, Feb. 23, 2003, p. 12.

Jalan, Bimal, Millennium Challenges for Management and Technology Towards India Inc.—Strategies for Competitiveness, New Delhi, All India Management Association (Amexcel Publishers Pvt. Ltd., New Delhi), 1999, pp. 185-91.

Mashelkar, Ramesh A., Innovation and Vision—Key to a Competitive Tomorrow, Towards India, Inc.—Strategies for Competitiveness, New Delhi : All India Management Association (Amexcel Publishers Pvt. Ltd., New Delhi), 1999, pp. 125-37.

Mashelkar, Ramesh, 1998, "Manufacturing Technology in India—The New Challenges".

Singh, K. Manmohan, India Can Do It—What Will it Take, Global Competitiveness, Delhi : All India Management Association, (Amexel Publishers Pvt. Ltd., New Delhi), 2000, pp. 49-59.

Suman, Shikha, R & D Mangement : Issues and Challenges, *Management Review*, June 2002, p. 30.

Terpstra Vera and Sarathy, Ravi, International Marketing, Fort Worth : The Dryden Press, Harcourt College Publishers, 2000, p. 713.

Toffler, Alvin, Tomorrow's Economy—India has to Leverage its Strength in IT to Cross the Final Frontier, *India Today*, March 17, 2003, pp. 28-30.

CHAPTER 8

Impact of Liberalization and Globalization : An Indian Perspective

SONIA CHAWLA

INTRODUCTION

The Sovereign Democratic Republic of India occupies a small proportion of India's long history—the half century since 1950. Within this short time span however, its economic regime has experienced two radical transformations. First, with the establishment of the Planning Commission in March 1950, India launched upon a unique experiment in state-led 'growth with social justice' within the constitutional framework of parliamentary democracy. However, this policy matrix came under significant pressure in the 1980s, culminating in the unprecedented balance of payments crisis in 1990-91. The Indian government responded to this crisis with an equally forthright policy regime grounded in a reform trinity popularly referred to as 'Liberalization, Privatization and Globalization' (LPG). These three economic concepts have necessitated a series of (ongoing) policy reforms by the Union and State Governments. Internationally, globalization has yielded impressive growth dividends, including for relatively poor developing countries. The term globalization as such denotes adjustment of national economy with that of the world economy. It refers to convergence of different economies of the world, which is given the name of global village. The liberalization process was initiated following a balance of payments crisis in 1990-91. India's economic reform program has emphasized gradualism and evolutionary transition rather than rapid restructuring or shock therapy.

EVALUATION OF INDIA'S ECONOMIC DEVELOPMENT FROM 1980-81 TO 2000-2001

These economic reforms have yielded the following significant benefits :

Unlike some other developing countries, notably those in East Asia, which transitioned to a liberalized framework in the three decades since 1950, India has been a gradual reformer. Continued reliance on state intervention created a highly regulated economy. The result was the absence of significant levels of competition either from imports or within the domestic economy. Industrial capacity restrictions, prohibitions in foreign trade, high tariff walls, prohibitions on technology transfer, inadequate patent protection, restrictive labour laws and administered interest rates severely limited the scope for the efficiency enhancing impact of markets.

During the post-1985 period, the economy grew at around 6% with an increase in real per capita income of around 4%. The incidence of poverty declined from 44% to 26% and the life expectancy at birth grew significantly from 48 years to 62 years. Literacy rate increased from 52% in 1990-91 to 65.38% in 2000-01.

The planned and tightly regulated development till the mid-1980s resulted in positive though moderate levels of growth. However, growth rates in the "early reformers" in East Asia were considerably higher as illustrated by the following table :

TABLE 8.1
GDP Growth (average % per year) : International Comparison

	1965-80	*1980-90*	*1990-2000*
China	6.4	9.5	10.3
Korea	9.5	9.7	5.7
Malaysia	7.4	5.2	7.0
Thailand	7.4	7.6	4.2
Indonesia	7.9	5.5	4.2
India	3.7	5.3	6.0

Not only was economic growth lower in India during the period 1965 to 1980 but unlike the East Asian economies, which aggressively sought export competitiveness for domestic manufactures, India sought self-sufficiency. The positive impact of economic reform in India is illustrated in table by the narrowing of the "growth gap" *vis-a-vis* East Asian countries during the period 1980 to 1990. In post-1990 the Indian economy has fared very well in comparison. Economic growth in India averaged 6% per annum during the decade of the 1990s. In comparison economic growth in East Asia, except in the case of China and Malaysia, was adversely affected by the financial crisis in the second half of the 1990s.

The insularity of the economy can be gauged from the fact that India's share in world exports reduced from 1.85% to 0.42% between 1950 and 1980. The results have been positive in the external sector during the period from 1980-2000 which was marked by an increase in the share of India's exports in World exports from 0.42 to 0.67%.

The ratio of external debt to GDP declined from 5.5% in 1990-91 to 2.6% in 2000-01. Similarly, the profile of external debt became more stable. The ratio of short-term external debt to total external debt declined from a peak of 10.2% in end March 1991 to 2.8% in end December 2001.

The level of Foreign Exchange Reserves increased from a level equal to 3 months import in 1990-91 to a level of over 8.5 months of import since 1993-94. By 2000 India's short-term external debt was only 8.5% of foreign exchange reserves, which is much lower than 10% in China, 15.5% in Malaysia, 45.6% in Thailand and 112.6% in Argentina.

Macro-economic stability and a higher degree of openness have also resulted in an increase in inflow of foreign investment (portfolio plus FDI) from a level of $ 113 million in 1990-91 to $ 14,294 million in 2000-01, though these are far below the potential inflow.

The productivity and efficiency of the Indian economy has been a traditional and much analyzed concern in India. Agriculture in the private sector appears to have responded the most favourably. Annual average growth in this sector increased from 3.9% during the period 1960 to 1985 to 7.2% in the reform period 1985 to 2000.

The pressure of increased competition in the domestic and in the present internationl market, improved managerial practices and better capacity utilization. These changes in the macro-environment have benefited business in general. The ratio of PAT to Net sales for private manufacturing increased to a peak of 9.1% in 1994-95 before declining to 6.2% in 1997-98. PSEs on aggregate continued to make losses in the 1990s. Aggregate loss was 4.5% of net sales in 1990-91. This increased to a peak of 6.9% in 1993-94 before declining to 3.9% in 1997-98. Clearly economy wide reform has benefited both the public and the private sector. In the public sector losses persist. Possibly, the beneficial changes in the macro-environment have not been matched by initiatives within PSEs, to increase their competitiveness, perhaps due to complex procedures within PSEs, due to their ownership structure.

Higher levels of investment will be key for acceleration of the growth rate to a level of 8%, which is estimated to be the minimum required to effectively tackle the problem of poverty. There is considerable evidence to show that an increase in investment levels sharply increases the rate of economic growth. Increase in productivity coupled with an increase in investment explains the acceleration in economic growth in many developing countries. Following table provides an inter-country comparison of incremental investments and increase in economic growth over the period 1980 to 1995.

TABLE 8.2
Investment and GDP Growth Rates; Cross Country Comparison (Average % per year)

	Change in Investment Rate		*Change in GDP Growth*	
	1980-90	*1990-95*	*1980-90*	*1990-95*
China	11	15.5	10.2	12.8
Malaysia	2.6	16	5.2	8.7
Indonesia	7	16.3	6.1	7.6
Thailand	9.4	10.2	7.6	8.4
Turkey	5.3	25.	3	3.2
Argentina	-0.3	5.7	-4.7	16
India	6.5	5.3	5.8	4.6
Venezuela	-5.3	3.8	1.1	2.4
Brazil	0.2	3.5	2.7	2.7
Philippines	-2.1	3.2	1	2.3
Egypt	2.7	-1.5	5	1.3
Poland	0.9	1.1	1.9	2.4

China, Malaysia (1990-95), Indonesia, Thailand, Turkey (1980-90) and Argentina (1990-95) are examples where a sharp increase in the rate of investment had a positive impact on economic growth. India has had consistent increases in the investment levels with resultant increases in economic growth as well. The low rates of economic growth in Venezuela, Brazil, Philippines, Egypt and Poland can be associated with the negative or low rates of change in investment levels. It has been estimated that India needs to increase its investment rate to 30% of GDP if it is to grow at 8% per year. This is considerably more than what has been achieved in the past. However, enhanced savings in the public sector coupled with increased usage of foreign savings can bridge the savings-investment gap in a manner consistent with macro-economic stability. FDI is one such stable, potential source of financing, particularly in the context of privatization.

Globalization is a complex process that is having a massive impact on living standards across both the developed and developing world. In short, the liberalization and global competition are both a challenge and opportunities.

COMPETITION POLICY—THE BASICS

Competition policy can be defined in many ways but basically it is the measure and instrument used by governments to determine the 'conditions of competition' between producers and suppliers of goods and services that operate in their markets—Competition (or anti-trust) law, is a subset of competition policy, and exists to combat anti-competitive business conduct. The key focus of competition policy in the North is to achieve efficiencies through enhanced inter-firm rivalry, by limiting anti-competitive behaviour in the private sector as well as prohibiting government-led market distortions. These efficiencies are assumed to result in lower prices and more choices for the consumer, better products and services and increasing opportunities for existing and new businesses. Thus, Shelton states : "The broad objective of competition policy is to help ensure that market economies deliver high and rising standards of living." Although market efficiency is often the key goal of competition policies, in practice, most governments take into account non-efficiency goals such as fairness, opportunities for small businesses, pluralism, technological development and employment, in the conduct of their domestic competition policies.

Developing countries are being urged to introduce competition policies and laws as part of the neo-liberal economic package and to demonstrate their commitment to open markets. There are two forces leading to a common interest in establishing multilateral cooperation in competition policy and law. First, economic globalization has resulted an increase in the volume of business operating across national borders. This means that the conduct of Transnational Corporations (TNCs) has significant international effects but all governments face huge challenges in dealing with them. Even where domestic competition policies are strong, there are difficulties with international inter-governmental access to information and legal jurisdiction. In these circumstances, international co-operation is required to prevent anti-competitive behaviour and restrictive business practices. Second, there has been a huge merger wave that began in the 1990s and is characterized by a large incidence of cross-border takeovers and mergers. Most cross-border amalgamations are taking place among the industrial countries and the largest proportion is within the US. However, during the last decade, a considerable proportion of Foreign Direct Investment (FDI) in developing countries has taken the form of acquisition of existing enterprises rather than Greenfield investment. The perceived risks from mergers and acquisitions have been a key factor in persuading developing countries that it may be necessary to have some form of competition policy. There is a danger that mergers and strategic alliances between firms will lead to a concentration of wealth and economic and market power, undermining local competitors without delivering greater efficiency. Such a situation requires action by competition regimes, at national as well as international levels.

1. Data reported in the *Financial Times* (*FT*, October 25, 1999) suggests that of the total world-wide merger activity of nearly $ 2.5 trillion, almost $ 1.6 trillion represented takeovers and mergers within the United States; much of the remaining activity occurred in other industrial countries.
2. UNCTAD (Trade and Development Report, 1999) data suggests that if China (which among developing countries has not only been the largest recipient of FDI, but most of this investment has also been greenfield) is excluded, the share of mergers and acquisitions in the accumulated FDI in developing countries rises from 22 per cent during 1988 to 1991 to an average of 72 per cent. The understanding of how competition policy might work to support developing economies is still evolving and requires more study.

SOME EXAMPLES OF ANTI-COMPETITIVE BEHAVIOUR AND RESTRICTIVE BUSINESS PRACTICES

Monopolies : A monopoly occur when one company has total control of the production or delivery of a particular product or service. As a sole supplier, monopoly companies can fix prices without reference to competitors. *Market Dominance* : A company has market dominance when it occupies a position of such strength in the market that it operates without effective constraints from competitors or potential competitors. *Cartels* : A cartel is a group of companies who agree (in writing, verbally or tacitly) to stop competing with each other. This usually involves agreed market allocation/market sharing, price fixing, eliminating non-cartel competition, and sometimes, collusive tendering. National competition law can deal with domestic cartels but export cartels often go unchecked. *Collusive tendering also called bid-rigging* : This involves members of a cartel colluding or arranging among themselves the prices and other conditions to be set in submissions to tender for contracts in order to avoid inter-company competition. *Differential pricing* : A supplier charges different prices to different buyers on a basis other than the quality or quantity ordered. *Transfer pricing* : It is practice of either under-invoicing or over-invoicing taking place between a parent company and its subsidiaries. The aim of under-invoicing is to lower the costs of the subsidiary so that its prices are reduced and it can eliminate its competitors from the market (disguised predatory pricing). The aim of over-invoicing is to increase costs artificially, in order to reduce profits and avoid taxation, or circumvent profit repatriation rules in the host country.

While it is important for trade and competition laws to be consistent, it is equally important for competition policy to be integrated into national development strategies and coherent with national industrial policy. Competition policies and laws should not prevent the promotion of economic growth through industrial policy measures, designed to foster concentration of local enterprises, or provide discriminatory support to infant industries. Furthermore, if developing countries lack a strong state, they may not have the institutional capacity to implement comprehensive competition policies and would be better focusing on a few simple rules. However, without any form of competition policy, developing countries are powerless to challenge anti-competitive behaviour that may inhibit their economic development. All governments should give serious consideration to what type of competition policy would be appropriate for their circumstances.

COMPETITION POLICY AND WTO

Existing WTO agreements do not address competition policy as such. However, the GATT agreements do have a number of provisions relating to areas of international competition. The most important of these are those dealing with enterprises owned by—states or enterprises with import monopolies or exclusive or special trading privileges; and with anti-dumping and subsidized trade. With respect to business conduct, the WTO barely addresses any conduct and competition problems, and as an inter-governmental forum, it has no authority to deal with private enterprises directly. The WTO Working Group on the Interaction between Trade and Competition Policy (WGTCP) was established at the Singapore Ministerial Conference in 1996. Since that time, the Working Group has received some 125 submissions from WTO Members. The WGTCP's mandate is "to study issues raised by members relating to the—interaction between trade and competition policy, including anti-competitive practices, in order to identify any areas that may merit further consideration in the WTO framework" and "to take the development dimension fully into account". The World Trade Organization (WTO) organized a Regional Workshop on Competition Policy, Economic Development and the Multilateral Trading System in 2000 at Phuket, Thailand. The most important question raised was how a competitive environment could serve to enhance rather than impair economic development. There was a good degree of agreement that industrial policy, if it was to be useful, had to be combined with competition policy even if the mix between the two policies needed to vary with the level of economic development. Competition law and regulatory tools are invoked mainly to take care of firm behaviour and market failures. Governments often intervene when markets fail but in the absence of a clearly defined competition policy and regulatory mechanisms, the intervention can be arbitrary and serve vested interests rather than the poor. In such a situation the absence of a competition policy and an adequate regulatory mechanism will simply mean the transfer of monopoly power from the public to the private sector. This is likely to harm the interests of consumers, especially the poor. Enforcement either lacked the necessary vigour or was carried out in a distorted manner. There was undue government intervention on many occasions, especially in Pakistan. In India, the law was made ineffective by manning the body charged with enforcement with inadequately qualified or experienced staff who was also too few in number.

CONCLUSION

- There is widespread consensus that national action on competition policy is insufficient and needs to be complemented by international cooperation.
- The first priority should be to build capacity at national level, so that national competition-promoting policies can be developed. Ideally, policies should have multilateral convergence in their objectives. Since there is no single accepted form for competition policy, and 'one size' does not fit all, each country will need to develop a policy that meets its needs and capacities.
- A synergy between the competition policy and other national policies on the one hand and coherence between the competition authority and other competent authorities on the other is necessary for the whole set-up to yield the desired benefits.
- A national competition regime bagged by adequate resources would allow the countries to investigate and prosecute anti-competitive behaviour.
- Cooperation agreements in the competition arena are best pursued in multilateral framework.
- More research and analysis is needed to assess the impacts of different forms of competition policy on economic development. In the meantime, there should be no multilateral disciplines obliging developing countries to have comprehensive competition policies or, indeed, any competition policy at all, if they do not think that its costs would outweigh its benefits.
- The WTO was established to liberalize trade, not to handle competition issues, and the two are philosophically quite different. A market-access approach targets trade maximization. A competition approach targets efficient resource allocations and welfare maximisation. UNCTAD and other bodies have greater expertise in competition policy than the WTO.
- If there is genuine international political will to establish a forum to manage anti-competitive behaviour, it would be preferable to establish a separate entity to help the development of national competition laws and their convergence. Many commentators believe that the best solution could be to establish an international competition authority, not dominated by the North and with

proper representation of the South in its governance, which had a positive attitude to participation by civil groups.

REFERENCES

Chaudhuri, Sudip (2002), 'Economic Reforms and Industrial Structure in India'.

Competition Policy : What Chance for International Rules? J. Shelton, OECD, 1998, p. 1 fhttp : www.oecd.org/daf/cip).

Department of Company Affairs, Government of India, 2000, Report of the High-level Committee on Competition Law and Policy (New Delhi, Government of India).

Economic Survey, 2001-02.

India Development Report, 2002.

Mehta, P.S., Competition Policy in Developing Countries : An Asia Pacific Perspective, CUTS, Center for International Trade, Jaipur, India.

SECTION II

MANUFACTURING SECTOR

Competitiveness of the Indian Garment Export Sector after Multi-Fibre Arrangement (MFA) Phase-Out

RAGHBIR SINGH AND LALIT MOHAN KATHURIA

Tracing the history of the Indian ready-made garment industry, it can be seen that in pre-independent India, clothing styles were dictated by the dress habits of the dynasties that ruled different parts of India from time to time. The long years of the birth rule in India had a definite influence on clothing patterns in urban areas. The decentralization of the textile industry witnessed the growth of power looms and small-scale processing units in India. Mass manufacturing of the garment industry began in India as an aftermath of the Second World War. The growing settlement of Indians in the US and UK during the late 1960s and 1970s who acted as importers of Indian cotton garments and also the socio-political events of the period led to a spurt in the growth of imports of garments from India. The need for mass production led to proliferation of several small-scale units. The various milestones in the growth of the garment industry include :

- Spurt in growth of garment exports from India during the 1970s.
- Setting up of Apparel Export Promotion Council (AEPC).
- Accelerated growth in late 1980s and early 1990s.
- Introduction of long-term quota distribution policies.
- Phasing-out of Multi-Fibre Arrangement (MFA) from 1995 to 2005.

The sixth round of General Agreement on Tariffs and Trade (GATT) negotiations called the 'Kennedy Round' held in 1962, with 62 countries attending, brought in the Long-term Agreement (LTA) regarding trade in the cotton textiles. This LTA lasted for 12 years from 1962 to 1974. As the imports of other fibre-based textiles and garments started increasing by the early 1970s, the LTA was replaced by the Multi-Fibre Arrangement. The MFA-I (1974 -77), MFA-II (1978-81), MFA-III (1982-85) and MFA-IV (1986-94) regulated the world trade in textiles and clothing through quantitative restrictions (quotas) till the implementation of GATT/94 with effect from January 1, 1995 (Koshy, 1997).

On April 15, 1994, the treaty to phase-out the MFA was endorsed. The treaty includes the Agreement on Textiles and Clothing (ATC), which sets out a time frame of 10 years between 1995 and 2004 for the phase-out of MFA quotas and integration into the World Trade Organization (WTO), thereby replacing GATT as given below :

TABLE 9.1
Phase-out of MFA Quotas

Phase 1	January 1, 1995	16% of the total 1990 Imports
Phase 2	January 1, 1998	17% of the total 1990 Imports
Phase 3	January 1, 2002	18% of the total 1990 Imports
Phase 4	January 1, 2005	49% of the total 1990 Imports

Table 9.1 shows that quotas under MFA are to be phased-out in four phases. Now, it in the last stage of the phase-out process and by January 2005, all the quotas will be abolished and free trade will become possible after January 2005.

PROFILE OF THE INDIAN GARMENT EXPORT INDUSTRY

The volume and character of the international trade has far reaching consequences in the case of developing countries like India. The contribution of the garment sector to the country's foreign exchange earnings and thus, the reduction in trade deficits confer a role of prominence to the garment sector.

Over the years, the export basket has shown a shift from low value added items to those with a higher value addition. The exports of commodities like textiles and garments increased their share in exports. The value addition in apparel exports makes it all the more important among other exported manufactured products. Ready-made garments have a value addition of as high as 70-80 per cent. This has given garments the unique status of being the highest net foreign exchange earner. The key features of the Indian garment industry are :

- Indian Textile and Clothing Industry contributes about 4% of GDP and 14% of Industrial output. This industry provides direct employment to 35 million people, second largest after the agricultural Industry.
- Largest net Foreign Exchange earner of India accounting for 35% of the foreign exchange.
- India's export of garments are primarily of cotton, almost 70% of the garment exports consist of this category. The share of synthetic garments is increasing but very slowly.
- India's share of world garment exports was 3.3% in 2001. In 2001, Global clothing trade was US $ 195 billion and India exported garments worth US $ 6.5 billion.
- Three-fourth of the garments exported are woven garments, balance is largely accounted for by knitted garments.
- Large dependence on North America and European Union as export destinations.
- More than half of the exports are accounted for by five product categories—women's dresses, blouses, skirts, men's shirts and knitted undergarments.
- Another feature of India's garment exports is the large number of exporters operating in the small-scale and unorganized sector through system of sub-contracting. The outsourcing level of India is 74% in case of Indian garments.

PERFORMANCE OF INDIAN GARMENT EXPORT SECTOR

USA and European Union (EU) are the major importers of Indian garments. In 2000, USA imported US $ 57.2 billions of garments with average unit value, equal to US $ 3.57 per square metre. While 56% of US imports valued at US $ 32.01 billion were cotton garments, only 34% of these were man-made fibre garments. The average unit value of cotton garments were higher at US $ 3.64 per square metre.

European Union imported US $ 42.5 billion worth of clothing. Out of the total textiles and clothing imports of US $ 65.9 billion, US $ 29.4 billion were from restrained suppliers, while US $ 20.9 billion were from preferential suppliers. In case of clothing, almost 43% and 36% originated in preferential and restrained sources respectively. This is explained by the increasing significance of Outward Processing Trade (OPT) between EU and its neighbouring regions. (Verma, 2002)

Table 9.2 shows that in US market, India's share, in 2000, grew at more than 10% in cotton dresses (Category 336), women and girls woven shirts (Category 341) and cotton skirts (Category 342). India operates in the low value segment in most cotton apparels in the US, i.e. in Categories 338, 347 and 348. Incidentally, US imports of these products are growing fastest among all cotton apparel categories. However, India has lost share in many categories during 1995-2000. In Category 347, its prices have grown

TABLE 9.2
Performance of Indian Cotton Garment Exports in US

Description	*Category*	*Growth rate in Market Share*	*Growth rate in Unit Value Realisation (UVR) of India*	*Growth rate of US Total Imports*
Baby Garments	239	113%	11%	85%
Dresses	336	28%	–6%	12%
Men & Boys (MB) Knitted Shirts	338	–19%	38%	88%
Women & Girls (WG) Knitted Shirts	339	–40%	26%	144%
MB Woven Shirts	340	9%	–2%	3%
WG Woven Shirts	341	10%	15%	31%
Skirts	342	–9%	3%	54%
MB Trousers	347	35%	74%	85%
WG Trousers	348	–7%	39%	140%

Source : Working Paper No. 94, Indian Council for Research on International Economic Relations, New Delhi, 2002, p. 10.

fastest among top ten suppliers. In cotton apparels, the countries like Indonesia, Malaysia, Hong Kong, Sri Lanka are competitors with India. India should try to increase the quality of its products, improve upon the delivery period rather than competing solely on price.

Table 9.3 shows that growth rate in UVR of imports of India in garment categories of knitted T-Shirts and Mens and Boys is more than the growth rate in UVR of imports of these garments from other suppliers. So, India is export competitive in these garment categories and stands to gain.

WORLD CLOTHING EXPORT SCENARIO AND INDIA

In the world clothing export scenario, out of the 15 leading exporting countries, eight are from Asia, viz. Turkey, Taiwan, Hong Kong, Thailand, China, Indonesia, South Korea and India. From all indications, China has become an undisputed leader from the point of view of market share and presence. China's garment export have reached a total value of US $ 35 billion in 2000 which are up by 47.7 per cent from 1994, at an annual growth rate of 6.7 per cent. This export value will reflect 65 per cent of the total textile exports of China and one-sixth of the world's clothing exports. Several studies indicate that China is expected to dominate the developed market through highly favourable quality-price performance and many experts forecast that China may appropriate about 60 to 80 per cent of the market share in the major destination markets after the MFA phase-out. (Koshy, 1997).

TABLE 9.3
India's Performance in the EU Clothing Import Market

Category Description	*Garment Category*	*Growth Rate of EU Imports*		*Growth Rate of Imports from India*	
		Value	*UVR*	*Value*	*UVR*
T-Shirts (Knit)	4	45%	16%	30%	23%
Jerseys, Pullovers (Knit)	5	42%	36%	56%	18%
M & B Shirts & Trousers	6	48%	3%	48%	13%

Source : Working Paper No. 94, Indian Council for Research on International Economic Relations, New Delhi, 2002, p. 13.

Why should a country, that is ranked among the top 15 competitive garment exporting nations in the world have to worry about the competition. Although, India is part of the global garment elite, its reputation rests on shaky foundations. It enjoys a garment trade surplus owing to the export quota regime guaranteed under MFA and because it's domestic high tariff barriers protect market, yet under WTO rules, India will find both these crutches jerked away quite soon. While the MFA will be phased-out by 2005, imports will soon be flooding the market and will become a deluge when the country is forced to lower its tariff barriers in a couple of years.

While a handful of firms are all set to conquer the world, India may not fare too well when its garment industry is pitched against the best. In the era of open markets and crumbling tariff walls, huge chunks of industry may be wiped out. The end of quota regime by the year 2005 is not a threat but an opportunity. A quota free market may throw up both a challenge and an opportunity for the clothing exports of India. In a quota free international market, some countries will have to vacate some of their shares because of high and increasing production costs, and India would need to quickly cash in on the emerging opportunities.

SWOT ANALYSIS OF INDIAN GARMENT EXPORT SECTOR

The implications of the MFA phase-out depend on the perceptions about India's strengths and weaknesses in garment sector. India's strengths in the sector can be identified as :

Strengths

- Easy availability of raw cotton. India has some of the finest qualities of the cotton in the world.
- Cheap Labour : Labour rate in India is US $ 0.56/hour whereas in Japan it is US $ 23.05/hour.
- Educated supervisory staff.

- Availability of Technical, Managerial and product development skills, as India is having Institutes like National Institute of Fashion Technology (NIFT).

Weaknesses

- Low Productivity in the garment-manufacturing sector. Our shirt manufacturing units produce between 9-12 shirts in eight hours shift whereas in China or Indonesia the production is between 18-20 shirts.
- Rejection level and rework level is between 5-20%, which is very high.
- Poor Infrastructure along with high cost of power and finance.
- Average lead time, from Product Development to final delivery in USA/EU, is between 4-6 months in India, whereas Far East suppliers deliver between 60-75 days.
- Outdated technology and low economies of scale.
- Outsourcing of cutting and sewing operations which causes quality problems like lot-to-lot variation and higher lead times.

Opportunities

- Global clothing exports will reach US $ 225 billion in 2005 whereas India's present share, in World Clothing Trade, is 3% which shows that there is a lot of growth opportunity available in clothing exports.
- Quota restrictions will be removed by the importing countries, so exporters will not have quantitative restrictions on the export quantities.
- Domestic apparel market will grow as 300 million middle class will grow to 520 million in next 5 years.
- Increasing share of non-quota countries like Japan, South Africa, etc.

Threats

- Intense competition from countries like China, Pakistan, Sri Lanka, Bangladesh and Nepal, China's share of world clothing trade jumped from 4% in 1980 to 16% in 2000, whereas India could manage to increase it from 1% to only 3%. In addition, India's unit value realization (UVR) is lower than that of China.
- Emergence of low cost manufacturing facilities in Vietnam and Mauritius.
- Lower import duty on imports from Pakistan by EU, which makes India's imports into EU unviable.
- Regional Trade Pacts and Bilateral Agreements, e.g., NAFTA, EU, APEC, ASEAN.
- Manufacturing facilities being established in new area like Mexico.
- Non-Tariff Barriers, e.g. use of Azo-free dyes, Social Accountability, Ethical Trading, etc.

Strategies for Increasing the Export Share

Following recommendations are made to improve the market share of India in the world clothing trade :

- Import duty on trims and fabrics should be removed which will make the price of Indian garments competitive in world markets.
- Modernization of ginning, processing, weaving sector should be undertaken immediately. Exporters should avail the cheap finance facility under 'Technology Upgradation Fund' scheme of Ministry of Textiles, Government of India. Process Management has to be improved in apparel manufacturing.
- Value addition should be increased in the garments. Latest designs and patterns should be followed. Products like swimwear, nightwear, uniforms and raincoats, etc. should be given the impetus. Technical textiles and industrial fabrics will gain more and more attention.
- Market Research studies should be conducted in the importing countries. The Indian garment exporters are hardly having any direct relationship with the ultimate consumer of the garment in the world markets.
- Supply Chain Management is the need of the hour. Strategic alliance between vendors, suppliers and manufacturers need to be established. The exporters should adapt Logistics Management.
- Indian companies should enter into strategic alliances with Multinational Corporations of U.S.A., Europe and East Asia, e.g. J.C. Penney, Marubeni, Wal-Mart and Sears, etc. so as to have buy back arrangements with these corporations. About 60 established brands control 85% of the world market in garments.
- Delivery of samples and garments should be improved. Exporters should react very quickly for want of samples by importers.
- The garment exporters should adapt EDI, ERP Systems and MIS.
- Smaller orders should be accepted by the garment exporters due to the changing needs of the customers.
- Lot size variations should be checked and wastages in the apparel manufacturing process should be curtailed so as to compete on prices and quality front.

In the context of India's overall international trade requirements and being the highest net foreign exchange earner, the garment export sector has to look at ways and means of achieving competitive advantage to sustain the growth and profitability in the quota-free trade of textiles and garments, to be brought in by the WTO. The garment industry will have to stand on its own feet after MFA phase-out and also safeguard its home market against cheaper imports as India will also have to open up its domestic market to the foreign suppliers after the phase-out. The route to a higher share lies in the production of more value-added products, collaborations and joint ventures. We have to change our mindset and see the world as one huge market and leverage our strengths accordingly.

REFERENCES

Apparel Export Promotion Council (1999) : *Handbook of Export Statistics,* 1997, 1998 and 1999, New Delhi.

Anson, Robin (1999) : *Strategies for Global Competitiveness,* Textile Intelligence. Paper presented at CII's TEXCON, Chandigarh, December.

Chandra, Pankaj (1997) : *Competing through Capabilities : Strategies for Global Competitiveness of the Indian Textile Industry.* Paper presented at CII's TEXCON Conference, Chandigarh.

Indian Institute of Foreign Trade (1997) : *India's Competitiveness in Export of Garments in the MFA Phase-out and Post-MFA Phase-out periods,* Occasional Paper 10, New Delhi : Apex Printing House.

Koshy, Darlie O. (1997) : *Garment Exports,* New Delhi : Prentice Hall of India Ltd.

Koshy, Darlie O. and Sudhir K. Jain (1995) : *Effective Export Marketing of Apparel to USA, EU and Japan,* New Delhi : Global Business Press.

Stuart S., Keith (2002) : *Competitive Advantage in the Post-MFA Era.* Paper presented at International conference on emerging trends in Textiles, Chandigarh, November 14-16.

Verma, Samar (2002) : *Export Competitiveness of Indian Textile and Garment Industry,* Working Paper No. 94, New Delhi : Indian Council for Research on International Economic Relations.

Productivity Improvement of Industrial Sectors in Punjab

B.S. Rathore and S.K. Dhameja

INTRODUCTION

Concepts of productivity emphasize the importance of assessing the cost effectiveness of new equipment, processes or technologies meant to facilitate a higher rate of production prior to their introduction. To catch up with the developed countries of the world, the developing countries have to ensure a high rate of productivity growth. In spite of the destruction caused by World War II, Japan has built-up a good image of its industrial products. The Japanese are now the leaders in the field of electronics and many of their products are even superior to those manufactured in the USA or West Germany. During the decade 1970-79, Japan had the highest rate of investment (33%) of gross fixed private and non-defence government investment as a percentage of GNP. During the very same period, it was 23.1% in France and West Germany, 22.7% in Canada, 20.2% in Italy, 18.8% in UK and only 17.5% in the USA. According to the figures available for 1981, the per capita GNP of India was just 2.03% in relation to the USA, while it was 104.91% in West Germany, 78.63% in Japan and 35.49% in the USSR. A country's development lies mainly in improving its productivity to such an extent that it may be able to contribute more and more to the GNP.

The growth rate in total factor productivity was only 1.3% per year in India during the period 1966-67 to 1979-80, according to the information furnished by Ahluwalia. According to her, for the same period the growth rates of total factor productivity for Korea was as high as 5.7% per year, that for Japan, Turkey and Yugoslavia, 3.1%, 2.0% and 0.8% respectively. She has also brought to the fore the fact that though labour productivity has improved at the rate of 2.5% per year in the country, the growth was mainly a spin-off of higher contribution of capital inputs per worker. According to a study conducted by Brahmananda, though labour productivity had registered a growth of 2.5%, the growth rate of labour productivity had declined from 2.8% per year in the decade ending 1960-61, to 2.5% per year in the decade ending 1970-71 and declined further to 0.95% per year in the decade ending 1980-81.

As per his study, the capital-output ratio was only 2.77 in 1950-51, as against 4.08 in 1980-81. Incremental capital-output ratio was 2.79 in the decade ending 1960-61, 4.45 in the decade ending 1970-71 and 6.22 in the decade ending 1980-81. Though developing countries have to resort to massive investments, unless the rate of output increases to a greater extent than the rate of capital investment, it would only weaken the economy further.

In this chapter, four major industrial sectors of Punjab, namely, Bicycle and Bicycle Parts Industry, Agro and Food Processing Industry, Textile and Hosiery Industry and Electronics Industry have been dealt in detail in terms of their present status and pitfalls in present technology adopted by them. Suitable Strategies for future development of these sectors including their productivity improvement have also been suggested.

THE INDUSTRIAL SECTOR IN PUNJAB

At the time of independence, Punjab had only a few hundred industrial units mainly processing foodgrains, cotton ginning and brick kilns. Most of the manufactured items of even common use came from outside. During the post-independence period, industrial development in Punjab took place in phases. Thus, in the fifties the cycle-parts and hosiery industries took their roots, while in the sixties, with the advent of the green revolution, agriculture-related industries like farm machinery manufacturing came up. The main focus in the seventies was on such industries as auto-parts and electronic items and during the eighties on such resource-based industries as food processing, vanaspati, edible and non-edible oils and sugar in a big way. A table depicting share of manufacturing sector in GDP of the state and country is given in Table 10.1.

We can see from Table 10.1 that the share of the manufacturing sector at constant prices has always been higher than at current prices, indicating that prices of manufactured goods are not rising at par with the prices of other goods. The share of the manufacturing sector in the Gross National Domestic Product at current as well as constant prices has always been higher than in the State Gross Domestic Product, which indicates that Punjab is still comparatively less industrialized.

Table 10.2 shows major industrial sector-wise break-up of industry in Punjab as on 31 March, 2000. The important sectors in terms of production,

TABLE 10.1
Percentage Share of Manufacturing Sector in Gross Domestic Product

Year	*At Current Prices*		*At Constant Prices*	
	Punjab	*India*	*Punjab*	*India*
1980-81	11.61	17.70	11.61#	17.70#
1985-86	13.51	17.90	14.40#	19.40#
1990-91	15.05	18.60	16.58#	21.10#
1995-96	15.76	18.10	15.80#	17.90#
1996-97	15.23	17.70	15.58*	18.20*
1997-98	15.04	16.70	15.88*	17.70*
1998-99	14.04	15.60	15.99*	17.00*
1999-2000	14.44	15.40	15.84*	17.10*

Statistical Abstract of Punjab ESO, Government of Punjab.
Note : (#) At 1980-81 (Constant) Prices, (*) At 1993-94 (Constant) Prices).
Source : National Accounts Statistics, CSO, Government of India.

investment, employment and export potential are bicycle and bicycle parts and automobile and components (transport equipment and parts), agro/ food processing (food products and beverages), textiles and hosiery, basic metal, metal products, machinery other than electrical and electronics industry. These sectors have contributed about 70 per cent of the total industrial output.

The main industrial centres in Punjab are Ludhiana, Jalandhar, Amritsar, Mandi Gobindgarh, Batala and Mohali. Ludhiana is known for the production of hosiery and readymade garments, bicycles and components, sewing machines and parts, machine tools, auto-parts, industrial fasteners, electrical and electronic goods. About 21 per cent of the total industrial units in Punjab are located in Ludhiana district. Famous for hand tools, pipe fittings, valves and leather products. Jalandhar is well-known for its sports-goods too. Mandi Gobindgarh, popularly known as the 'Steel-Town' of Punjab, hosts more than 300 steel re-rolling mills despite being situated far from the sources of raw materials. Batala is famous in the country for its castings and machine tools, while Amritsar is known for food products, paper machinery and textiles. Mohali near Chandigarh, which attracted a number of 'sunrise industries', thanks to its locational advantage and infrastructure, seems to have lost its momentum for growth in recent years.

District Ludhiana leads Punjab in industrialization. More than 28 per cent of the industrial output of Punjab comes from Ludhiana, which has the highest number (166) of large and medium units. While Amritsar and Jalandhar were traditionally more advanced, Sangrur, which was one of the centrally declared Backward Districts and Patiala, have become fast growth areas.

TABLE 10.2
Major Sector-wise Statistics of Industry as on 31 March 2000

NIC Code	*Name of the Industry*	*Units*		*Employment*		*Fixed Investment*		*Production*	
		(No.)	*%**	*(No.)*	*%**	*Rs. Lakh*	*%**	*Rs. Lakh*	*%**
20-22	Food Products & Beverages	9765	4.89	97704	8.73	273139	14.72	752769	18.66
23-26	Textiles, Hosiery & Garments, etc.	14556	7.29	190337	17.01	528706	28.29	668973	16.9
27	Wood Products	11623	5.82	39472	3.53	11509	0.62	30353	0.75
28	Paper Products	3527	1.77	23055	2.06	70258	3.79	87758	2.18
29	Leather & Leather Products	14488	7.26	38242	3.42	10241	0.55	33356	0.83
30	Rubber & Plastic Products	4567	2.29	43537	3.89	53317	2.87	183483	4.55
31	Chemical & Products	4022	2.01	36792	3.29	252516	13.61	444896	11.03
32	Non-metallic Mineral Products	2556	1.28	31684	2.83	24387	1.31	52243	1.30
33	Basic Metal Products (Forging, Re-rolling & Casting)	5645	2.83	69837	6.24	119858	6.45	477530	11.84
34	Metal Products (Hand Tools)	20579	10.31	103505	9.25	39465	2.13	150958	3.74
35	Machinery & Parts except Electrical (Machine Tools)	10644	5.33	67691	6.05	53143	2.86	226415	5.61
36	Electrical Machinery and Parts (Incl. Electronics)	4438	2.22	32657	2.92	123238	6.64	147942	3.67
37	Transport equipment and parts (Automobiles and parts Bicycle and parts).	6955	3.48	105574	9.43	167151	9.01	506915	12.57
38	Misc. Industry (Sports Goods)	3030	1.52	16615	1.48	51958	2.80	51965	1.29
74-99	Repairing and Serving	36984	18.52	82996	7.42	26883	1.45	41358	1.03
	Non-SIDO Industries	46303	23.19	139300	12.45	50179	2.70	176185	4.37
		199682	100	1118998	100	1855948	100	4033099	100

Note : (*) % Indicates the share of the sector to total industry.
Source : Director of Industries, Punjab.

Districts Bathinda, Ferozepur, Gurdaspur, Hoshiarpur, Kapurthala and Moga, each contributes two to five per cent share to the state's Industrial production; while Faridkot, Mansa and Muktsar each contributes less than one per cent share. These districts are industrially backward and 'A' category incentives are provided to industry coming up in them under the Industrial Policy, 1996.

During 1999-2000 the total value of exports from Punjab was Rs. 4,062 crores. The major sectors, which have made significant contribution towards exports from the state are woollen textiles, bicycles and parts, hosiery goods, hand tools, leather products, and sports goods. The trend of exports has not been uniform and has been nearly stagnant of late.

Table 10.3 depicts the concentration of types of industries in various districts of Punjab.

TABLE 10.3
District-wise Distribution and Types of Industries in Punjab

District	*Concentration of types of industries*
Amritsar	Power Loom Weaving, Wood and Machine Screws, Radio and Transistors, Agricultural implements, Paints and Varnishes and Dyes, Electric fans, Pharmaceuticals, Printing machinery, Textiles, Chemicals, Soap, Acids.
Bathinda	Cotton ginning and processing, Pharmaceutical, Flour mills.
Faridkot	Agricultural implements, Cottonseed oil, Rice bran oil.
Fatehgarh Sahib	Steel re-rolling, Pump parts, Sewing machine parts, Truck body building.
Ferozepur	Cotton ginning and processing, Grey board, Flour mills, Agricultural implements, mill board.
Gurdaspur	Agricultural implements, Conduit pipes, Machine tools, Soap and Chemical Products, C.I. castings, Brassware.
Hoshiarpur	Rosin and Turpentine oil, Paints and Varnish, Sugar, Agricultural implements, Pressure cookers, Paper and Paper board.
Jalandhar	Surgical instruments, sports goods, Hand tools, Automobile parts, Cocks and valves, Pipe fittings, Bus body building, Leather tanneries, Ball bearings, Publication, switch and switch-gears and Rubber goods.
Kapurthala	Agricultural implements, Pressure cookers, Fans, Wood and Machine screws, Electrical goods, Rice Mills, Rubber Goods, Bolts and Nuts and Diesel engines.
Ludhiana	Bicycles and bicycle parts, Automobile parts, Hosiery goods, Sewing machine and parts, Home appliances, Machine tools, Readymade garments, Hosiery needles, Rubber goods, Labels (Metal and Cotton), Chemical goods, Oil engines, Agricultural implements, Electronic goods, Tractor parts, Cycle tyres/tubes, Plastic goods
Mansa	Agricultural implements, Cotton spinning
Moga	Agricultural implements, Milk products.
Muktsar	Cotton yarn, Rice Bran Oil, Paper.
Nawanshahar	Light Commercial Vehicles, Pharmaceutical, Yarn and Sugar.
Patiala	Automobile parts, Sewing machine parts, Enamelled copper wire, Electrical goods, Bakery machinery, Cutting tools, Biscuits, Shoes.
Rup Nagar	Agricultural implements, Pharmaceuticals, Tractors and Parts, Electronic Components, Electrical Compoments.
Sangrur	Agricultural implements, Tractor parts, Cycle parts, Sewing machine parts, Milk products, Chilled Rolls.

Source : Director of Industries, Punjab.

Four major industrial sectors of the state have been discussed below with a view to highlight their technological status, human resource development and other factors that impinge on their potential for growth. Suggestions have been put forward to improve the productivity of these sectors.

A. Bicycle and Bicycle Parts Industry

1. *Present Status*

The second largest manufacturer of bicycles and bicycle parts in the world, India produced 13.1 million bicycles in 2000, while China produced 52.2 million. The Ludhiana cluster produces about 60 per cent of the total bicycles manufactured in the country in the large and small-scale sector and more than 80 per cent of the parts and components in the small and tiny sector. The first indigenously owned bicycle-manufacturing unit, Atlas Cycles, was established at Sonepat in 1951 in the SSI sector in undivided Punjab. Hero Cycle Ltd. commenced production of complete bicycles in 1956 as an SSI unit in Ludhiana and became the world's largest producer of bicycles in 1989, with a record production of 29,36,076 units and entered the Guinness Book of World Records.

Though the bicycle industry originated in Kolkata, Punjab became the most fertile ground for its evolution and growth. The unique feature of this industry of Punjab is that the components and parts (numbering 300) are manufactured in about 4,000 small and tiny units for both domestic as well as export markets. Table 10.4 presents the status of the industry for the last five years (SSI including tiny sector and the large and medium), showing time-series data on the number of units, number of employees, production and investment. Production has increased at an average annual growth rate of 12.8 per cent during 1995-96 to 1999-2000.

The capital-output ratio of the SSI and tiny sector is consistently declining as shown in Table 10.4. The Industry is largely primitive, neither replacing the existing obsolete machinery, nor adopting the latest and improved technology. On the other hand, in the large and medium sector the capital-output ratio has been continuously improving during the same period. The investment in the SSI sector per employee has increased from Rs. 20,000 in 1995-96 to Rs. 27,000 in 1999-2000; in the large and medium sector it has increased to Rs. 3,80,000 from Rs. 1,87,000.

The export value of bicycles and parts in Punjab in 1995-96 was Rs. 43,611 lakh, which increased to Rs. 70,643 lakh in 1996-97 and to Rs. 88,956 lakh in 1997-98. Exports declined sharply during 1998-99 to Rs. 46,243 lakh. During 1999-2000 it increased to Rs. 51,620 lakh and remained at the same level in 2000-01.

2. *Pitfalls in Technology*

(i) The ordinary bicycle comprises of as many as 300 individual components and over 1,500 operations are performed to

TABLE 10.4
Status of Bicycle and Bicycle Parts Industry in Punjab

Year	Units (No.)			Employment (No.)			Investment (Lakh)			Production (Lakh)		
	SSI	L&M	Total	SSI	L&M	Total	SSI	L&M	Total	SSI	L&M*	Total*
1995-96	3538	7	3545	43433	10476	53909	8770	18755	27524.93	91531	100013	131536
1996-97	3615	8	3623	43898	9773	53671	952219	22295	31824.27	109053	112170	153921
1997-98	3703	8	3711	44564	10843	55407	10178	31168	41345.91	133040	98532	172453
1998-99	3753	6	3759	45335	10475	55810	11314	35158	46472.47	152485	110448	196664
1999-2000	3773	8	3781	45730	11011	56741	12296	41752	54048.27	170034	120520	218242

Note : Only 40% (value added) of the production of L & M sector is added.
Source : Director of Industries, Punjab.

manufacture it. Various manufacturing techniques prevalent in our country are not only time consuming, but also causing extensive raw material wastage.

(ii) Most of the components of our cycles are made from mild steel, with the latest introduction of plastics and aluminium for the export market only. Even the steel of desired specifications and quality is not available at reasonable rates.

(iii) Quality control system is generally poor. The component manufacturers, being mostly in the tiny sector, have very inadequate quality control systems. Even at the assembly stage and in retailers and shops, the mechanics are not adequately trained and aware of the importance of various alignments, etc.

3. Strategy for Future Development

A well-defined strategy has to be formulated to sustain and accelerate the present growth rate and increase the market size, both domestic and export, against the back drop of stiff competition from China. Listed below are some strategic interventions, which can help in improving the quality, productivity and overall growth of this industry.

1. The trade associations related to bicycle and component industry should join hands and form a consortium/nodal agency to obtain the maximum advantage of partnership. This agency should work to safeguard and promote the interests of the industry in domestic and international markets, for procuring raw materials at reasonable prices, dissemination of trade information and liaison with government, financial, and other developmental institutions.
2. Ludhiana and the area around it have emerged as a natural cluster for the bicycle industry, with medium, small and tiny industrial units, using traditional and modern techniques of production, but not well organized and systematic. These units are located in a haphazard manner causing considerable environmental degradation and other problems. A common effluent treatment plant is absolutely necessary in the existing cluster, to provide a pollution-free environment. Better infrastructure facilities are essential for efficient material movement. The concept of 'flatted factory system' should be introduced in selected planned areas, provide more industrial accommodation and factory space. Unless a systematic and planned cluster approach is followed, further development of the industry and even the present trend of growth will not be sustainable.
3. Wide technology gaps have been observed between the technologies that are used in the developed countries and in India and it is necessary to bridge them by new developments in the designs of bicycles, parts and components. As it is beyond the capabilities of the existing small-scale sector it is absolutely

necessary to restructure and strengthen the Research and Development Centre for Bicycles and Sewing Machines at Ludhiana.

4. Training the workforce of the industry is necessary for upgrading their skills to adopt the latest manufacturing technologies, management techniques and quality management systems enabling them to compete in the international markets. Study visits to the developed countries should be conducted to give exposure to new developments taking place in the global arena.
5. The mindset of the consumer has to undergo a sea change. Bicycle is considered a poor man's transport. Population with higher income avoid riding a bicycle because it is a typical roadster model and does not suit their tastes and status. For overcoming this mindset it is suggested that new fancy models should be developed and offered to the public for free test ride and trade fairs and bicycle racing should be popularized.
6. As a part of policy and institutional support more specialized SSI bank branches may be opened to provide financial assistance to the SSI sector, finance should be made available at a reasonable cost, e.g., at a interest below or equal to prime lending rate (PLR) and financial evaluation procedures for lending should be made more objective and transparent and made public.

B. Agro/Food Processing Industry

1. Present Status

The food-processing sector covers a wide spectrum of products and is one of the largest in terms of production, consumption, export and growth prospects. The vast potential of agricultural resources available in Punjab can be better exploited and utilized by preserving and processing. At present, the agro-processing industry is mainly limited to traditional processing of agricultural raw materials, such as atta chakkies, oil mills, cotton ginning and rice shelling, etc., using a basic, low-grade technology. Only less than two per cent of the fruits and vegetables produced is processed, compared with 80 per cent in Malaysia. Therefore, there is scope for setting up processing units in the state, on a priority basis, using indigenous technologies as well as the latest technologies from abroad. The present status of the food and beverages industry in Punjab is shown in Table 10.5.

By using better techniques of farming, high yielding and hybrid seeds, agro-processing units could enhance farm income very substantially. Reports indicate that in the case of Pepsi Foods Limited, Hoshiarpur, the tomato yield increased by 200-266 per cent and income from farming increased by 230 per cent.

According to the assessment of Mckinsey (1997), packaged atta, packaged milk, fresh poultry, bakery, Indian dairy products and confectionery will grow faster with high volumes as these are mass-

Table 10.5
Status of Food and Beverages Industry in Punjab

Year	Units (No.)			Employment (No.)			Investment (Lakh)			Production (Lakh)		
	SSI	L&M	Total	SSI	L&M	Total	SSI	L&M	Total	SSI	L&M	Total
1995-96	8972	103	9075	50872	33952	84824	29260	141899	171159	132527	305835	438362
1996-97	9159	108	9267	52825	34855	87680	32829	164714	197543	154515	320804	475319
1997-98	9301	114	9415	54318	35482	89800	37260	195533	232793	173856	405214	579070
1998-99	9443	123	9566	56952	38165	95117	43941	220707	264648	192145	543721	735866
1999-2000	9644	121	9765	59950	37754	97704	53694	219445	273139	219750	533019	752769

Source : Director of Industries, Punjab.

consumption items. The projected volume of business turnover in different categories of food processing industries, according to this study is given in Table 10.6.

TABLE 10.6

Projected Volume of Business Turnover of Agro-processing Industry in India (2005)

Sl. No.	Food category and sub-category	Likely volume of business in 2005 (Rs. in crore)
1.	**Bold Volume and Growth**	
	(i) Packaged atta	15000
	(ii) Packaged milk	36000
	(iii) Fresh Poultry	27000
	(iv) Bakery	10000
	(v) Tea and Coffee	7400
	(vi) Confectionery	6500
	(vii) Soft drinks	10500
	(viii) Processing Meat and Poultry	9000
	(ix) Indian dairy products	7300
2.	**High growth and low volume**	
	(i) Frozen vegetables	350
	(ii) Puree, Jam, Sauces	1000
	(iii) Fruit drinks	2000
	(iv) Fresh vegetables	1200
	(v) Value-added dairy products	4700
3.	**Low growth and high volume**	
	(i) Sugar	24000
	(ii) Oil	50000
	Total	211950

Source : Mckinsey and Company (1997).

2. *Pitfalls in Technology*

Large gaps exist in the industry at different stages of operation, such as raw materials, technology and machinery, processing techniques, quality control and packaging. Most of the food processing units are in the small and tiny sector, using old inefficient, uneconomical machinery and technology and lacking infrastructure because of financial and other constraints. At present, workers do not have basic ideas of food processing and unskilled workers and supervisors work in the industry. Personal hygiene is also very poor in most cases.

3. *Strategy for Future Development*

To emerge as a leader in the agro-processing industry, a well thought-out co-ordinated, growth-oriented, multipronged strategy covering the following aspects need to be implemented :

1. Agri-Export Zones (AEZs) and Parks should be set-up product-wise, after examining their viability. This will facilitate building centralized and modern infrastructure.
2. Multinational companies (MNCs) should be attracted to invest in agro/food processing industry in Punjab. This will facilitate upgradation of the entire infrastructure for achieving the benefits of large-scale vertical integration of different activities across the agro-business chain.
3. The state government should carefully examine the schemes of the Government of India for the promotion of agro/food processing and adopt and implement expeditiously only those schemes which will facilitate the achievements of its objectives.
4. Training programmes on personal hygiene, quality control packaging, etc. need to be conducted regularly for floor level workers and other concerned personnel.

C. Textile and Hosiery Industry

Ludhiana is famous world-wide for its hosiery and knitting industry. The history of hosiery in Ludhiana can be traced back to 1902-03, when the first unit manufacturing woollen socks was set-up. During the years that followed this industry in Ludhiana progressed steadily. Till recent years our main trading partner for the export of hosiery knitwear, was the erstwhile USSR. However, after its disintegration, exports have diversified to other markets, viz. Europe, USA and other advanced countries.

1. *Present Status*

Production in the textile and hosiery industry in the Eighth Five Year Plan (FYP) achieved an impressive average annual growth rate of 26 per cent. It, however, declined sharply during 1995-96 to 1999-2000 as shown in Table 10.7.

The capital-output ratio of the SSI and the L & M sectors increased from 0.17 to 0.21 and from 0.81 to 1.01 respectively as shown in Table 10.7 during 1995-96 to 1999-2000. Investment per employee in the SSI sector nearly doubled from Rs. 0.19 lakh to Rs. 0.36 lakh while in the L & M sector it increased from Rs. 3.51 lakh to Rs. 5.70 lakh during 1995-96 to 1999-2000. Production per employee in the SSI sector increased from Rs. 1.15 lakh to Rs. 1.74 lakh and in the L & M sector from Rs. 4.31 lakh to Rs. 5.67 lakh. The export from textile and hosiery industry was to the tune of Rs. 141519 lakhs during the year 1997-98. It went up by 12.13 percent during the year 1999-2000. The year 2000-01 saw a decline in exports. The fall was 2.34 percent as compared to 1999-2000 year figures.

TABLE 10.7

Consolidated Data for the Textile and Hosiery Industry

Year	Units (No.)			Employment (No.)			Investment (Lakh)			Production (Lakh)		
	SSI	L&M	Total	SSI	L&M	Total	SSI	L&M	Total	SSI	L&M	Total
1995-96	13395	110	13505	94003	73199	167202	18164	257089	275253	107992	315759	423751
1996-97	13721	142	13863	96342	78999	175341	20298	316933	337231	120354	424831	545185
1997-98	13984	158	14142	98509	77440	175949	23484	362802	386286	141089	475679	616768
1998-99	14182	154	14336	101864	75864	177728	32246	471045	503291	157745	500835	658580
1999-2000	14380	176	14556	104184	86153	190337	37817	490889	528706	180902	488071	668973

Source : Director of Industries, Punjab.

2. Pitfalls in Technology

The textile and hosiery Industry in Punjab can be classified into two groups, viz., hosiery and readymade garments and textiles. The hosiery and readymade garments industry is highly labour-intensive. There exists a 'technological dualism' in this industry as, on the one hand, it uses state-of-the-art technology, manufacturing high value-added fashion garments and on the other, it relies on conventional, locally manufactured and fabricated machinery and equipment, well suited to the capabilities of the untrained and illiterate labour force. The dyeing processes at present are highly energy-consuming, inefficient and polluting and in-house testing facilities for colour-matching and colour-fastness are not available in most of the units. Designs normally are copied from magazines, journals, or samples provided by the buyers. The majority of the units have not adopted Computer Aided Designing/Manufacturing.

Machinery being used in the industry are flat-bed machines, circular knitting machines and imported reconditioned knitting machines. To cater to the requirements of western countries, it is essential to improve the technology not only to manufacture hosiery products, but also the basic machinery. The industry is still not using laser and other modern techniques for cutting the fabric. Knitwear is stitched on multi-thread lock-stitch, chain-lock, flat-lock and over-lock machines, either manufactured indigenously or imported. Embroidery, patchwork, printing and beadwork are done with indigenous machinery and the quality of embroidery is not acceptable in the international market. However, some of the progressive units have imported computerized multi-head embroidery machines, which can create intricate logos on T-Shirts and other garments.

3. Strategy for Future Development

1. With the addition of the latest models of machinery and equipment, the industry needs a trained workforce to handle these efficiently and effectively. A training centre needs to be set-up to impart training on electronic gadgets and systems, computer-aided designing and manufacturing, handling of testing equipments, etc. Apart from these technical training facilities, the industry also needs specialized trained professionals in different managerial, marketing, and financial areas, to make the units sustainable and internationally competitive.
2. An exclusive Centre for Research and Development for hosiery and knitted garments, to develop appropriate modern technologies and processes is required at Ludhiana. The Centre should act as a show-window of modern technology, by installing various machinery and equipment.
3. A full-fledged National Institute of Fashion Technology, on the pattern of such Institutes at New Delhi, Hyderabad, Tirupur, Kolkata and Mumbai, should be established at Ludhiana to train professionals in designing, marketing, quality control and

manufacturing of knitwear. The institute could help in creating awareness among the local entrepreneurs by organizing exhibitions, fashion shows, seminars, etc. The IITs/universities in the country, having textile technology as a branch of study, should be entrusted with special projects for developing and transferring eco-friendly, lesser energy and water-consuming technology for wet dyeing of yarn/fabric.

4. Textile parks with ultra-modern facilities are required to be developed near Ludhiana for hosiery and knitted garment units. The layout of the complex should be such that dyeing and processing units are clubbed together, so that a Common Effluent Treatment Plant is feasible.
5. Facilities for Air Cargo Services in or around Ludhiana need to be set-up. Such a facility will facilitate exports.
6. Machine-building facilities and capabilities within the country should be upgraded and updated, either through foreign collaborations or by assigning special projects to various institutes engaged in R&D, such as MERADO (Ludhiana) and CMTI (Bangalore). Creation of such facilities would not only help in developing the hosiery and readymade garments manufacturing units, but would also save foreign exchange, as well as earn it through exports.
7. The hosiery and knitwear manufacturing industry at Ludhiana can not compete with the multinational companies in the quantum of production, types, styles, designs and quality of products. Some Tie-ups with some of the larger established brands for manufacturing as well as marketing in the international market are essential for increasing India's share of foreign trade in this area.
8. For modernization and technology upgradation of the cluster, it is essential to provide finance at rates of interest comparable with internationally prevailing interest rates. This will help the small-scale units to purchase modern machinery and components required to produce products of acceptable quality.

D. Electronics Industry

The evolution of technology has led to increasing use of electronics in a variety of applications. Today, the electronics hardware industry spans a whole gamut of products and the entire spectrum of the value chain. Newer applications and better ways of doing things are fuelling growth. Electronics gadgets and tools being used in India are fast catching up with the world in terms of penetration. This can lead to an enormous domestic demand for these products, giving the necessary critical mass for global competitiveness. Such a base will also be a stabilizing factor for manufacturers to target the international market.

The major segments of the electronics hardware industry are information technology (comprising computers and computer peripherals), telecommunications (comprising switching equipment, transmission equipment and customer premises equipment clocks and watches), control instrumentation, industrial electronics, strategic electronics and the electronic components industry which supplies components to these segments. It will be appropriate to integrate these segments into one industry—Electronics Hardware Industry (EHI).

The growth rate of the electronics hardware industry has been slower than that of the software and service industry during the Ninth FYP. This trend needs to be reversed into a growth path by introducing a set of policies conducive to the growth of the electronics hardware industry. The sector-wise production of the electronics hardware industry during the Ninth Plan in India is given in Table 10.8.

TABLE 10.8
Production in Electronic Hardware Manufacturing Sector during Ninth Plan in India

(Rs. in crore)

Sector	*1997-98*	*1998-99*	*1999-2000*	*2000-01*	*2001-02(E)*
Consumer	7600	9200	11200	11550	13000
Industrial	3150	3300	3750	4000	4500
Computers	2800	2300	2500	3400	4000
Comm. & Broad Eqpt.	3250	4400	4000	4500	5000
Strategic	900	1300	1450	1750	1900
Components	4400	4750	5200	5500	6000
Total	22100	25250	28100	30700	34400

Source : Ministry of Information Technology (MIT) Report, Tenth Five Year Plan.

On the assumption that an electronic hardware growth-oriented policy, similar to the software policy, would be introduced, the Ministry of Information Technology, Government of India, has projected the production of the electronics hardware industry sector-wise, as shown in Table 10.9.

TABLE 10.9
Sector-wise Projected Production by 2007

Sector	*Production by 2006-07 (Rs. in crore)*	*Compound annual growth rate*
Consumer Electronics	38100	24
Industrial Electronics	6600	8
Computers H/W	14900	30
Communication and Broadcasting	12500	20
Strategic Electronics	3800	15
Components	15000	20
Total	90900	22

Source : MIT Report, Tenth Five Year Plan.

1. *Present Status of Electronics Hardware Industry in Punjab*

During 1985-90, SAS Nagar (Mohali), was the hub of electronics hardware industry and the second largest centre after Bangalore with top-grade units in communications, computers and peripherals, electronic components including picture tubes, semi-conductor devices, active components, etc. However, during recent years there has been an overall decline of the electronics hardware industry and it seems to have lost its momentum. Table 10.10 shows the growth rate of the electrical and electronics industry in the state.

Besides a few major units like M/s. Punjab Communication Ltd., Mohali, M/s. Semi Conductor Complex Ltd., Mohali, M/s. Bharat Telecommunication Ltd., Ludhiana (Beetel), and M/s. Telephone Cables Ltd., there are a large number of units in the SSI sector, manufacturing PCs, power supplies, industrial electronic equipment, TVs, Radios, UPS, electronic instruments, electronic test zigs, tools and components, etc. The domestic market is expected to expand. The electronics hardware industry has a very good employment potential, as mostly ancillary units, particularly in the SSI sector, are run by self-employed graduate engineers, diploma holders, ITI's in engineering and graduates/post-graduates from the science stream.

2. *Strategy for Future Development*

To achieve accelerated growth of the electronics hardware industry in the state the following measures are suggested :

1. State government should give priority-sector status to the electronics hardware industry at par with software and service industries.
2. An Electronic Hardware Technology Park (EHTP) in Mohali with world-class infrastructure will greatly boost the small-scale sector and attract new entrepreneurs and foreign investors. More Electronic Hardware Parks in the state on private initiative and with government support are necessary.
3. There is a need to train and develop quality manpower suitable for evolving innovative designs and the development of manufacturing, assembly and quality control techniques.
4. Research and Development, Designs and Quality Control Centres need to be set-up in participation with industry, with financial and technical assistance from international agencies.
5. Provide appropriate facilities and incentives to MNCs, to set-up manufacturing plants in each sector of the electronics hardware industry in the state. An investment climate comparable to Taiwan, the Philippines, Singapore, Korea and Malaysia need to be created to drive maximum competitive advantage from the twin factors of low cost high quality knowledge workforce and a fast growing domestic market.

TABLE 10.10

Status of Electrical and Electronics Industry in Punjab

Year	*Units (No.)*			*Employment (No.)*			*Investment (Lakh)*			*Production (Lakh)*		
	SSI	*L&M*	*Total*	*SSI*	*L&M*	*Total*	*SSI*	*L&M*	*Total*	*SSI*	*L&M*	*Total*
1980-81	977	10	987	5437	4445	9932	655	1635	2290	2073	5804	7877
1985-86	2167	23	2190	10841	5742	16583	1827	11446	13273	4510	6694	11204
1992-93	3633	27	3660	17495	8852	26347	4521	35552	40043	12809	53859	66668
1996-97	4113	28	4141	20696	9448	30144	6609	65453	72062	26427	187719	214146
1997-98	4223	33	4256	21947	10221	32168	8322	83765	92087	31388	252362	283750
1998-99	4301	34	4335	22436	10487	32923	8731	92193	100924	33056	170823	203879
1999-2000	4403	35	4438	23203	9454	32657	9379	113859	123238	36193	111749	147942

Source : Director of Industries, Punjab.

CONCLUSION

Small scale industries in the state of Punjab, the backbone of its industrial economy, are currently producing by and large low-value items, including hosiery and woollen textiles, bicycles, it's parts and other products. The level of technology in use in these industries is quite low, which results in low industrial productivity and quality of products, leading to a competitive disadvantage both in domestic and global markets. Upgradation of technology is the crying need of the hour for the very survival of most of the SSI units in the state. The Research and development facilities available are on the one hand woefully inadequate and out-dated and on the other seldom put to optimum use. With the process of the integration of the Indian economy with the global economy and the consequent far-reaching structural changes taking place, small-scale industries have to adapt and adjust themselves to the demands of the time, requiring them to become internationally competitive. They have to transit from a protected to a competitive environment. At the same time the WTO regime opens up a window of opportunities for small-scale industries to grow and flourish with acess to wider global markets. Upgradation of manufacturing processes and management practices, through the induction of technology, modern machines and adoption of international quality standards, are essential prerequisites for taking advantage of the emerging opportunities.

References

Ahluwalia, I., Industrial Growth in India, Oxford Press, 1985, p. 134.

Brahmananda, P.R., Productivity in the Indian Economy, Himalaya Publication, 1987, pp. 143.

Chhabilendra Roul, Bitter to Better Harvest Post-green Revolution : Agricultural and Marketing Strategy for India.

National Accounts Statistics, 1985, Central Statistical Organisation, Government of India.

National Accounts Statistics, 2001, Central Statistical Organisation, Government of India.

Statistical Abstract of Punjab, 1985-86, 1990-91 1995-96, 2000-01; Economic and Statistical Organisations, Government of Punjab.

Statistical Abstract of India, 2000, Central Statistical Organisation, Government of India.

Industrial Policies of 1987, 1989, 1992 and 1996 of Government of Punjab.

Sixth, Seventh, Eighth, Ninth and Tenth Five Year Plans, Government of Punjab.

State Development Reports on Industrial Development, Small Industries Service Institute (SISI), Ludhiana, Government of India.

Data on Employment, No. of Units, Investment and Production of Industrial Sector, Director of Industries, Punjab.

Report on Traditional Rural and Tiny Industry, Director of Industries, Punjab.

Ministry of Information Technology (MIT), Government of India, Tenth Five Year Plan Report.

Note on Agro-Processing Industry, Punjab Agro-Industry Corporation (PAIC).

Economic Survey of Punjab, 2000-01, 2001-02.

Ernest & Young India; The Hardware Opportunity.

Extent of Competitiveness and Performance of Some Indian Industries

KULDIP KAUR AND AMANDEEP KAUR

The Structure Conduct Performance (S.C.P.) framework has been widely used to explain the relative performance of firms/industries. A simple version of this approach assumes that basic exogenous conditions determine market structure and that there is a unidirectional flow of causality from market structure through conduct to performance. The S.C.P. approach rests fundamentally on the postulate that independent structural variables are comparatively immutable variables determining in the long-run the values of the dependent variables (Bain, 1970). Public policy towards industrialization is a significant determinant of the Structure, Conduct and Performance of industry.

The new economic policies adopted by the government of India in recent years are aimed at making the manufacturing sector more competitive through deregulation. The genesis of a measure of industrial deregulation can be traced in the modifications effected in Industrial Licensing Policy in 1973 when larger industrial houses, with assets more than Rs. 20 crores and foreign concerns were declared eligible to participate in the core industrial sector, provided it was not reserved for public or small industrial sectors. However, it was only after the path breaking recommendation of the Narsimhan Committee on Industrial Licensing (1987) that in the true sense trend towards deregulation and decontrol of industry began. To carry out the programme of industrial deregulation, the Industrial Licensing Policy of 1988 declared that non-MRTP and non-FERA Companies would no longer be required to obtain industrial licences under

IDRA for projects involving fixed investment upto 50 crores, if located in centrally declared backward areas and upto Rs. 15 crores if located in non-backward areas.

However, half-hearted attempts at reforming licensing system and deregulation during the eighties remained symbolic only. The 1990 industrial policy further extended deregulation policy for collaboration between foreign and Indian manufacturers. Further in 1991, Prof. Manmohan Singh did away with the major—

(I) Entry barriers, i.e., the system of capacity licensing.
(II) Growth, consolidation/diversification, etc. barriers by withdrawing relevant chapter from MRTP Act and instituting/accelerating export promotion measures.
(III) Barriers to competition from foreign trade and foreign competition by liberalizing foreign trade and adopting a friendly FDI policy.
(IV) Ending the areas of exclusivity for public and private sectors etc.

Now the question is, has the set of industrial reforms aimed at releasing, reducing, removing various barriers to growth etc. had any favourable effect on market structure conduct and performance? For answering this question the study attempts to evaluate :

(I) The extent of competitiveness in major industries of India in order to see whether there is a greater degree of competition in industrial sector as compared to the beginning of 1990's.
(II) How far the performance of these industries in terms of capital productivity and profitability been affected by the competitiveness in these industries.

DATA BASE AND METHODOLOGY

For the desired analysis time series data for the period 1991-2001, for 12 major industries and for different variables have been collected from various reports published by Centre for Monitoring Indian Economy (CMIE). The Industries covered are : (I) Drugs and Pharmaceuticals, (II) Textile Processing, (III) Marine Foods, (IV) Dairy Products, (V) Food and Beverages, (VI) Vegetable Oils and Products, (VII) Consumer Electronics, (VIII) Readymade Garments, (IX) Automobiles, (X) Metals and Metal Products, (XI) Computer Hardware and Software, and (XII) Machinery.

Three measures of extent of competitiveness have been used by this study. The first one pertains to number of companies producing under a particular industry during a particular year. The greater the number, the greater the degree of competition and *vice versa*. Second measure pertains to size inequality. Greater the inequality in size, the lesser the degree of competition and *vice versa*. Net sales have been used as an indicator of size. Third measure of extent of competitiveness used by the study is concentration ratio, measured by individual industry net sales divided by total net sales of all industries in a particular year (method used by Rotewin, 1964). After counting the number of industries in which the concentration increased over time and comparing it with the number in which it decreased, it can be concluded whether the competition has increased or not. If the former number exceeds the latter, concentration is deemed to have increased and *vice versa.* Increased concentration indicates lesser degree of competion and *vice versa.*

Two indicators of performance have been used in the study. First being the profitability computed in two ways. Profitability (P_1) is operating profits as percent of net sales and profitability (P_2) is operating profits as percent of gross fixed assets. Second measure of performance is capital productivity and is computed by dividing net value-added by gross fixed assets. All the financial variables have been taken at constant prices (1993-94=100).

For analyzing the effect of competitiveness on profitability and Capital Productivity, simple regression equations have been fitted. Profitability (P_1 and P_2) has been taken as dependent variables and coefficient of variation of net sales and number of companies (measure of size inequality and hence competitiveness) have been taken as independent variables.

RESULTS AND DISCUSSION

Table 11.1 shows the degree of competition via number of companies producing under different industries over the study period. It can be seen from the table that highest number of companies throughout the study period was in case of Machinery Industry followed by Metal and Metal Products and Food and Beverages. Lowest Competition was in case of Marine Food followed by Dairy Products. Number of companies in all the industries have increased over the study period, suggesting thereby that the extent of competition has increased in the recent years over the 90's.

Table 11.2 also depicts the similar picture. Number of industries where the concentration ratio has decreased is more as compared to number of industries where concentration ratio has increased over the study period. Table 11.3 also shows that majority of industries fell in low concentration (less than 10 percent) category over the study period. This is a clear indication of decreasing levels of monopoly in Indian industries.

Other objective of the study is to analyse the nature and extent of relationship between concentration and performance of the industry. There are two schools of thought in industrial economics which interpret concentration profitability relationship differently, namely, traditional and revisionist. Based upon the empirical relationship between profit rates and market concentration, the traditional view says that high concentration or lesser competition leads to collusion between the firms in an industry which manipulate price or restrict supply in such a way as to earn higher profits. The revisionist, on the other hand, suggest that the observed positive

TABLE 11.1
No. of Companies in Sample Industries

Name of Industry Year	*Drug and Pharma-ceuticals*	*Taxtile Processing*	*Marine Foods*	*Dairy Products*	*Food and Beverages*	*Vegetable Oils and Products*	*Consumer Electronics*	*Ready-made Garments*	*Automobile*	*Metal and Metal Products*	*Computer Hardware and Software*	*Machinary*
1991-92	101	20	3	8	241	55	21	8	24	261	21	359
1992-93	126	37	5	10	276	72	22	14	25	304	27	409
1993-94	158	61	17	14	359	93	21	20	24	378	43	500
1994-95	212	93	42	25	505	139	29	36	50	456	78	656
1995-96	254	Nil	51	32	616	159	35	52	56	507	107	737
1996-97	259	98	49	31	636	145	29	51	56	485	131	768
1997-98	243	84	38	26	579	116	27	24	58	442	155	765
1998-99	244	75	33	26	551	103	24	55	57	432	169	755
1999-00	247	76	31	25	581	103	30	56	56	451	235	831
2000-01	245	75	32	24	559	98	28	58	56	434	273	859

TABLE 11.2
Change in Concentration Ratio over the Study Period

Concentration Ratios (No. of Industries)

Year	*Increase*	*Decrease*	*Constant*
1992-93	7 (58.3%)	4 (33.4%)	1 (8.3%)
1993-94	9 (75%)	3 (25%)	—
1994-95	11 (91.7%)	1 (8.3%)	—
1995-96	6 (50.0%)	6 (50.0%)	—
1996-97	5 (41.7%)	7 (58.3%)	—
1997-98	6 (50.0%)	6 (50.0%)	—
1998-99	7 (58.3%)	5 (41.7%)	—
1999-00	4 (33.4%)	7 (58.3%)	1 (8.3%)
2000-01	5 (41.7%)	7 (58.3%)	—

Note : Figures in brackets are respective %ages.

TABLE 11.3
Frequency Distribution of Industries as per different Categories of Concentration

Category Year	*Low Concentration Less than 10%*	*Medium Concentration Between 10% to 20%*	*High Concentration More than 20%*
1991-92	9	—	3
1992-93	9	—	3
1993-94	9	—	3
1994-95	8	2	2
1995-96	8	2	2
1996-97	8	2	2
1997-98	8	2	2
1998-99	8	2	2
1999-00	8	2	2
2000-01	8	2	2

relationship between profitability and concentration results from firm level efficiencies that elevate both the market share and profits of large firms. In brief, the traditional view lays emphasis on collusion while revisionist view emphasizes on the efficiency of the firms in explaining the profit concentration relationship.

Table 11.4 shows the results of four regression equations fitted to test the relationship between competitiveness and profitability of the sample industries. The results show weak positive association between the two

TABLE 11.4
Impact of Measures of Competitiveness on Industrial Performance (1991-92 to 2000-2001)

Equation No.	*Equation*	r^2	*Correlation Coefficient (r)*
1	P_1=4.97+.07X_1 (2.60) (1.60)	.20	.45
2	P_2=8.95+.22X_1 (1.31) (1.50)	.18	.42
3	P_1=4.37+.09X_2 (2.07) (1.72)	.23	.48
4	P_2=6.24+.33X_2 (.84) (1.74)	.23	.48

where :
P_1 = Operating profits as percent of net sales.
P_2 = Operating Profits as percent of Gross fixed assets.
X_1 = Coefficient of Variation of Net Sales.
X_2 = Coefficient of Variation of Number of firms.
Note : Figures in the brackets are respective values.

variables. Value of r^2 ranged between .18 to .23, suggesting thereby that only 18 to 23 percent of the total variations in profitability (P_1 and P_2) are explained by the extent of competitiveness in these industries. Regression coefficients in all the equations are also non-significant though positive.

Table 11.5 shows the relationship between capital productivity and concentration ratio over three points of time 1991-92 and 1996-97 and 2000-01. Table depicts that during years 1991-92 and 1996-97, maximum number of sample industries fell in low concentration category, suggesting more competition. During these years however their capital productivity was not highest. However, these industries fell in medium capital productivity category. Over the year 2000-01, eight out of 12 industries again recorded low concentration hence high degree of competition does not ensure high capital productivity.

With the adoption of New Economic Policy, competition in industrial sector has increased and levels of structural monopoly have come down. Hence, the survival of firms would be the outcome of a fierce struggle and this would improve their efficiency in resource allocation. Though low profitability in low concentration industries can be considered as a welcome preliminary sign of improved allocative efficiency but low capital productivity in these industries is disheartening. Hence, the need of the hour is that Indian firms should concentrate upon improving the efficiency in resource allocation through research and development and technological improvements. The process of increasing competition in the manufacturing sector, the government has to be conscious of the fact that the new economic

TABLE 11.5
Relationship between Concentration Ratios and Capital Productivity

CAPITAL PRODUCTIVITY

Concentration	*High Capital Productivity*			*Medium Capital Productivity*			*Low Capital Productivity*			*Total*
	1991-92	*1996-97*	*2000-01*	*1991-92*	*1996-97*	*2000-01*	*1991-92*	*1996-97*	*2000-01*	
High Concentration										
1991-92	1			1			1			3
1996-97					1			1		2
2000-01			0						2	2
Medium Concentration										
1991-92										
1996-97		0			2					2
2000-01			0			0			2	2
Low Concentration										
1991-92	2			7						9
1996-97		1			4			3		8
2000-01		2				3			4	8

rules create a level playing field, rather than discriminating against those firms that are where they are, simply because they responded to government inducements in the past.

References

Bain, J.S. (1970), "The Comparative Stability of Market Structure", in J.W. Markham and G. Papanek (eds.), *Industrial Organization and Economic Development,* Houghton and Mifflin, Boston.

CMIE (2000 and 2001), *Corporate Sector,* EIS.

George, K.D. and Carry, B. (1983), "Industrial Concentration : A Survey", *Journal of Industrial Economics,* Vol. XXXI.

Gokarn Subir and Rajinder Vaidya (1993), "Deregulation and Industrial Performance—The Indian Cement Industry", *EPW,* Vol. 30, No. 34, pp. M. 33 to M. 41.

Government of India (1987), *Report of Narsimhan Committee.*

Rotewin, E. (1964), "Economic Concentration and Monopoly Power in Japan", *Journal of Political Economy,* June, pp. 262-77.

Export Competitiveness of Indian Manufacturing Industry

NAVJOTE KHARA AND DEEPENDRA SINGH GARCHA

Organizations are in the midst of a paradigm shift : that of changing business scenario from industrial age to information age. During the industrial age firms strived to achieve excellence from mass production and economies of scale. Though technology had a role to play, it was the quality of physical assets that offered efficient mass production of standardized products. The increasing dependence on technology by organizations in the twentieth century made obsolete many of the assumptions of the industrial age. Firms can no longer gain competitive advantage by improving the physical assets alone. Now, it is the intangible assets that enable an organization to develop customer relationships, innovate products and services, and produce them at low costs with short lead times.

OBJECTIVES OF THE STUDY

This Chapter aims to provide insight into the concept of export competitiveness of Indian manufacturing industry. The Chapter fulfils the following objectives :

1. Understand the impact of globalization on a nation and a firm's competitiveness.
2. Present a conceptual framework and factors influencing of export competitiveness.

3. Analyse the Indian exports scenario since 1950s in reference to manufacture exports.
4. Examine the export competitiveness of Indian manufacturing industry in relation to other industrializing Asian countries.
5. Suggest policy measures to boost export performance of the manufactured goods.

GLOBALIZATION

As information technology breaks down the barriers of time and location, the boundaries between domestic and foreign markets are increasingly getting blurred. Consequently, the last century has witnessed an increase in globalization of business. Globalization has been impacted by falling political and tariff barriers, rise in regional groupings and trade pacts.

Porter (2001) has identified environmental triggers to globalization. These are increased scale economies, decreased transportation and storage costs, changed distribution channels, changed factor costs, reduced government constraints and narrowed national economic and social circumstances.

Globalization is transforming the world at a breathtaking pace. There has been a phenomenal growth in international trade and capital flow across national boundaries. This growth has been more pronounced after World War II. World exports increased from $ 61 billion in 1950 to $ 3447 billion in 1990. The share of world exports in GDP also rose from approximately 6% in 1960 to 16% in 1990. Over 50% of GNP of most industrial countries (except Japan) is now directly affected by international demand changes. However, the expansion in Foreign Direct Investment (FDI) has been more than that in international trade, especially in the last two decades. The direct FDI increased from less than $ 5 billion in 1960 to $ 171 billion in 1992. In the foreign exchange market trading increased from $ 15 billion per day in 1973 to $ 900 billion per day in 1992. The ratio of worldwide transactions in foreign exchange to world trade rose from 9:1 in 1973 to 90:1 in 1992.

Hall *et. al.* (1992) define globalization as a process that cuts across national boundaries, integrating and connecting communities in new space-time combinations.

Globalization is characterized by :

- Tightly linked financial markets,
- Global sourcing of inputs, marketing and distribution of production and manufacturing of products and final products,
- Increased pressure for improved quality and reduced product price, and
- Evolution of business towards more comprehensive and continuous global co-ordination and integration.

COMPETITIVENESS AND PRODUCTIVITY

Liberalization in terms of flow of goods and services and factors of production has resulted in aggressive competition in global market. The survival in global markets has made it necessary for firms to improve productivity and produce high quality goods at competitive prices. This concern of the firms has led to their shifting focus from comparative advantage to competitive advantage. The essential difference between both is, that, whereas the former is derived from resource endowment of the economy and is external to the policy system, the latter is factor performance and technology driven, which can be altered through policy changes and managerial action.

Porter (1990) highlighted the two major sources of competitiveness, viz. efficiency in use of resources (or productivity which leads to cost competitiveness) and product differentiation. He further emphasized that through product differentiation, it is possible to neutralize cost disadvantage and that this strategy has been effectively pursued by industrialized countries.

However, the concept of competitiveness is a much broader concept than those of cost competitiveness and productivity. It encompasses the relative costs at which products are produced and sold. In an open economy the prices at which goods are sold are determined by prices of factors and intermediate inputs, profit margins and exchange rates. Movements in any of these variables influence the competitiveness of a product in the global markets. Other qualitative determinants of competitiveness at the global level include customization of products and after sales services. In general, it is observed that countries that have been competitive at the global level are those, which have improved productivity and lowered cost levels. Mere product differentiation is not of much use. In fact, improvement in productivity extends the scope for competitiveness.

Competitiveness in simple terms means the ability to compete or do the same things that one's competitor does. Competitiveness can take place at various levels. At the highest level we can speak about national competitiveness. This indicates the ability of the entire national economic system to operate in the global sphere. Then comes industrial competitiveness, which implies the ability of firms in an industry to compete in the global market against firms from all other countries. At the basic level is firm competitiveness, which speaks about a firm being competitive relative to other firms in its line of business.

CONCEPTUAL FRAMEWORK OF EXPORT COMPETITIVENESS

Export competitiveness refers to a country's market share in world output. This ignores the influences of differing natural growth rates and of distortions arising out of subsidies, taxes or regulations. Export competitiveness depends critically on supply side factors such as productivity and costs. While measures like devaluation as a means of boosting exports have their limitations, increasing productivity and improving quality consciousness can provide a real boost to exports and make firms as well as industries competitive.

Gokarn (1999) says that the factors affecting export competitiveness can be categorized as macro-economic and micro-economic factors. The effect of macro-economic factors is represented by the movement of the Real Effective Exchange Rate (REER), which aggregates the movements of the domestic currency against the currencies of major trading partners. Other things remaining the same, depreciation in the REER results in an increase in the competitiveness of all industries.

There are three factors underlying REER, viz. nominal exchange rate, domestic inflation and inflation outside control of policy-makers. When studying competitiveness from a macro-economic perspective, the nominal exchange rate and domestic inflation are referred to. The former is the price of domestic currency in terms of basket of foreign currencies, and the latter is the price of the currency in terms of basket of goods.

The micro-economic factors are collectively represented by the notion of unit costs. This measure is specific to each industry. Other things remaining same, a decrease in unit costs results in an increase in competitiveness of a specific industry. A variety of inputs are utilized in the production process, e.g. wages, capital, materials. The cost of production depends on the efficient utilization of the same.

Figure 12.1 gives a conceptual framework of competitiveness. The bottom layer lays out policy issues at macro-economic level on the left and micro-economic level on the right. Both components of REER are under the

FIG. 12.1
Competitiveness Framework

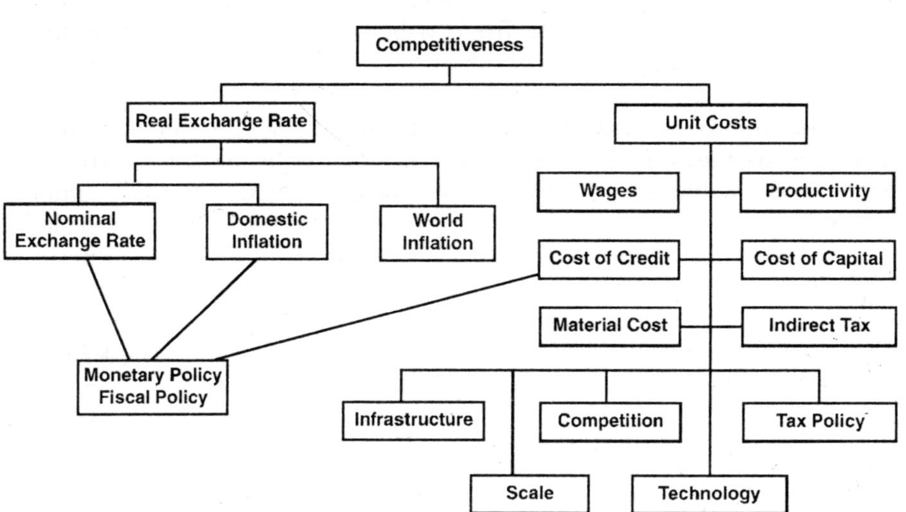

influence of the domestic policy control and are directly affected by the stock of money in the market. The figure also shows a link between the macro-economic policy and cost of capital under unit costs. This link reflects the role of interest rates, which emerge out of macro-economic policy.

The role of the micro-economic policy is to create an environment in which the resources flow. There are five micro-economic factors that determine the environment in which producers operate, viz. infrastructure, scale of economies, competition, technology and indirect taxes.

The increase in exports can be due to a variety of factors. We limit this study to competitiveness alone, which may be in price as well as non-price factors. Competitiveness can improve or decrease not solely on the basis of price but also on characteristics of goods and after sales service. Non-price competition is as important as price competition in deciding the competitiveness of an economy.

INDIAN EXPORTS SCENARIO IN MANUFACTURING INDUSTRY

In 1950, India's share in world exports was 1.9 percent. This compared favourably with 0.9 percent in China and 1.4 percent in Japan. By 1965, however, the share had dropped to 1 percent and it continued to fall progressively to 0.45 percent in 1980 and recovered marginally in 1997 to 0.62 percent. This was in sharp contrast to Japan and China's experience. The Chinese share in world exports, after initially falling to a low of 0.7 percent in 1977 increased to 3.2 percent in 1997 while Japan's share increased from 1.4 percent in 1950 to a peak of 10.3 percent in 1986. Their rapid growth was achieved by China's change in policy towards progressive integration with the world economy since 1978 and Japan's emphasis on export orientation to industrialization. India, on the other hand, persisted with its inward orientation in the policies till 1991 with a gradual change towards globalization. While there was some change in emphasis on exports, reflected in the ratio of exports to GDP that rose from an annual average of 3.41 percent in the 1960s to 3.68 percent in the first half of the 1970s and to 5.26 percent in the latter part of the 1970s, import substitution primarily dominated the development strategy until the end of the 1970s. More recently, the export to GDP ratio has grown to almost 8.5 percent (Table 12.1).

Even though an increasing trend is observed over the period 1960-61 to 1999-2000, real aggregate exports grew at lower rates till the mid-eighties from when they are on a high growth path. India's manufactured exports also followed a similar trend path. However, exports are found to have lowered during the couple of years ending with 1997-98.

Figure 12.2 shows that the growth path, being demarcated into three distinct phases, comprised of initial phases of low to moderate export growth till the mid-eighties and a phase of high growth thereafter. The period-wise growth rates point to such evidence. Table 12.2 shows that

TABLE 12.1
India's Share in World Exports and Ratio of Exports to GDP

Year	*Share (%)*	*Ratio of Exports to GDP*
1951	2.10	6.10
1960	1.13	4.08
1970	0.68	3.35
1980	0.45	4.65
1990	0.53	5.73
1995	0.60	9.00
1999	0.66	7.93

Note : Numerator is Exports in Rs. crore terms. Denominator is GDP at current prices in Rs. crore terms.

Source : IMF International Financial Statistics Year Book and Economic Survey (various issues).

FIG. 12.2
Trends in Indian Manufacture Exports

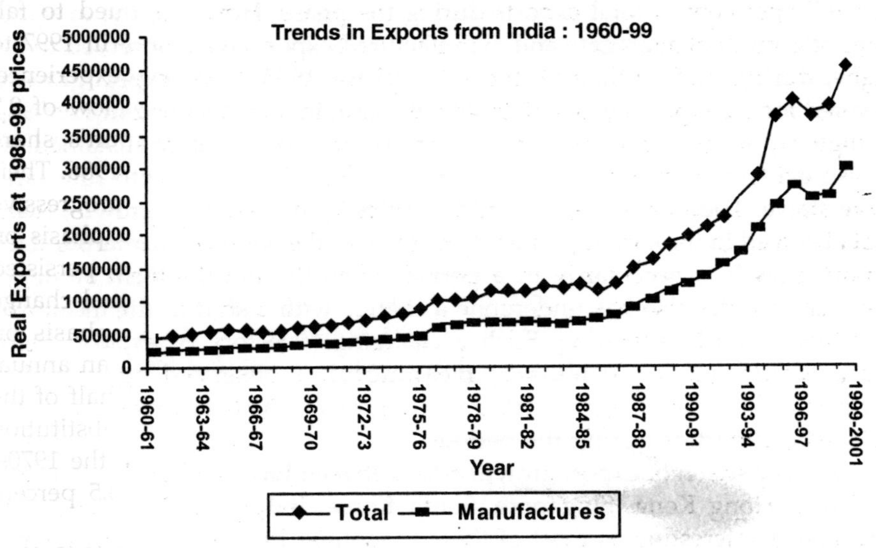

aggregate exports at constant prices, during 1960-61 to 1972-73, grew at a low of 4.71 per cent. In sharp contrast, during 1985-86 to 1999-2000, aggregate exports registered significantly higher annual average growth of 9.73 per cent with a number of years witnessing unprecedented high growth.

Certainly, such high average growth supported a significant break in trend of real exports in 1985. The time path of manufactured exports witnessed changes almost similar to that of aggregate exports with the manufactured exports growing at an average rate of around 6 per cent during the first two phases.

TABLE 12.2
Period-wise Growth Rates of Exports : Aggregate and Manufactures

(in %)

Product Groups	*1960-72*	*1973-84*	*1985-95*	*1985-99*
Aggregate Exports	4.71	5.29	11.44	9.73
Manufactured Exports	6.05	6.19	12.91	11.33
Share of Manufactures in Aggregate Exports (average)	48.07	54.41	70.54	71.96

Note : The growth rates for each phase are average annual percentage change.
Source : Government of India, Monthly Statistics of Foreign Trade in India (various issues).

The trends in manufactured export growth show a turnaround of above 11 per cent during 1985-99, as a result of which manufactures account for above 70 per cent of total exports during the phase. However, the average rates of growth of aggregate and manufactured exports were observed to be higher during 1985-95 than for the entire phase, 1985-99. As export growth lowered for a couple of years after 1995-96, and, in fact, declined in 1997-98, so high export growth during trade liberalization could not be sustained. It is also evident from Table 12.2 that periods with higher growth rates are more stable. The phase after the mid-eighties witnessed high growth, than that observed in the earlier phases. Nonetheless, the observed turnaround in export growth is necessarily in a period when the development strategy pursued in India also has undergone a change with a shift in the incentive structure towards exporting. Such a changing trajectory of exports from India would seem particularly meaningful if observed against the performance of select industrializing countries, which have emerged as successful exporters during the period.

A comparison of export growth rates between India and such countries as China, Hong Kong, Singapore, South Korea, Indonesia, Malaysia, and Thailand is interesting as most of these economies have undergone regime transformation towards trade liberalization sometime during 1980's or even earlier. Moreover, going by the export share in world market India does not vary much from other Asian nations. Therefore, we include major Southeast Asian nations to compare changes in India's external competitiveness.

Table 12.3 brings out that exports from all these countries grew at high rates in the post-1985 period irrespective of their performance in the earlier phases. India's high rates of export growth rate during the liberalization phase are thus no exception.

TABLE 12.3
Average Annual Growth of Manufactured Exports Across Industrializing Economies (From 1960-99, in Percent)

Country	*1960-72*	*1973-84*	*1985-99*
India	4.22	5.73	10.65
China	6.22	6.61	15.07
Hong Kong	15.19	8.41	13.31
Indonesia	-0.44	5.20	9.11
Malaysia	7.27	7.29	13.45
Singapore	7.44	10.46	12.57
South Korea	35.37	18.80	13.16
Thailand	9.14	9.17	13.43

Source : Calculated from World Bank, IMF International Financial Statistics (Various issues).

EXTERNAL COMPETITIVENESS OF INDIAN EXPORTS

We examine two sources of external competitiveness, viz. domestic inflation and nominal depreciation. Table 12.4 brings out the movements in external competitiveness in the Asian nations. With the start of the Southeast Asian currency crisis in 1997, many countries in this region were forced to devalue their currencies substantially. India lost its competitiveness to these countries despite maintaining a low inflation rate.

TABLE 12.4
Movements in External Competitiveness

Country	*Inflation (CPI)*			*Exchange Rate (% Change)*			*External Competitiveness#*		
	1995	*1996*	*1997*	*1995*	*1996*	*1997*	*1995*	*1996*	*1997*
India	10.0	9.2	6.5	3.4	9.3	2.5	6.6	−0.1	4.0
China	17.1	8.3	2.8	−3.1	−0.4	−0.3	20.2	8.7	3.1
Indonesia	9.5	7.9	6.6	4.1	4.2	24.2	5.4	3.7	−17.6
Malaysia	3.4	3.5	4.0	−4.6	0.5	11.8	8.0	3.0	−7.8
Singapore	1.7	1.4	2.0	−7.2	0.5	5.3	8.9	1.3	−3.3
South Korea	4.5	4.9	4.5	−4.0	4.3	18.3	8.5	0.6	−13.8
Thailand	5.8	5.9	5.6	−0.9	1.7	23.8	6.7	4.2	−18.2

Note : # Inflation less percentage change in nominal exchange rate. Minus sign indicates rise in competitiveness.

Source : International Financial Statistics, 1998; Asian Development Outlook; World Economic Outlook, 1998.

MANUFACTURE EXPORTS COMPOSITION POST-LIBERALIZATION

India's latest phase of economic reforms was initiated in mid-1991 with a primary focus on trade policy reforms. The underlying rationale lay in the appreciation of the fact that the earlier restrictive and inward looking import substitution-oriented policy regime created an anti-export bias. These could be addressed by introducing competition, both through liberalizing imports and changing the industrial licensing procedure. Research has shown that free trade and higher growth has focused on the positive impact of trade on innovation through economies of scale, technological spillovers and elimination of replication of R & D. Free trade provides access to a large international market, state of art technology, which in turn leads to new product innovation. Developing countries with limited R & D stock can boost productivity with a more developed country having a large stock of knowledge from its cumulative R & D activity. The operation of free market forces allows reallocation of resources according to the nation's comparative advantage.

TABLE 12.5
Share of Manufactures in Total Exports

Country	*1990*	*1997*
India	72	74[a]
China	73	86.7
Hong Kong	96	95.6
Indonesia	36	55.4
Malaysia	55	78.5
Singapore	73	86.9[b]
South Korea	93	88.1
Thailand	61	73.3

Note : [a] 1996, [b] 1998.
Source : Drawn from Tables A4 and A5 of Major and Wood (2000).

The export composition of the Asian countries has been over the period changing in favour of manufactures. Bhattacharya (2001) explains this movement in the industry to low land/labour ratio, scarcity of other natural resources, complemented with a large skilled and unskilled labour. Another distinct trend is visible in the manufacturing sector. An increasing proportion of the region's exports are being accounted by products, which have a higher level of technology and science.

An exercise was carried to determine the effect of reforms on change in composition of manufactured exports. The major manufactured products have been categorized according to their technological characteristics. There are three broad categories. Firstly, resource intensive products whose major competitive strength is access to natural resources (e.g. aluminium smelting, oil refining, etc.). Secondly, labour-intensive products whose major competitive strength is cost of skilled and semi-skilled labour (e.g., garments, footwear, toys, etc.). Thirdly, knowledge and technology-intensive products. This category consists of scale intensive products whose major competitive strength is length of production runs (e.g. steel, chemicals, automobiles, paper, etc.), differentiated products whose competitive strength is customization (e.g., machine tools, power generating equipment) and science-based products whose competitive strength is rapid application of science and technology.

A summary result of this classification is given in Table 12.6.

The share of technology and knowledge intensive exports has increased from 18.50 percent of total exports in 1991-92 to 23.70 percent of total exports in 1997-98. The share of labour-intensive exports has gone down from 24.70 percent of total exports in 1991-92 to 31.85 in 1997-98. The share of resource-intensive exports to total exports did not depict any definite trend over the years. In conclusion, India's exports of manufactures have shifted to more value-added product categories.

Table 12.6
Manufacture Exports Composition from 1991-92 to 1997-98

	1991-92	*1994-95*	*1997-98*
Resource-based			
Total (Rs. mn.)	166,305	306,398	647,142
Percent of total exports	48	43	50
Labour-based			
Total (Rs. mn.)	110,464	217,023	320,616
Percent of total exports	32	31	25
Technology-based			
Total (Rs. mn.)	64,162	173,685	307,734
Percent of total exports	19	25	24
Total Exports (Rs. mn.)	340,931	697,646	1,275,492

Source : CMIE, India Trade Database and DGCI & S (figures in approximate).

In global market the growth rate of technology and knowledge-intensive exports was the highest. The trend growth rate of resource-based, labour-based and technology and knowledge-based exports were 25 percent, 17 percent and 26 percent respectively. Thus, the Indian experience is consistent with the global trend.

As mentioned earlier that the international comparisons of levels of competitiveness and productivity have mainly focused on labour productivity and unit labour costs. Cost competitiveness is often replaced by unit labour costs, which is defined as the ratio of labour costs to labour productivity. The rationale of this measure being, an increase in labour costs will increase the unit costs, as the industrial prices are cost determined. This results in higher prices leading to decrease in competitiveness. Table 12.7 compares the growth of Real Product Wage in India (annual emoluments per employee deflated by price index for manufacturing). It is evident that the growth in real product wage is highest in India.

TABLE 12.7

Annual Growth Rate in Real Product Wage (RPW) from 1979 to 1989

Country	*Growth Rate in RPW*
India	3.9
Australia	0.4
Belgium	1.2
Canada	1.2
Germany	0.8
Japan	2.1
USA	0.6

Source : Applebaum and Schettkat (1995).

It is observed that labour productivity along with labour costs provides a clearer picture of competitiveness. Table 12.8 presents the growth rate of manufactured exports and value-added per worker of some of the industrializing countries. The growth of value-added per worker is the lowest in India.

TABLE 12.8

Growth of Manufactured Exports and Value-Added Per Worker

Country	*Exports*	*VA per worker*
India	5.62	2.12
China	9.9	4.5
Singapore	16.38	2.58
South Korea	18.44	5.71
Thailand	21.15	3.09

Source : Cooper (1995).

Apart from comparing competitiveness on the basis of unit labour costs, the main factors influencing differences in global competitiveness are technological competitiveness and the ability to compete on delivery. Investment in production capacity play a crucial role in determining competitiveness and in this context comparison of R & D activities among nations becomes relevant. Table 12.9 shows India's investment in R & D, receipt of patents and the contribution of private and public sector towards R & D is evident from the table that nearly 88 percent of funding is provided by the state whereas it is only 21 percent in Japan.

Table 12.9
International Comparison of R & D

Country	*Total R & D Expenditure (As % of GDP)*	*Business Expenditure on R & D (As % of Total Expenditure)*	*Public Funding As % of Total R & D Expenditure)*	*Patents#*
India	0.909	13.05	88.07	0.06
France	2.308	59.77	59.39	16.68
Germany	2.791	74.18	37.66	24.42
Japan	2.85	66.02	21.46	40.52
South Korea	1.63	29.6	19.00	1.12
Thailand	0.342	13.85	69.57	0.02
USA	2.658	70.33	45.88	16.72

Note : # Average number of patents granted per 1 lakh inhabitants, 1985 to 1987.
Source : Prakash Chandra and P.C. Shukla (1994).

POLICY MEASURES TO IMPROVE EXPORT COMPETITIVENESS IN MANUFACTURING INDUSTRY

Bhattacharya (2001) has suggested certain policy measures that the government can initiate to speed up exports of manufactured goods from India :

1. In order to access global technology market a liberal technology import policy is required. The Government of India has taken steps to liberalize the technology import policy, which allows domestic firms to enter into joint ventures or go for outright purchase of technology. Either way, it facilitates access to global technology market.
2. FDI plays a significant role in promoting the exports of a nation and the technology import policy should be complemented by a liberal FDI policy.
3. Along with import of technology and accessing the same through the FDI route, the country should also commit resources to local R & D efforts.
4. Reforms are required in the labour market to promote rapid expansion of firms, which are interested to modernize or enter into more profitable sectors.

5. Along with acceleration of new technology and FDI, the skill level of labour will also require simultaneous upgradation. This implies a reduction in demand for unskilled labour and a rise in demand for semi-skilled and skilled labour. Failure to meet this demand will lead to an increase in labour cost, resulting in a loss of competitiveness.
6. Exporting firms require support in form of information and intelligence from the government in areas of techno-commercial aspects, intellectual property rights, etc. Government support to these firms will help them concentrate on their core business activity of manufacturing.
7. The "made in" factor, which is currently negative for India, needs to be countered and this can effectively take place at national level.
8. Access to information technology can influence the country's competitive strength. Telecommunications, including internet, provide the backbone of international commerce. The quality and quantity of access as well as the costs are critical components of global competitiveness. Issues related to the digital divide have to be addressed.
9. The domestic policy initiatives must be supported by international action by ensuring continued and increased market access in the developed countries for manufacture exports from India.

CONCLUSION

India's export growth witnessed long-run stagnancy till the mid-eighties, from when a turn-around was seen as a result of liberalization. With changing growth performance over the period, the Asian developing countries emerged as important destinations of India's exports. The ratio of exports to GDP increased from 6 percent in 1950 to almost 8 percent in 1999. Manufacture exports also showed a similar trend increasing from 6 percent in 1960 to 11 percent in 1997. They now account for more than 70 percent of the total exports. Whereas the share of technology and knowledge-intensive exports in manufacturing has increased, the share of labour-intensive exports has gone down. On the other hand, the share of resource intensive exports to total exports does not depict any definite trend over the years. An increase in labour unit costs and low growth value-added per worker has declined the competitiveness of the sector. Firms require spending more on R & D in order to gain technological competitiveness. Low land/labour ratio, scarcity of other natural resources, along with a large skilled and unskilled labour has provided a competitive edge to the Indian manufacturing industry. Still initiatives are also required from the government to boost the exports of the sector.

REFERENCES

Banik Nilanjan, An Analysis of India's Export during 1990s, *Economic and Political Weekly,* Volume XXXVI, No. 44.

Bhattacharya, B., Export Performance : Increasing Competitiveness through New Sources of Productivity Growth, *Occasional Paper 18,* Indian Institute of Foreign Trade, 2001.

Gokarn, Subir, National Competitiveness Policy : An Overview, *Productivity,* Volume 40, No. 1, April-June 1999.

Mohan, Ravi, Competitiveness—Factors and Framework for Measurement, *Productivity,* Volume 40, No. 1, April-June 1999.

Nayyar, Deepak, *Globalization : The Game, The Players and The Rules,* Gupta, 1997.

Porter, Michael, *Competitive Strategy,* Free Press, 2001.

Prakash, Chandra and Shukla, P.R., Manufacturing Excellence and Global Competitiveness in Indian Manufacturing Industry : A Fresh Look, *Economic and Political Weekly,* February 26, 1994.

Saxena, K.B.C. and Sahay, B.S., World Class Manufacturing and Global Competitiveness, *Productivity,* Volume 40, No. 1, April-June 1999.

Sharma, S.S., Nair, N.K. and Barman, A.K., India's Performance in the World Competitiveness Scene, *Productivity,* Volume 40, No. 1, April-June 1999.

Sharma, S.S. and Nair, N.K., Economic Reforms in India and Competitiveness, *Productivity,* Volume 40, No. 3, October-December 1999.

Suresh, Babu M., Trade Liberalisation and Export Competitiveness of Indian Manufacturing, *Productivity,* Volume 40, No. 1, April-June 1999.

Upadhyay, V., The Political Economy of Globalization, *Productivity,* Volume 40, No. 1, April-June 1999.

www. rbi.co.in , Dua, Pami and Banerji, Anirvan, *A Leading Index for India's Exports.*

www. rbi.co.in, *Productivity in Major Manufacturing Industries in India : 1973-74 to 1997-98.*

Process-based Management Systems and Productivity

AKEPATI S. REDDY

An organization can be considered to include a multitude of processes. Each of the processes takes in inputs, transforms them into outputs and delivers product(s) or services to either an internal customer or an external customer. A process can be defined as comprising of a set of interrelated and interacting activities and operations. Within the process, the set of activities and operations are used in specific sequence for realizing a product or service from the transformation of inputs. Product realization from a process involves use of resources of the organization, such as manpower, work environment, physical resources (like infrastructure and facilities) and technological and information support.

A process can be schematically shown as below :

All outputs of a process cannot be delivered as products and/or services to customers. Some of them are undesirable and wastes from the angle of the process in question. These require separation from the products, collection, treatment and disposal. Otherwise, these can affect both the organization and the environment in which the organization exists and operates. Some of the outputs are unintended, but have economic value and can be put to beneficial uses. Such outputs can be considered as by-products. Transformation of inputs into outputs is rarely 100% efficient. Further segregation of products from the unintended and undesirable outputs and residual inputs is also rarely 100% efficient.

Productivity can be considered as the rate of realization of a product/service per unit of inputs from a process. This can be enhanced through :

- Improving input quality and finding appropriate (relatively cheap and/or less hazardous) alternatives and substitutes,
- Improving product to incorporate customer requirements and expectations,
- Increasing availability factor of organizations resources,
- Ensuring consistency through appropriate monitoring and control of activities and operations of the process,
- Minimizing wastes through source reduction and recycling and reuse of wastes,
- Considering wastes as resources and making efforts to transform them into by-products, and
- Improving the process through modifications and changes to the technologies, management practices and procedures.

Management systems that strive for achieving the organization's objectives through managing various processes of the organization can be called as process-based management systems. ISO-9001-based Quality Management Systems (QMS), ISO-14001-based Environmental Management Systems (EMS), and OHSA-18000-based Occupational Health and Safety Management Systems (OH & SMS) are examples for the process-based management systems. Each of these systems is used by the organization for achieving a distinct objective : QMS for ensuring product/service quality and customer satisfaction; EMS for ensuring improved environmental performance and compliance with relevant legal and other environmental requirements; and OH & SMS for ensuring health and safety to the employees and minimizing risks and liabilities. But none of these systems has productivity enhancement as its objective.

All the above-mentioned process-based management systems follow almost a common set of management principles for guiding organizations towards improved performance. Quality management principles described in ISO-9000 : 2000 are given on next page :

- Customer focus
- Leadership
- Involvement of people
- Process approach
- System approach to management
- Continual improvement
- Factual approach to decision-making
- Mutually beneficial supplier relationships

By critically looking at these management principles one can understand that the QMS while ensuring achievement of its purpose (ensuring quality of product/service and customer satisfaction) will also simultaneously contribute to the productivity enhancement.

For ensuring consistent and predictable outputs, documented procedures, competent manpower and proper monitoring and control of key activities and operations of the process may be required. The procedures should be sufficiently specific for ensuring technical adequacy, for economic optimization and for consistent interfacing of related operations and activities. Further, the procedures should have enough flexibility to allow regulated use of alternate options for performing the tasks related to the process. The personnel performing the tasks should be competent on the basis of appropriate education, training and experience. Important activities and operations of the process should be monitored for key parameters and controlled through factual decisions (made on the basis of analysis of reliable and accurate data and information obtained through monitoring and measurement activities). In other words, consistent and predictable outputs/results demand application of at least the following three management principles :

- Process approach
- System approach to management
- Factual approach to decision-making

In order to keep up competitiveness and increase revenue and market share, an organization should strive to improve effectiveness and efficiency of its processes quicker than its competitors. Such strivings can help the organization in ensuring fulfilment of customer requirements, minimization of rejects, wastes and reworks, and reduction of costs. Continual improvement can provide the organization the needed flexibility for speedily responding to the changing market and for quickly reacting to the market opportunities.

An organization should adopt an attitude that there is always a scope for improvement. Organizations improvement efforts should engulf, in addition to the improvement of the process in question, even the product(s)/service(s) of the process, and the resources of the organization that support the process. Further, efforts should also be made to actively involve suppliers of the process inputs through building mutually beneficial relationships with them. Active involvement of suppliers is considered as very important for increasing the flexibility and speed of the organization to respond to the changing market.

Improvement of a process can follow both reengineering and kaizen approaches. The former may require tracking of relevant scientific and technological advancements/developments, and revision and revamping of the existing process. Kaizen is conducted within the existing process and it is based on the belief that many small increments, which are easy to implement, will result in large gains. Improvements to a process could be both reactive and proactive. In case of a reactive improvement, a known weakness of a process is removed and the process is improved through Deming's PDCA cycle or its variants, which could involve the following steps :

1. Collect and analyze data, and find root causes for the known weakness,
2. Identify options/solutions for removing or minimizing the weakness,
3. Evaluate effects of implementation of different options/solutions identified and selecting an option or solution for implementation,
4. Implementation and standardization of the selected option/ solution, and
5. Evaluation of the effectiveness and efficiency of the process after implementing the solution.

In case of proactive improvement, efforts are made for improving the process very systematically along a chosen direction. Here the direction for improvement may be provided by the requirements and expectations of the customer. One approach recommended for the proactive improvement is mapping of the process in question in order to assess the current situation and identifying a list of prioritized opportunities for process improvement, and then exploiting each of the opportunities while following the above mentioned five steps.

The above discussion indicates that continual process improvement demands application of at least the following four quality management principles :

- Continual improvement,
- Customer focus,
- Mutually beneficial supplier relationships, and
- Factual approach for decision-making.

Management/Availability of organization's resources is essential for the monitoring and operation of processes and realizing desired products and services from them, and for assessing and improving both processes and products/services in the light of the requirements and expectations of the customer. Organization's resources that need management include the following :

- People/manpower/human resources,
- Work environment of the people,
- Physical resources such as infrastructure and facilities, and
- Technological and information support.

Responsibilities and authority should be assigned to only those people who are competent, knowledgeable and experienced for performing the relevant tasks. Training needs should be identified, training should be provided and effectiveness of the training should be assessed. Further, people should be aware of their roles and responsibilities and of their contribution towards achieving the organization's objectives. Work environment of the people should be such that they are fully involved, committed and motivated in achieving the organization's objectives. Further, it should support effective use of their innovation, creativity and other abilities for furthering the organization's objectives. Infrastructure and facilities required for carrying out the process should be identified and provided. Management of organization's resources, essentially demand the application of at least following two management principles :

- Leadership, and
- Involvement of people.

This chapter has tried to discuss 'how process-based management systems, in the process of achieving the specific purpose, work for enhancing productivity and ensuring organization's competitiveness. Process-based management systems are using almost the same set of management principles for achieving their specific purpose. This indicates that these systems can be integrated into a single system. Benefits accrued from such integration on the productivity enhancement front may be more pronounced. Currently, at least in India, these systems are not seriously implemented and made sufficiently functional. Sole objective behind implementing these systems has been to obtain third party certification/ registration, rather than getting benefited through improved performance and enhanced productivity.

CHAPTER 14

Productive Efficiency of Indian Textile Industry : A Non-Parametric Analysis

RUCHI TREHAN AND SUNIL KUMAR

The efficient and productive use of the existing resources is one of the most important sources of growth and development of an economy. A dynamic analysis of the productive efficiency of an industry helps the policy-makers to assess whether the industry is adopting the 'best practices' or not. Besides this, efficiency analysis aids the policy formulators to chalk out the future strategy for the growth of the industry.

This chapter aims to analyze the productive efficiency of Indian textile industry using time series data for the period 1973-74 to 1997-98. For the purpose of this study, a non-parametric estimation is used to estimate the scale and technical efficiency of textile industry instead of the parametric approach owing to several reasons. Firstly, the input-output regression estimated by Ordinary Least Squares (OLS) method results in average or expected level of outcome given certain inputs, instead of the desired maximum achievable outcome (Soteriou, *et. al.*, 1998). Moreover, econometric approach for evaluating efficiency is based on the assumption that all decision-making units are operating efficiently and would not be appropriate if technical efficiency assumption is dropped (Fukuyama, 1993).

Second, non-parametric analysis does not require *a priori* functional specification of the unknown technology or distribution assumptions about the error term that may cause potential specification error. The multiple outputs and variable return to scale of production provide meaningful technical and scale efficiency measures for each decision-making units without having data on input price or costs. Third, non-parametric approach also identifies sources of production growth, hence provides recommendation for performance improvement (Fukuyama, 1993; Grabowski *et al.*, 1994). Non-parametric analysis also avoids the problem arising from multicollinearity among variables (Elyasiani and Mehdian, 1993; Chen and Yeh, 1997). Basically, a non-parametric approach uses linear programming technique to measure efficiency of operating units with the same objective. It measures efficiency based on the concept of technical efficiency, where efficient firms are those that use less of every input to produce the given amount of output or produces much more of every output given the amount of inputs as compared to other firms or linear combination of firms.

The remainder of this chapter has been structured in the following way. Section I discusses non-parametric model to measure technical efficiency of Indian textile industry. Section II presents the data base and measurement of the relevant output and input variables. The empirical results have been discussed in the Section III. Finally, a summary of empirical results has been presented and conclusions drawn have been discussed along with their policy implications in Section IV.

Section I

THE MODEL

This section specifies the mathematical programming technique to measure the extent of technical inefficiency of textile industry in India.[1] We use the deterministic frontier approach based on Farrell's (1957) concept of technical efficiency for analyzing the productive efficiency. The non-parametric frontier approach allows us to decompose technical inefficiency into : (i) scale inefficiency (i.e. not producing at constant returns to scale); and (ii) pure technical inefficiency (operating off the iso quant). In the discussion of the methodology which follows, it has been assumed that $x \varepsilon R^n+$ represents a vector of inputs, $y \varepsilon R^m+$ represents a vector of outputs and $k = 1,...K$ represents observations (years) of x and y. A linear programming technique has been used to construct a number of production frontiers which encompass the observations on x and y.

The first type of best practice frontier has been constructed on the basis of assumption of prevalence of constant returns to scale. The construction of such a frontier is illustrated in Figure 14.1 with x on horizontal axis and y on the vertical axis. Movements to the right along the horizontal axis represent equi-proportional increase in all inputs. One, two and three represent observations *only* and x for years one, two and three, respectively.

The best practice production frontier has been constructed by using only data for the current year and all previous years. So, for example, at time period one there is only one observation and thus the best practice frontier (I) passes through one (1) and the observation must be efficient. At time

FIG. 14.1

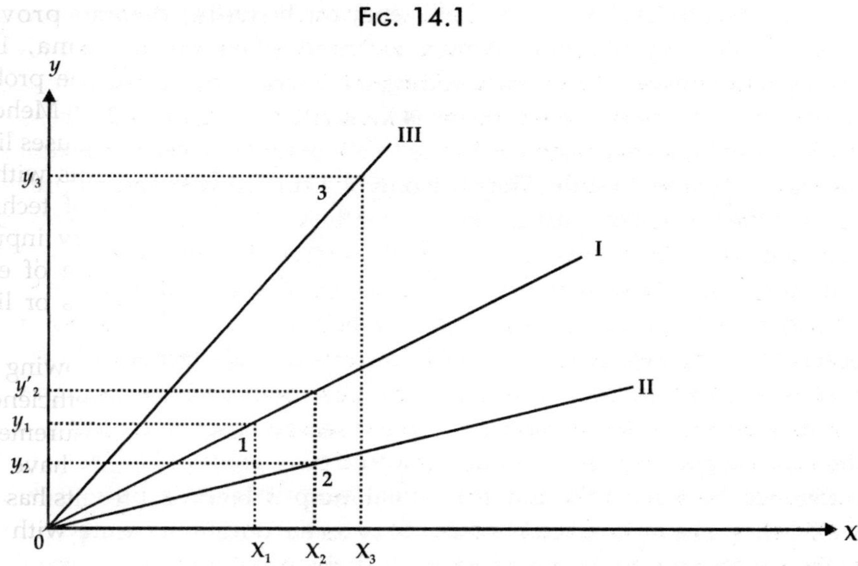

period two we construct the frontier using the data for periods one and two. In this case, the best practice production frontier will not pass through two (2), but through one (1). Thus, observation two is technical inefficient and one can determine what could have been produced in time two using X_2 inputs, if technical efficiency exists, by moving up the frontier to *y*\. The ratio of actual output (*y*^) to potential output (y'_2) is defined as λ and λ always lies between zero and one. For observation three, the best practice production frontier is ///. In this case, observation three is efficient, i.e., $\lambda = 1$. This is the overall measure of technical efficiency. The linear programming (LP) problem that is used to construct the frontier and calculate overall technical efficiency, λ, is stated as :

Min λ

Subject to

$$y \leq zY$$
$$\lambda x \geq zx$$
$$z \; \varepsilon \; r^k +$$

where λ is a scalar value representing a proportional reduction in all inputs such that $0 < K < \lambda$. In this problem y is the m dimensional vector of output produced in a particular year; x is the n dimensional vector of inputs used in a particular year; Y is the $(k \times m)$ matrix of output where k represents the number of observations (i.e. years); X is the $(k \times n)$ matrix of inputs and z is the vector of intensity parameters or weights attached to each of the observations or years in the determination of overall technical efficiency.

The overall level of technical efficiency can be further decomposed into (i) scale efficiency (θ); and (ii) pure technical efficiency (φ). In order to distinguish between these, two additional frontiers are constructed. The construction of one of these frontiers is illustrated in Figure 14.2. These best practice frontiers are constructed so as to allow for increasing, constant and decreasing returns to scale. They use only the current year and all previous years in the process of constructing the frontiers. With respect to observation one, the variable returns to scale best practice frontier is x_1IC and the constant returns to scale frontier is *I*. Thus, the first period observation lies on both frontiers, i.e., there is no technical inefficiency. For the second period observation the best practice variable returns to scale frontier is x_1IC (the best technology is that represented by year one) and the best practice constant returns to scale frontier is *I*. If the second observation had been on the variable returns to scale frontier it would have produced y''_2 output. The difference between this and the actual output level is pure technical inefficiency. The ratio of actual output to potential output (measured relative to the variable returns to scale frontier) is defined as φ and lies between zero and one. Thus, when an observation is purely technical efficient then φ = 1. Finally, for year three the best practice frontier would be $x/$ 13*D*. Evaluating year three relative to this frontier indicates that this year is purely efficient, i.e., φ = 1.

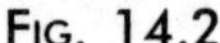

Fig. 14.2

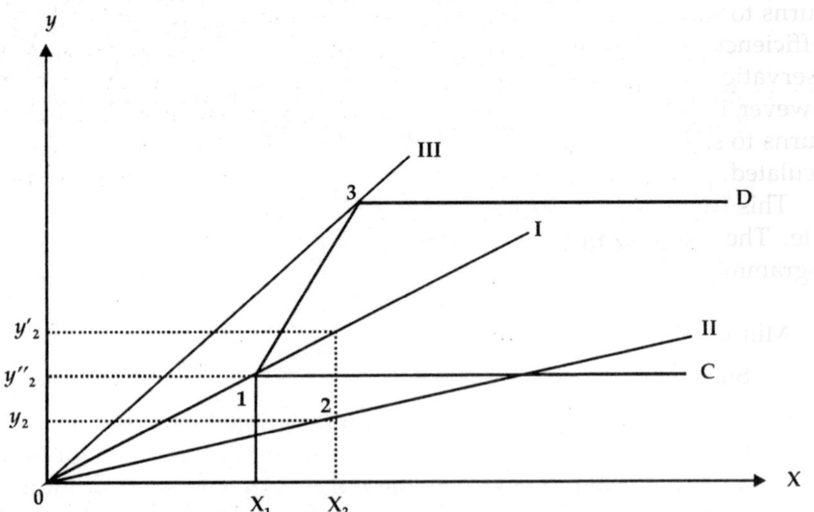

The linear programming problem that has been used to solve for φ is written as :

Min φ

Subject to

$y \leq zY$
$\varphi x \geq zX$
k
$Z_i = 1$
$i = 1$
$z \in R^k+$

In the above problem φ is a scalar and the constraint $\sum_{i=1}^{k} z_i = 1$ allows variable returns to scale.

Referring again to Figure 14.2, if the observation for period two is operating at constant returns to scale (frontier/), the output will be y'_2. For observation two, the total output lost as a result of overall technical inefficiency is $y'_2 - y_2$ with $y''_2 - y_2$ due to pure technical inefficiency and $y'_2 - y''_2$ due to scale inefficiency. Alternatively, we could measure scale efficiency as :

$$\theta = \lambda / \varphi$$

This measures the proportional reduction in input usage that is achieved if the firm is operating at constant returns to scale. For constant returns to scale the value φ equals 1, and all values less than 1 reflect scale inefficiency. Calculating φ allows us to determine whether a particular observation is operating at constant or non-constant returns to scale. However, it does not allow us to determine whether increasing or decreasing returns to scale prevail. In order to do this, a third type of frontier is to be calculated.

This frontier is constructed so as to impose non-increasing returns to scale. The third frontier is constructed by solving the following linear programming problem :

Min ψ

Subject to

$y \leq z\,Y$
$\psi x \geq zX$

$$\sum_{i=1}^{k} z_i \leq 1$$

$z \in R^k+$

It can be proven that $\sum_{i=1}^{k} z_i \leq 1$ impose non-increasing returns to scale and φ is a scalar.

If $\theta \neq 1$ and $\psi \neq \varphi$ then decreasing returns to scale exists as the *t//* calculation is based on a non-increasing returns to scale frontier. Alternatively, if $\theta \neq 1$ and $\psi \neq \varphi$, then increasing returns to scale is indicated.

Section II

DATA AND MEASUREMENT OF VARIABLES

The required data have been culled out from the various issues of Summary Results of Annual Survey of Industries (Factory Sector). The present study is confined to the period from 1973-74 to 1997-98. In the present study, we considered only one output (gross value-added at constant prices) and two inputs (gross fixed capital at constant prices and number of employees).

All monetary data have been deflated by using appropriate price deflators.[2] The gross value-added figures at constant price have been utilized as an index of output. Following Jayadevan (1995) and Goldar (1986), we preferred gross value-added as an index of output in place of net value-added because depreciation charges in the Indian industries are known to be highly arbitrary, fixed by income tax authorities and seldom represent true/actual capital consumption.

In the present study, we use the gross fixed capital stock as a measure of capital input. The standard practice of perpetual inventory method has been followed here to generate the series of gross fixed capital stock at constant prices. This requires a gross investment series, an asset price deflator, a depreciation rate, and a benchmark capital stock. We followed the procedure adopted by Martin and Warr (1990), Austria and Martin (1995), Wu (1997), Fan *et. al.* (1999) and for getting an estimate of initial value of capital stock. This procedure involves the following steps :

Step 1 : The gross real investment (I_t) has been obtained by using relationship :

$$I_t = (B_t - B_{t-1} + D_t)/P_t$$

where

B_t = Book value of fixed capital in the year t;

D_t = Value of depreciation of fixed assets in the year t; and

P_t = Price index of machinery and machine tools in the year t.

Step 2 : The logarithm of gross real investment was first regressed against a time trend to obtain its average growth rate (ω) and a trend value of investment at the beginning of the same, i.e. I_0.

Step 3 : Making the conventional assumption that the capital stock grows at a steady state at time t_0, the value of capital stock for initial year (K_0) has been then estimated as :

$$K_0 = \frac{I_0}{\omega + \delta}$$

where
K_0 = Gross value of initial capital stock;
ω = Estimated growth rate of investment; and
δ = Annual rate of discarding of capital.

In the present analysis, we have taken annual rate of discarding of capital equal to 5 percent.

Step 4 : After obtaining the estimate of fixed capital for the benchmark year, the following equation has been used for the measurement of gross fixed capital series at 1981-82 prices :

$$K_t = K_{t-1} + I_t - \delta..K_{t-1}$$

where
K_t = Gross fixed capital at 1981-82 prices by the end of year t;
I_t = Gross real investment in fixed capital during the year $t\backslash$; and
δ = Annual rate of discarding of capital.

In the present study, the number of employees consisting both non-production and production workers has been taken as the measure of labour input.

Section III

EMPIRICAL RESULTS

This section presents the empirical results obtained by applying above outlined method for the data of textile industry for the time period 1973-74 to 1996-98. Table 14.1 presents the estimates of overall technical efficiency (λ), pure technical efficiency (φ) and scale efficiency (θ) for textile industry. An attempt has also been made to assess the impact of liberalisation process of Indian economy on the technical efficiency of textile industry. Following Dutt (1993), Fujita (1994), Kaplinsky (1997) and Swamy (1997), we trifurcated the whole study period into distinct sub-periods; (i) Pre-liberalisation period (1973-74 to 1979-80); (ii) Mild-liberalisation period (1980-81 to 1990-91); and (iii) Intensive-liberalisation period (1991-92 to

TABLE 14.1
Estimates of Overall Technical (λ), Pure Technical (φ) and Scale (θ) Efficiency Scores in Textile Industry in India; 1973-98

Year	λ	φ	θ	*Returns to Scale*
1973-74	0.66695	1.00000	0.66695	irs
1974-75	0.63012	0.95815	0.65765	irs
1975-76	0.76456	1.00000	0.76456	irs
1976-77	0.74912	0.96449	0.77670	irs
1977-78	0.72337	0.91607	0.78964	irs
1978-79	0.74949	0.90627	0.82701	irs
1979-80	0.59969	0.75574	0.79352	irs
1980-81	0.64238	0.80374	0.79925	irs
1981-82	0.70427	0.84772	0.83079	irs
1982-83	0.69714	0.84761	0.82248	irs
1983-84	0.65116	0.79559	0.81846	irs
1984-85	0.80756	0.90621	0.89115	irs
1985-86	0.62796	0.86031	0.78465	irs
1986-87	0.70739	0.92810	0.76220	irs
1987-88	0.58467	0.84144	0.69484	irs
1988-89	0.71466	0.90832	0.78680	irs
1989-90	0.75808	0.85351	0.88820	irs
1990-91	0.79171	0.89776	0.88187	irs
1991-92	0.81649	0.95836	0.85197	irs
1992-93	0.79318	0.88835	0.89286	irs
1993-94	1.00000	1.00000	1.00000	crs
1994-95	0.89045	1.00000	0.89045	drs
1995-96	078897	0.79338	0.99445	irs
1996-97	0.75413	0.75822	0.99461	irs
1997-98	0.69906	0.70812	0.98720	irs
Mean (1973-98)	0.73250	0.88150	0.83393	
Mean (1973-80)	0.69762	0.92867	0.75372	
Mean (1980-91)	0.69882	0.85730	0.81461	
Mean (1991-98)	0.82033	0.87235	0.94451	

Note : 'irs', 'drs' and 'crs' represent increasing, decreasing and constant returns-to-sc respectively.

Source : Author's Calculations.

TABLE 14.2
Results of Kruskal-Wallis Test for Comparing Non-Pair-wise Efficiency Scores between Pre- and Mild-liberalization Periods

	Test Statistics	*Inference*
Overall Technical Efficiency (λ) $H_0 : \mu_\lambda^P = \mu_\lambda^M$	0.018	Accept H_0 *at 5* percent level of significance
Pure Technical Efficiency (φ) $H_0 : \mu_\varphi^P = \mu_\varphi^M$	4.739	Reject H_0 *at* 5 percent level of significance
Scale Efficiency (θ) $H_0 : \mu_\theta^P = \mu_\theta^M$	3.119	Reject H_0 *at* 10 percent level of significance

Notes : (1) μ^P and μ^M and /j.% represent mean of overall technical efficiency (A) scores for Pre- and Mild-liberalization periods, respectively;

(2) //£ and *ju^* represent the mean of pure technical efficiency *(cp)* scores for Pre- and Mild-liberalization periods, respectively; and

(3) */j.0* and *fj.%* represent the mean of scale efficiency (0) scores for Pre- and Mild-liberalization periods, respectively.

Source : Author's Calculations.

TABLE 14.3
Results of Kruskal-Wallis Test for Comparing Non-Pair-wise Efficiency Scores between Mild- and Intensive-liberalization Periods

	Test Statistics	*Inference*
Overall Technical Efficiency (λ) $H_0 : \mu_\lambda^m = \mu_\lambda^l$	5.760	Reject H_0 *at* 5 percent level of significance
Pure Technical Efficiency (φ) $H_0 : \mu_\phi^m = \mu_\lambda^l$	0.180	Accept H_0 *at* 5 percent level of significance
Scale Efficiency (θ) $H_0 : \mu_\phi^m = \mu_\theta^l$	9.763	Reject H_0 at 5 percent level of significance

Notes : (1) μ^m and //{ represent the mean of overall technical efficiency (/1) scores for Mild- and Intensive-liberalization periods, respectively

(2) *jUy* and p^1 represent the mean of pure technical efficiency *(<p)* scores for Mild- and Intensive-liberalization periods, respectively; and

(3) *fj,'$_e$* and */jg* represent the mean of scale efficiency *(0)* scores for Mild- and Intensive-liberalization periods, respectively.

Source : Author's Calculations.

1997-1998).[3] During Pre-liberalization period, the averages for λ, φ, and θ have been noted to be 0.69762, 0.92867 and 0.75372, respectively for Indian textile industry. This indicates that the levels of overall technical inefficiency, pure technical inefficiency and scale inefficiency are in order of about 31 percent, 7 percent and 24 percent, respectively.[4] This reflects that during Pre-liberalization, technical inefficiency was primarily driven by scale inefficiency (i.e. not working on optimal scale) rather than inefficient operations. Thus, pure technical inefficiency was foremost source of overall technical inefficiency and scale inefficiency was scant source of overall technical inefficiency during Pre-liberalization.

During the Mild-liberalization period, the averages for λ, φ, and θ have been found to be 0.69882, 0.85730 and 0.81461, respectively for textile industry in India. This result indicate that the levels of overall technical inefficiency, pure technical inefficiency and scale inefficiency were in array of 31 percent, 14 percent and 18 percent, respectively. This reveals that during Mild-liberalization period, both inefficient operations and working on sub-optimal scale were more or less alike culprits in explaining overall technical inefficiency.

The comparative analysis of technical efficiency scores between Pre-liberalization and Mild-liberalization reveals that :

1. The overall technical efficiency remained invariant during Mild-liberalization period;
2. The average of pure technical efficiency scores, which symbolizes the ability of management to convert the inputs into outputs, reduced from 0.92867 during the Pre-liberalization period to 0.85730 during Mild-liberalization period; and
3. The average scale efficiency of Indian textile industry improved during Mild-liberalization period since the average of scale efficiency scores increased during Mild-liberalization to 0.81461 from 0.75372.

On the basis of these observations, we can infer that during Mild-liberalization period the managerial inability enlarged and at the same time a movement towards most productive scale size has taken place in Indian textile industry. Besides this, scale inefficiency remained a leading source of overall technical inefficiency than pure technical inefficiency. In order to determine whether efficiency scores for Pre- and Mild-liberalization periods are statistically different, we applied Kruskal-Wallis test.[5] The Kruskal-Wallis test here compares the distribution of efficiency scores for two groups (time periods). Based on Kruskal-Wallis test, it can be safely inferred that overall technical efficiency of Indian textile industry remained almost unchanged (relative to Pre-liberalization period) with the start of process of deregulation and decontrol in Indian economy in general and in Indian industrial sector in particular during 1980s. However, an increase in pure technical efficiency (relative to Pre-liberalization period) has also been observed to be statistically significant. In addition, a statistically significant decline in scale efficiency (relative to Pre-liberalization period) has also been observed.

It is worth mentioning here that the decade of eighties may be characterised as the period of technological innovation. The rate of technical progress in Indian manufacturing was positive during this period and a

U-shaped 'turnaround' in the growth pattern of technical progress has taken place in the early eighties [Ahluwalia (1991)]. Overall, the process of diffusion of best practice techniques of industrial production has initiated in early 1980s. Moreover, this period coincides with the establishment of a variety of programmes aimed at deregulations and decontrols of Indian industrial sector by breaking down the financial and technical barriers. During this period, a significant invariance of average of overall technical efficiency scores which indicates the inability of textile enterprises to 'catch up' in the sense of using 'best practices' industrial techniques. This also reflects the failure of textile industry to switch over to new 'best practice' techniques.

During Intensive-liberalization period, the averages for λ, φ, and θ have been observed to be 0.82033, 0.87235 and 0.94451, respectively in Indian textile industry. The comparative analysis of Mild and Intensive-liberalization periods reveals that a U-turn in technical efficiency and its components has taken place in Indian textile industry during Intensive-liberalization period. Alternatively, the technical inefficiency, pure technical inefficiency and scale inefficiency all turned down during Intensive-liberalization period in comparison of Mild-liberalization period. The result of Kruskal-Wallis test implies that during Intensive-liberalization period, the increase in both overall technical and scale efficiency was statistically significant. On the other hand, the increase in pure technical efficiency has been observed to be statistically insignificant. On the whole, the findings indicate that overall technical efficiency of textile industry improved due to "Reforms by Storm" in Indian industrial sector since July 1991. The direct policy implication of these results is that Indian textile industry was able to 'catch-up' in the sense of using best practice industrial techniques during Intensive-liberalization period.

Looking at the study period as a whole, we observed that except 1993-94, the Indian textile industry remained inefficient in utilizing inputs. The averages for/I, <*p*, and *9* for study period as whole have been observed to be 0.73250, 0.88150 and 0.83393, respectively. The result implies that by adopting 'best practices', Indian textile industry could have reduced inputs of labour and capital by about 27 percent. Also about 16 percent of technical inefficiency identified above has been observed due to operations of the industry at sub-optimal scale. The extent of managerial inefficiency, which is reflected, by pure technical inefficiency has been observed to be about 11 percent. Except a few exceptions, which occurred during Intensive-liberalization phase, the Indian textile industry has been found to have operated in the zone of increasing returns-to-scale. This reflects that efficiency of Indian textile enterprises can be further enhanced by increasing their scale of operations.

Tobit Analysis

In order to determine whether the process of Capital deepening specified by growth in capital intensity affected the technical efficiency of textile industry or not, we utilized left-censored tobit regression. The choice of tobit regression model over simple linear regression model encountered in most text books is governed by the fact that the ordinary least squares (OLS) estimation procedure is not appropriate for explaining variations in a dependent variable which is limited in the range (e.g. a variable measuring relative efficiency, which can only take values between zero and one). We, therefore, estimated the following tobit regression model.

$$(1-\lambda) = \beta_0 + \beta_1 (K/L) + \varepsilon$$

It should be noted that in above model, we are explaining 'inefficiency' rather than efficiency. A positive sign of β_1, now indicates that the increase in capital intensity may increase the technical inefficiency of the textile industry. It is possible to estimate the regression coefficients in the tobit model in several ways. In this chapter we utilized the econometric software package SHAZAM Version 7 to estimate the parameters by the method of maximum likelihood. The estimated regression model is given below.

$$(1 - \lambda) - 0.35077 - 0.030264(K/L)$$
$$(5.2973)^* \quad (-2.1018)^*$$

Note : * represents that coefficients are significant at 5 percent level of significance.

The results of tobit regression indicate that increase in capital intensity significantly reduced the technical inefficiency in Indian textile industry. Alternatively, we can safely infer that the process of capital deepening had a positive affect on the overall technical efficiency of Indian textile industry.

SECTION IV

SUMMARY AND CONCLUSIONS

The present study evaluates the productive efficiency of textile industry in India by applying mathematical programming technique on the time series data for the period 1973-74 to 1997-98. The empirical results suggest that Indian textile industry has been, for the most part, technically inefficient. That is, the textile industry has not produced the maximum attainable output given the inputs of capital and labour and the available existing technology during the study period. Also, technical inefficiency has been found due to both inefficient operations as well as by operating on a sub-optimal scale. The tobit regression analysis confirmed that the process of capital deepening had a positive affect on the overall technical efficiency of Indian textile industry.

It has also been found that barring few exceptions, the textile industry has operated mostly in the zone of increasing returns to scale. This indicates that textile industry has some inherent advantages of economies of scale and has potentials to improve efficiency by increasing scale of operations. During 1980s, as new technology diffused throughout the industrial sector, technical efficiency remained invariant in textile industry as compared to Pre-liberalization period. This reflects an inability of this sector to switch over to new technologies and adopt 'best practices' which emerged during the Mild-liberalization phase of industrial reforms. Since 1991, textile industry had adjusted to the new technologies, which are evident from an ascent in technical efficiency during the Intensive-liberalisation phase. A straightforward implication of the above mentioned empirical results is that in India, textile enterprises are now more flexible in responding to changes in technology, product lines and markets, and thus are able to catch up with the changes in economic environment. Therefore, it is expected that any change in Industrial Development Policy for promoting textile industry would bring desired results in terms of augmenting growth and efficiency of resource utilization.

Notes and References

1. Much of the discussion here is based on Fare, Grabowski and Grosskopf (1985); Fare, Grosskopf and Lovell (1985); Grabowski and Pasurka (1988); and Aly, Grabowski, Pasurka and Rangan (1990).
2. The net investment and depreciation figures have been deflated by the 'wholesale price index of machinery and machine tools' with base 1981-82=100. The current price figures of net value-added have been converted into constant price figures by using 'wholesale price index of manufactured products' with base 1981-82=100.
3. The first phase of economic liberalisation so-called "Mild-liberalisation phase" in India began in 1981 with the SDR 5 billion loan from the International Monetary Fund. The loan was conditional on an "adjustment programme" which aimed at mitigating the constraints against the growth of private sector; and to increase the leverage of the foreign sector. Because of these conditions, the government liberalised imports, relaxed price controls, deregulated industrial production, oriented industrialisation towards the export market, and toned down budgetary support for the public sector. These policies were consolidated in 1985 by sharply reducing taxes (income and wealth taxes were slashed and estate duty was abolished), introducing modified value-added tax (MODVAT), raising the MRTP limit, and liberalizing the terms and conditions for foreign capital. The Mild-liberalisation phase that began in 1981 with the IMF loan of SDR 5 billion, continued in a sporadic manner until 1990. In July 1991, the Rao's government started to liberalize the Indian economy with greater intensity by adopting a coherent programme focusing on the investment regime, trade policies, financial sector, deregulation of domestic industry, taxation and public enterprises. The economic measures initiated in 1991, closely monitored by the IMF and World Bank under 'Structural Adjustment Programme (SAP)', constituted the second phase of liberalisation so-called 'Intensive-liberalisation phase'. By abandoning the "caution and hesitation" that defined earlier efforts at liberalisation, the Rao's government embraced the philosophy of liberal economic reforms. "Reforms by Storm" has supplanted the "Reforms by Stealth" of Mrs. Gandhi's time and the "Reforms with Reluctance" under Rajiv Gandhi regime. The reforms package resulted a 180-degree change in very policies governing different aspects of the Indian economy. The policy-makers successfully engineered a thorough transformation of India's economic policies by paying full attention on liberalisation and globalisation.

4. The sum of scale inefficiency and pure technical inefficiency may not turn out to be exactly equal to overall technical inefficiency due to the presence of the rounding errors. Kruskal-Wallis test (*H* test) is a non-parametric test whose null hypothes is that *k* samples come from an identical continuous population, that is, the sample means of the technical efficiency scores by *k* sub-sample are equal. Where *n* is the full sample size, *k* is the number of sub-sample, n_i is the size of sub-sample *i*, and R^2 is the square of the rank indices of sub-sample /'. It is approximated closely with a chi-square distribution with $k - 1$ degree of freedom. The null hypothesis of equal means is rejected when *H* exceeds the critical value.

REFERENCES

Ahluwalia, I.J. (1991), *Productivity and Growth in Indian Manufacturing,* Oxford University Press, New Delhi.

Aly, H.Y., R. Grabowski, C. Pasurka and N. Rangan (1990), "Technical, Scale and Allocative Efficiencies in U.S. Banking : An Empirical Investigation", *Review of Economics and Statistics,* pp. 211-17.

Austria, M.S. and W. Martin (1995), "Macroeconomic Instability and Growth in Philippines, 1950-87 : A Dynamic Approach", *The Singapore Economic Review,* Vol. 40, No. L, pp. 65-81.

Chen, C.H. and Yeh, T.E. (1997), "A Study of Efficiency Evaluation in Taiwan's Banks", *International Journal of Service Industry Management,* Vol. 9, No. 5, pp. 402-15.

Dutt, R. (1993), "New Economic Policy and its Impact on Industrial Relations and Employment in India?", *The Indian Journal of Labour Economics,* Vol. 36, No. 1, Jan. March, pp. 66-76.

Elyasiani, E. and Mehdian, S. (1993), "Measuring Technical and Scale Inefficiencies in the Beer Industry : Non-parametric and Parametric Evidence", *The Quarterly Review of Economics and Finance,* Vol. 33, No. 4, pp. 383-408.

Fan, S., X. Zhang and S. Robinson (1999), *Past and Future Sources of Growth for China,* EPTD Discussion Paper No. 53, International Food Policy Research Institute, Washington, D.C., U.S.A.

Farrell, M.J. (1957),"The Measurement of Productive Efficiency", *Journal of the Royal Statistical Society,* Series A, 120, pp. 253-81.

Fare, J., R. Grabowski, and S. Grosskopf (1985), "The Technical Efficiency of Philippine Agriculture", *Applied Economics,* Vol. 17, No. 2, pp. 205-14.

Fare, J., S. Grosskopf, and C.A.K. Lovell (1985), *Measurement of Efficiency of Production,* Kluwer Nijhoff, Boston.

Fujita, N. (1994), "Liberalization Policies and Productivity in India", *The Developing Economies,* XXXII-4, December, pp. 509-20.

Fukuyama, H. (1993), "Technical and Scale Efficiency of Japanese Commercial Banks : A Non-parametric Approach", *Applied Economics,* Vol. 25, pp. 1101-12.

Goldar,-B.N. (1986), *Productivity Growth in Indian Industry,* Allied Publishers, New Delhi.

Grabowski, R. and C. Pasurka (1988), "The Technical Efficiency of Japanese Agriculture, 1878-1940", *The Developing Economies,* Vol. XXVI-2, No. 2, June, pp. 172-86.

Grabowski, R., Rangan, N. and Rezvanian, R. (1994), "The Effect of Deregulation on the Efficiency of US Banking Firms", *Journal of Economics and Business,* Vol. 46, pp. 39-54.

Jayadevan, C.M. (1995), "Inter-State Variations in Employment Growth Rates : Evidences from Organised Industry in India ", *Indian Journal of Regional Science,* Vol. XXVII, No. 1 & 2, pp. 41-56.

Kaplinsky, R. (1997), "India's Industrial Development : An Interpretative Survey", *World Development,* Vol. 25, No. 5, pp. 681-94.

Martin, W. and G. Warr (1990), *The Declining Economic Importance of Agriculture,* Invited Paper to the 341 Annual Conference of the Australian Agricultural Economic Society, Brisbane, Feb. 12-15, Soteriou, A.C.

Karahanna. E., Papanastasiou, C. and Diakourakis, M.S. (1998), "Using DEA to Evaluate the Efficiency of Secondary Schools : the Case of Cyprus", *International Journal of Educational Management,* Vol. 12, No. 2, pp. 65-73.

Swamy, D.S. (1997), "The World Bank and Globalisation of Indian Economy", in George, K.K.,V.S. Nair and J. Jacob (ed.), *Economic Development and the Quest for Alternatives,* Concept Publishing Company, New Delhi, pp. 102-35.

Wu, Y. (1997), *Productivity and Efficiency : Evidence from the Chinese Regional Economies,* Discussion Paper No. 97-18, Department of Economics, University of Western Australia, Australia.

Transforming Public Enterprises in India into Intelligent Organizations

V.K. Kohli

INTRODUCTION

A major part of the Public Sector in India is known to be working inefficiently, charactering low productivity levels, poor competitiveness and high operating losses. Various prescriptions have been recommended for improving their performance. In this chapter an attempt has been made to examine the need for creating learning culture in public enterprises in order to improve their performance.

Organization development is a unique organizational improvement strategy that emerged in the late 1950s and early 1960s. Originally based on in sight from group dynamics and on theory and practice related to planned change, the field has evolved into an integrated framework of theories and practices capable of solving or helping to solve most of the important problems confronting the human side of organizations. Technology has a shelf life of about five years. That means obsolescence occurs at the rate of about 20 per cent per year. The organizations that succeed in this highly competitive environment will be those that recognize that the only constant thing is change. Dealing with change as the constant demands that we rethink the way we develop the people who will manage and contribute to that change. Constant learning and relearning are critical to be competitive. The ability to think, to analyze and to learn better and faster than the competitor becomes our discriminator. Dealing with change as the constant, demands that we create learning organizations that acknowledge the changing nature of knowledge. Every plan to grow and every plan to stay alive in the competitive environment must be a transition plan. How we plan transition, will determine whether we can compete. If our workplace is not a learning organization, it will die. Only the ability to change can provide stability. The longer we resist change, the farther behind we get, and the more difficult catch-up becomes. In the knowledge Economy of today, the Learning Organization alone will survive. For only its abilities to learn, create, codify and utilize knowledge faster than its rivals—and quicker than the environment changes—will provide tomorrow's corporation a competitive advantage that is externally sustainable. Indeed, since the core competence of any organization is nothing but the individual and collective learning of all its people—and the value chain it creates, will itself only be a domain of learning—the 2020 corporation must be built of, around, for and by people.

The importance of learning was put forward by a Chinese philosopher, Confucius (551-479 BC). He believed that everyone should benefit from learning. "Without learning, the wise become foolish; by learning, the foolish become wise." "Learn as if you could never have enough of learning, as if you might miss something." *The new economy has ushered in great business opportunities—and great turmoil. Not since the industrial revolution have the stakes of dealing with change been so high. Most traditional organizations have accepted, in theory at least, that they must either change or die.*

What is a Learning Organisation?

"An organization is skilled at creating, acquiring, and transferring knowledge, and at modifying its behaviour to reflect new knowledge and insight," Peter Senge in his book, The Fifth Discipline, described a learning organization as "a place where people continually expand their capacity to create results they truly desire, where new and expensive patterns of thinking are nurtured, where collective aspiration is set free and where people are continually learning how to learn." Thus a learning organisation . . . .

- is an active philosophy; not merely an organizational system,
- believes that its only competitive advantage is learning,
- encourages people to learn to produce the results they desire,
- nurtures creative and innovative patterns of collective learning,
- promotes exchange of information between employees hence crating a more knowledgeable work force,
- develops fresh organizational capabilities all the time, and
- produces a very flexible organization where people will accept and adapt to new ideas and changes through a shared vision.

CHANGE MANAGEMENT A STRATEGY FOR LEARNING ORGANISATION

Change may be regarded as one of the few constants of recorded history. Often society's 'winners both historical and contemporary, can be characterized by their common ability to effectively manage and exploit change situations. Individuals, societies, nations and enterprises who have at some time been at the forefront of commercial and/or technological expansion have achieved domination, or at least 'competitive' advantage, by being innovative in thought and/or action. They have been both enterprising and entrepreneurial. Management and change are synonymous : it is impossible to undertake a journey, without first addressing the purpose of the trip, the route you wish to travel and with whom. Managing change is about handling the complexities of travel. It is about evaluating, planning and implementing operational, tactical and strategic journeys—about always ensuring that the journey is worthwhile and the destination is relevant. Change is inevitable in the history of any organization. Organizations that do not change or keep pace with the changing environment suffer from entropy and soon become defunct. Organizations have an internal environment but exist in an external environment. The internal environment is in terms of the task, structure, technology, social (people) and economic variables, while the external environment is in terms of the larger terms of large social, political, economic and cultural factors. To function effectively organizations have to achieve equilibrium within the internal variables in active interactions with each other and also with the external environment.

However, this equilibrium is not static but dynamic. Hence, organizations have to modify and change to adapt to the changing internal and external environment. A short list is given below regarding some of the changes, which affected almost all organizations in the past few decades.

1. Technological innovations have multiplied and products and know-how are fast becoming obsolete.
2. Basic resources have progressively become more expensive.
3. Competition has sharply increased.
4. Communication and computers have reduced the time needed to make decisions.
5. Environmental and consumer interest—groups have become highly influential.
6. The drive for social equity has gained momentum.
7. The economic interdependence among countries has become more apparent.

Above and many other changes compel organizations to cope with the environment and become more adaptive. If they do not adapt to the circumstances they become extinct. Change is a complex process. Social scientists have suggested a number of models about change; one model suggests that change takes when the forces favouring a particular innovation become stronger than those opposing it. Another model suggests that changes results when an individual, a group of people or an organization recognizes a problem and succeeds in finding a solution. Another model suggests that change occurs through the borrowing of ideas and practices from people of other societies or cultures. Still another is that, within an organization, group or society, some people or institution moves out ahead of the rest who, eventually, imitate the innovators and general change occurs. Undoubtedly, these and other models of the change process are descriptive of the complex dynamics of change, all of the processes operating simultaneously in various segments and on several dimensions of society. Regardless of the model of change dynamics that seem appropriate in each situation, the task of the sponsor or manager of change is to stimulate, reinforce and promote those social forces and activities, which seem to promise successful movement in the direction of proposed change, and to discourage those, which do not. To do this, those involved in planned change the knowledge and understanding of the dynamics of change.

Implementation Strategies

A learning organization can be created by :

- keeping the company in a state of constant change,
- cultivating diversities in the functioning of an organization,
- creating mechanism to unlearn old and obsolete knowledge,
- building settings where people collectively learn and take decisions, and
- disseminating learning throughout the organization systematically.

To acquire and inculcate these traits in people—and, thus, envision an organization that is continuously expanding its capacity to create its future—will, however, require a shift of mind. In its quintessence, Peter Senges' five discipline of learning organization (Senge, 1990) are helpful in creating a learning organization. These are :

- Team Learning
- Shared Vision
- Mental Models
- Personal Mastery
- Systems Thinking

Team Learning

The most challenging of all the disciplines, team learning is different from team building. While the former include improving team members' skill and communication skills, this is about enhancing a team's capacity to think and act in synergistic, coordinated and united ways because the members know each other's hearts and minds. Teams, not individuals are the fundamental learning units. Unless a team can learn, the organization can not learn.

Shared Vision

To create a shared vision, large number of people within the organization must draft it, empowering them to create a single image of the future. As opposed to a vision statement from the top, such a vision is a vehicle for building a shared meaning of the organization's future in every employee's mind, particularly where none earlier existed. With a shared vision, people will do things because they want to, not because they have to.

Mental Models

Individuals act according to the true mental model that they subconsciously hold, not according to the theories which they claim to believe. If team members can constructively challenge each other's ideas and assumption, they can begin to perceive their mental model, and to change these to create a shared mental model for the team. This is important as the individual's model will control what they think can or cannot be done.

Personal Mastery

Personal Mastery is the process of continuously clarifying and deepening an individual's personal vision. This is a matter of personal choice for the individual and involves continuously assessing the gap between their current and desired proficiencies in an objective manner, and practicing and refining skills until they are internalized. This develops self-esteem and creates the confidence to tackle new challenges.

Systems Thinking

Systems thinking is the ability to see the bigger picture to look at the internal relationships of a system as opposed to simple cause-effect chains; allowing continuous processes to be studied rather single snapshots. Effectively, it means that every employee in the organization must learn to acquire peripheral vision. Systems thinking is fundamental to any learning organization; it is the discipline used to implement the disciplines. Without systems thinking each of the discipline would be isolated and therefore would not achieve their objective. The fifth disciplines integrates them to form the whole system, a system whose properties exceed the sum of its parts. However, its converse is also true-systems thinking cannot be achieved without the other core disciplines : Personal Mastery, Team Learning, Mental Models and Shared Visions.

Why do we Need Learning Organizations?

The factors which focus on the need of Learning Organization are :

Being Competitive

The child who cannot or does not learn cannot grow. The child that cannot grow cannot mature and cannot compete with peers. The organization that cannot learn cannot grow. The organization that cannot grow cannot mature and cannot compete. The bottom line is we must be competitive. A new paradigm is needed here. A TV show recently talked about U.S. firms outsourcing programmers to India, Ireland, Australia, and the Philippines to develop software for use in the United States. The September 1994 issue of ED Yourdon's Newsletter, Guerilla Programmer was devoted entirely to the software industry in India. He defines a Stage 1 industry as an industry that is "selling bodies", and a Stage 2 industry as an industry that sells the expertise of the company in managing an entire project. Stage 2 companies are now emerging in India. Motorola in Bangalore, India, is a Software Engineering Institute Capability Maturity Model (SEICMM) Level 5 organization with about 200 software engineers. Yourdon claims that several other Indian companies are almost as good. Yourdon also identified Peru, Chile, and South Africa as developing emerging software industries. Thus, the organization which is able to quickly learn and then innovate its work will be able to change its work practices to perform better in the constantly changing global environment.

Institutionalizing the Learning Process

Although we recognize the responsibility of the individual to learn and to be competitive in the market place, individual learning may make them competitive with peers, but it cannot save the organization. To be competitive as an organization, we must institutionalize the learning process. What does it mean to institutionalize? When you wake up this morning, did you debate whether you would brush you teeth? Did you wonder if every one would know about it, if you had not? Did you think about whether you could "get away with it"? Probably not, you just did it. To brush your teeth is a habit. You have institutionalized brushing your teeth. How do you institutionalize a practice? Again, brushing your teeth as an example, think of how your children acquired the habit. First, perhaps they watched you brush your teeth—you led by example. Then, you brushed their teeth. Next you helped them brush their teeth—you were teaching them how to do it. Then, you watched them do it alone—this is on-job-training. When you were satisfied that they knew how to brush their teeth, you reminded them every morning and every night and checked to make sure that they brushed their teeth. Occasionally, you send them back to the bathroom when they failed the breath test. This is quality assurance—when practices are instituted and before they become institutionalized.

Process Improvement

Process improvement and the creation of a learning organization are closely linked. Learning Organizations see process improvement as a normal part of the maturing process. These organizations expect change, they institute change, and they are capable of institutionalizing change. Who has the responsibility to create the learning organization? The leader of that organization. An organization's ability to improve is directly proportional to its leader's commitment to create a culture that not only invites learning but also demands continuous learning. Learning organization must be led by learning leaders—people who are actively committed to their own learning. Learning leaders attend the training with or before their employees. These leaders define the goals for their organization, then commit the resources to make it happen. These leaders understand that the only competitive organization in the information Age will have its ability to learn faster than its competitors. Organizational change is blocked unless and until the major decision-makers learn together, share common beliefs and goals and make the commitment to take the necessary actions for change. These leaders make the commitment to spend the money required for training, but only after they make sure that the training is linked to their business strategy; they don't waste training dollars.

Training

Who has the responsibility to train? The organization. But to the extent that, it is the responsibility of the organization to train, it is the responsibility of every employee to learn.

Who should pay? Every one who benefits—the employee, the organization, and the customer. A few examples of how employees might pay are, they could be required to attend classes half on company time and half on their time, homework assignments performed on their time could account for some percent of the total effort, books read could be prerequisites to attend formal training, or completion of scored computer-based instruction could be prerequisites for formal classroom training.

The Main Advantages Associated with the Learning Organization

- It uses only knowledge as a competitive advantage for survival.
- It constantly tries to attain total quality in every sphere.
- It builds evolutionary bonds with Costumers and Vendors.
- It is best suited to cope with incessant global change.
- It creates energized work force that evolve with the organization.

Learning Organizations are Skilled at Five Main Activities

- systematic problem-solving,
- experimentation with new approaches,
- learning from their own experience and past history,

- learning from their experiences and best practices of others, and
- transferring knowledge quickly and efficiently throughout the organization.

Intelligent Organisation and Managing the Future

Managers, organizations and the societies they serve would be foolish, fatalistic, if they failed to realize the necessity of planning of the future. Planning for planning's sake must be avoided. The ultimate failure of centralist planning initiatives, such as those adopted by the Soviet Union and China, and by many corporations in the 1960s and 1970s illustrate the need to be responsive. Plans must be flexible and in tune with the environment in which they are implemented. Operating environments, in the broadest sense of the term, need to be understood and managerial actions need to reflect their complexities and intentions. There is no evidence to suggest that the rate and the nature of change are likely to alter dramatically. Technologies, industries and societies will continue to converge. Organizations will continue to seek strategic supply chain. Managers and employees in general will be judged, as they are now, on their ability to cope with and manage change. Adaptability, continuous improvement, lifelong learning and sustaining competitive advantage remain the watchwords. Corporate winners, whether public or private enterprises will have fostered and maintained a desire to succeed through progressive, dynamic and challenging initiatives. Strategies and cultures that welcome, address and imaginatively manage change will continue to triumph. We will return to the need to maintain a competitive edge. The first law of the jungle is that the most adaptable species are always the most successful. In the struggle for survival, the winners are those who are most sensitive to important changes in their environment and quickest to reshape their behaviour to meet each new environmental challenge.

CONCLUSION

The process of change assumes qualitatively different dimensions in large and complex organizations. There are demands by the external environment and varying pressures from internal groups. In complex organisation, with rapid change in the environments, the process of change is one of transition from the present to the future. In such a case vision becomes an important process of collectively creating models of the future, and helps most people to move towards these models. Changes are complex, involving the structure, systems, processes, and new norms and behaviour. Continuous monitoring is needed. Change has to continuously balance innovation with stability. When an organization undertakes to respond to a new challenge, to complex and changing environments, it needs to re-examine and redefine its mission, create a vision for the members of the organization and develop broad strategies of mobilizing energies of most members of he organization to move into the future. Such a change will be called transformational change. Bechhard (1989) suggests four types of changes as transformational : a change in what drives the organization, a fundamental change in the relationship between and among organizational parts, a major change in the ways of doing work and a basic change in means, values, or reward systems. Many managers will readily accept the overall argument for a need to change organization structures and management styles for more effective performance. They emphasize a collaborative, participative approach centered on team processes. They demonstrate a commitment to the creation of shared vision of the future direction of the company and the necessary steps, structural and behavioural, to achieve that vision. They stress a proactive approach to learning, creating new experiences with which to challenge the *status quo* and a culture that encourages continuous experimentation and risk-taking. In brief, implementing change in the effective manner needs the Knowledge, Professional skill to implement the knowledge and techniques (Change models) for the organizational development. It is the art to implement the change in the era of uncertainties. For this purpose specialized change agents or professionals are required. Learning Organization is just a means to a business goal, created to improve productivity and most importantly profit. Learning Organization will herald a transformation in the way companies do business and perceive human society. For, it could create an era when customers will be offered value—not quality. And people will be managed—not human resources. Resources are disposable; for the Learning Organization, people are not. The most successful people in the next five to ten years will not necessarily be the smartest today, or who know the most. Success in the Information Age will be defined not by what you know at any given moment, but by your ability to learn. Knowledge will quickly become obsolete, and the only survivors will be the life long learners. The critical skills we need are the abilities to think, to analyze, and to learn. The best learners are becoming the most valuable people in our organizations. Life long learning is becoming the single most important ingredient for success, and the responsibility for learning begins with the individual. In today's global competitive market place, where continuous change and adaptation is the only way to survive, organizations to become intelligent and learning organizations should keep their minds open for all ideas.

References

I.S.F. Irudayaraj, "Organisational Culture", *South East Asian Journal of Management*, 1994.

Hussey, D.E., "How to Manage Organisational Change", Kogan Page, 1996.

Michal, Beer and Nitin Nohria, "Cracking the Code of Change", *Harward Business Review*, May-June 2000.

Nadler, Feedback and Organisation Development, pp. 22-29.

F. Mann, "Studying and Creating Change", in the *Planning of Change* eds.

Calvert, G., Mobely, S. and Marshal, L., "Grasping the Learning Organization," Training 48, No. 6 (June 1994), 38-43 (ERIC No. EJ 484475).

Garvin, David A., "Building a Learning Organization", *Harvard Business Review*, July-August, 1993, pp. 78-92.

Senge, P.M., The Fifth Discipline, The Art and Practice of the Learning Organization, New York, Doubleday, 1990.

Watkins, K.E. and V.J., "The Learning Organisation San Francisco : Jossey, Bass, 1993.

Gaining Global Competitiveness : Lessons from Successful Companies

Sanjeev K. Sharma and K.K. Uppal

A. INTRODUCTION

The business techniques, technologies and opportunities now exist globally. The emerging business scenario lays less thrust upon economic value generation through production of material goods and more on creating and harnessing the information, knowledge and ideas. This is creating a knowledge economy. In order to thrive in a wired world, organizations have to continuously innovate. Innovation and creativity are key attributes of great companies.

During the 1980s the United States saw some of its economic competitiveness weakened by Japan and European imports. Japanese cars that during the 1970s were regarded as mediocre quality now proved to be better than those produced by United States auto giants. Leather goods and ceramic tiles from Italy gained world renown, and the German Printing press industry proved to be the best in the world. At the same time, the United States maintained its lead in main frame computers and micro-processor chips, continued to be the best in the world in manufacturing passenger air craft and started to make serious headway in the development of high quality television, an area in which Japanese were too far ahead to be caught.

Quite clearly, economic competitiveness is in continual state of flux.

B. MAINTAINING ECONOMIC COMPETITIVENESS

The United States has lost its position in some areas of business domain but has obtained a well entrenched position in others. So what accounts for the competitive advantage that nation enjoys? The most important determinants of competitiveness are labour costs, interest rates, exchange rates and economics of scale and research says that the best way to achieve competitive advantage is with innovation. Quite often this is accomplished through on-going improvements of goods and services. For example, "Volvo", the Swedish auto-maker has continually striven to improve auto safety, as safety has become a more important factor in the consumers car buying decisions, thus Volvo has increased its competitive advantage.

Another way international firms maintain their competitive advantage is by making their innovation obsolete, i.e., they develop a new product that replaces the old one. For example, "Raychem", a United States firm that for years has focused on supplying technology-intensive products to industrial customers. One of its best selling products was a system for sealing splices in telephone cables. The product generated over $ 125 million annually and customers were happy with it. However, Raychem introduced a new splice closure technology that tremendously improved performance. Today the firm is converting customers to the new technology and has stopped manufacturing the old product. As a result, competitors who were working on developing a product to compete with Raychem's original product have found that they must start all over again.

Thirdly, as the competitive environment varies by industry, company and country and therefore international strategies differ substantially from one company to another and the means to implement them from one company to another. For example, companies in industries with relatively homogenous products, such as copper tubing or newsprint, compete more on price than companies in industries that differentiated and innovative products, such as branded toothpaste or state of the art computer chips. Thus, the operating strategies for the former are usually more influenced than the latter by cost savings, such as developing more productive equipment and operating methods, producing on a large scale to allocate fixed costs over more units and locating to secure cheap labour materials. But companies within the same industry also vary in their strategies, such as "Volkswagen" being more concerned with reducing costs of automobiles than "Rolls Royce", thus explaining why the former has recently moved much of its automobile production to Brazil to take advantage of lower labour costs, whereas the latter has not.

Fourthly, the size of company and the resources it has relative to its competitors, also affects the competitive advantage. For example, a market leader such as Coca-Cola has resources for many more international options than a smaller competitor such as Royal Crown. Also, leadership in one market does not guarantee leadership in all. For example, in most markets Coca-Cola is the leader with Pepsi-Cola in the strong second position, however Pepsi outsells Coke in Assa and "Inca-Kola" outsells both of them in the native Peru. Thus, the challenge before the international companies is to mould the pricing of the products within the framework of the size of the company, so that their international marketing objectives can be achieved.

C. GAINING INTERNATIONAL COMPETITIVENESS

Why are some firms able to innovate consistently while others cannot?

According to "Michael E. Porter", the answer rests in four broad attributes that individually and interactively determine national competitive advantage. These factors may vary in terms of their magnitude due to the industry characteristics, size and spread of the company, etc.

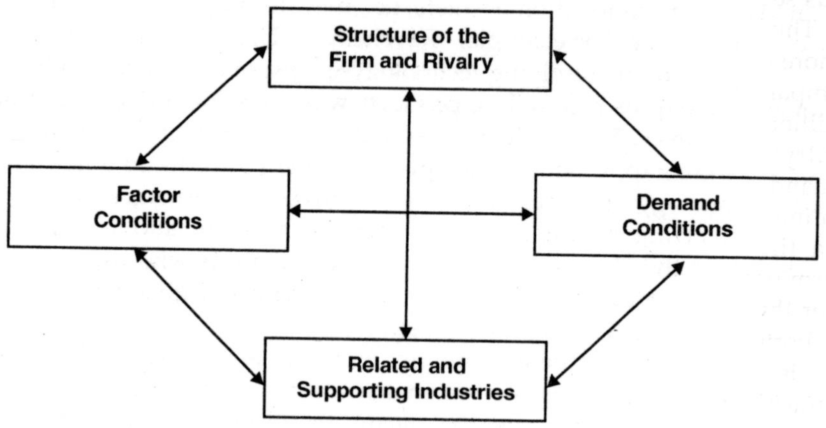

Source : Adapted from M.E. Porter (1990) : The Competitive Advantage of Nations (New York : Free Press, 1990, p. 72.

The factor conditions include land, labour and capital. For example, if a country has a large, relatively uneducated work force, it will seek to export goods that are highly labour-intensive. On the other hand, if the workforce is highly educated, the country will seek to produce goods and services that tap the intellectual abilities of these people. Then in order to maintain a competitive position, a country must continually upgrade or adjust its factor conditions. For example, Denmark has two hospitals that specialize in studying and treating diabetes.

Denmark also is world-leading exporter of insulin. By creating specialized factors and then working to upgrade them, the country has maintained its premier position in the health case field. Similarly, the Netherlands, world-leading exporter of flowers, has created research institutes in the cultivation, packaging and shipping of the flowers. As a result, no one has been able to dislodge that country's foothold in international flower industry.

Sometimes nations may develop the factor conditions they need. Italian steel-makers in northern Lombardy; for example, found that they were unable to compete because of high-energy costs, high capital assets and lack of local raw materials. So they pioneered technologically advanced mini-mills that use less energy, require only modest capital investment, permit producers to locate source of scrap and end use customers, and are efficient at small scale. These Italian firms are now both important mini-mills operations and world leaders in selling equipment for mini-mills.

Another example is of Japan, this country has to import many raw-materials, but by developing just in time production methods, major Japanese manufactures have been able to reduce the amount of resources they need to minimum and to increase their overall productivity at the same time. This has helped gain world market share in the auto and consumer goods sector.

Thus, gaining competitive advantage depends on an ability to use one or more of the four determinants in tandem. For example to be innovative, a company must often have access to people with the necessary skills (factor conditions) as well as domestic competitors who create pressure to innovate (rivalry); customers who demand a better or less expensive product (demand conditions) and suppliers (supporting industries) who provide both innovative suggestions and the low cost materials. It is also necessary for a firm to commit itself to the industry (firm strategy) and to be determined to find a way to solve the problem through innovative effort rather than to look for an easy way around the disadvantage.

Porter states that a nation's competitive advantage is strengthened if there is strong local demand for the good and services. This demand provides a number of benefits. First, it helps the seller understand what buyers want. Second, if changes become necessary, such as customers desires for a product that is smaller, lighter or more fuel efficient, the local seller has early warning and can adjust or innovate for the market before more distant competitors can respond. In fact, the more sophisticated the local buyers, the greater the advantage to the local seller. For example, one reason the Japanese firms pioneered small, quite air conditioning units is that many Japanese live in small houses and apartments where loud noise can be a problem. The firms also developed units that were powered by energy saving rotary compressors because customers complained that the price of energy was very high and they wanted a fuel-efficient unit. As a result, the Japanese now dominate the world market for small air conditioners.

Similarly, Sweden, long concerned with helping the disabled, has now spawned a competitive industry that focusses in the special needs of these people, and Denmark's environmental concern has resulted in Danish companies developing highly effective water pollution control equipment and wind mills. In the United States, consumers helped to develop a highly efficient fast food industry and as the desire for this cuisine spread worldwide, United States franchisees like McDonald's and Pizza hut that have been able to tap international demand for their products.

Another determinant of the national competitive advantage in the presence of related and supporting industries that are internationally competitive. These are mainly service industries. When supplies are located near the producer, these firms often provide lower cost inputs. These are not available to the producer's distant competitor. In addition, supplies typically know what is happening in the industry environment and are in a position to both forecast and react to these changes. By sharing this information with the producers, they help the producer maintain its competitive position. The Italian shoe industry is an excellent example. Shoe producers interact on a regular basis with leather manufactures, exchanging information that is useful to make both competitive. Thus, such interactions are mutually beneficial to both the parties.

Porter's fourth broad determinant of national advantage is the context in which firms are created, organised and managed, as well as the nature of domestic rivalry. Management practices vary across countries. In Italy, for example, successful firms typically are small or medium sized enterprises serving small market niches and operate in fragmented industries such as lighting, furniture, footwear and packaging industries. In Japan, successful firms are often those that require cooperation across financial lines and that demand the management of complex assembly operations. National goals are equally important. Domestic rivarly in another determinant of nation's competitive advantage. Nations having world leaders tend to have strong local rivals. Switzerland enjoys competitive advantage in the pharmaceutical industry because of rivalry among Hoffman's, Ciba-Geigy and Sandoz. In Germany, bayer, BASF help the country to remain ahead in chemicals.

The Government of any country can influence its multinational business significantly. For example, the government intervention for the purpose of protecting domestic industries usually result in less movement of goods and services across borders. A government's major role in global business may stem from its being a world trade negotiator. Many people believe that governments should limit competition from foreign goods in the interest of protecting local business and the jobs they offer. In the United States, people question why the Japanese are allowed to set-up auto plants in the United State while the country's farmers cannot sell rice in Japan even though imported rice would cost less than Japanese produced rice. They also fume at newspaper headlines such as "As United States Automakers shut plants, Toyota is expanding aggressively". They ask why are Americans not allowed to do business in Japan as easily as Japanese firms can do business here?

D. DEVELOPING AN INTERNATIONAL PERSPECTIVE

Firms operating in cross-border markets need to develop an international perspective. This requires attention in three areas :

(a) Experience

One way to create an international perspective is to hire individuals with international experience. A company cannot become a true MNE without sending its managers overseas. The primary benefit of such experience is that it helps managers learn how to evaluate situations and this process is often different from that used at home.

For example, one of the most frequent criticisms of United States Managers is that they rely too heavily on scientific strategic planning, overemphasize qualitative models and overlook the artistic, diplomatic and humanistic aspects of international business. Greater international experience will help managers avoid such tendencies.

(b) Focus

The second way to develop an international perspective is by emphasizing global orientation to human resources activities such as hiring, remunerating; performance appraisal, promotion, etc.

(c) Attitude

The third way to develop an international perspective is by changing the attitude that many managers have toward their work. Companies should screen the conditions carefully for the overseas assignments and put only individuals with the right attitude.

E. MANAGING DIVERSITY OF INTERNATIONAL BUSINESS

Diversity is the outcome of globalization, Workforce of any MNC comprises people from different countries. Within this diversity of national origins, there is even wide diversity of cultures, religions, language and dialects, educational attainment, skills, values, ages, races, senders, and other differentiating variables. Managing such a cosmopolitan workforce is a challenging task for any executive.

Problems associated with management of diversity :

(a) Among the primary problems associated with diversity is the likely absence of cohesion among workers, where group lacks cohesion, members become less productive, and it is difficult to create a work environment that is conducive for efficiency and effectiveness.

(b) Another problem of diversity relates to inaccurate communication which may result from different meanings assigned to words and different interpretations assigned to situations.

(c) Yet another problem resulting from diversity relates to sexual harassment. Many women are victims of sexual harassment in the workplaces. Sexual harassment consists of any unwanted sexual behaviour, inclusively but not limited to suggestive looks, sexual jokes, touching or pressure for sexual favours.

(d) Finally, earning gaps exists in multicultural work groups. An American or a German is paid much more in an MNC than his/her counterpart from the host country.

There are also hosts of benefits to be gained from diversity :

(a) Cultural diverse groups can enhance creativity, lead to better decisions and result in more effective and productive performance.
(b) A significant benefit from diversity relates to prevention of group link, which is a Social conformity and pressures on individual members of a group to conform and reach consensus.
(c) Another benefit of diversity stems from the possibility of generating more and better ideas. Because group members come from a host of different cultures, they are able to create greater member of creative and unique solutions and recommendations.

Thus, to reap the benefits listed above, the challenges of International managers is to focus on the following :

(a) *In the entry stage,* the focus should be on building trust and developing team cohesion. This can be a difficult task for diverse teams, whose members are accustomed to working in different ways.
(b) *In the work stage of development,* attention needs to be directed more towards describing and analyzing the problem or task that has been assigned.
(c) *In the action stage,* the focus is to shift to decision-making and implementation. This can be a difficult task, as it demands consensus building among members. By achieving this objective, experienced managers work to help the diverse group recognize and facilitate the creation of ideas with which anybody can agree.

F. COPING WITH CHANGING POLITICAL ENVIRONMENT : THE IMPERATIVES

The political environment effect MNE in many ways. For example, all major triad groups have trade barriers that are designed to limit the sale of foreign goods in their countries. This in turn typically result in trade negotiations that are designed to open up these markets or to reduce trade deficits. Protectionism trends are particularly treacherous because they are psychological as well as legislative, i.e., even the trade barriers are covered, there is a tendency for people to be protectionist and to buy local.

International firms say that they are open for free markets; but does the political environment of particular country supports that Political decisions involving domestic foreign policy can have direct effect on a firm's international market success. For example, U.S. government placed a total ban on trade with Libyans to condemn Libyan support for terrorist attacks, imposed restrictions on trade with South Africa to protest apartheid and placed total ban on trade with Iraq, whose actions constituted a threat to national security of U.S. and its allies. In each case the international marketing programme of U.S. companies, whether it was IBM, Exxon, or Hawg Heaven Bait Company, were restricted by these political decisions. Thus, these international firms have a challenge to maintain effective relations with other countries. So that their survival does not come at stake.

G. CHALLENGE OF COPING WITH CHANGING ECONOMIC ENVIRONMENT

The change in the economic environment of a particular industry effect the trade of that country with regard to other countries, in which the former has international marketing operations. Also as internal economic conditions deteriorate restrictions against foreign investment and purchasing may be imposed to strengthen the domestic economy. For example, the most pressing conditions affecting the U.S. trade during the mid-1980's was the relative strength of the dollar in the world markets. Because the U.S. dollar value was high compared with the most foreign currencies, U.S. goods were expensive for foreign buyers.

H. CONCLUSION

In an increasingly competitive, complex and unpredictable world, many business enterprises are seeking competitive advantage by strategic management of their human resources and their knowledge base. In an environment where technologies are rapidly becoming obsolete, intellectual capital of the human resources has come to represent the primary source of value creation and advantage for the organizations. It is this mutually complementary Management of technology and human resources, which will be the basis of sustainable competitive advantage. All these developments make it imperative that Indian enterprises shift their thrust from internally focused management to competitive mapping. The mantras of benchmarking, customer relationship, total quality management, building a brand equity, creating a dedicated and knowledge-based work force can help companies in their quest for excellence in the borderless world. *The challenge before Indian business is to be lean, clean and green.*

Section III

SERVICE SECTOR

Challenges and Strategies for Competitiveness, Productivity and Globalising Indian Insurance Market

RAVINDER VINAYEK AND RAVI KUMAR GUPTA

INTRODUCTION

The circle is complete. Privatization to nationalization and back to privatization. It has been quite a journey.

The private sector-dominated Indian life insurance sector was nationalized by the Union Government in 1956. The great national brand : Life Insurance Corporation of India (LIC) was established with the idea to weld together a dynamic and vigorous organization capable of taking insurance to every sector of people, throughout the country and mobilizing their savings while affording to them complete security together with efficient service. The non-life insurance business was nationalized in 1972, under the aegis of General Insurance Corp. (GIC), which established four 100% subsidiaries, National Insurance Co., New India Assurance Co., Oriental Insurance Co. and United India Insurance Co. Soon after, GIC insured the big things (satellites and so on), while the four subsidiaries were supposed to compete with each other in the market for non-life insurance (industrial machinery, vehicles and so on). Somehow, the 'competition' failed to turn the market efficient.

The very reasons for which the insurance sector was nationalized are now being given for its privatization. The current reasoning : the sector needs to grow, for which it needs genuine competition (not fake competition between four arms of the same establishment). Yes, competition of the kind that might manage to build a reputation of efficiency and fair play and thus reposition the concept in consumer minds as a hugely beneficial service, not a sort of must pay tax, the benefits of which may never come. The sector is perhaps the worst case in India of a monopoly gone terribly wrong.

As one segment of India turns 'Net-savvy', we still hear harrowing stories of embattled widows having to struggle with the system to lay a finger on their policy claims. Yet, the concept has thrived. This is because it has been a 'forced choice', a policy is mandatory in some cases (car insurance) and by tax breaks in others (life insurance). American insurers in contrast, seem almost enthusiastic about paying up (instantaneously too, almost without verifying the claim's validity), simply because this pleases customers, which generates positive word-of-mouth, which attracts more policy-holders and high volumes in this business help spread risks even wider, allowing a lowering of rates and raising of profits. That's how statistics work. On a bigger base, the probabilities settle down to predictable levels and with system-wide risks balanced out (and volatility eliminated), profits improve.

OPENING-UP THE INSURANCE SECTOR FOR PRIVATE COMPANIES

In December 2001, the private insurance companies started their operations, and since then, country has seen the entry of 12 new life insurance and eight non-life players in India. This is the right time to think about what has been achieved in this short period and ponder about the road ahead. Although it is difficult to clearly define the trends that are likely to emerge in the future, listing the key issues today with focus and strength will definitely go a long way to make the liberalisation of this sector a true success. The new private life insurers have infused approximately Rs. 2,000 crore as capital so far, and although the figures are still less than what was initially expected by Insurance Regulatory and Development Authority (RDA), (both in terms of number of players and capital infused), it is no mean achievement in this short span. The fact that a lot of players are still waiting in the wings for a revision in the capital infusion structure from 74 : 26 to 51 : 49, also throws up the possibility of a lot more action in the next year. However, there is still a long way to go before the private insurance companies can, even collectively, make a dent into the market share of the state monolith, i.e., the Life Insurance Corporation of India (LIC). However, in this financial year, the private players have succeeded in garnering 4.28 per cent of regular premium individual new business, 8.16 per cent single premium new business, and 51.5 per cent of the pension market in terms of number of policies. In Taiwan, entrants took only a 3 per cent share within seven years of opening up, while in Korea their share was barely 1 per cent after 20 years. The achievement of private insurers in India has been impressive indeed by those standards. Still, the life insurance premium as a percentage of GDP is only 1.3 per cent, which is very low compared to 5.2 per cent in the USA, 6.5 per cent in the UK and 8 per cent in South Korea. In the next 4-5 years, the affect of liberalization may see this grow up to as much as 8 per cent of the GDP.

Although this target ignores the difficulties of approaching the widespread population, new entrants will have to find ways to cater to the demands despite having to cover large distances or high costs relative to returns. In order to achieve such targets, specific steps are required both from the Government as well as the insurers.

Hence, the opening up of insurance sector to private insurance has put a great responsibility on them to ensure a very fast growth of insurance so that India can come to the level of the developed countries of the world in the penetration of the insurance.

CHALLENGES BEFORE THE INDUSTRY

The new as well as the old insurers are facing a number of challenges in the liberalized market.

1. New Insurers

The new insurers are to invest a minimum Rs. 100 crores as capital. The insurance business does not produce profit in the first five years as the generation of profits normally starts in the sixth year. Hence, the new insurers have to be ready for locking up the capital for 5 years, without earning any profit. Besides, they are facing problems regarding shortage of the trained managerial cadres for insurance industry. Even the setting up of various offices and the distribution channel is a time consuming process.

Further, the new insurers have to compete with the established insurers like LIC and GIC which have created their corporate image over the years, have a big net-work of branches and agents, have a pool of experienced managers and vast financial resources. Further, life fund of the LIC continue to be guaranteed by the government. Hence the new insurers have to assure the policy-holders about the safety of the life fund to win their confidence. The foreign insurers who are the partners of the Indian Insurers will have expertise of the international market. It will help in establishing corporate image in the market. But foreign insurers lack experience and knowledge about Indian insurance market that can prove to be a major handicap. The Indian insurers mostly will be from manufacturing industry and they may have some knowledge of the consumers for non-financial products. This may help in the marketing of the insurance products.

2. Existing Insurers

The existing insurers, LIC and GIC, have created a large group of dissatisfied customers due to the poor quality of services. Hence, there is a shift in large number of customers from LIC and GIC to the private insurers.

LIC may face problem of surrender of a large number of policies as they will be wooed by new insurers by offering innovative products at lower prices. Even the corporate clients under group schemes and salary savings schemes may shift their loyalty from LIC to the private insurers. There is a likelihood of exit of young dynamic managers from LIC to the private insurers, as they will get higher package of remuneration. Further; LIC has over-staffing and with the introduction of the full computerization, a large number of the employees will be surplus. However, they cannot be retrenched. Hence, the operating costs of LIC will not be reduced. This will be a disadvantage in the competitive market, as the new insurers will operate with lean office and high technology to reduce the operating costs.

GIC and its four subsidiary companies are going to face still more challenge. Their management expenses are very high due to surplus staff and they cannot reduce their number due to service rules. Their management of claims is also not upto the mark. This will put strain on their financial resources. Further they have been depending upon the premium income of the corporate clients mainly and have not developed business in the personal line. There is a danger that GIC and its four companies will very soon lose corporate clients. Hence, they are likely to be in real trouble.

Hence, LIC and GIC have challenges to effect radical restructuring of the organizations so that they become more competitive, lean and may operate at low operating costs. However, the biggest challenge before LIC and GIC is the change in mindset of all employees from top to bottom so that they become more responsive to the customers and the market.

3. Expectation of the Consumers

Today LIC has more than 60 products in its kitty. Even GIC has more than 180 products. But most of them are outdated as they are not suitable to the needs of the customers. Hence, old as well as new insurers will have to offer innovative products to the consumers. The consumers are particularly awaiting good Pension Plans, Health Insurance, Term Insurance and Investment Products like Unit Linked Insurance from the life insurers. Similarly, the customers expect innovative products from the general insurers for managed Healthcare, Property Insurance, Accident Insurance and other products related to the personal line of insurance.

The consumers also expect reduction in the premium of life insurance products as the longevity of the Indian life has improved three times in last 50 years. The price of the existing life insurance products is much higher and there is scope of reduction of premium to the extent of 30% by the life insurers on the basis of improved mortality However, it is possible only if the efficiency of the insurers improve considerably in future. Similarly, there is scope for reduction of premium for fire insurance, which should be. The prices of all products of general insurance deserve reduction of around 20% but it is possible only if the management expenses are reduced considerably by the existing as well as new general insurance companies.

Further consumers expect better yield on the life insurance policies.

The existing yield on most of the life insurance policies is around 6% which is much lower than the yield in the market for other financial instruments. The rise in the yield is possible by more prudent management of the investment of the life fund and reduction in the management expenses.

Besides, the consumers expect improved quality of services in the liberalized market. At present, policy-holders are very much aggrieved by the sub-standard services of LIC and GIC, particularly in the area of settlement of claims, issue of new polices, transfer of the polices and revival of policies. The new insurers will have to be more particular to meet this expectation of the consumers. Hence, the existing as well as the new insurers will have to meet all expectations of the consumer for innovative products, reduction of premium, better yield on policies and radically improved quality of service to the consumers.

Distribution Channels

In the liberalized insurance market there are multi-distribution channels, which include agents, brokers, corporate intermediaries, bank branches, affinity groups and direct marketing through telesales and internet. Some channels are cheaper than others. Hence, there will be competition among the channels. The new insurers operate with the help of the multi-distribution channels but the existing insurers may be forced to operate only with the help of Agents. Hence, intense competition will grow among the old and new insurers in the market to win the consumers

Consumer Education

The market in the recent past has been flooded by a large number of products, by a fairly large number of insurers operating in the Indian market. Even with limited range of products offered by LIC and GIC, the consumers are confused in the market. Their confusion will further increase in the face of a large number of products in the market. The existing level of awareness of the consumers for insurance products is very low. It is so because only 62% of the Indian population is literate and less than 10% well educated. Even the educated consumers are ignorant about the various products of insurance. Hence, it is necessary that the extensive plan for education of consumers should be undertaken by all the insurers. The consumer organizations and the media can also play very important role in educating consumers. This will result in expansion of the insurance market and will also keep the needy consumers to purchase appropriate products.

Consumer Grievance Redressal

The insurers have to face an acute problem of the redressal of the consumers regarding grievances for deficiency in products and services. IRDA has already appointed Ombudsman for looking into the grievances of the policy-holder and its judgment will be binding on insurers. Further under Consumer Protection Act (CPA) 1986, the consumer courts are "operating at District, State and the National level. In the competitive market, awareness level of the consumers will increase and it will help consumers to fight for their legal rights for deficiency in services. Hence, the number of legal cases filed by the consumers against insurers is likely to increase substantially in future. This will be a challenge to the insurers.

STRATEGIES FOR COMPETITIVENESS, PRODUCTIVITY AND GLOBALISING INSURANCE MARKET

The major strategies to be adopted in shaping the future of the insurance market can be broadly outlined as :

1. Product Innovation

As is natural, with the liberalization of any sector, customer expectation get build-up for better products and services. Till now, the major focus of most of the new entrants have been to offer products that can cater to as large a target audience as possible. Innovations have been in terms of rider benefits like critical illness, hospital cash, surgical benefits, options to purchase paid-up additions, etc.

Also, the market has seen the launch of unitized products and unit linked products with various investment options. As the market matures, more new products will be introduced, offering various dimensions of risk, return and flexibility. Unit-linked products, inflation protection products, products designed specifically for loans like housing finance, auto finance, credit cards and consumer loans are likely to flood the market in the near future. Specific products that will sell and products suited to some alternate distribution channels are also likely to be offered. Even in the pension products, the returns might be tied to index-linked funds or equity/debt funds. Buyers will also have the option to switch funds before the annuities begin and to invest different amounts at different times. As the market develops, and competition increases, one key differentiator between companies will be the product range and the prices at which they are offered.

2. Distribution—The Key to Success

Distribution will be the most important factor for all insurance companies. LIC already has a wide reach and presence, which cannot be duplicated easily. Building a distribution network from scratch is expensive and time-consuming. Yet, if insurers are to take advantage of India's large population and reach a profitable mass of customers, new distribution avenues and alliances will be imperative. This would call for substantial shift in the distribution of insurance in India. Worldwide, insurance products have gradually moved away from service to being commodity products that can be sold through the medical shops, groceries, novelty stores, etc. Expansion through the traditional agency force is not only costly, but also a time-consuming affair. It is imperative that alternate channels are utilised to reach out to the customers as fast as possible. The alternate channels will also bring down the cost of distribution, which will benefit the customers in the long-run. With the amendment of the IRDA Act with regard to corporate agent/brokers, the necessary thrust on development of these alternate channels is expected. Apart from this, the bancassurance channels also has tremendous potential, given the fact that India has a widely spread banking network that reaches every nook and corner of the country. The alternate distribution channels that are likely to be used extensively include brokers, independent intermediaries and corporate agents, bancassurance, direct channels (Tele-marketing, Direct Mailers, Internet Sales), societies, co-operatives and gram panchayats.

3. Bancassurance—An Effective Channel

Bancassurance could be one way for new players to take on the might of the public-sector players who have set-up their own extensive branch network. Bancassurance would also facilitate insurance companies to shift focus from highly competitive markets to markets where the competition has not yet caught up. The Asia-Pacific markets have been adopting successful European ways and customising it to the local conditions. Bancassurance is one such attempt, which is gaining popularity in Asia, more particularly in India. Issues related to the operationalization of bancassurance agreements are many and depend on the current state of parties to the agreements : banks and insurance companies. However, some of the issues relating to customer ownership and impact of like deficiencies in insurance products on existing relationship need to be clearly understood by many banks before adopting this system.

4. Competition—More Companies to Venture into Insurance

Prior to nationalization in 1956, there were 245 life insurers carrying out business in India and catering to a population of 36 crore. Today, because of advances in communication and information technology, the requirement may not be of such a large number but it is generally felt that the sheer size of the Indian market can provide comfortable room for many more players. USA has more than 2,200 insurance companies and the UK has more than 500. However, since liberalisation, only 12 new companies have started operations in India. Another factor that can help more companies to venture into insurance is the capital requirement of new companies. While the Rs. 100 crores capital is good enough for a player planning a pan India presence, still the Government can contemplate a smaller capital to the tune of Rs. 30-40 crores for allowing regional players in specific markets only.

5. Building Trust and Customer Confidence—With Long-Term Objectives

Market surveys have repeatedly shown that the building trust and faith is of paramount importance for any new insurance player. Life insurance as a category enjoys tremendous confidence as safe savings a trust primarily created by LIC. Therefore, the major challenge before the private insurers is to create confidence in customers that they are present with a long-term objective. While brand and company image building will be the focus for some time, the conservative Indian psyche demands that there should be some safety-nets for the customers. Although IRDA has taken adequate steps to avoid any crisis arising out of insolvency, but it would be prudent for the insurance companies to allocate a small percentage (1-2 per cent) of the premium towards a Policy Holder's Protection Fund. This would not only help in building confidence, but also help in the stability of the industry in the long-run. Moreover, with the proposed reforms in the tax sops insurance is more likely to be sold on grounds of protection than on investment. This will be a significant shift for the Indian market, and we may see a trend emerging in the future that smoothens the business more evenly during the year rather than cramping too much in the last quarter. This will be a healthy sign because in this manner, resource utilization can be optimized by the companies throughout the year.

6. Insurance Education and Training

Over the next 3 to 5 years, the Government expects over 30 Life Insurance Companies in the Indian market. All these insurers will need qualified insurance professionals. Apart from that, the aggressive expansion plans of the new private sector players will also demand a lot of quality manpower. The number of people required to man suitable posts at the branch and regional offices will also be stupendous. The battle for talent has already begun and the recurrent recruitment advertisements in the newspapers bear testimony to that. Till now, insurance companies have been tapping talent from the FMCG, finance and hospitality industry. However, this cannot be sustained in the long-run and therefore some steps are required immediately. There is a pressing need to start specialized insurance program both short-term and long-term that can be offered as independent stand alone course by management institutes. In terms of training of agents, IRDA has already accredited 14 insurance training institutes spread across Mumbai, Pune, Chennai, Secunderabad and Warangal. These schools will churn out approximately 1,500 students annually, who will be the primary distribution channels for insurance companies. The capacity of these training institutes will have to be increased dramatically to ensure a smooth supply of training agents in the long-run.

7. Thrust on Usage of Information Technology

Information technology will be used extensively to service large number of customers efficiently (Customer Relationship Management) and bringdown costs. IT has to complement or supplement distribution channels in a cost-effective manner. Faster and better service will be provided to the customers right from issue of policy, to like payment of premium, revival, grant of loan, transfer of policy and settlement of claims. The road ahead is certainly not an easy one for the new entrants. While the government IRDA can provide the necessary impetus through various policy measures, the companies have to execute the groundwork so that the industry can provide "more for less" to the customers.

8. Pension Market—Next Big Bang Reform

The potential consumers of Pension services are those people who have a latent need for it and can also afford it. About 1/3rd of the population is defined as working population who are earning some form of income. This group comprising of nearly 314 million workers as estimated by the Dave Committee (on the basis of 1991 census) has identified that only about 10% of them have access to some form of retirement benefit and/or pension arrangement. The remaining 90% of this work force or about 283 million are potential consumers of pension products. The potential size of the pension market has also been estimated through studies conducted by Mr. R. Ramakrishnan, a distinguished Actuary and retired Executive Director of LIC and Prof. R. Vaidyanathan of IIM, Bangalore. Mr. Ramakrishnan estimates the 'Returned Income' from employees other than those in Government and corporate sector, to be of the order of Rs. 1,25,000 crores in 2000-2001. He further estimates that 5% of this could be directed towards premium under pensions. However, even if the companies are able to bring in only 1% of this under pension during the first year, the premium could be Rs. 1,250 crores. He further estimates that within 15 years it could grow to Rs. 150,000 crores. Prof. Vaidyanathan has separately estimated through an analysis of reported income of Bhagidari sector that the accumulated pension fund in year 2005 could be Rs. 326,000 and has suggested the following strategies for effectively tapping the Pension Market :

- To undertake projects to understand the pensions market, consumer profile, different types of pension products, etc. for meeting the different and diversified needs of various segments of society.
- To share their experiences in India and in other countries to help evolve a realistic database in relation to mortality and morbidity statistics to help in better understanding of product design, pricing, packaging of pensions, etc.
- To present to the Government and the Regulator, i.e. IRDA, a case for some regulatory reforms to maximize the return on pension funds and a package of tax incentives for the prospective consumers of pension market.

9. Health Insurance—Unhealthy Yet

The current healthcare market is estimated at Rs. 100,000 crores and is expected to grow to Rs. 262,000 crores by 2012. The private health care expenditure is almost 75 per cent. Still, the health insurance coverage is negligible, with only about 10 per cent of the market being tapped today. Healthcare costs are rising dramatically and private expenditure may not be able to cope with it. With Mediclaim having failed to penetrate to the desired levels, life insurance companies have a tremendous potential to supplement the general insurance companies in providing better health insurance services. The life offices can offer level premium long-term health products as riders attached to the basic products. Coupled with a better servicing network, this sector could see a tremendous boom for the life companies in the near future.

What really has kick started the whole gamut of healthcare management is its massive business potential in a country like India with over 100 crore population. With the per capita income of Indians increasing lifestyle diseases are projected to replace infectious diseases as the major health problem in the country, says the healthcare study carried out by the Confederation of Indian Industry (CM) in association with McKinsey & Co. At least 40 per cent of the out-patient spending would be concentrated on lifestyle diseases like heart ailments, asthma, cancer and nervous and circulatory disorders by the year 2012, according to the findings of the study. The report also brings out the link between development and hospitalizations— if in 2001, when the GDP per capita was $ 2,100; there were 31 hospital admissions per 1,000 people then there are expected to be 39 hospitalizations per 1,000 people in 2012, when the GDP per capita would be around $ 3,600. In comparison, Thailand, with a GDP per capita of $ 5800, the number of people hospitalized in 2001 were 61 per 1000 while in US, where the per capita income is $ 22,000, 113 people per 1,000 population were hospitalized. In the much more developed Singapore, with a per capita income $ 25,000, the number of hospitalizations in 2001 were 127 per 1,000 people. While the study estimated the level of hospitalizations in the country, it is also found that at the present rate, there would soon be a dearth of hospital beds besides there will not be enough specialized physicians. At present, there are 1.5 beds per 1,000 population or 1,500,000 beds, and the number of physicians is 0.5 per 1,000 people. By 2012, there would be a 50 percent rise in the demand for beds, or/and additional requirement of 7,50,000 beds. According to the report, seven disease groups would drive the growth in number of out-patients with cancer, heart ailments, circulatory and nervous disorders, musculoskeletal diseases, ailments of the sensory-organs and asthma—with infectious diseases taking a backseat. Globally, the major reasons for the immediate growth of healthcare is a rapidly aging society, progress in medical technology, increasing health awareness, changed lifestyle and finally increasing budget deficits in almost all countries and India is no exception. Healthcare insurance is only a means to provide the required funds to pay for medical care. Effectively, health insurance is not an end in itself but a potent driving force to provide and generate healthcare facilities for the masses. However in India, the health insurance sector was completely neglected by the public sector non-life companies for whom this portfolio was a loss-making one.

Though the product Mediclaim was simple, the policy-holder was having a tough time in going through the claims settlement processes of the insurance companies. This may be the reason why not many people really bought Mediclaim though it was a necessity. The market in terms of product and the total premiums was very small. Things are changing after the sector has been opened up for the private sector. Both the new and old players are able to realise the large potentials in the health insurance segment, which will be a part of their booming retail business. The total amount of premium is going to increase from the currently meagre, Rs. 400-Rs. 500 crore to Rs. 10,000 and Rs. 15,000 crore in the next 5-6 years, with the number of policy-holders expanding to five to six crore from the present 25 lakhs. The Insurance Regulatory and Development Authority (IRDA), the insurance regulator, has also tried to bring about both structural and operational changes in the health insurance market promoting health insurance as a social security measure. To begin with, IRDA recently issued licenses to 20 third party administrators (TPA), which will only be organizing the whole gamut of medical services for the policy-holders and also smoothens out the claims settlement process. These TPAs will enter into an agreement with domestic non-life insurance companies, to offer health services to the policy-holders for remuneration. The insurers will forward the list of Mediclaim policy-holders to the TPA, which will then issue identification cards to the policy-holders. Customers will have access to a 24 hours help line, whereby the TPA will respond immediately and send a doctor when required. If needed, the policy-holder will be sent to a hospital nearby. The TPA will issue an authorization letter to the hospital, pay for the treatment and get reimbursed by the insurance company. TPAs will be a boon to the lower strata. The rich class can afford medical treatment while the poor cannot. Their tendency is to delay treatment till it becomes a chronic problem or go to a small nursing home where charges are low but qualified doctors and sophisticated equipment are few. Things may change soon. The National Insurance Company (NIC) has already tied up with many hospitals in Bangalore, Chennai and Delhi. Banks including State Bank of India (SBI) and Union Bank are extending facilities for funding the hospital treatment, who will later be reimbursed from the customer's health insurance policies. All the four state non-life insurance companies are in the process of appointing TPAs for launching health insurance products. TPAs will revolutionise the administration of insurance policies with regard to a cashless hospitalisation and benefits thereof. Sometimes it so happens that as there is no governing regulator for hospitals therefore they charge as per their whim. As a result, hospitals fleece the patients and insurers, says Dr. Nayan Saha, Managing Director, Paramount. So, as far as manipulations in health insurance are concerned, they will continue since service providers (hospitals) will inflate the bill and recommend unnecessary tests with prolonged length of stay. There are several filters which insurance companies can implement to prevent such manipulations. This is where health TPAs can play an important role, provided there is cooperation among them. The total investment needed to bridge the gap between supply and demand of healthcare management in the next decade could be Rs. 1,00,000-1,40,000 crore, of which only Rs. 30,000 crore would come from the Government and international agencies. The remainder will have to come in the form of private investment.

References

Dua, Gaurao (2001), "Health Insurance—Unhealthy Yet", *Investor Business Standard,* September, 24.

Jha, R.N. (2000), "Challenges Before Insurance Industry", *Proceedings of Keynote Address* delivered at a seminar as part of AD Shroff Birth Centenary Celebration on 19th February in Mumbai.

Josh, N.N. (2001), "Pension Sector Reforms : Some Concerns", *Proceedings of Seminar on Developing Pensions Market in India,* July 3rd by FICCI, New Delhi.

Parekh, Ashvin (2002), "Bancassurance an Effective Channel", *The Financial Express,* January 20.

Rangachary, N. (1999), "The Indian Insurance Industry", *Proceedings of Annual Public Lecture* delivered under the auspices of the AD Shroff Memorial Trust on 19th January in Mumbai.

Saloner, Garth, Spepard, Andrea, Pondolny, Joel (2001), *Strategic Management,* John Wiley and Sons, Inc., N.Y.

Singh, Pritam (2002), "New Age Assurance", *The Financial Express,* November.

Srinivasan, K.K. (2002), "Globalizing Indian Insurance Market—Nationalized Firms Fit to Face Competition", *The Financial Express,* November.

Swain, Sitanshu (2002), "Health Insurance Set to Revive with TPAs' Aid", *The Financial Express,* November.

Tripathi, Rishi Roop (2000), "All in it Together", *A&M,* January 15, pp. 38-45.

Achieving Global Competitiveness through Service Excellence and Total Customer Satisfaction

Urvashi Makkar and Ashok Shukla

In recent years, sociologists have questioned whether the marketing concept is an appropriate philosophy towards market in an age of environmental deterioration, resources—shortages, explosive population growth, world-hunger, poverty and neglected social service. The marketing concept rests on *four pillars—target market, customer needs, integrated marketing and profitability*. But this concept side steps the potential conflicts among consumer wants, consumer interests and long-run societal welfare. These situations call for a new concept that enlarges the marketing concept, i.e., the *Societal Marketing Concept or Humanistic Marketing Concept.* This concept holds that the organization's task is to determine the needs, wants and interests of target markets and to deliver the desired satisfaction more effectively and efficiently than the competitors in a way that preserves and enhances the consumers' satisfaction and the ethical considerations into their marketing practices. To achieve *Total Customer Satisfaction,* the needs, wants and priorities of the customers must be incorporated in the design and development, manufacturing and service stages of the product.

A sound understanding of customer behaviour is essential for the long run success of any marketing programme and it is seen as a cornerstone of the *Societal Marketing Concept.* An integrated strategy with *Value System* as hub of all the marketing activities will be most effective in achieving a firm's objective through customer satisfaction. Here, the value system is an in-built mechanism which distinguishes the right from wrong, do's and don'ts of any action, even when no one is looking. This right or wrong is not in any absolute metaphysical or moral sense but only in the context of the social environment in which a person lives and acts.

In India, we have borrowed almost all the marketing concepts from the highly materialistic society of west, where the value-system ingredients are entirely different. This is one of the major reasons behind the lack of synchronization between the soul of Indian organizations and soul of our country.

It can be observed that most of our organizations have deviated from the path of 'common good' to 'self good' resulting in the deterioration of societal marketing concept and 'value crises'.

Reshaping of the consumer behaviour studies, with special reference to value system and customer satisfaction is needed. Theoretically, it is quite easy to say that we should link consumer behaviour with societal marketing concept, but a question arises, how? And certainly one way to do so is on the basis of the principals of Value-system and Total Customer Satisfaction.

Another problem is that we have failed to implement these concepts in some of the important services resulting in declined quality of services and unhealthy dissatisfaction among the consumers.

Therefore, it becomes necessary for us, not only to modify the prevalent practices going against values, but also to find suitable way out for implementation of these redefined principles in the sectors. This will definitely lead organizations to generate maximum level of satisfaction among consumers and long-run success.

> *"In the 1970s, consumers were ready to pay 'more for more', and luxury goods flourished. In the 1980s, consumers began to demand 'more for the same', and the discounting era grew strong. Today's consumers are demanding 'more for less' and the winners will be super value marketers".*
>
> —Phillip Kotler

TOTAL CUSTOMER SATISFACTION MANAGEMENT

All business firms have realized that marketing is a core element of management philosophy and the key to its success lies in focusing more and more on the customer. That is, it will be the customer who will decide where the firm is heading. Thus, the challenge before the marketers is to ensure that they satisfy every customer. Adam Smith in his, 'The Wealth of Nations', has said that *"Consumption is the sole end and purpose of all production and the interest of the producer ought to be attended to, only so far as it may be necessary for promoting those of the consumer."*

This quotation only reiterates that the purpose of production is consumption and one's own purpose will be served only if the consumers' interests are attended to. Here then arises a very vital question. How can marketers ensure that his/her firm is able to respond to their customers' requirement quickly? The answer to this question lies in the quality of services it is offering to its customers. This again will depend upon the consumer expectations from the product or service. No doubt, the quality of the product or service will decide whether it matches the consumer expectation or not, but the firm and marketer must make all efforts to ensure that consumer satisfaction is achieved.

CUSTOMERISATION

Today consumer is looking out for *"value for money"*. The challenge before the marketer is to identify what value would appeal and convince the consumers. Marketers are trying to enhance the concept of value through unique delivery methods. They have realized that product service characteristics, customer's aspirations and perceptions and the availability of competing alternatives can be used to enhance customer value.

But the focus and challenge before every firm is to rebuild itself around its customer. It should be able to perceive, interpret, serve and satisfy the customer with the type of products and services he/she desires and arm itself so as to gain competitive edge of customerisation.

Customerisation refers to the process wherein all the employees of the firm are required to interact directly with the customer and end user. They can have access to every person and function within the organization, who may be involved in designing and fine tuning key products and processes, and turn every interaction with the customer into a platform of interactive communication, so as to add value and increase customer satisfaction.

Customerisation will help a firm in :

- Providing quality of service to match the customer requirement.
- Help to focus on consumer needs so as to add value and offer benefits to the customer.
- To identify new customers, new market segments and new applications for existing products.
- Work towards total customer satisfaction and maximum customer delight.

However, it may be noted that consumer satisfaction is a relative rather than an absolute measure. Further, very often satisfaction after the purchase is dependent on expectations held before the purchase of the product or service.

Expectations

Consumer expectations though may look realistic but are very often built-up on a very high platform. Therefore, the quality of the product or service may not match the expectations, which again will affect the consumer's satisfaction level.

So as to reduce the level of dissatisfaction amongst the customers, the marketing decision-maker could adopt an approach wherein he can classify markets in relation to the degree of opportunity to deliver customer satisfaction. He could establish a list of common factors and then evaluate each market opportunity against these. The most probable factors that influence consumer behaviour are :

- Market size.
- Rate of growth of the market.
- Stability of demand.
- The due importance attached to price by the consumer before making a purchase decision.
- Consumer emphasis and the due importance given to the quality aspect.
- The consumers' expectations of pre and post-purchase service.
- Customers desire for product innovation.
- The level of competition (inclusive of both existing and potential competition).
- The firm's competitive strength in terms of price and product performance.

The above aspects will help the firm to assess the various factors, which can help them in building consumer expectations and then delivering customer satisfaction accordingly. Of course, there are other sources of information, which may also influence the consumer's expectations. These may be the consumer's own experience (if he had exposure to the product or services before) the experience of friends, neighbours and colleagues, price—as an indicator of quality and corporate image.

WORKING TOWARDS ENHANCING CUSTOMER SATISFACTION

In the existing business environment, where markets are turbulent and customer needs are fast changing, companies should opt for ways to add value for their customer by offering products or services just the way they want it. When the customer has to choose from a large and bewildering number of options, features, pricing structures and delivering methods, offering a unique product to every individual customer will go a long way in adding value to the consumer decision-making process.

Customer satisfaction is a continuous process, which does not begin or end with purchase. It covers the entire ownership experience from selecting a product, to purchase, through aftercare to repeat purchase. Clearly, there are three phases in the Customer Satisfaction Process, namely :

1. *Pre-Sales* : During this stage, the customer's expectations are developed through the various information sources like advertising, word of mouth and so no.

2. *During Sales* : When the customer is engaged in experiencing on how the seller deal with enquiries and sell products.
3. *The After Sales Period* : This refers to the period when the customer has started using the product.

Thus, customers' expectations and their experience will together determine the level of satisfaction.

From the above discussion it is seen that consumer satisfaction goes beyond the core product or service offering. Marketing decision-makers have to start by trying to understand the elements, which together will determine the satisfaction levels. Then listing the elements in a proper sequence, so as to identify what is to be done so as to increase the customer's satisfaction level. This can be done only if the marketers involve a system which facilitates interaction with their customers. These interactions will prove to be as important as the quality of the core product or service offered by the company in the long-run.

IMPORTANCE OF REGULAR RESEARCH

Regular research is necessary to keep a track of the changing levels of customer satisfaction. Market research will give excellent clues to the firm about what the existing or prospective customers think. At the same time, they will also provide information on how they rate one's competitor. This will indirectly indicate where the firm stands. In short, market research will help the firm to enter into a dialogue with their customers and also help in avoiding losing sight of them. Very often companies find themselves in deep trouble for neglecting the very reason for their business, i.e. the customer.

There are many cases of brands and companies, which have witnessed a downward swing in their business only on account of forgetting their customers and not doing anything to enhance their customer satisfaction. A classic case referred to world over is that of the automobile giant—The Ford Motor Company , which got into deep trouble twice for not listening to their customer. By providing the no frill, low priced Model T, Ford had revolutionized the American markets and the top automobile-makers for 17 years. However, after 17 years the same customers rejected 'Ford' in favour of options available from General Motors. This was because Ford failed to recognize the new value providers or the change in customer's choice.

Alyque Padamsee, Chief Executive, A.P. Association had opined that, *"Companies are not making products today, they are making customers. A brand's success can no longer be evaluated on the basis of its market share, but has to be measured by the share of the customer's wants and to do market research and try to understand the consumer choices and what is the value for money that buyer look out for, will ultimately have to be satisfied in best possible manner. With the constantly changing consumer choices, the firm must understand the real customer satisfaction indicator-value, which is said to be unique".*

In today's competitive scenario, with plenty of modern and economical alternatives available, the marketers should provide value-added services to ensure customer satisfaction. They can do this by offering superior value products at lesser price than their competitors or by providing benefits that more than offset a higher price.

Regular researches can enable marketers to become aware of the changing consumer satisfaction levels. For instance, the car manufacturer could mail a customer satisfaction survey form to their new car buyers twice—the first time a month after they have bought the car and then after around eighteen months after the purchase. Such a research or exercise will help the firm to assess whether satisfaction levels have changed as the customer 'lives with the product'. Added to this the manufacturer can also keep their dealers informed about the customer satisfaction levels by providing periodic reports, so that they can respond immediately to any changes in level.

FEEDBACK

Many of the companies are encouraging their customers to give a feedback and use this as a means of maintaining regular contact and dialogue. Having realized the importance of obtaining a feedback from their customers, companies are encouraging their customers to talk. Feedback helps the marketers and firms to get an idea about the customer's viewpoint on their products or services and further this information helps them to take action and deal with any problem immediately.

Various methods can be used to obtain information on the customer satisfaction levels of the product purchased or service provided.

It has been rightly said, *"Design delivers value"*. Good marketers have always worked towards channelising their customer's feedback into their product development in order to establish a link between product features and customer requirements. In the words of N. Jayaraman, Executive Vice-President (Sales and Marketing) Colgate Palmolive, *"When you look at the development of a product design, you have to first identify the consumer need that has to be fulfilled. It can be a latent need, but you can also create a need. That's where an understanding of the consumer is critical. We conduct studies constantly in every category on consumer usage and attitude"*.

When Samsung India was seeking customer feedback before designing its TV set, it used its questionnaires to probe deep into its target customer's wish fulfilment notions. They discovered that he/she would love to watch a video film that doesn't have creepy-crawly advertisements running across the bottom. So Samsung India added a facility to its TV sets that allowed viewers to zoom the picture, cutting the commercials out of frame.

THE VALUE CREATION STRATEGY—A WIN-WIN GAME

The term value creation simply means continuously doing newer and newer things that gives increasing and continuous returns to the people, who are directly or indirectly associated with the organization. Value creation is closely related to innovation; innovation of processes, products and way of doing the business. It also implies shifting focus from 'stealing away other's market share to creating newer markets', identifying newer customers and inventing newer ways of marketing, implementing and distribution, i.e., continuously designing and implementing newer ways of serving the people. Organizations like Amazon.com, Dupont, NEC, and Infosys have done it successfully.

Imagine the shift in the concept of consumer satisfaction to consumer delight. Satisfying the customers on the basis of bare expectations of the consumers was considered good enough, but the real challenge lies in providing an added support to the product so that consumer is absolutely delighted and feels that his money is spent in an intelligent proposition. This results in providing a clear edge to the organization doing so. 3M, Motorola, Wal-mart and Baron International were able to delight their customers through innovative products, services and pricing propositions.

Customer delight can seldom give an edge over the others in the competitive scenario. What if every body finally decides to delight the customers in their own way so as to have an edge over each other? If we have Xerox and Intel on one hand, then we also have Canon and AMD on the other hand, respectively, who are ultimately up against each other by continuously trying to delight their customers. This calls for moving ahead of times and thinking on the lines of a concept, which could do much more than delight the customer. We insist on calling this proposition as "Customer Ecstasy". Once committed to value creation, these organizations are able to progress by taking quantum leaps leaving the competitors gasping for breath and making the customers ecstatic in its true sense. The concept of consumer orientation is a new management buzzword, rather it is the supreme state of satisfaction, which is attained after actually acquiring the product or service and realizing that it is way beyond one's expectations. Smart managers, who are more Y2K compliant, will not stop at sales rather they will break the barriers of tangibility and place the product well enough so that the consumer attains a state of complete ecstasy. Only then brand equity can be redefined.

Value again can be constructed in different ways. That is to say that Japanese consumer-durable-product customer will at no point settle for any thing less than a Sony, while for an average Asian customer, a low priced, efficient enough set of AIWA or Akai will solve the purpose better.

Value will be the determining factor for upward trend of any company in the next millennium. The Lever's in India revised a beautiful strategy to uphold and maintain a bay against their competitors by closely studying the nitty-gritty of the consumable goods market. The HLL point of view doesn't leave space for myopia, without loosing the focus on their current goods, their strategy is purely based on taking a quantum leap by diversifying into a completely new domain to operate in, while further strengthening its current customer base. The launch of HLL's Annapurana brand Atta was a marvel strategy (Quantum leap) in this respect.

But, paramount is the need to create value through innovation. Innovation is a paradigm of a Co's R & D department. Not every product/ variant can be called an innovation. This rules out the possibility for the competitors to create a niche or simply segregate the market.

This brings out another important aspect of the concept of value creation strategy. This strategy calls for a gradual shift in the focus. The organizations must shift their focus from structure, strategy and system to People, Purpose and Processes.

MEETING THE SUPER VALUE CHALLENGE

The strategies of successful companies towards total consumer satisfaction are difficult to achieve when consumers actively interact with products. As cited by *Phillip Kotler,* consumers wanting more for less expect super value products. To add on to the changes in the consumer needs and desires, the information flood and lack of differentiation among competing brands have converted products into services. Today's marketing scenario has thrown before the managers of Consumer's Driven Organizations, the task of designing and marketing products and services with attributes that maximize consumer satisfaction. But the question is how do corporates achieve this end when products are almost transferred into services.

ADD VALUE THROUGH EFFECTIVE PRICING

Pricing is another sensitive issue. Marketers should use the entire pricing issue so as to have a long-term relationship with the customer. In the competitive pricing scenario, the manner in which the product or service can add perceived value will determine what the consumer is willing to pay and whether this will add to customer satisfaction.

At times supple pricing can generate considerable value for the customer when the firm is offering a range of products or services in a mix and match formulation. This is what the ITC group of hotels that runs the Welcome group chain of hotels did to add value to customer satisfaction by adopting a suitable flexible pricing policy.

By allowing the customer to choose the price to be ultimately paid, the company is contributing towards enhancing the value they would derive from the price.

CREATE DISTRIBUTION EQUITY

Marketers have realized that with greater availability of goods that are close substitutes of competing brands, having good distribution channels can actually prove to be the differentiating factor in determining customer value, satisfaction and hence their loyalty also.

FIG. 18.1
Consumer Behaviour Model for Achieving Customer Value

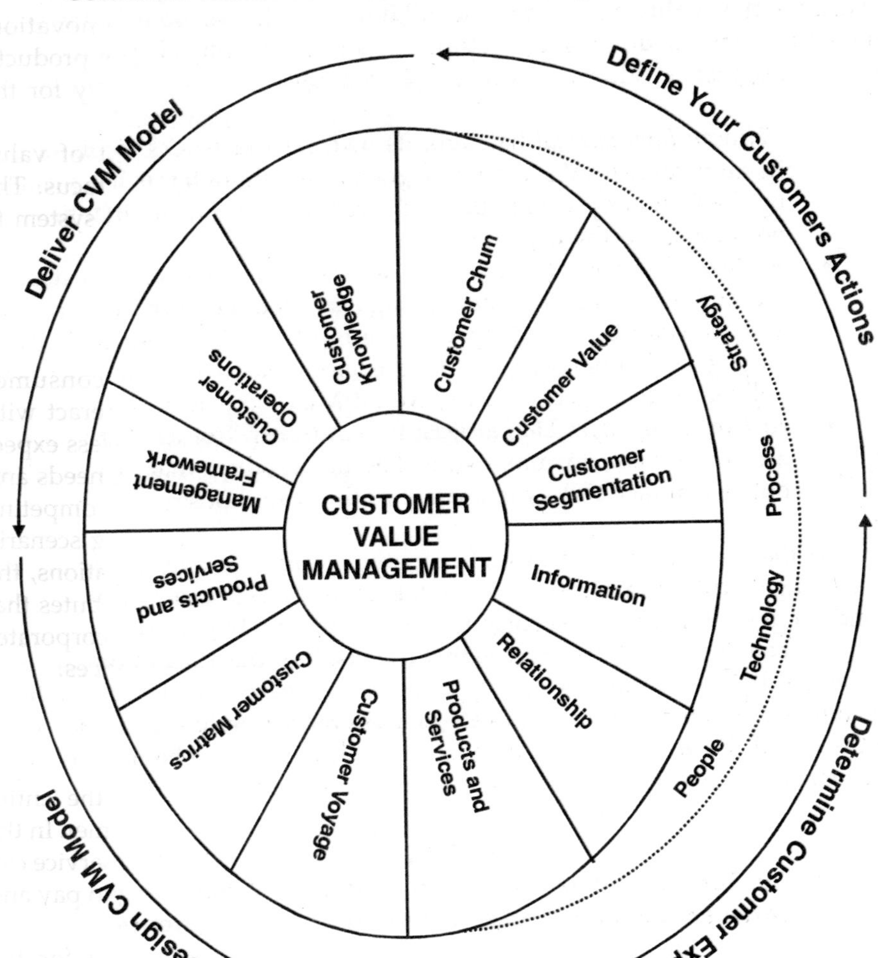

Also, while it will be easy for companies to match product technologies and prices, it will not be easy to duplicate an effective distribution system offering a value chain of quality of services. Wipro Infotech had built a network of 15 C & F agents and 400 dealers to enable it to keep its inventories low as well as peg a high turnaround time for products and the dealer's investments. Added to this, having a wide network of distributors also kept the company close to the customers. Shri K. Purushotham, the Business Manager (Channels), Wipro Infotech says that "*What configurations the customer orders is critical to us, and given the complications of assembling a customer-specific configuration, our objective is that we should be able to service an order between six to 48 hours*".

Today, firms are going all out to enhance customer satisfaction and value and also increase their distribution equity by monitoring and sustaining the quality of their product till it reaches the customer's doorstep. Such firms try to do this by getting closer to the physical activity of distributing their products. To quote few examples :

- *Videocon International* has built its own fleet of trucks to distribute its high value CTV's and white goods even though this has pushed up the Company's costs. But such sealed trucks ensure that there is no damage to the delicate goods.
- *At Maruti Udyog Ltd.*, the four key elements that are constantly measured are transit time, damage to product, turnaround time and transporter rating. In the words of the Ex. CEO of Maruti Udyog, R.C. Bhargava, "If a transporter has a regular record of delivering damaged vehicles, we (at MUL) get rid of him".
- *At Hindustan Lever Ltd.*, at least two in-transit test-runs of product are undertaken to make sure that the product that reaches the outlet is intact and stored safely at the ware-house.

As the market place gets tougher by the brand, it is only the presence of a strong distribution equity which will eventually determine or be able to stand the test of consumer satisfaction and hence the brand equity.

As seen in Fig 18.2, we can see that the result of the attribution process influences the perception of quality and the degree of satisfaction. When customers are satisfied, they are likely to make more purchases and be loyal to the brand. While in case of dissatisfaction, it is more probable that they may make complaints or take action against the supplier.

FIG 18.2

The Subsequent Behaviour, on Account of Discrepancy between Customer Expectation and Actual Experience

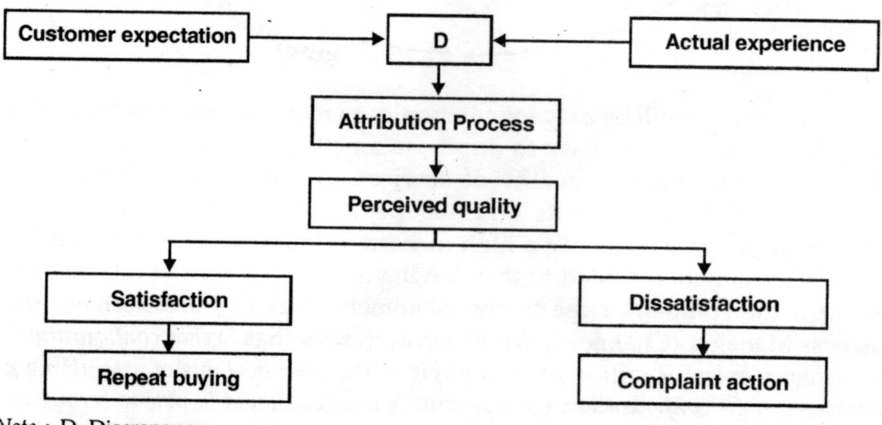

Note : D=Discrepancy.

Sometimes the consumer may undergo stress, feel anger, tension and frustration when he realizes that the cause of dissatisfaction is attributed to the supplier and at the same time perceives it to be under his or her control. In such cases, the tension will reduce only if he or she resorts to taking private or public actions.

BUILDING COMMITMENTS

Keilty, Goldsmith and Boone have performed extensive research in identifying and defining the qualities that make managers successful and helping their clients apply those qualities within their own corporation or organisation. As frequently happens, some individuals are admired and respected for the way they manage others, but the reasons for their success are not always apparent. Building on the work of McKinsey and Company, the internationally respected management consulting firm and through their experience with many excellent companies and managers, they have developed valuable insights and a very useful model concerning managerial excellence known as the Five Key Commitments Model, shown in Fig. 18.3. The essential qualities and relationships necessary for successful management can be explained and understood in terms of commitment, a characteristic common to all individuals recognized for managerial excellence.

Fig 18.3
The Five Key Commitments Model

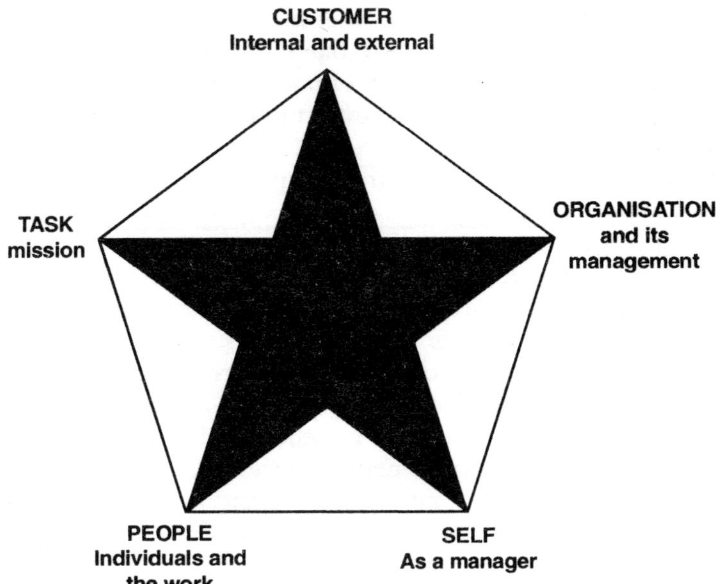

Managers carry out their tasks in an interpersonal world. Other people continually view the manager's manners, bearing, and conduct. From their observations, they form impressions of the manager's values, beliefs and attitudes. Excellent managers make a powerful and positive impression on others because they blend a set of positive beliefs with an equally appropriate set of positive behaviours. These beliefs and actions form "commitments." The most effective manager shares a fundamentally similar set of five commitments. These are :

- Commitment to the customer.
- Commitment to the organisation.
- Commitment to the self.
- Commitment to the people.
- Commitment to the task.

Separately, each commitment is extremely important to effective management. Together, these commitments form the essential framework for long-term achievement of managerial excellence. True excellence seems to result from genuine dedication and positive service in all five areas of commitment.

COMMITMENT TO THE CUSTOMER

The first and probably most important management commitment focuses on the customer. Excellent managers strive to provide useful service to customers. A customer is defined as anyone who rightly should benefit from the work of a manager's unit. For some managers, their work directly affects the external customer. For other managers, the essential customer is internal. For example, employees in one unit of an organization often serve members of another unit in same organisation. Whether the customer is primarily external or internal, the key to this commitment is service. The two primary ways in which an excellent manager demonstrates strong commitment to the customer are serving the customer and building customer importance.

Serving the customer boils down to consistent and conscientious dedication to customer needs. This requires responsiveness to customers through continually encouraging and listening to input from the people who use the manager's services or products.

Building customer importance means presenting the customer in a positive manner to those who actually provide service to the customer. The customer is not always appreciated by others within an organisation. In fact, some employees view the customer as a necessary evil. To these employees, the customer is the source of most problems and is often viewed as someone to be tolerated.

Excellent managers build customer importance by : (1) clearly communicating the importance of the customer to employees, (2) treating the customer as top priority, and (3) prohibiting destructive comments about the people who use their work group's products or services.

Robert Wayland and Paul Cole offer the following examples of principles which an organisation should adopt to acquire and retain loyal customers :

- Customers are assets : Understand, nurture, and protect their lifetime value.
- Products come and go : Customers are forever (you hope!).
- Know what you are really selling : Focus on the total customer experience, not just the sale.
- Customers relate to people not companies : Empowered employees excite customers.
- Expectations are more important than explanations : Point your customer information system forward, not backward.
- Customers are known by the company they keep : Build a strong brand.

Length of the relationship between the customer and firm will be determined by opportunities for mutual gain. It is the responsibility of the business firm to do research of its customer on an ongoing basis and process this information and use it so as to build-up the reputation as the "service provider model" for its competitors. This requires significant investments in data-base management and also along with its demographic data, segment-wise profiles and needs, satisfaction survey details, forward positioning surveys and front-line employee feedback.

From the Fig. 18.4, we can see the characteristics exhibited by new clients (current asset) and existing (long-term asset) customers. The characteristics exhibited by the long-term customers are such that they and

Fig. 18.4

Customer Satisfaction Relationship Portfolio

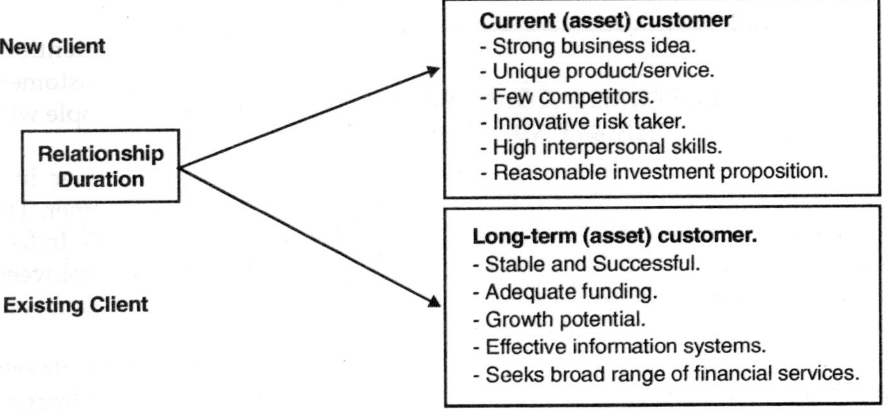

the firm providing the product or services enjoy a long-term relationship. Eventually some of the small business customers may go on the decline. So the firm is now required to add continuously to their pool of asset customers. It will be they who will enable the firm to grow and become successful and also form the next generation of long-term customers.

RELATIONSHIP MARKETING

The other strategy followed by marketers to capture, cultivate and captivate consumers is Relationship Marketing. Relationship Marketing focuses on 'caring of consumers'. Corporates today search for avenues for direct contact. However expensive it may be, they are attending to consumer complaints religiously, listening to the response with rapt attention, designing products which they need and trying to build relationship with them. Chairmen and CEOs of big corporates are walking out of their offices into the market place or inviting consumers in search of a touchy feely sense of what motivates buyer behaviour. Fig. 18.5 elaborates few key factors which are essential for Relationship Marketing.

FIG. 18.5
Laws of Relationship Marketing

LAWS OF RELATIONSHIP MARKETING
1. Track consumer satisfaction levels, continuously. 2. Try becoming a consumer of your own company. 3. Empower employees to take any necessary steps for consumer satisfaction. 4. Dramatically improve the services associated with the product. 5. Let consumer determine specifications of all new products. 6. Shift focus from marketing and production to consumer satisfaction.

CUSTOMER COMPLAINT AND FEEDBACK (CC&F) MANAGEMENT SYSTEM

"One of the strongest signs of a bad or declining relationship is the absence of complaint from the customer. Nobody is ever that satisfied, especially not over an extended period of time. The customer is either not being candid or not being contacted", said Theodore Levitt.

Each customer complaint should be treated like an unpolished gem; a gem that needs to be captured, examined, and polished. Your company or organisation can only be richer and wiser as it collects and polishes each of the gems of insight and wisdom. Having a system that captures these gems of wisdom and polishes them is extremely important.

Many Indian organisations don't keep this in mind, hence there is deterioration in service. Ultimately, it results in decline in profits, firing of people, and customers go elsewhere. To a company that understands that service and customer satisfaction are essential elements for success, a customer complaints and feedback management system is must. Deteriorating customer service is visible in Indian organisations viz., public transport, and airline, banking and retail stores. It is also a common feature in other sectors in Indian economy.

Every company or organisation in India is always receiving complaints. The difference between one and other organisations is the frequency and intensity of complaints. Some organisations will ignore the complaints while others with a well-informed and educated workforce will ensure that complaints are attended to. But this alone is insufficient.

The better organisation must keep a record of these complaints—the frequency, the intensity, the location and so on. It is vital for the workforce to record most, if not all, complaints. This must be followed by resolution of the complaints and elimination of root cause of each complaint.

Figure 18.6 shows a flow chart of a Customer Complaint and Feedback System. This flow chart is simple and self-explanatory. The key points include the following :

1. Complaints must be collected from all sources, viz. Letters, phone calls, meetings and verbal inputs.
2. Data should be collected via customer complaint and feedback (CC&F) form and a formal corrective action request (CAR) form must be used.
3. Complaints must be resolved as quickly as possible and customers must be contacted and informed.
4. All customers must get a response within 15 days which may be a simple 'thank you' or a solution for a complaint.
5. Issues which are generated locally, must be resolved locally, preferably on the complaint site.
6. Issues beyond the control of the local entity must be resolved at the central coordinator or analyst level that will further analyse the issue and propose a solution.
7. On a regular basis, data must be analysed and systematic issues must be identified, resolved and eliminated. Otherwise, there will be an impact on future purchases by current and potential customers. This may result in lost business and reduced market share.
8. Performance measures must be identified and monitored.
9. There must be regular promotion and facilitation system for constant nurturing of complaints. Following methods of promotion must be used : (a) promotion during monthly departmental meetings, (b) promotion during new employee training and

FIG. 18.6
Customer Complaint Flow Chart

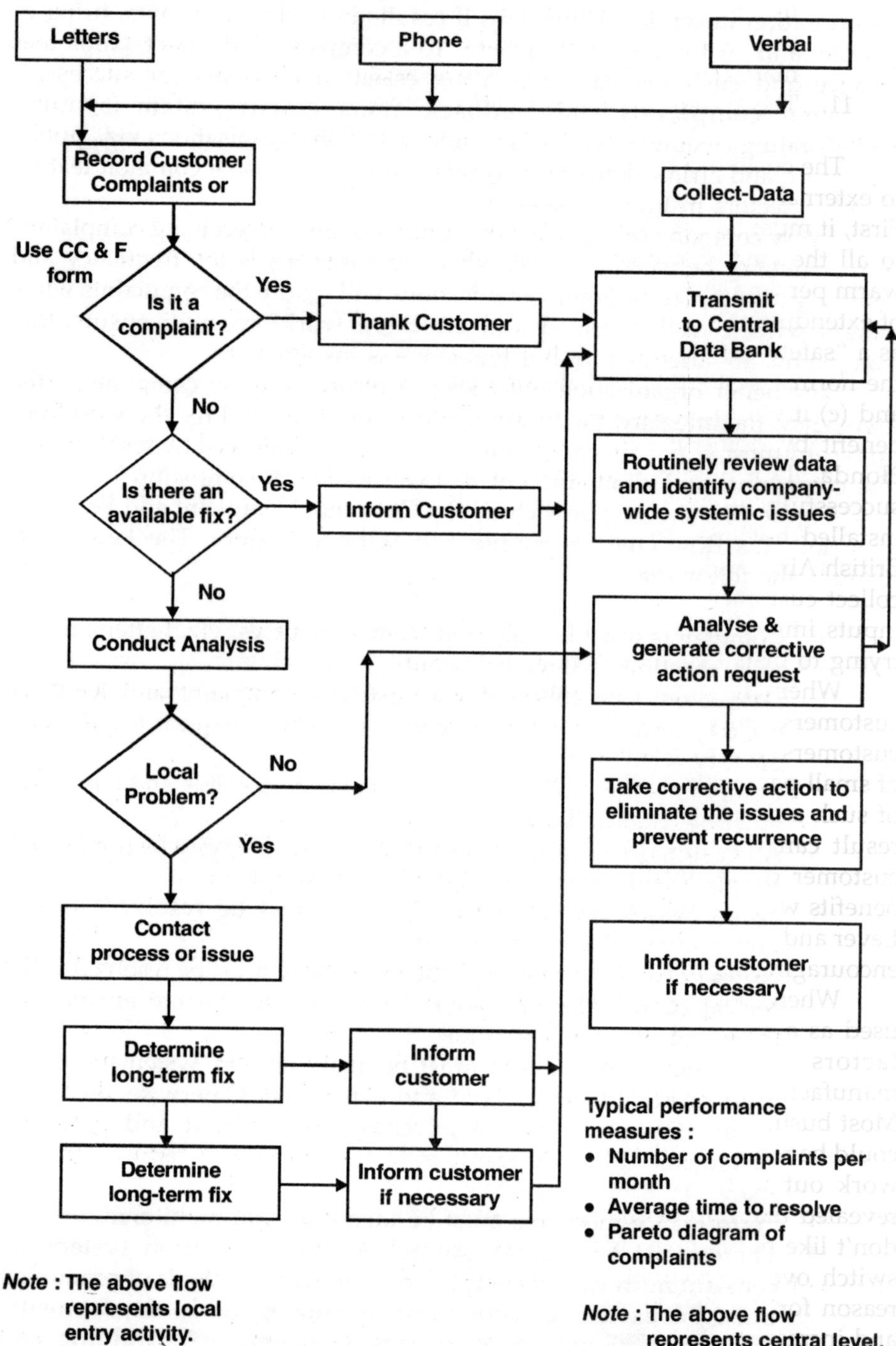

(c) encouraging managers to use the system and become role models for their employees.

10. Managers must help to manage the entire process by promoting the use of the system at all levels and at each entity within the organisation. They must develop a foolproof complaint management system in their organisations.
11. The system must be extended to customers.

The customer complaint and feedback system (CC&F) can be extended to external customers but only after it is working well inside the company. First, it must be extended to preferred customers and later can be provided to all the customers. The customer complaints must be attended to by a warm person. The quality department can manage this service. The benefits of extending the system to customers include the following : (a) it will serve as a "safety net" to catch customer complaints that are managed poorly by the normal system, (b) it will convince customers that the company cares, and (c) it will give a competitive advantage. Even the best companies will benefit by doing this. Some companies like Telco, Maruti Udyog, Hero Honda, TVS Suzuki, Eicher Demm, Escorts, etc. have implemented it successfully in India. Marriot Corporation and American Express have installed hot lines to collect customer complaints in the USA. In Britain, British Airways has installed video booths at London's Heathrow Airport to collect customer complaints . This is very innovative way to collect "hot" inputs immediately after the trip. Indian Airways and Air India are also trying to install such systems to satisfy their customers.

When the customer complaint and feedback system is extended to customers, employees should be encouraged to go out of the way to help customers. A way of doing this is to empower employees to make decision of small payments on the spot to handle dissatisfied customers. The impact of such a decision would be electrifying to customers and employees. The result can lead to a quantum jump in customer satisfaction. After the customer complaint management system starts functioning smoothly, the benefits will be enormous. To some extent Procter and Gamble, Hindustan Lever and Godrej are using it in India. It is observed that the results are very encouraging for both the customers and the companies.

When consumers complain and express their dissatisfaction, it could be used as a feedback for better or newer products. Figure 18.7 explains the factors affecting customer interaction resulting into developing, manufacturing, marketing and delivery of customised products/services. Most businesses lose around 25 percent of their customers annually. If this could be reduced by at least five percent, the profit impact of this saving can work out to be very high even on a per customer basis. Studies have revealed that approximately 70% of customers switch brands because they don't like the human side of service or product provider. When customers switch over to competitor's brands, the firm must try to understand the reason for the defection. Figure 18.8 explains the process of adding value and increasing consumer satisfaction level.

FIG. 18.7
Factors Affecting Customer Interaction

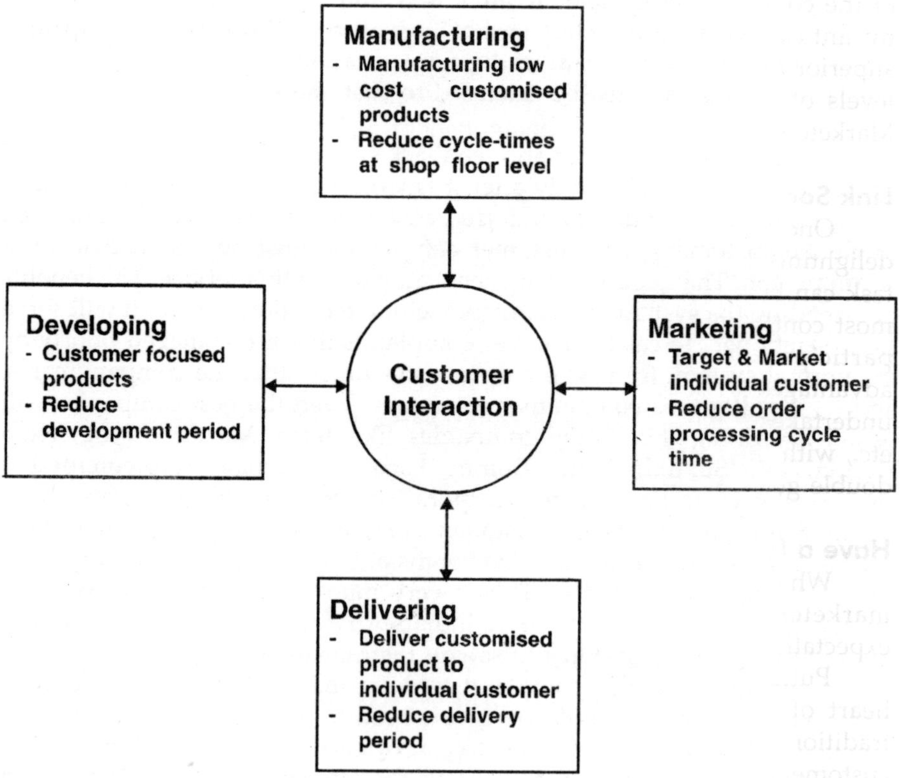

Manufacturing
- Manufacturing low cost customised products
- Reduce cycle-times at shop floor level
Developing
- Customer focused products
- Reduce development period
Customer Interaction
Marketing
- Target & Market individual customer
- Reduce order processing cycle time
Delivering
- Deliver customised product to individual customer
- Reduce delivery period

FIG. 18.8
Process of Adding Value and Increasing Consumer Satisfaction Level

Firm
Identify Individualised customer need requirement
Identify & work toward customising those levels
Make the customisation Plans viable
Customise product
Customised service
Customised delivery
Increase in customer value & satisfaction

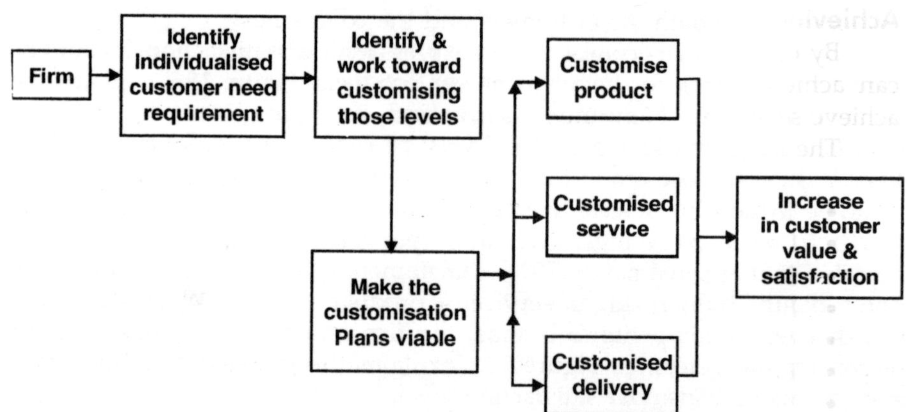

DELIGHT MARKETING

Delight marketing is yet another mantra that fosters value in the minds of the consumers. Delight marketers move beyond consumer expectations by anticipating their needs and then surprising them with constantly superior products or services. Delight is not a one-time offering to gain the levels of satisfactions but at each encounter with the consumer, Delight Marketers provide a human touch benefit.

Link Social Responsibilities at Most of the Contact Points

One major focus is that the customer's delight can be achieved by delighting customers at both related and interrelated contact points. This task can be strategically achieved if marketers link social responsibility at most contact points to their advantage. For example, advertisements and participation in fairs are mandatory for any computer dealer. The advantages of the same can be achieved in a cost-effective way if the dealer undertakes some services like maintaining the roads, parks, the bus stops etc., with their contact address. By performing this, the dealers satisfy the double goals of social responsibility and result in creating awareness.

Have a Holistic View

What is delight to a customer today is an expectation tomorrow, so marketers should modify their strategies from time to time on the expectations of the customers.

Putting the customer first or achieving customer satisfaction is at the heart of total quality management (TQM). This principle supports the traditional notion that the "*Customer is King*". If a company cannot satisfy its customers, another company will. Processes and products must be designed with one thing in mind—satisfying the customer. Companies must move from a "product out" mentality (i.e., pushing the product or service out) to a "Customer in" attitude (i.e., providing a product or service that customers expect, or better yet, beyond what they expect).

Achieving Global Competitiveness

By combining Service Excellence and Total Customer Satisfaction, we can achieve Global Competitiveness. But the question arises : How to achieve service excellence/service quality?

The answer lies in the following actions :

- Top management commitment.
- Determine customer requirements/needs.
- Set goals.
- Become customer-driven.
- Motivate employees.
- Empower and train.
- Improve continuously.

Fig. 18.9 explains aptly how to achieve global competitiveness through service excellence and total customer satisfaction A company must start with understanding customers' requirements—most importantly with their problems. Identifying customers' requirements is not an easy task and requires much diligence. But some useful tools include surveys and research, customer contact, warranty performance records and customer complaint records. One successful method to organize customer requirements and identify gaps in performance is to use customer need analysis.

Fig. 18.9

Achieving Global Competitiveness through Service Excellence and Total Customer Satisfaction

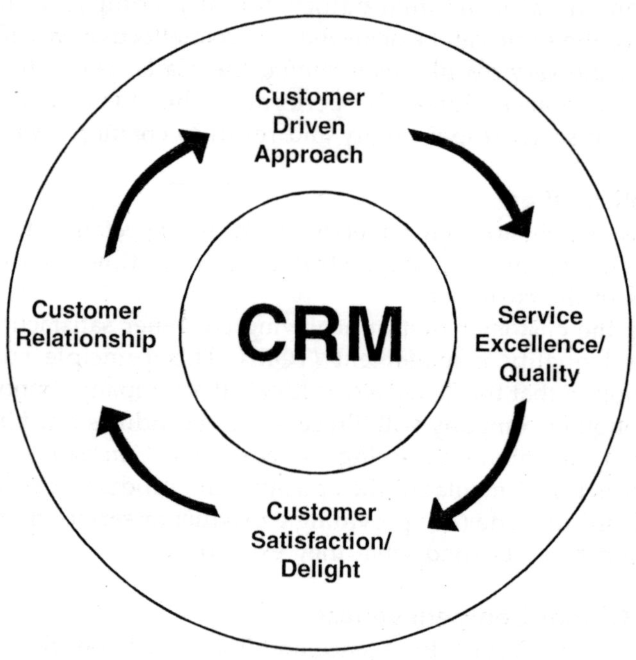

References

www.crmcommunity.com.

META Group in www.exchangeinc.com.

Customer Relationship Management—The What, Why & How, *TAG, Quarterly Journal*, Volume 4, December, 2001.

Fox, Tricia, Stead, Steve, Customer Relationship Management : Delivering the Benefits, White Paper by Customer Relationship Management (UK) Ltd. & SECOR.

Cosulting Ltd.

Gupta, S.L., *Consumer Behaviour*, S. Chand, New Delhi, 2001.

Nair, Suja R., *Consumer Behaviour*, APH, Delhi, 1999.

Bennett, Peter D., *Consumer Behaviour*, Prentice Hall of India, New Delhi, 1998.
Engel, James F., *Consumer Behaviour*, Dryden Press, Philadelphia.
Houdon, D.L., *Consumer Behaviour*, UPSD Publisher, New Delhi, 2002.
Schiffman, Leon G., *Consumer Behaviour,* Prentice Hall of India, New Delhi, 1999.
Kessler, Sheila, *Measuring and Managing Customer Satisfaction*, Wheelar Publisher, New Delhi, 1998.
Bank, John, *Essense of Total Quality Management*, Prentice Hall of India, New Delhi, 2002.
Bagade, S.D., *Total Quality Management*, Himalaya Publication House Mumbai, 2000.
Bestefield, Dale, H., *Total Quality Management*, Pearson Education, New Delhi, 2001.
Arora, K.C., *TQM and ISO 1400 (is 13967)* S.K. Kataria, Delhi, 2000.
Berk, Susan, *Total Quality Management*, Excel Books, New Delhi, 1995.
Joseph, *Total Quality Management*, Excel Books, New Delhi, 1995.
Sharma, D.D., *Total Quality Management* (Sultan Chand, New Delhi), 2000.
Wakhlu, Bharat, *Total Quality Management* (Wheelar Publisher, New Delhi), 1994.
Noori, Hamid, *Production and Operation Management : Total Quality and Responsiveness*, McGraw Hill, New Delhi, 1995.
Canine, Joan Koob, *Keeping Customer for Life*, American Management Association Publications Service, New York.
Sarazen, J. Stephen; Salter II, James M., *Managing the Customer Satisfaction Process*, American Management Association Publications Service, New York.
Murthy, B.N., *Consumer Quality*, New Age International Publisher.

CHAPTER 19

Productivity in the Banking Industry with Special Reference to State Bank of India Group

SANJAY KAUSHIK

India, like the whole world has witnessed a sea change in the economic and banking environment during last decade. The operating environment for banks in India has undergone a rapid change. There has been increased opportunities for banks to increase their revenues because of on-set of liberalisation measures. But at the same time, banking industry is facing stiff competition because of new players entering in the market. It has resulted into a direct impact on profitability of banks. Customers are becoming more demanding. Keener competition is forcing the banks to be on their toes.

Productivity is the key to competitiveness, which in turn is an indicator of a country's potential for economic growth in short to medium-term. Productivity is not a mere rationalisation or reducing consumption of resources but is concerned more with making available products and services that enhance the quality of life and accelerate economic development.

The success of an organisation/industry/economy depends upon its people. According to Gunnar Myrdal,[1] "The people in India, work perhaps not too much more than half the number of hours a year, compared with what people do in a developed country and what the Indian people must come to do if the country shall become developed. And when they work, their efficiency is low. The paramount imperative in India's situation, if it wants to advance substantially and rapidly is to raise labour productivity".

In the final instance, Indian economic planning will succeed or fail will depend on this human factor, whether India can get its population to work more to better and to produce more. Productivity is a vital indicator of economic performance. It is a complicated but key indicator of a nation's well-being and future economic development.

The concept of productivity is understood in different ways by different people. It is the output and manpower for a personnel functionary, while for an engineer output per machine unit is synonymous with productivity. Productivity although is a "technological relationship between inputs and outputs but it cannot, and indeed should not be treated independently from the socio-economic environment which the concept permeates into the policy framework of national development either as a means to accelerate the process of material advancement or as an end."[2] A clear recognition of the differences in the socio-economic environment among nations is important because of the fact that, explicity or implicity, the approach to productivity is governed by the respective national objectives and priorities, which again are derived from the environment.

According to Kopleman,[3] perhaps the most widely accepted definition of productivity is the physical process conceptualization used by many economists. He said that "productivity is the relationship between physical output and one or more of the associated physical inputs used in production. Broadly conceived—it is a systems concept; it can apply to various entities, ranging from individual or machine to a company, industry or national economy".

Profitability of banks is dependent upon two factors : (i) internal, and (ii) external. While the internal factors relate to banks resources like manpower, funds, etc. and also systems and procedures. The external factors relate to interest rate structure, stipulations pertaining to lending, and branch licensing policy, etc. of the controlling authorities, viz. RBI and government of India. The operational efficiency of the banks is mainly related to internal factors. The word productivity which is normally used as an indicator of the efficient use of resources can thus be synonymous to operational efficiency in banks. It may therefore, be remarked that productivity in banks can not be judged only by their profitability. In fact, both need not necessarily move in the same direction. For instance, while the productivity might increase, profitability may decrease because of the increase in Statutory Liquidity Ratio and Cash Reserve Ratio. Similarly, while the productivity may have decreased but the profitability might increase. While productivity indicates use of resources, profitability of banks in India is determined, apart from use of resources, by the interest.

It will not be possible to increase profit without improving efficiency and productivity. As emphasised by PEP Committee, "Banks being business organisations, profit should continue to remain an important consideration. At no time should their operations result in a loss and act as a drag on the Government revenue. The net result of the promotional activities which they are being called upon to undertake should not partake the nature of subsidy grants",[4] therefore, under the given circumstances profit can be improved by improving productivity.

SOURCES OF PRODUCTIVITY

Productivity is affected by a large number of determinants. Any factor which reduces waste in any form or increases efficiency can be called a source of productivity. The notable sources of productivity might relate to improvement in technological knowledge, changes in capital/labour ratio, improvement in managerial knowledge, changes in hours of work, reallocation of resources, changes in quality of land, education, hours of work, regulations, increased specialisation, economies of scale, entrepreneurship, social attitudes, changes in business environment, etc.

Organisations productivity is greatly influenced by technical and human factors. Sutermeister[5] has summed up most of the factors effecting productivity at micro/organization/individual level in a diagram. The diagram given in Fig. 19.1 explains such factors.

In reading the diagram it should be kept in mind that :

1. The diagram consists of a series of concentric circles, each divided into segments.
2. The size of segment does not reflect its relative importance. The relative importance, in fact, may differ for each organization and even each individual employee.
3. It is deemed that the factor in each segment of each circle affects or determines the factor(s) in the corresponding segment of the next smaller circle.
4. The factors in each segment of each circle frequently affect and are affected by factors in some of the other segments in the same circle.
5. The factors in each segment of each circle may also affect factors in segments elsewhere in the diagram.
6. All factors in the diagram are subject to change with time, especially individual's needs and formal organization.

American Bankers' Association in the light of the opinion that "effective use of productivity measurement and improvement techniques requires a comprehensive, total productivity model", developed a "Bank Office Total Productivity Model" (as shown on page no. 211) and suggested measures of total factors productivity. However ordinarily, partial productivity indicated by per employee, per office and some financial indicators can be relied upon. In fact, these are popular all over the world. According to Cunnigham,[6] the universal yardsticks of banking economies are, profit per square foot and profit per employee.

To quote PEP Committee, "There is no such thing as a single index of operational efficiency of banks. It has many facets, which are complimentary as well as substitutive. The emphasis laid on each will also keep on changing

FIG. 19.1
Factors Influencing Productivity

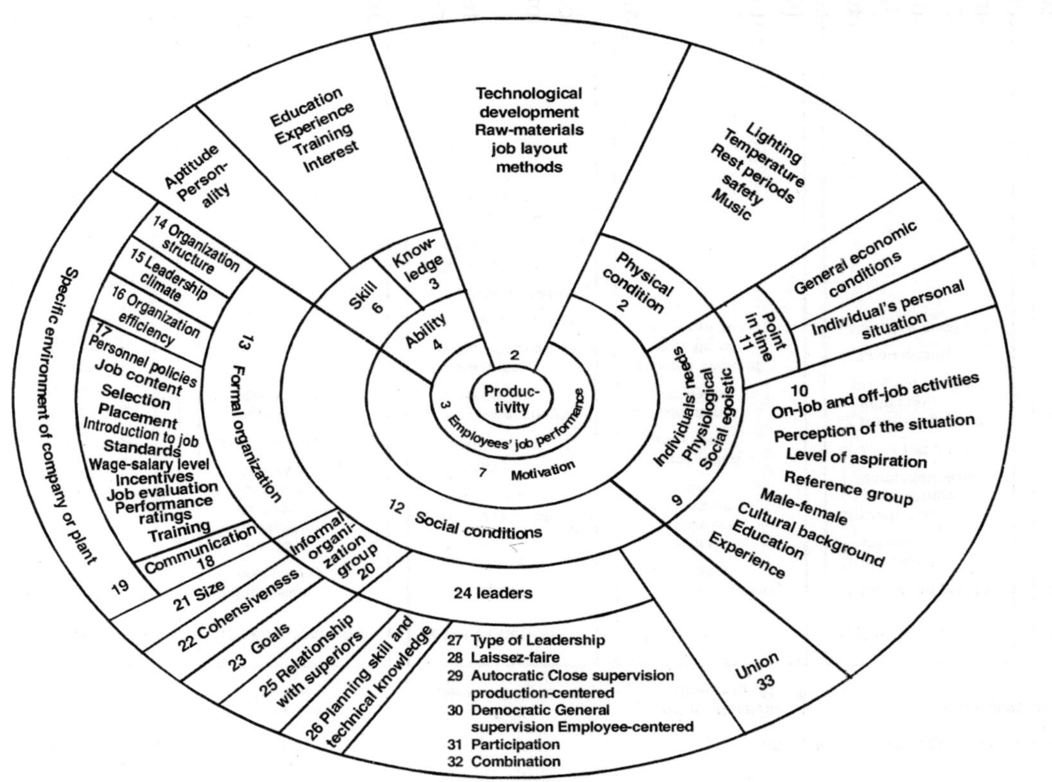

Source : Sutermeister, A. Robert, *People and Productivity*, McGraw Hill Book Company (2nd ed.), London, 1969, (Inner Cover).

Bank Office Total Productivity Model

SERVICE "PRODUCTION" PROCESS			PRODUCTIVITY MEASUREMENT PROCESS			
Resource Inputs	Bank Office Functions	Transacton Process	Product/ Service Outputs	Partial Productivity Measures	Total Productivity Measurement	
Input Costs ❑ Branch staff costs ❑ Branch facility costs ❑ Equipment costs ❑ Other costs	**Teller Functions** ❑ Paying ❑ Receiving ❑ Notes **Platform Functions** ❑ New accounts ❑ Loan ❑ Services (customer inquiries) ❑ Credit Card **Administration** ❑ Audit ❑ Supervisor ❑ Marketing	**Bank Operations** ❑ Policies & procedures ❑ Structural (central/ decentralized functions, location) ❑ Technology ❑ Work methods, procedures	**Teller Functions** ❑ No deposits ❑ No Checks cashed ❑ No traveler, etc. Redeemed **Platform Functions** ❑ No new accounts opened ❑ Customer inquiries/answers ❑ Saving certificate ❑ Travelers' checks ❑ Safe deposit box transactions ❑ Food stamps processing	**Efficiency** ❑ Staff hours/work processed ❑ Function costs/work processed in function ❑ Transaction volumes ❑ Work items processed ❑ Dollar value of work items processed	**Net Impacts** ❑ Increased profits ❑ Increased deposits ❑ Customer satisfaction/ complaint levels ❑ Error reduction ❑ Non-compliance with Fed. Regs./citations ❑ Loan quality ❑ Service quality	**Total** ❑ Efficiency + net impacts and composite of partial measures in total productivity

Source : Exhibit 4.1 of *Productivity Improvement for the Banking Office—A Comprehensive Guidebook*, American Bankers' Association, Washington, D.C. 1983.

with reference to time, to attempt reducing them into one dimension will be devoid of content and may at times be misleading".[7]

INDICATORS OF PRODUCTIVITY

Indian Banking industry is labour-intensive and manpower cost is not insignificant.

Since it is difficult to measure labour productivity in a service industry like banking, various economists have suggested different productivity indicators to indicate level of productivity. These indicators can be classified into two groups :

(i) Qualitative, and
(ii) Quantitative.

A. Qualitative Indicators

Some economists have suggested a few qualitative productivity indicators, viz. quality of lending, recovery of loans, state of internal housekeeping, morale of employees, etc. But none of them has used these qualitative indicators in measuring productivity.

B. Quantitative Indicators

Some economists have suggested and used these productivity indicators, which can be classified as follows :

1. Income-Statement ratios :
   (a) Profit and Loss Account Ratios.
   (b) Balance Sheet Ratios.
2. Physical Work Unit Ratio.

1. *Financial Statement Ratios*

Information regarding input or output or both is taken from published income statements, i.e. profit and loss account and balance sheet of a bank, viz.

Balance Sheet Ratio

- per employee deposit ratio,
- per employee credit ratio, and
- per employee deposit + credit ratio.

Profit and Loss Account Ratios

- per employee profit or per employee operating profit,
- per employee establishment expenditure, and
- per employee spread ratio.

2. *Physical Work Unit Ratios*

In this case physical work unit is taken as a base for quantification of output of banking industry, viz.

per employee deposit accounts,
per employee credit accounts,
per employee deposit and credit accounts, and
per employee vouchers.

Productivity index is supposed to give feedback to the concerned authority to improve performance in the next period. In other words, productivity index serves as a basis for improvement.

Thus, one can conclude that productivity in banks has deemed to have improved only if—

(I) The quantitative indicators mentioned earlier reflect a significant increase and not only a marginal increase during a period of say 10 years. The increase should result in offering higher rates to depositors and the charging of a lower rate to borrowers.

(II) The quality of customer service offered has also improved due to changes in technology, adoption of innovative methods in systems and procedures and improved employee maturation and involvement.

(III) There is an improvement in internal housekeeping inspite of an increase in the volume of business.

(IV) Improvement in recovery rate, i.e., gradual decline of overdue advances to total advances.

While devising indicators for productivity measurement, certain criteria need to be fulfilled. Such criteria can include :

(I) Regard shall have to be given to all factors of production rather than manpower alone.

(II) The qualitative aspects shall need due consideration *vis-a-vis* the quantitative aspects.

(III) Indicators may comprise both favourable and adverse features referring to producivity.

(IV) The devised indicators should be simple and understandable to staff at all levels, so that their computation and comparison are possible. Staff resistance to such improvement can also be minimised.

(V) The productivity norms shall be capable of being related to individual performance appraisal so that discrimination between better and poor performers is facilitated.

PRODUCTIVITY IN STATE BANK OF INDIA GROUP

The present study to analyze the productivity of State Bank of India group has been conducted on the basis of 15 indicators. These indicators have been divided into three categories. One set of indicators measure output in terms of input of number of employees, i.e., labour productivity. Another set of indicators measure branch productivity. The last set of indicators depict productivity on the basis of certain financial ratios. These set of indicators are as follows :

Per Employee Indicators (Labour Productivity)

1. Credit per employee. (Cr/E)
2. Deposit per employee. (D/E)
3. Total earnings per employee. (TER/E)
4. Total expenditure per employee. (TEXP/E)
5. Establishment expenses per employee. (ESTB/E)
6. Spread per employee. (SPR/E)

Per Branch Indicators (Branch Productivity)

1. Credit per branch. (Cr/Br)
2. Deposits per branch. (D/Br)
3. Total earnings per branch. (TER/Br)
4. Total expenditure per branch. (TEXP/Br)
5. Establishment expenses per branch. (ESTB/Br)
6. Spread per branch. (SPR/Br)

FINANCIAL RATIOS MEASURING PRODUCTIVITY

1. Total Earnings as percentage of total credit. (TER%TCR)
2. Establishment Expenses as percentage of Total Expenditure. (ESTB%TEXP)
3. Establishment expenses as percentage of total earnings. (ESTB%TER).

Table 19.1 shows the inter bank comparison of growth rates in various indicators of productivity of SBI group, i.e., State Bank of India and its subsidiaries, namely, State Bank of Hyderabad (SBH), State Bank of Bikaner and Jaipur (SBBJ), State Bank of Patiala (SBOP), State Bank of Mysore (SBM), State Bank of Saurashtra (SBS), State Bank of Indore (SB Indore), and State Bank of Travancore (SBT), Growth rate per employee, Growth rate per branch, and Growth rate as financial indicators have been shown in the table. The rate of growth for SBI and its subsidiaries for different years from 1990-91 to 2000-01 has been worked out separately in Appendix 19.1 to Appendix 19.8. Based on these appendices the rate of growth during 1990-91 to 2000-2001 for SBI and its subsidiaries has been shown in Table 19.1. Table 19.1 depicts the following :

TABLE 19.1
Inter-Bank Comparison of Growth Rates in Indicators of Productivity of SBI Group

Bank	Per Employee						Per Branch						Financial		
	Cr/E	*D/E*	*TER/E*	*TEXP/E*	*ESTB/E*	*SPR/E*	*Cr/Br*	*D/Br*	*TER/ Br*	*TEXP/ Br*	*ESTB/ Br*	*SPR/ Br*	*TER% TCR*	*ESTB% TEXP*	*ESTB% TER*
SBI	11.82	14.84	17.76	17.48	17.19	25.23	10.71	16.57	16.67	16.34	15.90	24.27	5.86	1.22	0.81
SBH	14.87	16.83	20.84	20.31	16.75	27.22	13.94	15.66	19.94	19.46	15.75	26.67	5.50	-1.60	-2.10
SBB&J	14.02	15.30	18.75	18.10	17.26	26.37	11.95	13.22	16.48	15.79	14.99	23.63	4.63	-0.24	-0.72
SBOP	11.77	12.42	19.96	19.79	20.28	45.75	9.32	9.79	17.43	17.30	17.20	43.58	8.40	2.53	2.42
SBM	16.54	16.37	19.15	19.07	19.47	20.34	14.18	14.05	16.86	16.72	16.92	18.08	2.76	0.37	0.26
SBIN	16.38	17.29	22.22	22.99	16.49	22.64	13.75	14.58	17.31	20.64	14.04	20.74	3.14	-0.63	-1.42
SBS	16.75	17.99	20.31	19.73	16.45	22.40	15.04	16.71	19.90	19.30	15.76	22.63	4.42	-1.88	-2.46
SBT	17.48	16.83	18.83	18.19	17.74	22.29	16.21	15.67	17.67	17.06	16.78	20.86	1.85	0.16	-0.38

Source : Derived from rates of growth during 1990-91 to 2000-01 for various banks as shown in Appendices 1 to 8.

Per Employee Indicators

Table 19.1 shows that growth rate in Cr/E has been highest for SBT, i.e., 17.48 percent, while SBOP has the lowest growth in Cr/E (11.77 per cent) and D/E (12.42 per cent), while SB Indore has the highest growth in D/E (17-99 per cent). TER/E and TEXP/E recorded highest growth rate for SBS, i.e., 22.22 per cent and 22.99 per cent respectively, while for SBI it has been lowest, i.e., 17.76 and 17.48 per cent respectively. SBOP has the highest growth rate for ESTB/E and SPR/E, i.e., 20.28 per cent and 45.75 per cent respectively. SB Indore has the lowest growth rate in ESTB/E, i.e., 16.45 per cent, while SBM has the lowest growth in SPR/E, i.e., 20.34 per cent.

Per Branch Indicators

SBT has the highest growth rate in Cr/Br, i.e. 16.21 per cent, while SBOP has lowest growth in CR/Br, i.e. 9.32 per cent. SBOP has lowest growth in D/Br also, i.e. 9.79 per cent while SB Indore has the highest growth in D/Br. SBI has the lowest growth in TEXP/Br, i.e. 16.34 per cent, while SBS has lowest growth in ESTB/Br. SBOP has the highest growth in ESTB/Br and SPR/Br, i.e. 17.20 per cent and 43.58 per cent respectively. SBM has the lowest growth in SPR/Br, i.e. 18.08 percent.

Financial Indicators

Highest growth in TER%TCR has been noted of SBOP, i.e. 8.40 per cent while SBT has lowest growth in it, i.e. 1.85 per cent. ESTB%TEXP has been negative for SBH (–1.60 per cent), SBBJ (–.24 per cent), SBS (–0.63 per cent) and SB Indore (–1.88 per cent). ESTB%TER growth rate has been negative for all banks except SBI (0.81 per cent) and SBOP (2.42 per cent), SBM (0.26 per cent).

STRATEGIES TO IMPROVE PRODUCTIVITY

One among several positive fallouts of the Indian economic reforms of the 1990s is the rediscovery of the idea of productivity. Although the concept was known in the 1950s and the National Productivity Council was set-up, yet the efforts generated were not whole-heartedly pursued. Increasing productivity has emerged as a new national priority, where the efforts of all concerned are to accelerate the process of economic growth and raise the standard of living. For the total economy to be highly productive, the route is to raise the productivity of each major resource—capital, material, human and leadership productivity.

In the customer friendly marketing environment, productivity has assumed all the more importance. Banking, being service-oriented industry needs big improvement in employee productivity. Banks need to rationalize their staff and office network including regional and zonal offices. Redeployment strategies should be adopted which would include positioning staff in branches for non-fund-based business, recovery efforts, new business area like selling insurance and mutual fund products to new and potential customers would help reduce transaction costs. All this requires greater customer orientation and awareness, that has to the imbibed by employees along with a change in the banks' work culture to make employees more productive.

The SBI group banks are yet to match the private sector banks. The following suggestions are given to improve productivity of SBI and its Group :

- The first step to make employees more productive is to communicate the need for change throughout the organization and build commitment at all levels.
- Reward, recognition and incentives to employees who perform will send the right signal, ensuring job satisfaction, boosting employee morale and building employee commitment.
- The employees must be trained and developed to reduce the avoidable waste of time and energy.
- Raising the skill bar at entry level is another step to ensure that people with the requisite skills get into banks.
- There should be no political and administrative interference.
- The present system of dual control over the banking system between RBI and the banking division of ministry of finance should end. RBI should be the primary agency for the regulation of banking system.
- Banks should be given more freedom in their decision-making and day-to-day working so as to increase the potential productivity growth.
- There should be written job descriptions for improvement of staff productivity.
- Establishment expenditure should be brought down. Overstaffing should be avoided and employees must deliver the goods effectively.
- Invest in technology for better MIS, product development (including derivatives), risk management, funds management and customer service.
- Team spirit should be developed.
- Employees need to be fit in body and mind. The banks should organise on an ongoing basis stress management programmes, yoga, etc. This will encourage physical fitness in employees and they will be at their productivity best.
- It is recommended that all the banks should set-up effective productivity cells. These cells should monitor the productivity and its growth continuously on the basis of key indicators. Productivity improvement programmes should be developed and implemented.
- Productivity audit should be introduced as an essential element in the annual reports of the companies.

Notes and References

1. Gunnar Myrdal, Productivity, *Journal of Productivity,* Vol. 1 (Aug.-Sep.) 1960, p. 481.
2. Country Report (India), Factors which Hinder or Help Productivity Improvement, Asia Productivity Organisation, Tokyo, 1980, p. 1.
3. Kopleman, Richard E., Managing Productivity Organisations, McGraw-Hill Book Company, New York, 1986, p. 3.
4. Report of the Productivity, Efficiency and Profitability Committee on Banking, (Mimeo) headed by J.C. Luther, Reserve Bank of India, 1977, para 4.2.
5. Sutermeister, A. Robert, People and Productivity, McGraw Hill Book Company, (2nd ed.), London, 1969 (inner cover).
6. Cunnigham, C.W.W., Regional Director South Asia, Annual Report, Grindlays Bank (India Branches), 1985.
7. PEP Committee on Banking, RBI, 1977, para 4.16.

References

Report/Statistical Publications

Government of India, *Economic Survey,* New Delhi (issues of relevant years).

Indian Banks Association, Financial Analysis of Banks, Bombay (issues of relevant years).

Reserve Bank of India, *Reserve Bank of India Monthly Bulletins,* Bombay (issues of relevant years).

Indian Banks Association, *IBA Bulletins,* Bombay (issues of relevant years).

Appendix 19.1
Productivity Indicators—State Bank of India

Year	Per Employee						Per Branch						Financial		
	Cr/E	D/E	TER/E	TEXP/E	ESTB/E	SPR/E	Cr/Br	D/Br	TER/Br	TEXP/Br	ESTB/Br	SPR/Br	TER% TCR	ESTB% TEXP	ESTB% TER
1990-91	18.25	22.53	3.01	2.96	0.61	0.62	472.51	583.50	78.03	76.78	15.89	16.06	16.51	20.70	20.36
1991-92	19.56	26.74	4.86	4.78	0.70	1.53	510.23	697.72	126.71	124.68	18.28	39.95	24.83	14.66	14.43
	7.18	**18.69**	**61.46**	**61.49**	**14.75**	**146.77**	**7.98**	**19.57**	**62.39**	**62.39**	**15.04**	**148.75**	**50.38**	**-29.16**	**-29.16**
1992-93	21.08	29.32	4.93	4.84	0.83	1.31	545.96	759.12	127.71	125.28	21.39	34.00	23.39	17.07	16.75
	7.77	**9.65**	**1.44**	**1.26**	**18.57**	**-14.38**	**7.00**	**8.80**	**0.79**	**0.48**	**17.01**	**-14.89**	**-5.81**	**16.45**	**16.10**
1993-94	18.11	33.35	4.69	4.57	0.86	1.27	470.93	867.07	121.95	118.83	22.34	33.09	25.90	18.80	18.32
	-14.09	**13.74**	**-4.87**	**-5.58**	**3.61**	**-3.05**	**-13.74**	**14.22**	**-4.51**	**-5.15**	**4.44**	**-2.68**	**10.70**	**10.11**	**9.37**
1994-95	20.91	36.69	5.46	5.15	1.13	1.70	549.04	963.02	143.39	135.29	29.86	44.84	26.12	22.07	20.82
	15.46	**10.01**	**16.42**	**12.69**	**31.40**	**33.86**	**16.59**	**11.07**	**17.58**	**13.85**	**33.66**	**35.51**	**0.85**	**17.40**	**13.68**
1995-96	25.67	41.37	6.74	6.38	1.43	2.03	673.33	1084.91	176.88	167.51	37.72	53.26	26.27	22.52	21.33
	22.76	**12.76**	**23.44**	**23.88**	**26.55**	**19.41**	**22.64**	**12.66**	**23.36**	**23.82**	**26.32**	**18.78**	**0.59**	**2.03**	**2.41**
1996-97	26.34	46.86	7.44	6.87	1.40	2.26	700.19	1245.51	197.94	182.76	37.38	60.29	28.27	20.45	18.88
	2.61	**13.27**	**10.39**	**7.68**	**-2.10**	**11.33**	**3.99**	**14.80**	**11.91**	**9.10**	**-0.90**	**13.20**	**7.61**	**-9.17**	**-11.45**
1997-98	30.97	54.70	7.80	7.02	1.48	2.25	831.79	1468.81	209.51	188.65	39.86	60.56	25.19	21.13	19.03
	17.58	**16.73**	**4.84**	**2.18**	**5.71**	**-0.44**	**18.79**	**17.93**	**5.85**	**3.22**	**6.63**	**0.45**	**-10.90**	**3.31**	**0.75**
1998-99	34.67	71.17	9.42	8.99	1.74	2.55	916.94	1882.00	249.02	237.85	46.17	67.50	27.16	19.41	18.54
	11.95	**30.11**	**20.77**	**28.06**	**17.57**	**13.33**	**10.24**	**28.13**	**18.86**	**26.08**	**15.83**	**11.46**	**7.82**	**-8.13**	**-2.55**
1999-00	42.02	84.31	11.03	10.16	1.91	2.96	1084.83	2176.50	284.97	262.29	49.51	76.61	26.27	18.88	17.37
	21.20	**18.46**	**17.09**	**13.01**	**9.77**	**16.08**	**18.31**	**15.65**	**14.44**	**10.28**	**7.23**	**13.50**	**-3.27**	**-2.76**	**-6.29**
2000-01	52.87	88.47	13.97	13.22	2.79	3.83	1251.26	2674.90	330.70	313.03	66.22	90.85	26.43	21.15	20.02
	25.82	**4.93**	**26.65**	**30.12**	**46.07**	**29.39**	**15.34**	**22.90**	**16.05**	**19.34**	**33.75**	**18.59**	**0.61**	**12.07**	**15.26**
Rate of Growth during 1990-91 to 2000-01	11.82	14.84	17.76	17.48	17.19	25.23	10.71	16.57	16.67	16.34	15.90	24.27	5.86	1.22	0.81

Note : Rate of growth for the period is given in bold figures.
Source : Worked out from various issues of IBA bulletins.

Appendix 19.2
Productivity Indicators—State Bank of Hyderabad

Year	Per Employee						Per Branch						Financial		
	Cr/E	D/E	TER/E	TEXP/E	ESTB/E	SPR/E	Cr/Br	D/Br	TER/Br	TEXP/Br	ESTB/Br	SPR/Br	TER% TCR	ESTB% TEXP	ESTB% TER
1990-91	12.23	21.30	2.16	2.10	0.50	0.55	227.26	395.98	40.23	39.04	9.35	10.21	17.70	23.95	23.24
1991-92	14.02	23.38	3.56	3.47	0.57	1.37	267.65	446.47	68.00	66.21	10.84	26.13	25.41	16.37	15.94
	14.64	**9.77**	**64.81**	**65.24**	**14.00**	**149.09**	**17.77**	**12.75**	**69.03**	**69.60**	**15.94**	**155.93**	**43.52**	**-31.64**	**-31.41**
1992-93	16.37	28.23	4.06	3.94	0.66	1.18	307.27	529.93	76.26	73.93	12.30	22.11	24.82	16.64	16.13
	16.76	**20.74**	**14.04**	**13.54**	**15.79**	**-13.87**	**14.80**	**18.69**	**12.15**	**11.66**	**13.47**	**-15.38**	**-2.31**	**1.62**	**1.18**
1993-94	17.53	35.07	4.47	4.30	0.73	1.32	309.48	619.24	79.02	75.87	12.91	23.30	25.53	17.02	16.34
	7.09	**24.23**	**10.10**	**9.14**	**10.61**	**11.86**	**0.72**	**16.85**	**3.62**	**2.62**	**4.96**	**5.38**	**2.88**	**2.28**	**1.29**
1994-95	23.70	39.93	5.43	5.11	0.89	1.72	430.07	724.47	98.56	92.83	16.14	31.38	22.92	17.39	16.38
	35.20	**13.86**	**21.48**	**18.84**	**21.92**	**30.30**	**38.97**	**16.99**	**24.73**	**22.35**	**25.02**	**34.68**	**-10.25**	**2.18**	**0.23**
1995-96	27.64	43.44	6.80	6.44	1.24	2.16	497.56	782.02	122.46	116.04	22.46	38.89	24.61	19.36	18.34
	16.62	**8.79**	**25.23**	**26.03**	**39.33**	**25.58**	**15.69**	**7.94**	**24.25**	**25.00**	**39.16**	**23.93**	**7.40**	**11.32**	**12.00**
1996-97	28.62	51.26	7.80	7.43	1.26	2.46	505.12	904.88	137.71	131.15	22.39	43.51	27.26	17.07	16.26
	3.55	**18.00**	**14.71**	**15.37**	**1.61**	**13.89**	**1.52**	**15.71**	**12.45**	**13.02**	**-0.31**	**11.88**	**10.77**	**-11.80**	**-11.35**
1997-98	32.44	60.61	8.44	7.76	1.37	2.68	556.51	1039.49	144.89	131.41	23.56	46.13	26.04	17.93	16.26
	13.35	**18.24**	**8.21**	**4.44**	**8.73**	**8.94**	**10.17**	**14.88**	**5.21**	**0.20**	**5.23**	**6.02**	**-4.50**	**5.02**	**0.01**
1998-99	36.48	72.63	9.68	8.92	1.91	3.18	623.62	1241.52	165.61	152.63	32.74	54.38	26.56	21.45	19.77
	12.45	**19.83**	**14.69**	**14.95**	**39.42**	**18.66**	**12.06**	**19.44**	**14.30**	**16.15**	**38.96**	**17.88**	**2.00**	**19.64**	**21.58**
1999-00	41.25	84.98	11.86	10.99	1.70	3.52	695.76	1433.29	200.11	185.46	28.71	59.49	28.76	15.48	14.35
	13.08	**17.00**	**22.52**	**23.21**	**-10.99**	**10.69**	**11.57**	**15.45**	**20.83**	**21.51**	**-12.31**	**9.40**	**8.30**	**-27.83**	**-27.43**
2000-01	47.83	100.11	13.36	12.35	2.16	4.12	807.63	1690.43	225.74	208.65	36.56	69.58	27.95	17.52	16.20
	15.95	**17.80**	**12.65**	**12.37**	**27.06**	**17.05**	**16.08**	**17.94**	**12.81**	**12.50**	**27.34**	**16.96**	**-2.82**	**13.19**	**12.88**
Rate of Growth during 1990-91 to 2000-01	14.87	16.83	20.84	20.31	16.75	27.22	13.94	15.66	19.94	19.46	15.75	26.67	5.50	-1.60	-2.10

Note : Rate of growth for the period is given in bold figures.
Source : Worked out from various issues of IBA bulletins.

APPENDIX 19.3
Productivity Indicators—State Bank of Bikaner and Jaipur

Year	Per Employee						Per Branch						Financial		
	Cr/E	D/E	TER/E	TEXP/E	ESTB/E	SPR/E	Cr/Br	D/Br	TER/ Br	TEXP/ Br	ESTB/ Br	SPR/ Br	TER% TCR	ESTB% TEXP	ESTB% TER
1990-91	10.70	18.99	2.12	2.08	0.52	0.51	216.30	383.99	42.93	42.14	10.61	10.30	19.85	25.18	24.71
1991-92	10.98	18.42	3.06	2.99	0.61	1.15	215.06	360.94	59.98	58.63	11.98	22.47	27.89	20.43	19.97
	2.62	**-3.00**	**44.34**	**43.75**	**17.31**	**125.49**	**-0.57**	**-6.00**	**39.72**	**39.13**	**12.91**	**118.16**	**40.52**	**-18.84**	**-19.18**
1992-93	11.69	19.98	3.03	2.96	0.64	0.78	241.40	412.74	62.68	61.20	13.23	16.13	25.97	21.62	21.11
	6.47	**8.47**	**-0.98**	**-1.00**	**4.92**	**-32.17**	**12.25**	**14.35**	**4.50**	**4.38**	**10.43**	**-28.22**	**-6.90**	**5.80**	**5.68**
1993-94	12.12	23.40	3.27	3.22	0.70	0.78	242.27	467.91	65.29	64.41	14.05	15.57	26.95	21.81	21.52
	3.68	**17.12**	**7.92**	**8.78**	**9.37**	**0.00**	**0.36**	**13.37**	**4.16**	**5.25**	**6.20**	**-3.47**	**3.79**	**0.91**	**1.95**
1994-95	13.81	26.38	3.63	3.58	0.86	0.98	286.49	547.06	74.44	74.35	18.00	20.32	25.98	24.21	24.18
	13.94	**12.74**	**11.01**	**11.18**	**22.86**	**25.64**	**18.25**	**16.92**	**14.01**	**15.43**	**28.11**	**30.51**	**-3.58**	**10.99**	**12.37**
1995-96	16.24	30.94	4.72	4.56	1.18	1.54	328.01	624.66	95.44	92.09	23.86	31.09	29.10	25.91	25.00
	17.60	**17.29**	**30.03**	**27.37**	**37.21**	**57.14**	**14.49**	**14.18**	**28.21**	**23.86**	**32.56**	**53.00**	**11.98**	**7.02**	**3.39**
1996-97	19.97	35.80	5.73	5.46	1.22	1.79	394.21	706.50	113.18	107.89	24.25	35.43	28.71	22.48	21.43
	22.97	**15.71**	**21.40**	**19.74**	**3.39**	**16.23**	**20.18**	**13.10**	**18.59**	**17.16**	**1.63**	**13.96**	**-1.33**	**-13.25**	**-14.30**
1997-98	24.32	43.36	6.73	6.13	1.42	2.08	477.24	850.76	132.13	120.34	27.97	40.92	27.69	23.24	21.17
	21.78	**21.12**	**17.45**	**12.27**	**16.39**	**16.20**	**21.06**	**20.42**	**16.74**	**11.54**	**15.34**	**15.50**	**-3.57**	**3.41**	**-1.20**
1998-99	25.65	51.71	7.52	6.92	1.67	2.20	492.43	992.43	144.48	132.82	32.17	42.30	29.34	24.22	22.27
	5.47	**19.26**	**11.74**	**12.89**	**17.61**	**5.77**	**3.18**	**16.65**	**9.35**	**10.37**	**15.02**	**3.37**	**5.97**	**4.21**	**5.18**
1999-00	29.78	61.40	9.04	8.22	1.79	2.53	559.21	1152.98	169.75	154.51	33.67	47.52	30.36	21.79	19.84
	16.10	**18.74**	**20.21**	**18.79**	**7.19**	**15.00**	**13.56**	**16.18**	**17.49**	**16.33**	**4.66**	**12.34**	**3.46**	**-10.03**	**-10.92**
2000-01	38.59	77.10	11.24	10.46	2.44	3.40	652.52	1303.78	190.15	176.89	41.41	57.57	29.14	23.41	21.78
	29.58	**25.57**	**24.34**	**27.25**	**36.31**	**34.39**	**16.69**	**13.08**	**12.02**	**14.48**	**22.99**	**21.15**	**-4.00**	**7.43**	**9.79**
Rate of Growth during 1990-91 to 2000-01	14.02	15.30	18.75	18.10	17.26	26.37	11.95	13.22	16.48	15.79	14.99	23.63	4.63	-0.24	-0.72

Note : Rate of growth for the period is given in bold figures.
Source : Worked out from various issues of IBA bulletins.

Appendix 19.4
Productivity Indicators—State Bank of Patiala

Year	Per Employee						Per Branch						Financial		
	Cr/E	*D/E*	*TER/E*	*TEXP/E*	*ESTB/E*	*SPR/E*	*Cr/Br*	*D/Br*	*TER/ Br*	*TEXP/ Br*	*ESTB/ Br*	*SPR/ Br*	*TER% TCR*	*ESTB% TEXP*	*ESTB% TER*
1990-91	13.21	25.06	2.08	1.96	0.41	0.37	284.57	540.08	44.76	42.20	8.92	8.01	15.73	21.14	19.93
1991-92	14.02	22.14	3.73	3.49	0.50	1.78	305.91	482.94	81.42	76.24	10.82	38.93	26.62	14.19	13.29
	6.13	**-11.65**	**79.33**	**78.06**	**21.95**	**381.08**	**7.50**	**-10.58**	**81.90**	**80.66**	**21.30**	**386.02**	**69.21**	**-32.86**	**-33.32**
1992-93	15.89	26.11	3.84	3.69	0.56	1.35	347.53	571.20	83.97	80.61	12.19	29.55	24.16	15.12	14.52
	13.34	**17.93**	**2.95**	**5.73**	**12.00**	**-24.16**	**13.61**	**18.28**	**3.13**	**5.73**	**12.66**	**-24.09**	**-9.22**	**6.55**	**9.24**
1993-94	16.57	33.74	4.28	4.06	0.62	1.45	352.97	718.68	91.07	86.40	13.15	30.92	25.80	15.22	14.44
	4.28	**29.22**	**11.46**	**10.03**	**10.71**	**7.41**	**1.57**	**25.82**	**8.46**	**7.18**	**7.88**	**4.64**	**6.78**	**0.65**	**-0.53**
1994-95	20.38	38.94	4.67	4.43	0.80	1.75	433.17	827.69	99.37	94.20	17.05	37.24	22.94	18.10	17.16
	22.99	**15.41**	**9.11**	**9.11**	**29.03**	**20.69**	**22.72**	**15.17**	**9.11**	**9.03**	**29.66**	**20.44**	**-11.09**	**18.92**	**18.83**
1995-96	24.12	45.33	6.40	6.02	1.08	2.11	504.58	948.24	134.04	126.10	22.59	44.27	26.56	17.91	16.85
	18.35	**16.41**	**37.04**	**35.89**	**35.00**	**20.57**	**16.49**	**14.56**	**34.89**	**33.86**	**32.49**	**18.88**	**15.80**	**-1.02**	**-1.78**
1996-97	27.04	51.62	7.13	6.71	1.17	2.29	541.79	1034.24	143.02	134.58	23.56	45.95	26.40	17.51	16.47
	12.11	**13.88**	**11.41**	**11.46**	**8.33**	**8.53**	**7.37**	**9.07**	**6.70**	**6.72**	**4.29**	**3.79**	**-0.63**	**-2.28**	**-2.25**
1997-98	31.31	59.02	7.91	6.82	1.37	2.70	580.68	1094.40	146.83	126.60	25.56	50.15	25.29	20.19	17.41
	15.79	**14.34**	**10.94**	**1.64**	**17.09**	**17.90**	**7.18**	**5.82**	**2.66**	**-5.93**	**8.49**	**9.14**	**-4.21**	**15.33**	**5.67**
1998-99	36.72	67.49	8.77	8.00	1.45	2.92	676.12	1242.55	161.51	147.33	26.82	53.79	23.89	18.20	16.61
	17.28	**14.35**	**10.87**	**17.30**	**5.84**	**8.15**	**16.44**	**13.54**	**10.00**	**16.37**	**4.93**	**7.26**	**-5.53**	**-9.83**	**-4.61**
1999-00	43.86	77.34	10.14	9.15	1.60	3.55	808.82	1426.05	186.97	168.76	29.55	65.54	23.12	17.51	15.80
	19.44	**14.59**	**15.62**	**14.38**	**10.34**	**21.58**	**19.63**	**14.77**	**15.76**	**14.55**	**10.18**	**21.84**	**-3.23**	**-3.81**	**-4.82**
2000-01	38.59	77.10	11.24	10.46	2.44	3.40	652.52	1303.78	190.15	176.89	41.41	57.57	29.14	23.41	21.78
	-12.02	**-0.31**	**10.85**	**14.32**	**52.50**	**-4.23**	**-19.32**	**-8.57**	**1.70**	**4.82**	**40.14**	**-12.16**	**26.06**	**33.69**	**37.79**
Rate of Growth during 1990-91 to 2000-01	11.77	12.42	19.96	19.79	20.28	45.75	9.32	9.79	17.43	17.30	17.20	43.58	8.40	2.53	2.42

Note : Rate of growth for the period is given in bold figures.
Source : Worked out from various issues of IBA bulletins.

Appendix 19.5
Productivity Indicators—State Bank of Mysore

Year	Per Employee						Per Branch						Financial		
	Cr/E	D/E	TER/E	TEXP/E	ESTB/E	SPR/E	Cr/Br	D/Br	TER/ Br	TEXP/ Br	ESTB/ Br	SPR/ Br	TER% TCR	ESTB% TEXP	ESTB% TER
1990-91	9.64	17.15	1.95	1.92	0.51	0.56	192.79	343.08	39.03	38.46	10.21	11.28	20.24	26.55	26.16
1991-92	10.60	17.50	2.61	2.58	0.59	0.90	213.75	353.01	52.74	51.98	11.99	18.26	24.67	23.07	22.73
	9.96	**2.04**	**33.85**	**34.38**	**15.69**	**60.71**	**10.87**	**2.89**	**35.13**	**35.15**	**17.43**	**61.88**	**21.88**	**-13.11**	**-13.09**
1992-93	12.84	21.80	3.19	3.15	0.66	0.84	256.99	436.22	63.81	63.03	13.27	16.73	24.83	21.05	20.80
	21.13	**24.57**	**22.22**	**22.09**	**11.86**	**-6.67**	**20.23**	**23.57**	**20.99**	**21.26**	**10.68**	**-8.38**	**0.63**	**-8.73**	**-8.52**
1993-94	12.77	24.92	3.55	3.53	0.72	0.92	261.19	509.82	72.61	72.16	14.64	18.83	27.80	20.29	20.16
	-0.55	**14.31**	**11.29**	**12.06**	**9.09**	**9.52**	**1.63**	**16.87**	**13.79**	**14.49**	**10.32**	**12.55**	**11.96**	**-3.63**	**-3.05**
1994-95	16.60	30.34	4.03	4.00	0.79	1.19	339.31	620.22	82.41	81.85	16.25	24.38	24.29	19.85	19.72
	29.99	**21.75**	**13.52**	**13.31**	**9.72**	**29.35**	**29.91**	**21.65**	**13.50**	**13.43**	**11.00**	**29.47**	**-12.63**	**-2.14**	**-2.20**
1995-96	18.82	35.07	5.31	5.07	1.20	1.69	378.29	704.63	106.86	102.04	24.11	34.13	28.25	23.63	22.56
	13.37	**15.59**	**31.76**	**26.75**	**51.90**	**42.02**	**11.49**	**13.61**	**29.67**	**24.67**	**48.37**	**39.99**	**16.31**	**19.01**	**14.42**
1996-97	21.70	39.37	6.19	5.83	1.28	2.07	432.10	783.88	123.34	116.12	25.54	41.28	28.54	21.99	20.71
	15.30	**12.26**	**16.57**	**14.99**	**6.67**	**22.49**	**14.22**	**11.25**	**15.42**	**13.80**	**5.93**	**20.95**	**1.05**	**-6.91**	**-8.22**
1997-98	23.46	42.51	6.32	5.87	1.37	2.06	468.32	848.50	126.17	117.18	27.48	41.15	26.94	23.45	21.78
	8.11	**7.98**	**2.10**	**0.69**	**7.03**	**-0.48**	**8.38**	**8.24**	**2.29**	**0.91**	**7.60**	**-0.31**	**-5.62**	**6.62**	**5.18**
1998-99	26.10	48.74	7.14	6.84	1.64	2.15	515.71	962.86	141.10	135.23	32.46	42.48	27.36	24.00	23.00
	11.25	**14.66**	**12.97**	**16.52**	**19.71**	**4.37**	**10.12**	**13.48**	**11.83**	**15.40**	**18.12**	**3.23**	**1.56**	**2.36**	**5.62**
1999-00	32.62	58.07	8.44	8.02	1.95	2.46	628.16	1118.38	162.56	154.46	37.60	47.38	25.88	24.34	23.13
	24.98	**19.14**	**18.21**	**17.25**	**18.90**	**14.42**	**21.80**	**16.15**	**15.21**	**14.22**	**15.83**	**11.53**	**-5.42**	**1.41**	**0.54**
2000-01	43.00	76.31	10.89	10.64	2.81	3.14	710.94	1261.69	180.09	175.95	46.60	52.07	25.33	26.48	25.88
	31.82	**31.41**	**29.03**	**32.67**	**44.10**	**27.64**	**13.18**	**12.81**	**10.78**	**13.91**	**23.94**	**9.90**	**-2.12**	**8.80**	**11.87**
Rate of Growth during 1990-91 to 2000-01	16.54	16.37	19.15	19.07	19.47	20.34	14.18	14.05	16.86	16.72	16.92	18.08	2.76	0.37	0.26

Note : Rate of growth for the period is given in bold figures.
Source : Worked out from various issues of IBA bulletins.

APPENDIX 19.6
Productivity Indicators—State Bank of Saurashtra

Year	*Per Employee*						*Per Branch*						*Financial*		
	Cr/E	*D/E*	*TER/E*	*TEXP/E*	*ESTB/E*	*SPR/E*	*Cr/Br*	*D/Br*	*TER/ Br*	*TEXP/ Br*	*ESTB/ Br*	*SPR/ Br*	*TER% TCR*	*ESTB% TEXP*	*ESTB% TER*
1990-91	10.94	18.77	2.13	2.07	0.53	0.56	248.69	426.58	48.45	47.12	11.94	12.83	19.48	25.34	24.64
1991-92	11.67	17.35	3.26	3.19	0.57	1.08	285.34	424.19	79.81	77.98	13.94	26.34	27.97	17.88	17.47
	6.67	**-7.57**	**53.05**	**54.11**	**7.55**	**92.86**	**14.74**	**-0.56**	**64.73**	**65.49**	**16.75**	**105.30**	**43.57**	**-29.45**	**-29.12**
1992-93	13.88	21.86	3.54	3.48	0.65	0.90	310.76	496.71	80.51	79.06	14.83	20.53	25.91	18.76	18.42
	18.94	**25.99**	**8.59**	**9.09**	**14.04**	**-16.67**	**8.91**	**17.10**	**0.88**	**1.38**	**6.38**	**-22.06**	**-7.37**	**4.93**	**5.46**
1993-94	13.73	25.69	3.56	3.50	0.69	1.01	315.75	590.74	81.97	80.44	15.76	23.29	25.96	19.59	19.23
	-1.08	**17.52**	**0.56**	**0.57**	**6.15**	**12.22**	**1.61**	**18.93**	**1.81**	**1.75**	**6.27**	**13.44**	**0.20**	**4.45**	**4.38**
1994-95	19.02	32.50	4.61	4.44	0.95	1.60	415.44	709.75	100.81	97.01	20.86	34.95	24.27	21.50	20.69
	38.53	**26.51**	**29.49**	**26.86**	**37.68**	**58.42**	**31.57**	**20.15**	**22.98**	**20.60**	**32.36**	**50.06**	**-6.53**	**9.75**	**7.62**
1995-96	22.56	39.12	6.00	8.86	1.35	1.91	480.90	833.68	127.85	188.85	28.91	40.84	26.59	15.31	22.61
	18.61	**20.37**	**30.15**	**99.55**	**42.11**	**19.38**	**15.76**	**17.46**	**26.82**	**94.67**	**38.59**	**16.85**	**9.56**	**-28.81**	**9.28**
1996-97	26.89	46.15	4.06	6.17	1.32	2.22	567.18	973.59	148.97	130.25	27.98	46.86	26.27	21.48	18.78
	19.19	**17.97**	**-32.33**	**-30.36**	**-2.22**	**16.23**	**17.94**	**16.78**	**16.52**	**-31.03**	**-3.22**	**14.74**	**-1.21**	**40.33**	**-16.94**
1997-98	30.01	49.97	7.45	6.48	1.56	2.36	624.67	1040.28	155.23	134.89	32.47	49.24	24.85	24.07	20.92
	11.60	**8.28**	**83.50**	**5.02**	**18.18**	**6.31**	**10.14**	**6.85**	**4.20**	**3.56**	**16.05**	**5.08**	**-5.39**	**12.06**	**11.37**
1998-99	33.37	58.62	8.47	8.16	1.76	2.73	680.25	1194.75	172.75	166.50	36.00	55.75	25.40	21.62	20.84
	11.20	**17.31**	**13.69**	**25.93**	**12.82**	**15.68**	**8.90**	**14.85**	**11.29**	**23.43**	**10.87**	**13.22**	**2.19**	**-10.18**	**-0.37**
1999-00	38.07	70.99	9.97	8.87	1.75	2.96	791.08	1428.96	200.74	178.71	35.39	59.65	25.38	19.80	17.63
	14.08	**21.10**	**17.71**	**8.70**	**-0.57**	**8.42**	**16.29**	**19.60**	**16.20**	**7.33**	**-1.69**	**7.00**	**-0.08**	**-8.41**	**-15.40**
2000-01	47.99	89.00	11.74	11.57	2.26	3.36	883.53	1638.32	216.21	213.02	41.76	61.91	24.47	19.60	19.31
	26.06	**25.37**	**17.75**	**30.44**	**29.14**	**13.51**	**11.69**	**14.65**	**7.71**	**19.20**	**18.00**	**3.79**	**-3.56**	**-1.01**	**9.56**
Rate of Growth during 1990-91 to 2000-01	16.38	17.29	22.22	22.99	16.49	22.64	13.75	14.58	17.31	20.64	14.04	20.74	3.14	-0.63	-1.42

Note : Rate of growth for the period is given in bold figures.
Source : Worked out from various issues of IBA bulletins.

APPENDIX 19.7
Productivity Indicators—State Bank of Indore

Year	Per Employee						Per Branch						Financial		
	Cr/E	*D/E*	*TER/E*	*TEXP/E*	*ESTB/E*	*SPR/E*	*Cr/Br*	*D/Br*	*TER/ Br*	*TEXP/ Br*	*ESTB/ Br*	*SPR/ Br*	*TER% TCR*	*ESTB% TEXP*	*ESTB% TER*
1990-91	12.11	20.36	2.19	2.14	0.53	0.62	210.43	353.77	37.99	37.21	9.12	10.75	18.05	24.51	24.01
1991-92	12.48	19.12	3.26	3.22	0.60	1.16	246.58	377.79	64.50	63.53	11.83	23.01	26.16	18.62	18.34
	3.06	**-6.09**	**48.86**	**50.47**	**13.21**	**87.10**	**17.18**	**6.79**	**69.78**	**70.73**	**29.71**	**114.05**	**44.89**	**-24.02**	**-23.60**
1992-93	13.82	22.33	3.37	3.32	0.64	0.84	272.61	440.52	66.47	65.51	12.64	16.51	24.38	19.29	19.02
	10.74	**16.79**	**3.37**	**3.11**	**6.67**	**-27.59**	**10.56**	**16.60**	**3.05**	**3.12**	**6.85**	**-28.25**	**-6.79**	**3.62**	**3.68**
1993-94	15.38	26.51	3.89	3.83	0.70	1.13	289.08	498.34	73.12	72.09	13.22	21.31	25.29	18.34	18.08
	11.29	**18.72**	**15.43**	**15.36**	**9.37**	**34.52**	**6.04**	**13.13**	**10.00**	**10.04**	**4.59**	**29.07**	**3.74**	**-4.96**	**-4.92**
1994-95	14.37	30.70	4.51	4.37	0.94	1.53	355.11	584.09	85.79	83.23	17.89	29.26	24.16	21.49	20.85
	-6.57	**15.81**	**15.94**	**14.10**	**34.29**	**35.40**	**22.84**	**17.21**	**17.33**	**15.45**	**35.33**	**37.31**	**-4.49**	**17.21**	**15.34**
1995-96	21.77	36.50	5.45	5.27	1.17	1.89	408.33	684.72	102.22	98.88	21.94	35.55	25.03	22.19	21.46
	51.50	**18.89**	**20.84**	**20.59**	**24.47**	**23.53**	**14.99**	**17.23**	**19.15**	**18.80**	**22.64**	**21.50**	**3.62**	**3.23**	**2.93**
1996-97	23.59	41.06	6.32	6.07	1.25	2.18	431.97	751.92	115.81	111.22	22.94	40.02	26.81	20.63	19.81
	8.36	**12.49**	**15.96**	**15.18**	**6.84**	**15.34**	**5.79**	**9.81**	**13.29**	**12.48**	**4.56**	**12.57**	**7.09**	**-7.04**	**-7.71**
1997-98	27.83	49.31	7.02	6.61	1.39	2.31	501.75	888.86	126.62	119.31	25.17	41.70	25.24	21.10	19.88
	17.97	**20.09**	**11.08**	**8.90**	**11.20**	**5.96**	**16.15**	**18.21**	**9.33**	**7.27**	**9.72**	**4.20**	**-5.87**	**2.28**	**0.35**
1998-99	30.91	58.74	8.51	8.05	1.73	2.84	547.80	1040.82	150.90	142.63	30.74	50.38	27.55	21.55	20.37
	11.07	**19.12**	**21.23**	**21.79**	**24.46**	**22.94**	**9.18**	**17.10**	**19.18**	**19.55**	**22.13**	**20.82**	**9.16**	**2.16**	**2.48**
1999-00	41.02	73.55	10.01	9.36	1.91	2.71	710.50	1261.38	173.50	162.25	33.25	47.00	24.42	20.49	19.16
	32.71	**25.21**	**17.63**	**16.27**	**10.40**	**-4.58**	**29.70**	**21.19**	**14.98**	**13.76**	**8.17**	**-6.71**	**-11.35**	**-4.91**	**-5.92**
2000-01	52.24	102.10	13.29	12.31	2.36	3.56	837.89	1637.65	213.20	197.55	37.89	57.21	25.44	19.18	17.77
	27.35	**38.82**	**32.77**	**31.52**	**23.56**	**31.37**	**17.93**	**29.83**	**22.88**	**21.76**	**13.95**	**21.72**	**4.20**	**-6.41**	**-7.26**
Rate of Growth during 1990-91 to 2000-01	16.75	17.99	20.31	19.73	16.45	22.40	15.04	16.71	19.90	19.30	15.76	22.63	4.42	-1.88	-2.46

Note : Rate of growth for the period is given in bold figures.
Source : Worked out from various issues of IBA bulletins.

Appendix 19.8
Productivity Indicators—State Bank of Travancore

Year	Per Employee						Per Branch						Financial		
	Cr/E	D/E	TER/E	TEXP/E	ESTB/E	SPR/E	Cr/Br	D/Br	TER/ Br	TEXP/ Br	ESTB/ Br	SPR/ Br	TER% TCR	ESTB% TEXP	ESTB% TER
1990-91	10.96	20.16	2.27	2.24	0.47	0.53	219.32	403.66	45.54	44.88	9.33	10.62	20.76	20.79	20.49
1991-92	12.21	22.32	3.09	3.05	0.53	0.93	243.71	445.62	61.73	60.90	10.67	18.49	25.33	17.52	17.28
	11.41	**10.71**	**36.12**	**36.16**	**12.77**	**75.47**	**11.12**	**10.39**	**35.55**	**35.70**	**14.36**	**74.11**	**21.99**	**-15.72**	**-15.63**
1992-93	15.34	25.95	3.81	3.75	0.62	0.92	308.34	521.69	76.88	75.37	12.38	18.56	24.93	16.43	16.10
	25.63	**16.26**	**23.30**	**22.95**	**16.98**	**-1.08**	**26.52**	**17.07**	**24.54**	**23.76**	**16.03**	**0.38**	**-1.56**	**-6.25**	**-6.84**
1993-94	17.85	31.73	4.48	4.41	0.66	0.95	357.18	634.69	89.62	88.14	13.22	18.92	25.09	15.00	14.75
	16.36	**22.27**	**17.59**	**17.60**	**6.45**	**3.26**	**15.84**	**21.66**	**16.57**	**16.94**	**6.79**	**1.94**	**0.63**	**-8.69**	**-8.39**
1994-95	24.56	37.62	5.38	5.22	0.84	1.23	484.05	741.48	106.19	102.94	16.71	24.30	21.94	16.23	15.74
	37.59	**18.56**	**20.09**	**18.37**	**27.27**	**29.47**	**35.52**	**16.83**	**18.49**	**16.79**	**26.40**	**28.44**	**-12.57**	**8.23**	**6.68**
1995-96	26.05	42.19	6.85	6.65	1.06	1.70	514.43	833.17	135.33	131.33	21.04	33.64	26.31	16.02	15.55
	6.07	**12.15**	**27.32**	**27.39**	**26.19**	**38.21**	**6.28**	**12.37**	**27.44**	**27.58**	**25.91**	**38.44**	**19.92**	**-1.31**	**-1.20**
1996-97	28.17	49.75	7.95	7.64	1.28	1.90	559.52	988.33	157.93	151.78	25.54	37.83	28.23	16.83	16.17
	8.14	**17.92**	**16.06**	**14.89**	**20.75**	**11.76**	**8.77**	**18.62**	**16.70**	**15.57**	**21.39**	**12.46**	**7.30**	**5.03**	**4.02**
1997-98	30.65	57.23	8.66	8.17	1.16	2.05	606.18	1131.52	171.28	161.69	22.96	40.63	28.26	14.20	13.40
	8.80	**15.04**	**8.93**	**6.94**	**-9.38**	**7.89**	**8.34**	**14.49**	**8.45**	**6.53**	**-10.10**	**7.40**	**0.11**	**-15.61**	**-17.11**
1998-99	32.12	65.42	8.85	8.53	1.30	1.79	640.36	1303.91	176.50	170.00	26.05	35.84	27.56	15.32	14.76
	4.80	**14.31**	**2.19**	**4.41**	**12.07**	**-12.68**	**5.64**	**15.24**	**3.05**	**5.14**	**13.46**	**-11.79**	**-2.45**	**7.91**	**10.10**
1999-00	39.61	78.61	10.45	9.94	1.70	2.17	769.26	1526.88	202.99	193.10	33.13	42.27	26.39	17.16	16.32
	23.32	**20.16**	**18.08**	**16.53**	**30.77**	**21.23**	**20.13**	**17.10**	**15.01**	**13.59**	**27.18**	**17.94**	**-4.26**	**11.96**	**10.58**
2000-01	52.55	95.08	12.40	11.60	2.27	3.24	953.35	1724.73	225.03	210.43	41.88	58.86	23.60	19.90	18.61
	32.67	**20.95**	**18.66**	**16.70**	**33.53**	**49.31**	**23.93**	**12.96**	**10.86**	**8.97**	**26.41**	**39.25**	**-10.55**	**16.00**	**14.03**
Rate of Growth during 1990-91 to 2000-01	17.48	16.83	18.83	18.19	17.74	22.29	16.21	15.67	17.67	17.06	16.78	20.86	1.85	0.16	-0.38

Note : Rate of growth for the period is given in bold figures.
Source : Worked out from various issues of IBA bulletins.

CHAPTER 20

Trends in Operational Poductivity of Commercial Banks in India

MONIKA AGGARWAL

In India, a radical restructuring of the economic system consisting of industrial deregulation, liberalization of policies, public enterprise reforms, reforms of taxation system, trade liberalization and financial sector reforms have been initiated since 1992-93. Banking sector reforms were undertaken by the Reserve Bank of India in order to improve the financial health and soundness of banks through capital adequacy norms, income recognition norms and provisioning requirements, etc. Indian banks gained the benefits of prudential regulations and re-capitalization. This is reflected in the relatively clean and healthy balance sheet of the banks. But there is need to further improve the financial soundness so that the banks can cope up the increasing competition brought by the process of liberalization and globalization.

Moreover, the increasing scope of bank activities, the range of services offered by banks, the continuous technological changes, impact of globalization and liberalization, entry of new players both domestic and foreign, government controlled and regulated environment, all have redefined the business of banking. The business of banks has transformed from the traditional banking to the social and development banking, from brick or mortar banking to that of anywhere banking. Now the survival of banks depends on the efficiency with which they use their inputs and the effectiveness of their output. In this changing scenario analysis and comparison of its operational productivity could bring the necessary improvements in the banking system.

DATA BASE AND METHODOLOGY

The present study deals with the objective to study the trends in operational productivity of commercial banks in India. For this purpose, the commercial banks were divided into three categories, namely, public sector banks, private sector banks and foreign banks. The data was collected for the period of 1980 to 2000-2001. The various sources of data were, the Data Bank on Indian Commercial Banks published by the Indian Banks' Association, the Statistical Tables Relating to Banks in India published by the Reserve Bank of India for various years, the website of the Reserve Bank of India and the various issues of Indian Economy published by the Center for Monitoring Indian Economy (CMIE). For the period 1988-89 the data was annualized.

The operational productivity refers to how efficiently a bank manages its business. The following ratios were considered under this category of productivity :

1. Interest Income/Average Working Funds.
2. Non-Interest Income/Average Working Funds.
3. Operating Expenses/Operating Income.
4. Cost of Deposits.
5. Spread/Average Working Funds.

For calculating trends, the straight-line method of least square of trend analysis was used.

Formula : $Y_0 = a+bx$

where 'Y_0' is used to designate the trend values to distinguish them from actual 'Y' values, 'a' is the intercept and 'b' represents the slope of trend line. 'X' represents the time. In order to determine the values of constants 'a' and 'b' the following two equations were solved :

$$\Sigma Y = Na + b\Sigma x$$
$$\Sigma xy = a\ \Sigma x + b\Sigma x^2$$

where 'N' represents the number of years.

The Compound Growth rate was also calculated using the following formula :

$$R = P[1 + R/1001]^T$$

For calculating trends, averages and standard deviations, the MS EXCEL software for windows 98 was used.

HYPOTHESES

The following hypotheses were constructed for the present study :

H_1 — The operational productivity of foreign banks is higher than the private sector banks.

H_2 — The operational productivity of private sector banks is better than the public sector banks.

ANALYSIS

Table 20.1 indicates the operational productivity ratios of public sector banks operating in India for the years 1980 to 2000-2001. As stated earlier, five ratios were considered under this parameter. In the year 1980 the interest income/average working funds of the public sector banks was 6.49 percent. It increased up to 7.13% in the year 1984. Then in the year 1985 it showed a slight decrease when the ratio was 7.12 percent. Again it followed an increasing trend and increased to 10.18% in the year 1991-92. Then it followed a declining trend till 1993-94 and became 8.56 percent. After that, it showed a sign .of improvement and reached up to 9.69% in the year 1996-97. But again it declined and finally reached 8.84% in the year 2000-01. In case of the non-interest income/average working funds, in the year 1980 the ratio was 0.76% but after that it started declining and reached to 0.62% in the year 1984. Then it showed an improvement and in the year 1990-91 it increased to 0.81 percent. But subsequently it showed a decline and reached to 0.72% in the year 1991-92, again it followed an increasing trend in the year 1995-96 and became 0.87 percent. After that, it showed a significant decline and reached to 0.64% in the year 2000-01. The operational expenses/operational income in the year 1980 was 90.63 percent. It started declining and became 87.44% in the year 1982. Thereafter, it increased and in the year 1984 it reached to 91.47 percent. Again it started declining and became 77.76% in the year 1988-89. In the year 1989-90 it increased to 97.58 percent. Then it showed a declining trend and reached to 83.20% in the year 1991-92. After that, it showed an increase and in the year 1992-93 it became 90.67 percent. Then it showed a declining trend and reached the level of 83.95% in the year 1997-98. Then with slight fluctuations, the ratio reached up to 85.55% in the year 2000-01. The cost of deposits in the year 1980 was 5.75 percent. It increased to 5.93% in the year 1981 and then fell down to 5.77% in the year 1982. It increased up to the year 1985 and became 7.23 percent. Then it showed a significant decline in the year 1986 and became 6.23 percent. But after that it increased again and reached up to 8.14% in the year 1990-91. In the year 1991-92 it showed a decline and became 7.22 percent. Again it increased to 7.74% in the year 1992-93 but subsequently declined and reached to 6.43% in the year 1994-95. In the year 1996-97, it improved and became 7.44 percent. But again it declined and reached to 6.79% in the year 2000-01. Similarly, the spread/average working funds of

TABLE 20.1
Public Sector Banks

(Percentages)

Years	Interest Income/ Average Working Funds		Non-Interest Income/Average Working Funds		Operational Expenses/ Operational Income		Cost of Deposits		Spread/Average Working Funds	
	Ratio	Trend	Ratio	Trend	Ratio	Trend	Ratio	Trend	Ratio	Trend
1980	6.49	6.68	0.76	0.68	90.63	90.24	5.75	6.19	1.71	1.56
1981	6.74	6.83	0.72	0.69	87.57	89.99	5.93	6.25	1.69	1.64
1982	6.78	6.98	0.67	0.69	87.44	89.75	5.77	6.32	1.67	1.71
1983	6.78	7.13	0.62	0.69	87.51	89.51	5.92	6.38	1.76	1.79
1984	7.13	7.29	0.62	0.70	91.47	89.26	6.19	6.45	1.95	1.87
1985	7.12	7.44	0.65	0.70	90.17	89.02	7.23	6.51	1.94	1.94
1986	7.13	7.59	0.67	0.71	89.23	88.77	6.23	6.57	1.86	2.02
1987	7.19	7.75	0.67	0.71	89.18	88.53	6.44	6.64	1.81	2.09
1988-89	8.01	7.90	0.73	0.72	77.76	88.28	7.17	6.70	1.96	2.17
1989-90	8.56	8.05	0.74	0.72	97.58	88.04	7.75	6.77	2.03	2.25
1990-91	8.69	8.20	0.81	0.73	97.37	87.79	8.14	6.83	1.97	2.32
1991-92	10.18	8.36	0.72	0.73	83.2	87.55	7.22	6.90	3.22	2.40
1992-93	9.55	8.51	0.73	0.74	90.67	87.30	7.74	6.96	2.39	2.47
1993-94	8.56	8.66	0.78	0.74	89.23	87.06	7.09	7.03	2.36	2.55
1994-95	8.61	8.82	0.83	0.75	85.08	86.81	6.43	7.09	2.92	2.62
1995-96	9.2	8.97	0.87	0.75	85.26	86.57	6.84	7.16	3.08	2.70
1996-97	9.69	9.12	0.82	0.75	84.74	86.32	7.44	7.22	3.16	2.78
1997-98	9.09	9.27	0.77	0.76	83.95	86.08	7.13	7.28	2.91	2.85
1998-99	9.02	9.43	0.74	0.76	85.53	85.83	7.16	7.35	2.81	2.93
1999-00	8.92	9.58	0.71	0.77	84.51	85.59	7.13	7.41	2.7	3.00
2000-01	8.84	9.73	0.64	0.77	85.55	85.34	6.79	7.48	2.84	3.08

public sector banks in the year 1980 was 1.71 percent. It declined and reached to 1.67% in the year 1982. After that, showing an increasing trend it became 1.95% in the year 1984. Again it declined and reached the level of 1.81% in the year 1987. Then it touched the level of 3.22% in the year 1991-92. It declined till 1993-94 and became 2.36 percent. After that it showed an increasing trend and increased to 3.16% in the year 1996-97. Again it showed a declining trend and reached up to 2.70% in the year 1999-2000. In the year 2000-01 the ratio improved and became 2.84 percent.

Table 20.2 shows the compound growth rate, average, standard deviation and coefficient of variation of the operational productivity ratios of public sector banks. The Compound growth rate of the interest income/average working funds in the whole period under study was 1.48 percent. Whereas, the non-interest income/average working funds showed a negative growth rate of 0.81 percent. It means that these banks were not concentrating on the non-interest income though it could also give good returns and improve the financial soundness of banks. The operational expenses/operational income of public sector banks showed a negative growth rate indicating a good sign of progress. It means that their operational expenses as compared to operational income have decreased. The cost of deposits showed a positive growth rate. The spread/average working funds showed growth of 2.45 percent. Overall, it can be said that the operational productivity of public sector banks has increased over the period of study, but the increase was less in comparative terms and in view of liberalized environment.

TABLE 20.2
Public Sector Banks

(*Percentage*)

	Interest Income/ Average Working Funds	*Non-Interest Income/ Average Working Funds*	*Operational Expenses/ Operational Income*	*Cost of Deposits*	*Spread/ Average Working Funds*
Compound Growth Rate	1.48	-0.81	-0.27	0.79	2.45
Average	8.20	0.73	87.79	6.83	2.32
Standard Deviation	1.13	0.07	4.53	0.69	0.55
Coefficient of Variation	13.78	9.59	5.16	10.10	23.70

Table 20.3 shows the operational productivity ratios of private sector banks. The interest income/average working funds in the year 1980 was 6.69 percent. It improved till the year 1984 when the ratio was the highest, i.e., 10.88%. It declined in the year 1985 and became 7.38%. After that, it started improving and reached to 9.44% in the year 1989-1990. Again showing a

TABLE 20.3
Private Sector Banks

(Percentages)

Years	Interest Income/ Average Working Funds		Non-Interest Income/Average Working Funds		Operational Expenses/ Operational Income		Cost of Deposits		Spread/Average Working Funds	
	Ratio	Trend	Ratio	Trend	Ratio	Trend	Ratio	Trend	Ratio	Trend
1980	6.69	7.43	0.54	0.54	92.87	94.62	5.24	5.29	2.41	2.84
1981	7.01	7.56	0.54	0.55	91.07	93.78	5.28	5.42	2.55	2.83
1982	7.01	7.69	0.52	0.56	91.01	92.94	5.46	5.55	2.49	2.82
1983	7.22	7.81	0.49	0.56	92.27	92.11	5.65	5.68	2.51	2.81
1984	10.88	7.94	0.58	0.57	95.73	91.27	5.64	5.80	3.98	2.81
1985	7.38	8.07	0.57	0.58	93.52	90.44	5.84	5.93	2.53	2.80
1986	7.55	8.20	0.54	0.58	91.79	89.60	6.01	6.06	2.46	2.79
1987	7.84	8.32	0.59	0.59	90.56	88.76	6.33	6.19	2.46	2.78
1988-89	8.36	8.45	0.59	0.60	76.55	87.93	6.9	6.32	2.59	2.77
1989-90	9.44	8.58	0.68	0.61	95.53	87.09	6.99	6.45	3.1	2.77
1990-91	8.89	8.71	0.69	0.61	96.28	86.25	6.88	6.57	2.85	2.76
1991-92	9.71	8.83	0.66	0.62	79.39	85.42	6.04	6.70	4.01	2.75
1992-93	9.39	8.96	0.65	0.63	86.44	84.58	6.95	6.83	2.89	2.74
1993-94	9.07	9.09	0.62	0.63	81.26	83.75	6.38	6.96	3.01	2.74
1994-95	8.95	9.21	0.63	0.64	77.87	82.91	6.23	7.09	3.08	2.73
1995-96	9.97	9.34	0.78	0.65	78.58	82.07	7.39	7.21	3.12	2.72
1996-97	10.51	9.47	0.76	0.66	79.34	81.24	8.24	7.34	2.91	2.71
1997-98	9.72	9.60	0.64	0.66	78.14	80.40	7.93	7.47	2.44	2.70
1998-99	9.66	9.72	0.6	0.67	84.17	79.57	8.39	7.60	2.09	2.70
1999-00	8.69	9.85	0.59	0.68	78.7	78.73	7.14	7.73	2.13	2.69
2000-01	8.87	9.98	0.61	0.68	80.28	77.89	7.14	7.86	2.33	2.68

decline in the year 1990-91, it improved in the year 1991-92. In the year 1991-92 it was 9.71%. Again it declined and in the year 1994-95 it became 8.95 percent. After that, it showed the signs of improvement and reached as high as 10.51% in the year 1996-97. Again showing a declining trend in the year 1999-2000 it became 8.69 percent. Then it improved in the year 2000-01 and reached to 8.87 percent. The non-interest income of the private sector banks in the year 1980 was 0.54 percent. In the year 1983 it declined to 0.49 percent. It improved in the year 1984 and became 0.58 percent. Again it declined till the year 1986 and reached the level of 0.54 percent. Then it started improving and increased to 0.69% in the year 1990-91. Till the year 1993-94 it decreased. Thereafter, it improved and reached 0.78% in the year 1995-96. Then it showed a declining trend and reached as low as 0.59% in the year 1999-2000. Again in the year 2000-01 the ratio showed a little improvement and became 0.61 percent. The operational expenses/ operational income of private sector banks in the year 1980 was 92.87 percent. Showing a slight decline, it reached to 91.01% in the year 1982. It improved and became 95.73% in the year 1984. Then it followed a declining trend till the year 1988-89. In this year, the ratio was 76.55 percent. It showed improvement till 1990-91 when it became 96.28% but again in the year 1991-92 the ratio fell to 79.39 percent. In the year 1992-93 it increased to 86.44 percent. Then it declined to 77.87% in the year 1994-95. Again, it started increasing and in the year 1998-99 it became 84.17 percent. It fell in the year 1999-2000 and became 78.7% but subsequently increased in the year 2000-01 and became 80.28 percent. The cost of deposits in the year 1980 was 5.24 percent. It followed the increasing trend till the year 1983 and reached the level of 5.65 percent. Then it showed a slight decline and came down to 5.64% in the year 1984. Again it followed an increasing trend till the year 1989-90. In this year the ratio was 6.99%. After that it started declining and reached to 6.04% in the year 1991-92. It increased in the year 1992-93 and became 6.95%. Again it declined and in the year 1994-95 it became 6.23 percent. Thereafter, it increased significantly and became 8.24% in the year 1996-97. In the year 1998-99 the ratio increased to 8.39% and subsequently showed a decline. In the year 2000-01 it became 7.14 percent. The spread/ average working funds in case of private sector banks in the year 1980 was 2.41%. It increased to 2.55% in the year 1981. Then with a slight decline in the year 1982 it increased to 3.98% in the year 1984. Following a declining trend, it became 2.46% in the year 1987. Then it improved and became 3.1% in the year 1989-90. Again showing a declining trend till the year 1990-91 it improved significantly and became 4.01% in the year 1991-92. In the year 1995-96 it increased to 3.12 percent. After that it went down and reached 2.09% in the year 1998-99. Finally, it showed an improvement and became 2.33% in the year 2000-01.

Table 20.4 shows the compound growth rate, average, standard deviation and coefficient of variation of the operational productivity ratios of private sector banks for the period 1980 to 2000-01. The compound growth rate of interest income/average working funds was 1.35%. The non-

TABLE 20.4
Private Sector Banks

(*Percentages*)

	Interest Income/ Average Working Funds	*Non-Interest Income/ Average Working Funds*	*Operational Expenses/ Operational Income*	*Cost of Deposits*	*Spread/ Average Working Funds*
Compound Growth Rate	1.35	0.58	-0.69	1.48	-0.16
Average	8.71	0.61	86.25	6.57	2.76
Standard Deviation	1.22	0.07	7.11	.94	0.51
Coefficient of Variation	14	11.48	8.24	14.31	18.48

interest income/average working funds also showed a positive growth of 0.58% unlike the public sector banks. Whereas, the operational expenses/ operational income showed a negative growth rate of 0.69 percent. This was also a good sign. The cost of deposits of these banks showed a positive growth of 1.48% and the spread showed a negative growth rate of 0.16 percent. It means that although the interest income and non-interest income of these banks increased at a good rate yet they were unsuccessful to check their increased interest expenses and high cost of funds.

Table 20.5 shows the operational productivity ratios of foreign banks. The interest income/average working funds of foreign banks in the year 1980 was 6.46%. It improved till 1984 and increased to 7.32 percent. Then, it fell down to 6.97% in the year 1985. Again it started improving and in the year 1990-91 the ratio increased to 12.17 percent. But in the year 1991-92 the ratio declined to 11.70 percent. In the year 1992-93 it increased to 11.72 percent. It declined to 10.10% in the year 1994-95 and then improved till the year 1996-97. In this year, the ratio was 11.17 percent. Again showing a declining trend it became as low as 9.30 percent in the year 2000-01. The non-interest income/average working funds of foreign banks in the year 1980 was 1.60 percent. It increased to 1.69% in the year 1981. Then it started declining and in the year 1984 it became 1.32 percent. It again improved in the year 1985 and in 1989-90 it increased to 2.06 percent. But then it showed a declining trend and in the year 1993-94 it became 0.99 percent. After that, it started increasing and became 1.56 percent in the year 1997-98. But then again it decreased and reached the level of 1.26% in the year 2000-01. The operational expenses/operational income of foreign banks in the year 1980 was 73.76 percent. The ratio declined till the year 1982. In the year 1982 it was 66.93 percent. Then, it showed an increasing trend and became 77.12% in the year 1987. It fell down significantly in the year 1988-89 and became 69.93 percent. Again it increased and in the year 1990-91 became 87.05 percent. But in the year 1991-92 it fell to 65.10 percent. It increased in the year 1992-93 and became 84.15 percent. After that it declined and reached

Table 20.5
Foreign Banks

(Percentages)

Years	Interest Income/ Average Working Funds		Non-Interest Income/Average Working Funds		Operational Expenses/ Operational Income		Cost of Deposits		Spread/Average Working Funds	
	Ratio	Trend	Ratio	Trend	Ratio	Trend	Ratio	Trend	Ratio	Trend
1980	6.46	7.16	1.60	1.62	73.76	72.54	4.90	5.73	3.01	3.14
1981	6.79	7.37	1.69	1.60	67.93	72.58	5.15	5.84	3.41	3.19
1982	6.79	7.57	1.55	1.59	66.93	72.61	5.27	5.95	3.52	3.23
1983	7.01	7.78	1.55	1.58	69.70	72.65	5.47	6.06	3.26	3.27
1984	7.32	7.98	1.32	1.56	72.95	72.69	6.01	6.17	3.18	3.32
1985	6.97	8.19	1.38	1.55	72.67	72.73	5.89	6.28	2.88	3.36
1986	7.52	8.39	1.42	1.54	72.56	72.77	5.81	6.39	3.13	3.40
1987	8.45	8.60	1.71	1.52	77.12	72.81	6.32	6.50	3.34	3.45
1988-89	9.04	8.80	1.81	1.51	69.93	72.85	8.52	6.61	3.11	3.49
1989-90	11.29	9.01	2.06	1.50	84.79	72.89	9.73	6.72	3.62	3.54
1990-91	12.17	9.22	1.84	1.48	87.05	72.93	10.92	6.84	3.79	3.58
1991-92	11.7	9.42	1.28	1.47	65.10	72.97	5.72	6.95	3.94	3.62
1992-93	11.72	9.63	1.09	1.46	84.15	73.00	7.12	7.06	3.59	3.67
1993-94	10.1	9.83	0.99	1.44	67.69	73.04	5.70	7.17	4.24	3.71
1994-95	10.1	10.04	1.25	1.43	66.15	73.08	5.69	7.28	4.34	3.75
1995-96	10.52	10.24	1.37	1.41	72.24	73.12	7.19	7.39	3.76	3.80
1996-97	11.17	10.45	1.52	1.40	71.55	73.16	8.50	7.50	4.16	3.84
1997-98	10.39	10.65	1.56	1.39	68.79	73.20	7.78	7.61	3.92	3.88
1998-99	8.85	10.86	1.46	1.37	78.13	73.24	8.58	7.72	3.47	3.93
1999-00	9.87	11.06	1.42	1.36	71.16	73.28	7.09	7.83	3.85	3.97
2000-01	9.3	11.27	1.26	1.35	71.11	73.32	6.18	7.94	3.64	4.02

to 66.15% in the year 1994-95. Then it increased in the year 1995-96 to 72.24 percent but again fell down and came to 68.79 percent in the year 1997-98. The position of foreign banks in case of the operational expenses/ operational income worsened in the year 1998-99 when the ratio increased to 78.13% but after that it started declining and reached to 71.11% in the year 2000-01. The cost of deposits in the year 1980 was 4.90 percent. It showed an increasing trend till 1984. In the year 1984 it was 6.01 percent. After that, it fell and in the year 1986 it became 5.81 percent. Then it showed an increasing trend and in the year 1990-91 it reached as high as 10.92 percent. But in the year 1991-92 it fell significantly and became 5.72 percent. Then it increased to 7.12% in the year 1992-93. It fell down and reached to 5.69% in the year 1994-95. Again it increased to 8.50 percent in the year 1996-97. Then it declined to 7.78% in the year 1997-98. In the year 1998-99 it increased to 8.58 percent. Then it followed a declining trend. In the year 2000-01, it declined to 6.18 percent. The spread/average working funds was 3.01% in the year 1980. It increased to 3.52 percent in the year 1982. Then it fell down and became 2.88 percent in the year 1985. Then it increased to 3.34% in the year 1987. Again it fell down to 3.11% in the year 1988-89. Showing an increasing trend it then increased to 3.94% in the year 1991-92. Then it declined to 3.59% in the year 1992-93. After that it showed an increasing trend and in the year 1994-95 it increased to 4.34 percent. It again declined in the year 1995-96 to 3.76%. In the year 1996-97 it increased to 4.16% and subsequently declined thereafter. In the year 1998-99 the ratio reached to 3.47 percent. It again improved in the year 1999-2000 and became 3.85%. But in the year 2000-01 it declined to 3.64 percent.

Table 20.6 shows the compound growth rate, average, standard deviation and coefficient of variation of operational productivity ratios of foreign banks. The compound growth of the interest income/average working funds was 1.75 percent for the period of study. Whereas, the non-interest income/average working funds showed a negative growth of 1.13 percent. The operational expenses/operational income showed better

TABLE 20.6
Foreign Banks

(Percentages)

	Interest Income/ Average Working Funds	*Non-Interest Income/ Average Working Funds*	*Operational Expenses/ Operational Income*	*Cost of Deposits*	*Spread/ Average Working Funds*
Compound Growth Rate	1.75	-1.13	-0.17	1.11	0.91
Average	9.22	1.48	72.93	6.84	3.58
Standard Deviation	1.88	0.25	6.13	1.63	0.41
Coefficient of Variation	20.39	16.89	8.41	23.83	11.45

results. Its growth rate was also negative, i.e. 0.17 percent. The cost of deposits was high with growth rate of 1.11 percent. The spread/average working funds was 0.91 percent. It means that the foreign banks, unlike private sector banks were keeping their eye off the non-interest income. They also raised their funds at a higher cost, which adversely affected their operational productivity.

CONCLUSIONS

From the foregoing analysis, the following conclusions can be drawn :

- The compound growth rate of the interest income/average working funds in case of the foreign banks was much better as compared to the public sector banks and the private sector banks. The public sector banks showed better performance as compared to private sector banks. The averages of this ratio shows that the performance of foreign banks was better as compared to public sector banks and private sector banks. But here the public sector followed the private sector.
- The compound growth rate of the non-interest income/average working funds showed that the private sector banks were concentrating more on earning the non-interest income. On the other hand, the public sector banks and foreign banks were ignoring it. These banks should also try to concentrate on raising their non-interest income so that their operational productivity could improve. The growth rate of this ratio was positive for private sector banks and negative for both the public sector banks and foreign banks. On an average, the position of foreign banks was much better as compared to public sector banks and private sector banks. The private sector banks followed by foreign banks.
- The operational expenses/operational income of all the three sectors showed a negative growth, which is a good sign. This ratio indicates that the performance of private sector banks was the best; followed by the public sector banks and then the foreign banks. The average of this ratio indicates that the foreign banks had better performance followed by the private sector banks.
- The cost of deposits of all the three sectors showed a high positive growth. The growth rate of the cost of deposits was the highest for private sector banks and the lowest for the public sector banks. Hence, on this account the performance of public sector banks was best; followed by the private sector banks and the foreign banks respectively.
- On an average the ratio of the spread/average working funds of foreign banks was better as compared to public sector banks and private sector banks. The public sector banks followed the private sector banks. The compound growth rate of spread/average

working funds in case of the public sector banks and the foreign banks was positive. The private sector banks showed a negative growth rate.

- On an average, the overall operational productivity of foreign banks was better as compared to private sector banks and public sector banks. The private sector banks followed the public sector banks. The analysis of compound growth rates and the averages showed that the operational productivity of public sector banks is increasing at a higher rate as compared to private sector banks and foreign banks. The private sector banks followed the foreign banks. Thus, the first hypothesis (H_1) is accepted and the hypothesis number 2 (H_2) is rejected.

References

Data, Bank of Indian Commercial Banks, published by the Indian Banks' Association.

Various issues of Indian Economy, published by the Centre for Monitoring, Indian Economy.

Various issues of the Statistical Tables Relating to Banks in India, published by the Reserve Bank of India.

www.reservebankoflndia.org.in.

Insurance Sector in India in Post-Liberalisation Period : Challenges of Change

B.S. Bhatia and Swati Kumaria Puri

A thriving insurance sector is of vital importance to every modern economy. First, because it encourages the savings habit, second, because it provides a safety net to rural and urban enterprises and productive individuals and most importantly it generates long-term funds for infrastructure building. The nature of the insurance business is such that the cash inflow of insurance companies is constant while the payout is deferred and contingency-related. This characteristic of their business makes insurance companies the biggest investors in long-gestation infrastructure development projects in all developed and aspiring nations. This is the most compelling reason why domestic sector and foreign companies should spread the insurance habit in the society.

The insurance landscape in India is undergoing a major change. Closed to foreign competition since nationalization in 1956, the insurance industry had been protected from competitive pressures. Now with the passing of the Insurance Regulatory and Development Authority (IRDA) Act, 1999, the Indian Insurance sector is opened to private competition and several new players have entered the scene. The bill allows foreign equity stake in domestic private insurance companies to a maximum of 26 per cent of the total paid-up capital and seeks to provide statutory status to the insurance regulator. It provides for the establishment of an authority to protect the interests of the holders of insurance policies, to regulate, promote and ensure orderly growth of the insurance industry and amend the Insurance Act, 1938, the Life Insurance Act, 1956 and the General Insurance Business (Nationalization) Act, 1972.

This project undertakes the study of insurance industry in India and the new techniques and trends adopted by insurance players to face the global competition.

OBJECTIVES

This study broadly aims at examining the key issues in the insurance industry in India after liberalization. These issues present themselves as possible trends, opportunities and challenges for both existing and new companies. The specific objectives of the study are :

- To examine the structure of Indian Insurance Industry.
- To identify and analyse the inadequacy and weaknesses of Insurance Industry in India.
- To identify broad trends in Insurance Industry in India.
- To determine future prospects of industry.

Scope of the Study

- The study is based on the various insurance companies in India, which includes both public and private players in the insurance sector.
- The study includes analyse of companies offering both life insurance and general insurance.

Research Methodology

The study is based largely on secondary data, which has been collected from books, journals, magazines and various websites.

STRUCTURE OF INDIAN INSURANCE INDUSTRY

Since long, the two state-owned monoliths—*Life Insurance Corporation (LIC)* and *General Insurance Corporation (GIC)* have run the insurance industry in India. As a result of the policy of liberalization we have seen some structural changes in the industry in the past few years, after the new private players began offering their services. The biggest change has been the development of world-class regulatory framework for the proper development of the country. In a bid to make the industry more competitive and aggressive, an eight-member committee chaired by R.N. Malhotra was constituted in 1993. The committee took a year to submit its report. The main thrust of its recommendations were : open up the insurance sector, improve the service standards of Indian insurance players, and extend insurance coverage to a larger section of the Indian population. Floodgates of competition opened up by the privatization of insurance industry did throw a challenge to the well-protected nationalized sector and it seems that they have picked up the gauntlet. LIC and GIC, both are trying to reposition themselves by having re-engineering done on the structure and operations of their respective organizations.

Life Insurance

With privatization of Insurance sector in 2000, 12 new entrants have made their presence in about 40 cities across the country, represented by more than 5000 agents. Liberalisation has expectedly been followed by a plethora of launches, each event laying claim to some variant of the "new, improved" product. Ever since the nationalization of Life Insurance in 1956, Indian consumers have lived with a state owned monopolist as the sole provider of life insurance.

Life Insurance Corporation of India

One of the main companies in India providing Life Insurance is Life Insurance Corporation of India (LIC). LIC came into being in 1956 after amalgamation of 245 Indian and foreign insurance companies by an Act of Parliament. LIC was set-up with business mission of spreading life insurance, maximizing mobilization of people's savings, conducting business with the utmost economy and meeting various life insurance needs. It took off in 1956-57 with new business of just around Rs. 200 crore sum assured. In 2001-02, it issued 23.2 million policies for a total sum assured of Rs. 192,572.31 crore, generating a first-premium income of Rs. 14843.32 crore. Today, LIC is a multi-dimensional organization offering individual life insurance, group insurance, pension and gratuity schemes. It also operates in countries like Fiji, Mauritius, UK, Nepal, Bahrain and Sri Lanka.

It has computerized all 2,048 branches, of which 1,463 are connected by metropolitan area networks (MANs) and wide area networks (WANs). Today, LIC has more than 50 different products that address the need of each and every Indian from a newborn to a 70 year old. LIC did a commendable job of developing the life insurance market-penetration premiums to the GDP of 1.3%; LIC has achieved this by leveraging its phenomenal brand and its widespread distribution network. These efforts made it possible to offer protection to more than 100 million policy-holders, but even this is only 23% of the insurable population. This indicates the potential available for expansion of the insurance market and the fact tempted the private players to enter the market on the opening up of the sector.

The performance of *Private companies* has been a mixed bag. Potential private entrants therefore expect to score in the areas of customer service, speed and flexibility. They point out that their entry will mean better products and choice for the consumer. Critics counter that the benefit will be slim, because new players will concentrate on affluent, urban customers as foreign banks did until recently.

Some of the important private players are mentioned below :

ICICI Prudential with more than 12,500 policies in force, premium income in excess of Rs. 150 crore, and 16,000 agents enrolled, is a clear leader amongst the new entrants. Aggressive distribution, leveraging existing customer base and detailed implementation planning have helped the company in achieving its goal.

Next, *Max New York Life, HDFC Standard Life and Birla Sun Life* combines are all reportedly in the Rs. 50-60 crore premium ranges and in the second rung of new entrants. These companies are in the phase of building strong presence and are pushing sales aggressively through the distribution network.

The third rung of strong performers includes *TATA AIG, Kotal Old Mutual and Bajaj Allianz*, with premium incomes reportedly in the Rs. 30 crore range. These players are marginally behind their competitors in the second rung. The other ventures are currently establishing their presence and will take more time to make an impact on the industry landscape.

The private players have introduced 70 odd "new" products in all. A portfolio scan shows up two important things—Firstly, endowment and money-back products constitute almost half of the total and secondly, much of the actual business transacted has been through their assured return, single premium policies. In distribution, the trust of every new entrant has been on building up a sizeable agency force. Untapped potential in India in terms of life insurance is shown in the following table :

TABLE 21.1
Insurance Potential in India

Indian Population	1 bn.
GDP as on 2000 (Rs. bn.)	20,000
Gross domestic savings as a % of GDP	23%
NCAER estimate of insurable population	240 mn.
Estimated market by 2005 (Rs. mn.)	650

Source : Indiainfoline.com and NCAER.

General Insurance

The general insurance industry in India has currently about Rs. 12,000 crore of premium income, with a 5 year compounded annual growth rate in the 11% range. General Insurance Company, which ruled the general insurance sector before liberalization was not doing well and not considered profitable. However, now that new companies are making an entry, companies are likely to target lines of business that are profitable.

General Insurance Corporation commands the general insurance sector along with four of its fully owned subsidiaries viz.—New India Assurance

Company Limited; United Indian Insurance Company, Oriental Insurance Company Limited; and National Insurance Company Limited. Currently, these companies control 30%, 25%, 23% and 22% of the market, respectively. India, which accounts for around 8% of Asia's gross domestic product (GDP), contributes to only 2% of the region's non-life business (with a premium base of about Rs. 110 billion as in 2001-02), which in fact points to a large untapped business potential. But now with the opening up of insurance sector a variety of options have been opened to reach customers.

A comparison of the performance of the four non-life insurance companies in India is presented in the table below :

TABLE 21.2
Performance of Non-life Insurance Companies

	New India	*United*	*Oriental*	*National*
Rating for claims paying ability	IAAA	IAAA	IAAA	IAAA
Market share in terms of GDPI*	34%	23%	22%	21%
Claims Incurred Ratio	74%	87%	84%	82%
Net Underwriting expenses including claims incurred/ Net premium written	97.8%	113.4%	109.6%	107.7%
Operating Ratio	67.%	86.4%	84.4%	84.6%
Yield on Investments	13.8%	12.7%	13.5%	13.0%
PAT/Average Assets Deployed	8.4%	4.0%	4.9%	5.0%
PAT/Net Worth	24.0%	17.9%	21.2%	18.7%
Net Premium/Gross Premium	72.3%	71.5%	72.3%	77.2%
Premium Written/Adjusted** Net Worth	39%	65%	47%	48%
Technical Reserves/Adjusted** Liquid Assets	42%	66%	52%	49%
Premium Written per Employee (Rs. lakh)	11.28	9.13	8.25	8.15

* Gross Direct Premium Income.
** Adjusted figures include excess of market value over book value of investments.

With the relevant legislative changes enacted by the Parliament, the stage is now set for entry of new intermediaries in the business. The new regulations allow for the formation of both corporate agents and brokerages that will represent the customers in an insurance transaction and will be free to source the best product, service and price arrangement from any insurance company in India. In the smaller $ 2.5 billion general insurance business, there are several new players. According to a FICCI-Mckinsey report by 2007, these private companies will capture a 40-50% market share.

The general insurance industry in India has currently about Rs. 12,000 crore of premium income, with a 5 year compounded annual growth rate in the 11% range.

The general insurance business is broken into three different product lines—fire and allied perils (25%), marine (10%) and miscellaneous (65%). Commercial insurance business is far more developed than the market for general insurance products sold to individuals. The largest book of business among such lines is the motor insurance business. The new entrants are going straight to the car manufacturers and their dealers and tying up with them to try and lock-in customers along with the purchase of new vehicles. This approach is likely to become increasingly important in the mix of available distribution options. The new private companies are liaisoning with banks, credit card companies and other such groups with an aim of providing better customer service.

INADEQUACY OF INDIAN INSURANCE COMPANY

The insurance industry has been growing at 20%, but it lags far behind its global counterparts when it comes to insurance penetration. In India, Insurance awareness is low, term insurance plans are not promoted, unit-linked assurances are not available, insurance covers are expensive, returns from insurance products are low and there is a dearth of innovative and buyer-friendly insurance products. Some of the reasons for low penetration are, insurance products are not designed to suit the needs of the market, insurance companies are not responsive enough to insurance-buyers needs, the marketing network is weak, turnover of agents is very high, and training of agents is inadequate.

The following facts show how under-developed the Indian insurance business is due to state monopoly and lack of aggressive marketing of insurance policies. The low level of penetration of life insurance in India compared to other developed nations can be judged by a comparison of per capita life premium which is shown in the following table :

TABLE 21.3
Life Insurance Penetration in Selected Countries

Country	*Life Premium Per Capita US $ in 1994*
Japan	3,817
UK	1,280
USA	964
India	4

Source : Various Newspapers.

Thus, potential for growth is huge in the Indian insurance industry. The middle-income segment of the Indian population, is 312 million strong but LIC services less than 100 million policies. Only 65 million Indians have been introduced to insurance. All these figures work out to an average of 1.5 policies per person, which is a penetration of just six per cent. Insurance premia as a percentage of domestic savings is low in India which is an indicator of low insurance penetration. Currently, LIC and GIC collect just about 8.5 per cent of the domestic savings through selling insurance products. Researchers in the Pune-based National Insurance Academy have established that only 9 per cent of the livestock in India is insured and only 2 per cent of agricultural pumps are insured. Sadly, most general insurance transactions are generated by banks and financial institutions, which have a lien on assets of their borrowers. The above data shows that there is a lot of untapped potential in the Indian Insurance Industry.

Retail Segment or Personal Insurance, especially in general insurance is another unexplored area. Currently, personal insurance, including health, householders, shopkeepers, personal accident, travel insurance and professional indemnity covers, constitute only 12 per cent of Indian general insurance premium. This poor figure is largely due to lack of adequate distribution channels rather than lack of products. By tapping such under-served niches, new entrants can expand the market substantially. Since service and speed will be valued, a price premium is also possible. The story of *Motor Insurance* is no different. Only about 60 per cent of motor vehicles and only 46 per cent of two-wheelers are insured. All these are sure indicators of the untapped potential in the Indian insurance industry. *Health insurance* is another segment with great potential because existing Indian products are insufficient. By the end of 1998, GIC's MediClaim scheme covered only 2.5 per cent of total population. Indian products do not cover disability arising out of illness or disability for over 100 weeks due to accident. Neither do they cover a potential loss of earnings through disability. Studies have shown that in addition to increasing healthcare costs, the deterioration in performance of this business is because of a mix of healthcare provider—induced moral hazard and adverse risk selection.

While health insurance is an important issue for the government as well as IRDA, as long as irrational competition from the incumbent persists, private companies are likely to offer health insurance only to the extent required to complete mandatory requirements and that too by crafting products that are customer-oriented. GIC companies need to take a hard look at the features and pricing of MediClaim and reposition the product to make it profitable.

The *Huge Rural Segment* is another instance of untapped potential. Rural India's contribution is just about 54.7 per cent of total LIC policies and 47 per cent of LIC's total sum assured during 1998-99. Rural population constitutes 74.3 per cent of the country's population but the insurance companies still prefer the urban segment as the cost of procuring rural business is high.

Similar is the case with *Pensions*. The lack of a comprehensive social security system combined with a willingness to save means that Indian demand for pension products will be large. However, current penetration is very poor. By March 1998, LIC's pension premium was only $ 22 million. Making pension products into attractive saving instruments would require only simple innovations already common in other markets. For example, their returns might be tied to index-linked funds or a specific basket of equities. Buyers could be allowed to switch funds before the annuities begin and to invest different amounts at different times.

Insurance premia is also one of the factors that have caused the insurance potential to remain untapped. Premium rates are at present set most unscientifically with very little attempt to fine tune the risk attached to different categories of businesses. The result is that they penalize the low risk category, which is in majority. This can be seen in the failure to differentiate between smokers and non-smokers in fixing premium for life and personal accident covers or between flood-prone areas and dry lands for fire and allied perils cover. This results in a great deal of cross-subsidization. Low premium rates in one area necessitate higher premium elsewhere. Mortality tables are not revised for ages and no effort is made at all to re-evaluate the rating of other classes based on recent loss experiences. Indian insurance companies are too slow in revising their premia. Currently, LIC premia are determined by macro-inputs related to the years between 1991 and 1996. The last time LIC revised its premia, was after a gap of 12 years.

Same is the case for general insurance. There is no proper research on claims and thus premia are not scientifically determined. GIC is making profits in fire and marine insurance and incurring losses in motor insurance. This means there is cross-subsidization : GIC is charging lower premia for motor insurance and charging higher premia for fire and marine insurance. Motor insurance premia was revised upwards only during 1997, but the cross-subsidy still continues. However, there are signs to indicate that this is changing.

LIC has already taken the initiative by revising its premia downwards. LIC reduced premia for its without-profit plans between one and 33 per cent from May 1998. For endowment plans, premia reduction was between 22 per cent and 38 per cent. For whole life plans, premia reduction was between 23 per cent and 26 per cent.

Inefficient asset management and low investment yield are also responsible for the high premia charged by Indian insurance companies. On an average LIC could generate a yield of just 12.37 per cent on its investments during 1997-98. During 1998-99, the future was still lower at 11.96 per cent.

Investment restrictions have been responsible for low yields. LIC has to invest not less than 20 per cent of its life fund in central government securities, a minimum of 5 per cent in the National Housing Bank, not less than 25 per cent in state government securities including government—guaranteed marketable securities, and a minimum of 25 per cent in the social sector. The remaining 25 per cent can be invested in private sector and in loans to policy-holders.

GIC has its own restrictions on investments. It has to invest a minimum of 25 per cent in Central government securities, a minimum of 10 per cent in state government and PSU securities, a minimum of 35 per cent in loans to state governments, HUDCO and DDA, for housing projects and the remaining 30 per cent can be invested in equities, term loans and debentures.

No doubt, investment restrictions are there. But, LIC and GIC can enhance investment yields within the ambit of these restrictions by being more proactive in managing their investments. Insurance companies have not been able to satisfy the customer.

Poor Customer Service is also one of the reasons for lack of growth of the insurance sector. Most agents and development officers are interested only in procuring new business. Servicing existing customers satisfactorily has not been a priority for them as the incentives are based on new business generation and not on satisfactory servicing of existing customers. Moreover, LIC and GIC have no tied agents. Even existing agents are not buyer-friendly. They are always desperate to fulfil their quota of business and have little time to explain policy features to prospective customers. More than 10 per cent of LIC policies are surrendered or get lapsed every year. There is no market research worth the name and computerization is woefully inadequate.

The field staff and the agents of the GIC and its four wholly owned subsidiary companies have seldom bothered to venture out into the rural areas to sell any personal insurance. There is a *lack of penetration of the rural market* by life insurance and general insurance companies.

Other factors such as a very high concentration of insurable assets in few sectors and in large corporate entities, negligible penetration of retail commercial insurance, low insurance awareness, financing of assets through undeclared income, and poor experience with claims processing will also impede the pace of development of the insurance industry in general and alternate channels in particular.

FUTURE OF INSURANCE

All challenges listed above, can be viewed as opportunities. However, to convert opportunities into profits, new entrants in the insurance distribution need to make considered choices in selecting their customers, the portfolio of services they offer and the capabilities they need to acquire or build. The insurance market is likely to witness a change in the marketing mix, that is product, price, place and promotion. The IRDA, with its developmental and regulatory guidelines, is likely to promote competition, fairness, and reliability and at the same time, protect insurance against excessive, inadequate or discriminatory rates. The evolution of life insurance industry will happen in several fronts : products, distribution channels, technology, servicing processes and facilities. The focal point for this evolution will be customer.

The customer in India is increasingly becoming aware and is actively managing his/her financial affairs. People are looking not just at products but also at integrated financial solutions that can offer them stability of returns along with total protection. While the insurance sector is seeking to maintain a balance between acquiring customers and developing existing ones, customer acquisition is vital, as no retention strategy will entirely stem customer defection. The key to success therefore would be in providing insurance solutions, not insurance products. Service would focus on enhancing the customer experience and maximizing customer convenience.

Another key success factor would be finding the optimal mix of distribution channels. While insurance will continue to be sold through personal interaction, internet will be effectively used by companies for offering information and for doing comparison-shopping. Web sites will emerge which will provide this evaluation service comparing the products of different insurers. Evolution of independent brokers, providing insurance services, will also emerge. Substantial shift in the distribution of insurance in India is likely to take place. Many of these changes will follow international trends.

Corporate agents and Bancassurance can emerge as significant intermediaries. A sea change in the Indian financial services industry is imminent with banks and insurance companies increasingly realizing the strategic significance of Bancassurance in the future viability of their businesses. In the UK, almost 95% of banks and building societies are distributing insurance products today. In India too, banks hope to maximize expensive existing networks by selling a range of products. Various seminars and conferences on bancassurance are taking place and many bankers have clearly shown their inclination to enter insurance market by leveraging their strengths in the areas of brand image, distribution network, face to face contact with the clients and telemarketing coupled with advanced information technology systems. The mergers of Citibank with Travellers in USA and of Winterthur, the largest Swiss Co. with Credit Suisse are recent examples of the phenomenon likely to sweep India too.

Next thing to be taken into consideration is formulating a *marketing strategy*. Environmental factors such as macro-economic parameters, regulatory norms and themes, technology, infrastructure, legal set-up, competition and degree of globalization should be considered in framing the strategy.

Insurers will see a real opportunity for *sales in semi-urban and rural areas* and will design suitable for these markets. Since India has an agrarian economy, there are immense opportunities for the new entrants to provide for liabilities and risks associated in this sector like weather insurance, rainfall insurance, cyclone insurance, crop insurance, etc. Innovative products in line with rural needs and perception and an efficient delivery system are the two aspects that have to be developed in order to penetrate the rural markets.

Technology will play a crucial role in delivering the highest standard of services to both the end customer as well as the intermediary. Technology will also help in reducing the costs significantly and hence get reflected in the pricing of the products.

To develop the insurance market, *penetration in the small and medium establishments* is essential. Currently, this market is undeserved at all stages of the fulfilment cycle. Tapping into this potential will require an awareness campaign, creating targeted product development and distribution system that caters to the requirements of such customers.

There should be expansion of commercial insurance market related to *product emphasis*. An increasingly large part of economy is centered on knowledge and human assets, so more non-conventional products should be provided by the insurance companies. This is a gaping hole and the new entrants, with access to international product development expertise, are best positions to quickly fill this vacuum.

A new distribution system must be implemented. Companies should work with a multilayered distribution and support system that impedes quick decision-making. The industry should gradually move from traditional individual agents towards new distribution channels, with a paradigm shift in creating awareness and not just selling products. While tied agents will continue to play an important role in distribution, alternative channels like corporate agents, brokers, and bancassurance should be tapped.

Personal accident insurance is another area that can be developed into a sizeable sector. It provides cover, at a very reasonable cost, against a whole range of situations and is ideally suited for large cross-sections of the Indian society in the informal sector. The new entrants are focusing on tying up with banks, credit card companies and other such groups to access consumer directly. New entrants and GIC companies have to look at overall profitability and increase their market share.

Today, the focus is on designing and selling innovative products to existing customers to improve profitability. Customer-focused strategies require *CRM (Customer Relationship Management)* by insurance companies to help acquire customers through various touch points and translate operational data into actionable insights for proactively serving customers. While the CRM market in India is still nascent, bigger players such as ICICI Prudential Life Insurance Company are adopting it in a big way. The company was earlier using Gold Mines (a sales and marketing tool) and HEAT (an operational CRM solution) from Front Range Solutions. Players such as Birla Sun Life, Aviva, HDFC Life and Met Life are expected to adopt CRM tools as well in the near term.

Multinational insurers are indeed keenly interested in emerging insurance business because their home markets are saturated while emerging countries have low insurance penetrations and high growth rates.

International insurers often derive a significant part of their business from multinational. Several companies have entered into strategic alliances or are preparing to forge one like Allianz, Aegon, AIG, Allstate, AXA, CGU, Canada Life, Cigna, ING, Mitsui Marine, Munich Re, New York Life, Old Mutual, Prudential, Rothschild, Royal Sun Alliance, Standard Life, Sun Life, Tokio Marine, Witnerthur, Yasuda Fire and Marine and Zurich.

Insurance sector will be a dominant force in the financial sector over a 10-15 year horizons. Insurers have an enormous responsibility to support the reinstatement of a business ethic that shuns short cuts and unethical practices, and contributes to the development of a strong insurance industry in India.

RECOMMENDATIONS

Opening of the insurance market has helped the insurance companies to tap the various market segments profitably, while improving their product and service offerings. It has lead to drop in premia, improved service, deeper penetration of insurance and lower administrative overheads. In order to meet the growing competition and challenges, insurers in a liberalized Indian market will have to address a host of other issues. They will have to :

- Leverage information technology to service large number of customers efficiently and bring down overheads. Technology can complement or supplement distribution channels cost-effectively. It can also help improve customer service levels considerably.
- Use data warehousing and effective management to gauge the profitability and potential of various customer and product segments and ensure effective cross-selling. Companies should understand the customer better and design appropriate products, determine pricing correctly and increase profitability.
- Ensure high levels of training and development not just for staff but also for agents and distribution organizations. Existing companies will have to train staff for better service and flexibility, while all companies will have to train employees to cope up with new products and an intensive use of information technology.
- Build strong relationships with intermediaries such as agents. The agency force is an important customer interface and companies must partner with this group to reach customers and reach them effectively.
- Regulators will also have to play an important role in developing the Insurance sector. Currently, accounting norms do not allow insurance companies to defer any customer acquisition cost, which results in high up-front costs. The same should be altered as that insurance companies are able to search high solvency margins.

CONCLUSION

Competition in the insurance sector will surely cause the market to grow beyond current rats, create a bigger "pie", and offer additional options to the customer. Yet, at the same time, public and private sector companies will be working together to ensure healthy growth and development of the sector. Challenges such as developing a common industry code of conduct, contributing to a common catastrophe reserve fund, and chalking out agreements between insurers to settle claims to the benefit of the consumer will require concerted effort from both sectors. With the opening up of insurance sector new products, better packaging and improved service will be offered to the consumers. Both new and existing players will have to explore new distribution and marketing channels. Potential buyers for most of this insurance lie in the middle class. New insurers must segment the market carefully to arrive at appropriate products and pricing. Recognizing the potential, in the past three years, the nationalized insurers have already begun to target niches like pensions, women or children. Alliances related to distribution rather than to products or technology will prove most valuable in the long-run. Insurers both public as well as private have an enormous responsibility to support the reinstatement of a business ethic that shuns short cuts and unethical practices, and contributes to the development of a strong insurance industry in India.

REFERENCES

- *Business Today*, March 22, 2000.
- *Business Today*, November, 24, 2002.
- *Business Today*, December, 8, 2002.
- *Business Today*, December, 22, 2002.
- *Business Today*, June 8, 2003.
- *Business India*, April 14 to 27, 2003.
- *The Financial Express*, Think Tanks on Insurance.
- The Changing Face of Insurance : Madhu Suthanan (CII Library).
- "Make it a Policy", *Business Today*.
- "Insure for Life", *Business World*.
- *India's National Magazine*, Volume 19, Issue 01, Jan. 05-08, 2002.
- www.indiainfoline.com/bisc/insu/html.
- www.clickmymoney.com.
- www.hdfcinsurance.com.
- www.india_insurance.net.
- www.investmentmap.com/indianinsurance.html.
- www.idaindia.org.
- www.interlinkre.com/page1.html.
- www.licindia.com.
- www.sbilife.com.

Annexure I

CAR MANUFACTURERS : 2001 SALES

(Insurance Companies are rushing to partner with all major car manufacturers and their dealers)

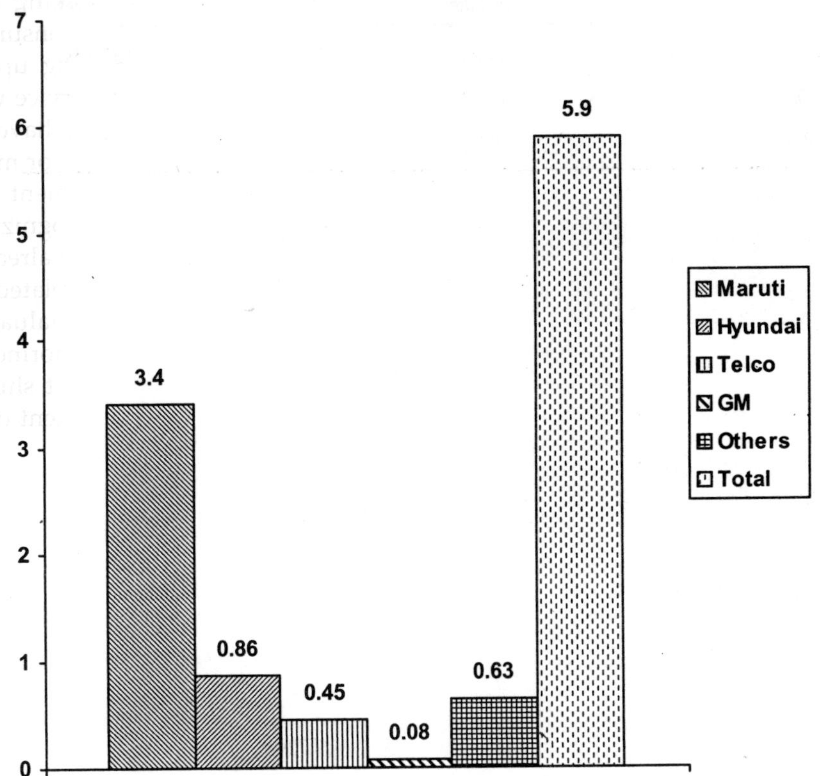

Note : Figures are number of units sold in lakh.
Source : GIC Financials, Monitor Estimates.

Annexure II (a)

CLAIMS SETTLED BY LIC DURING THE LAST THREE YEARS

Year	*Number (in lakh)*	*Amount (in crore)*
2000-01	75.86	11,637.98
2001-02	87.67	14,519.25
2002-03	95.34	16,952.34

Annexure II (b)

CLAIMS PERFORMANCE

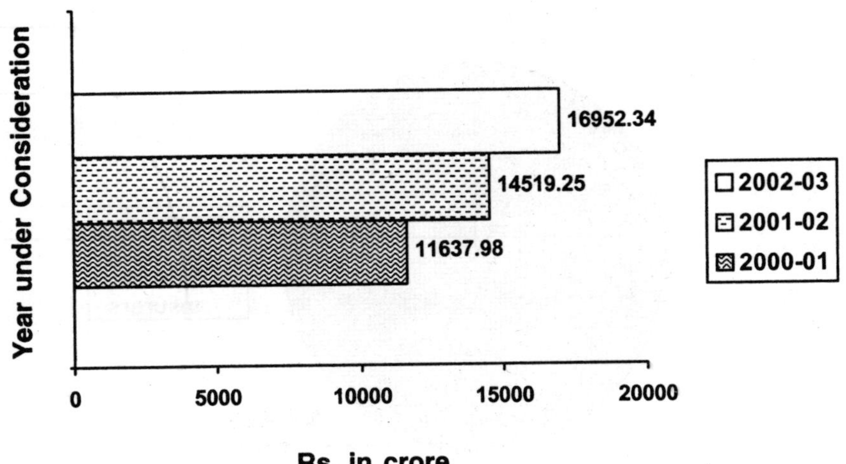

Annexure III

INDIVIDUAL NEW LIFE BUSINESS*

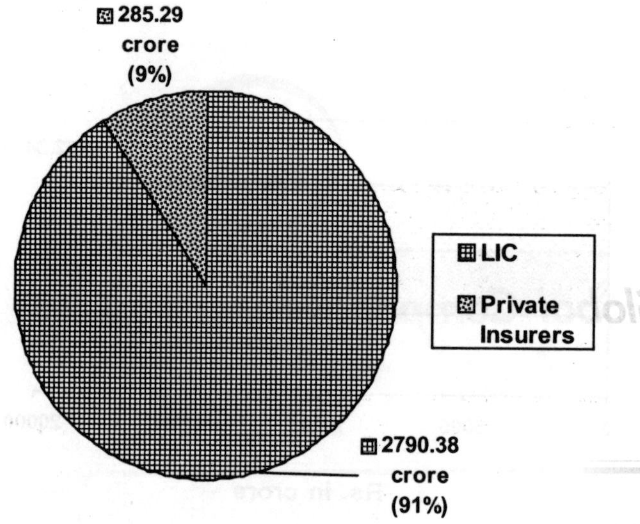

Note : Figures are for April to December 2002.
*Premium Income.
Source : *Business Today*, June 2003.

Global Competitiveness in Health Sector

SANTOSH GUPTA

Globalisation has made today's world market hyper competitive. With the advent of communication revolution and mass media information, the whole set of social aspirations are changing fast. There has also been gradual transference from the traditional morality-based concept to the development-based utilitarian theory of services.

The concept of patient satisfaction has encouraged the adoption of marketing culture in health service sector. The other factors that have necessitated a shift towards marketing approach are patient awareness, competition, purchasing power, etc. The strategy for patient satisfaction in healthcare service requires effective market plans, policies and the practices, to genuinely meet the needs of different strata of population (MacAlexander, 1993). This concept drew the attention of the service providers in advanced countries and became conscious of satisfying patients (Cooper, 1979, Kotler and Zaltman, 1970, Zaltman and Vertinsky, 1971 and Woodside, 1989).

In India, Government has spent vast amount of money on the infrastructure of hospitals, primary health centers and dispensaries, etc. but the quality of health care service has not improved and is still a neglected issue. Intensified competition, mushroom growth of private sector and global environment has added to patient's awareness. But cost factor, deteriorating ethics and attitude of doctors and paramedical staff has aggravated the problems. Because of the inherent presence of so many intangible features, it is very difficult to have a standardized and scientific measurement tool for services. Though quality service package is critical to the effectiveness of units, yet little research has been done.

In the present study, an attempt has been made to understand :

(a) Emerging issues in Health Service Sector.
(b) Objectives to be achieved.
(c) The Marketing Strategy.

EMERGING ISSUES

Some of the emerging issues in Health Service sector can be summarized as :

The Number Game

There is rapid growth of nursing homes and hospitals both in private and Government sector with tremendous variations in quality. With heightened awareness of quality issues, the consumer seeks ways to define and measure quality of medical services and accordingly make decisions about where to obtain the required expertise.

Competition

Under global environment there would be keen competition on value-oriented approach, therefore, the consumer is bound to ask for services in accordance with the money spent by him.

Ethics

Terms, which are gaining importance such as business ethics, medical ethics and legal ethics, are used to indicate the particular area of application. But to have a meaning, the ethics involved in each area, still refer to the value-oriented decision and behaviour of an individual. (Jones, Donald G).

Global Environment

The world is rapidly changing and this change is nowhere more evident than health consciousness.

Have and Have not

The expectations of consumers are rising, may they be rich or poor.

Attitude

Infrastructural facilities and qualification play an important role for good quality services but above all behaviour of Doctors and Medical Assistants is gaining momentum.

Quality of Administration

Administration, another dimension of health care service product is quite an effective component of health care service, especially in Indian situation where majority of staff from lower to upper level is not duty-conscious.

Infrastructure

This factor considers the physical environment of the health care unit. It plays a significant influence on the level of consumer satisfaction.

Evaluation of Health Services

Health services cannot survive and grow without a marketing friendly way. For better services there is need to revise programmes to meet the varying needs of different segments of the society. Flexibility is the key mantra (Rao, 1998).

OBJECTIVES TO BE ACHIEVED

In the light of above-mentioned emerging issues, an attempt has been made to develop the marketing strategy for globalising health services. The major reasons that have necessitated a shift towards marketing approach are intensive competition, patient awareness, increase in purchasing power of patients and availability of specialists (Yadav, 1993). The prime objectives based on primary and secondary sources are :

(i) Patient Satisfaction

The progress of service unit depends on the patient satisfaction and service quality in all developing and developed countries (Cronin and Taylor, 1992). This has been eloquently identified by a number of authors like Brown and Swartz (1989) and Parasuraman (1991).

(ii) Develoing Inter-Personal Skills

Many studies have considered staff behaviour as a common variable for different medical personnel (Mowen, 1993). Survey was also done in some socio-demographic groups on likert scale (1-5) (Table 22.1). It is evident that behvaiour of doctors and medical assistants is more important than other factors like Administration and Infrastructure.

TABLE 22.1
Variably in Demographic Groups

Variables	*Sex*		*Occupation*			*Mean*
	M	*F*	*B*	*S*	*D*	
1. Behaviour of Doctors	3.6	4.1	3.3	3.9	3.7	3.72
2. Behaviour of Medical Assistants	3.3	3.5	3.5	3.2	4.5	3.60
3. Administration	2.6	3.2	2.9	2.7	3.4	2.96
4. Infrastructure	3.2	2.8	3.1	3.1	3.1	2.44

B=> Business class.
S=> Service class.
D=> Dependents.

(iii) Corroborating the Customer's Perception and Selection of Unit

Respondents were asked to evaluate the criteria used to choose a particular health care unit. The attitudes used were efficiency, location, word of mouth, past experience, sanitation, time factor, etc. It was found that they gave first preference to efficiency of doctors and last to sanitation (Table 22.2).

TABLE 22.2
Selection Criteria of the Unit

Sl. No.	*Attributes*	*Ranks*
1.	Efficiency of Staff	1
2.	Past Experience	2
3.	Word of Mouth	3
4.	Infrastructure	4
5.	Time Factor	5
6.	Location	6
7.	Sanitation	7

(iv) Enhancing and Maintaining Quality of Health Service Packages

Quality of health service packages was studied under three heads : (a) Doctors and Medical Assistance; (b) Administration; and (c) Infrastructure.

Among doctors and medical assistants, competency and credibility of the doctor was rated higher than other factors like responsiveness and individual consideration. Under Administration, easy access was ranked first and high fee was ranked last, showing that patients don't mind paying for convenient and prompt services. Under infrastructure, well-equipped unit was the main criteria and parking space the last. It clearly shows that well equipped units and patient and attendant comforts are more important than parking space. (Table 22.3).

TABLE 22.3
Criteria for Health Service Delivery Package

Doctor & Other Staff	*Rank*	*Administration*	*Rank*	*Infrastructure*	*Rank*
Competence	1	Easy Access	1	Well-equipped Unit	1
Credibility	2	Reliability	2	Physical Facilities	2
Understanding	3	Communication	3	Staff Appearance	3
Courtesy	4	Suggestion & Grievance handling	4	Electricity & Water	4
Responsiveness	5	Security	5	Cleanliness	5
Individual considerations	6	Fee Structure	6	Building Appearance	6
—		—		Parking Space	7

(v) Curriculum

To acquire and retain professionals with requisite skills, attitudes and competence the curriculum of medical education needs to be revised in the changing socio-cultural economic scenario. Purpose is not to produce professionals only, but also a committed work force with knowledge.

The present curriculum lacks vigour to take up challenges of globalisation. Thus, a distinct design and content of the medical education programme is imperative, so that the basic awareness of demands and opportunities of global market can permeate.

(vi) Meeting Global Competition

Because of certain forces like technological, economic, social, political and cultural (Lakshmi, 1989), the present decade is witnessing phenomenal changes all over the world, establishing clearly that no nation can isolate itself completely from the rest of world and survive long (Rajan and Dhuna, 1998). Opinion of people was also surveyed. It can be concluded that there is need for making medical services more meaningful, vibrant and responsive to the changing needs, keeping economy of the country and global demands in mind.

THE MARKETING STRATEGY

Globalization has put forth a number of challenges. The strategy should be such that the institutes could deal effectively with different forces, like supplier power, buyer power, threat of substitutes and new entrants (Porter, 1994). In this context the marketing strategy is developed to help the health services in meeting the needs and requirements of the consumer. This includes analysis in detail :

1. Curriculum and contents of medical education and training process.
2. Consumer and health services imparting process.
3. Unit and their service quality delivery package.
4. Global environmental forces.
5. Gap analysis.

(i) Curriculum and Contents of Medical Education and Training Process

Though quality of professionals is critical to the effectiveness of any type of organisation, little research has directly examined the features of medical education from marketing point of view.

In order to achieve the objective of producing competent professionals with commitment and dedication, the following process can be adopted :

(i) To include in curriculum, medical ethics.
(ii) Greater emphasis on preventive measures.

(iii) To include in curriculum global contents.
(iv) Courses on analytical skills, stress management, value system, etc.
(v) To study relation between economy of the country and medical services.

(ii) Consumer and Health Services Imparting Process

Consumers epitomize an important step in the marketing strategy formulation in the model. In order to compete with global medical facilities, the local or national units must identify their target markets, recognize target market's needs and ferret out the criteria used by consumers in making choices.

To achieve the objectives of identification of the criteria used for differentiating the competing offers and in creating perceived differences between their offer and the competitor's offer, the process involves the inclusion of following issues :

Health facilities imparting process comprises of three phases : pre-encounter, encounter and post-encounter.
First phase is pre-encounter as customer's expectations begin to form before they encounter the providers. Expectations so formed are a function of information from advertisement, reputation and advice from relatives, friends (Parsuraman, Zeithamal and Berry, 1985).
The encounter, a period of time during which patients and doctors directly interact, offering personnel, physical and intangible services (Bitner, 1986).
In the post-encounter phase, patients evaluate comparisons of their expectations about total service package with their own experiences.

Therefore, it is important to understand and fulfil patient expectations of which services should be offered at different phases.

(iii) Units and their Service Quality Delivery Packages

The service package product is a unique combination of tangible and intangible benefits, salutary and productive for meeting the customer's individual needs. Therefore, to equip the professionals (both doctors and medical assistants) with vital skills, knowledge and competence to face existing situation and future challenges, the marketing strategy approach to be followed should suggest that the service quality packages should be fashioned in response to customer benefit concept. This can be achieved by designing and redesigning the service packages according to the demand of patients. It comprises three inter-related service benefit levels, namely, Crux Promote and Corroborate.

Cruxing Service Product

It is the nucleus of the total service package product, which provides Fundamental benefits to the consumer. Professional expertise and the accumulated experience represents the core resources needed for supplying crux benefits to the consumers (Kaushik, 1993). For this, it is suggested :

— Doctors and other supportive staff should be proficient enough to impart best service.
— Bilateral and multilateral exchange programmes of doctors and other staff will help in promoting awareness of global context.
— Sophisticated teaching techniques should be used, e.g. simulation for observing behaviour, brain storming for creative thinking, case study for analytical, problem-solving and decision-making skills, interaction and discussion for forming and molding attitudes and lecturing for knowledge in capsule form.
— Providing unique service advantage treatment to the patient.
— Adopting patient-oriented policies and procedures.

Promoting

The degree of service differentiation among different units depends on the type and quality of promoting services. For this it is necessary for the unit to provide internationalized promoting services, keeping the economy of country in mind and advertising in that fashion also.

Corroborating Services

The services, auxiliary to crux services are used for enhancing the value of core products, unlike promoting services which are used for facilitating the core services. For this, it is suggested that :

— Units must try to affiliate themselves with other reputed National/International units.
— Physical appearance, e.g. size, location cleanliness, parking space, brochure, etc. should be able to attract more customers.
— Financial consideration is an important factor, so it is important for the providers to explain to their patients the rationale behind the fee charged from them.

(iv) Global Environmental Forces

In order to develop awareness, attempts have to be made to impart knowledge for understanding cross-cultural, cross-technological and cross-social factors.

For this the following attempts should be made :

Explaining the reasons for providing/not providing facilities at par with international standards.

— A continuous evaluation system by introducing 360 Degree appraisal system.

— Injecting Global Environmental forces in their teaching and training programmes.

(v) Gap Analysis

The prominent conceptual model of service quality that has emerged in marketing literature is the gap analysis model proposed by Parsuraman, Zeithamal and Berry (1985). The service quality gap model is considered as a function of comparison between expectations and performance perception at the above mentioned levels. Therefore, delivery variable and output variables are important for measuring consumer expectations and performance. Effective outcome could moderate individual perceptions of service quality (Churchill & Supernant, 1982). Disappointing outcome could moderate an individual's perception of service quality even if the consumer evaluates the promoting and corroborating benefits above expectation. This can however be avoided by :

— Continuous evaluation and research to find out the reasons for gap and to take measures immediately. These may involve organizing seminars, symposia, group discussions and case studies for finding innovative ways for developing medical-facilities as per economy of the country.
— Exchange programmes to be introduced at National/International levels.

Lastly, it can be said that India is not an undeveloped but an under-managed country.

In such an economy attempts should be made in consonance with the Government to wipe out this service gap. There is also a need for an additional shift from the old approach of control and vigilance to the new paradigms of involvement and participation. This argument rests heavily on the philosophy of HRD, which nurtures a positive view of people and places emphasis on their wholesome development.

References

Bitner, Mary Jo (1986), 'Evaluating Service Encounters : The Effects of Physical Surroundings and Employee Responses,' *Journal of Marketing*.

Brown and Swartz (1989), A Gap Analysis of Professional Service Quality', *Journal of Marketing*.

Churchill (1982), 'An Investigation into Determinants of Customer's Satisfaction', *Journal of Marketing Research*.

Cooper, Phillip D., Richard, Maxilla and William (1979), 'Entry Strategies for Marketing in Ambulatory and other Health Delivery System in Phillip D. Cooper, 'Health Care Marketing, Issues and Trends', New York.

Jones, Donald G.A., 1977, 'Bibliography of Business Ethics,' *Virginia* (1977).

Kaushik, Madhulika (1993), *Marketing of Educational Services*' (ed.), 'Marketing of Services Concept and Applications,' IGNOU, N. Delhi.

Kotler & Zaltman (1970), 'Social Marketing—An Approach to Planned Social Change', *Journal of Marketing.*

Lakshmi, S. (1989), 'Innovations in Education', Sterling Pub., New Delhi.

Mac Alexander, 'Positioning Health Care Services', *Journal of Health Care Marketing.*

Mahajan, Vijay (2002), 'A Programme on Strategic Marketing Issues'.

Mowen, J. (1993), 'Waiting in the Emergency Room : How to improve Patient Satisfaction?' *Journal of Health Care Marketing.*

Parasuraman, A., Zeitham : V.A., Berry Leonard, (1985), "A Conceptual Model of Service Quality and its Implications for Future Research", *Journal of Marketing.*

Parasuraman, A, (1991), 'Refinement and Reassessment of the SERVQUAL Scale', *Journal of Retailing.*

Porter, M.E. (1994), 'Harvard Business School Press', Boston.

Rajan and Dhuna (1998), 'Globalisation and Management Education', *University News.*

Rao, Y.S.P. (1998), 'Re-engineering Management Education,' *University News,* India.

Sharma, R.D. (1999), A study of Patient Satisfaction in Outdoor Services of Private Health Care Facilities', *Vikalpa,* IIM, Ahmedabad, India.

Woodside (1989), 'Linking Service Quality, Patient Satisfaction and Behavioural Intention', *Journal of Health Care Marketing.*

Yadav, K. (1993), 'Health Services : The Indian Scene Marketing of Services—Concept and Applications', Indira Gandhi National Open University.

Zaltman & Vertinsky (1971), 'Health Service Marketing—A Suggested Model', *Journal of Marketing.*

Competitiveness of Public Sector Banks in India (Post-Liberalisation Scenario)

GAGANJEET KAUR

THE GENESIS

Public sector in Indian banking reached its present position in three stages—first, the conversion of the then existing Imperial Bank of India into the State Bank of India in 1955 followed by the establishment of its seven subsidiary banks; second, the Nationalization of 14 major Commercial Banks on July 1969 and last, the Nationalization of 6 more Commercial Banks on April 15, 1980. New Bank of India was later on merged with Punjab National Bank. Thus 27 banks constitute Public sector in Indian commercial banking. As at end March 2002, there were 296 Commercial banks operating in India. This included 27 Public sector banks, 31 Private banks, 42 Foreign banks and 196 Regional Rural banks. Also there were 67 Scheduled Co-operative banks consisting of 51 Scheduled Urban Co-operative banks and 16 Scheduled State Co-operative banks.

The Narasimham Committee on Financial Sector Reforms (1991) recommended the establishment of new banks in the private sector aimed at creating a more diversified profitable and efficient Banking system. Until 1991-92 all Public sector banks were fully owned by the government. After the reform process was initiated, these banks were allowed to access the capital markets to raise up to 49% of their equity. Till 2000-01 as many as 12 Public sector banks accessed the capital market and raised an amount aggregating Rs. 64 billion. The management of the Nationalized banks is under the purview of the Ministry of Finance, which has its representatives on the Board of Directors. The management of SBI is under the Reserve Bank of India, which has its representatives on its Board of Directors.

The objectives behind the setting up of the Public sector banks were manifold :

- Profit maximization and adding shareholder value,
- Allocation of credit to neglected sectors of the economy,
- Equitable economic growth, and
- Financial stability.

The financial crisis in Southeast Asia and Japan has brought to the fore the problems that weak and fragile domestic financial sector can pose for the economy. Every bank has to respect the forces of change sweeping across the financial sector and the answer is to tone up the banking sector by strengthening its capital base and asset portfolio.

OBJECTIVES OF THE STUDY

- To find out the challenges being faced by Public sector banks as a result of entry of Private and Foreign banks;
- To analyze the performance indicators of Public sector banks *vis-a-vis* Private and Foreign banks; and
- To suggest strategies for enhancing productivity in Public sector banks.

The fast pace of changes since the financial sector reforms initiated in 1991 have radically transformed the operational environment of the Banking sector in India. In their bid to be at par with the International norms, Indian Banking sector has seen the emergence of new Private sector banks along with foreign banks equipped with latest technology. This has lead to increase in competition and reduction in cost in the Indian Banking sector and thus emphasis on competitiveness, productivity and efficiency has gained momentum.

Entry of Private sectors and Foreign banks has lead to increased competitiveness in the form of :

- Better quality Banking services,
- Diversified and innovative products,
- Better Risk management techniques,
- Better regulation and supervision,
- Better Asset-Liability Management,
- Increased competition in domestic market,
- Better Accounting and Disclosure standards,

- Optimum use of state of the art Information Technology, and
- Focus on Customer Relationship Management by a team of highly experienced and motivated personnel.

On the contrary, these banks are destabilizing the economy by indulging in "Cherry Picking", i.e. less finance is available to the more disadvantaged segment. Most of the branches are located in urban and semi-urban areas whereas 70% of the Indian population lives in villages, so there is inequitable lending to different sectors of the economy but in urban areas these banks are playing a pivotal role and becoming dominant with their innovative products, i.e., phone banking, mobile banking, internet banking, any time banking, anywhere banking, use of smart cards, Electronic Fund transfer at the point of sale, ATM's, etc.

CHALLENGES FOR PUBLIC SECTOR BANKS—POST-LIBERALISATION SCENARIO

The major challenges for public sector banks are to protect the falling margins due to the impact of competition. Public sector have to meet the capital adequacy norms stipulated by the Basle Accord. Higher non-performing assets are the major cause of concern which arise mainly because of inability in the existing process of debt recovery, inadequate legal provision on bankruptcy and difficulty in the speedy execution of court decrees. There is spread of unhealthy trade unionism among the rank and file of Banking industry as well as lack of accountability. Highly unionized staff is also a contributing factor toward the low productivity of Public sector banks. Another major cause of concern is that Private sector banks have flatter hierarchical structure leading to faster decision-making in contrast to Public sector banks where there is over-staffing in all the branches. The infrastructure of Private sector is posing a major challenge to Public sector banks.

Private sector banks are marching in all spheres—New products, better technology, improved customer service, timeliness, promptness in providing services and better communication. The most important question to be answered is whether there is a better way of enabling Public sector banks to improve their performance while promoting Private banks compared to transfer of ownership and control from Public to Private sector banks? In India, mergers especially of the Public sector banks may be confronted with technology and trade union problems. Strong trade unions may prove to be significant obstacle for Public sector bank merger.

ANALYSIS OF PERFORMANCE INDICATORS OF PUBLIC, PRIVATE AND FOREIGN BANKS

The performance of public sector banks has become more responsive to changes in the market place with growing emphasis on profitability as an indicator of performance as opposed to non-commercial consideration in the pre-reform era. There was a distinct improvement in the net profit of the Public Sector Banks (from Rs. 4.6 billions in 1992-93 to Rs. 43.2 billion in 2000-01). The gross NPA's of Public sector banks as on March end 2001 was Rs. 54,773 crores as against Rs. 53,033 crores as on March end 2001 but the share of Public sector banks in total NPA's of SCB's declined to 85.7% from 87.8% during this period. Foreign banks operating in India have managed to increase their share of total net profit of the Banking industry from 13.3% to 14.7% during the year ended March 2001 but Foreign banks with one and two branch operations in India are expected to shut-down following the RBI guideline for capital adequacy norms for these banks. The following table shows a general comparison of three main classes of banks.

Parameters	*Public Sector Banks*	*Private Banks (Old)*	*Private Banks (New)*
Cost of Funds	Low	Moderate	High
Branch Network	Wide Spread	Regional	Low
Levels of Automation	Low	Moderate	High
NPAs	High	Low	Low
Capital Adequacy	Moderate	Low	High
Employ Productivity	Low	Moderate	High
Focus on Non-Interest Income	Low	High	High

Best Performers among Public Sector Banks during 1999-00

1. Highest rate of deposit growth	Andhra Bank
2. Highest rate of credit growth	State Bank of Indore
3. Highest growth of net profit	State Bank of Saurashtra
4. Highest growth in net profit	Syndicate Bank
5. Highest CAR	State Bank of Saurashtra
6. Highest return on assets	Corporation Bank
7. Highest percentage of interest income to working funds	Andhra Bank
8. Business per employee (Rs. Lakh)	Oriental Bank of Commerce
9. Highest staff productivity	Corporation Bank

Source : Bankers India.

The new Private sector banks continued to out perform the industry in several parameters such as asset growth ratio, operating profit growth and cost of intermediation. According to the RBI report on "Trend and progress in banking, the new Private sector banks recorded 52.8% of growth in assets—Old Private sector banks have grown by 18.7%, SBI by 17.7%, Nationalised banks by 14.5% and Foreign banks by 8.2% in 1999-00. In operating profits the new Private sector banks have recorded the highest growth rate of 81% whereas in Foreign banks it was 80.4% and Public sector banks with 23.7% during 1999-00. In intermediation cost (operating expense as a proportion of total assets) one of the main indicators of competitiveness, Private sector banks recorded the lowest with 1.42% while public sector banks had 2.52%.

On account of their high competitiveness, the new Private sector banks were in a position to operate at the lowest margin in the industry. Despite Public sector banks showing a marked improvement in the non-performing assets, new Private banks continue to be better. During 1999-00, the number of Public sector banks with net NPA up to 10% increased from 18 to 22. New Private banks have net NPA below 10%. The rate of gross NPA's to gross advances of Public sector banks declined from 15.9% in 1998-99 to 14% in 1999-00.

STRATEGIES TO BE ADOPTED BY PUBLIC SECTOR BANKS FOR ENHANCING PRODUCTIVITY

Rigorous Restructuring (operational, organizational and financial) is required in all Public sector banks and for this the foremost requirement is adequate infusion of funds. Public sector banks will have to sharpen the adaptive responses to competitive forces and thereby renew and reinvent the bank by changing procedures and processes. The need of the hour is consolidation and strengthening of these banks. Proper technological infrastructure is required in order to compete with new generation banks. Technology driven customer friendly products and services across different market segments will serve the purpose of strengthening the position of Public sector banks. There is over-staffing in almost all the Public sector banks so down sizing manpower will be a stringent measure to enhance productivity.

Non-performing assets contribute towards low productivity of these banks, so better recovery of NPA is required. The government has come to the rescue of the banking sector and recapitalization of the banks is the answer. Securitisation will require an overhauling of entire banking structure backed by a strong legal and regulatory framework. There has to be attitudinal change in the mindset of bankers. An element of timeliness, which reflects vital characteristics of corporate culture is lacking in Public sector banks, which needs to be revitalized. The employees should treat customers as customers of the bank and not customers of the branch.

Government and RBI have to decide to entrust the responsibility of governance in the hands of personnel who have the credentials and capability to provide leadership with a common vision and commitment and to evolve and enforce the discipline of new strategies. Government's role should be to act as a facilitator. Product diversification is required to compete with other banks and serve the needs of customers more effectively and efficiently than the competitors. Use of cards for financial transaction is recommended. The cost of servicing a transaction conducted through an

ATM or through an electronic mode such as Internet is less than a physical service to a customer from the counter of the bank.

There has to be effective cash management so that funds are available to the customer at the place of its deployment and for this centralization of the accounts of bank is necessary. The answer lies in standardization of hardware and operating system and application software to facilitate inter-connectivity of system across branches and an effective security policy to ensure confidentiality and integrity of transaction. The mechanism of Business Process Re-engineering (BPR) will help in strengthening Public sector banks and enhancing productivity and thereby efficiency of operations.

The following areas require focus for increasing competitiveness in Public sector banks :

- Better Asset liability management,
- Product differentiation,
- Strengthening of the capital base,
- Better credit assessment,
- Focus on retail banking,
- Building up MIS for decision-making,
- Improved appraisal criteria, and
- Multiple channels for delivery of the products.

By changing methods of marketing, advertising, designing, pricing and distributing financial products and services, Public sector banks can go a long way in serving the interest of the customers and for this aggressive and challenging work culture has to be provided. The Voluntary Retirement Scheme or the "Golden Hand Shake" that was introduced has reduced overheads by increasing profit per employee ratio and has enhanced productivity and now these banks have inducted fresh talent. Corporate governance system is of critical importance for stable, robust efficient and healthy banking system to be prudent in the pursuit of excellence. For weak banks, mergers may prove to be an effective remedial measure in a competitive environment. It is a means to consolidate the banks thereby paving the way for universal banking. Nevertheless with enhanced competition and deregulation of interest rates (for advances and deposits) the competition within Public sector banks has increased sharply. The government has already initiated the process for enabling the Nationalized banks to raise further capital through public issue and thereby allow reduction in government share holding up to 33%. Nationalized banks have been given autonomy (based on specified criteria) on creation, abolition, upgradation of post for their administrative offices up to the level of Deputy General Manager, recruitment of specialized officers, eligibility and entitlement for reimbursement of certain type of expenses. A system of half yearly review has been initiated with a view to get timely feedback about the financial position of the Public sector banks and take remedial measures for enhancing productivity.

CONCLUSION

Public sector have been exposed to increasing competitive environment through entry of Private banks, relaxation on the entry of foreign banks (the number of licenses granted are 12 per year), near total deregulation of interest rate structure and increased functional autonomy and operational flexibility in large number of areas for public sector banks. Banks are trying to cope with the competition by offering innovative and technology-based services to their customers. 7827 branches of Public sector banks were identified for computerization by March 2000 and 4620 had been computerized by March 1999.

PSB's are in the process of making huge investments in technology. The forces of competition are compelling banks to optimize resources used to attain pure technical efficiency and choose the optimal firm size including the quantity of various inputs and outputs so as to reap the maximum economies of scale.

References

Varshney, P.N., "Banking Law and Practice", Sultan Chand & Sons, New Delhi, 2001.

Anonymous, "Dominant Role of Private Sector in Banking", *Monthly Commentary on Indian Economic Condition*, January, 2001, pp. 12-23.

Kamesam, Vespa, "Indian Banking of Tomorrow," *Reserve Bank of India Bulletin*, February, 2002, pp. 123-26.

Ram Mohan, T.T., "Deregulation and Performance of Public Sector Banks", *Economic and Political Weekly*, February 2, 2002, pp. 393-408.

Rajaraman, Indira and Vashishtha Garima, "Non-Performing Loans of PSU Banks, *Economic and Political Weekly*, February 2, 2002, pp. 429-36.

Verma, Prashant, "The Sector to Watch," A & M, February 28, 2002, pp. 34-35.

Mathur, K.B.L., "Public Sector Banks in India – Should they be Privatized?", *Economic and Political Weekly*, June 8, 2002.

Ghosh, D.N., "Weak Banks : A Strategy for Self-Renewal," *Economic and Political Weekly*, January, 29, 2000, pp. 243-45.

Das, Abhiman, "Risk and Productivity Change of Public Sector Banks," *Economic and Political Weekly*, February 2, 2002, pp. 437-47.

Jalan, Bimal, "Indian Banking and Finance—Managing New Challenges," *Reserve Bank of India Bulletin*, February 2002, pp. 71-86.

www.bankersindia.com

www.shilpabichitra.com

www.actmindindia.org

TABLE 23.1
Profitability of Foreign Banks

(in percent)

Bank	*Return on assets*		*Return on equity*		*Non-Interest income to gross income*		*Staff expenses to operating expenses*		*Net profit margin*		*Net profit to deposists*		*Net profit to spread*	
	1998-99	*1999-2000*	*1998-99*	*1999-2000*	*1998-99*	*1999-2000*	*1998-99*	*1999-2000*	*1998-99*	*1999-2000*	*1998-99*	*1999-2000*	*1998-99*	*1999-2000*
(1)	*(2)*	*(3)*	*(4)*	*(5)*	*(6)*	*(7)*	*(8)*	*(9)*	*(10)*	*(11)*	*(12)*	*(13)*	*(14)*	*(15)*
ABN Amro	2.59	2.07	29.47	25.81	21.03	17.15	30.60	24.99	18.82	16.27	4.65	3.47	66.71	49.13
Abu Dhabi Commercial	0.37	0.52	8.48	11.84	14.59	12.09	39.52	38.61	3.16	4.18	0.44	0.59	16.51	24.92
Amex	0.25	0.92	2.36	10.97	25.11	31.94	38.45	41.34	1.77	6.22	0.47	1.95	8.99	26.00
Arab Bangladesh Bank	3.16	3.05	4.95	5.20	27.70	24.37	33.43	37.14	33.45	29.28	8.83	6.90	57.41	48.00
BNP	1.13	0.97	12.61	11.13	16.66	16.49	43.35	45.61	9.99	8.20	2.44	2.03	39.52	34.90
Bank Inter Indonesia	NEG	NEG	NEG	NEG	19.52	20.22	10.10	6.82	NEG	NEG	NEG	NEG	NEG	NEG
Bank Muscat Inti SAOG	NEG	0.65	NEG	1.81	12.57	17.97	26.73	32.04	NEG	6.34	NEG	0.66	NEG	21.35
Bank of America	2.04	2.36	23.23	23.05	10.48	23.63	31.38	50.84	14.07	17.53	4.12	6.08	45.04	58.10
Bank of Bahrain & Kuwait	0.76	0.97	10.43	11.01	11.77	16.04	29.18	36.19	6.12	7.43	1.20	1.37	64.13	57.92
Bank of Ceylon	2.33	3.01	6.27	8.83	20.85	25.23	23.36	23.41	16.45	22.79	6.87	8.19	35.61	52.60
Bank of Nova Scotia	2.32	1.68	23.82	15.67	19.46	19.35	27.05	30.75	15.56	14.55	3.49	2.74	68.01	5613
Bank of Tokyo-Mitsubishi	NEG	4.06	NEG	32.88	19.68	29.84	3.87	11.70	NEG	26.37	NEG	6.79	NEG	77.5
Barclays Bank	0.38	NEG	2.78	NEG	14.25	6.35	40.14	40.30	2.30	NEG	0.85	NEG	9.10	NEG
Chase Manhattan Bank	1.86	4.28	5.56	20.55	65.37	67.07	20.17	26.48	7.59	18.26	34.90	222.78	NA	371.79
Cho Hung Bank	4.68	0.51	13.05	1.87	20.38	16.92	23.67	29.27	33.27	4.68	5.81	0.81	51.19	6.30
City Bank	0.99	1.86	12.60	26.87	28.02	20.66	22.40	21.19	6.28	13.39	1.24	2.46	26.69	39.07

(Contd.)

TABLE 23.1 (Contd.)

(1)	(2)	(3)	(4)	(5)	(6)	(7)	(8)	(9)	(10)	(11)	(12)	(13)	(14)	(15)
Commerz Bank	0.29	0.45	1.82	2.87	20.71	12.66	39.26	42.66	2.34	3.50	0.51	1.54	8.81	15.10
Credit Agricole Indosuez	NEG	NEG	NEG	NEG	6.17	5.81	36.63	41.50	NEG	NEG	NEG	NEG	NEG	NEG
Credit Lyonnais	1.71	1.68	24.89	21.21	16.89	16.70	53.64	45.24	10.45	9.99	2.04	1.90	47.94	45.04
Deutsche Bank	1.28	1.12	9.51	9.89	23.41	28.70	29.97	31.75	8.78	7.74	2.33	2.36	22.59	21.97
Devp. Bank of Singapore	1.57	1.71	5.22	7.94	1478	14.25	34.41	35.35	9.57	14.76	2.60	8.68	43.68	43.17
Dresdner Bank	NEG	NEG	NEG	NEG	19.44	10.93	27.10	28.39	NEG	NEG	NEG	NEG	NEG	NEG
Fuji Bank	0.18	NEG	0.53	NEG	5.69	7.36	48.13	31.75	1.39	NEG	0.31	NEG	3.33	NEG
Hongkong Bank	0.65	1.11	6.61	15.02	20.00	20.45	37.94	33.88	5.64	9.75	0.84	1.39	21.72	34.96
ING Bank	0.04	NEG	0.25	NEG	16.15	29.45	32.62	38.02	0.27	NEG	0.11	NEG	0.95	NEG
KBC Bank NV	NEG	0.98	NEG	3.22	NEG	10.69	58.26	53.82	NEG	6.91	NA	0.88	NEG	19.54
Krung Thai Bank Public Co.	4.42	0.28	4.76	0.33	31.98	4.59	19.25	19.42	37.02	2.73	78.82	1.54	57.56	3.38
Mashreq Bank	NEG	NEG	NEG	NEG	10.20	13.73	27.94	32.16	NEG	NEG	NEG	NEG	NEG	NEG
Morgan Guaranty Trust	NEG	2.16	NEG	5.72	21.73	51.23	57.64	53.07	NEG	15.64	NA	19.41	NEG	98.75
OCBC Bank	4.84	NEG	6.34	NEG	28.48	20.17	35.35	38.01	34.46	NEG	16.15	NEG	60.52	NEG
Oman International	NEG	NEG	NEG	NEG	20.16	15.26	23.95	27.29	NEG	NEG	NEG	NEG	NA	NA
Sakura Bank	NEG	NEG	NEG	NEG	NEG	NEG	28.96	35.72	NEG	NEG	NEG	NEG	NEG	NEG
Sanwa Bank	0.96	0.13	4.05	0.49	12.31	11.62	2550	21.58	7.89	1.34	3.15	0.31	18.02	3.23
Siam Commercial Bank	2.52	2.42	8.91	8.95	8.27	12.40	17.20	17.38	2.14	17.32	5.49	6.32	43.18	39.98
Societe Generate	NEG	0.02	NEG	0.16	14.25	19.93	38.86	39.74	NEG	0.16	NEG	0.04	NEG	1.85
Standard Chartered Bank	2.61	1.80	29.76	21.34	17.15	19.28	44.09	40.10	13.87	13.74	2.46	2.71	47.51	41.31
State Bank of Mauritius	2.23	1.69	5.82	6.12	18.13	16.51	25.17	35.98	19.74	15.28	4.47	4.82	65.07	47.42
Sumitomo Bank	2.05	0.22	10.56	1.31	10.81	8.56	50.36	42.86	13.65	1,87	3.06	0.74	35.83	6.39
Toronto-Dominion Bank	4.00	3.58	4.51	5.63	4.47	11.53	27.10	32.07	28.87	29.35	NA	NA	30.26	38.06

TABLE 23.2
Financial Management of Foreign Banks

(in percent)

Bank	Average cost of assets		Average yield on assets		Average yield on advances		Average yield on investments		Spread to total assets		Capital adequacy ratio		NPA to advances	
	1998-99	1999-2000	1998-99	1999-2000	1998-99	1999-2000	1998-99	1999-2000	1998-99	1999-2000	1998-99	1999-2000	1998-99	1999-2000
(1)	(2)	(3)	(4)	(5)	(6)	(7)	(8)	(9)	(10)	(11)	(12)	(13)	(14)	(15)
ABN Amro	7.47	5.20	10.86	10.53	13.64	11.87	11.95	11.68	3.30	3.22	9.27	10.09	0.45	0.30
Abu Dhabi Commercial	8.29	9.13	9.99	10.98	11.57	12.04	11.35	15.76	1.93	2.09	10.01	10.61	3.59	2.10
Amex	9.30	6.53	10.63	10.10	13.36	11.98	13.31	11.53	2.78	3.91	9.25	10.09	2.32	4.32
Arab Bangladesh Bank	3.69	3.92	6.82	7.88	14.16	14.55	7.70	10.83	5.50	5.84	124.00	123.00	NA	6.07
BNP	9.40	8.97	9.43	9.93	14.17	14.13	11.53	11.37	2.67	2.70	9.09	9.55	0.63	0.08
Bank Inter Indonesia	8.75	8.80	9.67	10.17	14.83	14.71	8.82	12.25	2.75	2.78	57.26	59.92	10.53	48.78
Bank Muscat Inti SAOG	2.91	8.14	3.80	8.41	2.92	14.40	2.95	11.50	2.85	2.13	212.45	70.06	NA	2.38
Bank of America	11.55	8.42	12.99	10.29	16.58	12.47	11.87	10.64	4.41	4.63	9.26	12.93	NA	1.92
Bank of Bahrain & Kuwait	11.73	11.25	10.94	11.00	13.98	12.78	11.33	12.44	1.11	1.55	13.38	12.14	11.34	7.72
Bank of Ceylon	8.94	8.03	11.19	9.87	13.27	12.78	11.36	11.59	6.55	4.98	37.05	29.07	16.43	22.14
Bank of Nova Scotia	9.68	7.35	12.03	9.31	13.62	10.28	12.04	10.28	3.24	2.60	9.06	9.67	2.80	1.15
Bank of Tokyo-Mitsubishi	7.42	6.60	9.92	10.80	12.94	15.47	10.11	1.39	3.64	6.28	9.92	17.62	13.45	2.46
Barclays Bank	13.88	9.58	14.29	9.68	24.06	9.79	14.90	10.51	3.58	2.37	12.90	17.75	3.35	NA
Chase Manhattan Bank	2.14	36.75	8.51	7.72	0.94	16.63	8.03	7.39	-0.93	0.77	12.53	45.86	NA	NA
Cho Hung Bank	3.25	1.45	11.20	8.98	16.74	15.31	14.30	13.11	7.19	7.87	42.00	38.00	1.88	1.48
City Bank	9.58	7.17	11.41	11.04	16.66	15.67	12.97	12.34	3.44	4.54	10.00	10.58	2.08	1.05

(Contd.)

TABLE 23.2 (Contd.)

(1)	(2)	(3)	(4)	(5)	(6)	(7)	(8)	(9)	(10)	(11)	(12)	(13)	(14)	(15)
Commerz Bank	9.01	7.87	9.95	11.21	12.01	14.23	11.69	13.24	3.12	3.0	15.81	17.58	7.06	7.34
Credit Agricole Indosuez	9.79	9.14	11.67	1.26	13.87	14.45	15.71	13.15	2.83	2.91	8.56	11.82	24.75	6.13
Credit Lyonnais	10.31	9.70	13.62	14.00	21.62	22.63	9.78	9.50	3.63	3.52	9.90	9.70	NA	4.10
Deutsche Bank	6.30	5.08	11.20	10.35	13.45	11.19	12.48	12.66	4.93	5.00	9.50	10.44	NA	NA
Devp. Bank of Singapore	11.19	7.69	13.74	9.95	28.44	13.50	10.57	9.28	3.01	3.33	23.26	18.14	4.93	NA
Dresdner Bank	11.47	8.07	11.44	10.83	16.00	11.54	14.12	14.90	4.15	5.58	19.36	18.69	16.16	13.50
Fuji Bank	12.07	11.53	11.86	9.04	14.61	9.77	9.97	10.21	4.76	1.76	23.62	25.29	6.02	10.28
Hongkong Bank	7.75	7.03	9.19	9.08	13.17	11.24	11.36	12.49	2.69	2.75	9.31	10.30	0.91	1.04
ING Bank	19.74	9.74	11.48	11.38	18.95	14.37	10.70	13.96	3.56	6.24	12.79	21.15	5.67	13.26
KBC Bank NV	NA	1.95	0.99	12.73	NA	10.57	0.08	11.75	0.99	2.97	NA	18.51	NA	NA
Krung Thai Bank Public Co.	6.59	12.20	8.11	9.75	13.31	12.67	17.08	8.77	7.48	7.80	236.00	197.74	NA	NA
Mashreq Bank	10.45	9.01	11.44	9.89	16.61	12.36	9.96	11.34	2.35	2.23	12.13	9.04	24.21	20.96
Morgan Guaranty Trust	NA	0.09	1.45	6.74	NA	NA	1.54	8.34	0.60	2.01	413.00	89.0	NA	NA
OCBC Bank	3.03	4.96	10.05	9.83	3.50	13.76	11.60	11.23	7.24	7.16	94.00	98.34	NA	15.97
Oman International	12.03	12.68	9.61	9.41	12.21	10.11	10.45	12.71	-0.57	-0.46	9.07	11.08	38.03	33.79
Sakura Bank	7.98	5.78	12.57	11.60	15.02	13.30	9.62	10.76	6.81	6.37	10.29	15.01	12.59	16.49
Sanwa Bank	8.38	6.88	10.69	8.66	13.61	9.30	12.11	12.10	5.67	4.24	31.97	36.17	12.33	18.58
Siam Commercial Bank	4.59	8.67	11.47	12.25	14.58	15.06	11.69	10.80	6.34	5.62	39.00	28.00	10.51	5.17
Societe Generate	9.94	9.05	12.40	9.67	15.27	11.36	14.33	11.05	2.78	1.09	12.50	13.95	11.94	8.66
Standard Chartered Bank	12.36	7.44	15.61	10.58	20.16	13.28	17.50	11.82	3.63	4.29	8.67	10.21	1.72	1.03
State Bank of Mauritius	12.72	10.55	9.26	9.22	11.37	11.25	12.92	10.76	2.78	3.12	46.78	35.23	10.55	7.76
Sumitomo Bank	5.82	5.51	13.42	10.92	17.54	13.61	9.41	8.88	4.35	3.96	16.58	18.43	NA	1613
Toronto-Dominion Bank	NA	NA	13.23	10.78	15.77	11.45	16.72	18.25	11.49	7.61	74.23	51.98	NA	NA

TABLE 23.3
Profitability of Public Sector Banks

Bank	Return on assets		Return on equity		Non-interest income to gross income		Staff expenses to operating expenses		Net profit margin		Net profit to deposits		Net profit to spread	
	1998-99	1999-2000	1998-99	1999-2000	1998-99	1999-2000	1998-99	1999-2000	1998-99	1999-2000	1998-99	1999-2000	1998-99	1999-2000
(1)	(2)	(3)	(4)	(5)	(6)	(7)	(8)	(9)	(10)	(11)	(12)	(13)	(14)	(15)
Allahabad Bank	0.83	0.37	16.87	7.97	11.58	12.24	69.95	68.49	7.48	3.30	0.87	0.39	27.51	12.29
Andhra Bank	0.88	0.88	15.57	22.45	12.25	13.89	73.35	72.78	7.50	7.23	0.86	0.84	26.77	29.01
Bank of Baroda	0.86	0.91	15.15	16.40	10.71	10.94	70.03	68.78	7.80	8.58	0.94	0.98	26.78	29.34
Bank of India	0.40	0.31	8.52	7.03	11.11	14.22	72.24	71.55	3.89	3.13	0.45	0.36	14.26	13.36
Bank of Maharashtra	0.46	0.66	7.77	17.63	8.68	11.17	80.89	77.33	4.18	5.46	0.47	0.67	12.96	19.30
Canara Bank	0.49	0.46	9.55	9.43	12.46	14.49	71.46	70.46	4.23	4.15	0.54	0.49	14.75	16.42
Central Bank	0.46	0.40	8.41	8.15	9.61	10.45	75.64	79.76	4.03	3.60	0.48	0.42	13.94	12.29
Corporation Bank	1.47	1.47	21.06	21.94	13.16	14.44	60.94	58.31	12.35	12.40	1.52	1.63	51.62	50.72
Dena Bank	0.81	0.40	17.72	8.26	9.31	11.77	72.95	71.23	7.69	3.49	0.93	0.47	24.99	15.03
Indian Bank	NEG	NEG	NEG	NEG	10.90	12.66	76.33	78.16	NEG	NEG	NEG	NEG	NEG	NEG
Indian Overseas Bank	0.24	0.15	7.97	5.49	9.84	9.61	75.50	76.35	2.17	1.46	0.25	0.17	9.78	5.95
Oriental Bank of Commerce	1.37	1.29	19.80	20.95	8.48	8.26	58.49	54.03	11.25	10.40	1.37	1.26	39.46	39.09
Punjab & Sind Bank	0.59	0.55	9.67	15.45	10.20	12.04	69.27	72.10	5.12	4.78	0.59	0.58	22.24	21.99

(Contd.)

TABLE 23.3 (Contd.)

(1)	(2)	(3)	(4)	(5)	(6)	(7)	(8)	(9)	(10)	(11)	(12)	(13)	(14)	(15)
Punjab National Bank	0.86	0.81	20.77	19.42	10.91	12.37	77.68	77.68	7.45	6.94	0.91	0.86	22.52	25.25
State Bank of Bikaner & Jaipur	0.98	1.06	24.07	25.55	14.51	16.47	75.66	74.61	8.15	9.01	1.19	1.33	27.82	32.23
State Bank of Hyderabad	0.94	0.89	25.19	22.94	13.44	15.24	73.16	66.87	7.88	7.31	1.05	1.02	23.98	24.58
State Bank of Indore	0.69	0.81	17.17	21.16	15.21	19.3	70.57	69.24	5.32	6.52	0.77	0.89	15.96	24.11
State Bank of Mysore	0.53	0.64	14.59	18.41	14.69	17.03	76.43	78.96	4.11	5.00	0.60	0.73	13.65	17.16
State Bank of Patiala	0.98	1.13	1653	18.17	11.48	12.34	72.90	72.99	8.80	9.79	1.14	1.28	26.40	27.49
State Bank of Saurashtra	0.44	1024	6.32	18.94	13.20	14.06	75.21	74.00	3.67	10.66	0.53	1.50	11.39	35.83
State Bank of Tranvancore	0.43	0.57	11.81	16.31	13.02	14.37	72.07	75.23	3.69	4.91	0.50	0.65	18.16	23.57
State Bank of India	0.51	0.85	10.27	18.20	14.67	1385	70.34	71.13	4.59	7.96	0.61	1.04	16.95	29.61
Syndicate Bank	0.71	0.88	12.91	24.69	11.58	11.17	78.96	78.62	6.09	7.86	0.72	0.91	22.12	26.13
UCO Bank	NEG	0.18	NEG	4.33	9.96	11.18	81.29	81.04	NEG	1.65	NEG	0.20	NEG	6.63
Union Bank of India	0.56	0.31	9.83	5.90	8.39	8.28	65.56	70.77	5.12	2.80	0.57	0.33	19.27	10.58
United Bank of India	0.10	0.18	2.86	5.29	7.31	7.61	82.57	83.00	0.94	1.71	0.10	0.19	4.27	7.64
Vijaya Bank	0.30	0.45	7.25	9.18	9.83	8.89	69.14	71.84	2.73	4.02	0.31	0.46	9.53	13.61

TABLE 23.4
Profitability of Private Sector Banks

Bank	*Return on assets*		*Return on equity*		*Non-interest income to gross income*		*Staff expenses to operating expenses*		*Net profit margin*		*Net profit to deposits*		*Net profit to spread*	
	1998-99	*1999-2000*	*1998-99*	*1999-2000*	*1998-99*	*1999-2000*	*1998-99*	*1999-2000*	*1998-99*	*1999-2000*	*1998-99*	*1999-2000*	*1998-99*	*1999-2000*
(1)	*(2)*	*(3)*	*(4)*	*(5)*	*(6)*	*(7)*	*(8)*	*(9)*	*(10)*	*(11)*	*(12)*	*(13)*	*(14)*	*(15)*
Bank of Punjab	1.77	1.25	22.61	20.80	18.65	14.96	16.98	11.74	14.14	10.72	1.84	1.27	78.70	44.93
Bank of Rajasthan	NEG	0.32	NEG	16.26	11.07	11.78	68.52	70.34	NEG	2.66	NEG	0.37	NEG	12.90
Catholic Syrian Bank	0.02	0.26	0.89	12.24	8.72	12.97	68.80	73.97	0.14	2.04	0.02	0.27	0.84	10.51
Centurion Bank	0.92	0.82	14.04	17.86	10.13	16.70	9.10	10.49	4.88	6.46	1.00	0.89	21.75	42.75
Citi Union Bank	0.96	1.36	15.95	20.60	15.55	15.84	56.98	64.19	6.90	9.60	1.00	1.50	46.34	42.96
Development Credit Bank	1.03	1.02	9.65	12.11	14.76	20.32	42.91	43.25	8.43	8.77	1.13	1.05	44.14	51.30
Dhanalakshmi Bank	0.30	0.76	5.94	16.08	8.62	13.15	64.03	65.45	2.49	6.01	0.31	0.81	12.98	28.39
Federal Bank	0.03	0.59	0.73	13.55	11.62	13.05	61.16	66.68	0.26	4.57	0.04	0.72	2.88	25.72
Global Trist Bank	1.58	1.71	26.64	26.54	22.95	26.47	13.91	14.63	11.11	12.36	1.73	1.75	133.96	78.02
HDFC Bank	2.30	1.50	26.41	22.02	15.33	15.57	24.85	28.32	18.55	14.91	2.83	1.42	56.09	39.28
ICICI Bank	1.23	1.11	22.03	14.45	14.06	18.54	21.92	23.72	10.01	10.06	1.04	1.07	53.45	56.63

(*Contd.*)

TABLE 23.4 (Contd.)

(1)	(2)	(3)	(4)	(5)	(6)	(7)	(8)	(9)	(10)	(11)	(12)	(13)	(14)	(15)
IDBI Bank	1.09	1.54	18.00	25.58	8.92	11.51	20.32	22.47	9.50	12.73	1.12	1.77	47.98	66.90
Indus Ind. Bank	0.66	0.79	7.06	10.55	12.25	18.51	12.93	13.27	5.44	7.17	0.73	0.86	32.07	41.16
The J & K bank	1.30	1.33	24.28	25.13	5.84	10.62	63.53	56.36	11.60	12.14	1.33	1.28	32.52	41.96
Karnataka Bank	0.97	1.10	17.34	20.31	8.95	11.11	69.74	71.26	7.87	8.96	0.97	1.13	36.56	51.01
Karur Vysya Bank	1.31	2.07	20.81	31.25	10.77	12.15	58.87	62.89	9.79	14.95	1.46	2.30	40.83	51.91
Lakshmi Vilas Bank	0.84	1.26	15.07	23.64	17.12	21.16	55.97	60.00	6.56	9.34	0.93	1.34	34.09	43.98
Lord Krishna Bank	0.16	0.70	3.86	14.14	12.26	16.29	51.24	56.41	1.15	5.48	0.19	0.72	9.77	43.69
Nedungadi Bank	0.72	0.96	20.84	28.65	10.38	12.60	61.81	62.77	4.93	7.39	0.68	0.92	24.32	30.59
South Indian Bank	0.18	0.65	4.41	14.78	8.45	13.72	71.00	76.74	1.39	4.76	0.19	0.67	6.91	21.90
UTI Bank	0.88	0.96	17.00	22.80	11.10	15.87	23.55	23.59	7.40	8.87	1.02	0.89	42.77	56.33
United Western Bank	1.08	1.27	21.02	26.10	14.49	22.42	68.99	70.94	9.55	10.30	1.08	1.28	42.68	48.50
Vysya Bank	0.43	0.54	6.62	8.62	13.33	19.04	59.93	55.04	3.65	4.52	9.47	0.60	32.14	40.04

TABLE 23.5
Financial Management of Public Sector Banks

(in percent)

Bank	Average cost of deposits		Average yield on assets		Average yield on advances		Average yield on investments		Spread to total assets		Capital adequacy ratio		NPA to net advances	
	1998-99	1999-2000	1998-99	1999-2000	1998-99	1999-2000	1998-99	1999-2000	1998-99	1999-2000	1998-99	1999-2000	1998-99	1999-2000
(1)	(2)	(3)	(4)	(5)	(6)	(7)	(8)	(9)	(10)	(11)	(12)	(13)	(14)	(15)
Allahabad Bank	7.49	7.61	9.78	9.94	11.96	11.62	11.39	11.72	2.82	2.86	10.38	11.51	12.54	12.24
Andhra Bank	7.49	7.87	10.25	10.53	12.05	12.76	11.76	11.84	2.91	2.63	11.02	13.36	4.26	3.47
Bank of Baroda	7.35	6.78	9.83	9.42	11.67	11.39	11.92	11.57	3.01	2.92	13.30	12.10	7.70	6.95
Bank of India	6.92	6.64	9.16	8.61	11.54	11.29	10.69	10.47	2.61	2.31	10.55	10.57	7.55	8.61
Bank of Maharashtra	7.10	7.85	10.11	10.71	12.55	12.65	11.61	12.52	3.29	3.07	9.76	11.66	8.72	6.97
Canara Bank	7.48	7.19	1021	9.46	12.56	11.55	12.40	10.92	3.17	2.64	10.96	9.64	7.09	5.28
Central Bank	7.74	7.38	10.26	9.97	12.79	12.47	14.81	11.49	.97	2.96	11.88	11.18	9.79	9.84
Corporation Bank	8.76	8.30	10.33	10.12	11.49	11.46	13.00	12.01	2.49	2.73	13.20	12.80	1.98	1.92
Dena Bank	8.75	8.32	11.01	10.02	13.84	12.32	12.51	11.19	2.97	2.48	11.14	11.63	7.67	13.47
Indian Bank	8.34	8.05	9.22	9.96	10.87	11.84	10.55	11.41	0.92	1.61	NA	NA	21.67	16.18
Indian Overseas Bank	8.18	7.66	10.02	9.62	11.81	11.07	11.81	11.36	2.31	2.46	10.15	9.15	7.30	7.65
Oriental Bank of Commerce	8.51	8.83	11.16	11.35	13.30	11.87	12.28	14.09	3.10	2.90	14.10	12.72	4.50	3.80

(Contd.)

TABLE 23.5 (Contd.)

(1)	(2)	(3)	(4)	(5)	(6)	(7)	(8)	(9)	(10)	(11)	(12)	(13)	(14)	(15)
Punjab and Sind Bank	8.23	8.11	10.29	10.04	13.00	11.86	11.41	11.98	2.38	2.35	10.94	11.57	10.48	9.39
Punjab National Bank	7.05	7.63	10.33	10.26	12.44	12.08	11.46	11.89	3.57	2.99	10.79	10.31	8.96	8.52
SB of Bikaner and Jaipur	8.37	8.23	10.28	9.83	12.27	11.69	12.69	12.08	3.23	3.00	12.26	12.35	10.45	10.14
SB of Hyderabad	7.49	7.93	10.30	10.33	12.49	11.90	11.42	11.57	3.53	3.35	10.65	10.86	8.78	7.30
SB of Indore	7.83	7.67	10.93	9.97	13.01	1.54	11.53	11.30	3.92	2.99	12.35	11.26	10.10	7.55
SB of Mysore	8.18	8.00	10.94	10.55	14.42	13.67	12.37	11.99	3.58	3.39	10.23	11.50	10.55	8.12
SB of Patiala	7.47	7.16	9.89	10.11	12.10	11.53	12.01	11.59	3.53	3.86	12.47	12.60	8.23	6.09
SB of Saurashtra	8.31	8.40	10.36	10.02	12.63	12.22	14.01	12.66	3.49	3.20	14.35	14.48	7.70	7.87
SB of Travancore	8.98	8.73	10.20	9.96	11.52	10.97	12.24	12.10	2.20	2.27	10.27	11.09	10.80	8.58
State Bank of India	8.13	7.87	9.50	9.17	10.96	10.59	12.01	11.65	2.72	2.65	12.51	11.49	7.18	6.41
Syndicate Bank	7.63	7.23	10.24	9.94	13.18	12.31	11.64	11.85	2.94	3.04	9.57	11.45	3.93	3.17
UCO Bank	7.69	7.80	9.46	9.72	11.00	11.02	11.17	11.54	2.15	2.35	9.63	9.15	10.83	8.75
Union Bank of India	7.91	7.76	10.07	10.01	12.77	12.73	11.91	12.37	2.66	2.74	10.09	11.42	8.70	7.97
United Bank of India	8.25	8.11	10.05	10.00	11.46	11.38	11.91	12.19	2.00	2.10	9.60	9.60	14.70	12.70
Vijaya Bank	7.45	7.31	10.04	10.15	14.08	13.18	11.46	12.28	2.86	3.03	13.02	10.61	6.72	6.65

Section IV

AGRICULTURE SECTOR

Globalisation, Competitiveness and Productivity in Agriculture Sector

P.K. Vasudeva

INTRODUCTION

The characteristics of globalisation as it is unfolding now are multifarious. It is influencing culture as much as the economies of nation states. India is passing through a stage where there is no consensus on the globalisation. One school of thought considers this as the only path for accelerating economic growth and reducing poverty with the oncoming of foreign direct investments and the participating of multinational corporations in the economic development of the country. There are others who are equally vehement in condemning the moves towards globalisation, and consider it as a sure recipe for economic subjugation and path leading to further exploitation of the poor and the defenceless.

GOVERNMENT POLICIES

The Government initiated a policy of economic reforms in the early 1990s by stabilisation and structural adjustment programmes to attain the macro-economic stability and higher rates of economic growth. Export-led growth has been encouraged but it has not yielded the desired results after one decade of reforms. India's share at $ 46 billion is less than one percent of global exports. Exports will continue to be a residuary activity in the national economic policy framework till the important issue of labour, infrastructure and product quality is resolved.

The new export-oriented Exim Policy 2002-07 focusses on agricultural products, small-scale handicrafts and cottage industry and newly created Special Economic Zones (SEZs) to ensure "parity of rules and procedures in labour laws with international norms."

The mere fact that the country came out of the balance of payment situation after the 1991 crisis shows that the globalisation is beneficial to the country especially when it has been able to muster foreign exchange up to $ 75 billion now that is highly creditable and even the inflation rate remains less than 3 percent of the GDP for the last four years.

Whatever definition one selects, globalisation implies weakening of the restrictions imposed by or inherent in nation state. These restrictions had become more severe in the first half of the 20th century. The 19th century had seen the weakening of the national barriers, as the movement of goods and services and of capital, even of labour, was lot more easy. The 20th century saw progressive liquidation of the colonialism and corresponding rise in the powers of the nation state. The pendulum started to swing in the opposite directions since Second World War, and the move towards globalisation started gaining strength. In this period the mainspring of globalisation was the developments in information technology, which contributed more than anything else to the emergence of global village.

How the trends towards integration of the world economies are going to affect economies of the poor countries and the livelihoods of the poorer sections in these countries is a moot question.

LABOUR REFORMS

The second generation of economic reforms also envisages eliminating protective labour legislation. First, it must be noted that labour reforms cannot be successful without management responsibilities towards human resource development, legislative compliance and adequate provisions of infrastructure and work environment. Second, Indian industries must democratise to allow the flow of information and communication—internal and external, active and proactive and reactive in the organisation to discourage trade unionism. This also has productivity connotations.

Japanese industries such as Matsushita may receive over six million suggestions in a year; many are implemented on the floor shop itself. The top management awards its employees for contributing to the improvements.

In Toyota for instance, a suggestion to increase the productivity by 0.6 minutes will be implemented. Cannon saved $ 250 million in a year by implementing an employee's suggestion of replacing imported lens cleaning paper with local one.

It must be emphasized that India possesses the advantage of large labour force with skilled engineering and scientific industry. However, the labour market remains probably the most ineffective in the world because of deficiencies in infrastructure sector, which limits their productive capabilities. The Global Competitive Report 2001-02 has placed India at 69th position out of 75 countries ranked for telephone lines per 100 inhabitants; 73rd on road network outside major cities; 57th on port facilities and inland waterways; and 47th on air transport infrastructure. Export-oriented units are required to conform to international technical specifications such as British Standards (BS), German DIN, and American ANNSI.

Manufacturing units require uninterrupted power for producing uniform quality products. The manufacturing units in the states are closing down for the lack of adequate power.

GLOBALISATION BENEFITS

Theoretical case for free investment of goods, services, capital and labour across the border is fairly strong. Take for example free trade in goods and services. Benefits of free trade are reflected in specialization, expansion of the market, and economies of scale. International trade governed by comparative advantages benefits producers by allowing them to specialise in those products for which the local market is restricted and or can be soon saturated. Free trade also encourages competition leading to efficiency in production and eventually benefiting the consumers.

Similarly, a strong case can be built for free movement of capital especially if the objective is to have infusion of the outside capital in capital starved countries like India. If the capital comes with the superior technologies, the developing countries can further grow its economy to match the developed world. Generating technologies has now become a capital intensive, long gestating proposition where the poor countries are handicapped. The utility of infusing capital will depend on the investment portfolio. If the capital is invested in the speculative ventures, in takeovers, and mergers, or is extremely mobile it may do more harm than good. The resistance of the developing countries to a universal protocol for foreign capital investment in WTO negotiations in Doha must be understood.

PROFITABILITY AND COMPETITIVENESS OF AGRICULTURE

The science and practice of agriculture changes continually. Food production systems are challenged to deliver low cost, high quality, safe food produced in environmentally sustainable systems. Extension programs must evolve to assist people in agriculture as new technology is developed and implemented to meet these challenges.

The global pressures to increase volume and lower costs necessitate business-like procedures in many situations where traditional procedures, until recently, allowed satisfactory productivity and met societal expectations. New systems are required to have elevated efficiency and productivity in order to compete, but often have societal consequences which are unexpected or misunderstood. It is essential that extension keep pace with the changing constituencies to facilitate change in the most positive ways possible.

Technology transfer and application support from extension is essential for producers to be able to cope with change and compete. The competitiveness of U.S. agriculture and the resulting economic impact in balance of trade and jobs sustained are essential to this country. Even the most advanced agriculture systems benefit from extension education and applied research programs. The transition of much of agriculture to the modern competitive level makes re-training of people, re-structuring of business arrangements, and personnel issues critically important. The extension service has strength in these areas.

HARMONY BETWEEN AGRICULTURE AND THE ENVIRONMENT

Attention to the environment must be an integral part of any farm's production system—in both design and management. Environmental issues in agriculture include water quality, soil conservation, air quality, and odor-related issues. Extension plays a critical role in the integration of technological solutions with productivity.

Substantial reduction in the loading of agricultural chemicals to the environment by using cost-effective methods is very important to protect ground water and surface water. Adoption of appropriate technology by producers will require cropping and farming practices for particular soils and climates to enable producers to modify their pesticide and nutrient inputs, conservation systems, tillage and management practices to reduce the movement of agri-chemicals and waste products through soil.

Livestock manure handling is a potential source of pollution. Ventilation, sanitation, management practices, feed handling, and manure collection, treatment, storage, and utilization should be mutually compatible to ensure a safe environment. Phosphorus accumulation in soil is an emerging issue. Historically, phosphorus was thought to be bound with the soil and not move off farm fields in runoff water unless soil erosion occurred. Recent research has shown that the phosphorus in soils containing high levels of phosphorus becomes soluble and moves into water, thereby allowing the phosphorous to leave fields in runoff water. Soil phosphorus levels on livestock farms are high because manure has traditionally been spread with no regard to fertilizer value, and spread based on the nitrogen content and needs of the crop, resulting in an accumulation of phosphorus.

AGRICULTURAL SUSTAINABILITY

Sustainable agriculture does not refer to a prescribed set of practices. Instead, it challenges producers to think about the long-term implications of practices and the broad interactions and dynamics of agricultural systems. The general goals of sustainable agriculture are to develop economically viable, sustainable agricultural systems based on minimizing purchased agriculture inputs, mixing production systems, maximizing biodiversity, and preserving or improving water, soil, air, and food and fiber quality. Understanding agriculture from an ecological perspective that considers nutrient and energy dynamics as well as interactions among plants, animals, insects, and other organisms is critical to sustainability.

Farming methods that improve the sustainability of one farm may not be appropriate to a different farm or region. Each practice must be evaluated in a given farming system for its ability to achieve a set of economic, environmental, and social goals. Strong programs by the Extension Service can help evaluate systems, adapt new practices, and achieve the goals of lasting farm production, stewardship of land, water and wildlife, and improved quality of life for farmers, and rural communities.

PARTICIPATING IN THE GLOBAL MARKETPLACE

The revolution in American agriculture is having a significant impact on farm families, agri-businesses, and rural communities, requiring them to make major strategic decisions to be successful in the evolving agricultural industry. Increased globalization of markets provides more international opportunity as well as more competition in domestic and foreign markets. Dramatic changes in federal farm programs give producers greater flexibility in management decisions, and greater responsibility for marketing and risk management. Many extension programs have successfully assisted constituents in coping with these changes.

MACKINSEY'S REPORT ON AGRICULTURE IN INDIA

On Sepember 6, 2001, a team from the consulting firm McKinsey unveiled a road map to spur India's growth to 10%. At the end of the 2 hour presentation Prime Minister Vajpayee is said to have sighed : "But how is all this to be put through our polity?"

That difficulty may be the only one that stands between India's present 5% growth and the tantalising 10% that is said to be a panacea for all of India's social ills. There is nothing calamitous in the McKinsey prescription save in the eyes of those who see doom in letting in global winds of change.

Investment *vs.* Productivity

The McKinsey study is insightful in how, far from having to attract over 10 times the direct investment that India does now, the climb from 5% to 10% can be achieved by consciously tweaking the system to enhance productivity.

Now, productivity has to understand outside of the picture that first pops up in our minds. Most of us imagine it as a measure of work done in a unit of time. Yes, it is that but on a far wider canvas than the man-machine-conveyor belt image that we see.

Productivity is about putting in place systems that enable maximum yields from a given investment. Take the Indian power sector. Growing energy needs can be met in two ways : one by searching for the impossible dollars to create new facilities in the moribund state system or two by privatizing, to plug thefts, subsidies and waste, which will first yield more power and next attract fresh investments. Again, productivity-oriented reforms is about simplifying tax and excise tariffs that enhance compliance and competition.

The current focus on productivity as a driver for growth has largely been due to the work of Stanford Professor Paul Romer. Classically, economists have considered land, labour and capital as being in lock step with growth numbers. Then came the insight of Robert Solow who proposed that technical advances will get economies to start jogging. Finally comes Romer's assertion that focus on productivity will in fact cause economies to sprint.

When awareness, laws, enforcement, education and business climate of a country are conducive to competition and productivity, things automatically perk up : investment follows, infrastructure is created, global competitiveness is enhanced and steady growth is achieved. [India is well placed in the competitiveness race.]

In fact, the opposite is the case when mere investment is used to drive growth. This leads to over creation of capacity and supply and is hard to sustain. Paul Krugman predicted for this reason that the heady growth rates of Asian Tigers would not last. His hunch was that investment driven growth couldn't last unless backed by deep and wide reforms. Now Gordon Chang is prophesying the same for this and other related reasons.

The McKinsey Promise

Convinced of the primacy of productivity in driving growth the McKinsey Global Institute began a series of studies that covered 13 economies, among them Brazil, Korea and Germany. Hardheaded economists oversaw the studies. The conclusions were unmistakable : productivity and efficient markets yield more growth than capital alone can.

Armed with this knowledge, McKinsey turned to India. A study was undertaken by Amadeo M. Di Ludovico, William W. Lewis, Vincent Palmade and Shirish Sankhe, with inputs from India's econo-crats Montek Singh Ahluwalia and Rakesh Mohan.

According to the study a growth of more than 4% is denied to India by just three barriers : distortions in product-markets [2.3%], distortions in land-markets [1.3%] and state ownership of business [0.7%]. The study says these can be corrected by 13 initiatives. It asserts that what inhibits growth is not lack of capital or poor infrastructure. Indeed these will follow automatically as soon as distortions are removed.

If the 13 steps are taken, McKinsey promises a dream scenario : GDP growth rate will hit 10%; economy will touch $ 1.1 trillion; 75 million jobs will be created outside agriculture; fiscal deficit will fall from 10 to 6%; and

Indians will live in a prosperous economy. In how many years? Three, says McKinsey.

Let us consider Mckinsey's arguments.

The three Barriers

In the Indian product markets the following anomalies reign : unfairness and ambiguity [as in telecom license fees], poor enforcement [as in electricity revenue collections], reservations for small scale sectors [which stymy scaling potential as in the garment industry], restricted entry to foreign investments [as in retailing] and continued system of licensing [as for instance in the dairy industry, due to pressure from the co-operatives sector].

McKinsey holds out the success of the Indian auto industry following India's open door policy there : old clunky models died, better and cheaper cars arrived and employment soared 11% in the 8 years following 1992.

Turning to land-related issues McKinsey says, when seen in relation to GDP the cost of land per square meter in Indian metros is about 11 times that in Tokyo, 8 times that in Singapore and 16 times that in bustling Sydney. But why? Supply of land for development is way behind demand. Again, why? McKinsey says land records and delays in legal processes have tied up large tracts of land. Lacking clear titles, it is difficult to offer them as collateral for funding. Add to that high registration charges, poor tenancy laws and inflexible zoning and you have blocked opportunities waiting in construction and retailing industries, which are the greatest potential employers outside agriculture.

The third barrier is government ownership of business. McKinsey proves that the Indian worker is not naturally unproductive. Labour productivity in state units as against similar units in the private sectors are as follows : 3:27 in dairy; 10:20 in power generation; 0.5:3 in power transmission; 10:55 in banking and 25:76 in telecom. McKinsey says, "electricity boards lose a staggering 30 to 40 percent of their power, mostly to theft. By comparison, best-practice private power distributors lose only around 10 percent, mostly for technical reasons".

If the facts presented are compelling, the steps suggested for sweeping away all these ills are audaciously simple, given political will.

The 13 Steps and Life Thereafter

Here they are in MacKinsey's own words :

1. Completely eliminate the reservation of products for small-scale industry; start with 68 sectors accounting for 80 percent of output of reserved sectors.
2. Equalize sales taxes and excise duties for all categories of players in each sector and strengthen enforcement.
3. Establish an effective regulatory framework and strong regulatory bodies.

4. Remove all licensing and quasi-licensing restrictions that limit the number of players in affected industries.
5. Reduce import duties on all goods to the levels of Southeast Asian countries (10 percent) over five years.
6. Remove the ban on foreign direct investment in the retail sector and allow unrestricted foreign direct investment in all sectors.
7. Resolve unclear real-estate titles by setting up fast-track courts to settle disputes, computerizing land records, freeing all property from constraints on sale, and removing limits on property ownership.
8. Raise property taxes and user charges for municipal services and cut stamp duties (tax on property transactions) to promote the development of residential and commercial land and to increase the land markets liquidity.
9. Reform tenancy laws to allow rents to move to market levels.
10. Privatize the electricity sector and all companies owned by the central and state governments; in the electricity sector, start by privatizing distribution; in all other sectors, first privatize the largest companies.
11. Reform labor laws by repealing section 5-B of the Industrial Disputes Act, by introducing standard retrenchment-compensation norms and by allowing full flexibility in the use of contract labour.
12. Transfer the management of the existing transport infrastructure to the private sector; contract out the construction and management of new infrastructure to it.
13. Strengthen extension services to help farmers improve their yield.

This may generate political discomfort but how illogical or inhuman are these suggestions? Indians must reflect that though we are now cruising at about 5% growth, for the 40 years till 1990 we grew at the much derided 'Hindu rate of growth' of 2.5%. How did we get here? Economists agree India has attracted little foreign investment. So, how did India double its growth in 10 years? Obviously even the half-hearted lunges at piece-meal reforms in 90s have worked. Yes, there was the noise and heat of debates and protests, but we did it.

AGRICULTURE AND PRODUCTIVITY

Ever since the Agreement on Agriculture of the World Trade Organisation (WTO) began to be debated in the country, increasing agricultural productivity and improving food quality are being tossed as the only solutions for farmers' survival. Invariably, at every conference and seminar on WTO, the common refrain is that farmers are left with no choice but to increase productivity and thereby reduce the cost of production to remain competitive in a globalised world.

The productivity bug has bitten not only the agricultural scientists but also the policy-makers, planners and, of course, the politicians. So much so that even the President, Mr. A.P.J. Abdul Kalam, has urged agricultural scientists to work for doubling crop productivity in the next decade.

He was recently addressing a gathering of agricultural scientists at the 30th anniversary celebrations of International Crops Research Institute for the Semi-Arid Tropics (ICRISAT), near Hyderabad in Andhra Pradesh.

Within a fortnight of President Kalam's exhortation to agricultural scientists, farmers in Kurnool district in Andhra Pradesh, dumped cartloads of tomato on the streets. Excess production had resulted in a crash in tomato prices, with prices slumping to 50 paise a kilo (less than half a cent for a kg), farmers were left with no choice.

In Maharashtra, Uttar Pradesh and Punjab, irate potato growers have demonstrated their anger by throwing potatoes onto the highways. There are no takers for the bountiful potato harvest.

Not only crop failures, even bumper harvests have begun to push farmers into a vicious cycle of mounting debt and distress. Whether it is Andhra Pradesh, Karnataka, Tamil Nadu, Maharashtra or Punjab, farmers are increasingly becoming a victim of the new emerging phenomenon of "produce and perish".

Farmers have been misled to believe that diversification from staple grains to cash crops is the only way out to escape an uncertain future. At the same time, farmers are being asked to increase crop productivity to remain competitive in an era of 'free' trade.

Since the global trade parameters are being relaxed and phased out, increasing productivity is being touted as the new survival mantra. The high productivity refrain comes in handy for the biotechnology industry to bring in expensive and risky technologies, further compounding farmers' woes. In the bargain, it is the farmer who faces the brunt, often opting for the fatal route to escape the humiliation and distress that such half-baked advice brings in.

At every national and international conference, it is not unusual to see slide projections that point at the low productivity in India and, for that matter, in other developing countries. The projections for area and productivity under cereals, including wheat and rice, and crops such as sugarcane, cotton and vegetables, points to the prevailing dichotomy.

India ranks among the top five countries (often among the first two) having the largest area under crops such as wheat, rice, cotton, sugarcane, and vegetables. Its ranking in productivity brings it to the bottom of the chart, with per hectare yield or productivity hovering among the lowest five or ten countries. Increasing productivity will bring more income to farmers and, thereby, increase their presence and competitiveness in the international market.

Take the case of rice, the most important staple food crop of India. In the year 2000, India's rice paddy yield was hovering at 3,008 kg per hectare. In Thailand, the major rice exporter, paddy productivity stands at 2,329 kg.

In the US, the average yield per hectare was more than double at 7,037 kg. If productivity alone was the criteria, the US should have captured the entire world market in rice. And, at the same time, Thailand should not have been able to export rice considering that its average productivity is lower than even India. Moreover, even with such low rice paddy productivity, India had a record procurement of 20.9 million tones of rice in the 2001-02 marketing season.

The grain stock build-up over the last few years has seen India's rice and wheat surplus increase to an unmanageable level of 51.4 million tonnes in October 2002 (against a record 65 million tonnes in June 2001).

In fact, chief ministers of surplus rice-producing states of Punjab, Haryana, and Andhra Pradesh have been repeatedly asking their farmers not to produce more of rice as they have no place to stock it. The Centre too has been toying with the idea of getting out of food procurement leaving farmers to the vagaries of the market.

In the US, however, despite the high paddy productivity, farmers find its cultivation uneconomical. The US government, therefore, continues to subsidise its farmers.

Estimates point that the American farmers receive an average subsidy of $ 30,000 per farm per year. As if this is not enough, the new Farm Bill brings an additional federal support of $ 180 billion for the next ten years.

If high productivity is the criteria for global competitiveness, there is no plausible reason why the American farmers would depend on government doles for survival.

To ask the Indian farmers, therefore, to increase paddy productivity, is to merely push them into a death trap. Already, rice farmers in Punjab and Andhra Pradesh continue to suffer for producing more. For the past two years, with the Food Corporation of India (FCI) refusing to buy paddy under one pretext or the other, distress sale has become a common phenomenon. At many a places, a number of rice farmers preferred to commit suicide waiting endlessly for buyers in the markets. The scenario for wheat producers is no different. They too are faced with the 'produce and perish' syndrome.

In cotton, India has the dubious distinction of having the largest area under the crop and one of the lowest average yields. This prompted the multinational seed company, Monsanto, to hastily push in its genetically modified 'Bt cotton' variety, exploited paradox.

The Department of Biotechnology and the Indian Council of Agricultural Research (ICAR) too used the productivity yardstick to justify the approval granted to Bt cotton. By reducing pesticides use, Bt cotton was expected to reduce crop losses thereby increasing per hectare productivity.

The rise in productivity will help farmers get more for the produce, and also enable them to export.

While the impact—both negative and positive—of Bt cotton was too small to make any dent on the national production figures, the fact remains that cotton has lately emerged as the crop that has increasingly pushed growers into a death trap.

In 2002, more than 100 suicides were reported alone from 12 districts that constitute the Vidharva region of the eastern Maharashtra. Faced with mounting debt, a failed crop for the second year and government indifference, cotton farmers are resorting to suicides as a way out of misery. The Government's denial notwithstanding, more than 10,000 cotton growers have committed suicides throughout the country since 1987.

In contrast, the US remains the world's largest exporter of cotton. Armed with roughly $ 3.4 billion in subsidy, US farmers last year harvested a record crop of 9.74 billion pounds of cotton, aggravating a US glut and pushing prices far below the break-even price of most growers around the world, including India, China and West Africa.

In 2002-03, US cotton farmers are expecting to pocket even more, thanks to the Farm Bill signed by the US President, Mr. George Bush, in May 2002. The Government programme ensures farmers reap about 70 cents a pound of cotton by making up for any shortfall in the market with state support.

Although relatively small share of the farm population—just 25,000 of US 9,00,000 farming families actually raise cotton—their affluence and influence is legendary.

The average net worth of a full-time American cotton-farming household, including land and non-farm assets, is about $ 800,000, according to the US Department of Agriculture. And more than half of it comes from the government subsidies. The slump in world prices, therefore, has no impact on their lifestyles. But, in turn, brings misery to farmers in the majority world.

No wonder, US cotton continues to dominate the world market. Even if Indian farmers were to double the cotton productivity, how can they ever compete with the American cotton-producers who receive a lavish federal support?

More the cotton productivity in countries such as India, more would be the resulting crisis for the farmers and the country's food security and economy.

Furthermore, with the phasing out of quantitative restrictions on agricultural commodities, the import of cotton (from the US) has increased from 21,200 tonnes in 1999 to 48,805 tonnes in 2000.

It is strange that the government, which asks domestic farmers to improve productivity so as to attain global competitiveness, should allow highly subsidised imports so as to help the American cotton growers.

Let us move to another part of the world. Monica Shandu was adjudged the best small-scale sugarcane grower for 2001 in the Entumeni Hills of South Africa. She farms four acres with sugarcane, and the harvest brings her an equivalent of $ 200. Despite being a progressive farmer with high productivity levels, Monica lives in penury, barely managing to survive against all odds.

Far away in France, Dominique Fievez cultivates his farm of 400 acres with sugar beet. His is an average farm, which remains untouched by the price fluctuations in international market since 1984.

The reason : Fievez receives a huge subsidy support under the European Union's Common Agricultural Policy at the rate of $ 23,000 for each of the 33 acres that he grows with beet. Such heavy subsidies depress the international sugar prices, making it difficult for developing countries to export.

Monica Shandu gets a low price for her cane harvest because of the subsidies that farmers like Fievez in France continue to pocket.

To ask Monica Shandu in South Africa to work more for further raising the sugarcane productivity, therefore, is a sure recipe for disaster.

Similarly, asking the sugarcane growers in Uttar Pradesh and Maharashtra to raise productivity so as to be globally competitive is to further push them towards an uncertain future. And if you think that crop diversification may perhaps bail-out farmers, think again.

Even in the frontline agricultural State of Punjab, where diversification has been the goal since the early 1980s, it has been estimated that increasing the fruit and vegetable production by just one per cent will cause an unmanageable glut.

It is primarily for this reason that Punjab farmers have refused to diversify from the wheat-rice crop rotation despite the faulty recommendations of the agricultural scientists, year after year, and that too for the past 20 years!

There is something terribly wrong with the way developing country policy-makers continue to follow the economic prescriptions being doled out essentially to protect the massive subsidies being given to a few million farmers on either side of the Atlantic.

Equally more tragic is that it is the mainline economists and scientists in India and, for that matter, in other developing countries, who eagerly join the chorus.

Like the four blind men with an elephant, they continue to grope in the dark not knowing what actually ails agriculture. All they try to do is to fit the round holes in square pegs.

UNCTAD REPORT A WARNING

The United Nations Conference on Trade and Development (UNCTAD) has suggested a "strong demand stimulus" from all the major industrialised countries for the recovery to gain impetus and for developing countries to avoid difficulties in reaching their growth and development goals.

In its 2002 Trade and Development Report (TDR) the Geneva-based UN body was however, skeptical "about a more balanced global growth" this year with much of the world still riding on the performance of the US economy.

In a foreword to the 178 page report the UN Secretary General, Mr. Kofi Annan, said that even as the TDR saw some signs "of improvement in the world economy this year," it warned against complacency and emphasised the importance of policy coherence for sustained recovery and sustainable development.

Growth in the global economy slowed sharply in 2001, falling to 1.3 percent from 3.8 percent in 2000. International trade transmitted the slowdown in the industrial world to the developing countries, the report said, adding, "After growing by 14 percent in 2000, export volumes for developing countries grew by less than 1 percent in 2001.

For developing countries as a whole growth was 2.1 percent, down from 5.4 percent the previous year. The sharp deceleration of the growth of trade wiped out most of the current account surplus attained by the developing countries in 2001.

Unlike the recession of the early 1990s, the relaxation of monetary policy in the advanced countries had not triggered a shift of capital to emerging market.

In the context of slow global growth, improved market access could provide a boost to activity in the developing countries. While at the WTO Ministerial Conference in Doha, the concerns of the developing countries raised in Seattle were acknowledged the challenge now was to make the multilateral trading system "more development friendly."

Only by replacing imported skill and technology intensive parts and components with domestically produced ones there cannot be progress in capacity building and industrialisation, apart from increasing the domestic value-added content of exports. Such a strategy is crucial to prevent India from becoming graveyard for junk technology by the MNCs.

WTO AND GLOBALISATION

After seven protracted years during the Eighth Round of General Agreement on Tariff and Trade (GATT) known as Uruguay Round from 1986 to 1993 the Final Act was signed at Marrakesh in April 1994 for the emergence of World Trade Organisation (WTO) from January 1, 1995. It is for the first time in the history of GATT Rounds that 25 agreements were signed in which the Agreement on Agriculture (AoA), Agreement on Textiles and Clothing (ATC), Trade Related Aspects of Intellectual Property Rights (TRIPs), Trade Related Investment Measures (TRIMs) and General Agreement on Trade in Services (GATS) are prominent and have many implications on the developing countries.

The trading blocs represent bilateralism. In contrast WTO stands for Multilateralism. Had the Uruguay Round collapsed, the spectre of world trade conflicts and global depression would have been real. As international trade tension grew in 1980s, an increasing number of countries began to circumvent GATT rules. GATT became relatively powerless. This tended to hurt weaker countries more, as they were more susceptible to bilateral arm-twisting. It was clearly in the interest of the weaker countries like India (with 0.67% share of global exports) that the system tightened up and the rules straightened. This improvement in the rules of the multilateral system in the long-run will be a major gain for the developing countries including India.

On the issue of trading blocs, these are covered under Article XXIV of the GATT. They are thus not illegal under GATT, but have to abide by the disciplines that are set out in the Article. The Article is however, so full of ambiguities that it has very little effect on the way trading blocs have been formed. Under the Article the trade restrictions must be eliminated over a period not exceeding ten years. However, these cannot be reduced because of a principle of Most Favoured Nation (MFN) Clause.

So far India has gained a lot from the Ministerial Meetings especially at Doha Round. However, in the next development round in 2003, the developing countries including India has to safeguard their interest against the insistence of the developed countries to include some of the non-trade issues. For instance, there is a clamour on the part of some of the developed countries to bring in new issues in the next development round; the issues which are not strictly relevant for trading purposes, and for which other more relevant international organisations already exist. The labour and the environment clause (and also the clause on animal welfare) proposed by some of the developed countries are a pointer in this direction. These handicaps are likely to be enhanced with the emphasis on, what has been called 'market plus' agenda i.e., the provision of the competition policies, investment policies and so on. The balance may be tilted again in favour of the developed countries due to the superior bargaining powers of the developed countries.

India and other developed countries should unite on the issues on environment, AoA, TRIPs, TRIMs, GATS, sanitary and phytosanitary measures and so on. They should formulate a countervailing strategy on issues like 'sustainable living standards', food security, rural development and so on.

What should be India's Stand on the Cancun Round?

- Take a proactive role—not a responsive one;
- Insist on giving priority to food self-sufficiency, as long as 50 percent or more of workers depend on food production for their livelihood;
- Ask for better market access for tropical products;
- Ask for internationally determined norms on sanitary and phytosanitary safeguards;
- Resist introduction of hidden subsidies;
- Insist on closer scrutiny of the non-product specific subsidies in developed countries; and
- As a countervailing strategy bring issues such as 'sustainable living standards', rural development, food security and so on.

References

Walter, E., "Closing the UK's Competitiveness Gap" in *Europe Productivity Ideas* (European Association of National Productivity Centres, Brussels), 2/95, p. 1.

The World Competitiveness Report, World Economic Forum (IMD, Geneva), 1995, p. 26.

Pronk, J., Haq, M., "Sustainable Development : From Concept to Action", *Paper Presented at the Hague Symposium on Sustainable Development* (The Hague), 1992.

Daly, H., "The perils of free trade" in *Scientific American* (New York), Nov. 1993, p. 26.

Tolentino, A., *Productivity Improvement : Enterprises' Contribution towards Sustainable Development* (Geneva, ILO), 1994.

Stevens, C., "Do Environmental Policies Affect Competitiveness" in *The OECD Observer* (Paris), No. 183, Aug.-Sept. 1993, pp. 22-23.

APO, "Green Productivity Workshop Highlights Shifting Emphasis in Pollution Control" in *APO News* (Tokyo), June, 1994, p. 2.

World Development Report, 1995, "Workers in an Integrated World" in *Report No. 14086* (World Bank, Washington, D.C.)., June 1995, p. 74.

The Global Competitiveness Report, *op. cit.*, p. 33.

Gereffi, Gary : "Global Commodity Chains and Third World Development", *a paper for an Informal Workshop* (Geneva, ILO), 1995, p. 9.

D'Cruz, J.R., "Business Networks for Global Competitiveness" in *Business Quarterly* (University of Western Ontario, Canada), Summer, 1993, p. 93.

Goldman, Steven L., *et. al.*, *Agile Competitors and Virtual Organizations* (Van Nostrand Reinhold, New York), 1994.

Port, O., Cary, J., "This is what the U.S. must do to Stay Competitive" in *Business Week* (December 16, 1991), pp. 92-93; Port, O., "Moving Past the Assembly Line : 'Agile' Manufacturing Systems may bring U.S. Revival" in *Business Week* (McGraw-Hill, New York), October 23, 1992, pp. 177, 180.

MacCormack, A.D. *et al.*, "The New Dynamics of Global Manufacturing Site Location" in *Sloan Management Review* (MIT Sloan School of Management, Massachusetts), Summer 1994, pp. 69-80.

Yogendran, Radha, "Reaping the Benefits of Inter-company Exchanges" in *Productivity Digest* (National Productivity Board, Singapore), Nov. 1995, pp. 36-38.

Drucker, P. , "Trade Lessons from the World Economy" in *Foreign Affairs* (Council of Foreign Relations, New York), Jan.-Feb., 1994, Vol. 73, No. 2, p. 101.

"Asia's Competing Capitalisms : It is Southeast Asia, not Japan, that is Providing a Model for the Development of China and India" in *The Economist* (London), 24 June, 1995.

Vasudeva, P.K., *WTO : Global Business Policies*, Minerva Publishers, London, and New Delhi, 2001.

WTO and Indian Agriculture with Special Reference to Punjab

P.S. RANGI

After the Second World War, a meeting was held in Washington DC under which three institutions, viz., International Bank for Reconstruction and Development, International Monetary Fund and International Trade Organization were agreed upon to be established to monitor and supervise the development and trade flows among different countries of the world. In October 1947, about 23 countries including India agreed on different rules and regulations to govern trade and tariffs, which became effective in January 1948. Several rounds of negotiations were held later on and a number of countries kept on joining these organizations. These negotiations were concluded at Marrakesh in April 1994. India signed the General Agreement on Trade and Tariff (GATT) on 15th April, 1994 at Marrakesh. Consequent upon this, World Trade Organization (WTO) became effective on January 1, 1995 to formulate/modify rules and regulations governing free trade amongst member countries and monitor its implementation. Up to 1995, trade in agricultural commodities (except cotton and fiber) was not covered under GATT rules. Under the Uruguay Round, agricultural commodities have been covered under the multilateral trading system. At present, there are more than 150 member countries of WTO including China and almost 25 including Russia are waiting in the list to join it. It was envisaged that both developed and developing countries would benefit from the free trade. However, after eight years of implementation of various clauses of Agreement on Agriculture (AOA) under WTO, it is being felt that free world trade in agriculture has not benefited the developing countries including India particularly due to low productivity, poor quality and imperfectly competitive export market structure still continuing.

The articles in the AOA, which would affect agriculture most, are :

1. MARKET ACCESS

(a) Tariffication

Earlier agriculture imports were regulated through quantitative restrictions (QR) and import duties. Under WTO it has been agreed by all the member-countries to reduce/eliminate quantitative restrictions by April 2001. Instead of this, it was agreed to fix "bound" tariffs. Bound tariff rate acts as a ceiling rate. The countries bound themselves to some fixed levels of tariffs. India has bound its tariff rates at a very high level. For India, the tariff rates agreed were 100 per cent in case of primary products, 150 per cent for processed products and 300 percent in case of edible oils.

(b) Tariff Reduction

The commitments for reducing the tariffs starting since 1995 are as follows :

Developed Countries

On an average by 36 per cent in 6 years with a minimum of 15 per cent for each commodity.

Developing Countries

On an average by 24 per cent in 10 years with a minimum of 10 per cent for each commodity.

(c) Market Access

Under the Agreement, participating countries agreed upon their markets for imports within an agreed time frame. We are supposed to provide market access of three and five per cent by the years 2001 and 2005 respectively. The market access is based upon the consumption levels during 1986-88. This works out to about 5 million tonnes and 8.5 million tonnes respectively.

The Agreement on Agriculture (AOA) is closely linked to the agreement on application of Sanitary and Phytosanitary (SPS) measures which provide rights to the Government to restrict trade where necessary to protect human, animal and plant life and health.

2. DOMESTIC SUPPORT/SUBSIDIES

For the developing countries, the subsidies are to be lowered to a maximum level of ten per cent of the total value of agricultural production. The subsidies are termed as Aggregate Measure of Support (AMS) which include :

(a) Non-product Specific Subsidies

Such as subsidies on fertilizers, pesticides, irrigation water, credit, etc.

(b) Product Specific Subsidies

The gap between the domestic price of commodities and the international prices.

Amber Box subsidies are considered to be trade distorting and come under the progressive reduction commitments by member-countries.

At the time of signing of the agreement, AMS for India was negative because the domestic prices were lower than the international prices. But now the situation has changed since the international prices of food grains have gone down while the domestic prices have increased. For example, wheat prices in the world markets were US $ 236 per tonne during 1995-96 and now they are about 110 US $ per tonne. On the other hand, the minimum support price in India has increased from Rs. 330 to Rs. 620 in the same period.

Exemptions

Some expenditure incurred by the government is exempted from inclusion in the calculation of AMS. These exemptions are :

Green Box, which Includes Expenditure on

Research,

Pest and disease control,

Training services,

Extension and advisory services,

Marketing and promotion services, and

Infrastructure services.

All measures for which exemption is claimed shall conform to the criteria : (i) the support will be provided through a publicly support programme, and (ii) the support shall not have the effect of providing price support to producers.

Blue Box, which Includes Expenditure on

Public stock holding for food security,

PDS for targeted population at subsidized rates,

Direct income support to the producers as such decoupled income support,

Income insurance programme (keeping some areas uncultivated),

Relief for natural disasters,

Support to resource poor farmers, and

Payment under environmental programs.

Under public stock holding for food security, the government at current market prices shall purchase necessary food stocks.

Under income insurance and environmental programmes, producers will be eligible for such payments under clearly defined criteria in government programmes designed to assist the financial or physical restructuring of a producer's operations. Under the environmental programme, the payments shall be determined as a part of a clearly defined government environmental or conservation programme. The amount of payment in such a case will be limited to the extra cost or loss of income involved in compliance with the government programme.

3. EXPORT SUBSIDIES

Under the Agreement, there is commitment to reduce the Export Subsidies in 10 years as follows :

	Reduce subsidy by	*Reduce the quantity of Subsidized Export by*
Developed countries	36%	21%
Developing countries	24%	14%

Some developed countries like USA, EU and Canada provided 90-95 per cent export subsidy for wheat and 100 per cent in case of rice exports including Indonesia and Cambodia.

India is not providing any export subsidies except for some relaxations on the foreign exchange earnings. Developing countries are allowed to provide three of the listed export subsidies. These are reduction of export marketing costs, internal transport and international freight charges. We should use these relaxations to boost our agricultural exports, which are declining. Special stress has to be laid on the export of agricultural commodities that are fresh which are processed to capture the world market.

The export strategy has to be framed for the long-run and effectively carried out every year even if involving the simultaneous exports and imports of the same commodity during some years.

The green box and blue box subsidies are not included in the AMS. India does not spend much in these boxes, as we have not enough funds for these purposes and is arguing along with some other countries for clubbing all the boxes together into one AMS box. The developed countries have shifted some of their subsidies from AMS box to these boxes as given below :

	1986-88	*2000*
EU Total subsidies (US $ billion)	100	130
Green + Blue box subsidies	9	50
USA Total	50	60
Green + Blue box subsidies	24	51

Though developed countries claim that they have met all the reduction commitments on domestic support and export subsidies under AOA, yet the agricultural production in these developed countries is highly subsidized. For example, total agricultural subsidy has increased from 44 per cent of AGDP in based year 1986-88 to 49 per cent during 1999-2000. This ratio is 67 and 65 respectively for Japan. USA and OECD countries are giving the same level of subsidy during this period. Converted on per farm basis, on an average, the Japan farmer got US $ 26000 during 1999, which works out $ 11792 per hectare. Similarly, for USA, these figures were $ 21000 and 129 respectively. For E.C., these figures were $ 17000 and 831 and OECD $ 11000 and 218 respectively. For India, these were only $ 66 and 53 respectively.

The AMS in India has now been reported to have shifted from negative in 1986-88 to positive. Although international prices now are less than the domestic prices but any withdrawal of market price support system will beset the farmers in general and the resource poor farmers in particular more seriously, which will upset the social system of the country. Therefore, India should put up a strong argument for including Food Security/Social Security/Rural Poverty Box, as agriculture is a source of livelihood for a vast majority of poor population.

In further, negotiations to be held at Cancun (Mexico) during September 2003, India should argue :

- Replace AMS to producer support estimates (PSE), the negative product-specific support should be added to positive non-product specific support to get overall PSE.
- Put a cap on maximum PSE of say 40 per cent—the ceiling on product specific support may be 30 per cent and on non-product specific support at 10 per cent.
- Reduction commitments should be on each product line (wheat, rice, oils, etc.) and not on aggregate.
- Countervailing duties on imports should be permitted if the import is from the countries where PSE is higher than 10 per cent.
- Special safeguards enjoyed by other countries such as Peace Clause, SPS measure non-tariff barriers, etc. should be removed as these are against the very spirit of the AOA/WTO.

4. IMPACT OF WTO ON PUNJAB AGRICULTURE

To meet the national food demands, huge resources in terms of technical and financial have been utilized. New high yielding, high input responsive technology was developed, assured minimum support price and marketing was provided. Farmers responded very favourably. They invested heavily for improvements in land, creation of irrigation facilities and purchase of agricultural machinery for efficient and timely operations to achieve high yields. Punjab farmers played an important role in meeting an appreciable share of country's food deficit. Now when the country has become self-reliant or even surplus in terms of 'purchasable' demand, the

Punjab farmer is finding difficult to dispose-off his produce of wheat and rice. Under the proposed new policy, which was perhaps kept WTO agreement in view, the State Governments will be required to procure the food grains for PDS and FCI will procure for the food security system only and not as a price support measure.

Under WTO, the domestic support measures shall not have the effect of providing price support to producers. Under the same agreement, the public stock holding for security purposes is allowed. However, the process of stock accumulation and disposal shall be financially transparent and food purchases by the government shall be made at current market prices. The impact of both these measures will be very severe on the Punjab farmers, as their income will positively be reduced. Over a time if such a situation is allowed, this may cause social problems in the countryside.

To overcome these problems, we may seek from the Government of India the financial assistance which can be provided to the Punjab farmers to achieve the twin objectives of : (i) income insurance to the farmers; and (ii) environmental protection. Such assistance from the government to the formers is permissible under WTO.

In Punjab, wheat-paddy rotation is causing serious imbalances in soil fertility and ground water and also polluting the environment due to heavy use of chemicals. The suggested diversification may be accepted by the farmers if we ensure marketing as well as income. The State has to diversify 10 lakh hectare of rice to other crops, it will take enough time to multiply seeds for the suggested crops and an adjustment period of 7-10 years will be necessary. During this period, the farmers who change from rice and wheat to other crops should be provided direct income support. It will be necessary to create an Adjustment Fund for this, which can be given to protect environment degradation and income insurance to the farmers.

We should have a Punjab Chapter of World Trade Centre to study, evaluate, project, monitor and implement trading situations in the international market and take timely actions to safeguard the interests of the domestic producers (countervailing duties or anti-dumping measures).

To be competitive in the world market, it is essential to reduce transportation handling costs and loss of food grains. Silo storage and bulk handling of food grains will be effective to reduce post-harvest losses and increase productivity.

Farmers, extension workers and public need to be educated for improving productivity of agriculture, its quality, reduce cost of production, observe sanitary and phyto-sanitary standards for meeting the international standards of trade.

The State Government, Punjab Agricultural University and the farmers should join hands to provide necessary infrastructure for export-purposes, increase productivity of various agricultural products and production of quality products at low cost to be competitive in the world market. WTO is both an opportunity and a challenge to the Punjab agriculture and if corrective measures/timely actions are taken, it may prove very beneficial to the Punjab economy and the farmers.

Growth Performance of Productivity in Indian Agricultural Sector

SANJEEV GUPTA AND R.S. BAWA

I. INTRODUCTION

Agriculture is a driver of growth. All the three basic objectives of economic development of country, namely, output growth, price stability and poverty alleviation are best served by the growth of agricultural sector. When we look at state of agriculture at world's level we will find two distinct types of farming. In developed countries agriculture is highly efficient with substantial productive capacity and high output per worker results in permitting small number of population to feed entire population. Whereas in case of developing agrarian economies like India, productivity is very low and agricultural sector can barely sustain the farm population.

India has made a lot of progress in agriculture since independence and this sector has resulted in substantial increase in terms of growth of output, productivity and area under many crops. But, if we compare growth performance of Indian agriculture with the performance of agriculture of the developed economies, we will realize the fact that there is an urgent need to improve the productivity of this sector. A transition from extensive, low productivity agriculture to intensive, high productivity agriculture is a fundamental pre-requisite for the development of our agrarian economy. Productivity growth helps to reduce per unit cost of production and acts as a real indicator of progress in crop production activities.

A number of researchers like Rudra (1970); Dey (1975); Reddy (1978), Rao (1980); Nadkarni (1980); Dandekar (1980); Bawa and Kainth (1980); Ray

(1983); Chakraborti (1987); Jayalakshmi (1988); Achutan and Sawant (1995); Naik (1997); Alam (1997); Singh and Chandra (2001) and Gill (2002) have estimated the growth trends of principal crops at aggregate and disaggregate level, by using one or more of the conventional functional relationships. But the present study is more elaborative one; as many as ten alternative trend relationships are considered to study the long-term trends.

II. OBJECTIVES OF THE STUDY

Academicians, planners and policy-makers have stressed the need to understand the analysis of growth performance to frame a sound agricultural development strategy. In this chapter, an attempt has been made to study the growth behaviour of productivity of fourteen principal crops in order to make policy-makers aware and to have a more realistic understanding of the future prospects of Indian agriculture.

The specific objectives of the study were :

1. To analyse the growth performance of productivity of principal crops.
2. To study the impact of liberalisation on productivity of Indian agriculture.

III. DATA BASE AND ANALYTICAL FRAMEWORK

The study is based on 50 years secondary data covering the period 1950-51 to 1999-2000. The data relating to the productivity for fourteen principle crops for the above said period were pulled from various issues of 'Agricultural Statistics at a Glance' published by Directorate of Economics and Statistics, Ministry of Agriculture, Government of India, New Delhi. For the present analysis we have computed compound annual growth rates of productivity for entire period (P) [1950-51 to 1999-2000] and three sub-periods, viz., pre-Green Revolution (PrGr) [1950-51 to 1966-67], Green Revolution (Gr) [1966-67 to 1975-76] and post-Green Revolution (PoGr) [1975-76 to 1999-2000]. In order to analyse the impact of liberalization on growth performance, the period of post-green revolution was further sub-divided into pre-liberalization period (1975-76 to 1990-91) and liberalization period (1990-91 to 1999-00).

In order to fulfil the objectives of the paper compound annual growth rates of productivity were estimated by fitting an exponential function of the following form :

$$Y_t = \beta_0 \, \beta_1^t e^{U_t} \tag{1}$$

where Y_t is dependent variable, β_0 and β_1 are the unknown parameters, and U_t is the disturbance term. The equation (1) could be written in the logarithmic form as follows :

$$\log Y_t = \log \beta_0 + t \log \beta_1 + U_t \quad \ldots(2)$$

Above equation was estimated by applying Ordinary Least Square Method and compound rate of growth (gr_c) was obtained by taking antilog of estimated regression coefficient, subtracting 1 from it and multiplying the difference by 100, as under :

$$gr_c = (\text{A.L. } \hat{\beta}_1 - 1) \times 100 \quad \ldots(3)$$

where $\hat{\beta}_1$ is an estimate for β_1. The significance of growth rates was tested by applying t-test, given as follows :

$$t = \frac{\hat{\beta}_1}{s(\hat{\beta}_1)} \sim t\ (n-2)\ \text{d.f.} \quad \ldots(4)$$

where $\hat{\beta}_1$ is the regression estimate, s $(\hat{\beta}_1)$ the respective standard error. All statistically non-significant growth rates are treated as almost zero growth rates.

IV. RESULTS AND DISCUSSION

The results have been discussed in brief under the following sub-heads :

Growth Performance

Measuring agricultural growth has been one of the most extensively researched areas. The growth rate analysis helps in evaluating development programmes, which were launched with specific objectives over specific time. A positive growth rate reveals an increase-related aspect by its magnitude per annum, whereas *vice-versa* is case for negative growth rates. All the statistically non-significant growth rates indicate that there is no growth at all. Compound annual growth rates in respect of yield per hectare in case of 14 principal crops for overall (P) and sub-periods are shown in Table 26.1.

Perusal of Table 26.1 depicts that growth rate of productivity in case of food grains was 1.44% during PrGr and it increased significantly to 2.51% during GR and further showed acceleration to 2.69% during PrGr. For overall period of 50 years, productivity of food grain grew at the rate of 2.33%. In case of PrGr period productivity of rice increased at the rate of 1.86% and further showed an upsurge to 2.24 and 2.43% during GR and PoGr periods. For the overall period productivity of rice registered a growth rate of 2.01%. Productivity of wheat followed inverted U-path during three sub-periods. During PrGr, it grew at the rate of 1.50%, achieved significant

TABLE 26.1

All India Compound Growth Rates of Yield per hectare of Fourteen Principal Crops during different Time Periods

Crops	*1950-67*[I]	*1966-76*[II]	*1975-2000*[III]	*1975-91*[IV]	*1990-2000*[V]	*1950-2000*[VI]
(1)	*(2)*	*(3)*	*(4)*	*(5)*	*(6)*	*(7)*
Food grains	1.445 (4.264)	2.515 (3.314)	2.692 (20.672)	2.662 (7.957)	1.978 (9.097)	2.327 (37.228)
Rice	1.859 (3.838)	2.242 (2.864)	2.425 (13.429)	2.665 (5.641)	1.826 (6.573)	2.01 (26.304)
Wheat	1.503 (4.055)	3.531 (3.470)	2.88 (21.078)	3.445 (13.464)	1.827 (5.350)	3.197 (38.391)
Bajra	1.444 (2.735)	1.256 (0.440)*	2.159 (3.806)	0.576 (0.464)*	2.154 (1.231)	1.88 (10.252)
Jute & Mesta	0.224 (0.770)	1.276 (1.291)	2.306 (13.836)	2.364 (5.829)	0.916 (4.350)	1.282 (13.454)
Maize	3.158 (7.532)	0.4008 (0.298)*	2.281 (8.452)	1.968 (2.748)	1.236 (2.225)	1.78 (16.593)
Total Pulses	-0.34 (-0.714)	0.562 (0.424)*	1.07 (5.163)	0.98 (1.799)	1.02 (2.231)	0.52 (5.866)
Grams	-0.08 (-0.128)*	0.81 (0.468)*	0.947 (3.433)	0.2 (.284)*	1.69 (1.678)	0.71 (6.341)
Tur	-1.99 (-2.874)	2.908 (1.561)	-0.159 (-0.529)*	0.468 (1.095)	-0.359 (-0.258)*	0.021 (0.156)*
Nine Oilseeds	0.074 (0.167)*	2.264 (2.077)	2.355 (9.766)	2.051 (3.263)	2.076 (4.127)	1.362 (12.572)
Groundnut	-0.56 (-0.981)	2.61 (1.672)	1.12 (3.377)	0.88 (1.180)	1.43 (1.265)	0.81 (6.479)
Rapeseed & Mustard	0.625 (1.036)	3.056 (2.175)	3.02 (7.707)	4.4 (5.881)	0.34 (.292)*	2.058 (14.500)
Cotton	1.9 (4.186)	2.982 (2.678)	2.412 (7.275)	2.754 (4.209)	-1.04 (-1.217)	2.23 (21.180)
Potato	0.73 (1.454)	3.69 (3.774)	1.76 (8.814)	2.35 (6.655)	1.36 (1.727)	2.38 (23.035)

*Insignificant

Notes : Figures in parenthesis are the respective t-values.

I. Pre-green revolution period
II. Green Revolution period
III. Post-green revolution period
IV. Pre-Liberalisation period
V. Liberalisation period
VI. Overall period

acceleration to 3.53% during GR period, and decelerated to 2.88% during PoGr revolution. For entire period of 50 years it grew significantly at the rate of 3.25%.

Further it could be analyzed from the Table 26.1 that during PrGr growth rate of yield per hectare of bajra was 1.44% and decelerated to 1.25% during GR and further picked up during PoGr period and accelerated to 2.16%. For the overall period, productivity showed an acceleration of 1.88%. In case jute and mesta during sub-periods productivity showed continuous acceleration. It increased from 0.22% from PrGr to 1.28% during GR and further to 2.31% PoGr. For the overall period productivity of jute and mesta grew at the rate of 1.28%.

A further glance at Table 26.1 revealed that in case of maize, total pulses and grams during GR period growth rates were negligible and insignificant. All this happened due to neglect of these crops and implementation of modern techniques of production in case of rice and wheat. In case of maize, productivity grew at the rate of 2.28% during PoGr period and for overall period of 50 years it increased significantly at the rate of 1.78%. In case of total pulses negative growth of PrGr turned to be positive, significant, and accelerated to 1.07% during PoGR period. For overall period in case of total pulses, yield per hectare grew marginally at the rate of 0.52%. Productivity of grams followed the growth path similar to total pulses and showed meager growth rate of 0.71% for the entire period.

It can be further investigated that in case of tur (Table 26.1) negative growth of per yield during PrGr accelerated to 2.91% during GR and decelerated steeply and turned to be negative (–0.159%) during PoGr period. For the entire period of 50 years productivity of tur grew almost at the trifling rate of 0.021%. In case of nine oilseeds yield, per hectare showed continuous acceleration, it increased from 0.074% during PrGr to 2.26% during GR period and further accelerated to 2.35% PoGr period. For the entire period of study yield per hectare accelerated at the rate of only 1.36%. In case of groundnut, during PrGr period productivity depicted negative growth rate of 0.56%, but during GR period growth rate turned positive and depicted significant upsurge of 2.61%. The same growth path did not continue and it eclipsed to 1.12% during PoGr period. For the overall period of 50 years yield of groundnut showed marginal growth of 0.81%.

Further perusal of Table 26.1 conspicuously revealed that in case of rapeseed mustard, cotton and potato growth rates of yield depicted significant acceleration during GR period as compared to PrGr period but growth rates significantly decelerated in case of cotton and potato during PoGr period. In case of rapeseed mustard, yield per hectare followed almost same growth pattern during GR and PoGr period. For the entire period yield per hectare increased significantly at the rate of 2.06% in case of rapeseed mustard, whereas, in case of cotton and potato growth figures were 2.23% and 2.38% respectively.

Impact of Liberalisation on Growth of Productivity

Perusal of columns 5 and 6 from Table 26.1 indicated that productivity of food grains increased at the rate of 2.66% during pre-liberalisation period and decelerated to 1.97% during liberalisation period. In case of wheat, growth rate of yield that was 3.45% in pre-liberalisation moved down to 1.83% respectively in liberalisation period. In case of rice growth rates of yield followed the similar growth path as they followed in case of wheat. Further perusal of Table 2 revealed that growth rate of yield of bajra, increased at snail's pace of 0.57% in pre-liberalisation period and moved up to 2.15% in liberalisation period. In case of jute and mesta yield, per hectare which was 2.36% in pre-liberalisation period decelerated steeply to 0.92% in liberalisation period. Growth rate of productivity in case of maize was 2.28% during pre-liberalisation period decelerated to 1.24% during liberalisation, but in case of total pulses, productivity growth showed significant increase during liberalisation as compared to pre-liberalisation period. The growth rate of yield per hectare of grams, which was negligible in pre-liberalisation period, i.e. 0.20%, increased steeply to 1.69% during liberalisation period. It could be further analysed that in case of tur growth rate in term of yield was 0.47% during pre-liberalisation period but turned to be negative (–0.36%) during liberalisation period.

Compound annual growth rate of yield per hectare in case of oil seeds increased at the rate of 2.05% in pre-liberalisation depicted marginal increase in liberalisation period and reached at the level of 2.07%. Growth rate of yield of groundnut moved up from 0.88% during pre-liberalisation to 1.43% in liberalisation period. Further perusal of table conspicuously revealed that growth rates of yield per hectare of rapeseed and mustard have shown steep deceleration from 4.40% during pre-liberalisation period to 0.34% during liberalisation period. Yield per hectare of cotton increased at the rate of 2.75% in pre-liberalisation period but was replaced by negative rate of growth of –1.04% in the liberalisation period. In case of potato, growth rate of yield per hectare decelerated significantly from 2.35% during pre-liberalisation period to 1.36% during liberalisation period.

VI. CONCLUDING REMARKS

Analysis of growth performance indicates that during three sub-periods crops have shown different sort of growth behaviour. In case of certain crops like food grains, rice, wheat, etc. growth rate of yield per hectare depicted continuous acceleration, whereas in case of certain crops like groundnut, cotton, etc. growth path was an inverted U-shaped. In case of a few crops like bajra, maize, etc. growth rate of yield per hectare showed deceleration during the GR period and depicted acceleration during PoGr period. During liberalisation period performance of productivity represented the sad part of Indian agriculture because during liberalisation period productivity of most of the crops not only decelerated but also turned negative except in case of two crops. In case of only a few crops productivity showed marginal upsurge. All this happened because during reforms process central as well as state governments showed lukewarm response to the agricultural sector. Past trends and analysis of growth performance underscore that for better future we have to strengthen policies and programmes for further broadening the base for agricultural sector.

There is an urgent need to make collective efforts for promoting the productivity of Indian agricultural sector. Steps taken in isolation will not yield the desired results. What is needed is a well thought long-range strategy covering a package of initiatives as also legislation, wherever needed, to bring about a definite change in agricultural scenario in the country. Such a package should lay emphasis on R & D efforts, development of new variety of seeds, cutting costs, saving time and ensuring that the entire agricultural enterprise is more efficient accountable and productivity-oriented. On the other hand, necessary efforts for development of marketing infrastructure, effective crop management, training programmes, promotion of contract farming, strengthening of extension services, corporatization of agriculture and favourable public policy is necessary to improve productivity and efficiency and to compete in domestic and global markets. A significant upsurge of agricultural growth is vital for overall economic development and will make Indian agriculture a rewarding profession for the tillers of the soil, which is at par with the world leaders.

References

Achuthan, C.V. and S.D. Sawant (1995), "Agricultural Growth Across Groups and Regions : Emerging Trends Patterns", *Economic and Political Weekly*, Vol. 30, No. 20, (March 25), pp. A-2-A-13.

Alam, S. (1997), "A Quarter Century Experience of Crop Productivity Trends in Bangladesh : Implications for a Future Strategy," *Bangladesh Journal of Agricultural Economics*, Vol. XX, No. 1, pp. 15-27.

Bawa, R.S. and G.S. Kainth (1980), "A Time Series Analysis of Net National Product of India", *Margin*, Vol. 12, No. 3, pp. 51-80.

Dandekar, V.M. (1980), "Introduction to Seminar on Data Base and Methodology for the Study of Growth Rates in Agriculture", *Indian Journal of Agricultural Economics*, Vol. XXXV, No. 2, (April-June), pp. 1-12.

Dey, A.K. (1975), "Rates of Growth of Agriculture and Industry", *Economic and Political Weekly*, (June 21 and 28), Vol. X, Nos. 25 and 26.

Gautam, Virendra, K.N. Rai and Sudir K. Chaudhry, (1985), "Predicting Crop Acreage and Short–Term Production Credit Requirement in Hisar District", *Indian Journal of Agricultural Economics*, Vol. XL, No. 2, (April-June).

Gill, J. K. (*et al.*) (2002), " Growth Trends in Food Grains Production," *Productivity*, Vol. 43, No. 3, pp. 495-501.

Government of India (2000), *Agricultural Statistics at a Glance*, Ministry of Agriculture, Directorate of Economics and Statistics, New Delhi.

Government of India (2000), *Department of Agriculture and Cooperation : Annual Report 1999-2000 (Available at http ://www.nic.net.in).*

Government of India (2002), *Economic Survey, 2001-02*, Ministry of Finance, New Delhi.

Gujarati, D.N. (1995), *Basic Econometrics*, Singapore : McGraw-Hill, Inc.

Gyanendra Singh and Hukum Chandra (2001), "Growth Trends in Area and Productivity Affecting Foodgrains Production in Madhya Pradesh", *Agricultural Situations in India*, (Feb.).

Jayalakshmi, M. (1988), "Growth Rates of the Indian Economy : An Exercise in Methods", Unpublished Monograph.

Krishnaji, N. (1980), "Measuring Agricultural Growth", *Indian Journal of Agricultural Economics,* Vol. XXXV, No. 2, (April-June), pp. 31-41.

Nadkarni, (*et. al.*) (1980), "Measurement of Growth and Fluctuations in Crop Output—An Approach Based on the Concept of Non–Systematic Component", *Indian Journal of Agricultural Economic,* Vol. XXXV, No. 2, (April-June), pp. 21-30.

Rao, V.M. (1980), "Methodological Issues in Measuring Agricultural Growth : Lesson of Recent Indian Research", *Indian Journal of Agricultural Economics,* Vol. XXXV, No. 2, pp. 13-20.

Reddy, V.N. (1978), "Growth Rates", *Economic and Political Weekly,* Vol. XIII, No. 19.

Rudra, A. (1970), "The Rate of Growth of the Indian Economy" in E.A.G. Robinson and M. Kidran (eds.), *Economic Development in South Asia,* London : McMillan.

Natural Resource Management and Productivity Enhancement through Organic Agriculture

SUKHBIR KAUR AND HARPINDER SINGH

1. INTRODUCTION

Ever since the Industrial Revolution the processes of growth have been speeded up to produce more food for a growing population and to produce immense amounts of raw materials needed by the industries. For the past half a century the farms have become highly mechanized and specialized, as well as heavily dependent on fossil fuels, borrowed capital, chemical fertilizers and pesticides. Increasing specialization and economics of scale on farms have brought many benefits : high production levels, low prices for consumers and year round availability of many products. However, there have also been severe detrimental effects : declining soil productivity, deteriorating environmental quality, surface water pollution, soil erosion/ pollution, decrease in ground water table, loss of natural habitats, rise in pests and diseases, residue effect, and threats to human and animal health.

Modern agricultural research has taught the farmer to profiteer at the expense of posterity. In businesses such attitudes result in bankruptcy (Howard, 2000).

Organic Agriculture, with its concept of self-regulation, has shown new possibilities for farming in future. Organic agriculture is an agricultural production system in which yields are not only adequate economically but are also sustainable. Organic farming aims for optimal production under the conditions set by organic agriculture organizations.

Organic farmers stimulate production through fine-tuned management of the soil, water and other resources. The organic farmer's respect for nature is reflected in his/her actions, which are based on the self-regulating capacity of the various living organisms (IIRD, 2001).

The objectives of sustainability lies at the heart of organic farming and is one of the major factors determining the acceptability or otherwise of specific production practices. The term 'sustainable' is used in its widest sense, to encompass not just conservation of non-renewable resources (soil, energy, and minerals) but also issues of environmental, economic and social sustainability.

Sustainable agriculture will not only help to ensure that resources are recycled and maintained for the use of future generations but also aims at ensuring economic viability.

Organic products have a vast market potential especially in the overseas market as they provide a recognizable alternative for the health conscious consumers who seek food with little or no hemical residues. Organic products can also contribute to increased export and domestic market earnings by catering to specific market niches such as baby food.

"Organic farming is about adopting new thinking," says Gunar Rundgfen. A quiet revolution in organic lifestyles is changing the world. Maria odale'smagazine, *Organic Style,* talks about the new balance : "We believe the organic movement isn't just about seeds and weeds, but about health, beauty, food, home, garden, travel, work, family and soul."

This chapter aims at discussing the following issues :

1. The drawbacks of conventional agriculture in terms of decreasing productivity and diminishing natural resources.
2. The conceptual framework of organic agriculture and its relationship with productivity enhancement.
3. The status of organic agriculture worldwide and the scenario in Asia with special reference to India.
4. Suggested strategies for the promotion of organic agriculture.

2. DRAWBACKS OF CONVENTIONAL AGRICULTURE

The major criticisms of current agricultural practices are :

- It damages soil structure, soil fertility and also leads to soil erosion. Figures 27.1 and 27.2 describes the status of soil erosion and salt affected soils in Punjab.

It has lead to depletion of ground water table. The ground water table is going down by 30 cm per year in Punjab. It is declining in 77% of the area of the state where ground water quality is good and the canal water supply

FIG. 27.1
Problems of Soil Erosion in Punjab

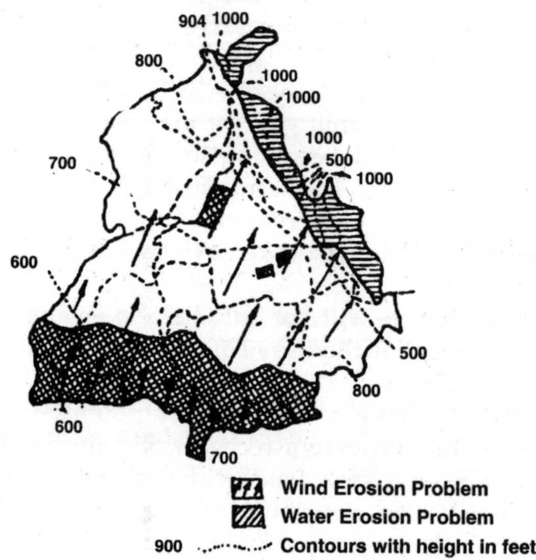

Source : State of Environment in Punjab First Status Report 1984.

FIG. 27.2
Salt Affected Soils in Punjab

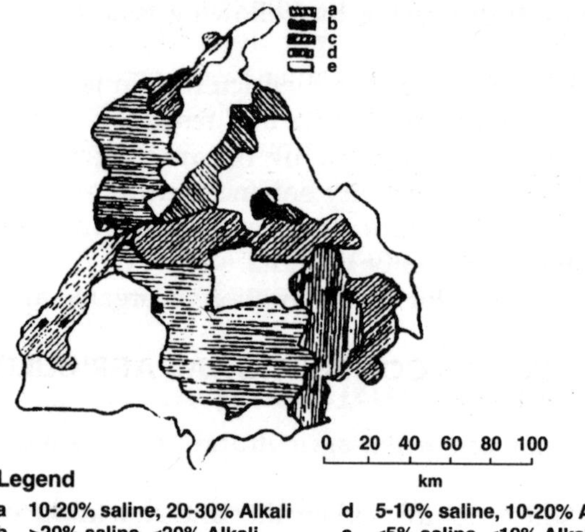

Source : Punjab environment : Status Report, 1995.

is limited. A critical water table depth of below 10 m has reached in 28% of the state. The following table shows the percent area under different water table depths in each hydrological zone of Punjab.

TABLE 27.1
Percent Area under different Water Table Depths (meters) in each Hydrological Zone of Punjab from 1973 to 2000

Year	*Foot-Hill Zone*			*Central Zone*			*South-West Zone*		
	<5	5-10	>10	<5	5-10	>10	<5	5-10	>10
1973	32	32	36	39	58	3	39	25	36
1990	23	57	20	9	66	25	39	49	12
1994	23	44	33	6	48	46	30	56	14
1996	37	35	28	6	69	25	45	47	8
1998	43	27	30	9	49	42	45	43	2
2000	30	47	23	6	41	53	41	50	9

- It damages the natural environment and traditional landscape.
- It creates potential health hazards in food that brings about a global decline in food quality. Reports indicate that the levels of DOT, BHC in human milk in Punjab are much higher than those in other countries. Ground water analysis in Ludhiana has indicated that about 90% of well water in the district contain more than 45 mg/l of nitrate. Similar results have also been obtained in Amritsar. High nitrate content leads to methaemoglobeneamia in the human and cattle population. (Punjab Environment, Status Report, 1995).
- It is an energy-consuming system. Natural farming produces 130 pounds of rice or 200,000 kilocalories of energy per man-day of labour, without any outside input. Ten times as much energy was expended in conventional farming, which used oxen and horse. The energy input in calories was doubled again with the advent of small-scale mechanization, and doubled yet another time with the shift to large-scale mechanization as shown in Table 27.2. (Fukuoka, 2001).
- It results in decrease in productivity as observed in Table 27.3.
- The conventional practices are leading to stagnation in agricultural production.

3. CONCEPTUAL FRAMEWORK

Definition

Organic farming covers agricultural systems that implements the environmentally, socially and economically sound production of food and fibers. Organic agriculture is a farming system which relies on crop rotations, the recycling of farm-produced organic material, i.e., crop residues, animal manure, legumes, green manure and off-farm organic wastes and on a variety of non-chemical methods for the control of pests, diseases and weeds. Synthetically compounded fertilizers, pesticides,

TABLE 27.2

Direct Energy Input in Rice Production, given as number of Kilocalories Required to Produce 1300 Pounds of Rice on a Quarter Acre in Japan

	Natural farming	*Farming with animals 1950*	*Small scale mechanized 1960*	*Medium scale mechanized 1970*	*Large scale mechanized 1980*
Human Labor	10-20	25	20	12	—
Animal Labor	0	6	4	0	0
Machinery	Hand tools	22	80	350	—
Fertilizer	0	40	75	54	—
Pesticides	0	11	25	72	—
Fuel	0	2	10	45	—
Total	10-20	96	214	533	1000
Energy Output	0.1-0.2	1	2	5	10
Energy Output/Input	100-200	20	10	4	2

Source : Fukuoka, 2001.

TABLE 27.3

Production of Cereals (per day) in India

Year	*Production (Grams per capita per day)*
1951	320.0
1961	427.3
1971	480.1
1981	473.5
1991	521.4
1997	531.2
2001	494.1

Source : Economic Survey of India, 2001-02.

herbicides, growth regulators and livestock feed additives are excluded or severely restricted. The products and methods of genetic engineering are also strictly prohibited.

Organic agriculture is defined as "an ecological production management system that promotes and enhances bio-diversity, biological cycles, and soil biological activity". It is based on minimal use of off-farm inputs and on management practices that restore, maintain, or enhance ecological harmony. The primary goal of organic agriculture is to optimize the health and productivity of interdependent communities of soil life, plants, animals and people. Organic agriculture has thus become an alternative to conventional farming (HRD, 2001).

The following five criteria could be a guideline for ascertaining the organic nature of a farm :

(1) *Productivity* : The system must be productive, it must yield food, feed and fiber, etc. Human input is equally directed at keeping the system itself intact. The system must be economically viable. This includes generating yields, but also conserving resources and minimizing risks of crop losses and soil damage.

(2) *Social Compatibility* : A farming system must be just and humane; it allows those operating as well as those managing it to live on and from it.

(3) *Preservation of the Environment* : The farming system must be ecologically sound. Farming always means interference with nature. Benign neglect does not suffice to keep a system intact. Natural resources, soil, and water must be maintained. The natural flora and fauna may not be destroyed through farming. Care must be taken to leave areas of refuge for natural plants and animals. Soil and other natural resources may not deteriorate through the yield extraction. Renewable energy resources are employed where feasible.

(4) *Nutrient Cycles* : Nutrient losses are minimized. Nutrients used for production of yields are as a rule produced in the system itself, not imported from outside. External fertilisers may only be used to balance deficiencies. The system must not be dependent on outside nutrient import.

(5) Farming techniques :

- *Crop rotation* : In an arable farming system, possibly including fallow, a balanced crop rotation results in yields, nutrient recycling to the soil, suppression of weeds and pests and allows the soils to keep their stability. Leguminous crops are important for nutrient recycling and for bringing nutrients into the system.
- *Inter-cropping* : In a system of perennials, it is desirable to have shade trees, often leguminous trees, possibly a system of inter-cropping to make the plants less susceptible to pests or hazards of weather.
- *Integration of crops and animal production* : Where livestock belongs to a farming system, stocking rates must be adapted to available fodder and water. Animal health kept up without constant use of veterinary drugs shows use of appropriate type of stock and stocking rates.
- *Bio-diversity* : The farming system promotes the existence of diverse species of life. The natural and local species of life is sustained in agro-systems.
- *Adaptability* : Farming systems that could adjust to changing conditions of population, market and policies.

Certification Requirements for Organic Agriculture

The environment and food quality benefits of organically produced food are not always immediately identifiable in the end product. Both consumer and producer interests are protected through certification programs, which consists of standards, inspection and certification. The certification programs vary per country or region because local conditions are different.

In countries like India, which are in the early stages of development of certified organic production, standards have to be developed from the broader perspective of promotion of organic agriculture, which covers different aspects of production, marketing, education, extension and research.

Based on the national standards developed through efforts of Institute of Integrated Rural Development (IIRD), a number of other organizations such as Spices board, Coffee board, Tea board and APEDA have come out with specific standards for various crops. Union Ministry of Commerce, Government of India, has also brought out standards for organic products and has announced a National Organic Plan.

4. STATUS OF ORGANIC AGRICULTURE

International

Organic production methods have developed in different countries, starting in 1924 with the bio-dynamic concept. The pioneers gave different names and are used throughout the world for what we call now "Organic Agriculture".

Global development of Organic agriculture is reflected by International Federation of Organic Agriculture Movement (IFOAM) membership figures : starting in 1972 with 5 founding organizations from three continents, growing to 100 member organizations in 25 countries, fifteen years later. In recent years membership exploded to 700 organizations in 130 countries, including 30 countries in Africa; 30 countries in Asia; 20 countries in Central America and the Caribbean; 10 countries in South America; 5 countries in Australasia and the Pacific; most countries in Europe; as well as the United States and Canada. These figures include at least 90 developing countries of which about 15 are LDCs (ITC Report, 2000).

European organic agriculture emerged in 1924 when Rudolf Steiner held his course on bio-dynamic agriculture. In the thirties and forties organic agriculture was developed in Switzerland by Hans Mueller, in Britain by Lady Eve Balfour and Albert Howard and in Japan by Masanobu Fukuoka.

In many other countries of the world organic agriculture was established because of the growing demand for organic products in Europe, United States and Japan. According to the Foundation Ecology and Agriculture (SOEL)—Survey, February 2002, (Figure 27.3) more than 17 million hectares are managed organically worldwide. Presently the major part of this area is located in Australia (7.7 million hectares), Argentina (2.8

Fig. 27.3
Continent-wise Organic Land Area

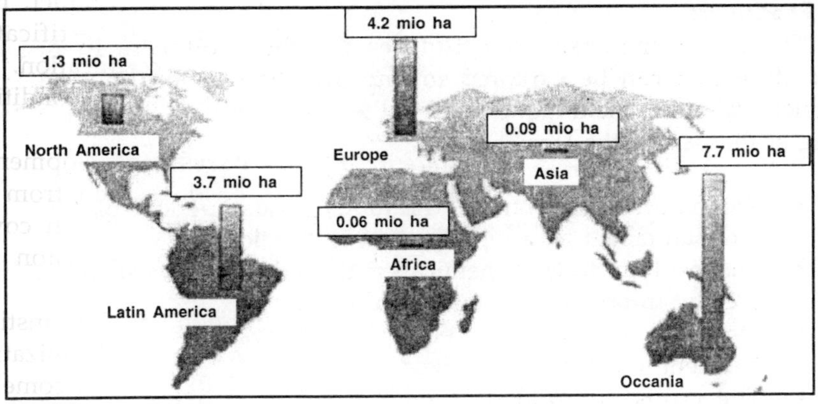

Source : SOEL, 2002.

million hectares) and Italy (more than 1 million hectares). Share of each continent of total organic area in percent is shown in Figure 27.4.

Scenario in Asia

In Asia the area under organic management is comparably small. The total organic area in Asia is now almost 100,000 hectares (0.55 percent of total area) (Figure 27.4). In eastern Asia significant organic producing countries are China, India, the Republic of Korea, Sri Lanka. India has only 2776 Hectares under organic management and there are about 1426 organic farms.

Fig. 27.4
Share of Each Continent of Total Organic Area in Percent

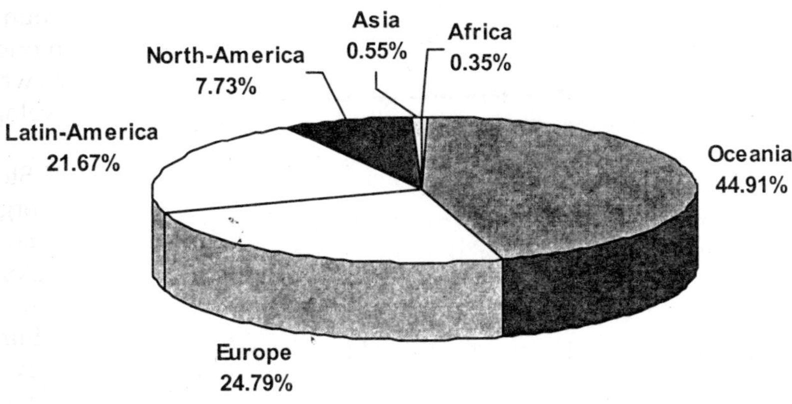

Source : SOEL, 2002.

5. OPPORTUNITIES FOR ENTREPRENEURS IN ORGANIC AGRICULTURE

For Producers

There are immense opportunities for the producers in organic agriculture that can be explored to improve the soil fertility and farm productivity and to yield higher returns thereby improving the standards of living at the part of the farmer.

- The natural environment, traditional landscape and bio-diversity are maintained by adopting organic practices.
- The residue effects of chemicals in the food products are minimized thereby improving the quality of food.
- Organic agriculture is an energy saving system.
- Nutrient losses are minimized.
- The crops are sold at premium prices and there is an ever increasing demand of organic products so these products are easy to market.
- One of the biggest benefits of organic farming is that it increases farm productivity in the long-run through enhancing soil structure and fertility and also minimizes the input cost as the expensive fertilizers and pesticides/herbicides are prohibited, thus increasing the profitability of the farm.

For Business Entrepreneurs

Since there are no official trade statistics, it is impossible to give a complete picture of world trade in organic products. However, it is clear that the European Union, the United States and Japan, are, by far, the largest markets, though there are smaller but interesting markets in many other countries, including some developing countries. The opportunities available for the business entrepreneurs are highlighted below :

- It is estimated that organic food and beverages market in 2002 was more than US $ 25 billion. Trade in organic food-stuff has indeed become a very important and global agri-business (OTA, 2002).
- The consumers' awareness is increasing regarding the chemical free food therefore the demand is increasing and there are opportunities for the traders to fill this gap.
- The organic trade is of particular interest in a development context because of the spectacular growth that has taken place in recent years, with growth rates of 10% and 40% (SOEL Survey, 2002).

The organic products are usually sold at premium prices. The price premium being paid in some of the Asian countries are listed in Table 27.4.

- Tropical, off-season, novelty and specialty products that are not

TABLE 27.4
Price Premiums on Organically Produced Products

Country	*Products*	*Price Premium*
India	All Kinds	100%
Philippines	Fresh Vegetables, Rice	30-50%
Thailand	Rice, Vegetables, Beans, Fruit	10-30%
China	Tea, Honey, Bamboo Shoots Peanuts, Rice, Beans	10-30%
Japan	Rice, Japanese Tea, Rice, Vinegar	20-50%

Source : SOEL, 2002.

produced in the major markets like cocoa, coffee, tea, spices, herbs, dry fruits, nuts, tropical fruits, etc., have high potential for traders.
- Organic customers have gone mainstream. In the past, most consumers were people with special health needs or members of religious groups. Today, consumers of organic foods are much broader based. The new target group is consumers in their 30's and 40's with higher education.
- There is whole range of organic products available in the market, that makes traders to diversify and make more profits.
- The organic sector is still a niche in the total food sector.
- Organic share in fruit and vegetable sales (higher than organic share in total food sales).
- Demand continues to exceed domestic supply. As demand for organic fresh produce is expected to continue to exceed production in developed countries, imports will be needed to meet consumers' demand.

6. BARRIERS IN ORGANIC AGRICULTURE DEVELOPMENT

Despite the vast potential of organic agriculture, it has not find favour with the growers, traders and the policy-makers. Some of the barriers in organic agriculture are discussed here :

- Growers are not aware of the technology and the benefits of organic production system.
- Farmers are mainly involved in conventional agriculture due to the importance and support being given by the governments.
- The conventional agriculture is highly subsidized by the governments.
- Market support is being given by the state in conventional agriculture system.

- Farmers are not aware of the drawbacks of conventional agriculture.
- It seems also clear—at least in the short to medium-term—that insufficient supply of organic products will be the main problem rather than lack of demand.
- Lack of organic processing industries.
- Long transport distances are one of the major hurdles in popularization of organic food products.
- Prices vary strongly among place, time and product group. Although there is a general lack of publicly available data on prices, some of the market surveys give some insight into this issue. For most countries, a sample of prices is given (mostly at retail level), but no price series or complete set of price data could be obtained. Since the organic sector in many countries is still dominated by a few traders, willingness to provide data has often been found to be limited, and market transparency is far from optimal.
- Lack of state regulation for organic agriculture makes it difficult in many countries to distinguish organic from low-chemical or even non-organic products.

7. THE SUGGESTED STRATEGIES FOR THE PROMOTION AND ADOPTION OF ORGANIC AGRICULTURE

The suggested strategies for the promotion and adoption of organic agriculture are discussed below :

- Generate awareness at the farmer's level regarding the technology and benefits of organic agriculture and drawbacks of conventional agriculture.
- Support from the state like the one that is provided for conventional agriculture.
- Government policy and support—most countries in western Europe have government policy and financial support for encouraging farmers to convert to organic production methods. In some countries, specific targets for organic agriculture have been set, e.g. to have 10% of the agricultural area under organic production by 2010.
- Potential producers/exporters should have a close look at likely future producer prices, as these are key in deciding whether to convert to organic farming, especially bearing in mind the conversion period of up to three years.
- AIDA (Awareness, Interest, Desire, Action) approach to be followed.
- Marketing support from the government.

- Generate awareness at the consumer's level regarding the benefits of chemical free food.
- Producers and traders should join a national/international organic agriculture/trade association to find out where the organic industry stands.
- Developing Marketing Channels—Internet, E-commerce, Home Delivery, Vegetarian Restaurants.
- Some organic marketing trends, like organic super markets, biodegradable packing organic food sales through public canteens and catering can be implemented.
- An important step is to establish national or regional organic standards and regulations and a reliable independent accreditation and control system to enforce those rules. Good post-harvest handling (e.g., cold storage), good infrastructure and logistics (including harbor or airports) will enable the fresh produce to arrive in good condition in the country of destination.

8. CONCLUSION

Organic farming is an approach to agriculture where the aim is to create integrated, humane, environmentally and economically sustainable agricultural production systems. Organic agriculture is the only solution for the sustainable development of agriculture and natural resources, which are being depleted by conventional methods. Green revolution has made us self-sufficient in food and other requirements but the need of the hour is to channelize our resources, skills and hard work for the sustainability of our agricultural system and limited resources so that the future of our progenies becomes secure.

Indian farmers have contributed a lot in making India self-reliant in food and fiber. If educated properly, they can contribute well for the conservation of our environment by adopting green enterprises like organic farming, dairy, poultry, etc., by respecting the natural resources. In business it is an utopian situation to hope for increasing productivity with minimal inputs, the wonder of organic agriculture is that it promises exactly that . . . long-term rise and continued productivity with decreasing inputs.

More sustainable agriculture will not only help to ensure that resources are recycled and maintained for the use of future generations but also help to maintain overseas market access as consumers increasingly demand that food be produced in an environmentally sustainable system. Organic products can contribute to increased export and domestic market earnings by supplying a particular market niche with the product perceived as high quality by environmentally aware consumers. Organic products provide a recognizable alternative for those consumers seeking food with little or no chemical residues.

The organic movement is small but it is making the difference and those who care for their children, their health, their planet and it's environment, should adopt this close to nature way of life.

References

Chaudhry, A.L. and Sharma, H.C. (1992), Natural Farming : Constraints and Prospects—Nature has given enough to fulfil our needs but not our greeds. Proceedings of the National Seminar on Natural Farming.

Concepts, Principles and Basic Standards of Indian Agriculture (2001), Institute for Integrated Rural Development (IIRD), Aurangabad.

Fukuoka, M. (2001), The Natural Way of Farming, Bookventure, Madras

International Trade Center Report (2000), Opportunities for developing countries in the production and export of organic horticultural products, Technical Center for Agricultural and Rural Cooperation, Food & Agricultural Organization of the United Nations. www.intracen.org.

Perng, C.M. (2000), Organic products finding a ready market on Taiwan, Report in the official website of USDA, www.fas.usda.gov.

Punjab Environment, Status Report (1995), Natural resources and environment, Punjab State Council for Science and Technology, Chandigarh.

Rudy Kortbech-Olesan (2000), Export opportunities of Organic Food from Developing Countries, World Organics 2000, A Conference organized by Agra, Europe (London) Ltd. www.intracen.org/mdds/sectors/organic/welcome.htm.

Rudy, Kortbech-Olesan (2000), World trends in consumption and trade of Exotic Food and Beverages—with emphasis on organic products, Sub-regional Trade Expansion in Southern Africa Buyers/Sellers Meeting on Exotic Food and Beverages, Johannesburg. www.intracen.org/mdds/sectors/organic/welcome.htm.

Rudy, Kortbech-Olesan (2002), Market Situation, Stiftung Oekologie & Landbau SOEL, Foundation Ecology & Agriculture. www.soel.de/oekolandbau/weltweit_infos.html

Sir Albert Howard (2000), An Agricultural Testament, Other India Press, Goa.

The official website of International Federation of Organic Agriculture Movement (www.ifoam.org).

The official website of Organic Trade Association of USA (www.ota.com).

The website of market and general information on organic farming (www.organicmonitor.com).

Yussef, M. and Witter, H. (2002), Organic Agriculture Worldwide 2002—Statistics and Prospects. Stiftung Oekologie & Landbau (SOEL, Foundation Ecology & Agriculture). www.soel.de/oekolandbau/weltweit_infos.html.

Agricultural Accounting : A Tool for Improving Productivity, Efficiency and Efficacy in the Agriculture Sector

DHARMINDER SINGH UBHA

INTRODUCTION

Agriculture is the most important sector of the Indian Economy. It provides us with food and our animals with fodder. It provides raw materials to our industries. It has been and continues to be the main source of livelihood in India because even today 2/3rd of the Indian population is directly or indirectly engaged in agriculture and allied activities. It also occupies an important place in the foreign trade of the country. Nearly one-third of the national income of our country originates from agriculture and allied activities. It will not be an exaggeration to say that agriculture is the real culture of the country and it has played and is playing an important role in the economy of the country. In spite of its relative importance in the economy of the country and its growing interrelationship with other sectors, agriculture has not received much attention from accounting researchers, practitioners, bodies and standard setters. Consequently, current accounting principles typically do not respond very well to the particular characteristics of agriculture business and the information needs of farmers and their stakeholders. Along with other reasons, like the illiteracy of farmers, the generally low level of managerial sophistication, decreasing size of holdings and fewer economic means in the sector, the unavailability of general accounting principles has led to a situation in which farmers are more reluctant to prepare accounting reports and make accounting records.

Agriculture, today, is passing through a critical phase in the country. It is believed that the arrival of World Trade Organisation regime will further aggravate the already miserable plight of the farmers. The politicians of the country, instead of preparing them to face the situation boldly, are creating unnecessary panic among the ignorant farming community about the possible consequences of the WTO policy. There is no denying the fact that with the entry of WTO in the agriculture sector and with the opening up of the economy, there will not be any smooth sailing for the Indian farmer and he has to equip himself with the global exposure in the field in order to face the stiff competition. It is in the fitness of things to mention right here that though we have achieved a green revolution and one more green revolution is being sought after, yet the status and position of our agriculture is much lower than it has been in the advanced countries of the world. The productivity and efficiency of the agriculture sector is deplorably low in all aspects and factors in comparison to the developed countries of the world. We still live at the mercy of God and the Government whereas in advanced countries the farmers have started running it on the prudent commercial principles. The farmers in those countries have started using highly sophisticated softwares for recording their agriculture transactions whereas we still have to make a beginning to make records even in the simple books.

PRODUCTIVITY OF AGRICULTURE SECTOR AND AGRICULTURAL ACCOUNTING

The term productivity, in general, means the total output per unit of the factor input. The productivity of the agriculture sector comprises the productivity of land, the productivity of labour and the productivity of real capital. The productivity of land means the output per hectare of land. The productivity of labour is taken to be the value-added per person. The marginal productivity of labour and real capital (Machinery, equipments, etc.) measures how efficiently these production factors contribute in the production process of the final product. The marginal productivity of real capital measures the increase in production volume associated with a unit increase in real capital, when all other factors are held constant in the production process. The marginal productivity of labour measures the increase in production volume associated with a unit increase in the labour, when all other factors are held constant in the production process. In economic theory, it is assumed that both the marginal productivity of labour and real capital is positive, but decreasing. The trends in the productivity of all the factors reveal that there has been some increase in productivity of agriculture over the years after independence but it is still very low as compared to that in other countries.

The reasons for this low productivity may be many but lack of accounting records by the farmers may be termed as one of the important reasons. They do not maintain any accounts relating to their agricultural transactions and as a result are not much aware of the inputs and outputs. It is a fundamental principle of management that better planning can be made and better control can be exercised if records of inputs and outputs are maintained in black and white. Indian agricultural sector is always accused of creating disguised unemployment, unplanned use of machinery and irrational cultivation of land. The records, if kept properly, present to the farmer the true picture of his state of affairs, sensitize him and compel him to take corrective measures in order to attain the desired productivity, efficiency and efficacy in his efforts. It is also believed that accounting can improve farm management and lead to better performance. Certain studies conducted in Europe revealed that the farmers who used agriculture accounting performed better in all respects than those who did not keep any systematic record of their farm operations. Accounting, thus, brings rationality to the efforts and endeavours of the farmers in carrying out their agricultural activities and enables them to have a cost benefit analysis of what they do.

It is evident that in order to match the global economy, we have to be in the fray and we cannot progress in isolation. It is altogether a different issue whether our farmer is in a position to face the competition or not and whether our government is sincere in giving him a proper lead in the matter. The farmers are totally indifferent to the agricultural costs. They neither have any cost benefit analysis nor do they believe in keeping any accounts. Whatsoever they get they simply call it their fate and wish that the lady luck would smile on them next year. As a result of small land holdings they cannot derive the benefits of economies of large scale. The cooperative movement has been unable to get the desired success in its mission. The false ego and pretensions of the farming community have also worsened their problems. The green revolution has turned the farmers lethargic and sluggish. The easy accessibility to bank loans has motivated them towards a luxurious life. All these factors when put together have created a vicious circle of problems galore for the farming community. Agriculture Accounting and costing can play a vital role in ameliorating the miserable plight of the farmers, can call upon them to improve the productivity and efficiency of the agricultural sector and can enable them to run their farming operations on commercial lines.

OBJECTIVES OF AGRICULTURAL ACCOUNTING

The basic objectives for adopting agricultural accounting can be as under :

- To analyse the records to make management decisions such as credit, government programme, what to grow and when, record production and diversify production;
- To get a true picture of the results of operations;
- To identify objectives and to classify them into short-term goals,

long-term goals and the priorities in each category);
- To list assets and liabilities and maintain their proper up to date records;
- To evaluate the fairness of operating arrangements;
- To analyse the alternate courses of action and to choose the best alternative; and
- To make decisions for capital asset replacement.

FARM ACCOUNTANCY DATA NETWORK IN EUROPE

In Europe, the Common Agricultural Policy (CAP) has been the cornerstone of the economic and political integration process, and to date the European Union's Directorate for agriculture still is the one, with by far the largest budget. The Farm Accountancy Data Network (FADN) was created in the context of Common Agricultural Policy by the European Economic Community in the year 1965. This network collects accounting information at the level of individual farms, and gathers every year data from a rotating sample of 60,000 professional farms across all member-states. FADN data are collected through a questionnaire from a variety of sources. The field of observation of FADN is that of commercial farms. The data relates to assets, liabilities, revenues and expenses of the farms in the sample and is summarized in reports similar to balance sheet and income statement. FADN uses market prices for valuation of non-monetary assets. Revenues are based on production, valued at end of period market prices. FADN distinguishes four broad categories of expenses. These are called specific costs, overheads, depreciation and external factors. Depending upon the type of farm, the specific cost refers to seeds and plants, fertilizers, crop protection and other crop specific costs, or feed and other live stock specific costs. Overheads include machinery and building costs, energy, contract work and other direct inputs. The external factors include wages, rent and interest. FADN does not consider the remuneration paid to the farmer and his family. The expenses not related to the farm activity are also not recorded as farm expenses. Both the specific cost and the overheads are determined on an accrual basis, but the external factors are valued on cash basis. Depreciation is calculated in accordance with the valuation of corresponding assets, that is normally replacement value. Consumption by the farm itself of livestock and farm output in general is valued at net realizable value. FADN has also given a format for the presentation of financial statements. It may be said that by doing so, FADN attempts to obtain something like a true and fair view of the financial performance and condition of the farms. It is alleged that FADN data is not obtained through book keeping procedures and it is inconsistent with basic Generally Accepted Accounting Principles (GAAP). However, it cannot be denied that FADN has created a lot of consciousness and awareness among the European farmers about agricultural accounting and has provided the methods for asset valuation, revenue recognition, expenses incurrence and presentation of financial statements. It has developed specific and general accounting guidelines. The Role of FADN can be said to be of a catalyst as for as implementation of agricultural accounting is concerned. The formats suggested by FADN for balance sheet and income statement are as under :

Structure of FADN Balance Sheet

Fixed Assets :	**Net worth :**
Land and permanent crops	Change in net worth
Buildings	Long and Medium term-loan
Machinery	
Breeding Live Stock	
Current Assets :	**Short-term loans**
Non-breeding live-stock	
Stock of agricultural produce	
Other Circulating capital	

Structure of FADN Income Statement

Total Output (by type of production)
+ Subsidies on production and costs
- Intermediate consumptions :
(a) Specific Costs :
  Seeds and plants
  Fertilizers
  Crop Protection
  Other crop specific cost
  Feed gazing livestock
  Feed pigs and poultry
  Other livestock specific cost
(b) Overheads :
  Machinery and building costs
  Energy
  Contract work
  Other direct inputs
- Taxes and VAT balance
= **Gross Farm Income**
- Depreciation
= **Farm Net Value Added**
+ Investment grants and subsidies
- External factors :
  Wages paid
  Rent paid
  Interest paid
= **Family Farm Income**

PROPOSED INTERNATIONAL ACCOUNTING STANDARD ON AGRICULTURE

The Proposed International Accounting Standard on Agriculture (PIASA) released by International Accounting Standard Committee provides the conceptual framework to agricultural accounting. Prior to PIASA, guidance for farm accounting could be found from the American Institute of Certified Public Accountants, 1996 and the Canadian Institute of Chartered Accountants, 1986. PIASA has recommended the model for definition, valuation and presentation of biological asset, agricultural produce and agricultural land. It has recommended that fair value is a better basis for the valuation of biological assets, agricultural produce and agricultural land than historical cost. It further concluded that market price is an indicator of fair value when active markets exist, and that market prices are more objective than allocations of historic cost. It also pointed out that for most agricultural assets relatively efficient markets exist and therefore fair value can be obtained easily. In the absence of active and efficient markets, the PIASA suggests to determine fair value based on the most recent market price for that class of assets, or market prices for similar or related assets. However, PIASA does not refer to the valuation of assets other than agricultural produce, biological assets and agricultural land, which means that these should be valued on historical cost basis. As for as revenue recognition is concerned, PIASA is of the view that it should be based on production and ending inventories of agricultural produce should be valued at fair value in their harvested state at the point of harvest. PIASA also requires that all of a farm's expenses should be reported on an accrual basis. PIASA has also made the presentation of financial statements simple and understandable. However, it is accused that PIASA is more useful to the professional accountants than the farmers. Thus, this proposed standard is a humble beginning in the field of agricultural accounting at the international level to make it more rational and useful.

APPLICATION OF AGRICULTURAL ACCOUNTING IN INDIA

Agriculture, in India, is still not undertaken on commercial lines and prudent business principles. The important reason for this is that our farmers neither keep the accounts relating to agriculture nor do they apply any techniques of accounting to control the agricultural costs. It is only with the help of accounts that we can have an optimum utilization of our frugal resources. Now agriculture is turning to be an industry and a profession. A number of farms have mushroomed around the cities where mixed farming is carried out. That is why it becomes imperative to apply all those accounting techniques and principles, which are applicable to industry and business. The account keeping will not only be helpful in determining the exact costs but will also be instrumental in controlling and curbing the costs and improving the productivity and efficiency of agriculture. The best crop cycle may be adopted by having the cost benefit analysis for each crop. A depreciation reserve may be created for the replacement of fixed assets like tractor, tubewell and thresher, etc.

Most of the agricultural transactions are exchange transactions. A worker may be given a part of the produce as a reward for his services. These kinds of dealings are to be converted into money value and then transferred to respective accounts. The cost concept of accounting can also not be applied in totality because assets like livestock are valued at market price. Similarly, self-produced goods are also valued at the market price. Some times goods from agriculture may be transferred to allied activities. The correct valuation of such transfers is also required. Fixed Instalment or Written Down Value method of depreciation may be applied on fixed assets. Agriculture is full of uncertainties and provision for the uncertain future is highly required. The crop insurance is still not undertaken on commercial lines. Record-keeping will encourage the insurance companies to come forward in the field of crop insurance. The produce used for personal use is also to be accounted for. The above may be the basis for agricultural accounting. The technique of Marginal Costing can be of great use in selecting the best crop mix by dividing the costs into fixed and variable costs. Budgeting may also be helpful for earning good profits in agriculture.

After a survey of several small and big farmers of the area it was found that most of them are ignorant about the agriculture costs and accounts. If a farmer is asked to tell about his income from agriculture, his immediate answer will be that he had a crop of Rs. 50,000 this time. He treats the whole receipt from the sale of produce as his income. Another version which is generally current is that the farmer first settles his old debt and then takes a new one at the time of the sale of produce and feels highly satisfied that now he has no outstanding payment of the previous years. So generally a farmer never thinks about the expenses incurred on the crop and if he thinks of something, it is only about the amount spent on buying the seeds, pesticides, manures and electricity. He never thinks about the costs of land and self-labour. He is totally ignorant about the concept of depreciation. So he does not keep into account the accounting assumptions and techniques relating to fixed assets.

The farmers are indulging in a rat race in the matter of buying modern agricultural equipment because of easy availability of bank loans. Even small farmers consider a tractor a matter of status and honour though it may be a white elephant for most of them. They never realize how will they pay the exorbitant interest. A fatal trend, which is perceptible now-a-days, is that the farmers sometimes get a tractor through bank loan to sell it immediately afterwards to spend the amount on useless luxuries of life. However, if a farmer maintains the proper accounts, he will have a proper analysis of the interest expenditure and hire charges if he hires the tractor instead of buying it. The disguised unemployment is another factor, which remains untouched because of non-maintenance of accounts. Most of the times the whole family of the farmer works in the fields directly or indirectly. But he never makes the evaluation of the services rendered by the members of the family. If a thorough analysis of the matter is made, he will find some of the members as economic burden on the institution. It is a fact that the efforts and outcome of the farmers are generally disproportionate.

No difference is generally found between the personal and agricultural transactions of a farmer. He normally keeps a common bank account from where he makes personal as well as business payments. In certain cases indigenous banking is still prevalent and all private and business expenses are paid in cash through the moneylender. The produce used at home is also not accounted for. Whatever is paid to the workers in the form of produce is not valued in money form and properly accounted for. The farmer does not bother about the concept of drawings and considers it below his status to account for the things used for domestic purpose. But this approach is against the concept of business. The business entity concept states that the entity of the business and the businessman is different and all transactions are recorded keeping the business in mind. Such an approach is needed in agriculture also if it is to be carried on commercial lines. Most of the farmers generally prefer cultivation of some particular crops because of status symbol though their costs of cultivation may not be fully recovered from them. They must have a cost benefit analysis of the crops and select those, which benefit the most at the least cost. Such an analysis is possible only through accounts.

Now the question arises how can the accounting techniques be implemented? Should all accounting techniques and principles be implemented immediately? No, in the beginning only such a system of accounting should be implemented as is easy to understand and simple to adopt. The beginning in this direction can be made by preparing simple cash book, account of each crop, account of live stock, account of expenses, net profit and loss account and finally the balance sheet. Most of the agricultural transactions are cash based and the receipts and payments can be entered in cashbook. Depreciation can be charged on farm machinery and building. Expenses incurred to make the land cultivable can be considered a part of costs of land. Expenses on insurance of crops and livestock may be there. The produce used at home and given to the workers may be treated like business accounts. Expenses may be categorized as per FADN basis. Similarly, the assets may be valued as per PIASA. The pattern of presenting the financial statements can be amended as per our own requirements. Thus, the principles of double entry system may be applied with a slight difference.

It is also suggested that cash system of accounting may be used, as it is simple to implement. When using this system, the income is recorded by the farming operation in the year in which cash is received, this may or may not correspond to the time when this income is earned. Expenses are recorded in the year in which they are paid, e.g. payment for fertilizer, seeds or repairs. This method of accounting is considered highly flexible because the farmers may influence the timing of the recognition of income and expenses. This system requires simpler records than accrual system and farmers may have cash available to pay expenses instead of having to use credit. It also promotes cash control and avoids the necessity of adjusting entries other than depreciation.

It can be said without an iota of doubt that once our farmers take to account keeping and become cost conscious, they will become truly commercial and agriculture will become a lucrative business. It will not only help in improving the productivity and efficiency of the agricultural sector but we shall also be in a position to face the music of the WTO more effectively. The government should play an important role in this direction by providing necessary training to the farmers regarding the maintenance of accounts. The government can also set-up a network on agricultural accounting on FADN pattern. The Institute of Chartered Accountants of India should also come forward in this field and issue certain accounting standards and guidelines as per the international standards. It should also be kept in mind that with the decrease in the size of land holdings, there would not be any choice except the cooperative farming which again will require the use of accounting techniques to make it a success. Farmers should be made to realise that the benefits of accounting outweigh the costs and the accounting information produced will not only be useful for external purposes but it will also be highly useful for better farm management. To conclude, it can be said that agricultural accounting may prove a panacea for the present ills of the farming community by turning them to be more commercially oriented.

References

Gupta, R.L., *Higher Accountancy,* Sultan Chand and Sons, New Delhi.

Josep, M. Argiles and Eric John Slof (2001), "New Opportunities for Farm Accounting", *European Accounting Review,* 10(2).

Slof, E.J. and Argiles, J.M. (1998), "An Analysis of the Accounting Principles Applied by the European Farm Accountancy Data Network", *European Accounting Review,* 8(4).

Sharma,V.P. and Others, *Corporate Accounting,* Unistar Books, Chandigarh.

SECTION V

INFORMATION TECHNOLOGY

Structure of I.T. Industry and its Policy Implications

INDERJEET SINGH

In conventional diffusion models developing countries were perceived to be passively engaged in the acquisition and use of technology that has been generated in industrialized countries, and available "off the shelf" in blueprints or codified knowledge. The technology acquisition and exploitation involves more than simply buying hardware and setting it to work. Technology is much more than the hardware; it also encompasses the knowledge, means and organization involved in applying science to the production of goods and services, i.e., the software.

The Information Technology industry is a typical example where an industry has shown a tremendous growth in terms of exports and has created vast employment opportunities as a result of liberalization. Upto 1984, Indian Software Industry had been nurtured in a protectionist environment guided by state managed system. The mid-1980s witnessed a phase of guided and guarded economic liberalization. This phase emphasized both greater access to imports and the promotion of software exports while still closely regulating the domestic computer and software industries. But the phase of 1990s, in fact, has been the real phase of economic liberalization. The IT industry over the years has been steadily moving up the value chain, the profile has evolved from coding, maintenance of legacy system and body shopping to high turnkey solutions and professional services. With the growing worldwide recognition of the Indian IT industry, the Indian professionals are today one of the most sought after global resource.

After the September crash and the controversial U.S. economic slow down, the Indian software sector in particular and the Information Technology industry in general has come into a trap of problems. Problems are manifested by reduced profit margins, reduced exports, less creation of employment, retrenchment of employees, closure of DOTCOM companies on a larger scale and so on. This chapter is an attempt to analyze the structure of the I.T. industry and derive a policy action program to bring the industry out of the current crisis.

SEGMENTATION OF THE I.T. INDUSTRY

IT industry can be segmented into hardware, software and training. Hardware has little synergy with software and very few companies are engaged in both the activities. Even where hardware companies provide 'total solutions', software is typically off the shelf software developed by specialized software companies. The characteristics, market requirements and economic dynamics of both the segments are vastly different. But on the other hand the software and training have a unique, but limited synergy between themselves. Training provides software development activity with the required programmers, while hands on experience gained in software development helps to develop better training inputs. It is therefore quite common to find a single company offering both software services/products and training.

The Indian I.T. industry continues to grow at an explosive pace. There is an increasing thrust by the private sector to have a connected and state of the art computing system. At the same time there is a growing awareness among the small and medium enterprises and small office and home office segment of the benefits of computerization. Over the past decade, the manufacturing sector in this industry is growing at an average annual rate of about more than 30 per cent. The IT industry, which was dominated by hardware industry, has experienced a shift towards software services. The share of hardware, which was 60 percent as at 1994-95, came down to 46 per cent by 1998-99 (Table 29.1).

TABLE 29.1
Break-up of Domestic IT Market (%)

Segment	*1994-95*	*1995-96*	*1996-97*	*1997-98*	*1998-99*
Hardware	60.0	61.0	58.5	48.0	46.0
Packaged Services	7.5	11.0	12.0	18.0	17.0
Services	25.0	22.0	23.0	29.0	33.0
Others	7.5	6.0	6.5	5.0	4.0

Source : Computed.

A look on the structure of the industry (Table 29.2) shows that industry derives the basic strength from software exports. An analysis of the composition of the exports may highlight the future opportunities and threats for the industry. But as indicated by the table, industry's major weakness lies on poor share of training component in the IT production basket. This implies industry is not investing on skill formation needed for meeting the challenges and obstacles of the future. Present export dependence due to sudden global demand coupled with low skill formation base for the future may lead the industry into a big crisis. Private sector is always interested in the immediate gains is thus least worried about future skill formation stocks of the industry. Here comes the role of Government intervention.

TABLE 29.2
Structure and Growth of the IT Market

(Rs. Million)

Segment	*1997-98*		*1998-99*	
	Total	*%*	*Total*	*%*
Training	8.6	4.8	11.9	5.0
System Integration	15.0	8.3	22.2	9.3
Maintenance	8.2	4.6	9.4	3.9
Packaged Software	19.6	10.9	22.5	9.4
Others	5.1	2.8	5.0	2.1
Networking	6.4	3.5	9.5	4.0
Peripherals	8.2	4.6	14.3	6.0
Systems	37.4	20.7	37.2	15.5
Exports	71.8	39.9	107.5	44.9
Total	180.2	100.0	239.6	100.0

Source : Dataquest.

Historically the industry has grown on the basis of nurturing and active buying support of the Government offices and public sector undertakings. But in the last decade, as also depicted by Table 29.3, the IT-related spending in percent share-terms has undergone a drastic shift in favour of the private sector. The role of Government as a buyer of this industry has significantly come down. The share of private sector has improved to 66.2 per cent in 1998-99 as against 53.0 per cent in the year 1995-96.

Thus out of the three segments of the industry, software segment has come to play a lead role in the last decade. The performance of the IT Industry is dependent on the performance of the software segment of the industry.

TABLE 29.3
Sector-wise Break-up of IT Spending

(% of Total)

Sector	1995-96	1996-97	1997-98	1998-99
Private Sector	53.0	51.0	76.0	66.2
Government	18.0	19.0	8.0	19.5
Public Sector	29.0	30.0	16.0	14.3
Total	100.0	100.0	100.0	100.0

Source : Computed.

HARDWARE SEGMENT OF THE INDUSTRY

The computer hardware market is a monopolistic competition type of market structure. Mostly computer hardware is sold like a commodity, i.e., there is a very little differentiation in terms of capabilities and performance. No single firm manufactures the entire system on its own. Each firm produces one or two parts, others are procured from outside and all these are assembled together and said as system. In the process, some companies have emerged as leaders for various products. For example, Intel for micro-processor chips, Malaysian and Taiwanese companies for printed circuit boards and other electronic parts. The process of commoditization of the hardware market has pushed down the margins drastically. Most of the producers operate on a wafer thin margin and rely on volumes to generate profits. Computer hardware industry can be further segmented into :

— Complete systems like mainframes, workstations, and personal computers;
— Peripherals like printers, plotters, modems, digitizers, etc.; and
— Consumables like diskettes, stationery, cables, wires, switches, etc.

According to an estimate, the industry has over 135 major hardware players supported by over more than 800 ancillary units and small vendors engaged in sub-assemblies and equipment manufacturing. Personal computers (PCs) constitute the largest share of the total computers and the peripherals market. Growth in demand for personal computers along with the rising popularity of the internet are the two major forces driving the growth of the domestic IT industry. During 1998-99, more than 8,20,000 PCs were sold in India which took the PC penetration to 3.2 PCs per 1000 persons. In India, 45 per cent of the buyers are the first time buyers, while rest are repeat buyers.

Brand-wise structure of the market shows that it is a market dominated by assemblers. Assemblers are small-scale industrialists who pick up discrete sub-assemblies and assemble them. The cost of production is relatively low because no testing is done and testing is basically done on hit and trial basis. In terms of number of units 57.5 percent market is with assemblers. Rest of the market is shared by branded equipment from multinational and Indian companies equally. Major chunk of profit goes to the assemblers because of low price and large customer base. Furthermore, assemblers are able to cut their costs by not paying levies, taxes and excise duties.

TABLE 29.4
Brand-wise Structure of Indian PC Market (1998-99)

Brand	*Share by No. of Units (per cent)*	*Share by Value (per cent)*
Assemblers (including GIDs)	57.50	44.90
MC Brands	21.90	38.10
Indian Brands	20.60	17.00
Total	100.00	100.00

Source : IDC India.

The price differential in products of branded and non-branded computers is very high. MNC brands are very costly in the market. Indian Brands are moderately priced. Unbranded, i.e., "others category" are priced at roughly one-third of that of MNC branded ones.

SOFTWARE SEGMENT

To understand the structure of the software industry, it would be imperative to understand the kind of value and thereby the profitability our companies are generating. Most of the work done by Indian companies is of the sub-contracting nature, executing assignments either onsite at client's premises or offshore at development centers in the country. A few of them have ventured into products of niche-segment. Indian companies are primarily operating at the low risk-low reward end of the product development. First area of operation is called the "body shopping", under which a local company acts like a placement agency. It picks up the candidates, sends them abroad and collects the fee from the overseas company or the candidates and sometimes from both. Second area is called an "onsite contracts". It is just similar to body shopping except that instead of programmers work is given as a contract to the contractors. The contractor is able to retain a major chunk of margin. The margin is quite high in this business channel. Thirdly, under "offshore contracts" the software development is transferred to local location. All investment in infrastructure facilities has to be met by the contractor. Here returns are high because of comparative cost advantage. So margins are higher than onsite contracts. Onsite and offshore are generally priced by the time and material spent method or fixed price method. Last area of operation is the area of "software products" that can be picked off the shelf and put to immediate use. These products can be of niche product type or mass product type. Profits from the products rely on volume of sales. Product development involves huge investment in research and development that means high risk and high return. Most of the Indian companies are operating on lower end of value chain, i.e., low risk-low return. Some companies are doing well in the area of systems integration. Systems integration, an area involving system study, analysis design and implementation of systems, still has higher margins and comparatively moderate risk level.

The software industry can be segregated into services and products. Services, generally user specific in nature, include body shopping, data processing, programming services, consultancy services, etc. where revenue is generated on the basis of time and material spent or on the basis of negotiated fixed contract price. Software products could be niche products or mass-market products systems software and application software products.

COST STRUCTURE OF THE SOFTWARE INDUSTRY

Cost structure for services is different from products. Services have a low fixed cost that can be recovered faster. Breakeven point comes quite soon in case of services but the total quantum and the life span of the profits is marginal. On the other hand, the product development has a substantially high component of fixed cost, which requires a relatively longer time to recover. The breakeven point comes quite later but the profit growth in products is exponential. In both the cases the major cost component is manpower followed by hardware, software and infrastructure costs. While the manpower, hardware, software and infrastructure could be considered as variable cost in case of service contracts, these must be classified as fixed costs in product development. In service contracts the recovery of these costs is immediate, while in products it takes a longer time. This is why Indian software industry is operating in low profile area of software market. If higher profits are to be earned and long-term stay of the industry is to be ensured, the companies must endeavour move up in the value chain, that is, from low risk-low returns to high risk-high return area.

As far as wages of different levels of software personnel are concerned, Switzerland has the highest wages in the world. This can serve as benchmark for cross-country comparisons of wage cost. A look on the Table 29.5 indicates that Indian salary cost is the minimum among the countries given in the table. All the salary costs are less than that of 30% of what is paid in Switzerland. On an average salary paid to computer professionals is 20.43 per cent of what it is paid in Switzerland and roughly one-third of that paid in USA. Another interesting point to be noted is that the variation among the employees of different ranks is the minimum. In Switzerland,

USA and Canada the variation, as displayed by the coefficient of variation, ranges from 10.45 per cent to 13.51 per cent. But in case of India the variation is quite pronounced, the coefficient of variation is to the tune of 36.74 percent. There is a big difference between the salaries of employees in different levels of hierarchy. Indian average wages are US $ 13583 as against the same US $ 46083 in USA. Historically this has been the fact responsible for developing India as a market from off-shore projects, especially for low value jobs. Also the larger wage differential between India and USA is the main factor that has been responsible for migration of Indian IT personnel to USA.

TABLE 29.5
Salary Cost Comparisons Across the Countries

(US$)

	Switzerland	*USA*	*Canada*	*UK*	*Ireland*	*Greece*	*India*
Project Leader	74000 (100.00)	54000 (72.97)	39000 (52.70)	39000 (52.70)	43000 (58.11)	24000 (32.43)	23000 (31.08)
Business Analyst	74000 (100.00)	38000 (51.35)	36000 (48.65)	37000 (50.00)	36000 (48.65)	28000 (37.84)	21000 (28.38)
Systems Analyst	74000 (100.00)	48000 (64.86)	32000 (43.24)	34000 (45.95)	36000 (48.65)	15000 (20.27)	14000 (18.92)
Systems Designer	67000 (100.00)	55000 (82.09)	36000 (53.73)	34000 (50.75)	31000 (46.27)	15000 (22.39)	11000 (16.42)
Development Programmer	56000 (100.00)	41000 (73.21)	29000 (51.79)	29000 (51.79)	21000 (37.50)	13000 (23.21)	8000 (14.29)
Support Programmer	56000 (100.00)	37000 (66.07)	26000 (46.43)	25000 (44.64)	21000 (37.50)	15000 (26.79)	8000 (14.29)
Network Analyst/ Designer	67000 (100.00)	49000 (73.13)	32000 (47.76)	31000 (46.27)	26000 (38.81)	15000 (22.39)	14000 (20.90)
Quality Assurance Specialist	71000 (100.00)	50000 (70.42)	28000 (39.44)	33000 (46.48)	29000 (40.85)	15000 (21.13)	14000 (19.72)
Database Data Analyst	67000 (100.00)	50000 (74.63)	32000 (47.76)	22000 (32.84)	29000 (43.28)	24000 (35.82)	17000 (25.37)
Metrics/Process specialist	74000 (100.00)	48000 (64.86)	29000 (39.19)	31000 (41.89)	—	15000 (20.27)	17000 (22.97)
Documentation/ Training Staff	59000 (100.00)	36000 (61.02)	26000 (44.07)	21000 (35.59)	—	15000 (25.42)	8000 (13.56)
Test Engineer	59000 (100.00)	47000 (79.66)	25000 (42.37)	24000 (40.68)	—	13000 (22.03)	8000 (13.56)
Average	66500 (100.00)	46083 (69.30)	30833 (46.37)	30000 (45.11)	30222 (45.45)	17250 (25.94)	13583 (20.43)
Standard Deviation	6946	6224	4278	5627	6844	4515	4991
Coefficient of Variation	10.45	13.51	13.88	18.76	22.65	27.92	36.74

Source : Rubin, H.A. *et. al.* (3996).
Note : Figures in parentheses are wages in a country as a percentage of wages paid in a highly paid country.

In the present phase of economic slowdown in USA and relatively improved wages in the IT sector in India, the wage differential is gradually narrowing down. This has got two implications :

— Migration of IT labour to USA will not be of the scale of late 1990s; and
— Increasing costs are gradually wiping out the comparative cost advantage that India has. The opportunity may slip into the hands of countries like China.

But the fact remains that India, a labour abundant economy, still offers and has the potential to offer IT labour at comparatively lower prices.

Table 29.6 gives the breakup of total cost for a developer with one to two years of experience for two kinds of projects : (a) On site work at client site, and (b) Offshore work done in India. In this table additional overheads are the additional administrative, managerial, communications and other costs, for onsite work there would be client's or agency's responsibility. The table gives the cost structure without taking taxes into account for both types of projects. Another assumption implied from the table is that there is no wage differential as far as basic Indian salary is concerned; it is only the allowances that make the difference. There is a big difference in total cost both onsite and off-shore. Salary component is 28.27 per cent (basic plus

TABLE 29.6
Cost Breakdown for Hiring Indian Software Labour with 1-2 Years of Experience

Cost Element	*Onsite work at Client site (US $)*	*Off-shore work done in India (US $)*
Overseas allowance	1900 (23.75)	n.a.
Overseas rent	1700 (21.75)	n.a.
Overseas local travel	300 (3.75)	n.a.
Overseas travel & other charges	450 (5.63)	n.a.
Local hardware use	n.a.	550 (11.96)
Basic Indian salary	900 (11.25)	900 (19.57)
Indian salary extras	400 (5.00)	400 (8.70)
Administrative, Financial overheads	650 (8.13)	650 (14.13)
Training overheads	300 (3.75)	300 (6.52)
Building & utility overheads	200 (2.50)	200 (4.35)
Additional off-shore overheads	n.a.	400 (8.70)
Profit	1200 (15.00)	1200 (26.09)
Total (Excluding taxes for onsite)	8000 (100.00)	4600 (100.00)

Source : Heeks, R. (1999).

extras) of the total cost in case of offshore work done in India whereas addition of allowances makes it to be more than 55 percent. Cost breakdown analysis indicates that in onsite projects more than 40 per cent of the cost is contributed by overseas allowances, rent and local travel which is non-existent in the off-shore work done in India. Further the rate of profit is only 15 per cent in case of onsite projects as against the same is 26.09 per cent in case of off-shore works done in India. This comparative cost advantage favoured the off-shore software development in India. But such an advantage is by nature a short-term phenomenon. Gradually with passage of time due to increasing wage rates and due to entry of more countries in the software production in the global arena this comparative cost advantage may not exist to the so high.

PATTERN OF DEVELOPMENT OF THE SOFTWARE INDUSTRY

Out of total software exports of Rs. 679994.15 lac in 1998-99, Tata Consultancy Ltd. share was Rs. 151832.00 lac. HCL Technologies Ltd., Wipro Ltd., Pentafour Software and the Infosys in order follow it. The software industry is a concentrated in the hands of few companies. The top most company, Tata Consultancy Ltd., has a share of 22.33 per cent in the total export of top twenty exporters. Out of the total exports of top twenty software exporters, 59.20 per cent of the business is with top 5 companies of India. The rest of the software industry shares remaining 40.80 per cent of the industry exports.

Most of the companies are mainly concentrated around big cities like Delhi, Bangalore, Mumbai, Chennai, Calcutta, etc. But among these cities the companies are not evenly distributed. Majority of the companies are concentrated in Banglore, Mumbai and the Delhi region. Basic reason for such a skewed pattern of distribution of software companies is existence of information-infrastructure in these areas. In initial phases of development of the software industry infrastructure facilities like Software Technology Parks (STP) and Export Promotion Zones (EPZ) were provided at these places. Later on location advantages and concession plans of governments further promoted the process of centralization of industry at these places.

As per an estimate of Electronics and Computer Software Export Council of India approximately 1000 companies have been engaged in export of computer software during the year 1998-99, out of which council has published statistics for more than 900 companies. Break-up of these exporters according to various exports slabs and the percentage share of each slab is given in Table 29.8. It may be seen from the Table 29.8 that there is a gradual up-gradation of the companies. As many as 20 companies have exported for more than Rs. 100 crore each and equal number of companies fall within the category of Rs. 50 crore to Rs. 100 crore. Number of companies in the category of Rs. 10 crore to 50 crore has also gone up from 32 in 1995-96 to 106 in 1998-99. Export analysis also reveals that share of these 146 companies in the export slab of Rs. 10 crore or above amounts to

TABLE 29.7
List of Top Twenty Exporters of Computer Software

Sl. No.	Company	(Exports/Rs. Lacs)	% Share
1.	Tata Consultancy Ltd.	151832.00	22.3
2.	HCL Technologies Ltd.	86200.00	12.68
3.	Wipro Ltd.	63250.00	9.30
4.	Pentafour Software & Exports Ltd.	53383.17	7.53
5.	Infosys Technologies Ltd.	50025.40	7.36
6.	NTTT Ltd.	39496. 00	5.81
7.	Satyam Computer Services Ltd.	37661.00	5.54
8.	IBM Global Services India Pvt. Ltd.	22900.00	3.37
9.	DSQ Software Ltd.	22432.00	3.30
10.	Tata Infotech Ltd.	22083.00	3.25
11.	Mahindra British Telecom Ltd.	17100.00	2.51
12.	Cognizant Tech. Solutions India Ltd.	16443.00	2.42
13.	International Computers (India) Ltd.	14493.62	2.13
14.	L&T Information Technology Ltd.	14255.71	2.10
15.	IMR Global Ltd.	13900.00	2.04
16.	Citicorp Information Tech. Industries	13581.56	2.00
17.	Patni Computer Systems Pvt. Ltd.	11873.18	1.75
18.	Complete Business Solutions (I) Pvt. Ltd.	10930.51	1.61
19.	Silver Line Industries Ltd.	10300.00	1.51
20.	HCL Perot Systems Ltd.	10054:00	1.48
	Total	679994.15	

Source : ESC India.

Rs. 10,380 crore which is 83.04 per cent of the total export of the software from the country. As many as 341 companies fall in the slab of Rs. 1 crore to Rs. 10 crore and their contribution is Rs. 1,169 crore which is 9.35 percent of India's exports. The analysis reveals that the companies in the segment of Rs. 10 crore export or less should be focused and targeted for extending the base to achieve higher growth. Number-wise this segment constitutes more than 80 percent of the industry. Over the years, in number terms, the share of this segment has been roughly above 80 per cent. It is possible for these small companies to expand their exports at much faster rate in comparison to the companies in the top segment.

TABLE 29.8
Slab-wise Number of Exporters in India (1995-96 to 1998-99)

Export Slab (Rs. Cr.)	*Number of Companies*							
	1998-99		*1997-98*		*1996-97*		*1995-96*	
	No.	*%*	*No.*	*%*	*No.*	*%*	*No.*	*%*
100 and above	20	2.19	13	2.08	5	.84	4	0.98
50-100	20	2.19	10	1.60	8	1.35	6	1.46
25-50	58	6.35	20	3.20	19	3.21	15	3,66
10-25	48	5.26	45	7.33	26	4.39	17	4.15
1-10	341	37.35	222	35.52	182	30.74	115	28.05
Up to 1	426	46.66	315	50.40	352	59.46	253	61.71
Total	913		625		592		410	

Source : ESC India.

STRUCTURE OF EXPORTS OF SOFTWARE INDUSTRY

The dynamic policy measures taken in the past by the Government of India would have acted as catalyst in further accelerating the export growth of India's software industry. The bold decision to exempt tax on the income of venture capital funds would lend vibrancy to the venture capital culture, which is an essential pre-requisite for the sustained growth of Indian software Industry. Export growth in relation to total exports is given in Table 29.9. Table shows that all commodity section has registered a growth of 20.45 per cent per annum during the period under consideration. In the same period software and related services segment has registered record growth of 57.08 per cent per annum. The share of software in the total export basket of the country has risen from meager 0.74 per cent in the year 1988-89 to 14.61 per cent in the year 2000-01. This share has grown at an average annual growth rate of 30.41 per cent per annum.

Until the mid-1970s Eastern Europe was the main destination of Indian software exports. But that has since changed, with the United States taking over as the main export market in the early 1980s with 75 per cent of the Indian exports geared to that market. This was because of the sheer size of the United States Market for software, which is much larger than any other market, as well as the long history of Indian engineers and computer professionals working in the United States. Some of them came back to India to set-up their own companies but maintained their contacts in the United States and were able to use these to penetrate the market. Indians who worked for large American IT multinationals also played a role in attracting attention to the software development work that was being done in India and to the level of skill and expertise. Further, India enjoys an advantage in

TABLE 29.9

Export Growth of Computer Software and Related Services in Relation to Total Exports in India (1988-89 to 1998-99)

Year	*Software Exports*				*Total Exports*		*Software Share*		*Exchange Rate*	
	(Rs. Cr.)		*(M. US $)*		*(Rs. Cr.)*		*in Total Export*		*(1 US $=)*	
1988-89	150.00	(—)	99.53	(—)	20232	(—)	0.74	(—)	15.07	(—)
1989-90	175.00	(16.67)	105.00	(5.50)	27681	(36.82)	0.63	(–14.73)	16.65	(10.48)
1990-91	250.00	(42.86)	139.35	(32.71)	32553	(17.60)	0.77	(21.48)	17.94	(7.75)
1991-92	508.00	(103.20)	206.00	(47.83)	44041	(35.29)	1.15	[50.20)	24.65	(37.40)
1992-93	740.00	(45.67)	260.00	(26.21)	53688	(21.90)	1.38	(19.49)	28.50	(15.62)
1993-94	1020.00	(37.84)	329.00	(26.54)	69751	(29.92)	1.46	(6.10)	31.00	(8.77)
1994-95	1474.00	(44.51)	475.48	(44.52)	82674	(18.53)	1.78	(21.92)	31.00	(0.00)
1995-96	2650.00	(79.78)	791.04	(66.37)	1063	28.64)	2.49	(39.76)	33.50	(8.06)
1996-97	4113.00	(55.21)	1158.59	(46.46)	118817	(11.72)	3.46	(38.93)	35.50	(5.97)
1997-98	6800.00	(65.33)	1813.33	(56.51)	126286	(6.29)	5.38	(55.55)	37.50	(5.63)
1998-99	12500.00	(83.82)	3012.05	(66.11)	141605	(12.13)	8.83	(63.940	41.50	(10.67)
1999-00	17150.00	(37.20)	4000.00	(.32.80)	176099	(24.36)	9.74	(10..33)	42.88	(3.33)
2000-01*	28350.00	(65.31)	6200.00	(55.00)	194048	(10.19)	14.61	(50.02)	45.73	(6.65)
Trend Growth Rate	57.08		43.56		20.45		30.41		9.50	

Note : Figures within brackets are simple year to year growth rates. • Estimated.

English, the main language used in development of software. During the 1980s, the software export market started to be more diversified. In the late 1980s, the United States share of Indian software exports was down to 60 per cent. In the 1994-95, the breakdown of markets for the Indian software exports was as : 58 per cent of exports went to United States, 20 per cent to Europe, 6 per cent to Southeast Asia, 3 per cent to Japan, 4 per cent to West Asia and the rest to other countries.

Destination-wise Indian software exporters have successfully penetrated into 85 countries during the year 1998-99 as compared to 66 countries during 1997-98. Thus, 19 countries have been added to the list of our export destinations that include small countries like Malta, Seychelles, Albania, and Lebanon, etc. Thus, good efforts have been made in market diversification of exports. North America (USA and Canada) continues to remain our largest market (Table 29.10) which has contributed Rs. 7683.49 crore (US $ 1.85 billion) which is 61.47 per cent of our export revenue in this sector during the year 1998-99 as compared to Rs. 3880 crore (US $ 1.03 billion) which was 57.06 during the year 1997-98. Thus, growth in this market in value terms is 98 per cent and the percentage increase is 7.73 per cent. Similarly, Europe (EC countries) continued to be our second largest market with our export of software estimated at Rs. 3180 crore (US $ 766 million) as compared to Rs. 1783 (US $ 475 million) during the year 1997-98. Percentage share of this market, however, has slightly gone down from 26.22 per cent in 1997-98 to 25.44 in 1998-99. It is interesting to note that our export of software to Japan and the Far East countries has grown to Rs. 558.88 crore (US $ 134.67 million) during the year 1998-99 and this market is now our third most important market. There is a need to increase our share in this second largest market after USA. Singapore, Hong Kong and other South Asian Countries have contributed Rs. 463 crore (US $ 111.73 million) and have become our fourth most important destination. Markets of Middle East, African continent and Russia are the new emerging markets and Indian companies have consolidated their position in these markets during the year 1998-99.

TABLE 29.10
Comparison of Major Destinations for Computer Software and Services Exports

Destination	1998-99 Value (Rs. Cr.)	1998-99 Sectoral Share (%)	1997-98 Value (Rs. Cr.)	1997-98 Sectoral Share (%)	Variation Share terms (%)
U.S.A. and Canada	7583.49	61.47	3880. 00	57.06	7.73
Europe (EC countries)	3189.53	25.44	1782.93	26.22	-2.96
Japan, Korea and Other Far East Countries	558.88	4.47	513.40	7.55	-40.78
Singapore, Hongkong and Other South E. Asian Countries	463.68	3.71	311.44	4.58	-19.01
Middle East Countries	234.42	1.88	81.60	1.20	56.28
African Countries	200.45	1.60	11.40	1.05	52.72
Australia and Other Oceanic Countries	114.24	0.91	144.84	2.13	-57.09
Russia and C.I.S. Countries	30.77	0.25	1.36	0.02	1130.80
Latin America	19,01	0.15	5.44	0.06	90.70
Europe (Non-EC Countries)	14.47	0.12	7.48	0.11	5.24
Total	12500.00		6800.00		
Indices :					
Coeff. of variation	186.19		174.02		
Herfindahl Index	0.4466		0.1192		

Source : ESC India.

The North America continues to be major destination for our software exports and this share has improved over a period of time. From marketing strategy point such over-dependence to the tune of more than 60 per cent on a single country or two is not viable proposition from long-term point of view. Any macro-economic problem of the destination country may affect the entire software industry of the country. Recent World Trade Center accident and the controversial US slow down have affected our export performance to greater extent immediately. What to talk of placement opportunities for software personnel in this region, even the retrenchment and process of under-employment has set on. This should be treated as an alarming bell by the Indian software industry. Software market should be diversified geographically to those areas where there is a greater potential in the future.

The domestic and the export market differ significantly as far as the product mix basket is concerned (Table 29.11). Turnkey projects, products and packages dominate domestic market. Both components, roughly constitute about 87.70 per cent of the total software traded. Professional services do not exist at all in the domestic software market. Consultancy, training and data processing component of the domestic market is very small, it is just 12.30 per cent of the domestic software activity. On the other hand, turnkey projects are totally non-existent in the software exports. Professional services category which is nil in domestic market constitutes 46.70 per cent of the total exports. It is followed by consultancy and training, the share of which is 27.40 per cent. Thus both domestic and export market have a diametrically opposite behaviour. For export-related software categories, there is no domestic market and *vice versa*.

TABLE 29.11
The Structure of the Production of Software Industry

Software Activity	*Domestic Market*		*Export Market*	
	Value	*%*	*Value*	*%*
Turnkey	2945	40.90	0	0.00
Professional Services	0	0.00	8009	46.70
Products and Packages	3370	46.80	1904	11.10
Consultancy and Training	497	6.90	4699	27.40
Data Processing	374	5.20	1887	11.00
Others	14	0.20	652	3.80
Total	7200	100	17150	100

Source : DOE, Govt. of India Reports.

Further the breakup of exports (Table 29.12) is an indicative of the fact that major share of the software exports is of off-site services. It is about 58.7 per cent of the total exports. Off-shore services share in the total software exports is 30.2 per cent. Off-shore packages share is only 11.1 per cent. So on the whole services dominate the software export market and still the products and packages are on the back seat. The proportion of onsite work will decline due to improvement in the telecommunications and the provision of infrastructure and facilities through Software Technology Parks and because of visa restrictions in the United States and Europe.

TABLE 29.12

Structure of Software Exports

Type of Service	*Exports*	
	Value	%
Off-site services	10067	58.7
Off-shore Services	5179	30.2
Off-shore Packages	1904	11.1
Total	17150	100

Source : DOE, Government of India reports.

Analysis of the product/service profile in the software sector reveals that there has not been much change in our basket of services. The Y2K opportunities were considered to be a big business of the order of at least five to seven billion dollars few years back has contributed approximately Rs. 2800 crore (US $ 675 million) which is 22.4 per cent of our total exports during the year 1998-99. Further, it is estimated that the accumulated Y2K business till March 1999 has contributed approximately US $ 1.2 to 1.5 billion. Although our performance in tapping Y2K opportunities can not be called very satisfactory, it suggests that Indian companies have been able to retain their due share in business other than that of Y2K in the major markets.

IT enabled services is another important area which is being focused by the Indian companies. It is estimated that IT enabled services has contributed approximately Rs. 1250 crore, that is, 10 per cent of the total basket. This new emerging area needs to be focused sharply because it is going to be a major foreign exchange earner in the coming years. Embedded software and e-commerce are other promising area. It is expected that the e-commerce itself would cross US $ 1.5 billion by the year 2003 that is presently at less than 5.0 million.

So, export growth of the Indian software industry have been skewed in many dimensions. Most of the skew patterns are responsible for the problems of today.

STRUCTURE OF EDUCATION AND TRAINING

Computer education and training industry, in India, composes of two categories. First, user-oriented training for basic awareness regarding hardware and software. Secondly, carrier-oriented training imparted to professionals that aspire to pursue a carrier in information technology and software development.

Computer education and training industry, in India, has come into being around 70s when few private institutes were set-up. In the beginning and even in the 80s the focus of training was on a low-end education for creating awareness about computers. High-end computer training was imparted only in IITs and engineering colleges and institutes. Most of the carrier-oriented professionals used to go abroad for training. The training segment of the industry got momentum in the late 80s and early 90s. During the last five years the industry has experienced an explosive pace of about 30-35 percent per annum. While the established training companies have maintained a high growth rate and hundreds of small companies have mushroomed in the last three years. Currently, the training segment of the industry is estimated to be a 12 billion in terms of revenue.

Basic computer education has become part of the school curriculum. Most of the recently mushroomed Private training institutes are imparting basic literacy in computers and low-end courses on a very large scale. Real training courses, relating to proprietary technologies and skill upgradation, are typically offered by leading IT companies. As per an estimate the total global market is estimated to be US $ 16 bn as compared to Indian market of US $ 0.35 bn. The unit cost of a training course in high-end and low-end is vastly different. Major concentration of training industry has been in USA because global companies of USA have been spending huge amounts to upgrade, motivate and retain their personnel. In this direction China is an emerging market.

India has more than 1900 institutions from which about 70,000 software professionals graduate each year. This is further supplemented by private training centers that supply about 50,000 students each year. With many students opting for further studies or other employment streams, it is estimated that India can supply about 75,000 software professionals each year. Despite the huge addition to the manpower base each year, the demand-supply gap is expected to remain tight during the next two years.

The domestic training has fairly a large number of scattered players. However, the top two (NIIT and Aptech) control around 70 percent of the market, which is estimated to be around Rs. 9.1 billion. Revenues are seasonal in nature, as 90 per cent of it comes from individual training and enrolment peaks during summer vacations. The key to profits is reducing the idle time of computers and tutors, which is generally around 25-30 per cent. Training institutes are perceived as high priced and low quality (barring a few top players).

Inspite of this, the segment grew by 34 per cent in 2000-01, driven by emerging career opportunities for high-end software packages and increasing penetration of computers.

POLICY IMPLICATIONS

Indian software industry has displayed a very high level of growth-rate both in terms of output and exports. Such a high growth performance can be sustainable only with continuous improvements in the product by improving the technology of production, by changing product mix, by investing more on research and development effort and by frequent upgrading of the human resources of the country.

Most of the software production done by the Indian companies was a sort of work sub-contracted by big software US companies. Work obtained by sub-contracting gives a relatively low margin and moreover the real working firm is unable to create its brand name in the market.

There is an urgent need to alter the composition of exports. Currently the Indian firms capture a low portion of the value-added in the world software industry. Most of the manpower is involved in tasks such as coding or testing software rather than in managing projects, the design of software, or the integration of different computer and software systems. Over the long term, Indian companies ran the risk of becoming stuck in the low technology and low value-added activities of world software production.

The share of services in the software exports has been continuously high. Indian firms have been basically operating as placement agencies, i.e., "body shopping" have been the main component Indian software exports. Indian software industry followed the easier option and operated in an area of exports where life span of the product is always small. This requires investment in software products, rather than services.

The sustainability of high growth rate, in production or in exports, always necessitates a huge investment in skill formation base of the country so that the future threats and challenges of the global market could be met. Private sector is always concerned about its immediate gain. Skill formation for the future of the industry is never and can never be part of its agenda. The skill formation base needs continuous investment in human resources, which is joint long-term responsibility of the government and the industry.

The salary structure analysis shows that during 1990s wages paid in India have been approximately one-fifth of that paid in Switzerland and one-third of that paid in USA. This wage differential has been the main cause of migration of Indian IT personnel to USA. Because of US slow down, tighter visa laws and relatively improved wages in India, migration may not be that lucrative now. Because of above referred wage differential and because of other costs India has a comparative cost advantage as compared to other countries. But this advantage is also a short-term phenomenon. Due to macro-economic conditions in US, the magnitude and nature of this comparative cost advantage may get adversely affected over time. So for the future course of action, the only way is to improve the efficiency and productivity in the Indian Industry.

The entire software industry is characterized by economic concentration in hands of few companies. In software exports, 59.20 per cent of the total business is with top five companies only and rest is shared by large number of odd units. Performance of the industry is basically the functioning of top five companies.

Training segment of the industry has registered a growth of 34 per cent per annum in the late 1990s. Most of the mushroomed IT institutes are imparting the basic computer literacy and low-end courses at a very large scale. Very few institutes are giving real training courses coupled with high-level skills relating to proprietary technologies. Preparing students to the level of product design and R & D, needs a training rigor that is presently in short supply. The unit cost of such high-end courses is very high. China and some other countries are spending a lot in this direction. These institutions cannot be opened by the industry alone. The industry-government collaboration can start such institutions. In the long-run both the industry and the state will gain from it.

Traditionally, the North America continues to be major destination for our software exports and this share has improved over a period of time. From marketing strategy point of view such over-dependence is not a viable proposition. Software market should be diversified geographically to those areas where there is a greater potential in the future.

Due to alarming rates of software piracy, foreign software companies are hesitant to enter, sublet, or sell their products in developing countries. This requires development of a stronger national and international protection for intelligence for intellectual property rights was also seen as essential to the development of the software industry.

To sum up, the present crisis of the Indian software industry needs a long-run plan for upgrading skill formation base, changing the production mix and market diversification in case of exports.

REFERENCES

Bauman, Adam (1994) : "FBI Arrests Father, Son in CD-ROM Piracy Probe; Software : Thousands of Counterfeit Computer Games are Seized in the First Major Case of its Kind", *Los Angeles Times*, 23 December, Business Section, page 4.

Elmer-Dewitt, Philip (1994) : "Nabbing the Pirates of Cyberspace", Time, Furger, Roberta (1995) : "Copy Protection, the Sequel : Coming to a PC Near You," *PC World*, January 1995, p. 33.

Hanna, N. (1991) : The Information Technology Revolution and Economic Development, W.B., Washington D.C.

Hanna, N. (1994) : Exploiting Information Technology for Development, W.B., Washington D.C.

Heeks, R. (1999) : India's Software Industry, IDPM, University of Manchester, UK.

Maggs, John (1995) : "Firms Target Three Nations for Piracy Proceedings", *The Journal of Commerce*, 15 February.

Mehta, Vinnie (2001) : "Glimpses of Indian IT Industry", An Address by the Director of MAIT on Independence Day (August 14).

Rubin, H.A. (1996) : World-wide Benchmark Project, Rubin Systems, Pound Ridge, New York.

World Bank (1993) : World Development Report, Washington D.C.

ERP Systems : Planning, Design and Implementation Model

Ashim Raj Singla and D.P. Goyal

INTRODUCTION

ERP has become a buzzword in the recent past because of its adoption by a large number of organizations. Whereas many organizations all over the world have already acquired ERP systems and many are at the threshold of acquiring these systems. ERP systems are highly integrated computer-based information systems, which help the organizations in planning, organizing and controlling of the resources.

More specifically, Enterprise Resource Planning (ERP) systems cover the techniques and concepts employed for the integrated management of business as a whole, from the viewpoint of the effective use of management resources, to improve the efficiency of an enterprise. ERP systems are integrated software (covering all business functions) systems, i.e. ERP is a set of application software that brings manufacturing, finance, sales, distribution, human resources and other business functions into balance. As the pace of change continues to accelerate and corporations around the world seek to revitalize, reinvent and resize in an effort to position themselves for success and keeping in view the new customer needs and resize market opportunities as they arise, high level of interaction and co-ordination along the supply chain will be key ingredient to their continued success.

The main objective of the ERP system is to integrate various functions/ departments/divisions within an organization to enable it to operate optimally so as to reduce cost, increase profitability and to achieve highest customer satisfaction.

Broadly the scope of the ERP systems is defined in all the functional areas of management, namely, Production Management, Financial Management, Marketing Management, Human Resource Management, and Warehouse Management, etc.

Some of the direct benefits of ERP systems include *Business Integration, Flexibility, Better Analysis and Planning Capability.*

In the case of ERP systems, the data of related business functions is also automatically updated at the time a transaction occurs. For this reason, one is able to grasp business details in the real time, and carry out various types of management decisions in a timely manner, based on the information.

Second advantage is that different languages, currencies, accounting standards and so on can be covered in one system, and functions that comprehensively manage multiple locations of a company which can be packaged and implemented automatically.

Another advantage is that by enabling the comprehensive and unified management of related business and its data, it becomes possible to fully utilize many types of decision support systems and simulation functions.

NEED OF THE STUDY

Almost all large-scale organizations are turning to some sort of Enterprise Resource Planning (ERP) systems as a solution to their information management problems. ERP systems if chosen correctly, implemented judiciously and used efficiently will raise the productivity and profits of the organizations dramatically. But some organizations fail in this because of choosing a wrong product, incompetent and haphazard implementation, inefficient or ineffective usage, or actual cost involved crossed the budget. ERP systems are definitely meant for large and medium size organizations because cost involved will definitely be high. Following questions that must be answered before an organization goes for ERP systems selection :

1. Should we buy the ERP systems? If yes, which package should it be?
2. What will be the costs involved?
3. What is the hidden cost involved?
4. How does one implement the package in the organization?
5. What changes should be made at the organizational level?
6. What are the hurdles and obstacles that one should be prepared for?
7. What is the role of consultants in the implementation and how should they be dealt with so that money is well spent?
8. How does one overcome the resistance of the employees?

The cost involved in implementing a ERP system is dependent on several factors like the package chosen, the technology used, whether the company is using the existing hardware/software infrastructure, how much training is needed, what are the resources available in-house for implementation, whether external consultants are required, and so on. So in some organizations (small and medium size) standard ERP application software will definitely be costly and more ever any software customization to standard package to fit the requirement of the organization will add more cost to implementation. It is better to develop the ERP systems itself on some proposed model if the organization needs are quite different from the readymade systems because readymade systems are highly generalized.

The discipline of ERP systems is in evolution stage. A survey of literature reveals that many researchers contributed in this area, but still a lot needs to be done. This has been highlighted through a review of related studies that is given below.

REVIEW OF LITERATURE

Valkoff, Olga (2001) in his study "Grounded process model of Enterprise System Implementation" developed a grounded process model of enterprise system (ES) implementation. As a part of this task it also considers the different forms that process model might take, and suggests a Format based on threads of continues process scripts instead of traditional 'sequence-of-events" type of process model; *Gattikar Thomrmationas Fredric (2000) in his study "ERP system in operational management : A model, instrument and an empirical test"* discusses a model of which costs and benefits arising from the implementation of the ERP system/has been developed and tested. This research on ERP implementation is associated with reliance on alternative (non-ERP) systems and with increased time required for managerial tasks is associated with negative overall plant impact; *Sena, Mark Philip (2001) in his study "Enterprise system for organizational decision support : An examination of objectives, characteristics and benefits"* stressed on Enterprise computing systems for the major section of intra-organizational sector of electronic commerce. The survey targets the adopters of four leading enterprise systems vendors, SAP, People Soft, oracle applications and J.D. Edward. It launches a new initiatives with in the decision support system field, give manager a new perspective on the decision support possibilities of enterprise computing and highlights the area where vendors may improve decision support facts of enterprise software offerings; *Startman, Jeffrey Keith (2001) in his study "Information integration for supply chain management; an empirical investigation of ERP systems in manufacturing industry"* examines the operational practices and procedures that are associated with effective use of integrated info systems and supply chain management *within the context of* the ERP used by North America's manufacturing firms. They have developed a rigorously validated measurement instrument to capture a firm's organizational aptitude and business performance related to the implementation and use of the ERP systems.

It emanates from the survey of literature that a little has been done in the area of design of ERP systems in general and design of ERP systems for small and medium scale organizations in particular. Keeping in view the research gaps and importance of study we have undertaken a study on planning and design model of ERP systems in Punjab Communications Limited (Mohali) with the following objectives in mind :

Objective of the Study

1. To study the planning, design, implementation and impact of ERP systems in Punjab Communications Ltd.
2. To develop a planning, design and implementation model for the low cost ERP system to be implemented in small and medium scale organizations.

Research Methodology

Secondary data for research is collected from related books, publications, annual reports, records of organization under study. For the primary data, questionnaire-*cum*-personal interview method has been used. For the collection of primary data, managers working at the three levels of management hierarchy of PCL were selected at a random basis and they were administered with the pre-tested questionnaire, which was designed on the basis of data collected from related books, publications, journals and from interviews with the experts in this area.

PROFILE OF PUNJAB COMMUNICATIONS LIMITED

PUNCOM is a semi-government company in telecommunication system. Among the major clients of the PUNCOM are Department of Telecommunication (Government of India), Indian defense department, etc. PUNCOM had implemented several types of telecommunication systems including VSAT multiplexers VSAT systems, fiber optics-based systems, and many more such systems. There are eight different departments including R&D, assembly, Transmission, ISD, switching, Q.A., marketing and PMD. PUNCOM has designed its own ERP system, which is assisting in various manufacturing activities.

Table 30.1 gives the people who participated in study from various three levels of management.

TABLE 30.1

Levels	*Punjab Communications Limited*
Level I	Managers, Head of Departments
Level II	Deputy Managers, Joint Managers
Level III	Engineers, Deputy Engineers

Table 30.2 gives the sample respondents selected for primary data collection from Punjab Communications Limited.

TABLE 30.2
Punjab Communications Limited

Levels	*Total Population*	*Sample selected*	*%age*	*Actual Response*
Level 1	25	12	50%	6
Level 2	35	12	50%	6
Level 3	108	27	25%	24

DISCUSSION

From the study of existing literature, discussions and primary data collection from PCL, various factors have been identified for *Planning, Design and Implementation* Model for ERP system.

The criteria set for identifying factors as extremely important factors is with an average score >=4.0. The average scores of the total data are used for this generalization, that are given along with the factors in the tables below. Further these factors are ranked (in descending order), based on the average scores, to facilitate the organizations to find those factors that are important for ERP design, so that management can consider these factors according to the importance attached to them. Since ERP cuts across the organizations, hence these factors that are determined for selected organization, can also be considered for all other type of organizations.

Table 30.3 gives extremely important factors (Avg. >= 4.0) in ERP system process design.

TABLE 30.3
ERP System Process Design

	Avg.
Identification of structured, semi-structured and unstructured tasks	4.1
Business processes should use models to evaluate or optimize a potential decision	4.3
Should broaden range of involvement with users	4.1
Identify functions required to support the goals and validate the same by means of goal/function matrix	4.3
For each function identify its role	4.1
Identify conventional and non-conventional processes of the system to fulfil the role	4.2
Structure the function by means of process structure diagram	4.1
For each process, develop a process model with the help of a flow chart	4.2
Classification of various data flows in various sub-processes	4.5
Classification of various internal and external constraint in various business processes	4.5
Identification of sequence of processes	4.1
Scheduling of processes	4.2
Identification of input and output processes	4.1

Table 30.4 gives extremely important factors (Avg. >= 4.0) in ERP system design from the viewpoint of information retrieved and user participation :

TABLE 30.4
Factors in ERP System Design

	Avg.
Provide information that is filtered, formatted and summarized	4.4
Verify source of information, provide information from preffered source and analyze information for bias	4.1
Information retrieval with minimum effort maintaining its legal and cultural appropriateness	4.1
There has to be appropriate level of summarization of information generated, i.e. comparison between the number of items in original data and number of items displayed	4.0
Information sharing between various processes	4.1
Less participants seems more efficient but it would not enforce quality and security standards effectively	4.1
Upper management able to see operational progress figures	4.3
Easy of learning and use	4.2
System should expect minimum user involvement	4.1
Should find a mismatch between an system goal and the way it tries to accomplish its goal	4.4

Table 30.5 gives extremely important general factors (Avg. >= 4.0) in ERP system design :

TABLE 30.5
Factors in ERP System Design

	Avg.
Understand markets and customers needs	4.3
Define long-term and short-term goals of the business	4.4
Develop vision and strategy for system design	4.2
Design product and its related services	4.0
Find the existing hardware and software support used with existing MIS software in use	4.3
Develop documentation and training needs	4.2
Plan quality management and security services	4.1
Provision for upgrading the old version with new version	4.1
Find how often change is required	4.2
Pre-specified change control form	4.2
Change control form's output is discussed with module leader and Team Leader	4.4
Identify significant assets of the system	4.08
Classification of data entities in the system	4.1
Carry out enterprise modeling using Entity-Relationship (E-R) approach	4.5
Rate of output can be increased by automating and systemizing some work	4.1
ERP is complete when user training is complete	4.1
Use password and other schemes to prevent unauthorized users from access	4.2
Periodically test firewalls and other security issues	4.5
Monitor intra, extra and internet for indicators of theft	4.4

Table 30.6 gives extremely important factors (Avg. >= 4.0) in design of components for ERP system from technical perspective :

TABLE 30.6
ERP System Design Factors

	Avg.
Develop system data architecture	4.3
Identify system's basic requirements	4.1
Design for implementation of data transaction	4.2
Develop decision concepts and decision tables for various processes	4.3
Create physical DFD for existing system	4.3
Create physical DFD of various processes and linkages between them	4.2
Create logical DFD, i.e., independent views of system, flow of data between processes, storage locations and people in system	4.3
Create data dictionary of system, i.e., name, description, aliases, contents and organizations	4.5
Create or identify data structure diagrams, i.e., pictorial description of relationship between entities in system	4.3
Formulate prototype plans. Construct and evaluate initial prototype	4.4
Access and discuss user reaction and make modifications as appropriate	4.25
Determine how to use information gained through the use of prototype	4.5
Use cyclic prototyping	4.3
Define coding standards and structural design	4.5
Database interaction design	4.5
Finalize the output design	4.1
Design of dialog to guide user	4.1
Strategy for input validation etc.	4.2
Techniques to ensure that transactions are complete	4.5
Validate data for accuracy	4.5
Run-time, Error handling, security and backup procedures	4.2
Output design in the form of Reports, documents, etc.	4.5
Identify and group the various reports according to Tabular Format, Graphics format, etc.	4.1
Identify system outputs and review logical requirements	4.2
Design, validate and test outputs	4.2
Make dialogue design strategy keeping in mind following parameters : paging, scrolling, user navigation, help system	4.2
Strategy for messages and comments on windows and screens	4.2
Avoiding bottlenecks should always be objective	4.25
Avoid extra steps of getting input from user	4.2
Keep the process of taking data simple	4.5
Develop function relationship, database design and unit testing plans for module relationship	4.1

Table 30.7 gives extremely important factors (Avg. >= 4.0) for client server architecture and transaction design for ERP system.

TABLE 30.7
ERP System Design Factor

	Avg.
Thin client implementation	4.2
Separate database server installed	4.6
Application server installed	4.4
Web-based application can be hosted	4.1
Three-tier or n-tier network implementation	4.4
Provide checks for transaction validations before actually processing the transaction	4.1
Apply various tests in checking the transaction data, e.g. existence test, limit and range test, combination test, duplicate processing, etc.	4.3
Use two phase commit to ensure consistency	4.5
Enterprise application architecture strategy	4.1
Network architecture	4.3
Process distribution and technology assignment	4.2
Implementation and strategy for transaction recovery by designing proper transaction with checkpoints	4.3
Implementation of two-phase commit in transactions	4.3
Design and implement transaction concurrency by database locking protocol	4.3

Table 30.8 gives extremely important factors (Avg. >= 4.0) in ERP system implementation.

TABLE 30.8
ERP System Implementation Factors

	Avg.
Manager's commitment	4.1
Commitment throughout the new organization	4.1
All participants understanding the benefits of new methodology	4.1
Committing resources for implementation	4.1
Creating an implementation plan	4.1
Understanding shortened process cycle after implementation	4.1
Personnel involved in training should have complete understanding of methodology	4.7
Training on tools supporting the methodology	4.1
Creating methodology-training material	4.2
Developing in-house training program	4.0
Developing different training paths for different types of jobs and techniques	4.2

Trainers experience with new methodology	4.09
Training on methodology approach, phases, tasks and deliverables	4.2
Hosting seminars to share ideas with personnel from other organization	4.2
Hosting training seminars to explore participants to the methodology	4.0
Top management education	4.09
Identifying functional heads/project leader	4.1
Appoint an outside ERP/BPR consultant	4.2
Formation of steering committee	4.2
Form the project core team	4.2
Spin-off tasks for various areas	4.3
Process mappings	4.2
Set BPR objectives and responsibilities	4.08
Hardware selection for implementation	4.6
Unit test/Integrated test/System test	4.5
Pre-evaluation screening of system	4.3
Package evaluation before implementation	4.3
Gap analysis with respect to actual needs	4.3
Reengineering the various processes	4.3
Configuration of the system	4.3
End user training on actual system	4.3
Steering committee meeting to be held weekly	4.1
New budget to be allocated in case of financial constraints	4.2
Steering committee member have to be permanent	4.1
Steering committee member changes according to module	4.1
Committee is independent of taking implementation decisions	4.1

Table 30.9 gives extremely important factors (Avg. >= 4.0) in ERP system design and implementation :

TABLE 30.9
Risk Factors in ERP System Design and Implementation

	Avg.
Inattention to work with the new system	4.11
Inadequate training to work with the system	4.1
Not solving enough problems to make change worthwhile	4.3
Operator error while executing transaction	4.25
Software bugs in system designed	4.3
Data errors while executing transactions	4.3
Upgradation of technology ease with package	4.1
Fragmentation of the processes	4.1
Every new versions changes processes	4.2

Difficulty in executing new processes	4.1
System is not up-dated as business needs change	4.08
System requires a great change from existing system practices	4.7
Unauthorized use of access codes and financial passwords	4.5
Failure to check unauthorized access to information	4.5
Theft by entering fraudulent transaction data	4.0

CONCLUSIONS

The various factors highlighted in the study for the planning, design and implementation of ERP system provide a general framework, which could be used for the development of low cost ERP systems. However, before a final model for such a system is suggested, there is a need to further investigate and validate the model; so that the model could be used by the researchers on one hand and by the system developers on the other hand. Once such a system is perfected to the desired benchmarks; it is expected that the model would go a long way in the development of low cost ERP systems; which in turn would be cost effective and would be employed for improving the efficiency of the small and medium scale organizations. This would help boost the economy of the nation at large.

References

Valkoff, Olga, "Grounded process model of Enterprise System Implementation." Dissertation abstract International. *Humanities and Social Science UML*; Vol 62; 2001, 248 pp. E.F. Peter Newson.

Negash Solomon, "Web-based Customer Support Interface." Dissertation Abstract International. *Humanities and Social Science UML*; Vol. 62; 2001, 216 pp.

Cotteleer, Mark J. D.B.A. "Operational Performance Following ERP Implementation." Dissertation abstract International. *Humanities and Social Science UMI*; Vol. 62, Harward University, 2001, 248 pp.

Navarrete, Carlos J., "Information Technology Expenditure with Organizational Value and Performance." Dissertation Abstract International. *Humanities and Social Science UMI*; Vol. 62, The Claremont Graduate University, 2001, 211 pp. Advertiser : Lome Olfman.

Gattikar, Thomas Fredric, "ERP System in Operational Management : A Model, Instrument and an Empirical Test." Dissertation abstract International. *Humanities and Social Science UML*; Vol. 62; 2000, 213pp. Directors : Dale H. Goodhue; K. Roscoe Davis.

Startman, Jeffrey Keith, Ph.D., "Information Integration for Supply Chain Management; an Empirical Investigation of ERP Systems in Manufacturing Industry." Dissertation Abstract International. *Humanities and Social Science UMI*; Vol. 62; 2001, 234 pp.

Melville, Nigel Patrick, "Information Technology Investment Impact and Industry Structure : Evidence from firms and Industries." Dissertation abstract International. *Humanities and Social Science UML*; Vol. 62; 2001. 141pp. Chair : Vijay Gurbaxani.

Sena, Mark Philip, "Enterprise System for Organizational Decision Support : An Examination of Objectives, Characteristics and Benefits." Dissertation Abstract International. *Humanities and Social Science UML*; Vol. 62; 2001. 194 pp.

Nichols, Denise Haskins, A Framework for IT Strategies Integrated with Business Strategies that Contributes to Successful Business Performance within an Organization. Dissertation Abstract International. *Humanities and Social Science UML*; Vol. 62; 2001. Director : Michael Lee Donnell.

Books

Daniel E. O'Leary; "ERP Systems; System, Life Cycle, Risks", Cambridge University Press. (2001).

Gary A. Langenwalter; "Enterprise Resource Planning and Beyond Integrating your Entire Organization," St. Luice Press. (2001).

Leon, Alex, "ERP Demystified", Tata McGraw-Hill Publishing Company Limited, New Delhi, 2000.

Garg, Vinod Kumar & N.K. Venkitakrishnan, "Enterprise Resource Planning" (Concepts and Practice), Prentice-Hall of India Pvt. Ltd. (PHI), New Delhi, 1998.

Sadagopan, S.; "ERP Management Perspective", TMH Publishing Co. Ltd., New Delhi, 1999.

Carrd, D; "Best Practice in Reengineerings," McGraw Hill, 1995.

Dewell; "Network Resource Planning for SAP R13", BaaN and People soft; TMH, New Delhi, 1999.

Garg, Vinod Kumar and Venkitakrishnan, N.K., ERPWARE—ERP Implementation Framework; PHI Pvt. Ltd., New Delhi, 1998.

CHAPTER 31

Role of Software Complexity Metrics in Productivity

RAJINDER SINGH

1. INTRODUCTION

In software engineering, various metrics have been designed in an attempt to measure the complexity of systems. Software complexity directly affects maintenance activities like software understandability, modifiability, and software testability. Estimates suggest mat about 40 to 70% of annual software expenditure involve maintenance of existing systems. Predicting software complexity can save millions in maintenance.[1-3] Clearly, if complexities could somehow be identified, men programmers could adjust development, maintenance., and testing procedures accordingly. As a result of this we can enhance productivity up to great extent. This concern has motivated several researchers to define and validate software complexity metrics.[4-8]

2. A NEW PROGRAM WEIGHTED COMPLEXITY MEASURE[11]

Different complexity metrics take into account different aspects of program complexity. Halstead's software science metrics[9] and McCabe's cycomatric number[10] are the two prominent contributions but account for different characteristics of a computer program. For Halstead's metric, the basis of detecting and measuring the complexity is the size of software module only and it does not take into account other characteristics of software systems such as program flow control, nesting and so on.[9,10]

Similarly, cyclomatic number measures the complexity due to program flow control only, but does not keep track of other features of software systems such as operators, operands, etc.

Complexity is also affected by design and inter-dependence of statements in a program. For example, an assignment statement involving some variables is dependent upon those statements in which values of these variables have been calculated. These statements may be located at different positions in the program.

In this chapter, we have attempted to take into account the complexities due to size of software modules, position of a statement in the logic of the program, type of control structures present in the module, and their nesting. The concept of weight is used to quantify these various aspects of complexity of software module.

A program is a set of statements, which in turn include operators and operands. Thus, the program statements, operators and operands are basic units of a program. The prominent factors, which contribute to complexity of a program are :

(i) Size

Large programs incur problem just by virtue of volume of the information that must be absorbed to understand the program and more resources have to be used in their maintenance.[4-5] Therefore, size is a factor, which adds complexity to a program.

(ii) Position of a Statement

We assume that the statements, which are at the beginning of the program logic, are simple and hence easily understandable and thus contribute less complexity than those which are at deeper level of the logic of a program. So we assign a weight (multiplier) 1 to first executable statement and 2 to second and so on. It may be treated as positional weight (Wp).

(iii) Type of Control Structures

A program with more control structures is considered to be more complex and *vice-versa*. But, we assume that different control structures contribute to the complexity of a program differently. For example, iterative control structures like while, do, repeat . . . until, for, to . . . do contribute more complexity than decision-making control structures like if . . . then . . . else. So, we assign different weights to different control structures.

(iv) Nesting

A statement which is at deeper level (higher nesting level) is harder to understand and thus contributes more complexity than otherwise. We take effect of nesting by assigning weight 1 to statements at level one, weight 2 for those statements which are at level 2 and so on. The weight for sequential statements is taken as zero.

By taking these assumptions into account, a weighted complexity measure of a program P is suggested as :

$Cw\ (P) = (\ W_t)i\ *\ (m)i$

where

Cw (P) : Proposed weighted complexity measure of program P,
(m) i : Count of unique operators (n^ and operands (n_2) in the ith executable statement of program module P,
j : Total number of executable statements in program P,
(W_t) i : Total weight of ith executable statement in program P,

where

$W_t = W_p + W_h + W_c$, here

W_p : positional weight, i.e. weight due to position of the statement,
W_h : weight due to nesting level of control structures and it is
= 0 for sequential statement,
= 1 for a control structure at outer level,
= 2 for a control structure at next inner level and so on.
W_c : weight due to type of control structures and it is
= 0 for sequential statement,
= 1 for decision-making control statements like if, then, else, case statements,
= 2 for iterative control structures like while, do, for, to, do, repeat, until statements,
Σ : Summation symbol,
i : Index variable.

In this complexity metrics we have taken into account different aspects of complexity : Halstead's size, McCabe's control structures, their nesting, and positional complexity of a statement in the logic of a program. In this metric the effect of these structures on complexity is quite significant.

3. COMPLEXITY METRIC BASED ON THREE TERM LENGTH ESTIMATOR[7]

Earlier programs length estimators were based on count of operators and operands only. Modern programming languages such as C, Pascal, M (xhila-2, Ada are rich in functions/procedures, keywords/reserved words and thus it seems logical to take a separate category for these tokens in addition to operators and operands categories. However, these tokens were treated as a part of operators category in all earlier theories.

Based upon the above justification, a new program length estimator [Ngr] is given as under :

Nr= nl log 2(n1) + n2 log 2(n2) + n3 log 2 (n3)
where,
n1 : Number of unique operators, which include only basic operators.
n2 : Number of unique operands.
n3 : Number of unique keywords/reserve words and functions/procedures/sub-routines.

Program vocabulary is :

n = nl +n2 + n3

By using these basic parameters of a program a complexity metric E is defined as

E = V/L
where V (volume) = N * Log_2 n.

4. APPLICATION OF SOFTWARE METRICS TO ADA[12]

In this paper, we have applied various complexity metrics to ada language and proposed some variations in counting rules used in earlier studies. By using these variations in counting rules, we have solved a contradiction about the language level of Ada. In earlier studies, it's level has been calculated as 0.27 placing it much below the assembly language.[19] In this study, we have calculated it's level as 1.47 which is higher man the levels of languages like Pascal, C and thus it proves mat Ada is a high level language.

The proposed variations in counting rules are as under :

In the earlier studies, parenthesis and quote marks used in any form have been considered as operators. But here parenthesis are ignored when used with functions like put-line() and quotes are ignored when used with sting constants or heading—Another variation is mat we have taken the separate category for reserved words and functions/procedures exclusively while in other studies these tokens were considered as a part of operators.

5. RELATIONSHIPS AMONG SOFTWARE COMPLEXITY METRICS, FAULTS AND TESTABILITY[8,14]

We have also established the relationship among software complexity metrics and suggested a criteria for the categorization of software systems as "decision bound" and "computation bound" systems.[8]

(a) Connection between Program Complexity and Faults[13]

In this work, we have established that fault rate is directly proportional to number of executable lines of code. If, somehow, we could predict/know executable lines of code in a module then we can estimate possible number of faults. Fault rates have been predicted as 0.0027, 0.0061 and 0.0067 for C, Fortran 77 and Pascal languages which may be used in future studies with real time data to give it further empirical support.

Relationship between complexity and faults has been established which is : more complexity, more possibility of faults, which seems true through intuition also.

(b) Connection between Program Complexity and Testability[14]

In this work we have proposed a method for calculating the testability amount of testing required to reveal expected faults by using the process of sensitivity analysis.[18] A relationship between complexity and testability has been established, which may be stated as :

More the complexity, less testability, more the amount of testing required to reveal expected faults and *vice-versa*. It agrees with intuition also. By knowing the testability of a program, we may utilize testing resources more effectively because a program with low testability requires more testing than a program with high testability. Thus, we may predict about its quality as well.

6. CONCLUSIONS

We have designed various complexity metrics, which take into account different aspects of complexity like Halstead's size, McCabe's control structures, their nesting, and positional complexity of a statement in the logic of a program. Our studies show that the effect of these structures on complexity is quite significant. We have also established relationships among software complexity, faults and testability. Here, the results agree with intuition. We have also proposed some variations in counting rules through which we have resolved a contradiction about the level of Ada language. By controlling, predicting, and measuring complexity, we can keep our systems easy and simple. We can utilize our resources and efforts more effectively. Thus, we can enhance our productivity upto great extent.

NOTES AND REFERENCES

1. W. Harrison, K. Magel, R. Kluezny and A. Dekock, "Applying Software Complexity Metrics to Program Maintenance," Computer, Vol. 15, pp. 65-79, Sept. 1982.
2. George, Stark, Robert C. Durst and C.W. Yowell, "Using Metrics in Management Decision Making," IEEE Computer, Sept. 1994, pp. 42-48.
3. Jonathan, M. Hops, Joseph S. Sherif, "Development and Application of Composite Complexly Models and a Relative Complexity Metrics in a Software Maintenance Environment," Elsevier, J., Systems Software, 1994, Vol. 31, pp. 157-69.
4. David LXanning and Taghi M. Khoshgoftaar, "Modeling the Relationships between

Source Code Complexity and Maintenance Difficulty," IEEE Computer, Sept. 1994, pp. 35-40.
5. S.D. Conte, Dunsmore, Shen, "Software Engineering Metrics and Models," The Benjamin/Cummings Pub. Company, Inc. 1986.
6. B. Mehndiratta and P.S. Grover, "Experimentation and Modelling in Software Complexity Metrics," Ph.D. Thesis, University of Delhi, 1990.
7. P.S. Grover, R. Singh, and N.S. Gill, Measuring Software Systems, published in the book "Operations Research : Theory and Practice", SPANIEL Pub. , New Delhi, 1994, pp. 71-93.
8. R. Singh and P.S. Grover, "Relationships among Software Complexity Metrics," Proc. International Conf. on SE Practices (CONSEG'95), Feb. 9-10,1995, New Delhi, India.
9. M.H. Halstead, "Elements of Software Science," New York : Elsevier North Holland, 1977.
10. T.J. McCabe, A Complexity Measure, IEEE Trans. On SE, Vol. SE-34, No. 3, pp. 187-94, 1976.
11. R. Singh and P.S. Grover, "A New Program Weighted Complexity Measure," International Conference on Software Engineering (CONSEG'97), Jan. 23-25, 1997, Chennai, India.
12. R. Singh, and P.S. Grover, "Application of Software Metrics to Ada," Proc. Annual Convention of Computer Society of India (CSI, 1994) Nov. 21-24,1994, Calcutta, India.
13. R. Singh, and P.S. Grover, "Connection between Program Complexity and Faults," Proc. National Conference on Software Engineering and its Application, Aug. 22-24,1996, Hyderabad, India.
14. R. Singh , D.R. Taneja and P.S. Grover, "Connection between Program Complexity and Testability," Proc. 31st Annual Convention of Computer Society of India (CST, 1996), Nov. 22-25, 1996, Bangalore, India.
15. Jeffrey Voas, Larry Morell and Keith Miller, "Predicting Where Faults can Hide from Testing," IEEE Software, March, 1991.
16. B. Mehndiratta, and P.S. Grover, "Software Metrics Applied to Ada," Proc. Software and Applications Conference (COMPSAC87), Tokyo, Japan, 7-9 Oct. 1987.

CRM—An Additive Tool for Competitiveness

DALBIR SINGH, NARENDER SINGH AND HAWA SINGH

"A customer is most important visitor on our premises. He is not dependent on us, we are dependent on him. He is not an interruption on our work; he is the purpose of it. He is not an outsider on our business, he is a part of it, we are not doing him a favour by serving him, he is doing us a favour by giving us an opportunity to do so." These are the words once said not by any company executive but by our father of nation Mahatma Gandhi. What a clear-cut vision of Gandhiji, which provides solution and competitive advantages to the companies when they are not able to achieve their objective in a competitive environment.

Relationships are as old as mankind. They have been studied by sociologists, socio-psychologists, anthropologists, philosophers and many others. Business organizations are also part of society so this subject matter is also of the same value like others. Traders and businessmen of yesteryears have earned profits and success by relying upon this relationship. In the early 90s, the concept of relationship management was formally introduced into the field of organizations marketing services, like financial institutions, airline, etc.

SIX-STAGE MODEL FOR RELATIONSHIP

It has been found that it is profitable to retain and reward the existing customers rather than running after new customer. The relationship management leads to the more use of company product by the customer.

They may charge more prices for the services they are offering. The same concept is also significant for industrial as well as consumer products. Relationship do not form over night but through the various stages as shown in diagram :

Six Stage Model of Relationship

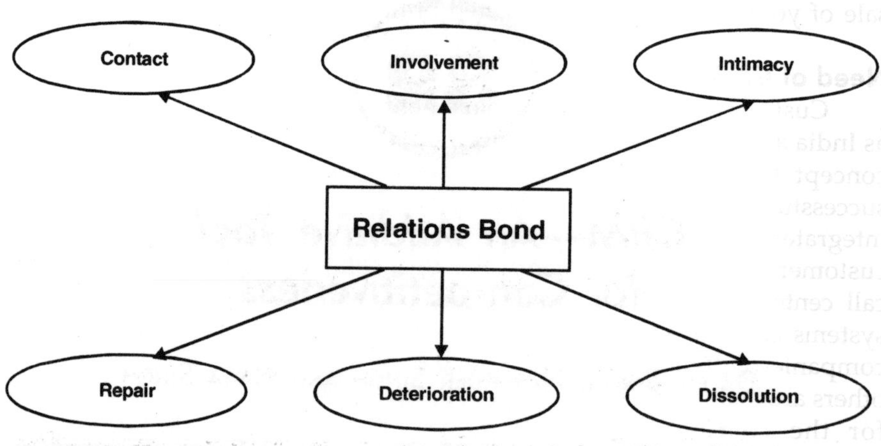

In the pre-liberalization era there was hardly any competition in the Indian market. It was not easily accessible to the multinational corporations. Most of the firms were operating in an uncompetitive environment and it was all sellers' market. Firms hardly required attention to create relationships with customers. In such situation, customer had no choice except that of cognitive dissonance and businesses were running without much 'caring' for them. In the beginning of the last decade of the 20th century, a new era of liberalization started. The market was open to foreign companies and products. The trade barriers were reduced in the form of decrease in custom duties. Approval of foreign direct investment, de-licensing and other measures were introduced to make the Indian market integrate with rest of the world.

The Indian firms faced the heat of competition in all business areas. MNCs with better products in terms of quality and technology have given tough challenge to most of Indian players. Many of foreign players who have already experienced with issues like customer relationship management in their previous markets, extended the same to the Indian market. This was the beginning of customer relationship management in India, forcing the Indian firms to start thinking in the same manner. In the present scenario, firms are facing customers who are more aware about choices available to them with regard to quality and price and they want value for their money.

Customer relationship management is a management function and the objective of this function cannot be achieved successfully without the cooperation, coordination and communication between all the levels of organization. CRM is also a social process which requires the skill and resource sharing within an organization as well as outside the organization. Sharing should be at all the points of contact with the customer. Now when the threats are there from the established brands, CRM has emerged as the solution. Having a very good relation with the customer, will increase the sale of your brand and other related brands of your company.

Need of CRM

Customers' relationship management is relatively a new concept as far as India and its Industries are concerned. Lot of companies are adopting this concept for gaining competitive advantage in the market. But, for the successful implementation of the concept CRM a company has to use a well-integrated computerized system, which can immediately respond to the customer queries and problems. For this, companies engage themselves in call centers from where a skilled person, with the help of computerized systems can immediately satisfy the customer's query or problem. So, the companies with enough resources have set-up, their own call centers while others are looking for outsourcing. This has given rise to lot of opportunities for the companies as well as for the other people looking for entrepreneurship or for a stable business. These companies or people can provide services (call centers) to the companies looking for outsourcing. This concept of call centers and customer relationship management has proven to be a stable and consistent business around the globe, but in India the business is showing the signs of downsizing even in the early stages of its evolution.

CRM is also acting as the medium for private advertising. CRM will take you at the stage which can yield a lot out of market on the basis of your relationship, as Nestle has done in its French Market. Nestle maintains a database of 2,20,000 of new mothers. On the basis of customer data-base, Nestle sends direct mails to these mothers related to information regarding the precautions during the pregnancy and on the birth of new baby. They also receive free sample of baby food. This has lead to increased sales of this category of food and it now boasts of 43% of total market share owned by the company (Adv. Age, Oct. 15, 1993, p. 16). Now some of the Indian companies are also maintaining customer data-base and Pharmaceutical companies like Cipla, Ranbaxy, Glaxo, etc., are taking a lead in this area.

Another thing, which makes it imperative for organizations to change their strategies and move towards Customer Centric Marketing, is the Pareto Principle. According to this 20% of the customers bring in 80% of the profits. By this it is not being suggested that you abruptly chuck away the rest 80% of your Customers. It is best to categorize ones customers, differentiate your service or outsource your unprofitable customers. That means, get in a third party to provide the bare minimum services to hold these 80% of the customers and since this party will be in the business of providing services it would be economical to serve these customers. Thus,

Customer Relationship Management should be the process of actively deepening the knowledge (not data) you have of your customers over time and then using that knowledge gained to customize your business and strategies to meet that customers individual needs.

CRM AS A COMPETITIVE ADVANTAGE

The firms by focusing on CRM can compete with the competitors, when it becomes difficult to compete on price alone. It is an important factor that takes the firm to a safe position in market.

CRM is also helpful in positioning the firm in the market as well as in customer's mind. When businesses are very good at customer relationship management, the strong bond will be there between firm and customers. All this will leads towards the brand and company loyalty. When you are effective in customer relationship management it will reduce the complaints as well as the barriers between organization and customers. It all leads towards :

(a) Brand loyalty,
(b) Brand extension, and
(c) Making consumer as advocates.

Impact of CRM on Sales and Marketing

To operate successfully in global market place, organizations have been moving to a customer centric focus and are being challenged to quickly and accurately deliver what customer is demanding. CRM with its customer centric focus, places the customer needs first and involves the following fundamental steps :

(a) Understanding the customer completely,
(b) Utilization of organizational capability to improve delivery of perceived value, and
(c) Facilitating the information flow inside and outside of organization.

Impact of CRM on Organizational Competency

Organizations moving to different sales methodologies need to align with the technologies they have chosen to employ. Sales people once had the luxury of functioning in any way they saw fit. With a shift to team selling everyone involved in value chain needs to be thoroughly versed in process and understand their unique role. Each member of the team needs to know what to expect along the continuum of the sale process.

Impact of CRM on Customer

Organizations are developing CRM culture norms and eventually all the sales and customers service representative will see team selling, knowledge-based selling as the only way to do business. The CRM norms are to be followed by all sellers. Customer competency may become a competitive advantage specially for value-added sellers. Pushing information and investigation of the information are also comparative advantages.

Impact of a CRM on Suppliers

Tying the new suppliers to customers will be technology and the internet. Core competency will help build technology-based distribution system to serve the customer. This will most likely involve the ability to adopt the new technology. The role of distribution manager may well be one of tying into virtual distribution centers and will therefore dictate a new set of skills and competencies.

INFORMATION IS CRITICAL TO MAXIMIZING PROFITABILITY AT EVERY STEP OF THE CUSTOMER LIFECYCLE

A majority of CRM installations lack the critical piece of the customer information pie; internal customer data integrated with value-added external business intelligence. Source Information Services is one such organization which integrates access to real-time, relevant corporate, industry, and market intelligence, thereby maximizing the CRM return on investment. Information is the key to upgrading the average sales-person to a customer-savvy, sophisticated sales specialist, as it empowers sales-people with daily information on their customers, their markets, and their industries, so they can target customers more accurately, closing more profitable business faster, retaining customers, and expanding relationships within accounts. CRM provides companies with an excellent framework for managing customer relationships. Adding information as a care ingredients enables companies to achieve a deeper, truly strategic customer understanding, which transforms the sales process in high-impact ways, resulting in enabling force to :

- Identify and focus on higher-profit prospects,
- Keep up-to-date regarding changes in their prospects' accounts,
- Manage accounts to their full potential, not just short-term results, and
- Concentrate on the best accounts and build preferred supplier relationships.

A superior understanding of prospects and customers gives sales-people the competitive advantage that translates directly into success. In order to demonstrate how external information empowers CRM, analyze in detail the four steps of the customer lifecycle.

FIG. 32.1
The Four Steps of the Customer Lifecycle

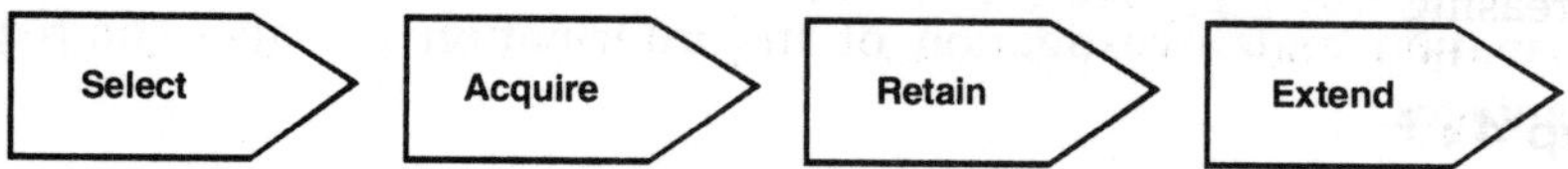

Step 1 : Selection

The customer lifecycle begins with prospect selection and identification. With accurate prospect knowledge, the sales team can focus on the best prospects for the company's products and/or services. It can find prospects based on the key attributes of prospects such as title, job function, industry, or numerous other criteria. Once the target prospects have been identified the company then empowers sales teams with knowledge to win, form corporate structure and financials to competitive details, market trends, industry news, key corporate decision-makers, and company news.

The business information integrated into the CRM system eliminates outdated information and inaccurate data, enabling the sales team to identify better, more qualified prospects. As a result, better prospects enter the sales process and effort is focused on more qualified opportunities. The results are increased sales, increased order size, increased revenues per sales-person, and decreased costs per qualified lead.

Step 2 : Acquisition

When a sales force is armed with greater prospect intelligence, it can demonstrate its product's unique value to each specific customer. This efficiency shortens the sales cycle while providing leverage against discounting and helps in monitoring trends and informing the sales staff of new legislation, revised product lines, and restructuring information that is essential in gaining an edge and standing out from the competitive crowd. With this the company can build more compelling proposals by demonstrating an intimate understanding of the client's business and improving call-to-sale conversion ratios.

Step 3 : Retention

Retention is the critical stage in the customer lifecycle, given that it can cost three times or more to acquire a new customer as against retaining an existing customer. An ideal CRM will monitor customers, prospects, industries, and competitors to ensure that sales-people are proactively communicating with customers, and addressing their constantly changing needs and concerns. Such a CRM relies on accurate, timely, and integrated business-information.

It ensures knowledge of critical customer situations, such as changes in personnel, updating of financials, expansion plans and office moves, new clients and partners, and competitor information. Armed with this knowledge the sales-people can proactively return to customers to solidify relationships, address new needs, and deepen the relationship across buying groups. Such proactive customer relations decreases loss rates, while increasing the lifetime value of your customers.

Step 4 : Extension

This final stage of the customer lifecycle can have the largest impact. Once the business relationship with a customer is established the sales force can take advantage of cross-selling opportunities, extending the relationship across the corporate family or even to partners. It's more efficient to sell to existing, happy clients than to find new ones. The key to extension is identifying and penetrating your best accounts. The information helps the user to know their customer better and sell additional products and services within the organization. Business analysis and needs reassessment can identify opportunities to up-sell, cross-sell, and increase average order size. For example, a new partnership or merger may open the door for extension of your existing customer's contract.

By understanding the corporate structure, the sales-people can leverage existing customer relationships to penetrate the organization and reach the goal of becoming a standard across an enterprise.

SOME COMPANIES DO CRM NATURALLY

Some companies know next to nothing about their customers, that they have no name and address files or details of their purchasing habits. Yet they are able to meet their customers' needs precisely by managing product development, stock replenishment, channel delivery and customer service. Profitability in these companies has been shown to out-perform all other companies in their sector (e.g., Wal-Mart). Surely, these are companies that understand CRM even where active management is not present. In these companies, the marketing manager is not the only key player, as everyone takes some responsibility for managing relationships with customers. Many activities are customer facing and must contain a marketing element because someone has concerned themselves with presentation as well as content of the product (or service) and of the delivery channel and method. As a result, although roles may be clearly defined, they are bound to cross-traditional barriers, effectively raising the visibility of marketing, even where the operations do not take place within a traditional marketing department.

CRM effectively encompasses an organization's ability to :

- Find customers.
- Get to know them.
- Keep in communication with them.
- Ensure that they get what they want from the organization—not just in the product but in every aspect of the organization's dealings with them.

- Check that they receive what they were promised, subject of course, to it being profitable.
- Ensure that the customer is retained, even if the customer is unprofitable today, the goal is long-term profitability.

CRM is not about price. It is not about sending higher volumes of mail or making higher volumes of annoying phone calls to prospects. It is definitely not about using channels to drive customers to competitors. CRM provides the capabilities to generate products, services, responsiveness, individualization, mass customization, and customer happiness.

COSTS AND BENEFITS OF RELATIONSHIP MANAGEMENT

The benefits of customer relationship management are usually to be found in one or more of these areas :

1. Lower costs of recruiting customers by saving on marketing, mailing, contact, follow-up, fulfilment, services, and so on.
2. No need to recruit so many customers to maintain a steady volume of business (especially in business-to-business marketing environments).
3. Reduced cost of sales—usually existing customers are more responsive customers. Better knowledge of your channels or distribution, drives more effectiveness in the relationship. CRM will also reduce marketing campaign costs and provide higher ROI in marketing and customer communications.
4. Higher customer profitability larger wallet-share more follow-up sales, more referrals for higher customer satisfaction and services; ability to cross-sell or up-sell from present purchases.
5. Increased customer retention, as loyalty-customers stay longer, buy more, contact you for their requirements which increases the bonding relationships and such customer buy more often. CRM therefore increases the opportunities and accomplishment of real lifetime value.
6. Evaluation of customer profitability, knowing which customers are truly profitable, which customers should be changed from low/no profit through cross-selling/up-selling; which customers might not ever become profitable, which customers should be managed by external channels and which customers/drive future business.

CONCLUSION

CRM is now gaining wide acceptance among the business world. Customer retention has become most important. Indian companies are implementing applications of CRM in a phased manner. The first component they are implementing is establishing call centers and database management systems. As the IT infrastructure of Indian companies becomes more mature, the scope, will increase exponentially. The need for CRM should be more strategic in nature as this will result in change in the processes and ways in which companies operate. The process can be re-engineered by using CRM solutions, to become more competitive.

REFERENCES

Bendapudi, N., Leone, R.P., "Star Performer", *Harward Business Review*, Nov. 2001.

Bhattacharjee, P., "Burning A New Trail", *Business World*, Dec. 2001.

Biradar, R.D., "Emerging Trends in Services Marketing", *Indian Journal of Marketing*, Vol. XXXI, Sept.-Oct. 2001.

Brown, Stephen, "Torment your customers", *Haward Business Review*, Oct. 2001.

Chase, R.B., Basu, S.R.; "Use Behaviour Science", *Harvard Business Review*, June 2001.

De, P.K., "Trade in Services", Yojana, Sept. 2000.

Elumalal, K., "Turning Customer Services for Maximizing the Bank Profitability", *Public-Opinion Survey*, Vol. XL VII, No. 2, Nov. 2001.

Fitzsimmons, J.A., "Service Management Operations, Strategy and Information Technology", 1997, McGraw Hill.

Grover, B.K., "Strategic Marketing Through Customer Service", *Indian Journal of Marketing*, May-June 2000.

Hartline, M.D., Maxham III, J.G., Mckee, D.O., "Corridors of Influence in the Dissemination of Customer-Oriented Strategy to Customer Contract Service Employees", *Journal of Marketing*, Vol. 64 (April 2000), 30-35.

Henry, A.S., "Consumer's Behaviours and Marketing Actions", Asian Book Pvt. Ltd.

Johns Nick and Roos, P.L., "Research Methods in Service Industry Management", 1988, Cassell, London.

Meuter, M.L., Ostrom, A.L., Round Tree, and Bituer, M.J., "Self-Service Technologies : Understanding Customer Satisfaction with Technology-Based Service Encounters"; *Journals of Marketing*, Vol. 64 (July 2000) 50-64.

Omen, T.W., Summers, J.O., A. Frank, "Relationship Marketing Activities Commitment and Membership Behaviours in Professional Associations", *Journal of Marketing*, Vol. 64 (July 2000).

Pearson, Stewart, "Building Brands Directory Creating Business Value from Customer Relationship", MacMillan Business Press Ltd., London.

Saluja, M., "Nurturing Relationship", *Indian Management*, Jan. 2000.

Shantha Kumar, D.K., Xavier, M.J., "CRM : A Research Agenda", *Advt. & Mkt.*, March 31, 2001.

Singh, Deepali, Vasdan, M.S., Relationship Marketing—An Indian Perspective", *Indian Management*, May 1999.

Singh, Jagjit, "Customer Relationship Management", *Marketing and Management News*, Vol. 6, No. 8, Jan. 1988.

Singh, Jagjit, "CRM : Changing Perspectives", *Marketing and Management News*, Vol. 9, No. 11, April 2001.

Singh, P., "CRM—The Snail Mail of the Internet Age", *Information Technology*, July 2000.

S. Ramesh Kumar, "Marketing Nuggets", Vikas Publishing House (P) Ltd.

Sukmar, V., "Customer Satisfaction", *Indian Journal of Marketing*, Vol. XXXI, Nov.-Dec., 2001.

Toffler, A., "The Third Wave", Bantam Books, New York.

William, G.Z. and Michael, D.A., *"Marketing"*, West Publishing Company.

William, J.S., Michael, J.E. and Bruce, J.W., "Fundamental of Marketing," McGraw Hill Publication.

IT Solutions for Service Providers in Education : A TQM Approach for Global Competitiveness

H.J. GHOSH ROY

Today's business organisations face a rapidly changing business environment. These changes have occurred due to increased global competition, significant advances in international business and changes in political and economic systems around the globe.

There are many in the economically developed parts of the world who expect companies from developing countries like India to be inferior not only in their products and services but also in their overall managerial sophistication? It is this psychological barrier that is perhaps the biggest stumbling block, preventing Indian companies from starting on the transformational journey to become world class in their strategies, organization and management. Prof. Chris Christensen, Harvard's celebrated teacher, defended the case method by saying 'because wisdom cannot be taught', and it was further extended by Ghoshal *et. al.*, as if wisdom cannot be taught then courage certainly cannot, either. Almost every organisation in India is struggling with this issue : What to change and how to change :

> Crosby (1994) writes about the companies in emerging nations who do nol have to repeat the mistakes of their counterparts developed nations. The "emerged" nations went through a lot of wasteful, unnecessary and counter-productive efforts during their journey to the current

developed status. According to Crosby, the key to install its prevention lies in the hands of senior management. The culture they deliberately cause in the organisation, and the educational content they introduce, determine how quality will be. Quality is not a game, or toy, to be tossed out to the crowd for their pleasure. It is serious business. Making quality happen in a company requires senior management to understand and act on few basic things. They are : Policy, Education and Witness. If management is not serious about quality it is better not to issue a policy on the same for soon they will be embarrassed.

In fact, it is the attitude of mind, which is important. The present context every where is 'competitiveness and productivity' in Indian Business or Indian Economy. In today's competitive market no business can survive without satisfied customers. There is no other industry (Stamatis, 1996) in which people skills are as important as immediate behaviours. There is no other industry where information has to be translated over and over again. There is no other industry where all employees have the responsibility and the opportunity to deal effectively with the customer. There is no other industry where all employees must make the customer feel comfortable in the face of irate behaviour. There is no other industry where the employee must answer the same questions over and over again with a smile, always showing concern and courtesy. Indeed, when treated well, shown respect and kept informed customers respond more favourably and then perception of quality improves (Petrina, 1994). Productivity means different things to different people. But the definition given by European Productivity Council is most appropriate one from 'Customer Satisfaction' viewpoint. The council advocates 'Productivity is an attitude of mind. It is a mentality of progress, of the constant improvement of that which exists. It is the certainty of being able to do better than yesterday and continuously. It is constant adaptation of economic and social life to changing conditions. It is the continual effort to apply new techniques and methods. It is the faith in human progress.'

TQM has produced (Mekoth *et. al.*, 1995) wonderful results in organisations both in India and abroad. Some organizations have started questioning the newness of the concept as well as its utility to organizations without probably realizing that the weakness lies in the implementation and not in the concept. In service industry, it is rather the customer contact employees who are the source of TQM. Top level management should be in constant touch with these employees so that customer's expectation is taken care in service design as well. Parasuraman, *et. al.* (1988) designed the SERVQUAL instrument to be applicable across the spectrum of service environments with a minimum adaptation. It provides service managers and associated decision-makers not only with information on customer perceptions of current service delivery but also their expectation, thus enabling a closer matching of service delivery according to expectation and needs. If any management decides to go for TQM, they must be serious about it and must make concerted efforts for some years to make it a success. Situation in Indian industries is highly conducive to higher performance in quality as the workers (Sarkar, 1991) inherited from the families of high level craftsmen are intelligent. The need for training is required for all employees. Kanji (1991) supports this view and suggests that TQM practice is necessary to overcome the basic organisational quality problems. Deming's 14-point principles of management have significant merit for exploratory research in context of an educational system/settings. The study (Conzemius, 1993) examined fourteen schools and observed the need for a theoretical model designed to guide the implementation of change initiatives. Spence (1993), examined the perceptions of individuals from fifteen schools of Detroit, USA and observed that Quality models helped in transforming organizational systems into collaborative culture.

An interesting study compared TQM applications (Sanders, 1993), in 2-year colleges. One president persisted and today has total quality system, the other abandoned TQM. The study provides background and specific data for administrators who wish to explore the viability of incorporating TQM into management system. Similarly, Dellana (1993), Weekley (1993), Pallandini (1993), Sohn (1993), Andrews (1994), Greene (1994), Klien (1994), Saraph *et. al.* (1993), Jone (1993), Cotter (1993), Hehmeyer (1994), etc. have made valuable observations on TQM practices in industry as well as in schools. Analytically addressed the 'why' aspects of Kaizen at Toyota. The study substantiated that not improving quality is costlier, in terms of the firm's prospects for growth and survival. The EPC definition of productivity, which focusses on the attitude of mind is in fact supported and substantiated by the study of Kini (1994) on Toyota. The study proves that the Japan's obsession with zero-defect quality is not without economically sound underpinnings.

To compete effectively in a global market place, organizations must elicit commitment from every member of the organization for contributions to continuous improvement of the operations. The aim of the present chapter is to suggest workable IT solutions for quality education in the universities in particular and other colleges/schools in general. TQM in education services is need of the hour. The managers or the service providers of the education business have to focus on academic accomplishments, personality development, administrative facilities, involving alumni's (for placements), involving parents, interacting with community at large for future business, etc.

The internet-enabled educational infrastructure is the only way towards Total Quality Management in Educational services. The internet is now a reality—it's the new infrastructure. The service providers have to bring all the stakeholders together in the new learning environment, i.e., students, teachers, parents, alumni, etc. In this techno-savy environment, teachers will be able to considerably reduce their administrative work-load and also create academic support through comprehensive feedback. This system will also take care of individual students by providing personalized counselling by the experienced teachers.

As we all know that every department in an educational set-up needs a set of 'state-of the art equipment' for its computer lab/class-rooms, conference rooms, libraries, visual aids, audio-linguistic labs, etc., the internet-enabled infrastructure would certainly lower the operational and other costs. Every educational institute has to and should create a web site and develop softwares for all these activities to be offered as per the framework below :

Total Quality Model of Excellence in Management Education

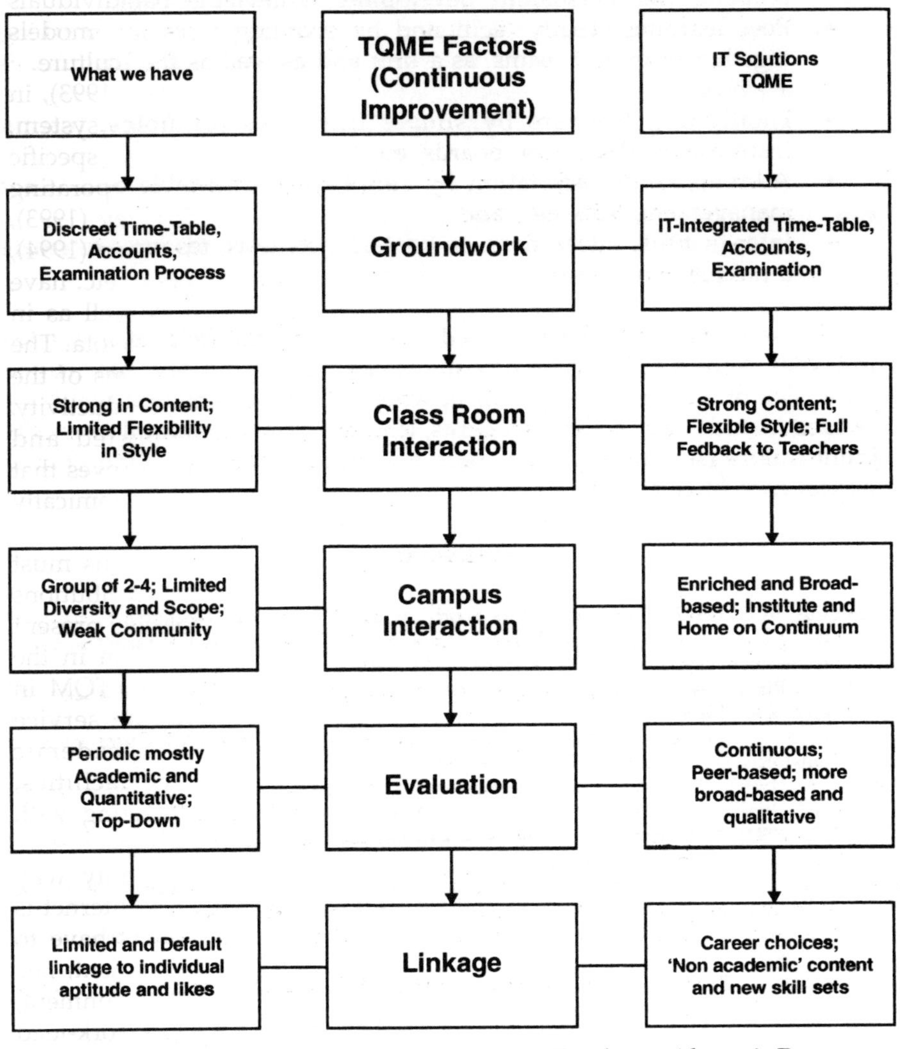

(Contributors : Teachers) (Contributors : Teachers, Alumni, Parents, Students, Community at large)

Quality education means providing all inputs at one window, with software infrastructure and integrating important facilities with the students, alumni parents and the community at large. The TQME framework would facilitate the service providers and have the following benefits :

- Stakeholders' integration by bringing teachers, students, parents, alumni into a tightly knit learning community,
- Better control over the progress of each student, e.g. in-depth analysis of performance, more feedback from parents, etc.,
- Enlarged resources available on-line, e.g. extensive academic, non-academic and personality development knowledge bank,
- Peer learning greatly facilitated by enabling tools for working together in project teams, as a unit and as well as the Institute as a whole,
- Facilitating teachers by simple interfaces for notes, testing instruments, discussion boards, etc.,
- Administrative facilitation by simplifying time-table and event management, MIS, etc., and
- Inter-Institute interactions on contents, contests, resource to create a unique experience.

The services would be provided on-line with the help of a TQME-Portal (See Annexure-I) where any interested person can get information with a click of a mouse. The platform where all the information would be provided include details about students, teachers, parents, alumni as well as administrators (see Annexure-II). Such an attempt would provide ground for excellence in education.

References

Conzemius, W.C. (1993), "An Exploratory Study of the Principles of Dealing's : Theory of Management in Public Schools Involved in Reform", Ph.D. Thesis : California School of Professional Psychology—Los Angeles, DAI, 54(4).

Crosby, Phillip (1994), "Quality Management in Emerging Nations", *Indian Management,* November, 30-34.

Ghoshal, S., *et. al.* (2001), "World Class in India—A Case Book of Companies in Transformation", Penguin Book, New Delhi, India.

Kanji, O.K. (1991), "Education, Training, Research and Consultancy—the way Forwards for Total Quality Management", *Total Quality Management,* Vol. 2(3), 207-12.

Kini, R.G. (1994), "An Economic Analysis of Conformance Quality, Ph.D. Thesis, Carnegie Mellon University, DAI, 56(2).

Klien, P.W. (1994), "A National Study of Quality Management in Baccalaureate Industrial Technology Programme," Ph.D. Thesis, Ohio University, DAI, 55(9).

Mekoth, N. and Hegde, S.G. (1995), "TQM and Service Organisations", *Indian Management,* Feb. 39-45.

Parasuraman, A., Zeithamal, V. and Berry, L.L. (1984), "A Conceptual Service Institute, Report No. 84-106, Aug. 9-24.

Saraph, J.W., Benson, P.G. and Schroeder, R.G. (1989), "An Instrument for Measuring the Critical Factors of Quality Management", *Decision Sciences,* Vol. 2(4).

Sarkar, B. (1991), "Total Quality Management Problem and Prospects in India", *Total Quality Management,* Vol. 2(3), 239-47.

Spence, D.L., "The Total Quality Model of Excellence : A Study of the Perceptions of the 1992-93 Participants", Ph.D. Thesis, Wayne State University.

Stamatis, D.H. (1996), *Total Quality Service,* St. Lucie Press, Florida, U.S.A.

ANNEXURE 1

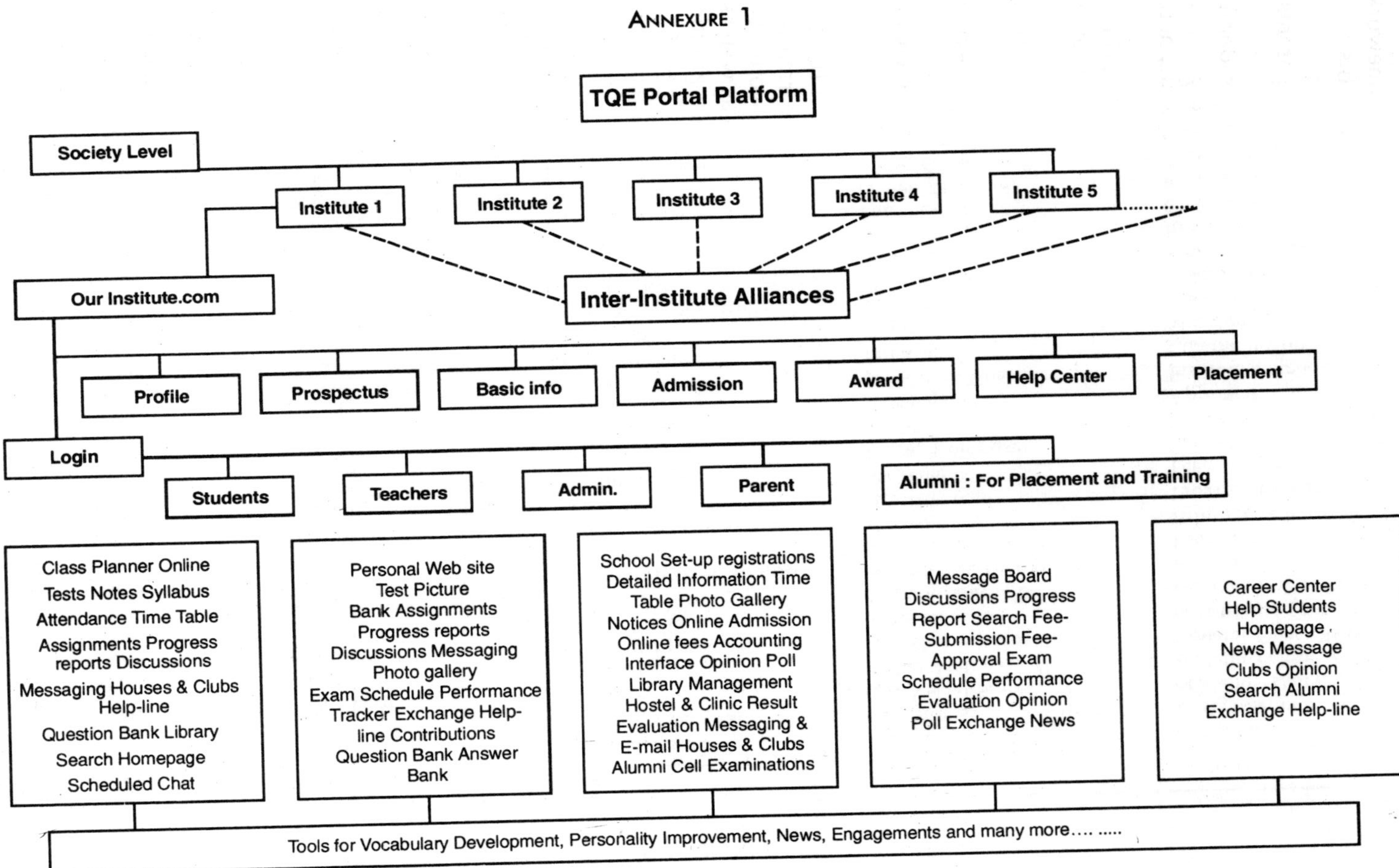

TQE Portal Platform
Society Level
Institute 1
Institute 2
Institute 3
Institute 4
Institute 5
Our Institute.com
Inter-Institute Alliances
Profile
Prospectus
Basic info
Admission
Award
Help Center
Placement
Login
Students
Teachers
Admin.
Parent
Alumni : For Placement and Training
Class Planner Online Tests Notes Syllabus Attendance Time Table Assignments Progress reports Discussions Messaging Houses & Clubs Help-line Question Bank Library Search Homepage Scheduled Chat
Personal Web site Test Picture Bank Assignments Progress reports Discussions Messaging Photo gallery Exam Schedule Performance Tracker Exchange Help-line Contributions Question Bank Answer Bank
School Set-up registrations Detailed Information Time Table Photo Gallery Notices Online Admission Online fees Accounting Interface Opinion Poll Library Management Hostel & Clinic Result Evaluation Messaging & E-mail Houses & Clubs Alumni Cell Examinations
Message Board Discussions Progress Report Search Fee-Submission Fee-Approval Exam Schedule Performance Evaluation Opinion Poll Exchange News
Career Center Help Students Homepage News Message Clubs Opinion Search Alumni Exchange Help-line
Tools for Vocabulary Development, Personality Improvement, News, Engagements and many more.... .....

Annexure II

Administrator	*Teachers*	*Students*	*Aiumini*	*Parrents*
Registration	Academic	My Course-ware	Administration	Academic
New Registration	Notes	Work at home (Assignments)	My Stores	Assignments
Update/Delete Reg.	References	Readings	My Visual Store	Students' Dairy
Club Request	Worksheet	Test Myself	Other Material	Bulletin Board
Reg. Requests	Assignments	Objective/Subjective	My Home Page (Create/View)	General Ques. Bank (Contribute Q's)
Information	My Question Bank	Comprehension	General Ques./Bank (Contribute Q/As)	General Q & A bank (Contribute Q/As)
Info Gallery (dynamically creating links for the homepage)	Class Question Bank	Doubts	Communication	Help-line
Popup Windows	Power Point Slides	Teaming up (worksheet)	E-mail	Administration
Time Table	Discussion (initiate)	Slide shows	Address book	Progress Report
Class-wise	Bulletin Board	Discussion (Limited to a class)	Message (View/Compose)	Fee
Teacher-wise	General Question Bank	Bulletin Board	Discussion (Participate)	Submit Fee
Replace readier	General Q & A Bank	My Class	Scheduled Chat	View Fee Deposition
Substitute Teacher	Class Planner	Class Question Bank	Interests	Approval
Substitute report	Student's Query	Time Table	Clubs	Institute Calendar
News	Evaluation	Class Planner	Web Magazine	Communication
Opinion Poll	Objective Paper (Compose/set for a class)	Progress Report	Opinion Poll	Message (View/Compose)
Holiday	Subjective Paper (Compose/set for a class)	Discussion (initiate/participate)	Services	Discussion
Profile (Teachers & students)	Comprehension	Our Campus	Stores	Scheduled Chat
Notice	Administration	Cubs	Question Bank	Interests
Thought of the day	Progress report	Houses	Search Members	Clubs Web Magazine (Contribute/View)
Bus Details	Performance tracker	Web Magazine	Photo Gallery	Opinion Poll
Institute Setup	Creale user	Opinion Poll	Change Password	Services
Add Class/Subject	Class time (able My time table)	Institute Calendar	Update Personal Details	Stores (Text/visuals/links)
Define Examination	Student list	Bus Details	Library Search	Question Bank
Define Class Teacher	Student's Attendance	Discussion (Participate)	Offer	Photo Gallery
Non-Acad. Categories	Institute Calendar	Contribution (Notes & News)		Change Password
Add Photo gallery		Communication		
		E-mail		
		Address Book		

Fee
Define Fee
Fee for Approval
Edit Fee Structure
Academic
Notes
(Add/Edit/Delete)
Assignments/Add/Edit/
  Delete)
Progress Report
Performance Tracker
Top 5 Students
Teacher's Performance
Teacher of the Month
My Question Bank
Add Links
Communication
Discussion
(Initiate /Participate)
E-mail
Address Book
Message
(compose/view)
Scheduled Chat
Interest
Clubs & Houses (new
  request/administer)
Opinion Poll
Add/Delete Alumini
News
  Services
Worksheet
Institute Calendar
Photo Gallery

Student's Dairy
Communication
Discussion
(Participate)
E-mail
Address Book
Message
(compose/view)
Scheduled Chat
Interests
Clubs
Houses
Opinion Poll
Services
Profile
Search Members
Photo Gallery
Stores
Question Bank
Change Password
Update Personal
Details
Library Search
Offers

Message (Compose/view)
Scheduled Chat
Search Stores
Question Bank
General Q & A Bank
Search Members
Photo Gallery
Dictionary
Help Line
Put Question
View Reply
Other's Question
View All Q & A
Library Search
Offer
Personal
Your Home Page
Change Password
Personal Details
My Visual & Text Store
Beyond Borders
Inter Institute
Society

Update Personal
Details
Offers

E-Governance for Productivity Improvement in Administration : An Indian Perspective

KULWANT KAUR

Now-a-days Internet and IT has entered into almost all activities of human life. It has created tremendous impact in the field of Banking, Tourism, Publishing, Trade and Commerce, Governance, Education, etc. This has redefined fundamentals and has potential to change mechanisms of delivery of service forever. It is in this context that the issues of SMART Governance need to be analysed.

Electronic Governance (EG) is the application of Information Technology to the processes of Government functioning to bring about Simple Moral Accountable Responsive and Transparent Governance. This chapter deals with major e-governance initiatives taken by Central and State Governments in India. It has been divided in three parts, i.e. Working Model of EG, Major initiatives taken by Central and State Governments and the benefits and threats of e-governance.

I. WORKING MODEL OF EG

EG through a technological innovation has changed the basic character of governance, operational methodology, functional style, ideological orientation even the spirit, heart and soul. IT offers a package of efficiency, time boundedness, cost effectiveness and transparency. Computer network and Internet are major tools of EG. In order to make government authorities more responsible and accountable we should require following initiatives at various levels :

- Identify *functional areas* in every Ministry/Department most necessary to be taken up as also those, which are easily assessable to EG.
- Make an *inventory* of existing applications/packages both domestic and international facilitating EG.
- Initiate moves to encourage Central and State Governments to *develop and link,* already *existing databases* to the public domain.
- Encourage both Central and State Governments to *prescribe knowledge of computers* as an essential qualification for recruitment/ promotion at various levels.
- Assist Central and State Governments in *identification* and implementation of suitable hardware and *software packages* for EG.
- *Establish links worldwide with institutions* engaged in similar activities so as to optimize and synergise benefits, by building sustaining platform for interchange of ideas and experiences.
- Initiate *amendments in Central and State Acts,* Rules and Regulations under various departments and ministries to put in place IT and Web enabled Citizen Services.
- Develop special pilot projects on *Paperless Government-on-Line* through electronics "Intelligent Government" concept by extensive use of Electronic Forms and Data Entry Interfaces through use of web and Internet technology.
- Build convergence into connected Services Delivery programs relating to the citizen devices.
- Identify measures for suitable protection of data during filling up, transmission and against alterations by using combination of security measures.
- Develop commercial and governmental systems for issuing and managing digital signatures/electronic signatures smart cards.
- Establish *Government Information Services (GIS)* and facilitate the setting up of National Information Infrastructure incorporating links with Government Information Infrastructure on one hand and State Information Infrastructure, District Information Infrastructure, Local Information Infrastructure (LII) and other networking systems on the other, so as to enable seamless transfer of information multilaterally between users and providers of information and services.
- Enable Ministries in Government of India as well as State Governments to formulate scheme for selected activities and suitable resource facilitation to encourage the same.

Operational Strategy

- Development of a suitable organisational structure : Once a decision is taken to implement and identify the Objectives of EG a team of officers headed by a Joint Secretary would drive the Operational Unit. With convergence of technologies being the essence of EG, other Divisions and officers would contribute from time to time. Secretarial help to the Unit would be essentially from the existing resources.

- Development of appropriate operational links : There would be three operational links to the above Project Team through :
- Interaction with the User Groups comprising of Industry, Citizen service dedicated organisations and eminent members of the public with interests in the subject. This could be the Citizen or *User Expert Groups*.
- Interaction through a *Steering Group* comprising of key departments/ministries represented at the respective Joint Secretary levels and identified initially for implementation of EG across their functional areas.
- The third expert group would comprise of solely Industry and Business representatives as inputs and interactions are strategically essential for giving industry focus to the Project. This would be the *Industry and Business Expert Group*.

CHALLENGES IN EG

I. Implementation Issues

EG is a big project so it should be implemented in phase-wise manner. Besides department related to public grievances, other sub-issues associated are :

(a) Technical Issues

(i) *Hardware issues* : As Hardware industry is changing rapidly it needs provision for upgradation by periodic replacement of computer elements.

(ii) *Software issues* : With respect to objectives, EG should take up software platform, which should provide application range from common man to government officials/staff. There should be single web based front-end for all government services to public. To use Internet and WWW based application, domain name standardization of various states must be done, as it is available for various countries.

(b) Standardisation : EG Demands Standards in all Areas

(i) Speed of carrying out transaction and delivery of a particular service,

(ii) Convenience and access,

(iii) Flexibility in options and time periods of service,

(iv) Empowerment by bringing services closer to the public and letting them choose as to how and when to carry out the transactions, and
(v) Providing better user interfaces.

(c) Social Acceptance Issues

Success of any new working model depends on its social acceptance. Besides awareness programs for computer literacy, stress should also be given on proper planning so that maximum interaction with public could be identified for the use of IT. Major areas can be Public Grievances (Electricity, Transport, Ration Card), Rural Services (Land Records), Police (FIR Registration, Lost and Found Valuables), Public Information (Pension, Registration of Licenses and Certification, Birth and Death Certificates), Agricultural Sector (Seeds Information, Crop Diseases, Fertilizers, Weather Forecast), Utility Payments/Billing (Electricity, water, telephone), etc.

(d) Legal Issues

EG demands amendment to existing laws. Besides that we need cyber laws. Amendment is needed in central as well as state laws.

II. Financial Commitments

In order to give the Project a specific focus, it should be financed through a separate budget head set-up for the purpose for coming financial years. Available budget heads would also be leveraged for addressing expenditures for the Project. This would also enable managing critical linkages and avoid rework and duplication.

III. Initiatives taken by various States and Central Governments

I. Andhra Pradesh : Implemented

(i) The Andhra Pradesh government's e-governance initiative is best known for APSWAN (Andhra Pradesh State Wide Area Network), a state-wide network for voice, data and video communication, which is the basic information highway for improving government-citizen and government-industry interface. In subsequent phases, APSWAN would be extended to all 'mandal' headquarters, other towns and eventually, to all villages. Prior to this, one of the first projects effectively taken up towards the implementation of e-governance was by the state's Department of Registration. It provides an easy and transparent process for registering and documenting immovable property. Perhaps the most daunting task for the Andhra Pradesh government was the compilation of the socio-economic classification of the state's residents and the preparation of a database of land records. These are the first stepping stones towards the issuance of multipurpose identity cards that would ensure better targeting for poverty alleviation programmes.

(ii) TWINS enables the citizens of Hyderabad and Secunderabad to access select services and information on Departments of the State and Central Governments. This is done by accessing integrated citizen service centres (ICSCs). The ICSC is a one-stop shop for key citizen services—such as payment of electricity, water and sewage bills, property tax, registration and issuing of birth and death certificates and many more. The government has also initiated the Secretariat Knowledge Information Management System with a view to exploit the power of computer networks, automate workflow in the Secretariat and to provide effective tools for performance evaluation.

(iii) SKIMS—Secretariat information system.

(iv) Lands and Registration Departments : The Andhra Pradesh Planning Department has put together a sophisticated Geographical Information System (GIS) which captures inputs from remote sensing satellites to create thematic data on road networks and community infrastructure.

II. Chandigarh

Initiated Project Telemedicine interconnecting three medical institutes, i.e. PGI–Chandigarh, AIIMS–Delhi and SGPG–Lucknow using ISDN. It has facilitated flow of information of research outcomes which will ensure better health care systems.

III. Kerala

(i) The first phase of the project for networking all the sub-treasuries in the State has been completed with five sub-treasuries and the extension counters in Thiruvananthapuram district being linked online. The second phase would test the capability of the VSAT architecture for networking. Even on completion of the first phase, the implications on proper resource planning at the Government level are fairly obvious. The project for linking the sub-offices, checkposts and other main nodes of commercial taxes department has completed the stages of systems study, techno-economic clearance and final tendering.

(ii) Co-operative banking network inter-linking State Co-operative Bank, 14 District Co-operative Banks, Primary Agricultural Co-operative Societies is being implemented in phases.

(iii) The Secretariat Wide Area Network linking the offices of all the ministers, secretaries and individual sections as well as office complexes housing the Heads of Departments are being put in place.

(iv) A common Web Portal for the Government of Kerala has been launched with the assistance of the local chapter of Computer Society of India.

IV. *Karnataka : Implemented*

(i) Computerised Constituency Management System,
(ii) Police net, and
(iii) Kannada Kacheri—Kannada Language Software Geographic Information System for Bangalore.

V. *Lakshdeep : Initiated*

(i) Training of officers and staff in basic concepts of computers and applications,
(ii) Entry Permit Holder Information System, and
(iii) Ship Ticketing.

VI. *Maharashtra : Initiated*

(i) Sales Tax department,
(ii) State Excise Department,
(iii) Registration and Revenue Department, and
(iv) General Administration Department.

VII. *Orissa*

(i) The Orissa Government deployed information technology towards the planning and development of land. The Bhubaneshwar Development Authority (BDA) has set-up kiosks at its office that map the city using a CIS. This has made life easier for citizens as they can check on existing schemes for housing, commercial and industrial projects without depending on middlemen. Citizens can also get accurate information on rates, vacancies and administrative procedures. Satellite earth station is functional for giving data connectivity to IT companies.
(ii) Internet services introduced by DOT for general public.
(iii) Orissa Centre of IBM Software imparting high-end software training.
(iv) B.Sc. (Hons.), Computer Science courses introduced in six Govt. colleges.

VIII. *Pondicherry : Proposed*

(i) To impart IT training by educational institutions.
(ii) To computerize all departments and provide facilities in outlying regions with Internet facilities.
(iii) Police net for networking of all Police Stations.

IX. *Punjab : Propose to set-up Hi-Tech Habitats*

X. *West Bengal : Initiated*

(i) *Finance Department* : NIC is preparing a software for implementing a model Value Added Tax Scheme (VAT) in the State of West Bengal. A Registration Project Card is running with the software prepared by National Informatics Centre for registration of documents relating to immovable properties in transactions involving sale, gift, mortgage, lease, partition, etc.

(ii) The Pension branch of the Pension Directorate has also been computerized. The software for The Pension Calculation and PPO Generation System for the Primary and Secondary School Teachers as well as employees of the Municipalities and Panchayats has been developed by the NIC and running since the last four years.

(iii) *Transport Department* : In the Transport Department, Smart Cards will be introduced for Registration Certificates and Driving Licenses. In several Motor Vehicle Offices computers are already being used online for work relating to registration, tax collections, issue of permit, etc.

(iv) *Land and Land Reforms Department* : It has been planned to put the Land records data retrieval system on KIOSK at Block Land and Land Reforms office at Thakurpukur/Metiabaruj in Kolkata as a pilot project. The software is accordingly customized to be operational at the Kiosk level. Land and Land Reforms Department has installed Computers in all the L.A. Offices and in the Offices of the Divisional Commissioners. In the Presidency Division, use of IT has been initiated in Arms Licenses Section, Accounts Section, Motor Vehicles Section, Certificate Proceedings Section, Zila Parishad, etc.

(v) Labour Department Computerization has been taken up in the Labour Department, for example, in Directorate of Employment, Directorate of Boilers, Directorate of Labour and Directorate of Shops and Establishments.

(vi) *Information and Cultural Affairs Department* : Department of Information and Cultural Affairs has taken up computerization on the basis of a study carried out by the Regional Computer Centre, Kolkata. The Kolkata Information Centre maintains a computerized database on the activities of the Department of I & CA and all other important departments of the Government, private organizations and individuals involved in cultural and related fields. Based on this data bank, two information kiosks including one touch screen kiosk and a Cyber net are being set-up in collaboration with Regional Computer Centre and West Bengal Electronics Industry Development Corporation Ltd. (WEBEL).

(vii) *Home Department* : Kolkata Police is expanding its computer network to cover all Police Stations in Kolkata. In Bidhannagar, computerization of the Police Control Room has been completed. A project for executing computerization of Detective Department of Kolkata Police has been completed.

(viii) *Public Grievance Monitoring* : A Public Grievance Monitoring system was successfully developed and initially implemented by the NIC District Centre at Burdwan about two and half years ago.

XI. Rajasthan : Initiated

(i) Vikas Darpan—GIS-based Planning and Decision Support System covers 40000 Tehsils on about 200 demograph and socio-economic indicators.

(ii) Rajasthan's Department of Information Technology has developed a state-wide intranet called 'raj SWIFT. This system uses the internet to facilitate online data, text and e-mail communication between the Office of the Chief Minister and the 32 District Collectors. Raj NIDHI, a web-enabled citizen-service information kiosk framework, is a modern, transparent and responsive system. The government aims to provide greater transparency in government-citizen interactions through projects such as 'Aarakshi' (which provides field officers with online information on criminals); computerisation of the Ajmer Collectorate (including grievance monitoring systems); computerisation of hospitals; computerisation of the Registration and Stamps Department; and networking of the Secretariat.

XII. Tripura : Initiated

(i) State government has launched its official website at : tripura.nic.in. We are in the process of further improvement of the site.

(ii) The Government has taken up the programme of training its officers and staff in basics and slightly more advanced concepts of computing.

(iii) The following major IT projects are at the implementation stage :

(a) Computerisation of Taxes.

(b) Computerisation of Treasuries and an Intranet for the State in various departments.

(iv) In addition to these projects, the system study is being done for the following projects :

(a) Transport MIS

(b) Computerisation and an Information System for Rural Infrastructure.

(v) The Government has also opened an Information-*cum*-Facilitation Centre (IFC) in the State Secretariat. This centre provides basic information on the activities of the various government departments of Tripura and uses a Database at the back-end to respond to all queries which may come up. This centre is also linked to the Internet so that information can also be got on national and global aspects.

(vi) The State Government is also in the process of finalizing the IT Policy of the State.

XIII. Gujarat

(i) Gujarat was in the limelight when it introduced the smart card-based driving license project. Each of the 22 Regional Transport Offices (RTOs) of Gujarat was equipped with state-of-the-art enrolment and issuance centres. The government has also implemented a state-wide WAN (Wide Area Network) project that connects its various office complexes and corporations and support services like voice, data and video traffic. The network provides a backbone for connectivity to any LAN establishment throughout the state.

(ii) Gujarat's State Road Transport Department's 'computerised check posts' project has reduced corruption at the 10 octroi posts to zero and has enhanced revenue earnings.

INITIATIVES IN DIFFERENT DEPARTMENTS OF GOVERNMENT OF INDIA

1. Department of Agriculture

(a) Website of this department is http ://www.nic.in/agricoop;

(b) DAC HQs and most of its attached and subordinate offices have been declared Y2K compliant and a report has been sent to Planning Commission. The remaining few offices will also be made Y2K compliant very early;

(c) A central sector scheme for strengthening IT apparatus in the DAC HQs. has been approved. Under the scheme, IT tools are being provided to all the offices in DAC. Under the aforesaid scheme, an Early Warning System is being established to monitor agriculture on real time basis directly from the fields by use of IT applications;

(d) Officers up to the level of Under-Secretary/Deputy Director have been provided with PCs and local area networking (LAN) has been established;

(e) The Plan is to provide with a PC and Internet connection upto the Section level;

(f) Video Conferencing facilities have been established in the DAC HQs. with the help of NIC;

(g) Officers are now using e-mail in their day-to-day working and the DAC has also been given the centralised e-mail address : agrindia@krishi.delhi.nic.in;

(h) Software programs are being developed keeping in view the functional needs of various divisions;

(i) An independent computer training room has been set-up where training is available on all working days during working hours to all officers and staff as per their needs and convenience;

(j) A central sector scheme for strengthening Information Technology and their horizontal and vertical networking with the DAC HQs. is under consideration and the proposal has been referred to Planning Commission.

2. Department of Posts

(a) On-going Computerisation in Post Office, Front offices, Money order services, Postal life insurance.

(b) Propose to connect Postal Directorate at Delhi, the N.E. postal circle and the Assam postal circle with internet as the link network, Computerisation of international mail and airlines accounts.

3. Department of Space

Technology-related activities mainly involve mission specific tasks configured around computer systems with/without networking for design, development, tests and simulation functions in various engineering discipline application software development and computerisation of administrative services and management decision support systems.

INITIATIVES IN DIFFERENT MINISTRIES OF INDIA

I. Ministry of Textiles

(a) The Ministry has set-up a Task Force on Information Technology to formulate the methodology of introducing IT in different aspects of textile sector.

(b) They have taken initiative to set-up a computer communication network for all its offices.

(c) As part of recommendations of IT Task Force, all organisations are taking up initiatives to establish E-mail facility for communication.

(d) Web site on internet is being installed in the Ministry as well as its attached/subordinate offices.

(e) Economic Research and Market Intelligence Unit (ERMIU) has been set-up at Office of Textiles Commissioner, Mumbai for collection and dissemination of information on production, designs, fashion, etc.

(f) As recommended by IT Task Force, all organizations under Ministry including attached/subordinate offices are directed to take up in house computerization for implementation of MIS in routine working.

II. Ministry of Parliamentry Affairs

Ministry of Parliamentary Affairs has appreciated the initiatives taken in the area of Electronic Governance. It has informed that it is in the process of computerising the working of the Ministry. It will seek expert advice of the concerned Department in application of IT in efficient Governance after completion of computerisation.

III. Ministry of Chemicals and Fertilizers

(i) The IT Plan for the Department was prepared about two years ago and the implementation has been phased over a period of five years. The hardware required for various Sections and the Offices

Senior Officer was procured in 1999 itself. PCs, provided up to the level of Section Officers have been connected on LAN. In-house Training Courses were organised by NIC for all the officials on Windows 98, Office 97, Internet browsing and E-mail. The various IT tools are being made use of by the officers of this Department.

(ii) A web site of the Department has also been launched, which was inaugurated in January 2000. The information required for updating the site is collected on the 5th of every month and passed on to NIC's main server machine.The Department is also operating a Facilitation Centre for providing information required by general public.

(iii) The Department is maintaining database on production Monitoring for the Chemicals and Petrochemicals on the Server machine installed at the NIC-C&PC Monitoring cell.

(iv) To implement the paperless office concept, the Office Procedure Automation (OPA) package has been put into use and its implementation is reviewed periodically. All the officers of the Ministry have been provided e-mail accounts for effective communication. It is also proposed that the PSU's/Organisation/ Attached Office of this department should have a VSAT connectivity for online communication both ways.

(v) The Department's IT plan is periodically reviewed by Secretary to ensure speedy implementation and to finally achieve the objective of integrating itself with the other Ministries/Departments through e-governance.

IV. Ministry of Civil Aviation

Ministry of Civil Aviation is using IT extensively in their office and necessary infrastructure has been set-up with the help of National Informatics Centre. Connectivity with various Government Departments is available including Internet connectivity, E-mail, video conferencing, etc. They have some packages like Office Procedure Automation (OPA), Parliament assurances, Monitoring System, Parliament Questions and Pay roll, etc. Through OPA, they have computerized the files and receipts handling and monitoring system since 1993. They have set-up a Felicitation Counter where information required by public is disseminated.

V. Ministry of Environment and Forests

Ministry of Environment and Forests has intimated that they have a web site where information/status on all important matters, e.g. environment and forest clearance is available. It is also in the process of setting up a LAN in the Ministry and has also drawn up IT Plan for the Ministry.

VI. Ministry of Finance

(i) All computers have been connected in a Local Area Network (LAN).

(ii) The LAN is connected to WAN (NICNET) though a Radio Frequency Link (2 mbps).
(iii) Internet and NICNET connectivity has been provided to all the clients (PC's) connected in the LAN.
(iv) E-mail has been provided to all the officers in DEA.
(v) Website for Ministry of Finance has been created three years ago and is being updated regularly.
(vi) File-Diary Monitoring System is functional in the office of Minister and Secretaries and is going to be implemented down section level.
(vii) All the officers and secretarial staff are being trained regularly on application softwares like MS Office, E-mail, Windows 98, etc.
(viii) Facilitation Centre had been set-up for the department for dissemination of the information to general public.
(ix) All the work activities of this office, namely, maintenance of loan-wise accounting, draw down of external assistance committed by various donors, debt service payment, budget preparation with regard to external assistance, amenable to complete computerization.

VII. Ministry of Labour

An IT Committee in the Ministry presently functioning under Additional Secretary (Labour) with participation of NIC Technical Director posted in this ministry formulates/recommends the computerisation proposals in consultation with users. The committee also monitors the implementation of approved projects and helps in removing the bottlenecks, if any, and speeding up the implementation. The IT committee finalizes and continuously review long-term and short-term IT induction plans in the ministry and its offices in consolation with the concerned officers.

Keeping the rapidly changing nature of IT in mind, the conceptual plan for implementing Integrated Labour Information System consisting of interrelated segments like, Social Security, Industrial Relations, Employment and Manpower, Industrial Safety and Health is being formulated accordingly. The Hardware, Software and Network components will be finalised at the time of execution keeping in view the availability of high technology equipment, project requirements and cost procurement.

The Directorate General of Factory, Advisor Service and Labour Institutes and Directorate General of Mines Sefety and Health, have computer infrastructure and are operating on computerised system. They are augmenting their IT resources.

Further to improve the quality of IT services from this Ministry, individual Bureau Heads have been instructed to submit revised IT plans based on working group on IT.

VIII. Ministry of Tourism

(i) Creation of thematic CD-ROM.
(ii) Creation of virtual reality CD-ROM on important monuments.
(iii) Data-base driven visitor query system at Tourist Office.

(iv) Putting up computer-based tourist information kiosks at airports, railway stations, bus depots, tourist offices, etc.

(v) One type of kiosk shall have a multi-media content providing information in an entertaining way and the other on Geographical Information System (GIS).

(vi) Developing MIS packages for various Divisions in the Ministry.

IX. Ministry of Communication

(i) Web site for DOT, WPC, MTNL, VSNL, TEC, C-DOT and TCIL.

(ii) Networking within DOT Training of DOT personal for computer usage.

(iii) Computerisation of Management Information System like, Personnel Section, Administration, Finance, Service matters, leave account, etc.

X. Ministry of External Affairs

(i) Government online international project of G-8 countries, Visa regulations of major countries (15), Back office automation activities which have Citizen Interface, RPO & E-mail project being implemented.

(ii) Eight regional passport offices have been fully computerized and networking between them is to be done.

XI. Ministry of Information and Broadcasting

IA Video tape on "Indian Electronics Industry and use of Computer in Day-to-Day work" has been provided to Directorate of Field Publicity, Ministry of I&B for creating awareness amongst users to enhance application of Information Technology.

XII. Ministry of Power

(i) A new plan scheme for computerisation has been introduced. The details of the scheme have been finalised which envisages procurement of hardware/software, providing training to the officers/staff of the Ministry, etc.

(ii) The Ministry of Power also has a website which has been functioning since 1996. All policy initiatives taken by the Ministry are available on the website. Separately, the website also has detailed information on the organisational structure of the Ministry, important notifications issued, especially those related to private power projects, status of reforms, restructuring programmes in various states, etc.

XIII. Ministry of Surface Transport

(i) Project on Development of Automatic Vehicle Counting, Classification and Axle Load Weighing System for Highway Applications.

(ii) Project on Intelligent Transportations System for Indian Conditions.
(iii) Committee for implementation of the scheme for Ancillary Development related to Ship-building and ship repair.
(iv) Networking of the lighthouses for DGLL.
(v) Advisory Committee on Introduction of Vessel Traffic Management System (VTMS) service in the Gulf of Kutch.

XIV. Ministry of Science and Technology

(i) Design, integration and implementation of an informative website of the Ministry/Department;
(ii) Application software development for internal processing and also for interactive public information system through Internet and stand alone basis; and
(iii) Formal customised training to all categories of officers and staff in DST.

References

R.P. Bhavsar & Dr. B.V. Pawar, "E-Governance in India : A Perspective", CSI Communications, June, 2001.
Electronic Governance—A Concept Paper; http ://www.bangaloreit.com.
http ://www.iiitb.ac.in.

CRM : Increasing Organisational Competitiveness

JASMINE BANSAL

"A little bit of quality will make the customers smile and a little bit of courtesy will bring them from a mile-Anonymous".

The so-called typical customer no longer exists and companies have been learning this lesson the hard way. Until very recently business was more concerned about the "is" than about the "who". In other words, companies were focused on selling as many products as possible, without any regard to "who" was buying them. Maximizing profitability with low cost was the real name of the game. But, with dwindling profits and increasing costs, the executives soon realized that these tactics were not enough to satisfy either the customers or share-holders. Moreover, customer's expectations rose by leap and bounds, thereby leaving no option for the marketer, but to introduce flexibility and ability in their operations and practice proactive marketing strategies to smoothen their position in the market. The increased number of customer defections forced organizations into taking measures to retain its customers, thereby making way for techniques like CRM, which mainly deals with retaining customers by ensuring their satisfaction. Also, the organizations soon realized certain important facts of business like, that the cost of acquiring new customers can be five time more than the cost of satisfying and retaining current customers and that a 5% reduction in the customer defection rate can increase profits by 25-85%, depending on the industry. As a result of this, Customer Relationship Management (CRM) emerged as core activity for businesses operating in fiercely competitive environment.

CRM : THE CONCEPT

Customer Relationship Management is a comprehensive approach which provides seamless integration of every area of business that touches the customer—namely, marketing, sales, customer service and field support—through the integration of people, process and technology, taking advantage of the revolutionary impact of the internet. CRM can also be defined as a management discipline, which aims at identifying the right customer and developing strategies for building and maintaining long lasting relationship with them. According to Ernest & Young, the consultancy firm, "CRM is the strategy for managing customers and customer relationships". In other words, it is the art of one to one marketing or loyalty marketing, which involves understanding the customer individually, interacting with them and customizing the products and services to suit their needs with the ultimate aim of retaining them for a long period of time. Thus, it starts with the process of attracting customers and continuing building relations with them, till the time they become an integral part of the organization (Fig. 35.1).

FIG. 35.1
The Customer Development Process

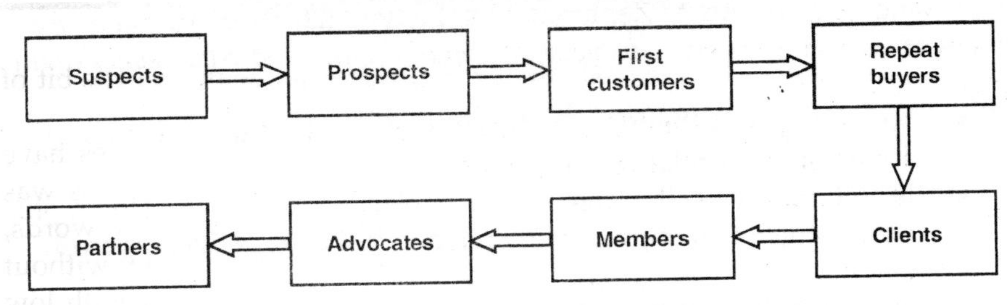

Source : Jill Griffin, Customer Loyalty how to earn it, how to keep it? New York : Lexington Books, 1995.

The starting point is including all the people who might conceivably buy the product or service (suspects). From these the company determine the most likely prospects, which it hopes to convert into first time customers and then into repeat customers and then into clients—people whom the company treats very specially and knowledgeably. The next challenge is to turn clients into members by starting a membership program that offers benefits to the customers who join in and then into advocates, customers who enthusiastically recommend the company and its products to others. The ultimate aim is to turn advocates into partners, people who will act as owners and will contribute in creating a niche market for the organization. Federal Express, the company having maximum number of loyal customers in the courier industry, has a Powership Programme, which installs computer terminals in the offices of high volume customers. It comprises of an automated shipping and invoicing system that saves customers' time and money while solidifying their loyalty toward FedEx. However, during this process some customers may drop out or shift to some other company. The challenge then is to reactivate these defectors through win back strategies like giving financial incentives or providing structural solutions to their problems. Here the relationship marketer need to offer only those value adding benefits that are difficult or expensive for the competitors to provide or those which are not readily available elsewhere, thus creating a strong foundation for retracting, maintaining and enhancing relationships.

CRM : A STRATEGIC INITIATIVE

Developing a suitable strategy for effective implementation of CRM is an important issue that needs to be examined very carefully by an organization, as the success of this tool depends to a large extent on the creation and evaluation of a suitable strategy for taking care of its customers. The strategy must be practical, relatively simple; easy to articulate and well disseminated at all the levels of the company. Though every company has its own way of taking care of its customers, still the company focus should always be on building strategy, which can enhance customer equity. Customer equity is the total of discounted lifetime values of all the firms' customers. So, the more loyal the customers, the higher will be customer equity. Rust, Zeithmal and Lemon (2000) distinguish three drivers of customer equity : *value equity, brand equity and relationship equity.*

- Value equity is the value of benefits of an offering as perceived by a customer, in relation to its cost.
- Brand equity is the customer's subjective as well as intangible evaluation of a brand over and above its objectively perceived value.
- Relationship equity is the customer's tendency to stick with a particular brand for a long period of time irrespective of the competitor's offerings.

Thus, the company needs to formulate a strategy that integrates all these equities in order to strengthen its payoffs and have a competitive edge. Along with this, the organization should also plan out a charter incorporating the following aspects :

The Mission

The purpose of an organization planning to implement the CRM techniques in an industry is to shift from being a transaction centric to customer centric business.

Objectives of Implementation

The need for adopting a CRM strategy may arise due to any of the following reasons (Pandit, Ajay and Sahni, A.K., 2002).

1. Rising cost of sales.
2. Increased Global Competition.
3. Dwindling Margins.
4. Constant need for more information.
5. Productivity.
6. Customer care.
7. Changing Paradigms.

Customer Expectations

Correct and timely identification of customer expectations acts as the lifeblood of effective implementation of CRM. Information may be collected regarding any of the following issues :

1. Customer identity and characteristics-basic data such as name, address, telephone numbers is must. Information regarding organization size, type of business, etc. (in case of business employees) and gender, family details, etc. (for individuals) are also important.
2. Information regarding products purchased and requests made.
3. Details regarding RFM, i.e., Recency (when customer last made a purchase), Frequency (how often) and Money (spending capacity).
4. Media and/or activity (telemarketing, direct mail, sales call, telephone call, advertisement, etc.) influencing the transaction.

Measurement Matrix

A parameter is drawn in order to measure the level at which the problems of the customer are taken into consideration by the company and what immediate steps a company would take in order to resolve those problems. Though organizations are different, their objectives may also differ but while implementing CRM, it is very important for a company to achieve the objectives that are set out to maintain its customers and build loyalty.

End Results Expected

The results expected with respect to :

1. Increase in life cycle of customer, i.e., increase in number of loyal customers.
2. Increase in sales due to positive word of mouth spread by loyal customers.
3. Cost benefit related to maintaining a current relationship as against building new ones.
4. Increase in revenue and organizational growth.
5. More scientific and systematic way of managing the business information.
6. Competitive edge.

7. Last but not the least, increase in service quality and customer satisfaction.

CRM DEVELOPMENT

Once an organization decides on implementing CRM as a tool for achieving core competency, the next step is deciding on a structured developmental process. This is to ensure that all the people involved in the process of implementing can anticipate and accurately scope various developments activities. Moreover, a sound development blueprint will ensure that implementers focus less on deciding the subsequent steps to be followed and more on the effective implementation of the valuable CRM functionality (Fig. 35.2).

FIG. 35.2
Process of CRM Development

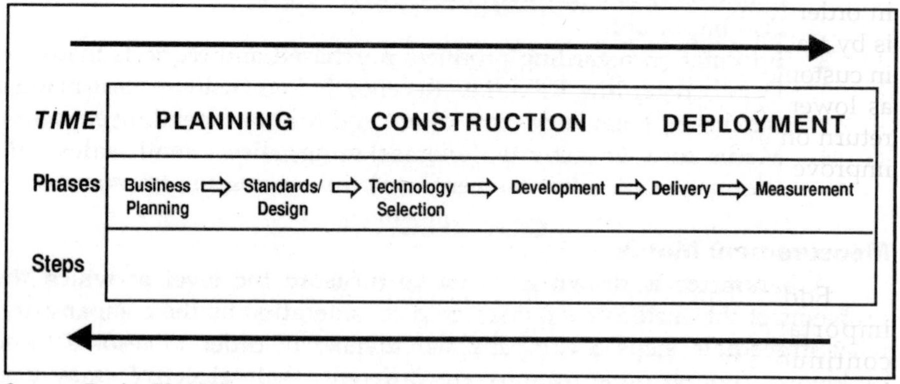

Source : Dyche Jil, 2000.

The first step in the development of a CRM model for any organization starts with formulating business plans keeping in mind the need and the objectives for adopting CRM. It includes making a CRM strategy encompassing the entire organization which can be leveraged at the time of CRM's inception to gain executive consensus and sponsorship. It can also be used as a focal point for requirements driven development and then after the deployment of the plan, a way to measure its success. The second step involves identifying the processes the CRM product will support. It involves formulating and communicating various standards and designs that will help in the implementation of the project. This step also includes a pre-implementation check of the organizational resources, both, which are available as well as the resources that may be required in future. The next step is a critical one as it involves selecting appropriate technology for implementation processes. It can be as simple as selecting an off the shelf product, i.e. a software solution or developing an in-house, traditional system of maintaining relationships by formulating effective strategies for the same. . . . Then comes the development stage, which involve the construction and customization of the CRM product, using specific features. It also deals with integrating various business processes with the CRM products. Process integration involves ensuring that identified business processes are tested with users to ensure not only that the business processes work, but also that technology features can be leveraged in order to refine them. In other words, the technological capabilities should improve, not compromise customer focused business processes. The delivery process is often overlooked into development. Basically, it involves the implementation of various strategies formulated at earlier stages after adequate user training has been imparted on the people responsible for implementation. Thus, training the people involved regarding the various techniques and technology is an imperative part of the delivery process. The training tools may include meetings, user guides, job aids and other documentation as well as online or web-based help to encourage implementers as well as users to make the most of CRM functionality. The measurement step brings the CRM process full circle as it evaluates its usage in order to refine CRM requirements. The best way to evaluate the process is by tracking the decrease in product defects and a corresponding increase in customer satisfaction. This measure can include value quantification such as lower support costs due to fewer support requests and thus increased return on investment. It also includes the incorporation of user feedback to improve CRM usability and business effectiveness.

CRM LIFECYCLE

Eddie Bauer Inc., the famous chain of retail stores, realized the importance of knowing the customer in early 90's and has been continuously working towards building a model for effective implementation of CRM and finding ways to retain their customers. In their Learning Relationship Model (Fig. 35.3) they describe the various stages in the process of development of the system of CRM, which helps in enabling

Fig. 35.3
The Learning Relationship Model

Gather Data
About the CUSTOMER

CRM OBJECTIVE
Building customer Value
(Revenue, profitability and customer satisfaction)

Convert Data to Information to DIFFERENTIATIVE CUSTOMERS

Use to CUSTOMISE each
- Offer
- Communication
- Interaction

Which build stronger CUSTOMER RELATIONSHIP

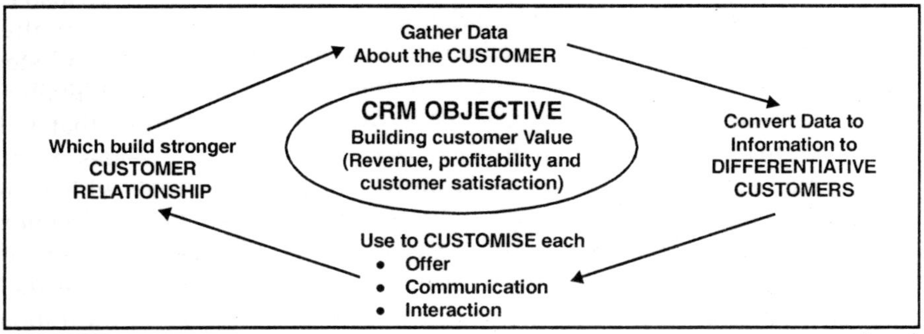

Source : Courtesy Eddie Bauer Inc.

a beneficial outcome for the organization. The model assumes that the organization has already developed a CRM strategy and has identified the various technologies and techniques to be used for the implementation of CRM product. It basically deals with issues that need to be handled during the construction phase including the development and delivery of the CRM product.

The model highlights that gathering adequate data regarding the needs and wants of customers is the first step for any organization planning to incorporate CRM in its system. This may be done through a large number of quantitative and qualitative research techniques, which will entail identifying in detail the demographic profile, buying pattern in terms of usage, frequency and repeat purchase, channel preferences of each and every customer individually. Such information should then be used for developing a central repository, accessible to all the employees as well as customers at all points of time. The information should then be adequately used to customize the offerings to the customers not only in terms of products and services meeting their needs but also with respect to the way of communication, choice of media and time of delivery. This exercise of customization will help the organization in building and strengthening long lasting relations with the customers, resulting in the achievement of organizational objectives.

For instance, Companies like IDBI have a system of centralized database, which can be accessed by both the internal (the employees) as well as the external customers of the organization The customers can not only get detailed information regarding the status of their transactions with the bank like the prevailing rates of interest, EMI, loan redemption period, etc. but can seek answers to queries too. Having spent around 20 crores on successful implementation of CRM project, IDBI is fast shedding its image of a product-oriented organization to a customer centric one.

ROAD BLOCKS

CRM may face lot many roadblocks on its way to success, some obstruct the beginning of the project during the business planning or requirement gathering that allows a CRM team to set things right. However, the commonest bottleneck still remains the resistance to change. Many a times, internal support of employees is not generated by the top-level management, at the time of deciding on implementing a CRM strategy. This forces the members to resist any change in the environment and they try to stick to their comfort zones, claiming to prefer "old way of doing things". And if the employees follow such stand then even with the best of technology, CRM cannot become a success story. In order to avoid this, it becomes important to communicate the who, when, what, why and how of the CRM project to all the members of the organization. Adequate training sessions should be organized in order to enable the employees to get used to the CRM way of working.

Another road-block may arise from the customers, who may not be interested in sharing information with the company. This can easily be removed by following a *quid pro quo* policy, where the customers know that they will receive something valuable in return for information given. (For instance : Customers of Taj Group of hotels, are given special package deals for their stay in any of the group's chain of hotels along with keeping them updated with all the new schemes introduced by the group from time to time). Apart from this, giving customers full access to all the information collected by the organization helps in building their confidence. Though this may be risky, but such a tactic makes the customer participation in managing his information, potentially enhancing his perception of the company as a partner. (For instance, ICICI bank's customers can log on to the company's website with a secure password and check their own profile maintained by the bank as well as general information regarding the bank).

Last but not the least, lack of coordination is yet another inhibitor to the success of CRM. This may be between any of the following factors :

- Company objectives and CRM objectives.
- Top level management and front office employees.
- Various departments of the organization.
- Geographically and organizationally distributed members of the delivery channel.
- Human factor and technology.

CRM AND COMPETITION

Though most of the companies adopting CRM look forward to improving customer service and increasing sales uplift through retrofitting existing technologies, investing in new hardware and software solutions and hiring management experts to bolster their strategies in preparation for a revolution in customer loyalty, their main aim is fighting the market competition. Being the market leaders therefore is the primary objective, achievable only by serving the customers in the best possible manner, which in turn is the only way to retain and refrain them from switching over to the competitor. For instance, Bharat Petroleum Corporation Ltd. (BPCL), the oil giant has successfully executed several CRM schemes over the past five years. It opened several channels of contact with the customers : introduced products like Petro Card and services like "Pure for Sure" and "Quality and Quantity" petrol pumps to address customer problems, things quite unheard of in case of a public sector company. The result was its sales are growing close to 3% that is almost double the industry average and over the past five years it has consistently boasted of 21% return on net worth, again the maximum in the industry. Seeing the immense advantage of following the customers closely, last year HP (Hindustan Petroleum) also introduced Club HP, a club exclusively for preferred customers buying products HP brand.

Thus, all transactions must be looked at as relationship building opportunities (Reicheld, 1993), aimed at increasing profitability and gaining competitive advantage, not by reducing the wages or increasing scale of production, but by formulating effective business policies for retaining customers. The management can therefore consider the following key points for successfully developing, deploying and maintaining CRM solutions :

Avenue

The first and most important step for any organization planning to implement CRM solution should be to enquire about related projects elsewhere in the company. An organization should understand that CRM is a team effort that requires participation from a range of players across the business. Therefore, exploring various avenues that can help in reducing cost should not be ignored.

CRM Relationships

Every organization should keep in mind that CRM is essentially about relationships and technology is just a support mechanism. Therefore, focusing on improving relationships enables the organization to develop more prospects into repeat customers, thereby increasing revenues, return on investment and productivity.

Proactive Executive Empowerment

Management involvement is critical for two reasons. As company leaders, management sets the overall strategic direction for CRM—including budget and delivery parameters and ensure that the culture of customer service is incorporated in the organization from top to bottom. Equally powerful is the management's empowerments of the employees to develop positive customer relationships and corresponding systems that support and enhance those relationships.

Blueprinting

No organization builds without a road-map but many organizations deploy CRM without understanding the business processes in place in the organization. Defining business processes, understanding departmental interactions and identifying bottlenecks enables in better management of CRM system by the employees.

Service Guidelines

Just as an organization needs a guide map for understanding the system of CRM; similarly it should also formulate a series of customer service guidelines for every customer-facing department. These can further be used, as a part of employee's performance evaluation and compensation package. In short, customer ownership will result in increasing efficiency and effectiveness of the employees.

Knowing the Users

The organization should not only consider the features of a CRM solution but should measure its benefits to the users. Thus knowing in detail the requirements of the user-employees as well as the customers will result in choosing the best CRM solution.

Internal Support

There is no point deploying a CRM solution that is not supported by the internal staff. Moreover, the solution should be one, which supports the existing infrastructure and resources (human, capital or technological) of the organization.

Small Successes

An organization will find itself in beneficial position if it introduces only a handful of CRM solutions during the start up stage, rather than many solutions. In most business environments change is difficult and it takes time for the employees to adapt to new business processes and tools. Smaller deployments will further reduce the risk of resistance to change. As users become more familiar with the change, they will begin focusing on how the CRM tools can be used to improve their customer relationships and overall productivity.

Ongoing Evaluation

As with most things in life, a CRM solution will only be successful if the organization is committed to long-term evaluation and maintenance. Developing a CRM steering committee, consisting of users across the organization is the best solution for this. The committee should be responsible for evaluating ongoing business requirements, customer requirements and productivity enhancements that will enable better and long-term relations with the customers. The evaluation will ensure that relationship development becomes the core competency of the organization and empowers the users to change their plans and tools according to changing need of the business environment.

CONCLUSION

An old Chinese proverb says, "Give a hundred year lease on a desert and it will become a garden; give a one year lease on a garden and it will become desert".

The point is that ownership and long-term commitment makes a lot of difference when it comes to dealing with important tasks, and customer relationships is a big deal. The field of marketing has transcended many paths from product marketing to mass marketing to niche marketing and all the way to marketing a memorable experience to the customers in the form of CRM. CRM is changing the entire outlook towards running a business and is driving revenues and profitability. It is motivating customers to buy additional products and services by raising their satisfaction scores and helping companies focus which customers they should focus on and which channels they should invest in. In short, despite the risk and cost associated with it, CRM is valuable, viable and revenue generator.

REFERENCES

Reichheld, F.F. (1993), "Loyalty-based Management", *Harvard Business Review*, March-April.

Jill Griffin (1995), "Customer Loyalty : How To Earn It, How To Keep It", Lexington Books, New York.

Dyche Jill (2002), "The CRM Handbook : A Business Guide to Customer Relationship Management", Pearson Education, New Delhi.

Pandit, Ajay & Sahni, A.K., (2002), "CRM : A Tool for Competitive Advantage", *Productivity*, April-June.

WEBSITE REFERENCES

www.crmfoundation.com
www.icicibank.com
www.idbi.com

E-Governance : A Tool for Increasing Government Productivity

DEEPAK KAUSHIK

I.T. is the buzzword in the world. The I.T. revolution is sweeping every corner of the globe. U.S.A., U.K., China, Hong-Kong all are using this technology in their various projects which benefit both government and the people. Good governance has entered the development lexicon even though how to achieve good governance remain debatable. The Government System should not only be user-friendly, responsive but transparent too. Complex procedures, lack of information and commitment, huge records all have made government user-unfriendly, inefficient and have decreased over all government productivity. Using Information and Communication Technology, the quality of services by government can be improved, making government procedures simple and user-friendly.

With the arrival of IT in a significance way in India, the manner in which products and services are now being delivered is undergoing a change. As with the all other institutes in the country, the Government too has to realign themselves in accordance with this shifting pattern where IT is becoming the enabling tool for reaching out to citizen of the country with speed and economy. The approach to public governance has been witnessing a fundamental shift in the concept, manner and method by which the State delivers its services. In its final stage, public governance may come to assume the form of Electronic Governance.

E-GOVERNMENT AND E-GOVERNANCE

Electronic governance is the application of information technology to the process of Government functioning in order to bring about simple, Morale, Accountable, Responsive and Transparent (SMART) Governance. EG is really E-enabled government, E-effective government and E-excellent government. E-government is government any-time any-where.

The term E-governance and E-government are often used in overlapping manner although the two are not exactly the same thing. Much of this is due to lack of a standard definition of E-governance and we in India have been using this term in a general sense. In the case of E-government the services and information are delivered to the citizen or clients through electronic medium while in case of E-governance, the interaction between the citizen and the government takes place through electronic medium and decisions are processed electronically. It is necessarily more interactive and goes beyond E-government.

Electronic governance involves transformation from being a passive information and service provider to active citizen involvement. Its dimension could include the following :

- Single source of information for citizen.
- Equality and ease of access.
- Optimizing resources of multiple organizations.
- Inter-governmental participation.
- Public Networks.
- Involving various stake-holders.
- Stimulating debates.
- Exchanging view and information.
- Increasing participation by citizens in decision-making.
- Public information feedback.

Information and communication technologies (ICT) can serve a variety of different objectives and the resulting benefits that emerge would be : Increased transparency, greater accountability, impact on corruption, greater convenience for workers as well as citizens, revenue growth and cost reduction and increased productivity and competitiveness.

Major Application Areas

Public Grievances and Distribution System (Electricity, Transport, Ration Card).

Rural Services (Land Records, Education, Employment).

Police (FIR Registration, Lost and Found Valuables).

Public Information (Pension, Registration of Licenses and Certification, Birth & Death Certificates, Immigration).

Agriculture Sector (Seeds Information, Crop Disease, Fertilizers, Weather Forecast, Marketing, Price of commodities, Export & Import).

Utility Payments Billing (Electricity, Water, Telephone).

Environmental Related Issues.

Tax Administration.
Social Issues (Pension, Rehabilitation & Compensation).

Pre-requisite for E-Governance

- Large scale computerization.
- Government process reengineering.
- Capability of use of local languages in the IT systems.
- Awareness and Commitment.
- Infrastructure.
- Standardization.
- Certification Authority.
- Availability of Sufficient Financial Resources.

Digital Governance Models

Digital Governance Models are still evolving and continuously improvising to fully harness the potential of knowledge networks. Some models have got shape and finding greater recognition and are being replicated. These are based on the inherent characteristics of ICT, which are enabling equal access to information to anyone who is a part of the digital network and de-concentration of information across the entire digital network.

The five basic models of E-governance are :

- Broadcasting/wider,
- Critical Flow Model,
- Comparative Analysis Model,
- Mobilization and Lobbying Model,
- Interactive Service Model.

Broadcasting/Wider Model

This model assumes that a more informed citizen is able to better understand the governance mechanisms and is more empowered to make informed choices and exercise its rights and responsibilities. It also assumes that if all citizens have equal access to information then government can't make biased decisions. It opens up an alternate channel for citizens to access information as well as validate information available in local domain. This model is the simplest model and is the first step toward more evolved models and works as the building block to better governance. The main drawback of this model is that it is loses its effectiveness without government encouragement and under tight government controls and censors.

Application

- Making legislation and law-related information and court judgments/judicial statements that are of value to common citizens and create a precedence for future actions online.

- Putting names, contact addresses, e-mails, fax of government officials online.
- Make information regarding government plans, budgets, expenditures and performances online.

Critical Flow Model

Unlike the last model this model channels information of critical value to some targeted audience through the use of ICT and converging media. This model requires the foresight to understand the importance of particular information and locating audience to whom the availability of particular information set would make a critical difference in initiating good governance. This model also suffers from all drawbacks with which last model suffered. It exposes the weakest aspects of governance and decision-making process.

Applications

- Making available information electoral constituency-wise about corrupt politicians or to the concerned authority about corrupt officials,
- Making available information regarding Human Rights Violation records to NGO and concerned citizens,
- Putting Environment-related information of specific areas on local networks for local communities, and
- Making available Research Studies Report/Government Plans to the affected parties.

Comparative Analysis Model

This model as the name suggests is based upon exploring information available in private domain or public domain and comparing it with known information sets to derive strategic learnings and arguments. This model continuously collects new information and uses it as a benchmark to evaluate, propose or influence changes in current government policies and actions. It can use before-after analysis or with-without analysis. Generally this model is not used but due to it's effectiveness, it is gaining popularity very speedily. This model can be used for checking performance records.

Application

- To find effectiveness of current government policies by comparing with policies in past, and
- In patent-related disputes, public goods, ownership rights resolution.

Mobilization and Lobbying Model

This model tries to group the people of same thinking together ultimately building strong virtual communities which share similar values and concerns, promoting active sharing of information between these communities to impact international as well as national decision-making. The strength of this model is availability of diverse ideas, expertise and resources in virtual communities. It can effectively overcome geographical, institutional and bureaucratic barriers. This model creates an effective deterrent for government bodies and individuals.

Application

- Amplifying the voices of marginalized groups who are traditionally marginalized from the decision-making process.
- Building-up global expertise on a particular theme.
- Formation of pressure groups to pressurize decision-makers to take their concerns into consideration.
- Encouraging public debates on global as well as local issues.

Interactive-Service Model/Government to Citizen to Government Model

This model is improved model of earlier models and make the direct participation of individual in government process possible. It fully uses the facilities provided by ICT saving time and cost in decision-making. This model is being used in developed countries and being proposed for developing countries, but it requires very advanced technology for the implementation.

Application

- Using video-conferencing for communication between Policy-makers and citizens.
- Using ICT for general utilities like election, income-tax return, payment transfers, public grievances for reducing delay and cost.

Since implementing any governance model will require total re-engineering and far-reaching changes of government processes, proper and cautious thought should be given before going for any model. Just replicating any popular model will not result in good governance, ultimately increasing the gap between government and citizens.

Benefits of Electronic Governance

- It would improve the shortcomings of the present system.
- Most importantly it would reduce the procedural/postal delays involved in the current system.
- To some extent it will control corruption.
- It will strengthen our democracy.
- Increase participation of people in policy decision process.
- Improve the degrees of communication between the government and public.
- Speed up the processes of Government functioning.

- Effective government.
- Improve transparency.
- Feeling of Equality in the public.

Challenges before Electronic Governance

1. Implementation of EG is not a simple task, it is very big and time-consuming. So it cannot be implemented in one step and will have to be implemented in phased manner.
2. Challenges related with Hardware Upgradation
3. Since EG is for common man so the software developed should be such that common man can easily and effectively use it.
4. There should be one simple, convenient, flexible interface for all government services through which public as well as officials can access the information.
5. Various standardization related with internet, domain names, etc. need to be done.
6. How to bring services closer to the public and letting them choose as to how and when to carry out the transactions?
7. How to achieve Social acceptance?
8. How to achieve social awareness among computer literate as well as computer illiterate?
9. How to generate financial resources?
10. How to tackle security-related issues?
11. How to handle excess staff and train the existing staff, recruitment policy, promotion-related issues?
12. How to generate political commitment?
13. How to get institutional support?

E-GOVERNANCE INITIATIVES IN INDIA

E-governance is not only the new but also the new-trend occurring in India. This is catching up speedily in the form of a movement and everybody is talking about it in eager expectation of the very many benefits flowing from its adoption. It seems like win-win for government as well as citizens. Most of the states have either started working in this direction or planning to work due to which there is no uniformity in the process and are at different levels of implementation. Central government has also started working in this direction. The first step toward this was the Information Technology Act, 2000. This Act is to provide legal recognition for transaction carried out by means of electronic data interchange and other means of electronic communication commonly referred as electronic commerce which involve one of the alternatives to the paper-based methods of communication and storage of information to facilitate electronic filing of documents with government agencies. Chapter III of the act deals with electronic governance, defining electronic form as any information generated, sent, received or stored in media, magnetic, optical, computer memory, microfilm, computer generated micro or similar device.

Through paras 4 and 5 of the Act, legal recognition of the electronic records and of digital signatures has been provided—which means that any information that used to be earlier in writing or in type written or printed form can now legally be "rendered or made available in an electronic form" and "accessible so as to be usable for subsequent reference".

To promote, facilitate and develop in an orderly manner the carriage and content of communications (including broadcasting, telecommunications and multimedia), for the establishment of an autonomous commission to regulate carriage all forms of communications, the Communication Convergence Bill, 2001 was enacted.

The National Task Force on IT and Software Development, constituted by the Prime Minister's Office, has established India emerging as an IT superpower in the world by 2008. The Task Force has already submitted its reports in 3 parts. Task force has set-up a target of US $ 50 Billion for software export from India by 2008. Domestic Software industry is targeted to reach the level of US $ 30 Billion by this time. A number of initiatives recommended in the report have already been implemented by the concerned department/ministries. The Task Force has also identified Citizen-IT interface as one of the key areas to service the information requirements of the citizen through deeper penetration of IT in society and through the extensive use of latest tools in the networked society.

Schemes Proposed in the Tenth Five Year Plan for Facilitating Convergence and E-Governance

(Some schemes may overlap the areas of Convergence and E-governance since E-governance is one of the prime areas of application of convergence).

Convergence

No.	*Scheme*	*Amount (Rs. in Crore)*
1.	Research Centre for Information Security	300
	(a) Technology for E-Commerce	
	(b) Information Security, Encryption, Digital Signatures	
	(c) Public Key Infrastructure	
	(d) Smart Cards	
	(e) Bio-metrics	
	(f) Digital Rights management	
2.	Centre of Excellence for Wireless Technology	360
3.	Test Bed Projects in Emerging Technologies	100
4.	Development and application of appropriate Tele-medicine Technologies suited to Indian condition	150
5.	Development and application of Tele-educational Technologies	150
6.	IT for masses (Support for multi-functional Application Community Centre)	700
7.	Setting-up National Standardization Institution for Convergence Standards	100
8.	National Institute of SMART Governance	15
9.	National Council of E-governance	5
	Total	1830

GOVERNMENT-WIDE INFORMATION INFRASTRUCTURE

1. Government-wide electronic information infrastructure should be created to simplify service delivery, reduce duplication, and improve the level and speed to the public. This would provide the public (business and individuals) with the opportunity to send and receive, over electronic terminals, the information that currently passes between them and the government on paper.
2. The government and the private sector would need to collaborate to put in place Electronic Fund Transfer (EFT) system, since this is critical to the successful implementation of Electronic Commerce, as well as direct service delivery to the citizens.
3. It is necessary that computers should be cheaper to increase their penetration. The possibility of procuring cheaper second-hand computers available elsewhere should also be explored. These can be channelised through ET&T, and NICSI by proper coordination with groups of NRI's abroad.
4. Re-engineering of the existing government processes and producers is essential to bring about transparency in working, reducing bureaucratic control, increasing efficiency and productivity, reducing cost of service, delivery, etc. Integration of projects across various departments to provide a single point of contact for citizens for delivery of service electronically is essential.
5. The Freedom of Information Act to be enacted which shall ensure right of citizen to have access to the information.
6. A National Institute of SMART Governance should be set-up to focus on all issues concerning IT-supported Governance (Recommendation No. 97). Electronic Governance Institutes throughout the world are concerned with public policy, cyber law, economic development, delivery of service to citizens, constituency relationship and replacing industrial age institutions with the electronic art of governance, i.e. through digital age technologies and networks.
7. A Transaction fee-based delivery of services system with involvement of private sector to harness the enormous capability of private enterprises.
8. Service Delivery Points (SDPs) should be set-up at the convenient location for citizens to access services. All STD/ISD booths should be converted into IT booths through whatever necessary steps required to do the same. They will operate as PTICs (Public Tele Info Centers).
9. Smart cards, stored value cards, Credit-Debit cards could be integrated in the framework of National Electronic Payment Systems for effecting payment of bills to Utilities.

10. Implement Government-wide Electronic Procurement and Settlement System to enable informed, transparent decision to be made with uniform terms and conditions.
11. Implement simple, electronic system for filing income tax return.
12. Development of User-friendly India Portal.
13. Start National Institute of E-governance/Council for E-Governance.

E-GOVERNANCE PROJECTS IN STATES

Andhra Pradesh

Apswan : Network for voice, data and video-communication throughout the state. Operational with 2 Mbps fibre optic links connecting State Secretariat with 25 centres.

Card Project : Manual system of registering and preserving documents of immovable property transactions replaced by simple and transparent system.

Multi-Purpose Household Survey Project : A World Bank aided project, to be implemented with an expenditure of Rs. 70 crore, MPHS will computerize all basic socio-economic data of all residents of the state and generate a database of land records.

Fully Automated Services of Transport : Provides services like issuance of learner driving licenses, vehicles registration through a comprehensive networked solution.

Secretariat Knowledge Information Management System : Generic product that efficiently manages information and knowledge of the Secretariat.

A.P. Development Monitoring System : Combines geographical information system with data from Remote Sensing Satellites. The system has created base maps of 1,122 'mandals', constituent revenue villages, and habitations.

Gujarat

Smart Card Project : 22 : RTOs of Gujarat equipped with state-of-the-art driving license evolvement and issuance centers.

Statewide Wan : To connect various office complexes of Gujarat government.

Disaster Management System : To maintain communication during natural disasters.

Karnataka

Computerization of Education Department : Established, with technical assistance from NIC, a computer center at the office of CPI to speed up work, automate routine jobs and spread computer awareness.

Computerization of Treasury : Rs. 30 crore have been invested to computerize Treasuries by November 2000. Comprising installations of around 250 VSATS all over the state to capture every single transaction accounting for over Rs. 20,000 crore at all 31 district treasuries and 184 'Taluk' treasuries, under this system, accounts are updated instantly.

Vidutnet for KPTCL : India's first VSAT-based communication network, Vidutnet—To support real time data applications for power generation and distribution in KPTCL. The network is also used for voice and fax communication.

Tamil Nadu

STAR : Simplified and transparent administration of registration across Tamil Nadu, a comprehensive IT package for all needs of the registrants.

School Project : To take computer literacy to 1300 higher secondary schools in the state.

Tele-Medicine Project : Allows doctors in remote areas to consult experts on special cases or for referral purposes through a direct ISDN link.

Computerization of Land Records : To eliminate corruption in the Department and for customers' proof of ownership.

Local Language Computing : Standardized keyboard and fonts, Tamil Virtual Library, Tamil Software Development Fund, and Tamil Internet Research Center.

Computerization of Transport Department : Data-entered and updated the historical data of one crore records of vehicles and drivers in the state. Project extended to prepare better infrastructure and ISDN connectivity with all offices in the state for speedy transactions.

West Bengal

GIS-Based Municipality Information System : Started as a map-based GIS pilot project in Mahesthala municipality, WEBEL has carried out similar projects in 20 more municipalities. When completed, the project will cover 10 percent of states population.

Web and Kiosk-Based Education Information System : To provide information to students on demand, based on specific needs, thereby saving time and energy. EDIS to act as a 'friend, philosopher and guide' to students and guardians.

Vernacular Interface Project : Facilitates using computer in rural and semi-urban areas, for access to information in Bengali regarding tax payments, electricity and telephone bills.

At the national level, the picture of E-Government or E-Governance presents a wide variation of the level of computerization and the use of IT enable applications within the government and for delivery of services and information. Also, in the Central Government itself, various ministries are at different levels of computerization and delivery of services. In spite of sustained efforts, the entire government machinery especially in the states has not yet become fully available for the use of computerization and other IT applications. Some of the states have advanced whereas others have lagged behind for various reasons. Since the early starters would have advantage of further growth at a faster rate, the digital divide will increase not only from one region to another but also from one organ of the government to another. Although, a minimum agenda has been devised for computerization of the government, there is no real total picture of the country or any marking of the level up to which IT is being used by Governments.

Role of ERP Systems in Increasing Productivity and Competitiveness

SHIKHA KAKKAR

INTRODUCTION

Information Technology is a buzzword today. Rapid advancements are taking place in the field of information technology. Generation, acquisition, dissemination and application of data, information, ideas and knowledge are vital for the development of all sectors. The essence of IT is the micro-processor, data storage devices, data transmission elements, etc. The IT services mainly include product support, hardware and software maintenance, training and education system integration, application development and IT consultancy.

With the advent of Internet—the world has got a technology, which connects a computer with millions of computers in world-wide network and the most significant achievement in the information and communication system.

With the advent of Internet, the access to information is almost free. This has induced increased competition among businesses leading to a perfect competition in the market, with water-thin profits. In such a scenario, cost containment has emerged as the main business driver. A manufacturing firm looks at lowering costs in its entire supply chain by either shortening throughput times, lowering inventory or by providing quality service. Companies are now looking forward to adopting new re-engineering practices that would give them the competitive edge. One such panacea that surfaced in 1990's is Enterprise Resource Planning (ERP).

ENTERPRISE RESOURCE PLANNING (ERP)

It is defined as a set of applications that automates all departments within a company and attempts to integrate all departments and functions across a company onto a single computer system that can serve all those different departments' needs. Finance (Cost Management, Accounts, Receivable/Payable, General Ledger), HR (Payroll, Personnel-Management), Manufacturing (Sales-order-entry Invoicing, Capacity Planning), Logistics, etc. to help enable enterprise wide management of resources. ERP includes management of every operation in a value chain to minimize cost and time. Till recently information technology developers were developing more of need-based, isolated systems that targeted only the existing applications and not the business functions.

Individual Business Unit—A Pre-ERP Scenario

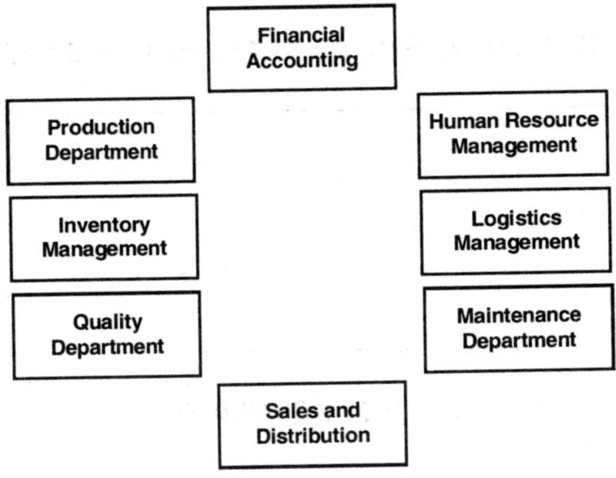

Post-EPR Integrated System

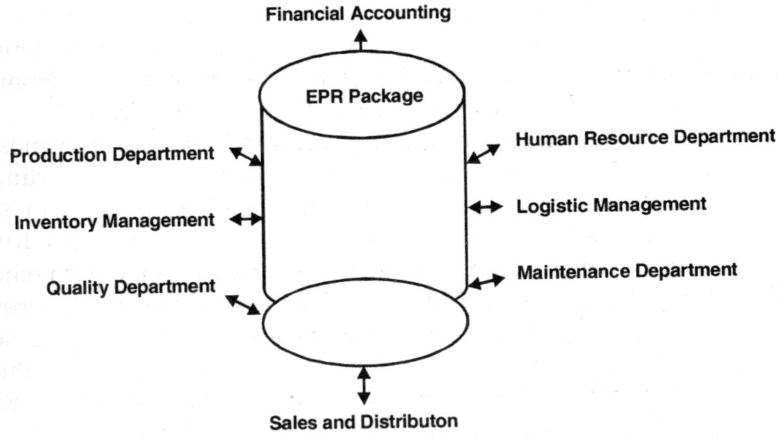

ERP facilitates seamless flow of information across all the departments, while optimally planning and managing all the resources of an enterprise. ERP today goes beyond the threshold of a singular segment of industry to diverse segments of corporate sector. As companies go global, there would be an increasing need for ERP systems with multi-sided management capabilities that ERP helps managers in reducing lead times, boost up productivity and improve customer satisfaction along with marketing support and post-sale field service that increase profitability.

ERP MARKET

AMR Research Inc., a leading industry analyst firm has predicted that ERP market is here to stay and would grow at compounded annual growth rate of 32% over next five years. The top five ERP vendors are SAP America, Oracle Corporation, People Soft Inc., JD Edwards and Company and Baan International Accounting for 61% of total ERP market revenue.

Total ERP Revenue (Actual and Forecasted) ($ billions))

1998	16.6
1999	20.2
2000	27.7
2001	37.4
2002	50.1
2003	66.6

INDIAN SCENERIO

Business enterprises in India are in the process of major transformation due to globalization and deregulation of Indian economy coupled with fundamental changes in the business models due to Information Technology-based business practices. Most of these enterprises in developing countries like India are in the process of implementing Enterprise Resource Planning (ERP) systems and process re-engineering initiatives. ERP systems promise benefits that range from increased efficiency to transformation of quality, productivity and profitability. However, its implementation poses some unexpected organizational challenges and changes that can be structural as well as cultural in nature. ERP helps to establish world class business practices and brings transparency in the organization but this demands for empowerment and flexibility in decision-making process too. The most promising argument is that, thrive in the e-commerce world, companies need to transform their internal business processes with the deployment of ERP systems. Hence, ERP is considered to be the backbone of e-commerce business. Recent trends in the industry indicate a slow down in the traditional ERP market. The slow down can be attributed to the saturation in the upper-end market and the stagnant world economy growth rates, which were as high as 40% per annum previously but have considerably slowed down to 15-20%.

Growth Rate of ERP in India

	Domestic (Rs. Mn.)	*Rate of growth (%)*	*Exports (Rs. Mn.)*	*Rate of growth (%)*	*Total*	*Rate of Growth*
1995-96	500.0		700.0		1,200.0	
1996-97	900.0	80.0	1,800.0	157.1	2.700.0	125.0
1997-98	2,800.0	211.1	3,400.0	88.9	6,200.0	129.6
1998-99	5,200.0	85.7	8,200.0	141.2	13,400.0	116.1
1999-2000	10,000.0	92.3	15,000.0	82.9	25,000.0	86.6
2000-01	11,001.0	80.0	28,000.0	86.7	46,000.0	84.0
2001-02	25,000.0	38.9	40,000.0	42.9	65,000.0	41.3

Now the market is also witnessing the emergence of SMEs (Small and Medium Enterprises) with a turnover of $ 50 to $ 500 million as a major ERP spender, with significant demand for module specific implementation. As the Fortune 500 market for product license revenue becomes saturated, larger ERP firms are shifting their focus to the middle market. The other areas like Supply Chain Management (SCM), Customer Relationship Management (CRM), extended ERP and web-enabled ERP are still evolving. The coming of Multinational Corporations on domestic soil is forcing suppliers and distributors to automate business processes. The survival of 100,000 odd SMEs that dot the Indian business scene, depend on how quickly they are able to integrate their operations with one another and the Internet. ERP segment is especially gaining popularity in the SME segment because of CRM, SCM and B2C in the business environment. Since the software cost of ERP vendors like SAP, Oracle, Baan, etc. normally runs into crores of rupees, sensing the presence of SMEs in India, some Indian software companies have come up with affordable branded solutions. Matrix ERP is one such software developed by Calcutta-based software company, Matrix Infosystems Ltd. The product has been priced at Rs. 7 lakh to 12 lakh. However, big operators seem to have woken up to the potential market of the SME sector. They are now providing individual modules at prices that are not too steep for the small companies.

REASONS FOR ADOPTING/INSTALLING ERP SYSTEMS

Installing an ERP system by an organization has many benefits, which form the major reasons for undertaking ERP systems by an organization. These includes :

Reduced Lead Time

One way of cutting cost is to reduce lead-time. Reduced lead time helps in reducing inventory cost. The ERP system improves the efficiency of the inventory management system by integrating the purchasing, planning and production departments. For example, if an order for 100 cars has been received, the ERP systems would first check the finished goods inventory, identifying the number of cars to be manufactured. Once this is done and the production plan is in place, the material management module of the ERP systems would prepare purchase order for each and every item taking into account their respective lead times. In case of non-integrated manual systems, this exercise would have taken days, which can now be achieved within a couple of hours. Therefore, quick access to information helps in reducing costs and achieving a high level of customer satisfaction.

Increased Customer Satisfaction

With the adoption of ERP systems, goods can be produced with the make-to-order approach that ensures highest customer satisfaction. With the web-enabled ERP systems, customers can place orders, track the status of their orders online and also pay online. Technical support if required is also made available online.

Integrate Financial Information

Finance has its own set of revenue numbers, sales has another version and different business units may each have their own version of how much they contributed to revenues. CEO in trying to understand the companies overall performance, faces different versions of the truth. ERP creates the single version of the truth that cannot be questioned because everyone is using the same system.

Integrate Customer Order Information

ERP systems have become the place where the order lives from the time a customer service representator receives it until the loading dock ships the merchandise and finance send an invoice. By having this information in one software system, rather than scattered among many different systems that can't communicate with one another, companies can keep track of orders more easily and coordinate manufacturing, inventory, shipping among many different locations at the same time.

Standardize and Speed-up Manufacturing Process

Companies with an appetite for mergers and acquisitions find that multiple business units across the company make the same widget using different methods and computer systems. ERP systems come with standard methods for automating some of steps of a manufacturing process. Standardizing those processes and using a single integrated computer system save time, increase productivity and reduce head count.

Leaner Hierarchical Structure

ERP systems provide the freedom to change manufacturing and planning methods as required, without reconfiguring the plant layout. ERP systems help companies reduce data transfer time, reduce errors and reduce design productivity through automated links between engineering and production department. One of the significant advantages of ERP system is its capacity-planning feature. The ERP systems have simulation capabilities that help the capacity and resource planners to choose the cheapest option, given the various capacity and resource utilization scenarios. This helps organizations in minimizing wastes as wastes only lead to increased costs and inefficiency.

So, to exploit the full potential of all the benefits companies must select software having the features given below or set these as criterion for ERP software selection :

- Functional fit with the business processes,
- Flexibility and Scalability,
- User Friendliness,
- Ability to support multisite planning and control,
- Amount of customization required,
- Cost to be incurred, etc.

CONCLUSION

ERP systems are not simple software systems that can be purchased and installed overnight but require organizational rethinking, restructuring and a business transformation that affects the entire organization. Since the information entered from anywhere in the organization affects all of the databases, in case wrong information is repeatedly processed in a wrong manner, it could result in chaos and disaster leading to decline of the organization. However, carefully planned and implemented systems are proving to be very useful tools. With the increasing availability and usage of Internet around the globe, web-based ERP is expected to gain wide usage in global manufacturing companies and in small and medium sized firms.

E-Business : A Must for Globalization

MANAV JINDAL, SANJEEV BANSAL AND RUCHI JINDAL

E-business is what happens when you combine the broad reach of the Internet with vast resources of traditional information technology systems. It uses the Web to connect together customers, vendors, suppliers and employees in a way never before possible. "Clicks and Mortar" refers to those companies that integrate their real-world, offline operations with an Internet, or virtual, presence

EVOLUTION THEORY—FROM BRICK AND MORTAR TO CLICK AND MORTAR

Is it about creating Web pages? Is it about putting up a form on your Website to order products? Is it about getting a costly consultant and even costlier hardware and software?

Unfortunately, none of these make up e-commerce. Let's propose a simple model for the business universe. Assume for a moment that your company is at the center of the universe. The rest of the universe can be divided into three distinct groups : your suppliers, your customers, and the environment that may or may not have interactions with you.

Phase 1 : In the beginning, we did everything manually, recording them on paper. In order to speed up the work, we computerized it. Then we set-up networks to share information pertaining to work. In our simple model of the business universe, the network first appeared within the organization. Interactions of this network with the outside world were almost zero. For any data to get added to or get out of this system, manual intervention was required.

Phase 2 : The next big Phase was the extension of access of this network to suppliers. This is widely known as EDI-Electronic Data Interchange. Now you could directly place an order on your supplier's Network access information regarding availability of stocks and raw materials at his end, and so on. You could plan better, reduce inventories, improve turnaround time, and so on. But the cost of setting up an EDI system can be prohibitive. So very few businesses could go in for such systems.

Phase 3 : The next logical Phase would be to extend your network to your customers also. But for most businesses, even for the really big ones, this was impossible, given the spread-out nature of the end customer. The best that could be achieved was to extend the network out to the distributor. But as said, only a few were able to implement such systems. Reasons for this included the high cost of connectivity, incompatible software and the high cost of making them communicate data across each other. And there things rested till the advent of open standards.

Phase 4 : The Internet has made it possible for business to interact directly with both the suppliers and the end-users without having to go in for heavy investments. And in the process, it re-wrote the basic rules of doing business. Anybody with a Web browser could directly make a purchase from any part of the world. Similarly, anyone with a Web server could run a multi-million-dollar business without having to invest in godowns, and other distribution and retail infrastructure. The story of Amazon.com is too well known to merit repetition here.

The actual e-Business operation can be described as follows :

1. The client uses the web browser on the local terminal to connect for the e-Commerce site via the Internet/Intranet.
2. The site presents the client with the products/services offered.
3. The client chooses to make an online transaction and the e-Commerce site requests the client browser to enable an SSL-protected link. The system offers high level of security to the entire process.
4. The e-Commerce site (also called the server), requests personal and financial information from the client that is relevant to the authentication and validation of the transaction in process. This is sent for validation to a transaction server connected to all the data-bases of all the supporting financial institutions. (For example, the authentication databases of Master Card, American Express or VISA), or the internal authentication data-base of an Intranet. Depending on the values returned to the transaction server by the authentication databases, the client's transaction process is further processed.

E-business really means, the extension of business systems and providing an easy-to-use interface between the external world and the organization, while increasing reach. Where one can complete the transaction online and integrate the supply chain into transaction management process.

E-Business Barriers

If e-commerce is so hot, Why has it still made no major impact in India? There are many reasons.

Internet Usage

The computer usage itself is insignificant. Internet usage is almost non-existent. The largest ISP, VSNL, has about two and a half-lakh subscribers. All the other ISPs put together may add an equal number. E-commerce happens over the Internet and low Internet usage results in low business. The government's role also seems useless when compared to forecasts which promise telephone lines to 15% of the country by 2010. But may be our internet usage will speed up due to the fact that industries, services, i.e. banking, insurance, etc. are being net based. Also, with the introduction of wireless application protocol and generalized radio services, Internet and other forms of electronic exchange will come onto the scene.

Bandwidth

The lack of bandwidth is a major cause for concern. Currently all international connectivity is through VSNL and is limited to a very slow speed of 165 megabits per second compared to other countries, e.g. in China the speed is of almost 2 gigabits per second. But there have been have several applications with the DOT by small ISPs to set-up their own gate-ways, which would definitely mean the introduction of newer and faster technology.

Cyber Laws

People have had problems of non-delivery of orders placed on Rediff on the Net. And it takes only one scam to shake the confidence from the system. Legal shelter is extremely imperative for confidence to build-up. Then there is the issue of insurance against fraud. Whether the centralized insurance agencies, which are opposed to the very idea of privatization, will provide low-premium insurance cover to a high-risk, totally intangible area like transaction indemnity is anybody's guess. The lack of a secure online payment mechanism and the continued debate on passing the Digital Signature Act are all major stumbling blocks.

Business-to-business sites are comparatively better off, as they normally have negotiated-contracts, with governing laws and jurisdiction set out clearly, also the transactions are normally between known entities that have, or are actively looking for long business relationships.

Digital Identity

How can you trust the site you are doing business with? Similarly, how does the site ensure that you are not using a stolen credit-card number? The answer to this is digital certificate. But, to issue a digital certificate, you need an extremely trustworthy agency issuing the certificate of identity.

Inter-state Goods Movement Regulations

Anyone involved in selling and shipping goods across the state borders will testify what a nightmare this can be. No two states have the same sales tax and excise-duty rules. The rates differ; the forms to be filled in, differ (so do the rates of bribe). And then there's octroi.

Set-up and Infrastructure Costs

In spite of what many vendors would want you to believe, e-commerce is not a one-man operation that can run from a couple of servers stashed away in a corner in a basement. Equally big is the cost of software, Web-hosting services, bandwidth, and proper security. All these could add up to quite a big amount, both in initial investments and in running costs. Though as industry progresses, several companies that offer specialized services have come into existence. E.g. Dynamic logistics offers in-bound as well as out-bound logistics for off-line companies that want to go online, SEEC will help online companies to adapt to new technology. New software like Screen Scrapping or Legal Wrapping, etc. has revolutionized infrastructure support system in India. A new concept of application service provider is coming-up under which application will be maintained, owned and developed by the service provider and users will lease the services of this application on payment of nominal fees and they will be relieved of all the technicalities in this process.

Advertising Costs

The Internet is often likened to a high-speed digital highway with millions passing by every minute. No way! It's more like a mess of alleyways that no one has ever mapped out. Having a cool Website will not bring in people. People come to a Website either by typing the URL directly in their browser, or by clicking on an interesting link seen on some other site. Either of these costs a lot of money.

Again, in the case of business-to-business sites, this may not be a major factor.

All these are applicable to business-to-consumer e-commerce. In case of business to business, the very high cost of building the systems is often the biggest stumbling stone. And it's often a Catch 22 situation, with everyone waiting for others to start off, so that they can see the results and then follow. Hopefully, some one will.

INDIAN OVERVIEW

The Indian private sector has already recognized the attractive economics of e-business. Clearly, the get onto the e-business power curve is really quite high. Needless to add, that the potential exists. The size of the transactions over the net at Rs. 10 crore by the end of 1999 approximately, a piddling size when compared to the world, is expected to cross $ 400 billion by the year 2003.

Unlike in the past, where existing attitudes have posed major challenges to adopting a new way of life, with the Internet it has been rather a smooth sailing, thanks to the extraordinary levels of Internet awareness in the country.

As a result of this, companies have been more open to taking studied chances, as is evident. Here, we are not just talking of companies that have static web sites but those which conduct commerce on the net like Color, India Book Shop, baba bazaar, Rediff-on-the-net and Shoppers Stop, selling from books and shirts to vegetables and soaps.

The lack of infrastructure was a serious impediment, but bottlenecks are soon being removed. With several private value-added networks (VANs) coming up and with the reach of Internet expanding, this is becoming less of a problem.

In fact, collective experience indicates that firms can deploy e-commerce solutions over the current infrastructure and realize significant benefits from them. To be fair, this is one area that has received focus from the highest levels and there is feverish activity to build bigger bandwidth and crucial payment gateways, which will enable online credit card authorization.

Indeed, there is much at stake for, say, an automobile company or a fast moving consumer goods company which has multiple offices with different manufacturing sites and warehouses, etc. across the country. Infact, Dynamix—a software infrastructure solutions company, is in the process of helping TELCO to replicate the Ford "just in time technology". The recent announcement of Hindustan Lever indicates that soon all of its cosmetic line will be made available only on the net, with one center in each city acting as demonstration/guidance center.

The country needs to get its legal, legislative, regulatory, infrastructure and manpower ready for e-business. We already see some of this readiness, and hence, India is ready to boom in e-business. While the air of optimism persists, the fact remains that in India Electronic Data Interchange (EDI) has not really taken off. Therefore, doubts persist whether corporate and government in specific will adopt and accept this as quickly as is made out.

In countries like India technology acts as a leveler that removes inequality between people of different income groups. For example, poorer people who visit banks for their regular banking activities feel that an unequal treatment is meted out towards them as against their richer counterparts, especially with the insignificant sums of their transactions;

while the same people feel more at ease with an ATM that shows no emotion and all clients are treated alike.

Internet Hits the Indian Banking Sector

Today you send an e-mail or pick-up a telephone and your banker lands at your doorstep. Welcome to the new invasion of technology in the Indian banking system. The liberalization and the technology-invasion have worked wonders for the banking sector, say bankers. If ICICI has shown what technology can do for banks, others have quickly realized the potential and are fast trying to catch up with it. Is technology then the new driver in the Indian financial system? When all the banks and financial institutions are offering the vanilla product, the differentiation had to come from service. This automatically put pressure on the institutions to adopt technology as their USP. According to industry estimates, some of these new banks on an average send out 500 e-mails on a daily basis regarding new products, services, or other routine matters.

Internet banking is fast catching up. Banking will never be the same again in India.

Welcome to the new invasion of technology in the Indian banking system. ICICI had announced a tie-up with a Compaq-led consortium for setting up the country's first payments gateway to facilitate secured on-line B2B and B2C e-commerce transactions.

This will be the first payment gateway tailored to meet Indian requirements and will not be subject to all the regulatory concerns that cloud other non-India-based payment gateways. The gateway offers the flexibility of multiple payment modes including credit, debit and smart cards, direct bank debits and e-cheques. The ICIC1 e-commerce payment gateway will launch a state-of-the-art internet payment system and is set to open the world of e-commerce to many more merchants, consumers and businesses in India by significantly lowering the cost and complexity of enabling secure transactions over the Net. The customer's credit card number will be protected through hardware cryptographic devises so that the only information available to merchants is a code. This will substantially reduce the capital costs of merchants.

MOVING "TOWARDS E-BUSINESS...."

The statistics show that 90% of all new businesses fail. We believe that is a direct result of the failure to plan. Take the opportunity to plan and increase your chances of success. While preparing for this topic there were several examples as well as case studies that we reviewed. These like most others left us starry-eyed. They seem to have this effect on most people of our age. But E-Business is not only success stories. There are several stumbling blocks that young entrepreneurs have to face. There are several start-ups that do not meet the "eye".

Here we have tried to explain the transactions that go into creating a structure e-business. We have made a comprehensive but necessarily an exhaustive e-business model.

There are 4 types of businesses that can be carried out over the Internet. They are :

1. B2B : that is Business to Business transactions that take place on line. For example, "dell.com". This company sells computers to several other enterprises via the internet thus eliminating the middlemen and reducing costs by a great deal.
2. B2C : that is Business to Consumer transactions that enable companies to get in touch with, service and make sales to their customers via the world-wide web. For example, "rediff.com". which sells everything right from music to books on the net.
3. C2B : that is Consumer to Business transactions where in the consumers specify their requirements and the business tries to meet them. Thus, the consumer gets the best bargain and businesses face fair competition, e.g. "priceline.com".
4. C2C : that is Customer to Customer transactions where in customers trade within themselves through auctions, e.g. Ebay.com"
5. With the changing times in the age of net, e-business cannot be just restricted towards being merely a B2B and B2C but with time it has also grown and is clearly even developing as C2C and C2B, e.g. ebay.com. and pricchnc used by various airlines like delta.com. The prices of tickets are no longer fixed but depend upon the place, time of booking, destination, etc. and not necessary that the price paid by the passenger boarding the flight will be the same as the rest of the passengers. Infact, now it is the customer who makes the offer and the organization has to make the counter offer.

The basic question to ask is whether to go online or offline?
You could judge your business on these criteria :

1. Whether the decision is an information intensive purchase decision?
   This will help in a way e.g. say a commodity like match-box there is hardly any need for any information before hand while purchasing one. Hence, e-would not be advisable.
2. Price, selection and frequency of change in the product ?
   A product like a personal computer, which keeps on innovating very fast it is extremely important to have latest information and hence e-business is important.
3. Will customization aid the user?
   In products where customization is important then business on the

net is very useful. Take the example of Levis jeans, they offer you the option of own jeans and have them custom made to your choice.

4. For sale of the products, is the touch and feel necessary?
5. Is there a need for new channels of distribution?
6. Is the product of the nature of a slow moving commodity?
   For products like antiques, paintings, etc. it is preferable to go on net since there are larger prospective customers that can be tapped at reduced costs.
7. What category of customer is the target?
   In India nearly 70% of the users are in the age group of 25-40 years. Hence a product that appeals to this segment e-business is the right option.

The First Move Towards e-business, "the Idea"

1. *You need a clear "Value Proposition"*

Unambiguous and clear picture of your idea helps reduce cost and cycle time, increase productivity and increase bottom lines. You have to analyze what are you offering your customer in terms of value. An idea which has no impact on society is not a good idea. A good idea is one which is :

(a) *Scalable* : this kind of an idea has a lot of scope and can expand across markets.
(b) *Malleable* : it can adapt to new markets and can forgo what it had initially started with. It allows you to move across related business with ease.
(c) It should not be averse to the constant addition of new features to attract eye balls.
(d) Unique and probably offers you "the first mover advantage".
(e) "Be distinct in the market place", you have to prove you are better than the others and in what way?
(f) Your idea should have a wide application.

2. *Create a Clear Revenue Model*

You should show source of revenues, whether it is from sales, advertising, franchise or whatever may be the case. The source must itself have growth powers at least for the next 10-15 years.

3. *"Keep HR Ratio Low ", i.e. Hype to Reality*

If you are unable to live up to the standards created your credibility is lost.

4. *Patent the Idea*

"The world is your oyster and entrepreneurs are global people". If not in India patent your idea with an international authority, it may cost a bit more but it is worth it as against the risk of losing your brainchild.

5. *Try and get a Digital Certification*

It helps you to certify the real identity of the merchant.

6. *Know your Client*

On the Internet it is very easy to lose customers. Your client would most probably be from a higher income group and therefore usually a well read and opinionated bunch. These are the kind of people who get you other customers by their word of mouth publicity. A single dissatisfied client can spell disaster as seen in the case of Walmart : the superstore. One dissatisfied customer started a site called "Walmartsucks.com." as a sign of protest against the company and to date this site has attracted the several aggrieved customers of the store and has a million hits a day!

7. *Know your Competition*

E-business faces competition from the real as well as the virtual world. Your competitor is just a click away. You have to be constantly alert and aware of the features being offered by him in order to keep your "critical mass" and retain your "first mover advantage".

8. *"Build a Good Team"*

Your team should have mutually exclusive and collectively exhaustive skills. Team members should be experienced, energetic and enthusiastic. Get members from every field to make up for each other's deficiency.

9. *The Team should have a Shared Vision*

"Aspirations that can be achieved asymptotically" Microsoft has a shared vision of one P.c. for every task. This is a vision, which also serves as a continuous ongoing ambition.

10. *Identify a Clear Leader*

There should be no diffused authority. There should be only one leader, some one who brings more value to the table than the others.

11. *Have a Clearly Defined Value System*

A value system is like the rudder in the ship to show you path in times of tribulation.

12 *The Most Important Decision*

Should you go in for venture capital?

Clearly identify what stage of funding you are at. Is your business a start-up, initial growth, positioning for going public, seeking a strategic partner, looking for near future acquisition or sale?

The options before you are :

Incubators

Incubators are those individuals who fund you from the very nascent stage right from the conception of the idea.

Angels

Angels are individual private investors who make up a large portion of "informal" venture capital home. They tend to invest small amount, and they can be difficult to locate because they usually don't belong to networks or trade associations. Angels are found among friends, family, customers, third party professionals, suppliers, brokers and competitors. For the most part, once they invest in two or three deals they are out of money.

Venture Capitalist

These investors are looking out for huge returns not just good ones. Venture capital is extremely hard to get and the competition is fierce. Venture capitalist fund only about 0.7% people, who come to them for funding.

Exit Strategy Funding Sources want to know how you plan to pay them back. Will the business generate a cash flow large enough to support the debt? Is the product or service so in demand that the company will go public? These questions and more will not only help determine your success, but they also narrow your search for the lender most likely to fund your request.

13. Prepare an aspirational model of what kind of wealth you want at each stage; right from the angel investor stage to the IPO stage. Having this model ready you are in a better bargaining position.

14. Make sure that your interests are protected. Should the venture capitalists appoint another CEO over you keep a 50% option vested the day after the CEO joins.

15. Do not shop around after you have finalized your venture capital. The venture capital community, especially in India is a small, close knit one and should this word spread no one will be willing to fund you.

16. Plan your supply chain. Online businesses also require huge external infrastructure support systems. The good part is that there are softwares companies like Euclid, SEEC, etc. which provide outward as well as inward bound logistics.

17. Hire a lawyer or a consultant to help you negotiate carefully.

IT in Agriculture : An Effort for Improving Global Competitiveness of Indian Farmer

MEERA BAMBA

It is common knowledge that there is an immense potential in Indian agriculture just waiting to be unleashed. The endemic constraints that shackle this sector and prevent the realization of its full potential are equally well known.

India's agricultural landmass spans 150 million hectares. But the fragmentation of agricultural land holdings makes it difficult to scale up the technology of cultivation and enhances the global competitiveness of Indian agriculture. The excessive dependence on the monsoon imposes its own limits on improving productivity of land and quality of crops. The variations between different agro-climatic zones through the country also toughen the challenge of evolving a common and standard approach to enhance agricultural yield and quality.

POOR EXTENSION MACHINERY

Indian agriculture has a strong research and development base. But the farmer is not able to apply the results to reap a richer and superior harvest because agricultural extension work lacks quality. There is a vast and hitherto untapped potential for agricultural exports. But inconsistent quality and uncompetitive prices make it difficult for the farmer to sell his produce in the world market. The irony of the situation is that while the market prices of agricultural products are exorbitant, the farmers get an un-remunerative return. A major chunk of the margin is eaten up by the large number of intermediaries or lost as avoidable wastage due to poor infrastructure.

From time to time, attempts have been made in different ways to tackle these myriad problems but none of them have been able to fully address the several constraints that Indian agriculture has had to cope with.

Limited Success of Efforts

The Union Government has for long tried to smoothen the ups and downs of Indian agriculture with subsidies. However, the problem with any subsidy is that it becomes difficult to sustain after a while. A solution that is often recommended, contract farming, is conceptually right. But it inevitably aggravates the feeling of vulnerability of the small farmers. It invariably makes small farmers, with their poor negotiating power, feel that they have got a raw deal. In fact, contract farming further skews the imbalance between the big and resourceful farmers and the small and poor farmers. Farmers also apprehend that contract farming will cause large-scale displacement of labour. Being fundamentally insecure in the Indian context, farmers also fear that they will be exploited by the more powerful corporate entities. Likewise any effort to corporatise farming invariably opens up a social-Pandora's box.

Another solution that India has experimented with is producers' cooperatives. Barring a few exceptions, the marketing expertise and effectiveness of these cooperatives is suspect. On the other hand, producers, consumers and the general public alike have had deeply ingrained and fundamental apprehensions about the basic operational efficiency and effectiveness of government corporations and cooperatives.

Each of these approaches has certainly helped up to a point in enhancing agricultural output, improving crop quality and reaching the produce to markets. But none of these has enabled the country to realize the full potential of its agriculture. A radically different and revolutionary approach to catapult the growth of the farm sector is an urgent imperative today.

Already the rapid globalization of the Indian economy and the advent of market reforms have intensified competition. The count-down has already begun for the World Trade Organization (WTO) framework to take effect on January 1, 2005. Indian agriculture, therefore, has to gear up to face international competition. What is more, there is a need to ensure that its growth path is equitable while being effective. It has been seen that the Government alone cannot shoulder the responsibility to improve the international competitiveness of the farmer. Prescribing readymade formula solutions cannot solve the problems of agriculture either. Against this background, ITC began to look at the rapid advances in Information Technology (IT) to resolve some of these chronic illnesses of Indian agriculture.

ITC'S IT-BASED INITIATIVES

ITC conceptualized and evolved its celebrated 'e-Choupal' project, the largest internet-based initiative in rural India by any corporate, based on the following tried, tested and observed capabilities of Information Technology (IT) :

> Information technology can be used to deliver real time information and customized knowledge to improve farmers' decision-making ability to better align farm output to market demand and improve productivity.

IT can aggregate the farmers' demand for inputs and services by creating, in effect, a virtual producers' cooperative. Farmers can leverage such a virtual cooperative to access farm inputs of the best quality and knowledge at lower cost.

IT is eminently capable of being used to set-up a direct marketing channel with more efficient price discovery and lower transaction costs in output marketing.

This multi-dimensional use of IT and the Internet to empower the Indian farmer, with readily accessible online knowledge and real-time linkage to world markets, is the essence of ITC's project 'e-Choupal'. This pioneering "click and mortar initiative" already reaches out to more than 6.50 lakh farmers in 6,500 villages and four states through 1,020 'e-Choupals'. Through crop-specific and customized web portals in local languages covering four products as yet—soya, wheat, coffee and aquaculture—these farmers can easily access real-time information on the local weather, knowledge about best farm practices and details of the prevalent commodity prices in Indian and international markets.

ON-LINE ACCESS TO EXPERTISE

Let us see how the 'e-Choupal' initiative is helping the Indian farmer in his daily life and work at the grass-roots level. Today the farmer has to embark on a wild goose chase and go to several sources to get information about the weather. The information may not be locally available at all. It may not be real-time information. It may not be specific to his geographical area and customized to his crop. Even if he is able to source some information, he may not be sure that it is reliable.

For an illiterate or semi-literate farmer in the rural hinterland who knows only his mother tongue, accessing knowledge about scientific practices specific to his crop and his land is an even more formidable and Herculean task. Even if he is able to obtain the required information, to source those prescribed agricultural inputs screened for right quality is another tall order. The source of supply of the requisite agricultural inputs is often a dealer, who has vested interest in selling products that give him best return, instead of making the prescribed best inputs available to farmer.

Project 'e-Choupal' places the technology, the Internet, at the need disposal of the farmer in his village. The farmer thereby enjoys the incredible facility of immediate on-line access to expert advice on agriculture, through either e-mail or the chat mode or the worldwide web. Very often this expert advice is from another progressive farmer elsewhere on the network. Based on such expert advice, the farmer can then order, on-line, the nutrient or the chemicals required.

Similarly, when the farmer has to sell his produce, he is normally constrained by the fact that he does not have the slightest idea about the price he can realise until he physically takes his produce to the *mandi*. The cost meter begins to tick as soon as he sets out for the *mandi*. He has to incur the transport cost and sundry personal expenses. Besides the high transaction costs at the *mandi* like commissions and handling charges, there are several other hidden costs in the *mandi* like cheating on weighment and delays in payment. Small farmers, who do not have the staying power to hold on to their produce till it fetches a remunerative price, inevitably have to sell in distress at whatever price that is offered.

On the other hand, the virtual *mandi* system that ITC's 'e-Choupal' creates, empowers the farmer to get reliable information about the prevailing prices and price trends in the domestic and world markets in the comfort of his hearth and home itself. It gives the farmer the technology and the tools to obtain all the market information. The farmer can also scan the analysis of the market and market trends done by experts and third parties. On top of all this, 'e-Choupal' gives the farmer the freedom and the ability to decide what to do with his produce. He can take it to the *mandi*, or he can sell his crop to ITC right at his farm gate at a given transparent price. What is more, the farmer can also access deferred pricing tools and de-link produce delivery, cash receipt and price fixation timings to obtain the most optimal deal for himself.

By creating an alternative and attractive direct marketing channel for the farmer, the 'e-Choupal' movement will stimulate the traditional *mandi* system to improve its efficiency. It will also help weed out some of the mal practices that taint the *mandi* monopoly. The 'e-infrastructure' that ITC is creating in rural India will also help conserve precious public resources that will otherwise need to be invested to expand and upgrade the *mandis*. This digital network will also serve as a strong foundation to evolve a vibrant futures market. The 'e-Choupal' model has the powerful potential to be adapted to all areas of agriculture—be it floriculture, sericulture, horticulture, poultry farming or animal husbandry.

BENEFIT TO FARMER AND CONSUMER

ITC's rural partnership is therefore enabling the Indian farmer to raise farm productivity, improve crop quality and plan and manage agricultural production on the basis of market demand. All these combine to help the farmer realize significantly higher farm prices. At the same time, the Indian and the international consumers are able to buy an agricultural product of a superior quality at a lower price. The cumulative macro-economic effect is to significantly contribute to the global competitiveness of Indian agriculture.

ITC has formulated clear plans and drawn up the path forward to rapidly scale up this 'e-Choupal' initiative. Over the next six to seven years, Project 'e-Choupal' will span one lakh villages, or one-sixth of rural India, and cater to a much wider range of crops. Some of the additional areas of agricultural activity that the company is seriously considering for coverage are horticulture, cotton and spices. ITC will roll out the 'e-Choupal' project in 15 States across the country.

Of course, the company has to surmount daunting problems in the implementation of this Internet initiative. Most serious among these are the major infrastructural problems of rural India. There is crippling power shortage. The lack of telecom connectivity and shortage of bandwidth are major roadblocks. Besides, the company constantly faces the challenge of training first time internet users to navigate their way through the worldwide web.

ITC has learnt invaluable lessons by finding creative local solutions to some of these apparently intractable problems. Solutions like the use of RNS kits in the telephone exchanges, or setting up VSAT to tide over connectivity problems, and using solar power as the back-up source of electricity.

It has also applied the template approach to management. It has also adopted special imaging techniques. All these help hasten download and optimize the farmer-usage of the Internet within the available bandwidth.

One of the most important features of the 'e-Choupal' movement has been the unstinting focus on ensuring that the agricultural community in the village evolve and coalesces around the lead farmer, called the 'Choupal Sanchalak'. This 'Choupal Sanchalak' maintains the Internet kiosk and helps other farmers find answers to their questions from ITC's proprietary crop-specific website that he can access and surf through.

The shared objective of using the Internet and customized knowledge-base created by ITC to enhance agricultural competitiveness strengthens this community-building process. For ITC, this community-building process has been as important as educating the farmer to use the Internet and Information Technology.

The 'e-Choupal' movement has significantly strengthened ITC's century-old relationship with the Indian farmer. It also serves as an inspiring model for other corporates engaged in agri-business in India as well as other developing countries.

Index

Achieving Global Competitiveness, 187, 205
Adding Value and Increasing Satisfaction Level, 204
  Process of, 204
Add Value through Effective Pricing, 194
Administration, 258
  Quality of, 258
Adopting/Installing ERP Systems, 431
  Reasons for, 431
    Reduced Lead Time, 431
    Increased Customer Satisfaction, 432
    Integrate Financial Information, 432
    Integrate Customer Order Information, 432
    Standardise and Speed-up Manufacturing Process, 432
    Learner Hierarchical Structure, 433
AEPC (Apparel Export Promotion Council), 85
Aggarwal, Monika, 228
Agricultural Accounting, 327
  Objectives of, 329
Agricultural Sustainability, 288
Agriculture and Productivity, 292
Agriculture and the Environment, 288
  Harmony, 288
Agriculture in India, 289
  Mackinsey's Report on, 289
Agriculture, 287
  Profitability and Competitiveness of, 287
Agriculture Sector and Agricultural Accounting, 328
  Productivity of, 328
Agriculture Sector, 285
  Globalisation, Competitiveness and Productivity in, 285
    Government Policies, 285
    Global Market Place, 289
Agro/Food Processing Industry, 101
  Present Status, 101
  Pitfalls in Technology, 103
  Future Development, 104
AMS (Aggregate Measure of Support), 301
Annan, Kofi, 297
Anti-Competitive Behaviour, 78
AoA (Agreement on Agriculture), 297, 300-01
Application of Software Metrics to ADA, 372
ATC (Agreement on Textiles and Clothing), 86, 297

Balance Sheet Ratio, 213
Bamba, Meera, 444
Banking Industry, 208
  Productivity in, 208
Bansal Jasmine, 406
Bansal, Sanjeev, 434
BATNEEC (Best Available Technology Not Entailing Excessive Cost), 30
Bawa, R.S., 306
Better Informed Customers, 4
Better Supply Chain Management, 7
Bhatia, B.S., 31, 240
Bhatnagar, Dyal, 53
BPCL (Bharat Petroleum Corporation Ltd., 413
Branch Productivity, 215
Bicycle and Bicycle Parts Industry, 98
  Present Status, 98
  Pitfalls in Technology, 98
  Future Development, 100
Building Commitments, 197
Building Trust and Customer Confidence, 181
Bush, George, 295
Business Process Re-engineering, 70

Cancum Round, 298
CAP (Common Agricultural Policy), 330

CAR (Corrective Action Request), 201
Cereals, 318
  Production of, 318
CFC (Codex Food Code), 50
Challenges in EG, 394
  Implementation Issues, 394
  Financial Commitments, 395
Changing Organisation, 156
Changing Political Environment, 170
Chawla, Sonia, 79
CMIE (Center for Monitoring Indian Economy), 229
Collusive Tendering, 78
Commercial Banks of India, 228
  Trends in Operational Productivity of, 228
Commitment to the Customer, 198
Companies Act, 1956, 32
Competition Policy, 77
Competition, 4
  Globalization of, 4
Competitiveness, 64
  Factors Affecting, 64
    Labour, 65
    Government, 65
    Exchange Rate, 65
    Technology, 65
    Cost of Capital, 65
    Management and Governance, 65
    Country-Specific Factors, 66
    Infrastructure, 66
Competitiveness of Nations, 9
Competitiveness, Productivity and Globalising Indian Insurance Market, 175
Competitiveness, Productivity and Globalising Insurance Market, 180
  Strategies for, 180
  Distribution, 180
  Bancassurance, 181
  Competition, 181
Competitors, 4
  Increasing Number of, 4
Confederation of Indian Industry, 184
Consumer Education, 179
Consumer Grievance Redressal, 179
Coping with Changing Economic Environment, 171
  Challenge of, 171
Computer Software, 348
  Top Exporters, 348
Consumer and Health Services Imparting Process, 262
Consumer Behaviour Model, 195
Conventional Agriculture, 315
  Drawbacks of, 315
Corporate Governance, 38
  Holistic Approach to, 38
CPA (Consumer Protection Act), 1986, 179
Create Distribution Equity, 194
Creating and Organising Knowledge, 69
CRM and Competition, 413
  Avenue, 414
  Productive Executive Empowerment, 414
  Blueprinting, 414
  Service Guidelines, 414
  Knowing the Users, 415
  Internal Support, 415
  Small Successes, 415
  Ongoing Evaluation, 415
CRM (Consumer Relationship Management), 250, 377, 407, 431
  Concept, 407
  A Strategic Initiative, 408
    Mission, 408
    Objectives of Implementation, 408
    Customer Expectations, 409
    Measurement Matrix, 409
    End Results Expected, 409
  Development, 410
    Process of, 410
  Life Style, 411
  Learning Relationship Model, 411
  Read Blocks, 412
  Need of, 377
  Concept, 407
  As a Competitive Advantage, 378
  An Additive Tool for Competitiveness, 375
  Increasing Organisational Competitiveness, 406
  Concept, 407
Crops and Animal Production, 319
  Integration of, 319
Cruxing Service Product, 262
Customer Complaint and Feedback Management System, 200
Customer Complaint Flow Chart, 202
Customer Development Process, 407
  Customer, 378
  Impact of CRM on, 378
Customer Interaction, 204
  Factors Affecting, 204
Customer Lifestyle, 380
  Steps of, 380
Customer Satisfaction Process, 190
  Pre-sales, 190
  During Sales, 200
  Aftersales Period, 191

Customer Satisfaction Relationship Portfolio, 199
Cyber Laws, 436

Delight Marketing, 205
Design Factor, 364-65
ERP System, 364-65
Daver, S.C., 64
Developing an International Perspective, 168
Experience, 169
Focus, 169
Attitude, 169
Developing Distinctive Competence, 6
Development of the Software Industry, 347
Pattern of, 347
Dhameja, S.K., 93
Differential Pricing, 78
Digital Governance Models, 419
Digital Identity, 437
Dogra, Balram, 3
Drucker, Peter F., 34

E-Business, 434
Barriers, 436
Bandwidth, 436
Advertising Costs, 437
Indian Overview, 438
A must for Globalization, 434
e-Choupal, 446-48
EDI (Electronic Data Interchange), 438
Education and Training, 354
Structure of, 354
Edward, J.D., 360
EFT (Electronic Fund Transfer), 424
E-Governance, 392, 417
Application Areas, 418
Pre-Requisite for, 419
Broadcasting/Wider Model, 419
Application, 419
Critical Flow Model, 420
Applications, 420
Comparative Analysis Model, 420
Application, 420
Mobilization, 420
Application, 421
Interactive Service Model, 421
Application, 421
Benefits, 421
Challenges, 422
Working Model of, 392
E-Governance Projects, 425
Andhra Pradesh, 425
Apswan, 425
Card Project, 425
Multi-purpose Household Survey Project, 425
Fully Automated Service of Transport, 425
Gujarat, 425
Smart Card Project, 425
Statewide Wan, 425
Disaster Management System, 425
Karnataka, 425
Computerization of Education Department, 425
Computerization of Treasury, 425
Vidutnet for KPTCL, 426
Tamil Nadu, 426
STAR, 426
School Project, 426
Tele-Medicine Project, 426
Computerization of Land Records, 426
Local Language Computing, 426
Computerization of Transport Department, 426
West Bengal, 426
GIS-Based Municipality Information System, 426
Web and Kiosk-Based Education Information System, 426
Vernacular Interface Project, 426
EHI (Electronics Hardware Industry), 108
Electronics Industry, 107
E-Government and E-Governance, 417
Electronics Hardware Industry in Punjab, 109
Present Status, 109
Future Development, 109
EMS (Environmental Management Systems), 135
Enhancing Indian Competitiveness through Knowledge, 64
Enhancing National Productivity and Competitiveness, 12
Strategies for, 12
Enterprises, 4
Competitiveness of, 4
EPZ (Export Promotion Zones), 347
ERP (Enterprise Resource Planning), 358, 428-29, 433
ERP in India, 431
Supply Chain Management, 431
ERP Market, 430
Indian Scenario, 430
ERP System Design, 362-63
Factors in, 363, 365

EU (European Union), 87
EVA as a Tool to Measure Productivity, 53
Excellence in Management Education, 387
Total Quality Model of, 387
Export Competitiveness, 122
Conceptual Framework of, 122
Export Subsidies, 303
Export Unit Value Index, 19

FADN Balance Sheet, 331
Structure of, 331
FADN (Farm Accountancy Data Network), 330
FADN Income Statement, 331
Structure of, 331
FCI (Food Corporation of India), 294
FDI (Foreign Direct Investment), 77, 121
Financial Ratios Measuring Productivity, 215
Financial Statement Ratios, 213
Firm's Competitiveness Strategies and Nation's Competitiveness, 11
A Model of, 11
First Move Towards e-Business, 441
Five Key Commitments Model, 197
Foreign Banks, 237, 273
Profitability of, 273
Financial Management of, 275
Fukuyama, 139
Future Comparative Advantage, 67
Indicators of, 67

Gaining Global Competitiveness, 164
Gaining International Competitiveness, 166
Gandhi, Mahatma, 375
Garcha, Deependra Singh, 120
GATS (General Agreement on Trade in Services) 297
GATT (General Agreement on Tariff and Trade), 49, 85, 297, 300
General Insurance, 243
GIC (General Insurance Corporation), 175, 241
Global Competitiveness, 47
Global Environmental Forces, 263
Globalization, 121
Globalization Benefits, 287
Government-wide Information Infrastructure, 424
Goyal, D.P., 358
Griffin, Jill, 407
Gupta, Ravi Kumar, 175
Gupta, Sanjeev, 306
Gupta, Santosh, 257

HACCP (Hazard Analysis Critical Control Point), 50
Health Insurance, 183
Health Sector, 257
Global Competitiveness in, 257
Health Service Delivery Package, 260
Criteria for, 260
Hindustan Lever Ltd., 196
Human Resource Management, 6

IBC (Imputed Bank Charges), 42
ICAI (Institute of Chartered Accountants of India), 37
ICAR (Indian Council of Agricultural Research), 294
ICRISAT (International Crops Research Institute for the Semi-Arid Tropics), 293
ICT (Information and Communication Technology), 68
ICWAI (Institute of Cost and Works Accountants of India), 37
IFOAM (International Federation of Organic Agriculture Movement), 320
Increasing Productivity and Competitiveness, 428
Role of ERP Systems in, 428
Increasing the Export Share, 91
Strategies for, 91
India and World Clothing Export Scenario, 88
India, 26, 32, 243, 266, 322, 422
E-Governance Initiatives, 422
Profitability Index of, 26
Present Reporting Framework, 32
Application of Agricultural Accounting, 332
Insurance Potential, 243
Competitiveness of Public Sector Banks, 266
Indian Agricultural Sector, 306
Growth Performance of Productivity in, 306
Indian Banking Sector, 439
Internet Hits, 439
Indian Cotton Garments, 88
Performance of, 88
Indian Economy, 40
Globalisation and the Changing Productivity Performance, 40
Indian Export Industry, 86
Profile of, 86
Indian Exports, 127
External Competitiveness of, 127
Indian Garment Export Sector, 87, 89

SWOT Analysis of, 89
Strengths, 89
Weaknesses, 90
Opportunities, 90
Threats, 90
Performance, 87
Indian Industries, 112
Competitiveness and Performance of, 112
Indian Insurance Company, 245
Inadequacy of, 245
Indian Insurance Industry, 241
Structure of, 241
Indian Manufacture Exports, 125
Trends in, 125
Indian Manufacturing Industry, 120
Export Competitiveness of, 120
Indian PC Market, 343
Brand-wise Structure, 343
Indian Textile Industry, 139
Productive Efficiency of, 139
India's Exports, 29
Industrial Licensing Policy, 1988, 112
Industrial Sectors in Punjab, 93
Productivity Improvement of, 93
Industry, 177
Challenges Before, 177
New Insurers, 177
Existing Insurers, 177
Expectation of the Consumers, 178
Distribution Channels, 179
Information Technology, 182
Thrust on Usage of, 182
Innovation-based Education, 69
Insurance Education and Training, 182
Insurance, 248
Future of, 248
Insurance Sector for Private Companies, 176
Opening-up, 176
Insurance Sector in India, 240
Intelligent Organisation, 161
International Business, 169
Managing Diversity of, 169
Inter-State Goods Movement Regulations, 437
Internet Usage, 436
Investment *vs.* Productivity, 289
IRDA (Insurance Regulatory and Development Authority), 185, 240
IT in Agriculture, 444
Poor Extension Machinery, 444
Limited Success of Efforts, 445
On-line Access to Expertise, 446
Benefit to Farmer, 447
IT Industry, 339-40
Segmentation of, 340
Structure and its Policy Implications, 339
IT (Information Technology), 445
IT Market, 341
Structure and Growth of, 341
IT Solutions for Service Providers in Education, 384

Jayaraman, N., 192
Jindal, Manav, 434
Jindal, Ruchi, 434

Kakkar, Shikha, 428
Kalam, A.P.J. Abdul, 293
Kaper, George, 31
Kaur, Gaganjeet, 266
Kathuria, Lalit Mohan, 85
Kaur, Amandeep, 112
Kaur, Kuldip, 112
Kaur, Kulwant, 392
Kaur, Sukhbir, 314
Kaushik, Deepak, 417
Kaushik, Sanjay, 208
Khara, Navjote, 120
Kohli, V.K., 154
Kotler, Phillip, 188
Kp (Capital Productivity), 58
Kumar, Sunil, 139

Labour Productivity, 215
Labour Reforms, 286
Learning Organization, 156, 160
Main Advantages Associated with, 160
Learning Process, 159
Institutionalizing, 159
Liberalization and Globalization, 73
Impact of, 73
LIC (Life Insurance Corporation), 175, 241-42
LPG (Liberalization, Privatization and Globalization), 73
LTA (Long-term Agreement), 86

MAI (Multilateral Agreement on Investment), 52
Maintaining Economic Competitiveness, 165
Makkar, Urvashi, 187
Malhotra, R.N., 241
Manufactured Exports, 130
Growth of, 130
Manufacture Exports Composition, 18
Post-Liberalization, 128

Manufactures, 22
  Export Unit Value Index, 22
Manufacturing Industry, 124, 131
  Policy Measures to Improve Export Competitiveness in, 131
  Indian Exports Scenario in, 124
Manufacturing, 22
  Relative Unit Labour Cost in, 22
Market Access, 301
  Tariffication, 301
  Tariff Reduction, 301
Market Dominance, 78
Marketing Strategy, 261
Maruti Udyog Ltd., 196
McKinsey Promise, 290
Meeting the Super Value Challenge, 194
Mental Models, 158
MANs (Metropolitan Area Networks), 242
MFA (Multi-Fibre Arrangement), 85
MFN (Most Favoured Nation), 298
Moving Towards E-Business, 439
Multi-Fibre Arrangement, 85
  Competitiveness of the Indian Garment Export Sector, 85
MVA (Market Value Added), 54

Nanda, Paramjit, 16, 47
Narasimham Committee, 266
Nationalization of Commercial Banks, 266
Nations, 9
  Competitiveness of, 9
Natural Resource Management, 314
Neelmeghan, A., 69
New Economic Policy, 1991, 16
New Scientific Fields, 5
  Advances in, 5
NIC (National Insurance Company), 185
Nine Box Diagram, 35
Non-Life Insurance Companies, 244
  Performance of, 244
Non-Product Specific Subsidies, 302
NTB (Non-Tariff Barriers), 49-50

OLS (Ordinary Least Squares), 139
OPT (Outward Processing Trade), 87
Organic Agriculture Development, 323
  Barriers in, 323
Organic Agriculture, 314, 322, 324
  Opportunities, 322
    Producers, 322
    Business Entrepreneurs, 322
  Certification Requirements for, 320
  Status of, 320
    International, 320
  Promotion and Adoption, 324
Organic Farming, 317
  Definition, 317
Organic Land Area, 321
  Continent-wise, 321
Organic Nature of a Farm, 319
  Productivity, 319
  Social Compatibility, 319
  Preservation of the Environment, 319
  Nutrient Cycles, 319
    Crop Rotation, 319
    Inter-Cropping, 319
    Bio-diversity, 319
    Adaptability, 319
Organizational Competency, 378
  Impact of CRM on, 378

Padamsee Alyque, 191
Pahuja, Anurag, 31
Pandit, A.J., 408
Patient Satisfaction, 259
Pension Market, 183
Personal Mastery, 158
Physical Work Unit Ratios, 214
PIASA (Proposed International Accounting Standard on Agriculture), 332
Post-Liberalization Period, 16
  Trends in Global Competitiveness of India, 16
Private Sector Banks, 233, 279
  Profitability of, 279
Process-based Management Systems and Productivity, 134
Product Innovation, 180
Productivity Accounting, 34
Productivity-Centric Global Competitiveness, 3
Productivity, 31
  Corporate Reporting on, 31
Productivity Improvement in Administration, 392
  E-Governance for, 392
Productivity, 213
  Indicators of, 213
    Qualitative, 213
    Quantitative, 213
Productivity Reports, 37
  Format of, 37
  Scope of, 36
Productivity, 210
  Sources of, 210
Product Specific Subsidies, 302
  Green Box, 302

Blue Box, 302
Profitability Index, 26
Profit and Loss Account Ratios, 213
Program Complexity and Faults, 373
Connection, 373
Program Complexity and Testability, 373
Connection Between, 373
Proposed International Accounting Standard on Agriculture, 332
Protecting the Knowledge, 70
Public, Private and Foreign Banks, 268
Analysis of Performance Indicators of, 268
Public Sector Banks, 231, 268-69, 277, 281
Financial Management of, 281
Profitability of, 277
Challenges for, 268
Best Performers, 269
Public Sector Banks for Enhancing Productivity, 270
Strategies to be Adopted by, 270
Punjab Agriculture, 304
Impact of WTO on, 304
Punjab Communications Limited, 361-62
Profile of, 361
Punjab, 316
Salt Affected Soil in, 316
Problems of Soil Erosion in, 316
Puri, Swati Kumaria, 240

QMS (Quality Management Systems), 135

Raikhy, P.S., 16, 47
Rangi, P.S., 300
Rathore, B.S., 93
Real Product Wage, 130
Annual Growth Rate, 130
Reddy, Akepati, S., 134
Regular Research, 191
Importance of, 191
Relationship Management, 382
Costs and Benefits of, 382
Relationship Marketing, 200
Relative Consumer Price Index, 17
Relative Unit Cost in Manufacturing, 18
Relative Unit Value Index of Exports, 17
Relative Wholesale Price Index, 18, 22
Restrictive Business Practices, 78
RPI (Relative Profitability Index), 18

Sahni, A.K., 408
Sales and Marketing, 378
Impact of CRM on, 378
SBBJ (State Bank of Bikaner and Jaipur), 215
SBH (State Bank of Hyderabad), 215
SB Indore (State Bank of Indore), 215
SBM (State Bank of Mysore), 215
SBOP (State Bank of Patiala), 215
SBS (State Bank of Saurashtra), 215
SBT (State Bank of Travancore), 215
SCP (Structure Conduct Performance), 112
SDPs (Service Delivery Points), 424
SEICMM (Software Engineering Institute Capability Maturity Model), 159
Sethi, Amarjiit Singh, 40
Shandu, Monica, 295
Sharma, Sanjeev K., 164
Shukla, Ashok, 187
Singh, Dalbir, 375
Single Factor Productivity, 44
Singh, Harpinder, 314
Singh, Hawa, 375
Singh, Inderjeet, 339
Singh, Manmohan, 64
Singh, Narender, 64, 375
Singh, Raghbir, 85
Singh, Rajinder, 369
Singla, Ashim Raj, 358
Six Stage Model of Relationship, 376
Smith, Adam, 188
Software Complexity Metrics in Productivity, 369
Role of, 369
Software Industry, 344, 352
Structure of the Production of, 352
Cost Structure of, 344
Software Segment, 343
State Bank of Bikaner and Jaipur, 222
Productivity Indicators, 222
State Bank of Hyderabad, 221
Productivity Indicators, 221
State Bank of India Group, 215
Productivity in, 215
State Bank of India, 220
Productivity Indicators, 220
State Bank of Indore, 226
Productivity Indicators, 226
State Bank of Mysore, 224
Productivity Indicators, 224
State Bank of Patiala, 223
Productivity Indicators, 223
State Bank of Saurashtra, 225
Productivity Indicators, 225
State Bank of Travancore, 227
Productivity Indicators, 227
STP (Software Technology Parks), 347

Strategies to Improve Productivity, 217
Suppliers, 379
  Impact of CRM, 379
Sustaining the Enterprise's Competitive Advantage, 8
Systemic Competitiveness, 10

TDR (Trade and Development Report), 296
Team Learning, 157
Technological Capabilities, 4
  Rapid Advances in, 4
Textile and Hosiery Industry, 104
  Present Status, 104
  Pitfalls in Technology, 106
  Future Development, 106
TFP (Total Factor Productivity), 40, 43, 45, 48
Tobit Analysis, 149
TPA (Third Party Administrators), 185
TQM (Total Quality Management), 205, 385-86
Transforming Public Enterprises in India into Intelligent Organizations, 154
Trend Co-efficient, 19
TRIMs (Trade Related Investment Measures), 297
TRIPs (Trade Related Aspects of Intellectual Property Rights), 297
Types of Industries in Punjab, 97
  District-wise Distribution, 97

Ubha, Dharminder Singh, 327
UNCTAD (United Nations Conference on Trade and Development), 51, 78, 296
Uppal, K.K., 164
Uruguay Round, 297

Value Creation Strategy, 192
VANs (Value Added Networks), 438
Varibales, 144
  Data and Measurement of, 144
Vasudeva, P.K., 285
Verma, Rajesh, 3
Videocon International, 196
Vinayek, Ravinder, 175

WANs (Wide Area Networks), 242
What is a Learning Organisation?, 155
Why Corporate Disclosures?, 32
Why do we Need Learning Organizations?, 159
  Being Competitive, 159
  Process Improvement, 160
  Training, 160
Working towards Enhancing Customer Satisfaction, 190
World Exports and Imports, 28
  India's Share in, 28
WTO and Competition Policy, 79
WTO and Globalisation, 297
WTO and Indian Agriculture, 300
WTO (World Trade Organisation), 52, 86, 292, 297, 300, 328, 445